D0212163

EX LIBRIS
SOUTH ORANGE
PUBLIC LIBRARY

AIR WARFARE

An International Encyclopedia

AIR WARFARE

An International Encyclopedia

VOLUME TWO, M-Z

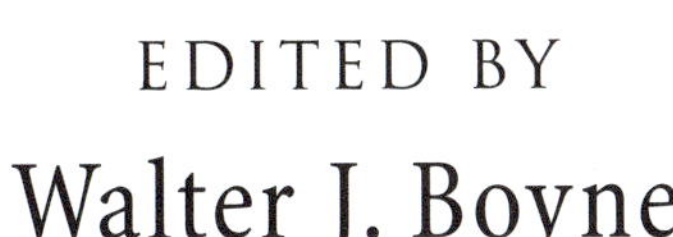

EDITED BY

Walter J. Boyne

ASSOCIATE EDITORS

Michael Fopp

Fred Johnsen

Stéphane Nicolaou

George M. Watson Jr.

FOREWORD BY

Michael J. Dugan

ABC CLIO

Santa Barbara, California Denver, Colorado Oxford, England

Library of Congress Cataloging-in-Publication Data
Air warfare: an international encyclopedia / edited by Walter J. Boyne ;
foreword by Michael J. Dugan.
p. cm.
Includes bibliographical references and index.
ISBN 1-57607-345-9 (hardcover : alk. paper) ISBN 1-57607-729-2 (e-book)
1. Aeronautics, Military—Encyclopedias. I. Boyne, Walter J., 1929–
UG628.A73 2002
358.4'003—dc21
2002002251

07 06 05 04 03 02 10 9 8 7 6 5 4 3 2 1

This book is also available on the World Wide Web as an e-book. Visit abc-clio.com for details.

ABC-CLIO, Inc.
130 Cremona Drive, P.O. Box 1911
Santa Barbara, California 93116-1911

This book is printed on acid-free paper.
Manufactured in the United States of America

CONTENTS

ALPHABETICAL LIST OF ENTRIES

MAPS

TERMS, ACRONYMS, AND ABBREVIATIONS

AA	antiaircraft
AAA	antiaircraft artillery
AAF	Argentine Air Force
AAMs	air-to-air missiles
AB	Agusta-Bell
ABCCC	Airborne Battlefield Command and Control Center
ABDA	American, British, Dutch, Australian
ABL	airborne laser
ABM	antiballistic missile
ACCS	Air Command and Control System; also: Airborne Command and Control Squadron
ACFC	Air Corps Ferrying Command
ACG	Air Commando Group
ACTS	Air Corps Tactical School
ACWP	Automotive Council of War Production
AD	Air Division
ADC	Air (Aerospace) Defense Command
ADRC	Air Documents Research Center
ADVON	Advanced Echelon
AEA	Aeronautical Experiment Association
AEF	Aerospace Expeditionary Force
AEW	airborne early warning
AF	Air Force
AFB	Air Force Base
AFC	Armed Forces Council
AFDD	Air Force Doctrine Document
AFM	Air Force Manual
AFMC	Air Force Material Command
AI	air interdiction
AIRCENT	Allied Air Forces Central Europe
ALAT	Army Light Air Force
ALCS	airborne launch-control system
ALERT	Attack and Launch Early Reporting to Theater
AMC	Air Mobility Command
AME	Aeronautica Militar Espanola
ANG	Air National Guard
ANR	Aeronautica Nazionale (National) Repubblicana
AOC	air officer commanding
ARM	antiradiation missile
ARPA	Advanced Research Projects Agency
ARRS	Aerospace Rescue and Recovery Service
ARVN	Army of the Republic of Vietnam
ASAT	antisatellite
ASC	Air Support Command
ASM	air-to-surface missile
ASTS	Air Service Tactical School
ASW	antisubmarine warfare
ATC	Air Transport Command
ATF	Advanced Tactical Fighter
ATGM	antitank guided missle
ATI	air technical intelligence
AVG	American Volunteer Group (Flying Tigers)
AWACS	Airborne Warning and Control System
AWPD	Air War Plans Division
BAe	British Aerospace
BAP	Bureau of Aircraft Production
BCATP	British Commonwealth Air Training Plan
BFW	Bayerische Flugzeugwerke
bhp	brake horsepower
BIS	British Interplanetary Society
BMEWS	Ballistic Missile Early Warning System
BNA	Bureau of Naval Aeronautics
BPF	British Pacific Fleet
BPR	bypass ration
CAB	Caproni Aeronautica Bergamasca
CACW	Chinese-American Composite Wing
CAF	Chinese Air Force
CAP	Civil Air Patrol; Combat Air Patrol
CAS	close air support
CAT	Civil Air Transport

CATF	China Air Task Force
CBI	China-Burma-India
CBO	Combined Bomber Offensive
CCP	Chinese Communist Party
CENTAF	United States Central Air Forces
CEO	chief executive officer
CETF	College Eye Task Force
CGS	Continental Ground Station
CIA	Central Intelligence Agency
CINC	commander in chief
CINCPAC	Commander in Chief, Pacific Fleet
CIS	Commonwealth of Independent States
CNAC	China National Aviation Corporation
CNO	Chief of Naval Operations
CNT	Cantiere Navale Triestino
COMINCH	commander in chief of the U.S. Fleet
COMUSMACV	U.S. Military Assistance Command, Vietnam
CONAC	Continental Air Command
CONAD	Continental Air Defense Command
CPTP	Civilian Pilot Training Program
CRAF	Civil Reserve Air Fleet
CRDA	Cantieri Riuniti Dell'Adriatico
CRT	cathode-ray-tube
CSAR	Combat Search and Rescue
CSAS	Comando Servizi Aerei Speciali (Special Air Services Command)
CTA	Centro Tecnico Aerospacial
CVE	escort carrier
DARPA	Defense Advanced Research Projects Agency
DASC	Direct Air Support Center
DATF	Desert Air Task Force
DCNO (Air)	Deputy Chief of Naval Operations for Air
DFC	Distinguished Flying Cross
DMSP	Defense Meteorological Satellite Program
DMZ	demilitarized zone
DNSS	Defense Navigation Satellite System
DOD	Department of Defense (U.S.)
DOS	Department of State (U.S.)
DRA	Democratic Republic of Afghanistan
DRV	Democratic Republic of Vietnam
DSC	Distinguished Service Cross
DSP	Defense Support Program
DVS	Commercial Pilot Training School
EAP	Experimental Aircraft Program
ECCM	electronic counter-countermeasures
ECM	electronic countermeasures
EDA	Ejército del Aire
EGNOS	European Global Navigation Overlay System
ELINT	electronic intelligence
EOP	Executive Office of the President
ER/ELINT	electronic reconnaissance/intelligence
ESM	Electronic support measures
ETO	European Theater of Operations
EVA	extravehicular activity
EW	Electronic warfare
FAA	Fleet Air Arm
FAC	forward air control/controllers
FAH	Fuerza Aerea Hondureña
FBW	fly-by-wire
FEAF	Far East Air Forces
FECOM	Far East Command
Fliegerkorps	Luftwaffe air corps
FM	Field Manual
FMA	Fabrica Militar de Aviones (Military Aircraft Factory)
FSTA	Future Strategic Tanker Aircraft
GCI	ground-controlled interceptor
GEO	geostationary orbit
GGS	Gyro Gun Sights
GHQ	General Headquarters
GHQ AF	General Headquarters Air Force (U.S.)
GIAP	Gvardeiskii Istrebitelnyi Aviatsionnyi Polk (Guards Fighter Air Regiment, Soviet Union)
GLONASS	Global Navigation Satellite System
GNBAP	Gvardeiskii Nochnoi Bombardirovochnyi Aviatsionnyi Polk (Guards Night Bomber Air Regiment, Soviet Union)
GNSS	Global Navigation Satellite System
GPS	Global Positioning System
GSDF	Ground Self-Defense Force
GvNBAP	Guards Night Bomber Aviation Regiment (Soviet Union)
Himmelbett	German radar system for night fighters
hp	horsepower
HQ	headquarters
HSA	Hawker-Siddeley Aircraft
HSD	Hawker-Siddeley Dynamics
HSU	Hero of the Soviet Union
HUD	head-up display
IADS	integrated air defense systems
IAF	Israeli Defense Force/Air Force
IAI	Israel Aircraft Industries
IAK	Istrebitelnyi Aviatsionnyi Korpus (Fighter Air Corps, Soviet Union)
IAP	Istrebitelnyi Aviatsionnyi Polk (Fighter Air Regiment, Soviet Union)
ICBM	intercontinental ballistic missile
IDSCS	Initial Defense Satellite Communications System
IFR	Instrument Flight Rules
IJN	Imperial Japanese Navy
IMAM	Industrie Meccaniche e Aeronautiche Meridionali
IOC	Initial Operational Capability
IQAF	Iraqi Air Force
IR	infrared

IRBM	intermediate-range ballistic missile
ItAF	Italian Air Force
JAAF	Japanese Army Air Force, Imperial
Jagdgeschwader	Luftwaffe fighter wing
Jagdstaffel (Jasta)	Luftwaffe fighter squadron
Jagdverband	Luftwaffe fighter unit
JASDF	Japanese Air Self-Defense Force
JATO	jet-assisted takeoff
JCS	Joint Chiefs of Staff
JNAF	Japanese Naval Air Force, Imperial
JPO	Joint Program Office
JSDF	Japanese Self-Defense Forces
JSF	Joint Strike Fighter
JSOTF	Joint Special Operations Task Force
Kampfgeschwader	Luftwaffe bomber wing
kph	kilometers per hour
Kriegsmarine	German Navy
LAMPS	Light Airborne Multipurpose System
Lichtenstein	type of German airborne radar
LORAN	long-range electronic navigation
LPS	Large Processing Station
LRP	Long-Range Penetration
Luftfahrtruppe	German aviation troops
Luftflotte	Luftwaffe air fleet
Luftstreitkräfte	German Air Service (World War I)
Luftwaffe	German Air Force (World War II)
MAAF	Mediterranean Allied Air Forces
MAAG	Military Assistance Advisory Group Vietnam
MAC	Military Airlift Command
MACV	Military Assistance Command Vietnam
MAD	magnetic airborne detection; mutual assured destruction
MAL	mat-landing
MANPADS	man-portable air defense system
MATS	Military Air Transport Service
MCM	mine countermeasures
MCT	Mobile Communication Terminal
MEO	middle-earth orbit
MGS	Mobile Ground System
MGT	Mobile Ground Terminal
MHz	megahertz
MIDAS	Missile Defense Alarm System
MIRACL	Mid-Infrared Advanced Chemical Laser
MIRV	Multiple Independently Targetable Reentry Vehicle
MIT	Massachusetts Institute of Technology
mm	millimeter
mph	miles per hour
MRBM	medium-range ballistic missiles
MRC	Military Revolutionary Council
MSDF	Maritime Self-Defense Force
MTU	Moteren und Turbine Union
NACA	National Advisory Committee for Aeronautics
NAF	Naval Aircraft Factory
NAP	naval aviation pilot
NASA	National Aeronautics and Space Administration
NASAF	Northwest African Strategic Air Forces
NATO	North Atlantic Treaty Organization
NATS	Naval Air Transport Service
NAVAIDS	aids to navigation.
NAVFE	Naval Forces Far East
NAVSTAR	Navigation Satellite Time and Ranging
NBAP	Night Bomber Aviation Regiment (Soviet Union)
NBS	National Bureau of Standards
NCO	noncommissioned officer
NEACP	National Emergency Airborne Command Post
NIAP	Nochnoi Istrebitel'nyi Aviatsionnyi Polk (Night Fighter Air Regiment, Soviet Union)
NLC	National Leadership Committee
NORAD	North American Air Defense Command
NPT	Nuclear Non-Proliferation Treaty
NRO	National Reconnaissance Office
NSA	National Security Act of 1947; also: National Security Advisor
NSC	National Security Council
NVA	North Vietnamese Army
NVAF	North Vietnamese Air Force
OGS	Overseas Ground Station
ONR	Office of Naval Research
OPEC	Organization of Petroleum Exporting Countries
OSS	Office of Strategic Services
PACAF	Pacific Air Forces
PACOM	Pacific Command
PAF	Pakistan Air Force
PAVN	People's Army of Vietnam (North Vietnamese Army)
PGMs	precision-guided munitions
PLAAF	People's Liberation Army Air Force (Chinese Communist Air Force)
PLSK	Pomonicza Lotnicza S-UBA Kobiet (Auxiliary Women's Air Force Service, Poland)
POL	petroleum, oil, lubricants
POW	prisoner of war
PPI	plan position indicator
PVO	Voiska Protivovozdushnoi Oborony (Antiaircraft Defense Forces, Soviet Union)
PWS	Podlaska Wytwornia Samolotow
PZL	Panstwowe Zaklady Lotnicze (National Aviation Establishments, Poland)
RA	Regia Aeronautica
RAE	Royal Aircraft Establishment
RAF	Royal Air Force
RAND	Research and development think tank
RCAF	Royal Canadian Air Force

REAF	Royal Egyptian Air Force
Reichsluftverteidigung	Air Defense of Germany
RFC	Royal Flying Corps
RGS	Relay Ground Station
Riesenflugzeug	giant aircraft
RLA	Royal Laotian Army
RLM	Reich Air Ministry
RN	Royal Navy
RNAF	Royal Norwegian Air Force
RNAS	Royal Naval Air Service
ROC	Republic of China
ROE	Rules of Engagement
ROTC	Reserve Officer Training Corps
rpm	revolutions per minute
RTAF	Royal Thai Air Force
RVN	Republic of Vietnam
RVNAF	Republic of Vietnam Air Force
RYAF	Royal Yugoslav Air Force
SA	selective availability
SAAC	Swiss American Aircraft Corporation
SAC	Strategic Air Commansd
SAGE	Semi-Automatic Ground Environment
SAR	search and rescue
SARH	semiactive radar-homing
SARTAF	Search and Rescue Task Force
SBIRS	Space-Based Infrared System
SBS	United States Strategic Bombing Survey
Schlachtstaffel	Luftwaffe battle flight
Schräge Musik	German upward-firing armament
SEAD	suppression of enemy air defenses
Seeluftstreitkräfte	German naval air force
Seenotdienst	Luftwaffe air rescue service
SEP	specific excess power
shp	shaft horsepower
SIAI	Società Idrovolanti Alta Italia
SIGINT	signals intelligence
SIOP	Single Integrated Operation Plan
SL	Schütte-Lanz airship factory
SLBM	submarine-launched ballistic missile
SNCA	Société Nationale de Constructions Aéronautiques (National Aircraft Building Company)
SOCONY	Standard Oil of New York
SOF	Special Operations Forces
SPS	Simplified Processing Station
SRBM	short-range ballistic missile
Staffeln	Luftwaffe squadrons
STC	Satellite Test Center
STOL	short takeoff and landing
SVAF	South Vietnamese Air Force
TAC	Tactical Air Command
TACAN	Tactical Air Navigation
TACC	Tactical Air Control Center
TBMs	tactical ballistic missiles
TEREC	tactical electronic reconnaissance sensor
TFA	Task Force Alpha
TOA	time-of-arrival
TOW	tube-launched, optically tracked, wired-guided missile
TsAGI	Tsentral'nyi Aero-Gidrodinamicheskii Institut (Central Aerodynamics and Hydrodynamics Institute, Soviet Union)
UAC	United Aircraft Corporation
UATC	United Aircraft and Transport Corporation
UAV	uninhabited aerial vehicle
UCAV	uninhabited combat aerial vehicle
UN	United Nations
USA	United States Army
USAAC	United States Army Air Corps
USAAF	United States Army Air Forces
USAF	United States Air Force
USAFE	United States Air Forces in Europe
USAFFE	United States Army Forces Far East
USMA	United States Military Academy
USN	United States Navy
USSR	Union of Soviet Socialist Republics
USTRANSCOM	United States Transportation Command
VC	Vietcong
VIP	very important person
VLF	very-low-frequency
VOR	Very High Frequency Omnidirectional Radio Station
VORTAC	a combination of VOR and TACAN
VSTOL	very short takeoff and landing
V/STOL	vertical/short takeoff and landing
VTOL	vertical takeoff and landing
VVS	Vozdushno-voennye Sily (Air Forces, Soviet Union)
WAAF	Women's Auxiliary Air Force
WAF	Women in the Air Force
WAFS	Women's Auxiliary Ferrying Squadron
WASP	Women Airforce Service Pilots
WDD	Western Development Division
WFTD	Woman's Flying Training Detachment
WPB	War Production Board
WRAF	Women's Royal Air Force
ZAT	territorial air zone
ZEL	zero-length launcher

AIR WARFARE

An International Encyclopedia

M

MacArthur, Douglas (1880–1964)

After his experience in World War I, Douglas MacArthur felt that the next war would be one of maneuver and movement, in which air superiority would be crucial. As air superiority grew in stature and importance, MacArthur's attitude evolved from skepticism to enthusiasm.

MacArthur formed and nurtured this attitude amid the controversy surrounding General Billy Mitchell and his probomber philosophy. As Army Chief of Staff, MacArthur exhibited a marked ambiguity toward aviation. On one hand, he acknowledged publicly and privately the importance of air supremacy for national defense, and he defended airmen against infantry and artillery officers hostile to the Air Corps and ignorant of airpower's potential. He also endorsed torpedo-planes, long-range bombers, and other innovations. On the other hand, MacArthur refused to consider creation of an independent air force, a separate promotion list for Air Corps officers, and increased appropriations for the Air Corps at the expense of other branches. MacArthur as yet had little understanding of airpower or what it could achieve.

MacArthur carried this ambivalence to his command as adviser to the Philippine army. From Manila, he pleaded for more aircraft while at the same time deemphasizing the advantage airpower might give Japan should it choose to attack the Philippines. MacArthur promised to use every cent he could spare from the Philippine defense budget to augment its air defenses, but when he received B-17s to reinforce the islands, he neither expanded existing airfields nor constructed new ones. MacArthur also did little to procure sufficient spare parts for the planes or to ensure their protection against Japanese attack—a decision that proved disastrous in January 1942 when Japan destroyed his air force on the ground. Having complete faith in Corregidor and his infantry, MacArthur took few steps to incorporate aircraft into his defensive scheme.

MacArthur's attitude toward airpower began to change during World War II. Under the tutelage of General George C. Kenney, his air commander, MacArthur came to realize that air supremacy held the key to all future operations. After his Guadalcanal and New Guinea experiences, MacArthur saw the war in the Pacific as a battle of logistics; his primary goal was the attainment of air superiority. Continuous, calculated application of airpower, he believed, would permit his land and sea forces to strike in swift, massive strokes, saving time and equipment and sparing American lives.

Once committed to this course, MacArthur educated himself about aircraft and pilots, learning what airmen could and could not accomplish, the impact of weather on air operations, and the effective range of his fighters and bombers. Kenney, Hap Arnold, and other prominent airmen believed that MacArthur acquired more knowledge about and made better use of his air units than any other field commander in the war.

By 1944, every MacArthur offensive centered on airpower. Barrages by B-17 bombers, defended by fighters, preceded each thrust. Seeking islands that could support air units, MacArthur urged his engineers to construct airfields and drones as soon as possible. MacArthur's enthusiasm for airpower became so strong that he eventually came to endorse the creation of a United States Department of Air Force—a reversal of his position when Army Chief of Staff.

MacArthur's confidence in airpower did not mean, however, that he believed that it alone would win the war against Japan. He remained committed to a combined arms philosophy; Japan could be defeated only by the integrated cooperation of land, sea, and air forces. Although acknowledging the contribution of air units to the war effort in the Southwest

Pacific, MacArthur doubted that strategic bombing, which remained unreliable, would succeed in breaking Japan's will or ability to fight. Securing air superiority, however, would position the United States for a land assault against Japan—an assault that MacArthur was convinced would be necessary to end the conflict.

Hiroshima and Nagasaki proved MacArthur wrong; he reacted to this ultimate extension of airpower with a combination of awe, disgust, and resignation. Atomic weapons promised to magnify the horrors of war beyond the limits of human imagination; the reality of nuclear annihilation made future wars unthinkable.

MacArthur became Supreme Commander of Allied occupation forces in Japan and was concerned about the growing power of communism in Asia. The Air Force was to be a central component of his strategy, but MacArthur's enthusiasm for airpower had not changed his conviction that, in the event of war, a combination of arms would win the day. The dropping of the atomic bomb shook, but did not topple, this faith.

When North Korea attacked South Korea, MacArthur did not share the confidence of the U.S. public and airmen who believed that the U.S. Fifth Air Force could stop the North Korean advance without the introduction of U.S. ground troops. Convinced that air action alone could not deter a mobile force determined to reach its objective, MacArthur urged the early deployment of U.S. Army units.

As commander in chief of the United Nations forces, MacArthur made effective use of air strength, working as he had during World War II to secure air supremacy before launching offensives. When China intervened, MacArthur recommended the bombing of bridges across the Yalu River and of Chinese bases in Manchuria—recommendations that ran afoul of the limited war envisaged by the Harry Truman administration and the United Nations. He later favored bombing China itself—a position that contributed to Truman's decision to remove him from command. Once back in the United States, MacArthur renewed his demands for strategic bombing against China. During the presidential election of 1952, MacArthur even proposed that the Air Force use atomic weapons against Chinese positions along the Sino-Korean border. MacArthur's proposal betrayed no real appreciation for the political, moral, military, or environmental consequences of nuclear attack and was ignored by president-elect Dwight Eisenhower and the Joint Chiefs of Staff. Yet it reflected the extent to which MacArthur's thinking about airpower had evolved over five decades of military service.

Daniel E. Worthington

See also

Air Superiority; Arnold, Henry H. "Hap"; Atomic Bomb; Bismarck Sea, Air Battle of; Eastern Solomons, Battle of; Guadalcanal; Hiroshima; Korean War; Mitchell, William; Nagasaki; Philippines; U.S. Army Air Corps; United States Army Aviation; World War II Aviation

References

Higgins, Trumbull. *Korea and the Fall of MacArthur: A Precis in Limited War.* New York: Oxford University Press, 1960.

Petillo, Carol Morris. *Douglas MacArthur: The Philippine Years.* Bloomington: Indiana University Press, 1981.

Schaller, Michael. *Douglas MacArthur: The Far Eastern General.* New York: Oxford University Press, 1989.

Macchi Aircraft (Aermacchi)

Originally Nieuport-Macchi, established in 1913 in northwestern Italy to build French Nieuport aircraft under license. During World War I, the company produced 840 Nieuport and more than 800 Hanriot fighters. Also manufactured were 731 seaplanes, including an outstanding single-seat fighter, 240 of which served in the Italian navy.

Emerging in the 1920s as Aeronautica Macchi, the company continued to emphasize seaplanes. In 1922, Mario Castoldi joined the company. Spurred by the Schneider Trophy competition, Castoldi designed a series of sleek racing seaplanes. Although completed too late for the final contest in 1931, the Macchi Castoldi 72 set a speed record in 1934 for piston-engine seaplanes (440.7 mph) that remains unbeaten.

In 1937, Macchi developed an all-metal monoplane fighter, the MC.200 Saetta (Lightning). Deliveries to the Italian air force began in the fall of 1939. Saetta production totaled 1,151. Armed with two 12.7mm heavy machine guns, the Saetta was exceptionally sturdy and featured outstanding maneuverability, finger-light control, and superb visibility. Maximum speed—312 mph at 14,750 feet—was limited by an 870-hp Fiat radial engine. The main Italian adversary in the Mediterranean Theater, the Hawker Hurricane, was faster than the Saetta but inferior to it in turn rate and diving speed.

Macchi turned to the German Daimler-Benz 601A liquid-cooled inline engine, which was eventually manufactured under license by Alfa-Romeo. Powered by this 1,075-hp engine, the streamlined MC.202 Folgore (Thunderbolt) entered service in November 1941. The Folgore, 1,005 of which were built, became the backbone of the Italian fighter forces. Production was severely limited by growing shortages of raw materials and difficulty in securing engines. As the conflict wore on, skilled Italian workers were drafted to labor in German factories. A maximum speed of 372 mph was attained at 18,370 feet. Maneuverability was superb and handling superlative. Armament remained light, although the twin heavy machine guns were augmented by two 7.7mm weapons in the wings.

The Folgore proved clearly superior to the Hurricane and the Curtiss Kittyhawk. The Italian fighter could even turn inside the Spitfire V, which could outclimb its opponent only above 15,000 feet.

Installation of a 1,475-hp engine enabled the MC.205 Veltro (Greyhound) to achieve 399 mph at 23,620 feet. Addition of two 20mm wing-mounted cannons brought armament to an acceptable standard. Only 262 Veltros were manufactured, of which 66 were in service when hostilities ceased.

Following World War II, Aermacchi became justly famous for a series of jet trainers and light attack warplanes. Designed by Ermanno Bazzocchi, the MB.326, powered by a Rolls-Royce Viper turbojet, entered service with the Italian air force in 1962. Some 800 MB.326s have served in 11 air arms and have been license-built in Australia, Brazil, and South Africa. A substantially improved MB.339 was developed in the 1970s, 100 of which are operational with the Italian air force. MB.339s are also in service in New Zealand, Argentina, Peru, Nigeria, Ghana, Dubai, and Malaysia. Aermacchi is indeed an illustrious and adaptable enterprise in the rich history of Italian aviation.

Sherwood S. Cordier

References

Braybrook, Roy. "Italian Excellence: A history of the Macchi/Aermacchi dynasty," *Air Enthusiast* (1993).

"Lightning from Lombardy." *Air Enthusiast* (January 1972).

"The Sprightly Saetta." *Air International* 13, 6 (December 1977): 284–291, 311–312.

MacDonald, Charles H. (1915–)

U.S. Army Air Forces colonel in the Pacific Theater during World War II. Holder of two Distinguished Service Crosses, MacDonald was the highest-scoring P-38 pilot (27 kills) to survive the war. He became the sixth-highest U.S. World War II ace and the fourth-highest AAF ace.

Charles Henry MacDonald, born in DuBois, Pennsylvania, was a 1938 graduate of Louisiana State University, where he studied philosophy. After taking an interest in flying, he joined the Army Air Corps; after training was assigned to fly the Curtiss P-36 with the 20th Pursuit Group, which was transferred to Hawaii before the Japanese attack on Pearl Harbor. MacDonald, leading a mixed unit of P-36s and Curtiss P-40s launched after the attack, was returning to Wheeler Field when shaken U.S. gunners fired flak at his group.

MacDonald was kept in Hawaii until 1943, when he was sent back to the United States to take over as commander of the 340th Fighter Squadron (flying Republic P-47s) of the 348th Group that was going to the South Pacific. In October 1943, MacDonald was assigned as executive officer of the Lockheed P-38–equipped 475th Fighter Group "Satan's Angels" after three uneventful months flying patrols with the 348th Group. On 15 October 1943, MacDonald and 50 P-38s engaged a large Japanese force attacking Allied shipping in Oro Bay. MacDonald attacked seven Aichi Val dive-bombers and shot down two for his first confirmed kills. His P-38 was badly damaged by a Mitsubishi Zero, and he was forced to make a belly landing back at the field. This battle cost the Japanese 36 aircraft without any losses to the Americans.

The events of 25 October 1943 earned MacDonald the first of two Distinguished Service Crosses. After all except his flight of eight P-38s turned back, the Consolidated B-24 force they were covering during a raid on Rabaul was attacked by Zeros. MacDonald's small flight saved a great many bombers from being shot down. MacDonald received one confirmed kill to bring his total to four. November 1943 saw Lieutenant Colonel MacDonald become commander of the 475th Group, a position he would hold for 20 months. By the summer of 1944, he was a double-ace.

During that time, Charles A. Lindbergh, the first person to solo across the Atlantic, made an extended visit to the 475th. Lindbergh's trip proved valuable because he showed the pilots that by setting the rpm low and the manifold pressure high the P-38s would consume less fuel and be able to extend their range by 50 percent, a procedure the Fifth Air Force widely adopted. By July Lindbergh had flown 25 missions with MacDonald, and they had become friends. On a 28 July "milk run," Lindbergh was nearly shot down, saved only by his skill as a pilot. Three days later, MacDonald shot down a Zero about to take out Lindbergh. General Paul Wurtsmith placed MacDonald on a 30-day punitive leave for endangering the American hero.

MacDonald returned to command the 475th Group in time for the liberation of the Philippines. On 7 December 1944, flying his P-38 *Putt-Putt Maru* on four sorties to protect Allied landing craft in Ormoc Bay, MacDonald shot down three Zeros in the first three sorties.

Between 10 November 1944 and 1 January 1945, MacDonald got 13 more Japanese kills and was able to score 27 confirmed before the war ended. (MacDonald finished second in terms of total victories in the 475th; Thomas B. McGuire had 38.) MacDonald retired as a colonel in 1966. He has been described as a rare combat leader, one who was able to inspire respect and loyalty from his troops while excelling in the air.

Scott R. DiMarco

See also

Consolidated B-24 Liberator; Lockheed P-38 Lightning

References
Frisbee, John L. "Super Ace." *Air Force Magazine* 76, 3 (March 1993).
Stanaway, John. *Possum, Clover, and Hades: The 475th Fighter Group in World War II.* Atglen, PA: Schiffer, 1995.

Mach, Ernst (1838–1916)

Philosopher-scientist. Ernst Mach was born in Chirlitz (today Brno in the Czech Republic) on 18 February 1838. He received a Ph.D. in physics from the University of Vienna in 1860 and taught at several universities in Austria-Hungary. In 1861, he proved the existence of the acoustical Doppler effect and suggested that it could help determine the relative speed of stars, thus ushering in the field of spectral astronomy.

His contribution to knowledge of the speed of sound carried on into the 1870s and concluded in 1886, when, having undertaken the study of fast-flying projectiles (he wondered about the apparent explosion of bullets after they left the cannon), he produced the first photograph of a projectile flying at the speed of sound. In the context of his life's work in physics, applied psychology, and philosophy, Mach's work on the speed of sound is small, yet it contributed greatly to the fields of speed photography, ballistics measurement, and aerodynamics. Mach retired from teaching in 1901 and moved to his son Luwdig's house at Vaterstetten (near Munich), where he died on 19 February 1916.

Guillaume de Syon

See also
Busemann, Adolf

References
Blackmore, John T. *Ernst Mach: His Work, Life, and Influence.* Berkeley: University of California Press, 1972.
Hoffmann, Dieter, and Hubert Laitko, eds. *Ernst Mach.* Berlin: DVW, 1991.

Magic

Name of U.S. project during World War II to break Japanese signal codes, specifically the so-called Purple, or diplomatic, code. The term has sometimes been applied to all attempts to break Japanese military codes and even (incorrectly) all World War II code-breaking.

The Purple code was broken in 1941 by the Army's Signal Intelligence Service, headed by William Friedman. Though revisionist history suggests that the Roosevelt administration knew (thanks to code-breaking) about the Pearl Harbor attack in advance, in fact military planners could only tell from code decrypts that Japan was about to make an aggressive move—but not what or where. Two well-known episodes where Magic code-breaking did have immediate operational impact took place early in the war. U.S. naval force commanders knew Japanese plans for the mid-1942 invasion of Midway (and Japan's hopes of luring out and destroying what remained of the U.S. fleet) thanks to the exhausting code-breaking efforts of Joseph Rochfort and his Hawaii-based Navy team. The ensuing battle, with great Japanese carrier and aircraft losses, was the turning point of the Pacific War. In April 1943, U.S. P-38 fighters, alerted by code-breaking of messages announcing his schedule and flight path, shot down the commander of the Japanese navy, Admiral Isoroku Yamamoto, as his aircraft neared a base in the Solomon Islands.

During and after both events, strong effort was made to divert Japanese suspicions regarding the sanctity of their codes. Japanese efforts against U.S. codes during the war were largely unsuccessful.

Christopher H. Sterling

See also
Signals Intelligence; Ultra

References
Budiansky, Stephen. *Battle of Wits: The Complete Story of Codebreaking in World War II.* New York: Free Press, 2000.
Kreis, John F., ed. *Piercing the Fog: Intelligence and Army Air Force Operations in World War II.* Washington, DC: Air Force History and Museum Program, 1996.

Magnetic Anomaly Detection

Detection of submarines from the air by the changes they induce in the earth's magnetic field. When present in or passing through an area, submarines distort the marine magnetic field; sensors track submarines by pinpointing and measuring these anomalies. Magnetic anomaly detection (MAD) is one of the most prevalent nonacoustic techniques of submarine detection.

Magnetic anomaly detection had its genesis during World War I. Seeking alternatives to hydrophones, U.S. scientists in 1917 began experimenting with magnetic detectors. In 1918, scientists and engineers at the New London Experiment Station tested a magnetic device attached to a naval vessel. These initial tests proved disappointing; the detector's range was too limited, and it experienced difficulty in divorcing itself from the towing ship's magnetic signature and, consequently, in distinguishing the source of magnetic variance. Navy officials deemed magnetic detection impracticable and shelved it in favor of sonar.

World War II revived interest in magnetic anomaly detection. Aircraft needed a way to track a submerged submarine; magnetic detection offered a possible means. Advances in electromagnetism promised to eliminate the technical limitations that had hampered World War I devices, and innovations in aerodynamics made a marriage between aircraft and magnetic detectors feasible. In June 1942, the U.S. Navy established Project Sail to undertake research and airborne testing associated with magnetic anomaly detection. Utilizing magnetometers designed for mineral exploration, scientists succeeded in developing the magnetic airborne (anomaly) detector. Early air trials proved promising; by the end of 1942, 200 sets of MAD gear were in service. By 1943, most antisubmarine warfare (ASW) patrol aircraft were equipped with MAD equipment.

Scientists and Navy officials believed that magnetic anomaly detection would supplant sonar as the primary means of detecting submerged submarines. Faith in MAD proved unfounded; magnetic detectors in practice were found to have limited usefulness. Essentially a shallow-water weapon, MAD devices worked well in the Mediterranean and the Straits of Gibraltar but had trouble detecting and tracking submarines in the deeper waters of the Atlantic. Limited range proved to be an insoluble problem; MAD gears were useful only when directly above or very near their targets, making it impossible to find moving U-Boats or stationary vessels at a distance. Magnetic detectors also found it difficult to determine the exact source of anomalies in the marine magnetic field—a difficulty shared by the post–World War II generation of MAD systems. By the war's end, Navy officials had joined MAD with radar and sonobuoys; MAD became secondary to sonobuoys in this configuration, the reverse of what experts had anticipated.

Magnetic anomaly detection has received considerable attention in the decades since World War II. Funding for research and development increased during the Cold War, with advances in system range, sensitivity, and effectiveness. Modern U.S. ASW aircraft are equipped with either the AN/ASQ-81 MAD system or the more sophisticated AN/ASQ-208.

MAD has as yet to supplant sonar, and its future does not appear promising. Intrinsically short-range systems, MAD sensors remain best suited for localization and targeting. Improving the detective range of MAD systems has proven difficult. Innovations in submarine construction, including the use of nonmagnetic metals and degaussing, threaten MAD's future as a useful detection device.

Daniel E. Worthington

See also

Antisubmarine Warfare; Radar

References

Price, Alfred. *Aircraft Versus Submarine: The Evolution of the Anti-Submarine Aircraft, 1912–1980.* London: Jane's Information Group, 1980.

Terraine, John. *The U-Boat Wars, 1916–1945.* New York: G. P. Putnam's Sons, 1989.

Malaya, Battles of (1941–1942)

As the probability of war with Japan grew in late 1941, the British moved the battleship *Prince of Wales* and battlecruiser *Repulse* to the Malayan base of Singapore to establish a significant, and hopefully deterrent, naval presence. It was intended that the capital ships be accompanied by the carrier *Indomitable,* but when Japan attacked Malaya in December, *Indomitable* was still undergoing repairs in Jamaica. Air defense of Malaya fell upon assorted RAF squadrons of Blenheim and Hudson bombers, Buffalo fighters, and obsolete Vildebeest biplane torpedo-bombers.

On 8 December, *Prince of Wales, Repulse,* and their escorts moved northward to intercept Japanese transports carrying troops to invade the eastern coast of the Malay Peninsula. RAF squadrons operating from land bases were to provide air cover, but this was poorly coordinated and ultimately failed. The Japanese 22d Naval Air Flotilla based in French Indochina found and attacked the British squadron with a force of more than 60 G3M2 Nell and G4M1 Betty bombers. *Prince of Wales* and *Repulse* took multiple bomb and torpedo hits and both sank, dealing a devastating blow to the British naval strength in the East.

The location of Allied bases was well-known; given the lack of an effective early warning system, many Allied aircraft were destroyed on the ground in a series of raids. Available RAF aircraft were no match for the advanced Japanese aircraft committed to the campaign, and Japan quickly won control of the air. Japanese forces advancing on the ground took over developed air bases in northern Malaya, such as at Alor Star, allowing Japanese air groups to base close to the front and in turn aiding further advances. Commonwealth forces were forced to move mainly at night and were quickly pushed down the peninsula.

RAF Hurricanes arrived as reinforcements in late January. These aircraft, with the remaining Buffalos, conducted defensive operations over Singapore, but attrition gradually reduced this force to insignificance. Commonwealth forces on Singapore surrendered on 15 February, ending the campaign.

The naval portion of the campaign highlights the difficulty of coordinating land-based air cover for surface fleets in World War II, as well as the futility of attempting surface naval operations in the face of enemy air superiority. The Japanese outperformed the Allies in the air in every way in Malaya and showed the high level of proficiency they possessed at this early point in the war.

Frank E. Watson

References

Falk, Stanley L. *Seventy Days to Singapore, 1941–1942.* New York: G. P. Putnam's Sons, 1975.

Malta, Siege of

British possession sitting astride the routes from Gibraltar to Alexandria and from Italy to Africa. Axis and Allied leaders recognized the importance of Malta early in World War II, and the Axis launched an effort to bomb it into submission. Fortunately for the Allies, the Regia Aeronautica (Italian air force) was assigned the task; it had no notable success, even though only three obsolete Gloster Gladiators defended the island. The fighters—*Faith, Hope,* and *Charity*—resisted stoutly while the Maltese climbed to their rooftops to watch the show. In early 1941, the Luftwaffe arrived to assist the Italians, and the Maltese quickly abandoned their rooftops for air-raid shelters. Hitler diverted Luftwaffe forces to the invasion of the Soviet Union, but in December 1941 the Germans returned. Casualties on Malta mounted while supplies ran short, and by July 1942 the island was nearing capitulation. Malta became the most heavily bombed place in the world.

The British made many attempts to reinforce Malta. On one attempt the British lost nine of 14 Hurricanes due to miscalculation of the fighters' range. The U.S. aircraft carrier *Wasp* ferried Spitfires to Malta in April 1942. Forty-six of 48 arrived, but the Luftwaffe and inadequate ground support virtually eliminated them. A second effort in May delivered 61 of 63 Spitfires, and improved ground support prevented the Luftwaffe from catching them on the ground. Though Malta now had an effective air defense, supplies continued to run low.

In June 1942, a resupply convoy was forced to turn back without delivering supplies to Malta, seemingly confirming German Field Marshal A. C. Kesselring's May announcement that Malta was neutralized. However, the British made one last major effort. In July, Operation PEDESTAL came through with enough cargo to keep Malta alive, even allowing Malta to take the offensive against Axis supply lines to Africa. With the British victory at El Alamein, momentum in the Mediterranean shifted to the Allies. Despite a renewed air offensive by Kesselring, the loss of its Libyan airfields crippled the Luftwaffe's efforts. The siege of Malta was officially raised in May 1943 following the surrender of Axis forces in North Africa.

Grant Weller

See also

German Air Force (Luftwaffe); Gloster Gladiator; Kesselring, Albert; Mediterranean Theater of Operations; PEDESTAL; Regia Aeronautica (World War II); Supermarine Spitfire

References

Cameron, Ian. *Red Duster, White Ensign.* New York: Doubleday, 1960.

Manned Orbiting Laboratory (MOL)

An ambitious U.S. Air Force program, canceled in 1969, to construct a manned space station. A dedicated launch site at Vandenberg Air Force Base (SLC-6) was completed before the program was canceled. The station was to be orbited from Cape Canaveral or Vandenberg by a modified Titan III launch vehicle. Crews would use modified Gemini space capsules to travel to and from the station. A mockup of the MOL station was launched from Cape Canaveral during the Titan III development flights to verify the flightworthiness of the design. The capsule used during the unmanned Gemini 2 mission was refurbished to the MOL configuration and relaunched on the same flight to verify the modifications did not effect its reentry characteristics.

Although it was expected that MOL would develop into an operational system, the first few flights were intended to demonstrate various technologies necessary for the Air Force mission. Experiments planned ranged from military reconnaissance using large optical cameras and side-looking radar, to interception and inspection of satellites, to exploration of the usefulness of man in space and the testing of manned maneuvering units.

After MOL was canceled, the basic structure and reconnaissance systems developed for the station were used in the design of the Keyhole 11 spy satellites. Some of the experiments originally designed for MOL were subsequently performed by NASA astronauts on the Skylab missions.

Dennis R. Jenkins

Mannock, Edward (1887–1918)

British World War I ace. Edward "Mick" Mannock started the war in an unusual way. He had been working as a civilian in Turkey and was interned. Repatriated because of his health, Mannock returned to England.

After a stint with the Royal Engineers, Mannock transferred to aviation, becoming James McCudden's pupil. In April 1917, he went to No. 40 Squadron but was slow to score. Once begun, however, his tally sheet climbed steadily, and he developed into an outstanding fighter pilot. In February 1918, with his score at 16, he was made a flight commander on No. 74 Squadron, flying SE.5as.

In Tiger Squadron, as it later became known, Mannock's abilities as a leader won him the undying loyalty of his men. This became important following the war, when controversy developed over the identity of the British ace of aces. Mannock had claimed 61 victories during the war, but his biographer and squadronmate, Ira "Taffy" Jones, elevated that number to 73, putting him one ahead of Canadian ace Billy Bishop. Given the debate over Bishop's score, the matter is still open to question.

Mannock was in command of No. 85 Squadron when he fell to ground fire on 26 July 1918. He was posthumously awarded the Victoria Cross.

James Streckfuss

References

Jones, Ira T. *King of Air Fighters.* London: Ivor Nicholson and Watson, 1934.

Shores, Christopher, Norman Franks, and Russell Guest. *Above the Trenches.* London: Grub Street, 1990.

Mao Tse-tung (1893–1976)

During the Long March (October 1934–October 1936), Mao Tse-tung's communist Chinese Red Army was assaulted by Nationalist (Kuomintang) airpower, and Mao learned that guerrilla forces needed protection from air attacks. Mao's views on airpower can be found in his numerous instructions to commanders and in the organization of the People's Liberation Army Air Force (PLAAF). After the Long March, Mao called for flight training in Xinjiang Province, where the pro-Soviet governor had a Soviet Russian air academy.

When Japan surrendered in 1945, Mao established his first air academy using captured Japanese aircraft and Japanese POWs. After founding the People's Republic of China in 1949, Mao established seven aviation schools. The Korean War was the PLAAF's first modern war and caused Mao to reflect on the importance of airpower and implement three principles of operation for the Chinese People's Volunteer Air Force, which were drafted by air force commander General Liu Yalou to reflect Mao's views: (1) Gain strength through the experience of war; (2) serve the land forces (all actions of the volunteer air force supported the victory of land forces, not vice versa); and (3) develop small encounters into large battles (use tactical air units from airfields inside Chinese territory; use opportunities to fight small engagements to gain experience; rotate air divisions for experience at the front; attain 100–150 operational aircraft; and deploy concentrated forces in air battle).

Attempts to provide forward airfields in North Korea were abandoned after repeated United Nations air attacks convinced Mao that control of the air was essential; in the Taiwan Strait Crisis of 1958, Mao called for greater attention to control of the air. After 1959, the Nationalist air force stopped bombing mainland coastal cities and began high-altitude reconnaissance over the mainland. Mao ordered interceptors and surface-to-air missile units to annihilate the enemy. Between 1959 and 1965, China shot down a total of 73 aircraft, including RB-57D, one P-2V, four U-2 reconnaissance aircraft and remotely piloted vehicles, and damaged another 173 aircraft.

Mao identified the basic tasks of the PLAAF as air defense and air support but never discussed an independent strategic air force. During the 41 years of Mao's leadership, he and the military high command rejected the strategic airpower theory of Giulio Douhet.

Hua Renjie with Richard C. DeAngelis

References

Lin, Hu. *The History of the Air Force.* Beijing: CPLA Armed Forces History, 1989.

Political Department of the Chinese Air Force. *The Blue Sky Voyage.* Beijing: no publ. avail., 1998.

Mareth Line, Battles of the (1943)

After defeat at El Alamein (October-November 1942) and Allied landings in French North Africa (November 1942) in Operation TORCH, Germany's Panzerarmee Afrika under General Erwin Rommel regrouped along the Tunisia-Libya frontier in old French fortifications called the Mareth Line.

In February 1943, Rommel attacked out of his Mareth Line positions but was soundly defeated by Allied armor and antitank forces, strongly supported by units of the Desert Air Force in the Battle of Medenine.

In March, units of Field Marshal Bernard Montgomery's Eighth Army outflanked the Mareth Line fortifications with a wide movement through the Matmata Hills in the south. This maneuver was possible in part because growing Allied air superiority hindered Axis air reconnaissance. Allied air interdiction also hampered the reaction of Axis armor to the flanking movement.

The battles at the Mareth Line saw the Desert Air Force, under Air Vice Marshal Harry Broadhurst, at the height of competence in support of ground operations. Hurricane

Mk.IID tank-busting aircraft were particularly effective in attacking German armor.

Frank E. Watson

See also

TORCH

References

Shores, Christopher. *Duel for the Sky: Ten Crucial Air Battles of World War II Vividly Recreated.* London: Grub Street, 1999.

Marine Corps

See U.S. Marine Corps Aviation

Marinelli, Jack L. (1917–1982)

U.S. Army colonel. Born in Ottumwa, Iowa, he joined the Iowa National Guard as a private in 1935, received his commission as a second lieutenant of cavalry in the Guard in 1938, and went on active duty two years later. Following training as a liaison pilot at Fort Sill, Oklahoma, in 1942, he served as the battalion air officer of the 72d Field Artillery in Italy and later as the artillery air officer of II Corps and U.S. Fifth Army.

In late 1945, he established the ground forces' first aircraft testing capability, the Light Aviation Section of Army Ground Forces Board No. 1 at Fort Bragg, North Carolina. As director he led the team of four pilots that qualified on the Bell Model 47 helicopter and conducted the testing when it was procured as the H-13. He became an enthusiastic proponent of the future of rotary-wing aircraft and their military uses. One of the senior officers he convinced was his next-door neighbor, Major General James M. Gavin. In 1947, Marinelli became the second officer to be awarded the rating of Master Army Aviator.

When the Korean War started, Marinelli was chief of Army Aviation in the Office of Army Field Forces. He played a large role in the acquisition and training of Army aviation personnel in the hasty mobilization that followed. He was heavily involved in the procurement of new aircraft, coordinated the activation and training of the Army's first transportation helicopter companies, and, to meet the urgent need for an organic aeromedical evacuation capability in theater, supervised the accelerated activation, training, and deployment of the first helicopter detachments, forerunners of the first helicopter ambulance companies. These detachments became famous for evacuating thousands of frontline casualties and established the utility and survivability of helicopters in combat.

In 1952, he became the aviation officer at General Headquarters, Far Eastern Theater, overseeing the creation of the 1st Division Aviation Company (Provisional). In 1955, he became the chief aviation staff officer in the Office of the Deputy Chief of Staff for Logistics on the Army Staff. Three years later he became president of the Army Aviation Board, a position that he held until his retirement in 1962. While president of the board, he qualified as a Navy jet pilot and was the first U.S. officer to fly and test the NATO Light Weight Fighter, the Fiat G-91.

A noted combat pilot in fixed-wing liaison aircraft during World War II, Marinelli became an advocate of helicopters not only to perform the traditional Army aviation missions but to transport men and materiel in the combat area. He was one of the central figures in the group of field-grade officers who attempted to expand the missions of Army aviation following World War II.

Upon retiring from the Army Marinelli became vice president for research and development for Beech Aircraft, where he continued his strong influence on new aircraft.

Edgar F. Raines Jr. and Robert R. Williams

Reference:

Bergerson, Frederic A. *The Army Gets an Air Force: Tactics of Insurgent Bureaucratic Politics.* Baltimore: Johns Hopkins University Press, 1980.

Cheng, Christopher C.S. *Air Mobility: The Development of a Doctrine.* Westport, CT: Praeger, 1994.

Raines, Edgar F. Jr. *Eyes of Artillery: The Origins of Modern U.S. Army Aviation in World War II.* Army Historical Series. Washington, DC: Center of Military History, Department of the Army, 2000.

MARKET-GARDEN (1944)

Allied code name for airborne operation to open a direct route through Holland and advance into Germany following the invasion of continental Europe. By the autumn of 1944, Allied forces had broken out of the beachhead established that June on D-Day and were making plans for a direct assault on the German homeland. British Field Marshall Bernard Montgomery had come up with a daring plan that called for an airborne assault to seize the bridges along the main north-south road through the Netherlands and open the door for a rapid ground assault by the British Second Army. The final objective was Arnhem—a 60-mile jump into German-held territory. Once across the bridge there, the British would be beyond the Rhine River, with open country between them and Berlin.

The operation called for the ground assault to be made by the British XXX Corps. In advance of the XXX Corps troops, the U.S. 101st Airborne Division was to be dropped on canal crossings between Eindhoven and Veghel, the U.S. 82d Airborne Division on the bridges over the Mass and Waal Rivers. The British 1st Airborne Division and the Polish 1st Airborne Brigade were to be dropped at Arnhem to capture the key bridges over the Rhine.

The massive airborne landings began on the morning of 17 September 1944. The two U.S. divisions largely accomplished their goals. However, the British paradrop and glider landing zones were too far from the Arnhem bridges, permitting an assault on only the northern end of the bridge. The remnants of 9th and 10th SS Panzer Divisions were refitting in the area and reacted quickly and violently. The British airborne troops soon found themselves surrounded by German troops. At the same time, XXX Corps failed to advance fast enough to link up with now beleaguered paratroopers, who held out for nine days and nights, a week longer than the plan called for. On 24 September, the order was given to withdraw.

Of more than 10,000 British troops parachuted and glider-landed at Arnhem, only 2,398 escaped across the river; some 1,400 died, and more than 6,000, half of whom were wounded, became prisoners of war.

MARKET-GARDEN was a failure because it depended on ground forces being able to attack on much too narrow a front, making it extremely vulnerable to German attacks from the flanks. The plan was overly ambitious and built around erroneous assumptions about German strength in the area. MARKET-GARDEN was a high-risk operation that in the end proved very costly for the Allied war effort and dashed hopes that the war could be finished in 1944.

James H. Willbanks

See also

Parachutes

References

Ryan, Cornelius. *A Bridge Too Far.* New York: Simon and Schuster, 1974.

Marseille, Hans-Joachim (1919–1942)

The most successful Luftwaffe fighter pilot in World War II. Even the legendary fighter pilot Adolf Galland called "Jochen" Marseille "the unsurpassed virtuoso among fighter pilots." An officer candidate before the war, his poor disciplinary record delayed his commission until 1941, despite moderate success in the Battle of Britain in 1940—he shot down seven RAF aircraft but was himself shot down four times. In early 1941, he was transferred to the 1st Group of Jagdgeschwader 27 (27th Fighter Wing) in North Africa, where an understanding commander gave him full rein to develop his talents. Marseille soon began to score regularly against the RAF and became renowned in the theater for total command of his aircraft and for his unerring aim. His skill as a deflection shooter allowed him to score as often as targets presented themselves—he could dive into the middle of a defensive circle of RAF fighters and totally destroy it. He once shot down eight RAF fighters in 10 minutes, a day in which he claimed 17 victories in three combat sorties. He was promoted to captain and given command of a *staffel* (squadron), whose primary mission was to fly high cover for Marseille. On 3 September 1942, he became the fourth member of the Wehrmacht to receive the Oak Leaves with Swords and Diamonds to the Knight's Cross of the Iron Cross from Adolf Hitler. Less than a month later he was dead. The engine of his new fighter seized while he was returning from a mission; Marseille struck its tail while bailing out and fell to the ground with an unopened parachute. His final victory total was 154 fighters and four bombers; all of his victims were from the Royal Air Force or the South African Air Force.

Donald Caldwell

See also

German Air Force (Luftwaffe)

References

Obermeier, E. *Die Ritterkreuztraeger der Luftwaffe, 1939–1945, Band 1: Jagdflieger* [Recipients of the Knight's Cross]. Mainz: Verlag Dieter Hoffmann, 1989.

Marshall Islands (1943–1944)

Site of air operations in preparation for and support of Allied amphibious invasion. Using newly won bases in the Gilbert Islands, Allied land-based airpower attacked Japanese installations in the Marshalls throughout December 1943 and January 1944. Carrier planes joined on January 29 operating from six heavy, five light, and numerous escort carriers. On 30 January, U.S. forces landed on the outlying islands of Kwajalein, the main atoll in the Marshall chain, and on Kwajalein proper on 1 February (Operation FLINTLOCK). The entire atoll was secure by 7 February with far lighter casualties than suffered in the Gilberts.

Allied carrier forces withdrew for other operations against Truk before the airfield on Kwajalein reopened and a Japanese air raid from Saipan caused much damage ashore.

Glenn L. Martin was always attentive to the needs of the U.S. Navy. Here a seemingly nonchalant parachutist stands on the wing of a T3M torpedo plane. (U.S. Navy)

Over several days, carrier-based attacks, combined with planes of Seventh Air Force in the Gilberts, destroyed Japanese bases on Truk and Ponape. Operations against Enewetak in the western Marshalls began on 17 February (Operation CATCHPOLE); preinvasion air bombardment seemed particularly effective. Islands not suitable for the construction of air bases were left in Japanese hands, as were islands with airfields whose operation could be suppressed from Kwajalein and Enewetak.

As in the Gilberts previously, in the Marshalls Japanese land-based airpower was unable to react to the concentration of carrier-based air strength in the time or force necessary to affect the outcome. Allied possession of the Marshalls penetrated the outer Japanese defensive line, compromised the major Japanese air and naval base at Truk, and paved the way for the reduction of that base and the invasion of the Marianas, themselves important as bases for beginning a strategic bombing campaign against Japan.

Frank E. Watson

References

Morison, Samuel Eliot. *United States Naval Operations in World War II, Volume 3: The Aleutians, Gilberts, and Marshalls.* Boston: Little, Brown, 1951.

Martin Aircraft

U.S. aircraft manufacturer. Glenn L. Martin taught himself to fly in 1909 at the age of 22 and set up his first aircraft company in 1912 in California. He was successful with a series of tractor-engine training types and was adept at attracting talented people to work for him, including Donald Douglas, Lawrence Bell, James S. McDonnell, Charles Day, Charles Willard, and James "Dutch" Kindelberger.

In 1917, Martin moved to Cleveland, where he built a new plant and on 17 January 1918 received a contract for a twin-engine four-place reconnaissance/bomber, the Glenn Martin Bomber. Although large orders were contemplated, only 10 were procured because of the Armistice. With two 400-hp Liberty engines, the aircraft had a top speed of 118 mph, which was far superior to the performance of either the German Gotha or the British Handley Page O/400.

The design was further developed into the MB-2 and subsequently the NBS-1, and 150 were procured. The aircraft gained fame due to its participation in the battleship-bombing trials led by Brigadier General William Mitchell.

Martin next developed a long line of aircraft for the U.S. Navy, including torpedo-planes, dive-bombers, and flying-boat patrollers. All of these were of conventional structure, but in 1932 the prototype of the revolutionary Martin B-10 bomber was rolled out. This twin-engine, all-metal cantilever monoplane had advanced features such as retractable gear, enclosed cockpits, and, later, the Norden bombsight. The B-10 became the most important bomber in the Army Air Corps, solidifying the concept of precision bombing and training most of the USAAF leaders of World War II.

Fame, if not financial success, was achieved with the beautiful Martin M-130 series of four-engine flying boats, led by the immortal China Clipper. Used by Pan American Airways, the Clippers established the first transpacific passenger service in 1935.

World War II saw Martin field a series of twin-engine bombers, including the Maryland, the Baltimore, and the Marauder. The latter initially had a bad reputation, but when modified and with proper training for pilots, it proved to be a highly capable combat aircraft, with the lowest loss record in Europe. Some 5,266 Marauders were built. During World War II, they flew 129,943 sorties, dropping 169,382 tons of bombs, but only 911 aircraft were lost in combat.

The firm also produced twin-engine PBM Mariner patrol planes that had a distinctive gull wing and twin vertical stabilizers. All of the Martin aircraft acquitted themselves well in combat. Martin also built 536 examples of the Boeing B-29 Superfortress.

The largest Martin piston-engine aircraft, the JRM-2 Mars, was produced in small numbers, but two are still in service as water-bombers fighting forest fires.

In the postwar years, Martin was less successful with its commercial airline and Navy designs. The 202 airliner had inherent design flaws that cut its career short, and the 404, though an excellent aircraft, failed to make money, with only 103 being produced. For the Navy, Martin built 152 AM Maulers, which resembled the Douglas AD Skyraider, and 21 four-engine P-4M Mercators, which resembled the Lockheed Neptune. Martin had greater success with the P-5M Marlin flying boat, of which 287 were built.

As he grew older, Glenn Martin became less politically adept and managed to alienate the Navy as well as the new U.S. Air Force. Two excellent designs, the P-6M Seamaster, a six-jet flying boat, and the XB-51, a three-jet attack aircraft, were not produced. The Seamaster fell victim to two accidents and the Navy's need to finance the Polaris program; the XB-51, despite its performance, did not find a role in the USAF. Instead, Martin was commissioned to build the English Electric Canberra as the B-57. It proved to be a long-lived, capable aircraft; 403 were built.

Martin then turned to the missile business and completed two major corporate mergers, becoming Martin Marietta and then Lockheed Martin. In October 2001, Lockheed Martin was awarded the largest U.S. defense contract in history—worth some $200 billion—to build the Joint Strike Fighter.

Albert Atkins

References

Wagner, Ray. *American Combat Planes.* London: MacDonald, 1960.

Martin B-10/B-12 Bomber

In the early 1930s, officials in the U.S. Army Air Corps contracted with the Glenn L. Martin Company of Baltimore to build a series of twin-engine, all-metal bombers with retractable landing gear. The resulting B-10/B-12 became the first modern bombers in the USAAC operational inventory. Faster than any fighters, they helped develop theories of unescorted precision daylight strategic bombing then germinating among U.S. airmen.

The prototype Model 123 first flew on 16 February 1932. Designated the XB-907, it reached speeds of 197 mph during July trials at Wright Field, Ohio. That fall it was returned to Martin for minor upgrades.

Following successful trials in October, the Army purchased the bomber on 17 January 1933 and designated it the XB-10. Army officials also ordered 48 production aircraft. The first 14 were YB-10s and had 675-hp Wright R-1820-25 engines. The YB-10s had transparent sliding canopies over the pilot's cockpit and over the rear gunner's position.

Martin completed delivery of 103 aircraft in August 1936. The B-10B had two Wright R-1820-33 775-hp engines. With a 71-foot wingspan and 45-foot length, it stood 15 feet high. Its gross weight was 16,400 pounds with a service ceiling of 24,200 feet and a range of 1,240 miles. Top speed was 213 mph, and it carried a bombload of 2,260 pounds.

The B-10/B-12s were popular among USAAC crews and a great success for Martin. In late 1932, Glenn L. Martin won the 1932 Collier Trophy for building the B-10.

The B-12As were powered by Pratt and Whitney R-1690-11 Hornet radial engines. The B-12, with its greater fuel capacity and ability to be fitted with large twin floats, took on the role of coastal defense.

In the late 1930s, the B-10/B-12s were generally replaced by Douglas B-18 Bolos and more modern four-engine Boeing B-17s. Although no USAAC B-10/B-12 ever saw combat, they did experience operational and public relations successes, such as Lieutenant Colonel Hap Arnold's B-10 Alaska survey mission of July 1934. They also set several aviation records for speed and range.

In August 1936, versions of the B-10 were demonstrated for foreign sale. Argentina bought 39 in 1936 and China bought six in 1937. Two of the Chinese planes made a

The designers at the Glenn L. Martin Company were initially slow to react to suggestions for a new bomber from Wright Field, but they eventually triumphed with the classic Martin B-10. (U.S. Air Force)

"leaflet" raid on Japan before all six were destroyed during the Japanese invasion in August 1937. The Soviet Union bought one, Siam (Thailand) bought six, and Turkey in 1937. Between September 1936 and May 1939, the Dutch bought 117 of the most modern versions for use in the East Indies. These saw combat against invading Japanese in the early 1940s.

Between 1933 and 1939, 189 export and 153 USAAC B-10/B-12/B-14s were produced and delivered. The only remaining B-10 was donated by the Argentine government to the U.S. government for display in the U.S. Air Force Museum in 1970. An export version, it was refurbished as a USAAC B-10B. It went on display in 1976.

William Head

References

Fahey, James C. *U.S. Army Aircraft, 1908–1946.* New York: Ships and Aircraft Books, 1946.

Jones, Lloyd S. *U.S. Bombers, 1928–1980s.* 4th ed. Fallbrook, CA: Aero, 1980.

Martin B-26 Marauder

U.S. bomber. In 1939, U.S. Army Air Corps officials ordered the B-26 Marauder medium bomber based on design alone. No prototypes were built prior to production. Martin's Baltimore plant built 201 of this original design. The first aircraft flew on 25 November 1940, and the 22d Bomb Group in Langley, Virginia, received the first four Marauders in February 1941.

The original B-26 was powered by two Pratt and Whitney R-2800 radial engines that generated 1,850 horsepower. It had a wingspan of 65 feet, a fuselage 56 feet long, 32,000-pound maximum weight, and a crew of seven. It had a maximum speed of 315 mph and a range of 1,000 miles with a maximum bombload of 3,000 pounds.

The Marauder had a troubled developmental history, due in part to a lack of pilot familiarity and unique features such as its small wing area. Although later models eventually overcame these minor design flaws and had a stellar career, early pilots called the B-26, among other derogatory things, the "Widowmaker."

Eventually, Martin produced 12 additional models, including the CB-26B cargo version and the TB-26B, TB-26C, and TB-26G trainers. The A model was essentially a minor revision of the B-26. The major change saw 109 of the 139 A models fitted with R-2800-39 radial engines and designated B-26A-1. Fifty-two A models were sold to the Royal Air Force.

The B models were originally purchased in four blocks, each having various and unique modifications, including armament upgrades, nose-gear improvements, and larger carburetor intakes. Later, 1,242 additional B models were also produced, adding among other things better forward armaments, longer wings (71 feet), and new R-2800-43 engines.

The B-26Cs were B-26Bs built in Martin's new Omaha, Nebraska, plant. The first B-26C Block 5 rolled out in August 1942 followed by 1,210 C models and 300 AT-26B trainers. The RAF received 123 C models. An additional 615 C models on contract when the war ended were canceled.

The F model was a modification of 300 B-26B-55-MAs that improved wing performance during takeoff. The RAF received 200 F models. The last production model was the B-26G. Martin built 1,100, including 57 TB-26G trainers for the USAAF and 150 for the RAF. This model was the same as the F model with minor internal changes. One XB-26H was built to test tandem landing gears. It was the last of 5,157 Marauders built by Martin by March 1945.

Although not as famous as its B-25 cousin, the B-26 served with distinction in every major theater of World War II as a first-rate medium attack bomber. During World War II, B-26s flew 129,943 sorties, dropped 169,382 tons of bombs, and downed 402 enemy aircraft; 911 B-26s were lost.

William Head

References

Gunston, William. *Bombers of the West.* New York: Scribner, 1973.
Swanborough, Gordon, and Peter M. Bowers. *U.S. Military Aircraft Since 1909.* Washington, DC: Smithsonian Institution Press, 1989.

Martin-Baker Aircraft

British aircraft firm established by James Martin in 1929 as Martin's Aircraft Works; in 1934, Valentine Baker joined the firm to create Martin-Baker Aircraft. The MB.1 was a two-seat cabin monoplane that flew in March 1935 but had no sales and was destroyed in 1938.

The MB.2 was a single-seat fighter designed for the British F.5/34 specification, powered by a Napier Dagger rated at 1,020 shp. It used tubular construction like the MB.1 and had fixed spatted landing gear. It mounted eight machine guns in the wings and had a top speed of 320 mph. Although the MB.2 had excellent maintainability and performance, no sales were obtained.

Three prototypes of the single-seat MB.3 started design in June 1939 to fighter specification F.18/39, featuring a six-cannon wing. The Rolls-Royce Griffon engine had been selected but was not made available, and Martin had to redesign the MB.3 for the Napier Sabre of 2,020 shp. Structure was bolted tubing and stressed skin, and steel was used in the fuselage structure, with spar/rib structure of duralumin in the wing. It flew on 31 August 1942; after that flight, a cut-down rear fuselage and bubble canopy were installed. It crashed on 12 September 1942, killing Valentine Baker.

The fuselage of the second prototype was significantly redesigned for the Griffon II engine of 2,305 shp with a contrarotating propeller. It used concepts from the P-51D Mustang but kept the same basic structure as the first prototype, with the same excellent maintainability. It flew on 23 May 1944 and, after an increase in fin, rudder, and stabilizer size, was considered by all that flew it to be the best-performing fighter aircraft in their experience. Flight testing continued into 1947, but none was procured.

Martin-Baker had sustained itself by taking contracts for miscellaneous aircraft equipment, and although it built no additional aircraft, it developed a line of ejection seats that gained a strong worldwide market.

Douglas G. Culy

References

Green, William, and Gordon Swanborough. *The Complete Book of Fighters.* London: Salamander, 1994.
Gunston, Bill. "Martin-Baker Fighters." *Wings of Fame* 9 (London: Aerospace, 1997), pp. 150–157.

Martini, Wolfgang (1891–1963)

Luftwaffe general; carries the unique distinction of holding a single position for the entire history of the Luftwaffe. Martini joined the German army as a telegraph officer in 1910 and was involved in communications for all of his 35 years of military service and an 18-year postwar career. He joined the still-secret Luftwaffe in 1933, became chief of its Signals Office in 1934, and retained that post until V-E Day. He reached his final rank of lieutenant general in 1941. He can fairly be judged to have been successful at his job. The Luftwaffe began and ended the war with the best radio navigation aids in the world and held its own in the radar wars with RAF Bomber Command despite a lack of resources and the well-documented fragmentation of its research efforts in all technical fields.

After the war, Martini played an important role in the reconstruction of West Germany's aviation and shipping industries, for which he was awarded the Great Service Cross in 1959 by the German government. He remained active in the German Society for Location and Navigation until his death in 1963.

Donald Caldwell

See also

German Air Force (Luftwaffe); Radar and How It Works

References
Theissen, B. "Lebenslauf General Martini" in German. Available online at http://mitglied.tripod.de/therapist/marti.htm.

Massive Retaliation

The concept of retaliating with nuclear weapons at a time and place of U.S. choosing in response to Soviet aggression during the Cold War. The prospect of such an asymmetrical response would, it was hoped, deter communist expansion around the globe without having to meet each individual threat via conventional means. Though the emphasis in public was on deterrence and retaliation, in private U.S. military officials also hoped that, should a war occur, the United States would be able to strike the Soviet Union so hard that a Soviet nuclear response could be severely curtailed or even prevented altogether.

The phrase *massive retaliation* was popularized during the furor in the press that followed a January 1954 address by Secretary of State John Foster Dulles to the Council on Foreign Relations. In his speech Dulles argued that "the way to deter aggression is for the free community to be willing and able to respond vigorously at places and with means of its own choosing," which would allow "our military establishment to fit what is *our* policy, instead of having to try to be ready to meet the enemy's many choices." This would therefore provide "more basic security at less cost," or what would later be called "more bang for the buck." Though Dulles's own thinking had actually become far less bellicose in recent months, one statement—that to accomplish all this the United States would have to "depend primarily upon a great capacity to retaliate instantly"—was interpreted by many to mean that the United States might use nuclear weapons in response to even a relatively minor provocation. In April, Dulles tried to clarify his message, and the Eisenhower administration's "New Look" at defense policy in general, in an article in the journal *Foreign Affairs.* In it he emphasized the importance of massive retaliation in deterring a general war with the Soviet Union and stated that while the threat should also prove useful in deterring localized aggression, in such cases the use of nuclear weapons would not be automatic. The article, however, received far less attention than the original speech had, and the phrase *massive retaliation* continued to connote to many a dangerous overreliance on nuclear weapons.

As the overwhelming U.S. strategic nuclear advantage of the early 1950s gradually withered away, criticism of massive retaliation within the policymaking elite grew. Though the nuclear playing field was still by no means level, as the Soviet capability to inflict massive damage on the United States grew, the threat that the United States would initiate nuclear war to prevent aggression on the periphery seemed more and more hollow. Crises such as those in the Taiwan Strait (1954–1955, 1958) seemed to confirm that U.S. nuclear brinkmanship might ultimately prove ineffective, reckless, or both. President Dwight D. Eisenhower reluctantly began moving toward larger conventional forces during his second term, and once John F. Kennedy assumed the presidency in 1961 the public emphasis on massive retaliation was over. Its role in deterring localized aggression was replaced by Kennedy's determination to "support any friend" and "oppose any foe," to be implemented by its new policy of flexible response. Massive retaliation's seat at the ideological core of nuclear deterrence was ultimately filled by the emerging concept of mutual assured destruction.

David Rezelman

See also
Atomic Bomb; Cold War; Missiles, Intercontinental Ballistic; Mutual Assured Destruction; Strategic Air Command

References
Bowie, Robert R., and Richard H. Immerman. *Waging Peace: How Eisenhower Shaped an Enduring Cold War Strategy.* Oxford, UK: Oxford University Press, 1998.
Dulles, John Foster. "Policy for Security and Peace." *Foreign Affairs* 32 (April 1954): 353–364.
Rosenberg, David Alan. "The Origins of Overkill: Nuclear Weapons and American Strategy." In Norman A. Graebner, ed., *The National Security: Its Theory and Practice, 1945–1960.* New York: Oxford University Press, 1986, pp. 123–195.

Mayaguez Incident

The last significant United States action of the long conflict in Southeast Asia. On 12 May 1975, elements of the Cambodian navy seized an American merchant ship, SS *Mayaguez,* in international waters off Cambodia's coast. Upon notification, U.S. President Gerald Ford insisted that this not become another *Pueblo* Incident—the international crisis that developed when North Korea seized the SS *Pueblo* in 1968.

As there were no significant U.S. military forces or warships in the area, the president ordered the carrier *Coral Sea* and destroyers *Holt* and *Wilson* to steam at full speed to the Gulf of Thailand. Meanwhile, U.S. Air Force and Navy planes from the Philippines took off to find the *Mayaguez.* The ship was sighted by the crew of a P-3. It was anchored off Koh Tang Island, 40 miles from the Cambodian shore.

An Air Force task force of HH-53 and CH-53 helicopters of the 40th Aerospace Rescue and Recovery Squadron and the 21st Special Operations Squadron was dispatched to U Tapao Air Base in Thailand, from Nakhon Phanom Air Base in the northern part of the country. The helicopters carried a large contingent of security policemen. En route, one of the helicopters crashed, killing all 23 men onboard.

Additionally, a battalion-sized Marine landing team was airlifted from Okinawa to U Tapao. As it arrived, the destroyer *Holt* was directed to seize the *Mayaguez* while the Marine force, airlifted and supported by the Air Force, was to rescue the crew, at least some of whom were believed to be held on Koh Tang.

On the morning of 15 May, 175 Marines were flown by helicopters from U Tapao to Koh Tang. They were met by a force of approximately 200 heavily armed Khmer Rouge troops, who shot down three of the first eight helicopters and damaged two others. About 100 Marines were put ashore. In immediate and constant contact with the enemy troops, they were supported by Air Force forward air controllers in OV-10s and air strikes from A-7s, F-4s, and AC-130s.

Strike aircraft from the *Coral Sea* hit targets on the Cambodian mainland. Subsequently, a fishing boat was seen approaching the destroyer *Wilson* with white flags flying. Aboard were the 39 crewmen of the *Mayaguez*.

With the safe return of the *Mayaguez* crew, the Marines on Koh Tang were ordered to disengage and withdraw. However, the Khmer Rouge troops continued to attack the Marine force. The battle raged throughout the day, and the last of the Marines were not evacuated until after dark. Inadvertently, four Marines and a Navy medic were left behind. They were taken prisoner by the Khmer Rouge and executed.

Four CH-53 and HH-53 crewmen (First Lieutenant Donald R. Backlund, First Lieutenant Richard C. Brim, Staff Sergeant John D. Harston, and Captain Rowland W. Purser) were awarded the Air Force Cross for their actions that day, the last awarded in that long and tragic war. One of the Americans killed in the action at Koh Tang Island, Second Lieutenant Richard Vandergeer, a copilot on one of the lost helicopters, is the last name etched onto the wall of the Vietnam War Memorial in Washington, D.C.

Darrel Whitcomb

References

Guilmartin, John F. *A Very Short War.* Austin: Texas A&M University Press, 1995.

McCain, John S. (1884–1945)

U.S. Navy admiral. Born on 19 August 1884 in Teoc, Mississippi, McCain graduated from the Naval Academy in 1906. He served in surface vessels until 1935 when, as a captain, he became a naval aviator. He subsequently commanded two shore stations and the carrier *Ranger.*

In January 1941, now a rear admiral, McCain became Commander, Aircraft, Scouting Force, in the Atlantic. Transferring to the Pacific, he then planned and directed all land-based air operations during the Guadalcanal campaign from May to October 1942. He next headed the Bureau of Aeronautics until August 1943, when he was promoted vice admiral and became deputy Chief of Naval Operations (Air).

McCain left Washington in August 1944 to command a carrier group in the Pacific, with which he participated in the Marianas campaign, the Battle of the Philippine Sea, and the Leyte Gulf operation. On 30 October, he replaced Vice Admiral Marc Mitscher as commander of Task Force 38, which he led until January. After returning to Task Force 38 on 28 May 1945, McCain led the fast carriers through the final month of the Okinawa operation and into Japanese waters for a series of devastating attacks on Japan's home islands that virtually eliminated the remaining warships of the Imperial Japanese Navy and, in concert with Army Air Forces raids, crippled industry and communications.

Hard service wore McCain down to barely 100 pounds. He flew home immediately after the Japanese surrender ceremony on 2 September but died on 6 September. He was promoted admiral posthumously.

Paul E. Fontenoy

See also

Bureau of Naval Aeronautics; Japan, Air Operations Against; Task Force 38/58; Tokyo Air Raids

References

Brown, J. David. *Carrier Operations in World War II: The Pacific Navies.* London: Ian Allan, 1974.

Morison, Samuel E. *History of United States Naval Operations in World War II.* 15 vols. Boston: Little, Brown, 1947–1962.

McCampbell, David S. (1910–1996)

The U.S. Navy's ace of aces. David S. McCampbell was born in Bessemer, Alabama, in 1910. He entered Georgia Tech, then received his appointment to the Naval Academy, from which he graduated in 1933. Due to the Great Depression, his commission as ensign was delayed one year. He completed Navy flight training in 1938 and served with the 4th Fighter Squadron before his transfer to USS *Wasp* as landing signal officer. After *Wasp* was sunk while on patrol off Guadalcanal in June 1942, McCampbell was returned to the United States. In August 1943, he was appointed commander of the 15th Fighter Squadron. After a training period, the squadron, made up of fighters, bombers, and torpedo-bombers, became the 15th Air Group and, on 10 April 1944, sailed for the western Pacific aboard USS *Essex.*

For the next seven months, the air group saw almost continuous combat, including two major air-sea battles. In June 1944, in the Battle of the Philippine Sea, McCampbell led his fighters, Grumman F6F "Hellcats," against a Japanese force of 80 carrier-based aircraft attacking the U.S. Fleet. McCampbell alone shot down seven of the enemy. The Japanese were routed. Later, in the Battle of Leyte Gulf, Commander McCampbell and his wingman intercepted a force of 60 land-based Japanese aircraft. After McCampbell shot down nine and his wingman five, the enemy abandoned the attack. The downing of nine enemy airplanes on one mission is unequaled in the annals of aerial combat. Immediately reassigned as target coordinator for a strike force of planes from three Third Fleet Task Groups, McCampbell's aircraft attacked the Northern Japanese Force, sinking four enemy aircraft carriers, one heavy cruiser, and one destroyer. By war's end, McCampbell's aerial victories totaled 34, with at least 20 more destroyed on the ground. He was awarded the Medal of Honor personally by President Franklin Roosevelt on 10 January 1945. Captain McCampbell continued his distinguished 31-year Navy career until his retirement in 1964. He died in Florida at age 86.

Charles Cooper

References

Georgia Aviation Hall of Fame, Museum of Aviation, Warner Robins, GA, 31099.

National Aviation Hall of Fame. "Archives." Available online at www.nationalaviation.org.

McConnell, Joseph C. (1922–1954)

Korean War jet ace. Joseph C. "Mac" McConnell was born on 30 January 1922 in Dover, New Hampshire. He enlisted in the U.S. Army as a private in 1940. He graduated navigator training and in 1944 flew 60 missions in B-24s.

After World War II, he stayed in the Army and again applied for pilot school, receiving his wings in February 1948. When the Korean War broke out in June 1950, McConnell applied for combat service, and in August 1952 he joined the 39th Fighter Interceptor Squadron, 51st Fighter Interceptor Wing, in Korea. Flying an F-86F named *Beauteous Butch* after his wife, Pearl "Butch" Brown, McConnell scored his first victory on 14 January 1953.

On 16 February, he became an ace after downing his fifth MiG-15. On 12 April, during heavy action over MiG Alley, his plane was hit by a MiG piloted by Soviet ace Semen A. Fedorets. Even though his plane was badly damaged, McConnell put the jet in a high-gravity turn, eventually coming up on the Russian's tail. McConnell made Fedorets his eighth victory. Fedorets ejected and survived the war. McConnell, his plane billowing smoke, made for the Yellow Sea, where he bailed out and was rescued.

The next day, he was back in combat in *Beauteous Butch II,* downing his ninth MiG. He became America's second triple-ace on the morning of 18 May, scoring two victories. That afternoon he scored his sixteenth and final kill. Fearing that their top ace might get shot down and needing McConnell at home to raise morale, the Air Force brought him home before the 27 July armistice ended the conflict.

After his tour in Korea, McConnell and his family moved to Edwards Air Force Base, California, where he served as a test pilot. On 25 August 1954, he was killed testing a North American F-86H.

Ironically, Hollywood filmmakers had just completed shooting *The McConnell Story,* starring Alan Ladd and June Allyson. With McConnell's death, the final scenes had to be reshot. When the film debuted in 1955, most reviewers considered it a generally accurate portrayal of McConnell's life. One critic described it as a "weepy yet effective fictional biography of the heroic test pilot."

To this day, McConnell remains America's top jet ace, hav-

The leading American ace of the Korean War, Joe McConnell, scored sixteen victories. (U.S. Air Force)

ing scored 16 victories in 106 sorties. He was also America's top Korean War ace and one of two triple-aces, the other being Major James Jabara. McConnell was awarded the Distinguished Service Cross and Silver Star for his service.

William Head

References

Boyne, Walter J. "The Forgotten War." *Air Force Magazine* 83, 6 (June 2000).
Dorr, Robert F. *Korean War Aces.* London: Osprey, 1995.
Futrell, Robert F. *The United States Air Force in Korea, 1950–1953.* Rev. ed. Washington, DC: Office of Air Force History, 1983.

McDonnell Aircraft

Major U.S. aircraft manufacturer. James S. McDonnell (1899–1980) founded the company in 1939 after working with several firms including Stout, Hamilton, and Martin. The company was intended to focus on military production of aircraft and parts. During World War II, it built subassemblies at its St. Louis plant. The XFD-1 Phantom prototype, ordered in 1943, first flew in January 1945. It became the first Navy jet ordered (March 1945) and was produced as the FH-1 60 in 1947–1948. This plane also accomplished the first jet landings and takeoffs in the carrier *Franklin D. Roosevelt* in mid-1946. A much improved version (larger engines and airframe), the F2H Banshee, first flew in January 1947, saw extensive service in Korea, and resulted in nearly 900 examples by 1953. The F3H Demon, though initially underpowered, was improved and saw more than 500 examples produced. The XF-85 Goblin was a tiny jet fighter designed to be dropped from a B-36. Two prototypes were built and flown as the world's smallest jet fighter (wingspan of but 21 feet and length of only 14 feet). The XF-88 Voodoo of 1948 seemed a failure until ordered into production in 1953, the first major McDonnell contract with the Air Force, as the improved F-101, which served for years in the air forces of the United States and Canada. They were the first USAF in-service aircraft to fly twice the speed of sound.

The F4H (originally F-110, later F-4) Phantom II first flew in 1958 and, thanks in part to Vietnam War needs, resulted in more than 5,000 manufactured when production stopped in 1979 in the largest non-Soviet fighter program since the F-86. The F-15 Eagle of 1972 led to more than 1,000 aircraft manufactured, as did the F-18 Hornet of 1978, but McDonnell lost contracts for the A-12 Avenger and F-23 projects. McDonnell took over Douglas Aircraft in 1967, becoming McDonnell Douglas, which in turn was taken over by Boeing thirty years later.

Christopher H. Sterling

See also

Boeing F/A-18 Hornet; Boeing F-15 Eagle; McDonnell F-4 Phantom II

References

Francillon, Rene J. *McDonnell Douglas Aircraft Since 1920.* 2 vols. 2nd ed. London: Putnam. 1979, 1988–1990.
Ingells, Douglas J. *The McDonnell Douglas Story.* Fallbrook, CA: Aero, 1979.

McDonnell Douglas Aircraft

When the McDonnell Douglas Corporation (MDC) came into being on 28 April 1967 as the result of the merger between the McDonnell Company and the Douglas Aircraft Company, it appeared to be a corporate marriage made in heaven. Unfortunately, the business partners had incompatible personalities. Their tumultuous 30-year union was finally dissolved in 1997 when, meekly, they were taken in as poor relatives by the huge Boeing family.

At the time of the merger the two partners had diversified and complementary strengths in the commercial sector (Douglas), the military aircraft sector (McDonnell and, to a lesser extent, Douglas), and the spacecraft-booster-missile sector (Douglas and McDonnell). It also had more limited strengths in the data-processing and electronic sectors as well as valuable design experience in the rotary-wing field. No other aerospace company in the world had a more balanced experience or enjoyed a better reputation.

In the commercial sector, the DC-8 had lost its initial lead (in terms of aircraft sold) to the Boeing 707 but was experiencing a strong revival as Boeing had been unable to match the stretched DC-8 Series 60 variants. Moreover, at the time of the merger the DC-9 was the world's best-selling twinjet (441 having been sold versus only 136 Boeing 737s). Yet Douglas never had the resources to come up with a competitor for the fast-selling Boeing 727 trijet and had misjudged the requirements of airlines for four-engine jumbo jets, thereby allowing the Boeing 747 to run away with the most lucrative segment of the jetliner market. Douglas was thus facing difficulties in managing and developing a smaller widebody aircraft to meet the requirements of American Airlines and other U.S. domestic carriers. Fortunately, McDonnell had the financial and managerial resources needed to see that program to maturity as the DC-10.

Faced with intense competition from Lockheed and its TriStar, the launching of the DC-10 program was complicated by the fact that James McDonnell and his advisers in St. Louis were not familiar with the peculiarities of the civilian market. A number of traditional Douglas clients were thus lost to Lockheed. Nevertheless, the DC-10 started pulling away from the TriStar after the initial domestic variant, the Series 10, was complemented in 1969 by two intercontinental variants, the Series 30 and 40. Moreover, in the late 1970s the Long Beach team was close to securing orders for stretched variants. Unfortunately, adverse publicity following two major accidents (caused by improper locking of an aft cargo door and unapproved maintenance practices) came at the same time as a downturn in the airline business.

Douglas, long the world leader in commercial transport aircraft, never got to develop another all-new jetliner as the conservative MDC senior management in St. Louis never fully supported proposals for twinjets such as the Advanced Medium Range Aircraft, Advanced Short-Medium Range Aircraft, and Advanced Technology Medium Range Aircraft. Thus, the only "new" jetliners to be placed in production after the DC-10 were nothing but modernized derivatives of the DC-9 and DC-10. The resulting MD-80 and MD-90 first flew in 1979 and 1993, and the MD-11 first flew in 1990. Another DC-9 derivative, the MD-95, flew only after MDC had been taken over by Boeing; this twinjet was then renamed the Boeing 717-200. The lack of all-new products was exacerbated by the marketing mistake of switching to MD designations instead of capitalizing on the strength of the long established Douglas franchise. Eventually, this led to the discontinuation of a long family of successful airliners; the final nail in the Douglas coffin was the Boeing takeover of MDC.

The merger of McDonnell and Douglas came at a time when the United States was heavily involved in the Vietnam War, a conflict in which two MDC products—the F-4 Phantom and A-4 Skyhawk—were the most numerous combat aircraft. Production of the A-4 and F-4 ended in the United States in 1979, but manufacture of the F-4 continued under license in Japan until 1981. By then, however, McDonnell Douglas had become the world's leading producer of combat aircraft, with development of the F-15 Eagle, F/A-18 Hornet, and AV-8B Harrier II having been authorized in December 1969, May 1975, and July 1976, respectively.

These successes were complemented by military contracts for two prototypes of the YC-15 STOL transport in 1972, for a KC-10 tanker derivative of the DC-10 in 1977, and for development of the C-17 Globemaster III airlifter and T-45 Goshawk carrier trainer in 1981. As all of these awards had been received before President Ronald Reagan took office, MDC was in an exceptionally strong situation when the new administration started an overdue buildup of U.S. forces.

Although in the 1980s MDC appeared to have a lock on the combat aircraft sector, it fell out of favor during the first half of 1991. First, the contract for the joint development with General Dynamics of the A-12 Avenger, a stealthy replacement for the carrier-based Grumman A-6 medium attack aircraft, was cancelled. Next, the Northrop/McDonnell Douglas YF-23 lost the Advanced Tactical Fighter competition to the Lockheed/Boeing/General Dynamics YF-22. MDC in St. Louis did get a consolation prize in June 1992 in the form of a development contract (followed later by production contracts) for its F/A-18E/F Super Hornet. Nevertheless, in order to keep production lines in St. Louis operating at satisfactory levels, MDC was forced to announce in late 1989 that responsibility for T-45 production would be transferred from California to Missouri.

The MDC military aircraft business suffered yet another major blow when the company failed to become, on its own, one of the contractors chosen to compete for development of the Joint Strike Fighter (JSF). In October 2001, partnered with Boeing Military Aircraft, the St. Louis team saw the X-32 lose the JSF competition to the Lockheed Martin X-35. The old McDonnell plant in St. Louis and the Douglas plant in Long Beach may soon follow the same path to oblivion as Douglas plants in Santa Monica, El Segundo, Tulsa, Chicago, and Oklahoma City.

Between April 1946, when its XHJD-1 twin-rotor helicopter made its first hover flight, and June 1961, when development work on its Model 86 skycrane was terminated, McDonnell had made several attempts to break into the rotary-wing sector. Seventeen years after the MDC merger, the company returned to that field when it acquired the helicopter business of the Hughes Corporation. Rights to the smallest (Model 269 and 300) of the three types of helicopters acquired from Hughes were sold by McDonnell Douglas Helicopters Company (MDHC) to Schweizer Aircraft in 1986. Conversely, MDHC continued manufacturing Models 500 and 530 light turbine helicopters and AH-64 Apache attack helicopters until the company was taken over by Boeing. In addition, MDHC designed the Model 600, an enlarged derivative of the Model 530, and the all-new Explorer, which was put into production in 1994. Boeing has since sold rights to the Explorer and to Models 500, 530, and 600.

In the United States, McDonnell had pioneered the design and manufacturing of manned spacecraft with the Mercury single-seat capsule, which first took a U.S. astronaut into space in May 1961. Its Gemini two-seat capsule last orbited the earth in November 1966, five months before the MDC merger. In August 1965, Douglas had won an Air Force contract for the Manned Orbiting Laboratory, which was to make use of a modified Gemini capsule. Unfortunately for MDC, that contract was terminated in June 1969 when funds had to be freed to cover the mounting cost of the war in Southeast Asia. MDC did win another spacecraft contract when NASA chose it to build Skylab. The first manned Skylab orbital mission was flown in May 1973. The third and

The top brass at McDonnell Aircraft were hoping for a production run of perhaps as many as 400 F-4 Phantom IIs when it was introduced. The Phantom went on to become the premier fighter of the west. More than 5,000 were built. (U.S. Air Force)

last Skylab mission ended in February 1974. Since then, MDC has been out of the spacecraft business as a prime contractor. However, it remained active in the booster and missiles field until taken over by Boeing in 1997.

René Francillion

References

Francillion, René J. *McDonnell Douglas Aircraft Since 1920.* Vol. 2. Annapolis, MD: Naval Institute Press, 1990.

McDonnell F-4 Phantom II

The primary Western fighter during the 1960s and 1970s. All told, 5,195 Phantoms were built in 17 major variants and were used in interceptor, fighter, bomber, reconnaissance, and defense-suppression roles. The F-4 was a highly capable aircraft for its time and was handicapped only by its large size and smoke footprint when in military power.

The Phantom II was designed and built to a U.S. Navy specification that called for a missile-armed Fleet Defense Interceptor and entered service in October 1961 as the F-4B. The U.S. Air Force adopted the Phantom as the F-4C in January 1964. Following experience in Vietnam, some F-4Cs were fitted with an SUU-16 Vulcan cannon pod and scored several kills despite the lack of an air-to-air gun sight. The F-4D entered service in March 1966 and had improved radar, weapons electronics, and a lead-computing optical gun sight. The F-4J entered service in December 1966 and was essentially an F-4B updated with many of the systems and structural changes found in USAF Phantoms. The F-4E was a significant revision of the basic F-4, achieving initial operational capability in October 1967. It had new solid-state radar and an internal 20mm cannon. Later F-4Es had wing leading-edge slats that greatly improved turn performance. The F-4F was built for the West German Bundesluftwaffe without Sparrow missile capability or leading-edge slats. F-4Gs were converted from F-4E airframes to perform the defense-suppression role and had the cannon replaced by Radar Homing and Warning equipment.

The F-4 saw combat in Vietnam, the 1973 and 1982 Arab-Israeli wars, the Turkish-Greek clash over Cyprus, and the Iran-Iraq war. The F-4B/C Phantom outclassed the MiG-17 in performance terms and was broadly comparable to the MiG-21F under typical combat conditions. It was, however, inferior to the MiG-19 in turns and acceleration to Mach 1.2.

The F-4K was built for the Royal Navy and first flew in June 1966. It was based on the F-4J but had updated systems and more powerful Rolls-Royce Spey turbofans, which required significant structural alterations. The F-4M was similar but was used by the RAF. It first flew in February 1967. The RF-4B, RF-4C, and RF-4E were reconnaissance versions of the standard F-4.

Andy Blackburn

See also

Aircraft Armament; Aircraft Carriers, Development of; BOLO; Gun Sights; Mikoyan-Guryevich MiG-17; Mikoyan-Guryevich MiG-21; Vietnam War

References

Boyne, Walter J. *Phantom in Combat.* Washington, DC: Smithsonian Institution Press, 1981.

Davis, Larry. *F-4 Phantom II in Action.* Carrollton, TX: Squadron/Signal, 1984.

Michel, Marshall L. III. *Clashes: Air Combat over North Vietnam, 1965–1972.* Annapolis, MD: Naval Institute Press, 1997.

McGuire, Thomas B., Jr. (1920–1945)

America's second-highest-ranking ace, with 38 aerial victories over the Southwest Pacific during World War II. Sharp, pugnacious, and "aggressive as hell," Thomas B. McGuire Jr. was born on 1 August 1920. McGuire attended Georgia Institute of Technology before enlisting as an aviation cadet in 1941. Graduating in February 1942, he served in the Aleutian Islands before joining the 431st Fighter Squadron, 475th Fighter Group, Fifth Air Force, in October 1943. In his first combat flying the Lockheed P-38 Lightning, McGuire shot down three Japanese aircraft over New Guinea; three days later he became an ace. Known for his spirited competition with Richard Bong for leading American ace, McGuire earned renown for shooting down three enemy aircraft in one day on five occasions. He also scored twin victories five times. On 25–26 December 1944, he downed three enemy aircraft over the Philippines, followed by four more the next day. For this remarkable exploit, he received the Congressional Medal of Honor. On 7 January 1945, less than a month before his scheduled return to the United States, McGuire banked his twin-engine Lockheed P-38 too tightly during a low-level dogfight, stalled, and crashed. A symbol of the brash, confident fighter ace, McGuire also provided leadership as a squadron commander and group operations officer. McGuire AFB, New Jersey, is named for him.

References

Bright, Charles D., ed. *Historical Dictionary of the U.S. Air Force.* New York: Greenwood Press, 1992.

Kenney, George C. *General Kenney Reports: A Personal History of the Pacific War.* Reprint. Washington, DC: Office of Air Force History, 1987.

Mediterranean Theater of Operations (World War II)

Important arena for airpower that played a critical role in the Allies' eventual victory over Germany. The air war in the Mediterranean theater lasted for five years. It began with low-key exchanges between British and Italian aircraft protecting their fleets. A high point, one that inspired the Japanese to adopt similar tactics in their attack on Pearl Harbor, was the attack on Taranto. German airpower proved decisive in the onslaught on the Balkans, swiftly overcoming all local resistance and driving the British out of Greece. The first airborne invasion of an island took place when the Germans invaded Crete.

Germany made a key mistake early in the war by declining to take Malta when it might readily have been taken. Instead, it was decided to bomb Malta into submission, and a long, bloody, and eventually fruitless campaign was waged to do so. All the while, Malta served as a key base in the Mediterranean and eventually proved to be the tool with which the Allies strangled the Axis supply lines to Africa.

The Mediterranean theater also included some of the biggest invasions in history—those of North Africa, Sicily, Italy, and southern France. All of this fighting was conducted on an enormous front, one that actually exceeded the Eastern Front, for it extended 2,200 miles from Gibraltar to the Suez Canal and averaged about 500 miles in width. It was also conducted with a minimum of resources on the part of the Axis, for while Germany faced some 360 divisions in the Soviet Union, it faced only about eight divisions in Africa and dispensed its resources accordingly.

In the early part of the war the brunt of the fighting on the Axis side was borne by Italy's vaunted Regia Aeronautica, the Italian air force and a symbol of fascist pride. The force was relatively small, with about 1,800 first-line aircraft, and few of those were comparable to German and Allied counterparts. Among the exceptions were the Savoia Marchetti SM.79 "Sparviero" (Sparrow Hawk); a fabric-covered trimotor, it was one of the best torpedo-bombers of the war. Italian fighter planes were initially obsolete in concept and underpowered and undergunned, but they were eventually supplemented by modern designs such as the Macchi-Castoldi MC.202 "Folgore" (Lightning), which were equivalent to their opposition.

When British victories in North Africa forced Germany to intervene on Italy's behalf, the Axis gained temporary air superiority. The German Messerschmitt Bf 109Gs fighters and Junkers Ju 87 and Ju 88 bombers enabled General Erwin Rommel's Afrika Korps to throw the British back once again to Egypt.

On the Allied side, the British began the war with a rag-

tag collection of fighters and bombers that included the Gloster Gladiator and Bristol Blenheim. These were soon reinforced with Hawker Hurricanes and U.S.-built Martin A-30 Baltimores. When the United States began its participation, Curtiss P-40s, North American B-25s, and other, more modern aircraft took part.

For the Axis powers, the situation altered drastically for the worse after the fall of 1942. In October of that year, the British won the decisive Battle of El Alamein, and on November 8 the United States effected a landing in North Africa.

By this time Allied airpower had overwhelmed the Axis air forces, with fighter-bombers and medium bombers harassing German tanks and fortifications on a continual basis. The Germans made futile attempts to resupply North Africa by air, using Junkers Ju 52/3m and Messerschmitt Me 323 transports, vulnerable even when escorted. The greatest loss occurred on 18 April 1943, the famous Palm Sunday Massacre, when 78 aircraft were shot down, including 51 transports.

Complete Allied air dominance made it possible for land forces to overcome the hard-fighting Afrika Korps and eventually resulted in victory when the Germans surrendered at Tunisia on 13 May 1943. The losses matched those at Stalingrad, with more than 250,000 prisoners being taken. Perhaps the most important consesquence of the air war in North Africa—aside from the German surrender—was the establishment of effective tactics of close air support.

Airpower also proved decisive in the invasions of Sicily (July) and Italy (September). The Germans virtually abandoned any attempt to resist the Allies in the air, instead allowing ground forces to fight on with only occasional air support.

Italy, which Benito Mussolini had envisioned as a huge aircraft carrier dominating the Mediterranean, now became host to a series of air bases for U.S. aircraft, enabling Fifteenth Air Force bombers to attack Germany from the south.

Although the use of airpower in the Mediterranean Theater of Operations has not received the attention given other theaters of the war, it was extremely important and may fairly be said to have been the decisive factor that made Allied victory possible.

Walter J. Boyne

See also

Alam el Halfa, Battle of; Crete, Battle of; Curtiss P-40 Warhawk;

Hawker Hurricane; Pantelleria; Regia Aeronautica (World War II); Taranto Air Attack

References

Boyne, Walter J. *Clash of Wings: World War II in the Air.* New York: Simon and Schuster, 1994.

Menoher, Charles Thomas (1862–1930)

The first chief of the Army Air Service, remembered for his conflict over military aviation's future with visionary airman Billy Mitchell.

Menoher graduated from West Point in 1886 and began a career in the artillery with duty in Cuba and the Philippines. He was promoted to flag rank in 1917 and commanded the 42d (Rainbow) Division on the Western Front in 1917–1918. Menoher was appointed director of the Army Air Service on 23 December 1918, though he lacked a background in aviation. His appointment can be seen as validating the Army view that aviation was to be supportive and therefore should be under the command of ground forces. Use of aircraft for observation was more important than pursuit or bombardment activities.

In early 1919, Brigadier General William "Billy" Mitchell was named assistant chief of the Air Service. Menoher, because of his own lack of air experience, assigned Mitchell most planning and training responsibilities. When Mitchell used these as a platform to promote his views favoring a strong and separate air arm, senior War and Navy Department officials pressed Menoher to restrict his subordinate. Menoher relieved Mitchell of most duties, but this merely left Mitchell with more time to speak and write. The two men were barely on speaking terms. As General Hap Arnold later put it, Menoher was "not only unable and wholly unwilling to cope with Mitchell's ideas, but he could not handle Billy Mitchell. Also, to make matters worse, he did not fly much." Menoher headed a War Department board that concluded in 1921 that "whatever may be the decision as to a separate Aeronautical Department, the military air force must remain under the direct control of the Army."

In early October 1921, by now a major general, Menoher resigned his Air Service post, finding it impossible to operate with Mitchell (who remained in place through 1925). After further tours of command in Hawaii and San Francisco, Menoher retired in 1926. He died in 1930 and was buried in Arlington National Cemetery.

Christopher H. Sterling

References

Arlington National Cemetery Website. Available online at http://www.arlingtoncemetary.com/cmenoher.htm.

Mercedes Engines

Engines originally produced by the Daimler-Motoren-Gesellschaft. Emil Jellinek, an Austrian diplomat and Daimler dealer, helped design a Daimler car in 1899 that was named after his daughter, Mercedes. The Mercedes name became a registered trademark of Daimler in 1902.

Before World War I, four manufacturers produced aircraft engines in Germany: Argus, Benz, Oberursel, and Daimler. Daimler's Mercedes led the way in production, first with a four-cylinder 85-hp engine, followed by a six-cylinder 100-hp model. To stimulate the growth of the industry, the German War Ministry held a competition among engine manufacturers in January 1913; the winner was a Benz four-cylinder 105-hp engine, with the Daimler a close second. Despite its second-place status, the Mercedes became the most widely used German aircraft engine throughout the war, with its 160-hp model found in almost every make of airplane. An eight-cylinder model was also produced, but its longer crankshaft tended to crack during normal operation.

One manufacturer who did not have a supply of Mercedes engines was Fokker. The War Ministry was not enamored of Fokker machines and assigned the Mercedes to factories such as Albatros. Anthony Fokker accused the ministry of favoritism and claimed that he could create an excellent fighter plane if he were given Mercedes engines. Manfred von Richthofen had faith in Fokker and helped arrange a series of competitions among aircraft manufacturers in 1918, the winner to be supplied with Mercedes engines. Fokker won the first of the Adlershof Trials, and his machine was produced as the Fokker D.VII, one of the best fighter planes of the war. In 1926, Daimler-Motoren-Gesellschaft and Benz & Cie merged to create Mercedes-Benz.

Suzanne Hayes Fischer

Mercury Space Program

Pioneering space program that helped Americans reach the moon. Shortly after taking office in January 1961, President John F. Kennedy asked his advisers to investigate the viability of a space program that would catch up to the series of successes the Soviet Union had achieved since 1957, when it first orbited a Sputnik satellite. In 1959, the Eisenhower administration had presented to the public seven astronauts who would train for Project Mercury, which aimed to put an American in earth orbit. When Kennedy was elected, he appointed an ad hoc committee led by MIT's Jerome Wiesner, which determined that a civilian space program would help rally public support: Not only would there be heroes, but the nonmilitary spinoffs would likely be substantial in such fields as communications and weather observation. Kennedy was very much taken with the first side of the argument.

Although not specifically interested in the space program, Kennedy understood the potential of its impact in terms of peaceful demonstrations of prowess against the Soviets. Thus, despite warnings that considerable technical problems were yet to be resolved, Kennedy gave the go-ahead for further funding of Project Mercury, which was expected to orbit astronauts by 1965.

The immediate challenge was to find an appropriate booster by identifying the type of ICBM that could be used as safely as possible. However, cosmonaut Yuri Gagarin's successful orbit of the earth on 12 April 1961 accelerated interest in Mercury. Alan Shepard became the first American in space when he carried out a 15-minute suborbital flight on 6 May 1961. This paled in comparison to Gagarin's 89 minutes in full orbit and led many observers to warn that the United States, though a military leader, still was far behind in space technology. As a result of this new challenge from the Soviet Union, Kennedy ordered a reevaluation of the space program and, three weeks after Shepard's flight, gave a public address in which he committed the United States to landing a man on the moon by 1969.

Project Mercury proceeded apace and sent five more astronauts into space. John Glenn became the first American to orbit the earth on 20 May 1962. Astronaut Donald K. "Deke" Slayton, grounded by a heart condition, was the only one of the first seven astronauts not to fly in Mercury. With the shift in priorities, however, it became clear that Mercury would be insufficient to prepare for a moon landing, and the program was replaced by Gemini. Mercury represented a new phase in American culture's fascination with technology, whereby the seven astronauts acquired the status of movie stars and Americans generally embraced their newfound status as a spacefaring nation.

Guillaume de Syon

References

Grimwood, James M., and Charles C. Alexander. *This New Ocean: A History of Project Mercury.* Washington, DC: NASA, 1966.

McDougall, Walter A. *The Heavens and the Earth: A Political History of the Space Age.* Baltimore: Johns Hopkins University Press, 1991.

Messerschmitt, Willy (1898–1978)

German aircraft designer. Willy Emil Messerschmitt grew up in Munich as the second son of a wine salesman. During World War I, he designed and built gliders (models S4 through S10) with the help of gliding pioneer Fritz Harth, a family friend. He later pursued his interests by studying engineering at the Institute of Technology in Munich.

In September 1923, he founded his own aircraft company in Bamberg and manufactured some of his gliders and several single-engine sportplanes (M 15, M 16, M 17). During this period, World War I flier and airline owner Theo Croneiss commissioned Messerschmitt to develop his first passenger plane, the M 18, which became his first all-metal plane, seating six. It was followed by the M 20 and M 24 models in the late 1920s, both of which were used by Lufthansa.

In 1927, Messerschmitt's company merged with the Bayerische Flugzeugwerke (BFW), based in Augsburg, Bavaria, which in turn led to the incorporation of the company with the financial help of family friends. In 1930, Willy Messerschmitt became a professor of aeronautical engineering at his alma mater in Munich. The worldwide economic depression caused a slump in German aircraft orders, forcing his factory to cut back on both design and production, although several projects already under way, such as the trainer M 27 and the postal M 28, were completed.

During that time, the BFW company survived in part thanks to small subsidies from the German Ministry of Transportation (then in charge of aeronautics). However, factory politics led to accusations of mismanagement against Willy Messerschmitt. In fact, the financial troubles of all German aircraft manufacturers make it difficult to support such charges (the main accuser, Fritz Hille, resigned his board membership to work for Heinkel). In the meantime, reorganization caused the complete incorporation of the Messerschmitt design bureau into BFW.

With the advent of the Third Reich, a new aeronautical structure was put in place that both served and hurt Willy Messerschmitt. He could count on the assistance of World War I ace and stunt pilot Ernst Udet, then in the new Air Ministry, but also had to deal with an unfriendly Erhard Milch, a former Lufthansa director who had canceled several Messerschmitt orders during the financial depression. As of 1935, the BFW factory was listed as the only holder of Messerschmitt designs; only in 1938 would the concern change its name to Messerschmitt.

During the Third Reich, Willy Messerschmitt served as acting president of the German Aeronautical Research Institute. During those years, he oversaw first the design of the Bf 108 Taifun, a four-seat civilian aircraft that was also one of the first German machines to incorporate retractable landing gear. It served as the basis for the development of the Bf 109 single-engine fighter (first used in the Spanish civil war). Other designs followed, some displaying Messerschmitt's remarkable design genius, such as the Bf 110 twin-engine fighter; others were ahead of their time, such as the Me 262, or far too impractical, from the Messerschmitt 264 long-range bomber to the Me 163 Komet rocket-glider fighter.

By the end of World War II, many German factories were producing Messerschmitt aircraft under license. Arrested in Murnau on 6 May 1945, Willy Messerschmitt was first flown to London, then back to Murnau, where he spent most of the following two years in camps or under house arrest.

After his release, Messerschmitt sought to diversify into new technological endeavors. Initially, a series of prefabricated buildings was sold as a way to deal with the housing shortage. Other projects included sewing machines and three-wheeled automobiles (with lowered gas consumption) affectionately known to Germans as "Isetta."

Offers to work with U.S. designers also came, but Messerschmitt declined them because of the Allies' refusal to allow him to regain control of his Augsburg factory to rebuild aircraft.

Messerschmitt also worked as an adviser to the Spanish aircraft industry and, together with aeronautical engineer Julius Krauss, oversaw three designs: the HA 100 training plane (roughly equivalent to the T-28 Trojan), the HA 200 jet trainer (used by both the Spanish and Egyptian air forces), and the HA 300 jet fighter. The latter was sold to Egypt, but Soviet interference interrupted further development of the project. After West Germany's admission into NATO in 1955, Messerschmitt was able to reopen the Augsburg factory. There he produced under license aircraft for Germany, France, and NATO, such as the Fouga-Potez CM-170, the Fiat G.91, and the Lockheed F-104G. A VTOL fighter project, the VJ 101, was also flight-tested in the 1960s but was canceled.

In 1968, Willy Messerschmitt was named CEO of the newly created Messerschmitt-Bölkow-Blohm aerospace concern, which helped produce the Panavia Tornado multirole fighter as well as several helicopter models. In 1973, he became chairman of the board; he died in 1978.

Guillaume de Syon

See also

German Air Force (Luftwaffe); Goering, Hermann; Heinkel Aircraft; Paris Air Agreement; Udet, Ernst

References

Ebert, Hans J., Johann B. Kaiser, and Klaus Peters. *Willy Messerschmitt—Pionier des Luftfahrt und des Leichtbaues* (Willy Messerschmitt: Pioneer of Aviation Design). Bonn: Bernard and Graefe, 1992.

Homze, Edward L. *Arming the Luftwaffe: The Reich Air Ministry and the German Aircraft Industry, 1919–1939.* Lincoln: University of Nebraska Press, 1976.

Messerschmitt Bf 109

The most famous fighter of the German Luftwaffe, produced in greater numbers (in excess of 30,000) than any other fighter aircraft. Created by Willy Messerschmitt and his chief engineer, Walter Rethel, the Bf 109 was the world's most advanced fighter at the time of its first flight in September 1935. A development of the very successful four-place touring Bf 108, the Bf 109 featured retractable landing gear, an enclosed cockpit, all-metal stressed-skin construction, heavy armament for the time, slotted trailing-edge flaps, and automatic Handley Page leading-edge slots.

Despite the pressures for ever-increasing production, the Bf 109 went through a long series of modifications, the last production version being the Bf 109K. In the process, horsepower was increased from the prototype's 695-hp Rolls-Royce Merlin to the 2,030-hp Daimler-Benz DB 605 engine in the Bf 109K.

The aircraft served in every theater in which the Germans fought and was used by many nations allied to Germany. In the early months of the war, it reigned supreme over the battlefield until it met its match in the Supermarine Spitfire. As the war progressed and new Allied fighters such as the Soviet Yak-3 and U.S. North American P-51 were introduced, it became increasingly difficult for the Bf 109 to compete on equal terms. Nevertheless, in the hands of a capable pilot it remained a dangerous weapon until the end of the war. Versions of the Bf 109 were produced in Czechoslovakia and Spain, and it fought again in the 1948 Israeli War of Independence.

Although it was the favorite mount of many top German aces, Allied pilots who flew test versions had mixed feelings. The cockpit was cramped, with visibility limited by the heavy frames of the canopy. By Allied standards, the control harmony was poor, a problem that was amplified by the inexplicable lack of a rudder-trimming device. At cruising speeds, the Bf 109 was generally considered delightful to fly, but its controls became very heavy as speed increased. The most notorious aspect of the Bf 109 was its appalling takeoff characteristics. An estimated 3,000 aircraft were lost during takeoffs in which the pilot lost control. Landing characteristics were also challenging, but the a skilled pilot could land in a relatively short distance, using heavy braking once the tailwheel was firmly planted on the ground.

Walter J. Boyne

See also

Meserschmitt, Willy

References

Brown, Eric. *Wings of the Luftwaffe.* London: Jane's Information Group, 1977.

Green, William. *Warplanes of the Third Reich.* New York: Galahad, 1990.

Messerschmitt Me 163 Komet

Tailless rocket-powered fighter conceived by Alexander Lippisch, whose design career began with the Zeppelin-Werke in 1918. Design of the piston-engine Lippisch DFS 194 tailless demonstrator aircraft began in 1938. Negotiations with Messerschmitt to take sponsorship of the program resulted in the DFS 194, and work on the Me 163 detail design was under way in September 1939. In February 1940, work on the Me 163 was shelved, and the DFS 194 design was revised to accept a Walter 882-pound/thrust rocket engine. Using hydrogen peroxide and potassium permanganate fuel, it flew in August 1940 at 342 mph.

The successful demonstration led to reprioritizing the Me 163 program, and work on the three prototypes resumed, powered by a 1,650-pound/thrust HWK 309 engine. Powered flights began in August that year, and ultimately a speed of 628 mph was achieved. A jettisonable two-wheel dolly was used for takeoff and a retractable belly skid for landing. Despite being unsatisfactory, this feature was carried over to the B production models.

A major redesign of the A model, the Me 163B prototype was rolled out in April 1942 and flew as a glider on 26 June 1942. Because of the unavailability of the engine, the first powered flight was not until 24 June 1943. The fuselage was as a two-piece metal monocoque construction, and the wings were all wood. Armament was two 30mm cannons. The fuel and engine systems were very unreliable. Leaking fuel could literally dissolve the pilots, and engines often failed.

A training unit was formed in late 1942, well before the first powered flight, operating from Peenemünde airfield. The first operational missions of the Me 163B were in May 1944, but its short range and low reliability did not allow actual engagements until August. The Me 163Bs never became a significant threat, although 279 Komets were delivered before the end of the war.

Douglas G. Culy

References

Green, William, and Gordon Swanborough. *The Complete Book of Fighters.* London: Salamander, 1994.

Messerschmitt Me 262

The first mass-produced operational jet fighter in the world. The aircraft looks advanced even today, with a streamlined fuselage, mildly swept wings, and two Jumo 004 turbojets mounted in nacelles under the wings. Initial flights of the airframe were conducted using a nose-mounted Jumo 210Ga piston engine and conventional propeller; the first flight under jet power took place on 25 March 1942, although the piston engine was still installed. Development continued among great political turmoil. Nevertheless, on 26 July 1944, Lieutenant Alfred Schreiber from Kommando Thierfelder shot down an RAF Mosquito reconnaissance aircraft in the first aerial victory by a jet fighter.

The Me 262 did not have a material impact upon the outcome of World War II. Less than 200 Me 262s were in operational service at any one time, despite the efforts of Messerschmitt to manufacture more than 1,400 of them in the last 18 months of the war. The Me 262 was produced in day-fighter, night-fighter, fighter-bomber, and reconnaissance versions.

Although the Me 262 was produced in day-fighter, night-fighter, fighter-bomber, and reconnaissance versions, less than 200 Me 262s were in operational service at any one time. (U.S. Air Force)

The problems lay not with the aircraft, or even with the questionable political decisions concerning its role and manufacture. The problem was simply one of technology: Junkers could not produce enough reliable engines to power all the airframes that Messerschmitt was capable of building. The Allies certainly influenced this problem; heat-resistant materials were difficult to obtain in Germany toward the end of the war, and constant bombing raids disrupted production and distribution of critical parts. Completed airframes were strafed and bombed even before they could be delivered. Simply put, even if Hitler had allowed the Me 262 to enter production without demanding that its role be changed from fighter to fighter-bomber, Junkers could not have produced sufficient engines to power them.

The Me 262 was actually very much a compromise aircraft, and its designers were not particularly happy with many aspects of it. The advanced swept wing was an inelegant solution to a late engine change that significantly altered the center of gravity, and the underslung nacelles were a solution to oversized and overweight power plants. The aircraft had precious little serious wind-tunnel time and a disappointingly low critical Mach number. In all, like many aircraft before it, the Me 262 was simply the best that could be built given the circumstances.

Dennis R. Jenkins

References

Jenkins, Dennis R. *Messerschmitt Me 262 Sturmvogel.* WarbirdTech Series Volume 6. North Branch, MN: Specialty Press, 1999.

Radinger, Willy, and Walter Schick. *Messerschmitt Me 262: Development, Testing, Production.* Atglen, PA: Schiffer, 1992.

Meyer, John C. (1919–1975)

World War II fighter ace; USAF vice Chief of Staff and commander of Strategic Air Command.

Born in Brooklyn, New York, he entered aviation training in 1939 and graduated in July 1940. He began his wartime career flying convoy patrols out of Iceland. In 1943, he took command of the 487th Fighter Squadron, 352d Fighter Group, Eighth Air Force.

From October 1943 through January 1945, Meyer flew 200 combat missions and logged 462 combat hours. During this time, he shot down 24 German aircraft in aerial combat and destroyed an additional 13 on the ground, making him the top-ranking U.S. ace in Europe in total aircraft destroyed. He ranked fourth in the Eighth Air Force in aerial victories and was the seventh-ranking U.S. Army Air Forces ace in World War II. His World War II combat career ended on 9 January 1945, after he sustained serious injuries in an automobile accident.

After the war, Meyer completed his college education at Dartmouth and in 1950 took command of the 4th Fighter Interceptor Group, which he took to Korea. In that conflict, he flew 31 combat missions in the F-86 Sabre Jet, downing two MiG-15s to add to his already impressive aerial victory total. In April 1951, he moved up to deputy commander of the 4th Fighter Interceptor Wing.

After the Korean War, Meyer continued to advance in rank, holding numerous key military positions until he attained his fourth star. In 1969, he was named vice Chief of Staff of the U.S. Air Force. He served in this post until 1972, when he assumed command of Strategic Air Command—only the second fighter pilot to hold that position. He retired from the Air Force in July 1974 and succumbed to a fatal heart attack in December of the following year while jogging.

Meyer's many decorations include the Silver Star with one Oak Leaf Cluster and the Distinguished Service Cross (DSC) with two Oak Leaf Clusters. He remains the only U.S. Air Force officer to have earned three DSCs. In 1988, Meyer's career was further validated by his induction into the prestigious National Aviation Hall of Fame in Dayton, Ohio. With a total of 26 aerial victories in two wars, General John C. Meyer is the ninth-ranking U.S. fighter ace of all time, an honor he shares with World War I ace Eddie Rickenbacker and World War II Marine Corps ace Joseph Foss.

Steven A. Ruffin

References

Bright, Charles D., ed. *Historical Dictionary of the U.S. Air Force.* New York: Greenwood Press, 1992.

Frisbee, John L. "Four-Star Ace." *Air Force Magazine* 72, 5 (1989): 172.

Midway, Battle of (1942)

The turning point that reversed Japanese military expansion in the Pacific during World War II. At Midway, the United States gained the strategic offense and never relinquished it.

The Doolittle Raid on 18 April 1942 settled a debate between Japanese factions over whether to take Midway. Because its duty was to protect the emperor, the military could not allow such a raid to happen again. Besides taking Midway, Japan planned to extend its reach north toward the Aleutians and south toward Australia. This led to the Battle of the Coral Sea, the first sea battle fought entirely through airpower. The U.S. lost the carrier *Lexington,* and Japanese aviators thought they had also sunk the *Yorktown.*

The Japanese expected that they could take Midway and then wait for the remaining two U.S. carriers to be lured into battle and destroyed. But the Americans had broken the Japanese code and planned an ambush of their own.

At Pearl Harbor, workers patched up the damaged *Yorktown* and got it into the fight at Midway, where four Japanese carriers were stalked by three U.S. carriers. In addition, Midway Atoll had torpedo-bombers, fighters, scouts, and bombers. From an aerial-resources standpoint, the fight was shaping up to be somewhat even. Surprise was on the U.S. side, but the Japanese had superior planes.

Early on 4 June 1942, Admiral Chuichi Nagumo launched aircraft to strike Midway, holding others back for protection against enemy ships. He had two objectives: knock out the Midway defenses, and sink any hostile ships, especially carriers. This double responsibility compromised Nagumo's ability to do either mission well.

U.S. scout planes sighted the Japanese carriers and aircraft headed for Midway, and all serviceable planes left the atoll. U.S. bombers and torpedo-bombers flew toward the carriers. Grumman Wildcats and aging Brewster Buffaloes headed for the incoming aircraft. The Japanese shot up these U.S. fighters, then bombed and strafed Midway.

Starting at about 7:00 A.M., four Martin B-26 Marauders, each carrying one torpedo, and six Douglas TBF Devastator torpedo-bombers attacked the Japanese carriers. Defending Mitsubishi Zeros shot down all but one of the torpedo-bombers and half of the B-26s. The few torpedoes the Americans launched missed.

Fourteen Boeing B-17s bombed from high altitude; all bombs missed as the ships maneuvered out of harm's way. Sixteen Marine dive-bombers made a glide-bombing attack because their pilots were not experienced enough for dive-bombing. Zeros shot down half of them, and the rest missed their targets. A similar fate befell the 12 older Vought Vindicators that went in next.

Nagumo ordered a second strike on Midway. This meant that deck crews had to switch general-purpose bombs for torpedoes and armor-piercing bombs. When the planes of the first wave returned to be retrieved and refueled, the crews had to take the second strike force below deck.

Unexpectedly, a search plane reported sighting a U.S. carrier within striking distance. Nagumo now ordered planes to be rearmed to attack the carrier instead of Midway. Crews switched torpedoes and armor-piercing bombs back for the regular bombs. There was not enough time to observe proper safety precautions. They stored gasoline tanks, bombs, and torpedoes all over the flight and hangar decks, making the Japanese carriers extremely vulnerable. Admiral Raymond Spruance launched his planes to where he thought the enemy carriers were.

However, Nagumo had turned his ships toward the Americans. When U.S. pilots did not find their quarry, they spread out in a search mode. Some eventually turned back because of low fuel; the rest arrived at their targets in piecemeal fashion. The Douglas TBD torpedo-bombers from the *Hornet* attacked first. Zeros from the combat air patrol dropped down on them, and eventually all were shot down; only one man, Ensign George Gay, out of 30 survived. The *Enterprise's* torpedo squadron saw smokescreens from the Japanese destroyers and headed toward them. They divided in order to attack from two directions, but this made them more vulnerable to the Zeros because the rear gunners' combined fire was diminished. Ten out of 28 men survived. The torpedo-bombers from the *Yorktown* arrived next. Again the defending Zeros were all over them. Carrying a torpedo, the Devastators could fly only at 100–120 mph and were sitting ducks. Only three persons survived out of 24 in this attack.

The Japanese appeared to be near victory. They were now ready to attack the U.S. ships. However, as their carriers swung into the wind, Douglas SBD Dauntless dive-bombers finally arrived at the battle—undetected. The Japanese carriers had no radar, and there was just enough cloud cover to hide the bombers from the lookouts. The Zeros were down low, finishing off the torpedo-bombers, and had not had enough time to climb to altitude.

The dive-bombers dove from out of the sun. Only two to four bombs hit each carrier but this was enough. The armed and fueled planes, as well as the munitions and gasoline containers scattered around, began exploding. The SBDs from the *Enterprise* hit the *Kaga* and the *Akagi,* while the *Yorktown* dive-bombers hit the *Soryu.* In five minutes, these three carriers were blazing infernos. The exploding torpedoes and bombs made it impossible to bring the fires under control. The fighting continued, and the carriers *Hiryu* and *Yorktown* were sunk later. The Japanese had been defeated, and the course of the war was irrevocably changed.

Emerson T. McMullen

See also

Coral Sea, Battle of the; Nagumo, Chuichi; Spruance, Raymond A.

References

Cressman, Robert J., et al. *A Glorious Page in Our History.* Missoula, MT: Pictorial Histories, 1990.

Fuchida, Mitsuo, and Masatake Okumiya. *Midway.* Annapolis, MD: Naval Institute Press, 1955.

Prange, Gordon W. *Miracle at Midway.* New York: McGraw-Hill, 1982.

MiG Aircraft

See Mikoyan-Guryevich Aircraft

Getting ready for takeoff, North American F-86s prepare for the trip up to MiG Alley. (U.S. Air Force)

MiG Alley

The 6,500-square-mile airspace in northwestern Korea where United Nations and communist jets fought for air superiority during the Korean War. On a map it resembled a parallelogram extending north to Suiho, south to Sinanju, west to Sinuiju, and east to Huichon. Most combat had an operational ceiling of 50,000 feet and was between U.S. Air Force F-86 Sabre Jets and Soviet-built Chinese MiG-15s from mid-1951 to mid-1953. Ultimately, the F-86s amassed 792 MiG kills and 78 losses.

Before the war began in June 1950, communist forces built a MiG base near the Manchurian border city of Antung (Dandong) to guard the important rail bridges over the Yalu River. This base and other targets in or near China became MiG havens.

On 8 November 1950, a USAF F-80 Shooting Star shot down a MiG-15 in the first jet-versus-jet combat. Even so, it soon became clear that the MiGs were better than the F-80s and F-84s, and U.S. officials deployed F-86s to Korea.

The MiGs possessed superior high-altitude characteristics, which the F-86s could overcome by high-speed dives that brought the dogfight to more favorable low altitudes. Moreover, USAF fighters were stationed in South Korea far from MiG Alley. They could not stay long for fear of running out of fuel. Being close to their bases, MiGs could loiter for long periods, choosing the time and circumstance of their attack.

With UN leaders concerned that the war might widen to include China and the Soviet Union, one of the most frustrating problems for USAF pilots was the politically imposed restrictions on attacking MiG bases and other targets in China or near its border. Bases like Antung were off-limits, although many F-86 pilots slipped across the border to engage and down enemy MiGs.

Another problem was the lack of F-86s. At the height of combat the USAF only had the 4th and 51st Wings, with 115 fighters in Korea. The enemy had nearly 500 MiGs at Antung. Keeping F-86 wings supplied and their aircraft airworthy was also difficult, and by early 1952 mission-incapable rates reached as high as 45 percent. Many F-86 missions faced three-to-one or four-to-one odds.

Later in 1952, the introduction of F-86Fs with more powerful engines, better wing and tail designs, and the A-1 radar-computed gun sight turned things decidedly in the USAF's favor. U.S. pilots were typically better trained and often had experience from World War II. Their more aggressive style meant that 37 F-86 pilots became aces. The top ace was Captain Joseph McConnell, with 16 kills.

The MiG pilots' abilities varied. Some, especially Soviet pilots, were excellent. U.S. pilots respected these men as the "honchos," but most others were not well trained and hence were called "nimwits."

One effective MiG tactic sent as many as 80 jets on a rapid sweep called a southbound "train." This proved deadly at first, but by late 1952 U.S. MiG combat air patrols began to employ countertactics that devastated MiG trains. The last combat over MiG Alley came on 22 July 1953, when Second Lieutenant Samuel P. Young shot down his first and only MiG-15.

William Head

References
Blair, Clay. *The Forgotten War: America in Korea, 1950–1953.* New York: Times Books, 1987.
Futrell, Robert F. *The United States Air Force in Korea, 1950–1953.* Rev. ed. Washington, DC: Office of Air Force History, 1983.
Sherwood, John Darrell. *Officers in Flight Suits: The Story of American Pilots in the Korean War.* New York: New York University Press, 1996.

Mikoyan, Artem I. (1905–1970)

Military aircraft designer of the former Soviet Union. Born the son of a carpenter in a small village in modern-day Armenia, Artem I. Mikoyan benefited, especially in the 1930s, from the career of his brother Anastas, who was a colleague of Soviet dictator Joseph Stalin and was a leader in the Communist Party and Soviet government. Meanwhile, Artem attended a village school and then high school in Tiflis (Tbilisi), Georgia. He completed his early education by taking a machinist course at a technical school in Rostov in 1923. The following year he worked as a mechanic in the local railway shop before moving to Moscow and being employed at the Dynamo factory. After finishing an obligatory tour of duty with the Red Army, Mikoyan entered the air force academy in 1931, where he learned to fly as well as design advanced aircraft. Graduating with honors in 1937, he became the Red Air Force permanent representative with the design bureau headed by Nikolai N. Polikarpov.

At the Polikarpov design bureau, Mikoyan eventually assumed responsibility over the production of the I-153 fighter. Mikhail I. Gurevich, who would prove to be his collaborator for 25 years, assisted Mikoyan in this effort. Members of the Soviet military and government, including Stalin, recognized that the Soviet Union needed a modern fighter different from the obsolescent, biplane-configured I-153. At the end of 1939, the Soviet hierarchy encouraged the formation of a new experimental department to create a modern fighter under the leadership of Mikoyan (chief) and Gurevich (deputy). Together they designed the I-200, a low-wing monoplane that first flew in March 1940. The new aircraft required extensive modification before it was ready to begin a small production run in December 1940. By then, the model name had changed to the MiG-1, a designation based on the initials of the last names of the designers separated by "i," the Russian word for "and." The most successful of the early planes was the MiG-3, which enjoyed a production run of 3,300 and provided interceptor defense for the Soviet Union's metropolitan centers during World War II. Other wartime MiG designs showed promise but were not significantly better than those fighter aircraft, such as the La-7 and Yak-9, that entered mass production.

After the war, Mikoyan and Gurevich examined German technology and merged two BMW 003 turbojet engines with the MiG-3 airframe to create one of the Soviet Union's first jet fighters in April 1946. The MiG-9 proved to be the successful precursor of a line of famous fighters, ranging from the Mig-15 to the MiG-31. Until a stroke disabled him on 27 May 1969, Mikoyan was manager and general constructor of the MiG OKB (Experimental Design Bureau). He received numerous awards and honors for his outstanding design achievements in military aviation, including membership in the Soviet Union Academy of Sciences in 1968.

James K. Libbey

See also
Gurevich, Mikhail I.; Lavochkin Aircraft; Mikoyan-Gurevich Aircraft; Polikarpov, Nikolai N.; Soviet Air Force; Yakovlev, Aleksandr S.

References
Belyakov, R. A., and J. Marmain. *MiG: Fifty Years of Secret Aircraft Design.* Annapolis, MD: Naval Institute Press, 1994.
Great Soviet Encyclopedia. 3rd ed. Vol. 16. New York: Macmillan, 1977.

Mikoyan-Gurevich (MiG) Aircraft

Soviet aircraft design bureau specializing in fighter aircraft. Artem Ivanovich Mikoyan joined with Mikhail Iosifovich Gurevich and in 1939 established an independent design bureau. The result of their first efforts was the MiG-3, one of the new fighters that was supposed to replace the old Polikarpovs by 1942. It did not perform well at the low altitudes where most air combat occurred on the Eastern Front and was considered a relative failure. Production ended prematurely in 1942 after only 3,322 were completed. None of MiG's other wartime efforts progressed beyond the prototype stage.

In 1945, MiG began to design the MiG-9 jet fighter, powered by two RD-20 engines copied from the BMW 003A. It first flew on 24 April 1946, with 664 being built. The next design, the MiG-15, made the acronym "MiG" synonymous with most all Soviet aircraft.

Design of the MiG-15 began in 1946 and used the RD-45 engine, a copy of the Rolls-Royce Nene shared by the British government (later versions used the improved VK-1). It first flew in May 1948, and by October the first MiG-15s were leaving the factories and entering service. With a top speed of 641 mph, a ceiling of 49,900 feet, and an armament of one 37mm and two 23mm cannons, it was the first Soviet fighter equal or superior to all its foreign competitors.

Just as the Zero was a nasty surprise to the United States in 1941, so was the MiG-15 when it appeared over North Korea in 1950. (U.S. Air Force)

The MiG-15 first saw combat over Shanghai in April 1950. As with the Japanese Zero a decade before, Western observers were not paying attention, and the appearance of the MiG-15 over Korea in November 1950 was a shock. The MiG-15 and the North American F-86 Sabre were roughly an equal match, the MiG slightly better in climb at altitude and in maneuverability in the vertical plane, the Sabre faster in a dive, with better horizontal maneuverability. The MiG had better weapons, but the Sabre had the better gun sight. Success depended on the skill of the individual pilots and the specific tactical situation. None of the other U.S. or British aircraft really had a chance.

After Korea, the MiG-15 saw further combat in the Middle East and was widely sold to all the Soviet Union's allies and to most of the newly emerging nations. Almost 10,000 were produced by the mid-1950s, including production by Poland and Czechoslovakia. In addition to the single-seat fighter, there was also a two-seat fighter-trainer, the MiG-15UTI, of which about 6,700 were built. The MiG-15UTI was even more widely sold than its single-seat brother and remained in use in the Soviet Union until the end of the 1980s.

From 1951 to 1956, the MiG-15 was supplanted in production with a modernized version, the MiG-17. Neither the MiG-15 nor the MiG-17 was capable of supersonic flight, which was finally achieved by the MiG-19 series (in production from 1954 to 1961). Only 3,700 MiG-19s were produced; it was sold widely, but it had the misfortune to appear between the exceptional and long-lived MiG-17 and the equally successful MiG-21.

Gurevich retired from the bureau in 1964; he died on 12 November 1976. Mikoyan died on 9 December 1970 and was succeeded by Rostislav Apollossovich Belyakov (b. 1919), who had long been MiG's chief designer. At this time, the MiG-23/MiG-27 family was entering production. Although the Sukhoi Su-17 was the first operational variable-geometry aircraft, the MiG-23 and MiG-27 were more distinctive, recognized first, and produced in greater numbers. From 1969 to 1982, 4,278 examples of the MiG-23, 910 MiG-27s, and 769 MiG-23UMs were produced. The MiG-23M and MiG-23P variants and derivatives were optimized for air combat and interception, respectively, and were distinguished by an ogival nose cone containing advanced radar systems. The MiG-23B variants and the MiG-27 were dedicated fighter-bombers, without air-to-air radar systems but with more flexibility for carrying bombs and rockets, and they had specialized ground targeting laser systems. These aircraft were distinguished by a sloping forward fuselage, which gave the type its Russian nickname, "Utkanos" (Duck-nose).

Too late for combat over Vietnam, the MiG-23 family has participated prominently in all the conflicts since then in the Middle East and Africa and has been exported to dozens of nations. By 1982, when Syrian MiG-23s tried to fight over Lebanon's Bekaa Valley, they were flown by pilots less experienced than the Israelis and were pitted against F-16s and F-15s, fighters of an entirely later generation. Also during the 1980s, MiG-23s had the misfortune to duel Pakistani F-16s over the Afghan border, which proved it was not merely Israeli skill at work over the Bekaa. The MiG-23 was retired from Russian service on 1 May 1998 but continues in service with former Soviet republics and other countries around the globe.

The cockpit of the MiG-17 may look somewhat primitive, but it was fully up to date at the time of its operational debut in late 1952. More than 6,000 were built, and it served throughout the Communist world. (U.S. Air Force)

Also entering service in 1969 was the MiG-25, a large interceptor capable of reaching Mach 2.8 at altitude. This aircraft was originally designed to counter the U.S. XB-70 and SR-71 and was produced in several reconnaissance variants. The MiG-25 (NATO code name "Foxbat") achieved notoriety in 1975 when Lieutenant Viktor Belenko flew an example to Japan, which allowed the United States to examine it thoroughly, revealing a curious mix of very advanced and antiquated technology. As a consequence, the Soviets introduced a drastically improved version, the MiG-25PDS, in order to restore their secrets. About 1,190 MiG-25s of interceptor, reconnaissance, and combat-trainer variants were produced by 1984. A further evolution of the basic MiG-25 design is the MiG-31. This aircraft is a highly modernized interceptor, with no reconnaissance or trainer variants included among the 500 or more produced between 1977 and 1986. In 1990, the further modified MiG-31M appeared, but the end of the Soviet Union and the decline of the Russian air force has prevented it from entering service.

The MiG-29 was the last MiG to be produced. The end of the Cold War and the collapse of the Soviet Union caused difficulties for most Russian arms producers, especially MiG. The political connections that earlier proved so advantageous now turned into a liability, as MiG was associated too closely with the old regime. At the same time, MiG was supplanted by Sukhoi, which experienced a flowering of design creativity and lacked the political baggage. In 1995, MiG was merged with the newly privatized aviation factories of the Moscow Area (Aircraft) Production Organization to become MiG-MAPO. A new design, the MiG-AT, has been offered in competition with the Yak-130 for the Russian air force's Advanced Trainer requirement.

George M. Mellinger

See also

Israeli-Arab Conflicts; Korean War; Mikoyan-Gurevich MiG-17; Mikoyan-Gurevich MiG-21; Mikoyen, Artem I.; North American F-86 Sabre; Polikarpov, Nikolai N.; Sukhoi Aircraft; Yakovlev, Aleksandr S.; Yom Kippur War

References

Belyakov, R. A., and J. Marmain. *MiG: Fifty Years of Secret Aircraft Design.* Annapolis, MD: Naval Institute Press, 1994.

Gunston, Bill, and Yefim Gordon. *MiG Aircraft Since 1937.* London: Putnam; and Annapolis, MD: Naval Institute Press, 1998.

Mikoyan-Gurevich MiG-17

In January 1949, the Soviet Mikoyan-Gurevich Design Bureau reassigned a large number of its aerodynamics staff to a new program in an effort to rectify basic deficiencies in the MiG-15 Fagot of Korean War fame. The 35-degree sweep of the MiG-15 was increased to 45 degrees. The empty weight was increased from 7,456 pounds for the MiG-15 to 8,664 for the first MiG-17. The speed was increased from 652 mph to 711 mph.

The MiG-17 proved to be a highly maneuverable aircraft. Coupled with its cannon armament, it became a formidable weapon, a fact attested to when it was first confronted during the Vietnam War. Returning U.S. fighter pilots demanded that guns be added to follow-on U.S. fighters.

Some 6,000 MiG-17Fs were produced by the Soviet Union. Under license, Poland produced about 1,000 LIM-5s (MiG-17Fs), and China made more than 2,000 of the aircraft.

The MiG-17 became one of the most numerous Soviet export fighters, bolstering air forces of Third World countries in Africa, Asia, and the Middle East, along with numerous Soviet bloc nations in Europe. As many as 40 nations operated the MiG-17. These aircraft have been in front-line service for more than 40 years—a testament to the reliability and maintainability of the basic design.

Alwyn T. Lloyd

References

Gunston, Bill. *Aircraft of the Soviet Union.* London: Osprey, 1983.

Stapfer, Hans-Heri. *MiG-17 Fresco in Action.* Aircraft Number 125. Carrollton, TX: Squadron/Signal, 1992.

Mikoyan-Gurevich MiG-21

Although the MiG design bureau had been progressing toward supersonic flight via the MiG-15, -17, and -19, the appearance of the MiG-21 was a lesson in contrast. Instead of continuing the series with another swept-wing aircraft, the design bureau opted for the delta wing.

Developed from the outset as a lightweight point defense fighter, experimental airframes were flown in 1955 using an axial turbojet. Initially, armament was limited to cannons. The appearance of guided missiles on Western aircraft (AIM-9 Sidewinder) led to home-grown development (K-13 Atoll) with the help of espionage. First deliveries in the Soviet Union took place during 1958, and Warsaw Pact forces followed. Exports were made to such countries as Egypt and Syria.

In common with other aircraft, the MiG-21 underwent continued development; the second series of aircraft featured blown flaps to which was added an enlarged spine containing avionics allied to an improved radar. Weapons capability was later increased by the addition of improved missiles and a ground attack capability.

This new variant saw widespread service throughout the Soviet sphere and remains in use today. Total production exceeded many thousands of all variants, including a two-seat trainer.

Kev Darling

References

Butowski, Piotr, and Jay Miller. *OKB-MiG.* Leicester, UK: Midland Counties, 1991.

Mikoyan-Gurevich MiG-29

Soviet fighter. The appearance of the MiG-29 confirmed that the Soviet Union was not lagging behind in aircraft development. This agile fighter, first developed in the mid-1970s, was the Soviets' answer to the Grumman F-14, McDonnell Douglas F-15, and General Dynamics F-16.

The prototype flew in October 1977 and was followed by a series of development airframes. These underwent various changes to help evolve the type; production began in mid-1982. The following year, MiG-29s were delivered to operational squadrons of the Soviet armed forces. A two-seat trainer (Fulcrum-B) entered service at the conversion and squadron levels. The most prolific version to enter use, both in Russia and overseas, is the Fulcrum-C. This features the humped spine aft of the cockpit containing increased avionics. The Fulcrum-C entered service in 1987.

Other experimental and preproduction MIG-29s include the Fulcrum-D (or K), intended for naval service aboard the Russian carrier *Tbilisi* and featuring a strengthened undercarriage, arrester hook, folding outer wings, and revised avionics.

Foreign operators of the Fulcrum include the Czech Re-

The MiG-29 was one of the most advanced aircraft in the world at the time of its first flight on 6 October 1977. Suitably updated, it remains a world-class fighter. (Big Bird Aviation)

public, India, Iraq, Germany, Poland, the Slovak Republic, Syria, and Yugoslavia. Other nations have ordered the aircraft in smaller quantities, including Cuba, Romania, and Iran. After the breakup of the Soviet Union, the supply of spares for these aircraft was initially spasmodic, although the situation was resolved for those countries paying in Western currency. The MiG-29 is destined to remain in service for many years as upgrades are proposed and implemented in weapons and avionics.

Kev Darling

References

Butowski, Piotr, and Jay Miller. *OKB-MiG*. Leicester, UK: Midland Counties, 1991.

Mil Aircraft

One of two Russian design bureaus specializing exclusively in helicopters. Mikhail Leontevich Mil was born in Siberia in 1909; after graduating from an engineering institute in 1931, he became involved in the development of autogyro aircraft and worked as an assistant to Nikolai Kamov. He formed his own design bureau in 1947, and his first design, the Mi-1, entered production in 1951. This small, two- or three-seat craft was the first helicopter in the Soviet Union to enter significant service, with about 2,700 being produced in the Soviet Union and Poland by the time it was replaced.

The Mi-2 successor was larger and much more powerful, using a turbine engine, and was able to carry up to eight passengers in addition to the pilot. Tremendously successful, the Mi-2 remained in production for 30 years, with 5,450 examples completed, primarily in Poland, which was licensed by Mil and the Warsaw Pact as the sole producer. The Mi-34 successor, dating from the 1990s, has proven unable to replace its predecessor.

The Mi-4, produced from 1953 to 1964, was the first Soviet helicopter to enter service with a significant load-carrying ability. With an appearance much like the Sikorsky S-55, the Mi-4 was able to carry 12 troops and also was produced in antisubmarine warfare (ASW), gunship, and civil transport variants. With 3,200 Mi-4s produced by 1964, it provided the backbone of Soviet helicopter forces until gradually replaced by the Mi-8 and was widely exported to Soviet clients.

The Mi-6 entered service in 1957 as the first Soviet heavy-lift helicopter. It was capable of carrying 90 troops or up to 8 tons of cargo, including small armored vehicles. It remained in production until 1980, and some of the 874 Mi-6s were sold to foreign countries, including Iraq and North Vietnam. Even bigger was the Mi-10, a flying crane; only 80 were produced during the 1960s.

The true successor to the Mi-6 was the Mi-26, capable of carrying up to 25 tons. Since 1983, 300 Mi-26s have been produced. Brief mention should also be made of the experimental V-12, flown in 1969 and easily the largest helicopter ever. This monster was powered by four turbine engines, mounted in pairs at the end of long, winglike sponsons, each pair driving a five-bladed rotor.

The most important helicopter was the Mi-8, which entered production in 1966 as a replacement for the Mi-4. With the nominal ability to carry 4 tons of cargo or seats for

24 troops, the Mi-8 often carried more. It also operated as an electronic warfare platform, and in one of its major armed configurations it was the most heavily armed gunship of all time, carrying four wire-guided antitank guided missiles and six pods of 32 57mm rockets, in addition to a heavy machine gun. By the mid-1980s, more than 8,600 Mi-8s (and the Mi-17 variant) had been built and were in service with every military that used Soviet weapons. During the 1990s, many updated and more heavily armored versions were offered, though the classic Mi-8 remained in wide service.

Equally famous has been the Mi-24 Hind dedicated attack helicopter, of which about 2,600 were produced by 1990. Entering service in 1969, it first saw combat in Afghanistan and quickly became prominent in the wars in the Middle East and sub-Saharan Africa. It even saw combat in Central America with the Sandinistas of Nicaragua and played a prominent role in the fighting in Chechnya.

The Mi-14 is unique among Mil helicopters in being a large, amphibious, land-based ASW helicopter. From 1976 to 1992, the Soviet, Bulgarian, and Polish navies received 270 examples, many of which remain in service.

Mikhail Mil died on 31 January 1970 and was succeeded first by Marat Tishchenko, who designed the Mi-24, and in 1992 by Mark Vineberg. In the post–Cold War period, Mil continues to design and sell military helicopters but also emphasizes a new line of helicopters intended for civilian use.

George M. Mellinger

See also

Kamov Helicopters

References

Everett-Heath, John. *Soviet Helicopters: Design, Development, and Tactics.* London: Jane's Information Group, 1983.

Gunston, Bill. *The Encyclopedia of Russian Aircraft, 1975–1995.* Osceola, WI: Motorbooks International, 1995.

Milch, Erhard (1892–1972)

The individual most responsible for the rapid formation, organization, and growth of the German Luftwaffe. Milch joined the German army in 1910, became an air observer in 1915, and ended World War I in command of a fighter wing. He joined the Lufthansa airline in 1920 and became its director in 1926. By 1933, when he joined the still-secret Luftwaffe as a colonel at the urging of his friend Hermann Goering, Lufthansa was the world's most successful airline. Milch next applied his energy to the organization of the new air force, with the full approval of Goering, who was preoccupied with his many other duties and the ongoing political intrigue within the Third Reich. Milch became Goering's deputy and the state secretary of the RLM (Germany's air ministry). He rose steadily in rank and was named a field marshal at the conclusion of the 1940 French campaign.

After the Battle of Britain, Goering devoted little time to the Luftwaffe, leaving executive control in Milch's hands. By 1943, Milch had added inspector general and director of air armament to his other titles. But his ambition to replace Goering as commander in chief became known, and Goering succeeded in taking away many of his responsibilities. In May 1944, Hitler accused Milch of deceiving him with respect to the Me 262 program and canceled a directive naming Milch as Goering's successor. Milch then withdrew into semiretirement at his hunting lodge and, in January 1945, was stripped of his last position and placed in the Führer Reserve.

In 1947, Milch was convicted of war crimes at the Nuremberg trials and sentenced to life imprisonment. His sentence was later reduced to 15 years, and he was released in 1955. He was employed as an adviser by several German industrial firms until shortly before his death in 1972.

Donald Caldwell

See also

German Air Force (Luftwaffe)

References

Corum, J. *The Luftwaffe: Creating the Operational Air War, 1918–1940.* Lawrence: University Press of Kansas, 1997.

Irving, D. *The Rise and Fall of the Luftwaffe: The Life of Field Marshal Erhard Milch.* Boston: Little, Brown, 1973.

Miles Aircraft

British aircraft manufacturer. Frederick G. Miles and George H. Miles helped form Southern Aircraft in 1925 for the purpose of rebuilding old airplanes. They designed and built the Martlet, a single-seat aerobatic biplane, in 1928–1929, selling five. In August 1932, Miles formed a partnership with Phillips and Powis. Their first design was the M.2 Hawk, a two-seat, open-cockpit, low-wing, single-engine monoplane intended as a successor to the de Havilland Moth for training and sport aviation, which flew in March 1933. This was succeeded by a side-by-side cabin-cockpit version, the M.3 Falcon, which evolved into the M.7 Nighthawk, the M.11 Whitney Straight, the M.16 Mentor, and the M.17 Monarch (1938), all seating two to four; the latter two models had limited production for use as navigational trainers.

The all-wood Magister primary trainer was a militarized and improved version of the Hawk and went into service in

October 1937. The Magister was used for all primary flight training in the RAF well into World War II; 1,293 were built. In 1936, Phillips and Powis Aircraft was bought by Rolls-Royce for the purpose of building a Kestrel-powered all-wood trainer, called the Miles M.9 "Kestrel" and Miles R.R. "Trainer," which flew in May 1937. The British Air Ministry ordered this design as an advanced trainer, which was in production from 1938 to 1942, with 3,450 being built.

In 1941, F. G. Miles bought Phillips and Powis Aircraft from Rolls-Royce and in 1943 renamed it Miles Aircraft. The M.28 Mercury prototype (put into production as the M.38 Messenger) was a twin-engine, cabin-cockpit, four-place, light, low-wing transport-trainer that flew in September 1942. The M.65 Gemini was a further improvement in this line; 250 M.38/M.65s were built.

Miles airplanes were prominent in air races in the 1930s and 1940s, and Miles had a reputation for aggressive and rapid experimental design. Miles proposed in 1936 and 1938 a blended-wing four-engine transport, the M.26 Miles-X. In 1941, Miles built a twin-engine scaled version of the X, the M.30 X-Minor, to demonstrate this design, which flew in February 1942. Two tandem-wing aircraft, the M.35 and M.39, flew as demonstrators in 1943. They were named "Libellulas" (Dragonflies), the M.35 being a single-engine pusher, the M.39, a twin-engine tractor.

In 1943, in spite of having no previous high-speed experience, Miles was asked to design and build Britain's first supersonic aircraft, the M.52, with the goal of reaching 1,000 mph, to be powered by the Whittle W.2/700 engine with afterburning. Miles made great strides, designing and wind tunnel–testing the optimum fuselage and designing and flight-testing a thin supersonic biconvex-airfoil wing. A mockup had been built when this program was canceled in February 1946, about six months before first flight, on the basis that its objectives were no longer needed. Data was given to Bell Aircraft for use in the design of the XS-1.

Miles continued to develop advanced aircraft, including the M.33 Monitor, a World War II twin-engine target-tow monoplane of 360-mph maximum speed; the M.57 Aerovan, a twin-powered, high-wing, pod-and-boom light transport of 120 mph maximum speed, that flew in 1946, with 48 being built; and the M.60 Marathon, a four-engine feeder liner that flew in 1946, with 42 being built. In 1947, Miles Aircraft was merged into Handley Page. Both F. G. and G. H. Miles continued design work on aircraft, associating with Airspeed, Hurel-Dubois, Beagle, and flight simulators (Link-Miles).

Douglas G. Culy

References

Gunston, Bill. *The World's Greatest Airplanes.* New York: Elsevier-Dutton, 1980.

Sturtivant, Ray. *British Research and Development Aircraft.* Yeovil, UK: Haynes, 1990.

Missiles, Air-to-Air and Air-to-Surface

Though widely used, air-to-air missiles (AAMs) have not yet replaced the gun as the primary air-to-air weapon. To establish and compare performance of various AAMs, a "launch envelope" is used to show minimum and maximum range against an aspect angle within which the missile can engage a target. The shape and size of the envelope will vary dramatically with target speed, altitude, and G-force as well as the firing aircraft's speed and altitude. For example, the maximum aerodynamic range at low altitude could easily be one-third of that at high altitude, and any maneuver by the target will collapse the envelope inward. A common failure is firing within the nonmaneuvering envelope; the target sees the missile and maneuvers to place the missile outside the maneuvering launch envelope. The missile then passes the target outside lethal range.

Infrared guidance is the technology of choice for small dogfight missiles (U.S. AIM-9 Sidewinder, Soviet AA-2 Atoll). The seeker homes onto the heat energy emitted by the target aircraft. The early generation of seekers operated in the 2–3 micron range and could home onto only the hot jet exhaust, but later seekers operate at longer wavelengths and can home onto the cooler parts of the target from the front. State-of-the-art seekers use imaging technology to select the precise point of impact.

Some early missiles (Fairey Fireflash, Raytheon Sparrow I, AA-1 Alkali) used beam-riding guidance. The fighter's radar emits a narrow beam that the pilot lines up on the target, and the missile steers toward the center of the beam. The first guided missile to enter operational service (the Hughes AIM-4 Falcon) used semiactive radar-homing (SARH). The fighter's radar locks onto the target and illuminates it; the seeker then homes onto the reflected emissions. Although SARH is inherently less accurate than infrared homing, the guidance laws used by the missile autopilot can be more sophisticated if the seeker is able to measure target closure rate.

A few of the larger AAMs use active radar guidance (Hughes AIM-54 Phoenix). The missile carries its own radar transmitter and homes onto the radar energy reflected off the target. Active radar guidance is now becoming practical for more moderately sized missiles (Hughes AIM-120 AMRAAM) and can be more accurate than SARH because range information is available to the autopilot.

The most influential missile ever is probably the AIM-9 Sidewinder infrared (heat-seeking) missile, originally devel-

U.S. Air-to-Air Missiles Since 1956

Year	*Name*	*Weight*	*Length*	*Range*	*Max. Speed*	*Capability*
1956	AIM-9B Sidewinder	155 lbs	9 ft, 3 in	2 miles	M=2.5	Narrow rear
1961	AA-2 Atoll	154 lbs	9 ft, 2 in	2 miles	M=2.5	Narrow rear
1963	AIM-4D Falcon	134 lbs	6 ft, 8 in	2 miles	M=4.0	Rear
1964	Red Top	330 lbs	10 ft, 10 in	7.5 miles	M=3.2	Limited all-aspect
1966	AIM-9D Sidewinder	195 lbs	9 ft, 5 in	5 miles	M=2.5	Rear
1975	Matra R550 Magic 1	198 lbs	9 ft, 1 in	1.9 miles	M=3.0	Rear
1977	AIM-9L Sidewinder	190 lbs	9 ft, 5 in	5 miles	M=2.5	All-aspect
1986	AA-11 Archer	232 lbs	9 ft, 6 in	4.6 miles	M=3.0 (est.)	All-aspect

oped by a small team operating on an equally small budget at the Naval Ordnance Test Station at China Lake, California. The AIM-9B achieved initial operational capability (IOC) in 1956 and was used in combat in 1958 by Nationalist Chinese F-86s. The U.S. Air Force employed the AIM-9B and AIM-9E in Vietnam, but they had problems at low level, in bad weather, or against maneuvering targets; the kill probability was a disappointing 15 percent. The AIM-9D was much better, and the later all-aspect AIM-9L achieved a kill probability of around 75 percent during the Falkland Islands War in 1982. The AA-2 Atoll (K-13A) bears a striking resemblance to the AIM-9B and is generally believed to be a copy. It has a similar performance to the AIM-9B and started to be replaced by the AA-8 Aphid from about 1976. The Hughes AIM-4D was also used in Vietnam, but it had serious operational problems requiring a complicated switching sequence to use; once armed, it had to be fired within two minutes.

One of the first missiles claimed to have an all-aspect homing capability was the de Havilland Red Top, which entered service in 1964. It was capable of homing onto a hot airframe from head-on if the target was supersonic.

The Matra R550 Magic 1, introduced in 1975, is the only European missile to compete with the Sidewinder family in the export market and is plug-in compatible with it. The later (1984) Magic 2 is an all-aspect weapon.

Probably the best infrared AAM in service today is the AA-11 (Vympel R-73) Archer. It is much better than the AIM-9M in acquisition, speed, electronic counter-countermeasures, and maneuverability.

Radar-guided missiles are another important variety. The world's first air-to-air guided missile to enter operational service was the Hughes AIM-4 Falcon, reaching IOC in mid-1956. Compared with its contemporaries, the radar-guided Falcon was a very effective weapon and was developed into multiple versions and exported widely, although the requirement for six missiles to fit within the internal missile bay of the F-102 interceptor meant that there was no room for a proximity fuse, and the warhead had to be very small.

The Fairey Fireflash was a beam-rider, the first air-to-air guided weapon to be deployed by the United Kingdom (August 1957). Operational trials discovered that the missile was effective against large cooperative targets, but it was too difficult for the average squadron pilot to use against maneuvering targets. It had a maximum speed of Mach 2 and could be fired at the rear of a target from a range of about 2 miles.

The first Russian missile to enter service was the AA-1 Alkali, probably in 1958. It had a range of about 3 miles. Guidance was achieved by riding a radar beam, and it was similar to the Fireflash in general performance and is likely to have shared many of the same problems.

The Raytheon AIM-7 Sparrow III was a semiactive radar-homer, with a range of about 25 miles. Used operationally by the United States during the Vietnam War, its performance was relatively poor because rules of engagement usually specified visual contact with the target. Only under unusual tactical circumstances was it employed in beyond-visual-range combat. A variant of the Sparrow, the British Aerospace Skyflash, used a monopulse seeker and demonstrated a remarkable performance during flight trials in 1975. There is some evidence to suggest that the accuracy of the later AIM-7M (used in the 1991 Gulf War) is comparable with tthat of he Skyflash.

The tactical limitations of SARH are that the fighter's radar must continue to illuminate the target until the missile hits, and only one target can be engaged at once. These restrictions are eliminated if the missile can illuminate the target using its own radar transmitter. The first active radar AAM to enter service was the Hughes AIM-54 Phoenix in 1974, with a range of about 115 miles.

Air-to-surface missiles (ASMs) have replaced bombs as the major airborne offensive weapon, particularly against heavily defended targets. The first air-launched guided missiles were built under programs managed by Siemens-Schuckert in Germany during World War I. Several missiles were tested; all were standoff glide weapons launched from aircraft or airships against shipping. The missiles were steered by commands sent through thin copper wires and were designed to split open near the target and deposit an airborne torpedo into the water. The Henschel Hs 293 became operational in summer 1943 and was probably the first successful modern ASM, with a range of about 18 miles. The missile was initially boosted ahead of the launch aircraft so that the operator could see the tracking flare, and it was guided onto the target using a two-axis joystick. Early versions were wire-guided, but a radio link was also used. The Hs 293 was used mainly in the Mediterranean Theater. The Hs 293D was probably the first missile to be television-guided, and about 70 test-firings were made before the end of World War II.

The U.S. Navy's Bat was the first antiship missile to use radar-homing; it was developed by the Navy Bureau of Ordnance in partnership with MIT, carried pulsed radar in the nose, and homed automatically onto radar energy reflected from the target vessel. With a range of up to 20 miles, from May 1945 it was very effective against Japanese warships and was used against bridges in Burma.

The Hughes AGM-65 Maverick is probably the most widely deployed ASM in the Western world and can be used against hard land targets, armored vehicles, and small ships. The AGM-65A and B are video-guided and lock onto a target nominated by the pilot, onto which they home automatically using the video image. Although the AGM-65A was used successfully in clear conditions during the 1973 Yom Kippur War, there have been instances of the seeker breaking lock and missing the target. Range varies between 10 and 25 miles, depending on the launch speed and altitude. Later versions (AGM-65C and -E) were used in a close-support role, homing onto reflected laser energy from a target designated by either an airborne pod or friendly infantry. The AGM-65E was similar to the -C but had a heavy-duty warhead, an improved laser tracker, and digital processing. The AGM-65D and -F used an imaging infrared seeker to home onto the target's heat image.

Although smaller antiship missiles use some form of command guidance (Aérospatiale AS.11), larger missiles usually have active radar guidance so that the launching aircraft can stay out of range of the target's defensive systems. The first post–World War II antiship missile to use active radar homing was the Saab RB 04, which entered service in 1958; it had a range of 20 miles.

Even though antiship missiles are small, fast targets, they can still be engaged successfully by many shipborne weapons systems; this led to the development of sea skimming ASMs. Sea skimmers have a radar altimeter, and the autopilot typically lets the missile down to the sea surface in stages, finishing a few feet above the water just before impact—the exact height varies with sea state. Most sea skimmers can be fired below the target's radar horizon and have a programmed popup to acquire the target before impact. Some can also perform dogleg course changes and a terminal maneuver to help defeat defensive systems. The Aérospatiale AM.39 Exocet is a typical sea skimmer; it entered service in 1977 and was used by the Argentine navy during the Falkland Islands War. It was developed from the ship-launched MM.38 and has a range of between 31 and 44 miles. An active-radar seeker provides terminal guidance.

Most airborne antitank guided missiles (ATGMs) are fired from helicopters and share many features with the equivalent infantry weapons. All have some form of shaped-charge warhead to penetrate the armor of a main battle tank, and some have a tandem warhead with a precursor charge to defeat reactive armor. Many helicopter-launched ATGMs are command guided using wires (AT-3 Sagger, GM-Hughes TOW), although the earlier AT-2 Swatter used an infrared seeker to home onto the target's heat source.

The Rockwell AGM-114 Hellfire is a helicopter-launched heavy antiarmor weapon and achieved IOC in 1984. The first three generations of Hellfire missiles used a laser seeker, and targets had to be designated by the firing helicopter or other friendly forces. The latest version, the Longbow Hellfire, uses a millimeter-wave radar seeker to provide adverse-weather fire-and-forget capability.

Andy Blackburn

See also

Bolo; Convair F-102 Delta Dagger and F-106 Delta Dart; Defense Suppression; Gulf War; Vietnam War

References

Gunston, Bill. *The Illustrated Encyclopedia of Aircraft Armament.* London: Salamander, 1987.

Jackson, Paul, ed. *Jane's All the World's Aircraft, 2000–2001.* London: Jane's Information Group, 2000.

Michel, Marshall L. III. *Clashes: Air Combat over North Vietnam, 1965–1972.* Annapolis, MD: Naval Institute Press, 1997.

Spick, Mike. *Designed for the Kill.* Shrewsbury, UK: Airlife, 1995.

Missiles, Intercontinental Ballistic (ICBMs)

The development of ICBMs commenced in the late 1940s and early 1950s with a program authorized by Congress under the direction of the Strategic Air Command (SAC). The first ICBM prototypes, the subsonic SM-62 Snark and the supersonic Boojum proposed by Jack Northrop in 1946, had a projected range of 1,500–5,000 statute miles with a speed of 600 mph and a 2,000-pound warhead. After experiencing difficulties with the performance of the guidance systems, Northrop suggested an inertial navigation system monitored by stellar navigation. Mechanical difficulties delayed testing

Solid rocket fuel made the Minuteman missile much easier to service and to launch. (U.S. Air Force)

until the 1950s. The U.S. Air Force also considered another early missile, the Navaho, but schedule delays and difficulties resulted in the elimination of the program.

The Atlas was the first-generation ICBM developed by the Convair Division of General Dynamics Corporation between 1956 and 1963. Continued research and development resulted in the construction of Atlas SM-65A through F missiles. Atlas A reached a maximum range of 600 nautical miles and an altitude of 57.5 nautical miles. Atlas B tests improved the range to 5,500 miles in 1958. The first successful operational use of the Atlas B occurred on 18 December 1958 with the launch of the world's first communications satellite. The Atlas D became the first fully operational missile used by Strategic Air Command. Model D, stored horizontally on above-ground launchers, had a maximum range of 6,500 nautical miles propelled by liquid fuel with 360,000 pounds/thrust with a radio-inertial guidance system. Improvements resulted in the Atlas E with an increased thrust of 389,000 pounds, an all-inertial guidance system, and a large warhead. The final version of the Atlas missiles, Model F, possessed most of the same characteristics as the Model E except for an improved thrust and quicker response time due to the storability of liquid fuel. The development of Minuteman missiles resulted in a decision to phase out the Atlas missiles. Under Operation ADDED EFFORT, Strategic Air Command retired the last of the Atlas missiles on 20 April 1965.

The Titan I, classified as a first-generation ICBM, with a range of 5,500 nautical miles with a radio and all-inertial guidance system, relied on its two-stage, liquid-fueled, rocket-powered design for propulsion. Stored in hardened silos until their retirement from Strategic Air Command in 1963, the Titan I was replaced by Titan II missiles under Operation ADDED EFFORT.

Like its predecessor, the second-generation Titan II missile had an effective range of 5,500 nautical miles. Improvements over the earlier version included reliance on an all-inertial guidance system, a larger warhead, and the ability of deploying from a hardened underground silo. Ordered by SAC in October 1959, the first Titan II reached operational capability on 8 June 1963. SAC continued to operate six Titan II missile units until three accidents resulted in the death of four airmen and the destruction of two missile sites. In 1981, the Department of Defense called for a safety investigation, after which the decision to retire the Titan II missiles resulted in their removal from SAC under a program called Rivet Cap. The last Titan II went offline on 18 August 1987.

The Martin Titan was the "Grand Slam" of American missiles, and served later as a booster for spacecraft. (U.S. Air Force)

In 1958, the Department of Defense approved the development of the Minuteman I missile. Designed to withstand a first strike, this three-stage, solid-propellant, rocket-powered ICBM also had an effective range of 5,500 nautical miles. The Air Force placed the Minutemans in hardened underground silos. In 1966, a modernization program required the retirement of Minuteman I missiles, a program completed on 12 February 1969.

The Air Force integrated the Minuteman II missile (effective range of 7,000 nautical miles) into the SAC program in 1965. Engineers also incorporated an improved guidance system, an increased payload capability, and a greater ability to withstand a nuclear strike in the Minuteman II. The operational deployment of 1,000 Minuteman ICBMs completed by April 1967 formed the backbone of the SAC program until the conclusion of the SALT Treaty, at which time the remaining Minuteman II missiles were deactivated and the silos destroyed.

The Air Force deployed more than 500 Minuteman III missiles during a modernization program in 1968. Designed as a multiple independently targetable reentry vehicle (MIRV), the Minuteman III contained three Mark 12 and Mark 12A MIRVs guarded by an improved computer memory. They were stored in hardened silos, and command-and-control safeguards included an ability for airborne control if communications failure occurs between command-and-control centers. Fifty Peacekeeper missiles deployed in 1982 replaced some of the earlier Minuteman missiles. Currently, the only land-based ICBM in the U.S. nuclear arsenal, the Minuteman III, has been reconfigured to hold only one reentry vehicle in accordance with a 1992 agreement. The Air Force intends to utilize the Minuteman III missiles through 2025.

Cynthia Clark Northrup

See also

Strategic Air Command

References

Miller, David. *The Cold War: A Military History.* New York: St. Martin's, 1999.

Missiles, Intermediate-Range Ballistic (IRBMs)

Land-based ballistic missiles, usually with nuclear/thermonuclear warheads and a range of 2,000–6,000 nautical miles. In a strategic sense, IRBMs were close to medium-

Ballistic Missiles (various countries)

Missile	*Country*	*Duration of service*	*Approximate range (miles/kms)*	*Warhead (MT)*
"Blue Steak" prototype	United Kingdom	1955–1960 project	1,512/2,800	1x3
SS-4 (Sandal)	USSR	1957–1991	1,080/2,000	1x1
SS-5 (Skean)	USSR	1961–1984	2,214/ 4,100	1x1
SS-14 (Scapegoat)	USSR	1965–not reported	2,160/4,000	no data
SS-15 (Scrooge)	USSR	Very limited deployment	3,024/5,600	no data
SS-20 (Saber)	USSR	1975–1991	2,214/5,000	3x0.15
Jupiter PGM-19A	United States	1958–1965	1,296/2,400	1x1.44
Thor SM-75	United States	1959–1964	1,296/2,700	1x1.44
Tomahawk BGM-109 GLCM	United States	1984–1990	1,555/2,880	1x0.20
Pershing II	United States	1983–1990	972/1,800	1x0.005
Dong-Feng 3/3A (CSS-2)	China	1971–	1,431/2,650	1x3
Dong Feng 4 (CSS-3)	China	1981–	2,430/4,500	1x3
S-2	France	1971–1983	1,782/3.300	1x0.12
S-30	France	1980–1998	1,890/3,500	1x1
Agni-2	India	developing	1,242/2,300	no data
Shahab-4	Iran	developing	1,080/2,000	no data
Jeriho-2	Israel	developing	1,080/2,000	no data
Ghauri-3	Pakistan	developing	1,926/3,566	no data
CSS-2	Saudi Arabia	developing	1,458/2,700	conventional

range ballistic missiles (MRBMs; 1,000–2,000 miles) and share some characteristics of historical significance.

MRBM/IRBMs were earlier types of ballistic missiles that laid the base for further development of missile technology and contributed to the initial steps of space programs. The whole history of MRBM/IRBMs revealed the dynamic and multifaceted interplay of military, technological, geopolitical, and diplomatic factors and trends. The MRBM/IRBM class remains the only one in the nuclear arsenal that was ever eliminated.

Due to their operational characteristics, MRBM/IRBMs were to be deployed in the same theater with the presumed targets. This emphasized the geostrategic disparity between the transatlantic alliance and the Soviet bloc. That is why MRBM/IRBMs emerged as highly provocative, instrumental tools for nuclear blackmail, bargaining, and pressure. Not accidentally, MRBM/IRBMs were involved in two major crises of the Cold War: the Cuban Missile Crisis (1962) and the Euromissile Crisis (1979–1985).

Soviet IRBMs were the bulk of the nuclear threat to Western Europe since the end of the 1950s. In order to ensure the confidence of European allies through U.S. nuclear guarantees, the United States deployed IRBMs (60 Thor missiles in England and 60 Jupiter missiles, divided equally, in Italy and Turkey). These were operated respectively by the RAF and Italian and Turkish air forces with nuclear warheads under USAF control.

The military value of these missiles diminished over time due to their vulnerability in the fixed and open launch sites. Nevertheless, they played a significant role, facilitating the greater European participation in NATO nuclear affairs, and were instrumental as a bargain tool to bring about a resolution to the Cuban Missile Crisis.

The arms-control limitations on ICBMs in the 1970s underlined the value of IRBMs in the strategic balance. The Soviet IRBM modernization (deployment of 800 SS-20s by 1988, capable of striking more precisely and deeply in Western Europe) challenged the transatlantic security link and ignited the second major missile crisis. Thanks to the endorsement of European allies and despite pacifist protests, NATO managed to deploy 464 Tomahawks in the United Kingdom, Germany, Italy, Belgium, and the Netherlands, as well as 108 Pershing IIs in Germany.

The new U.S. missiles, with superior operational characteristics, changed the balance in the field and placed a wide range of Soviet command, control, and communications targets under effective threat. Moscow and its allies were forced to concede. Under the 1987 Intermediate Nuclear Forces Treaty, all Soviet and U.S. MRBM/IRBMs were eliminated. Today some countries (Iran, Iraq, North Korea, Libya, and others) are trying to upgrade their ballistic missiles to the intermediate-range level.

Peter Rainow

See also

Cuban Missile Crisis; French Missile Production and Development; Missiles, Intercontinental Ballistic; Missiles; Multiple Independently Targetable Reentry Vehicle; Strategic Arms Limitation Talks; Strategic Arms Reduction Talks

References

Cartwright, John, and Julian Critchley. *Cruise, Pershing, and SS-20. The Search for Consensus: Nuclear Weapons in Europe.* London: Brassey's, 1985.

Miller, David. *The Cold War: A Military History.* New York: St. Martin's, 1998.

Missiles, Surface-to-Air

The first surface-to-air missiles (SAMs) were a byproduct of the German V-2 program. The Wasserfall (Waterfall) was a scaled-down version of the V-2 with a 200-pound warhead that utilized visual tracking and radio control to engage its target.

Strategic SAMs During the Cold War

The Wasserfall design led directly to the first Soviet SAM, the R-101, which was essentially a copy of the German system. Further improvements to the R-101 led to the R-113 (NATO designation SA-1 Guild). The SA-1 was the first SAM to effectively employ radars for onsite acquisition and fire control. Large numbers of the systems were deployed in a ring around Moscow beginning in 1954, but none was ever deployed elsewhere. The system remained in service until the mid-1980s, when it was replaced by more modern systems.

U.S. efforts reached fruition with the 1954 deployment of the first Nike-Ajax battalion. The Nike-Ajax was similar in performance to the SA-1 and was also deployed to protect key cities from strategic bombers carrying nuclear weapons. Approximately 300 permanent Nike sites were eventually deployed, with an upgrade already under way. The upgrade, the Hercules, extended range to more than over 75 nautical miles and increased the maximum altitude to more than 150,000 feet. The Nike system was exported to many U.S. allies during the Cold War but remains in operation in only Turkey and South Korea.

In the Soviet Union, the entirely new SA-2 Guideline utilized Fansong fire-control radar (range: 16 nautical miles; altitude 72,000 feet, with upgrades extending those numbers). The first command-guided SA-2s reached operational status in 1955 and by 1960 had claimed their first kill, a U-2 flown by Gary Powers. By mid-1965, the system had been deployed to Vietnam, where it gained fame by bringing down significant numbers of U.S. aircraft. Eventually, the SA-2 was deployed to many of Russia's allies, where it is still in service today. In fact, many countries have opted to upgrade their existing SA-2s with modern electronics and other enhancements as opposed to purchasing new systems. As a result, the half-century-old system remains a potent threat.

The need to protect against fast, maneuverable attackers led to the development of the SA-3 Goa in 1956, the inner layer of the Soviet defense umbrella, with the system reaching operational status in 1961. Like the SA-2, the SA-3 has been very successful in the export market. It has seen combat in every Middle Eastern conflict since 1970. In the 1990s, the SA-3 attempted to defend Serbia's airspace against NATO's Operation ALLIED FORCE with limited success.

The outermost layer of the Soviet Union's strategic air defense umbrella was the S-200 Angara (NATO designation SA-5 Gammon). Upon becoming operational in 1966, the system provided a quantum leap in the ability to engage strategic bombers and support assets before they could get close enough to become a threat. The SA-5 system combined an extremely long-range missile with sophisticated radars. The system utilizes the exceptionally powerful Square Pair radar to track targets and guide the missile. At its peak, the system was deployed in the Soviet Union at nearly 130 launch sites.

In 1967, work was begun on the system that would eventually become the S-300 (SA-10). The goal of the project was to develop a SAM with advanced capabilities to replace the obsolete SA-1 in the defense of Moscow. The system has seen constant updating. It uses the track-via-missile guidance technique, whereby the missile is simply command-guided until onboard sensors detect the target.

The United States did not develop a follow-on to the Nike until the modern Patriot system. Although work on the program was initiated in 1961, the U.S. Army was not able to deploy the system until 1982. The Patriot was designed as a mobile, all-weather air defense system providing long-range protection of key targets. The core of the system is the advanced planar phased-array AN/MPQ-53 radar, which is capable of tracking approximately 100 targets while guiding up to nine missiles utilizing the track-via-missile guidance technique. The Patriot has seen continuous improvement in computer technology, electronic countermeasures, radar versatility, and missile range. Patriot batteries gained fame by effectively countering Iraqi Scud attacks during the Gulf War. Several U.S. allies employ variants of the Patriot system, including Israel, Kuwait, and Saudi Arabia. Recent trends indicate that further deployments of the system are likely.

Russia's Almaz Central Design Bureau is hard at work on the next generation of strategic SAMs. For the Russians, the future lies with the S-400, designed to counter current and

The Boeing Bomarc was an extraordinarily sophisticated surface-to-air missile, designed to intercept incoming Soviet bombers. (U.S. Air Force)

future threats. It will employ several missile types to engage a variety of targets. As new threats emerge, so do new countermeasures; the cycle of improvement will inevitably continue.

Tactical SAMs

Tactical SAMs, along with mobile antiaircraft artillery (AAA), have a major role in defending ground personnel. Tactical SAMs can primarily be found in either a man-portable or vehicle-mounted configuration.

The first modern man-portable air defense system (MANPADS) was the U.S. Redeye, which became operational in 1964. This missile utilized an infrared (IR) homing system to lock onto an aircraft's exhaust. The Stinger replacement entered service in early 1981, utilizing a cooled-IR seeker that allowed ground troops to engage approaching targets rather than waiting until after they had been attacked and the aircraft was leaving the area. Like most other U.S. systems, the Stinger has seen constant improvement, primarily on the seeker head, making it more sensitive and more capable to reject IR countermeasures.

Tens of thousands of Stingers have been produced over the years, used by nearly 30 countries. In addition to the man-portable version, Stinger missiles have also been mounted on several ground vehicles and helicopters.

The first Russian MANPADS entered service in 1966. The SA-7, as it is known by NATO, was capable of engaging targets from directly behind the exhaust stream. Improvements were made to allow target acquisition up to 30 degrees on either side of the exhaust plume. In 1974, the SA-14 was brought into operational service, the first Soviet MANPADS to utilize a cooled-IR seeker. In addition to allowing forward-hemisphere engagements, the cooled-IR technology also greatly reduced the seeker's vulnerability to IR countermeasures. The SA-16 and SA-18 entered service in the early 1980s and featured improved resistance to IR countermeasures. The SA-18 can effectively discern even the most advanced countermeasures, such as pyrotechnical, blinking, and modulated IR decoys. It has the greatest range of any of the systems. All of these MANPADS have been produced in great quantities.

The only tactical SAMs produced by the United States that are not man-portable are the Raytheon MIM-23 HAWK (Homing All the Way Killer) and the Chaparral. Work began on the HAWK in 1952, and the system became operational in 1960. The HAWK was designed as a mobile, low-to-medium-altitude SAM intended to protect front-line ground forces from air attack. The system is mounted on trailers and is the exception to the vehicle-mounted trend. The missile utilizes semiactive radar-homing for guidance (the missile uses radar energy reflected off the aircraft to home onto the target). The radar providing the signal is a high-power illuminator, the fire-control radar for the HAWK system. After many upgrades, the HAWK is still in service in U.S. forces and has been a successful export.

The Chaparral was originally designed to provide close air support of field targets. Like many of the MANPADS, the system utilizes an IR seeker to engage targets out to a maximum range approaching 5 nautical miles. However, the system can lock onto many targets at nearly twice this range. Although phased out of the U.S. inventory, the system is still employed by a handful of countries.

The Soviet Union began working on vehicle-mounted tactical SAMs in 1958. The program led to the SA-4 Ganef, which entered service in 1967. The system is usually deployed 6–15 miles from the front. Very few remain in service today.

The second tactical SAM developed by the Soviets was the very successful SA-6 Gainful, which Bosnian Serbs used to down a USAF F-16 in 1995. The SA-6s are mounted on one tracked vehicle while the Straight Flush radar is mounted on another. Once the radars are activated and a missile launched, the round will home onto the reflected energy out to its maximum range and altitude.

A Soviet joint army-navy project was the SA-8 Gecko, in which both the missiles and radar would reside on the same chassis. Entering service in 1972, the six-wheeled all-terrain vehicle was able to move just behind the forward line of troops. The system was able to protect the troops within a radius of 5 nautical miles up to an altitude of 16,000 feet and has been exported to several countries, seeing combat in both the Middle East and Africa.

The SA-11 first entered service in 1979–1980. It is a tracked vehicle with four ready-to-launch Gadfly missiles located on the same chassis and designed to provide direct cover to the forward echelon of forces. The vehicle contains an additional four missiles that can be launched off the dual-role loader/launcher.

The most advanced Russian tactical SAM is the S-300V (SA-12 to NATO). The system's two missiles are known as the Gladiator and the Giant. Typically, an SA-12 battery will be a mix of both missile types, with the Gladiator engaging maneuvering targets, cruise missiles, and tactical ballistic missiles (TBMs) while the Giant concentrates on long-range aircraft and longer-range TBMs.

Probably the most advanced low-altitude tactical SAM is the SA-15 Gauntlet. This system, known in Russia as the Tor, was developed during the 1980s as a replacement for the SA-8. It was designed to defend against highly maneuverable aircraft, helicopters, precision-guided munitions, cruise missiles, and remotely piloted vehicles. The system comes mounted on either a tracked or wheeled vehicle, the wheeled version primarily intended for export. Mounted on the chassis are all the components required to make each vehicle an autonomous air defense cell. The system is slowly replacing the SA-8 in the Russian inventory and has been exported to a few countries.

The latest Russian radar-guided tactical SAM is the SA-17 Grizzly, designed to engage basically the same target set as the SA-15, only at a longer range (27 nautical miles) and higher altitude (82,000 feet) The system is in limited production and is being employed the Russian army. There are no known exports of the system.

The Russians also developed several vehicle-mounted IR systems. The first of these, the SA-9, was developed in the late 1960s and entered service in 1968. This system consisted of four IR missiles mounted on a BRDM-2 all-terrain reconnaissance vehicle. The system was replaced by the SA-13 in 1975, incorporating IR counter-countermeasures and allowing for all-aspect engagements. Both the SA-9 and the SA-13 have been successful on the export market and have seen combat in locations ranging from Africa to the Balkans.

The final tactical system is a hybrid gun-missile system known as the 2S6 Tunguska that was developed in 1970 as a follow-on to the ZSU-23-4 self-propelled AAA piece. The system first entered service in 1986 and was designed to fill the gap between the MANPADS and the SA-15. The Tunguska combines four 30mm cannons with eight command-guided SA-19 missiles. The missiles can engage fast maneuverable targets. The Hot Shot fire-control radar is mounted on the rear of the vehicle and provides the critical information required to engage with either the guns or the missiles. Additionally, the system is equipped with optical sites, which can be used to prosecute engagements with both weapons as well. The decision as to which weapon to use is left to the battery commander. The system is in service with Russian forces and has been exported to India as a replacement for their ZSU-23-4 guns.

As long as there is a credible air threat to troops on the ground, there will be a requirement for tactical SAMs.

Troy D. Hammon

See also

Defense Suppression; DESERT SHIELD; DESERT STORM; German Rocket Development; Missiles, Surface-to-Air; Wild Weasel; Yom Kippur War

References

Crabtree, James D. *On Air Defense.* Westport, CT: Praeger, 1994.
Cullen, Tony, and Christopher F. Foss, eds. *Jane's Land Based Air Defence.* Alexandria, VA: Jane's Information Group, 1999.
Schaffel, Kenneth. *The Emerging Shield: The Air Force and the Evolution of Continental Air Defense, 1945–1960.* Washington, DC: Office of Air Force History, United States Air Force, 1991.
Werrell, Kenneth P. *Archie, Flak, AAA, and SAM: A Short Operational History of Ground-Based Air Defense.* Maxwell AFB, AL: Air University Press, 1988.

Mitchell, Reginald J. (1895–1937)

British aircraft designer. Born on 20 May 1895 in Talke, Staffordshire, Mitchell trained as an engineer, joined Supermarine Aviation Works in 1916, and became chief engineer and designer in 1919.

Supermarine specialized in flying-boat construction. Mitchell produced a series of successful flying boats with wooden monocoque hulls for both military and civil use, including the Southampton and the Sea Lion, which won the Schneider Trophy in 1922.

Mitchell, however, was an early proponent of all-metal structure. In 1926, he designed a successful light-alloy hull for the Southampton that was stronger and lighter by some 900 pounds. A series of military and airliner boats followed that also attracted export orders.

Fame came Mitchell's way for his series of specialized racing seaplanes that competed for the Schneider Trophy. The unsuccessful wooden S.4 of 1925 was followed by the S.5, with a duraluminium monocoque fuselage, which won the 1927 contest. The all-metal S.6 won in 1929, and its developed successor, the S.6B, in 1931 gave the Schneider Trophy permanently to Britain.

Mitchell's experience with streamlining and monocoque structures led directly to high-speed fighter designs. The clumsy Type 224 was followed by the Spitfire in 1936. This design combined an elliptical wing planform to minimize drag with the powerful Merlin engine and a slender fuselage to produce the most successful British fighter of World War II. Some 22,000 Spitfires were built before production ceased in 1949. Mitchell himself did not witness this triumph; he died on 12 June 1937.

Paul E. Fontenoy

See also

Flying Boats; Supermarine Aircraft; Supermarine Spitfire

References

Andrews, Charles F., and Eric B. Morgan. *Supermarine Aircraft Since 1914.* London: Putnam, 1981.
Morgan, Eric B., and Edward Shacklady. *Spitfire: The History.* Stamford, UK: Key, 1987.

Mitchell, William "Billy" (1879–1936)

U.S. Army Air Service brigadier general and early advocate of American airpower. Born on 29 December 1879 in Nice, France, Mitchell grew up near Milwaukee, Wisconsin. He enlisted in the Army while attending George Washington University at the outbreak of the Spanish-American War in 1898. He became a Signal Corps officer and served in the Philippines. Afterward, he supervised the erection of a 1,700-mile telegraph line in Alaska. In 1905–1906, Mitchell was an assistant to the commandant of the Signal School at Fort Leavenworth, Kansas, where he developed a forward-looking lecture on military balloons.

After graduating from the Army Staff College, he returned to the Philippines and carried out a successful undercover reconnaissance of Japanese activities in the region. Subsequently, he served on the Army general staff until 1916, when he became deputy chief of the Aviation Section of the Signal Corps. He departed for Europe as an aeronautical observer in March 1917, weeks before the U.S. declaration of war.

In Europe, he planned the organization for the U.S. tactical air service and served as its operational commander. He presided over the largest air armada ever assembled for a specific mission at that time, during the Americans' 1918 Saint Mihiel Offensive. Upon returning to the United States, he became assistant chief of the Air Service and began his crusade for an independent air force and a unified department of defense.

Mitchell believed that airpower had made the naval battleship obsolete and substantiated his claims by sinking the German prize battleship *Ostfriesland* during an aerial bombardment test in July 1921. Mitchell publicly accused the War Department and Navy Department of incompetence and criminal negligence after the crash of the naval airship *Shenandoah* in September 1925. This led an army court-martial to convict him of insubordination.

Mitchell resigned on 1 February 1926 but continued his advocacy for airpower through numerous speaking tours, articles, and books. He died in New York City on 19 February 1936. His most famous publications include *Memoirs of World War I* (1928) and *Winged Defense* (1925), a reflection

General Billy Mitchell loved to fly, and in doing so won the respect of the men he led. (U.S. Air Force)

of his views on the military and the economic implications of aviation.

Bert Frandsen

See also
Saint Mihiel, Battle of; U.S. Army Air Service

References

Davis, Burke. *The Billy Mitchell Affair.* New York: Random House, 1967.
Hurley, Alfred F. *Billy Mitchell: Crusader for Air Power.* Bloomington: Indiana University Press, 1975.

Mitscher, Marc Andrew (1887–1947)

U.S. admiral and naval aviation pioneer. Mitscher was born in Hillsboro, Wisconsin, on 26 January 1887 and attended the U.S. Naval Academy, graduating in 1910. He spent five years assigned to various surface ships before being accepted for flight training. One of the navy's first naval aviators, Mitscher was at the forefront of that field for the next three decades. After tours with the aviation department on a cruiser and as commander of naval air stations on Long Island and Miami, Mitscher spearheaded the Navy's first attempt at transatlantic flight as command pilot of NC-1. Though he succeeded only in reaching the Azores, Mitscher earned a Navy Cross and the admiration of his peers. He later led Navy teams to the International Air Races of 1922 and 1923.

Following duty on USS *Langley,* the Navy's first aircraft carrier, Mitscher headed the Air Department on USS *Saratoga.* He subsequently served as executive officer on both ships. Ashore, Mitscher spent several tours at the Aeronautics Bureau and accepted sea assignments in command of an aircraft tender and Patrol Wing One. When war with Japan erupted, Mitscher was the commanding officer of the Navy's newest carrier, the *Hornet.*

Transferring to the Pacific, Mitscher and his crew carried Colonel Jimmy Doolittle's bombers to within range of Japan for their historic mission (April 1942). In May, he led his ship and aircraft into the decisive Battle of Midway, contributing significantly to the sinking of four irreplaceable Japanese carriers.

Promoted to rear admiral in July 1942, Mitscher took command of Patrol Wing Two and soon commanded Fleet Air during the campaigns for Guadalcanal (December 1942) and the Solomon Islands (April 1943). Commanding the Fast Carrier Task Force that supported, alternately, Admirals William Halsey and Raymond Spruance, Mitscher was just as successful in the Marshalls, Truk, Saipan, and the Battle of the Philippine Sea (June 1944), in which his aircraft decimated the Japanese air forces in the decisive Marianas Turkey Shoot. At the Battle of Leyte Gulf (October 1944), Mitscher's forces virtually eliminated the Imperial Japanese Navy as a fighting force. Throughout 1945, Mitscher's planes hammered Iwo Jima, Okinawa, and the Japanese home islands.

At the conclusion of the war, Mitscher served briefly as deputy Chief of Naval Operations (Air). Promoted to admiral in 1946, he subsequently served as commander of the Eighth Fleet and the Atlantic Fleet. Mitscher died at sea on 3 February 1947.

Michael S. Casey

See also

Doolittle, James H.; Guadalcanal; Halsey, William F.; Iwo Jima; Leyte Gulf, Battle of; Marshall Islands; Midway, Battle of; Okinawa; Philippines Islands, campaigns in 1944; Spruance, Raymond A.; Yamamoto, Isoroku

References

Coletta, Paolo E. *Admiral Marc A. Mitscher and U.S. Naval Aviation: Bald Eagle.* Studies in American History Volume 12. Lewiston, NY: Edwin Mellen, 1997.

Taylor, Theodore. *The Magnificent Mitscher.* Annapolis, MD: Naval Institute Press, 1991.

Mitsubishi A6M Reisen ("Zero")

Premier Japanese fighter of World War II. The Zero resulted from a navy proposal in May 1937 for a carrier aircraft to replace the Mitsubishi A5M Type 96 fighter.

A Mitsubishi design team led by Jiro Horikoshi drew upon combat reports from China to upgrade the specs. Horikoshi's team developed an all-metal, low-wing monoplane with a 780-hp Mitsubishi Zuisei engine, which first flew on 1 April 1939. Following initial tests, the two-blade propeller was replaced with a three-blade constant-speed unit, and a Nakajima NK1C Sakae 12 engine was fitted to surpass speed requirements. Production models of the A6M2 were deployed for combat in China in July 1940. With minor changes, including folding wing tips that reduced the span by 1 meter to accommodate carrier-deck elevators, the Type 0 Model 21 was manufactured at Nakajima and Mitsubishi facilities. The Zero led the attack and provided cover for Japanese bombers and torpedo-bombers at Pearl Harbor and the Philippines; Zeros ensured success in battle at Wake Island, Darwin, Ceylon, and the East Indies.

A series of variants began with the A6M3, powered by the supercharged Sakae 21 14-cylinder radial engine of 1,130 horsepower. Heavier armament, a shortened wing to eliminate the folding, fuel-tank reconfiguration, and other changes enabled the Zero to control airspace in the Pacific until May 1942. By mid-1942, captured Zeros were studied for weaknesses in performance and construction, and Allied fighter tactics were adapted accordingly.

Unable to compete with P-38s, F4Us, and F6Fs at higher altitudes, the Zero was modified in August 1943, employing a new wing design with heavier skins to increase diving speed; reworked exhaust stacks allowed more power. This A6M5, with the armament of the A6M3, could dive at speeds up to 410 mph. In early 1944, the A6M5b, even with even heavier wing skins, armored glass, fuel tank fire extinguishers, heavier armament, and a diving speed of 460 mph, failed to match the U.S. Navy F6Fs at Leyte Gulf and the Battle of the Philippines.

In late 1944, the ventral drop tank was replaced with a 250-kg bomb to be used as kamikazes, which sank the escort carrier *St. Lô* and damaged several others. Japan's defeat in the Philippines led to increased armament and use of the Nakajima Sakae 31 water/methanol-injected engine and self-sealing fuel tanks, which resulted in the A6M6c. Continued losses of carriers and aircraft and weak performance of the A6M series brought more extensive changes. Fitted with factory bombracks for use as a dive-bomber, stronger tail empennage, more armor, and wing drop tanks, the A6M7 Model 63 began production in May 1945. To deal with the increased weight, the more powerful Mitsubishi 1,560-hp Kinsei 62 engine was employed and yielded the A6M8 Type 0 Model 64 in April 1945, too late to be to produced before the war ended.

The name "Reisen" is a contraction of *rei sentoki,* (0 Fighter); Allied code names were "Zeke," "Hap," or "Hamp." The Zero, built in greater numbers than any other type of Japanese aircraft, remained Japan's first-line fighter until the end of the war. Estimates of total production figures are 10,449 of the A6M model in all variants.

Richard C. DeAngelis

See also

Horikoshi, Jiro; Mitsubishi Aircraft

References

Bueschel, Richard M. *Mitsubishi A6M1/2/-2n Zero-Sen in Japanese Naval Air Service.* Atglen, PA: Schiffer, 1995.

Francillon, Rene J. *Japanese Aircraft of the Pacific War.* Annapolis, MD: Naval Institute Press, 1995.

Horikoshi, Jiro. *Eagles of Mitsubishi: The Story of the Zero Fighter.* Trans. Shindo and Wantiez. Seattle: University of Washington Press, 1981.

Mitsubishi Aircraft

Japanese aircraft manufacturer. The Mitsubishi industrial complex originated during Japan's period of modernization following the restoration of the Japanese Meiji emperor in

1868. By the turn of the century, Mitsubishi was a large shipbuilding and shipping company. The Mitsubishi Shipbuilding and Engineering Company, Ltd., at its Oh-e-machi plant in the southern section of the port of Nagoya, produced Renault 70-hp aircraft engines as early as 1916. The following year, France licensed the company to manufacture the Hispano-Suiza engine. Mitsubishi aircraft interests date from 1918, when Dr. Kumezo Ito went to France to study aircraft manufacture in World War I. In May 1920, the Mitsubishi Nainenki Seizo KK (Mitsubishi Internal Combustion Engine Company, Ltd.) was separated from the shipbuilding operations and began manufacturing aircraft engines at its Nagoya plant.

During these early years, Mitsubishi filled an army order for its Type Ko 1 trainer based on the Nieuport 81 design and later the Type Ki 1 after the Hanriot HD-14 trainer. Upon securing a navy contract to produce carrier-borne aircraft, an engineering team under the direction of British engineer Herbert Smith, formerly of Sopwith Aviation of Great Britain, designed and produced planes for the Imperial Japanese Navy and Imperial Japanese Army. The company became solidly established as an aircraft manufacturer, and its designs reflected the British influence for more than a decade.

The company changed its name to the Mitsubishi Kokuki KK (Mitsubishi Aircraft Company, Ltd.) on 1 May 1928 and founded an engineering branch in Tokyo as Tokyo Kikai Seisakusho (Tokyo Engineering Works). The continued growth of ship, engine, airframe, and engineering divisions led to their amalgamation in 1934 under a reorganized company named Mitsubishi Jukogyo KK (Mitsubishi Heavy Industries Company, Ltd). In the period 1935–1940 Mitsubishi continued to expand aircraft and engine manufacturing facilities at the Nagoya Aircraft Works, located at the growing Oh-e-machi complex built on a dredged landfill in Nagoya Harbor.

By 1938, Mitsubishi's continued growth and production, including its expanded facilities at Nagoya (where 14-cylinder radial air-cooled Kinsei aircraft engines were manufactured), made Mitsubishi a leading contender in aircraft production with its rival Nakajima, which was founded by the Mitsui combine and produced more total units.

The growing ambition and power of army and navy militarists sought to create an aircraft industry that could be self-sufficient and based upon Japanese-designed airframes and engines. In order to become independent of foreign sources for machine tools, in January 1939 Mitsubishi opened a special plant at Hiroshima dedicated to machine-tool production. The Japanese government sought to maintain secrecy concerning the growth of its aircraft development and production and restricted the Japanese press in referring to Mitsubishi's aircraft manufacturing activity.

By 1940, Mitsubishi operated six airframe and 11 engine plants at manufacturing sites in Nagoya and other areas. The proliferation of designs and variants resulted in Mitsubishi's growing reputation as maker of some of the finest combat airplanes of the period and as one of Japan's leading aircraft and engine manufacturers, producing military aircraft for the navy and army and civilian aircraft in separate divisions of the company.

Throughout World War II, Mitsubishi played an important role in supplying Japan's armed forces with air assets for decisive battles. The company became the most significant aircraft producer in total weight produced; it was also the largest engine producer, making 38 percent of all Japanese combat aircraft engines in World War II. Figures from the U.S. Strategic Bombing Survey suggest that Japan's aircraft production peaked in 1944 with 28,180 aircraft. Japan produced some 50,000 fighters, bombers, and reconnaissance aircraft and nearly 70,000 aircraft of all types between 1941 and 1945, of which Mitsubishi produced 23 percent; Nakajima, its largest competitor, produced 37 percent.

Despite Japan's steadfast efforts, aircraft production declined sharply after 1944 due to the combined efforts of the U.S. Navy, which destroyed Japan's merchant fleets, and the aerial assault of U.S. B-29 bombers. The achievements of Japan's aircraft manufacturers during the period 1937–1945 had the effect of disproving the prevailing view in the West that the Japanese were capable of producing only poor-performing aircraft that would be mere imitations of obsolete Western designs. Many of Japan's aircraft in the early years of World War II were of exceptional quality and were surpassed by few contemporary machines.

Richard C. DeAngelis

References

Collier, Basil. *Japanese Aircraft of World War II.* New York. Mayflower Books, 1979.

Horikoshi, Jiro. *Eagles of Mitsubishi: The Story of the Zero Fighter.* Trans. Shindo and Wantiez. Seattle: University of Washington Press, 1981.

Mikesh, Robert C., and Shorzoe Abe. *Japanese Aircraft, 1910–1941.* Annapolis, MD: Naval Institute Press, 1990.

Sekigawa, Eichiro. *Japanese Military Aviation.* London: Ian Allan, 1974.

Mitsubishi G4M ("Betty")

Japanese light bomber. Mitsubishi's G4M (known as the Navy Type 1 attack bomber and code-named "Betty" by the Allies) was produced in larger numbers than any other Japanese bomber. The aircraft evolved from the Mitsubishi G3M series ("Nell" to the Allies), which originated with Admiral Isoroku Yamamoto's call for its development.

In September 1937, navy specifications were issued for a

One can only wonder what thoughts were going through the minds of these young Japanese pilots as they waited beside a Mitsubishi G4M equipped with the Okha suicide weapon. (U.S. Air Force)

land-based attack bomber to replace the G3M series, to be powered by a pair of 1,000-hp engines, able to carry a crew of seven to nine men, and have a top speed of 247 mph at 9,845 feet. The plane was designed for a range of 2,993 miles without a bombload, or 2,302 miles with an 800-kilogram torpedo or bombload.

To meet this performance, the aircraft's engines were later upgraded to Mitsubishi Kasei-14, an air-cooled, 14-cylinder radial engine capable of 1,500 horsepower. The G4M aircraft was distinguished by its cigar-shaped fuselage, which facilitated crew movements and mass production.

Defensive armament included a single 7.7mm machine gun in the nose, a flexible 7.7 mm machine gun in the dorsal blister, one 7.7 mm machine gun in each of the lateral fuselage blisters behind the wing, and one hand-held 20mm canon in the tail. The prototype first flew successfully on 23 October 1939, with only minor design changes called for; production was delayed due to the immediate need for the navy carrier fighter, the Mitsubishi A6M2, to escort the G3M bombers on raids deep into China.

Production of the G4M1 Model 11 began in 1940, and in the summer of 1941 the 1st Kokutai took the G4M1s on bombing raids of Chungking (Zhongqing). Additional G4M1s served in Indochina and on Formosa, where they joined in the sinking of HMS *Prince of Wales* and HMS *Repulse* and aided in eliminating U.S. airpower in the Philippines. G4M1s operated from bases in the East Indies, New Guinea, and Solomon Islands.

The weakness of the aircraft was its lack of armor to protect crew and critical components, as well as inadequate fuel-tank protection. High losses in combat were sustained due to the tendency of the aircraft to burst into flames when hit by enemy fire, earning it the tag "Flying Lighter" from Japanese troops and Allied forces. To remedy these deficiencies, the Model 12 was fitted with more powerful Kasei-15 engines, enabling higher altitudes to escape light antiaircraft guns. The fuselage side blisters were converted to flush panels, and rubber sheeting was added in the wing and fuselage tanks along with carbon-dioxide fire-extinguishing systems. The slightly reduced performance allowed the aircraft to sustain more battle damage, although losses remained heavy. Two G4M1s carrying Admiral Isoroku Yamamoto and his staff were shot down over Bougainville on 18 April 1943.

The later G4M2 Model 22 added yet more powerful engines, increased armaments and armor, and bomb-bay doors that were not used on the G4M1 model. In 1943, accelerated production of the G4M introduced several improved variants, but in small numbers. One version, the G4M2e, had the bomb-bay doors removed to carry the navy's suicide-pilot missile, the "Okha," however, these aircraft were heavy, had poor handling characteristics, and became easy prey for Allied fighters. Mitsubishi produced a total of 2,416 G4M aircraft of different variants, but only 60 units were of the later G4M3a introduced in January 1945. This model was powered by 1,825-hp Kasei-25 (MK4T) engines; some aircraft had minor armament changes, and some units were fitted with air-to-surface radar. The plane became known to the world on 19 August 1945 when two all-white G4M1s marked with green crosses transported Japan's surrender delegation to participate in the peace settlements of World War II.

Richard C. DeAngelis

See also

Horikoshi, Jiro; Mitsubishi Aircraft; Yamamoto, Isoruku

References

Francillon, Rene, and Ronald Percy. *Imperial Japanese Navy Bombers of World War Two.* Vol. 11. London: Hylton Lacy, 1969.

Francillon, Rene J. *Japanese Aircraft of the Pacific War.* Annapolis, MD: Naval Institute Press, 1995.

Moelders, Werner (1913–1941)

One of the outstanding leaders of the Luftwaffe fighter force. Werner "Vati" (Daddy) Moelders joined the Reichswehr as an officer candidate in 1931 and in 1934 was accepted for fighter training in the still-secret Luftwaffe. He was the most successful fighter pilot in the Kondor Legion in Spain, with 14 victories, but his greatest accomplishment in Spain was in the field of fighter tactics. He is credited with developing the basic two-aircraft (*rotte,* or "element") and four-aircraft (*schwarm,* or "flight") formations and tactics that were later adopted by most of the world's air forces. During the campaign in France, he became the first fighter pilot to be awarded the Knight's Cross of the Iron Cross, for 20 post-Spain air combat victories. During the Battle of Britain, he was the first of the younger generation of fighter pilots to be given command of a wing, Jagdgeschwader 51 (JG 51; 51st Fighter Wing), and engaged in a well-publicized scoring competition with Adolf Galland.

In mid-1941, JG 51 transferred east to take part in Operation BARBAROSSA, the Nazi invasion of the Soviet Union, and Moelders continued to score at a high rate. On 15 July 1941, he claimed his 100th and 101st victories. As the first German pilot to reach such heights, he was grounded from combat flying and awarded a new combat decoration, the Oak Leaves with Swords and Diamonds to the Knight's Cross of the Iron Cross, by Hitler. By now a colonel, he was named general of the fighter arm, a staff position within the Luftwaffe High Command. On 22 November 1941, while returning to Berlin from an inspection trip for Ernst Udet's funeral, he was killed in a plane crash due to bad weather, before he could have much effect in his new post.

Donald Caldwell

See also

German Air Force (Luftwaffe); Spanish Civil War

References

Obermeier, E. *Die Ritterkreuztraeger der Luftwaffe, 1939–1945, Band 1: Jagdflieger* [Recipients of the Knight's Cross]. Mainz: Verlag Dieter Hoffmann, 1989.

Moffett, William Adger (1869–1933)

The father of naval aviation. William A. Moffett was born in Charleston, South Carolina, on 31 October 1869. After graduating from the United States Naval Academy in 1890 and subsequently receiving his commission as ensign, he served in the cruiser *Chicago,* commanded by Captain Alfred Thayer Mahan. During the Spanish-American War, Moffett served in the armored cruiser *Charleston,* participating in the capture of Guam and at the Battle of Manila Bay. Moffett also saw duty as navigation officer in the armored cruiser *Maryland* and as executive officer of the battleship *Arkansas.* He won the Congressional Medal of Honor while in command of the cruiser *Chester* during the U.S. invasion of the Mexican city of Veracruz in 1914. Moffett's service as commandant of the Great Lakes Naval Training Station during World War I provided administrative experience and exposed him to the potential of aviation.

After the war, as captain of the battleship *Mississippi,* he oversaw the fitting of turret platforms used to operate gunfire-spotting and scouting aircraft. Largely through the influence of pioneer naval aviator Henry C. Mustin, Moffett became Director of Naval Aviation in March 1921 and in July, as rear admiral, assumed the position of chief of the new Bureau of Aeronautics, where he advocated the development of the aircraft carrier and initiated a program to equip nearly all battleships and cruisers with catapults and aircraft.

Moffett became embroiled in a controversy with Army General William "Billy" Mitchell and the advocates of a unified air force. It climaxed in 1925, when Mitchell criticized the naval leadership for "criminal negligence" in the failure of a flight to Hawaii and the fatal crash of the airship *Shenandoah.* Accusing Mitchell of irresponsible demagoguery, Moffett received satisfaction when a court-martial found Mitchell guilty of insubordination and forced his resignation from the Army.

Within the Navy, Moffett waged a decade-long battle to secure authority over aviation. He wrested control over aviation personnel from the powerful Bureau of Navigation and defended flight pay as one of the perquisites of flying officers and enlisted men. Moffett brought aircraft and engine procurement under the authority of the Bureau of Aeronautics and worked out a flexible system combining negotiated and competitive contracts for aircraft, engines, and equipment. His greatest accomplishment was 1926 legislation providing for the acquisition of 1,600 naval aircraft over 5 years.

He was less successful in the development of the small aircraft carrier and the flying-deck cruiser, a hybrid warship combining elements of the scout cruiser and aircraft carrier. Neither did the rigid airship prove to be a solution to the Navy's problem of reconnaissance in the Pacific. Neither *Akron,* completed in 1931, nor *Macon,* commissioned two years later, realized its potential in limited operations with the fleet. Ironically, Moffett died when *Akron* went down in a storm off the New Jersey coast on 4 April 1933.

A visionary and master of the art of compromise and public relations, Moffett understood that political activism was essential to meet the technological, bureaucratic, and economic challenges facing naval aviation. His energy and foresight created the foundation for what became the most powerful and efficient naval air arm in the world.

William F. Trimble

References

Arpee, Edward. *From Frigates to Flat-Tops: The Story of the Life and Achievements of Rear Admiral William Adger Moffett, U.S.N., "The Father of Naval Aviation."* Chicago: Lakeside Press, 1953.

Coletta, Paolo E. "The Apotheosis of Political Strategy: The Third Appointment of Rear Admiral William A. Moffett as Chief of the U.S. Bureau of Aeronautics." *American Aviation Historical Society Journal* 36 (Spring 1991).

Trimble, William F. *Admiral William A. Moffett: Architect of Naval Aviation.* Washington, DC: Smithsonian Institution Press, 1994.

Morane-Saulnier 406

The mainstay of the French air force at the beginning of World War II. The Morane-Saulnier MS 406 fighter, despite limited speed and armament, represented a new phase in French military aircraft development. The prototype 406 C1 flew for the first time on 20 May 1938.

The MS 406 marked an important change in French production methods from quasi-artisan style to conventional mass assembly. Unfortunately, the time required to produce an MS 406 was almost double that of the 8,000 hours required to build its German competitor, the Messerschmitt Bf 109. By December 1939, factory output was some 40 percent behind schedule, a problem accentuated by the delay in the production of the engine, the Hispano-Suiza 12Y of 860 horsepower.

Despite such production troubles, some 1,084 machines were produced. The MS 406 found a small export market in Turkey and Finland. After purchasing two French-built MS 406 C1s for evaluation, the Swiss Aircraft Factory manufactured a total of 74 machines under license, redesignating them as the D-3800; another 190, with heavy modifications by Swiss engineers, were redesignated the D-3801.

The MS 406, alongside the Curtiss H 75, became the main opponent of Luftwaffe fighters in the Phony War (September 1939–May 1940). It was the first French fighter to exceed 400 kph; training versions, the MS 430 and MS 435, were also developed. The fall of France, however, cut short the aircraft's career, although many continued to fly in French colonies as well as the Vichy and Free French air forces; a few were used by the Axis.

Guillaume de Syon

See also

French Aircraft Development and Production (World War I–Early World War II); Vichy French Air Force

References

d'Abzac-Epezy, Claude. *L'armée de l'air de Vichy.* Paris: SHAA, 1997.

Christienne, Charles, and Pierre Lissarague. *A History of French Military Aviation.* Trans. Frances Kianka. Washington, DC: Smithsonian Institution Press, 1986.

Morane-Saulnier Aircraft

French aircraft manufacturer during World War I. Morane-Saulnier was already a major part of the Aviation Militaire (French air force) when World War I began, the company's aircraft making up a significant portion of the strength of French escadrilles. However, the firm's first real mark in military aviation history began to take shape during the war's first winter when Raymond Saulnier collaborated with aviator Roland Garros on the design of a pair of steel wedges that would be fitted to the propeller of a Morane-Saulnier Type L parasol monoplane, allowing a machine gun to be fired through the propeller without damaging it. Garros tested the device the following spring with promising results, achieving three victories before falling prisoner behind enemy lines. Later that year, the great Georges Guynemer scored the first of 53 victories flying a Morane.

The Morane-Saulnier L continued to equip two-seater escadrilles doing reconnaissance and artillery regulation until gradually replaced by the Nieuport. But because the L had shown early promise as a fighter, Morane turned to the development of another monoplane, this one a shoulder-wing design known as the Bullet. The Bullet, like its parasol-winged stablemate, was rotary-powered; also like the L, it sported a Hotchkiss machine gun fixed in front of the pilot, steel wedges protecting the propeller from its fire. Unfortunately the Bullet, like the Parasol, also fell victim to competition from Nieuport, although it was the Type 11 Bébé that did in the latter Morane.

Morane-Saulnier also manufactured biplane designs during World War I, but none that achieved much fame or was built in large numbers. Its next, and last, wartime success came in the A-1, another parasol monoplane, which equipped a handful of fighter escadrilles toward the war's end. Wing failure led to the A-1's replacement.

James Streckfuss

See also
Garros, Roland

References
Davilla, James, and Arthur M. Soltan. *French Aircraft of the First World War.* Mountain View, CA: Flying Machines Press, 1997.

Mu Gia Pass

Site of U.S. interdiction campaign during the Vietnam War. On 30 September 1964, the U.S. Joint Chiefs of Staff implemented plans for cross-border air operations in Laos, including attacks on Mu Gia Pass. The objective was to stop the infiltration of enemy troops who, after leaving Mu Gia Pass, crossed over into Laos and made their way down the Ho Chi Minh Trail. A newly formed South East Asia group expressed unanimous agreement that U.S. participation in air strikes was essential if such operations were to have the desired military and psychological impact. The interdiction program of air strikes began on 14 October 1964. By 1966, more than 5,000 B-52 sorties had been flown to bomb the approach to Mu Gia Pass in Vietnam. The bombing campaign sometimes slowed but never halted the passage of troops through the pass and down the trail.

Albert Atkins

References
Foreign Relations of the United States, Volume 28: Laos. Washington, DC: Department of State, 1964–1968.

Muencheberg, Joachim (1918–1943)

Outstanding German fighter pilot and combat commander of Jagdgeschwader 26 (JG 26), considered to be the Luftwaffe's best fighter wing while under his leadership. A professional officer in the prewar Luftwaffe, Joachim "Jochen" Muencheberg was successful in the French campaign and in the Battle of Britain; he was awarded the Knight's Cross of the Iron Cross for 20 air combat victories. The squadron he led, Staffel 7/JG 26, was sent to Sicily in early 1941 as an independent command and given the mission of winning air superiority over Malta. Amazingly, this unit of 12 Messerschmitt fighters was totally successful in this daunting task, destroying Malta as an offensive base and causing the British to revise their strategy for the entire Mediterranean Theater of Operations. Staffel 7 spent six months in the theater, based in Sicily, Greece, and Libya, and was credited with 52 air victories without losing a single pilot, a record arguably unmatched by any squadron-sized formation in history when facing an opponent of nominally equal ability.

Upon his return to France, Muencheberg was given command of the 2d Group of JG 26 and led it from Abbeville during the period of the Luftwaffe's greatest ascendancy over RAF Fighter Command, whose respectful pilots called Muencheberg's group "The Abbeville Boys," a nickname that Western Allies would come to apply to any especially aggressive Luftwaffe fighter formation.

In mid-1942, Muencheberg was ordered to the Eastern Front to fill in for a wounded wing leader. He soon scored his 100th air victory, for which he was awarded the Oak Leaves with Swords to the Knight's Cross of the Iron Cross and promoted to major. He was given permanent command of JG 77 and led it to North Africa in October 1942. He increased his victory total to 135, including 102 against the Western Allies, but on 23 March 1943, while on his 500th combat mission, he collided with a Spitfire and crashed to his death.

Donald Caldwell

See also
German Air Force (Luftwaffe)

References
Caldwell, D. *JG 26: Top Guns of the Luftwaffe.* New York: Orion Books, 1991.
Obermeier, E. *Die Ritterkreuztraeger der Luftwaffe, 1939–1945, Band 1: Jagdflieger* [Recipients of the Knight's Cross]. Mainz: Verlag Dieter Hoffmann, 1989.

Multiple Independently Targetable Reentry Vehicle (MIRV)

By allowing a single missile to carry more than one warhead and sending each warhead to a different target, MIRVs make a single delivery vehicle far more flexible and dangerous. MIRV technology emerged in the 1970s. President Richard Nixon left it out of the initial Strategic Arms Limitations Talks, believing the Soviets to be far behind in MIRVs and hoping to secure the for United States a decisive advantage even while limiting the number of delivery vehicles. Nixon's estimates were incorrect, and both sides in the Cold War quickly developed and deployed MIRVs on both land-based ICBMs and submarine-based ballistic missiles.

MIRVs made nuclear deterrence less expensive by reducing the number of delivery systems needed to saturate the opponent with nuclear warheads, but many experts felt MIRVs were inherently destabilizing. Not only did MIRVs speed the arms race between the United States and the Soviet Union; they also introduced the use-'em-or-lose-'em factor. A leader facing unclear or unconfirmed evidence of a nuclear attack on his own nuclear assets might be inclined to launch immediately rather than wait for confirmation and risk a massive loss of weapons that might cripple the nation's nuclear war plan. The later Strategic Arms Reduction Talks focused on reducing or eliminating MIRVs.

Grant Weller

See also

Missiles, Intercontinental Ballistic; Strategic Arms Limitations Treaty; Strategic Arms Reduction Talks; Strategic Defense Initiative; Strategic Triad Concept

Mussolini, Benito (1883–1945)

Infamous as Italy's Il Duce, the fascist leader who restored international prestige to Italy but plunged the nation into World War II even though it was financially and militarily unprepared. Assuming power in 1922, he gradually consolidated dictatorial authority by obtaining control over military policy and becoming minister of all three armed services from 1925 to 1929 and again from 1933 to 1943.

Mussolini boasted that he would make Italian lakes of the Mediterranean and Adriatic. He consistently made rhetorical flourishes about Italy's destiny at sea—the rebuilding of the Roman Empire by foreign expansion. To effect this ideology required more than just bluster.

Possessing a tremendous sympathy for the air force, Mussolini thwarted the purchase of navy aircraft carriers by outwardly supporting the air force thesis that Italy was itself an unsinkable aircraft carrier. Sustaining this theory caused the navy in 1940 to have no effective air cover, because interservice rivalry dampened communication between the fleet and the air force's land-based bombers. Although some argued that Mussolini's military policy was based on bluff, between 1935 and 1939 the air force ordered about 8,700 warplanes and almost 3,000 trainers, a sizable fleet by international standards. Its aircraft compared favorably to those of the French in 1939–1940 but not to those of British or German design. Its mainstay fighter, the Fiat CR.42 biplane, despite its maneuverability, had less armament than its British counterpart, the Gloster Gladiator, and was no match for the British Hurricane and Spitfire.

The Italian bomber force was better off. Its mainstay, the Savoia-Marchetti S.79, was by most accounts an excellent aircraft but was difficult to control in inclement weather. The Italian air force's dominant ideology was misconstrued. It professed the theories of strategic air warfare as advocated by General Giulio Douhet, hoping that it would ward off the jealous efforts of the army and navy from throttling the young air arm if not outright reabsorbing it. The air force continued to demand the right to conduct its own war independent of the other services while building forces of medium and light bombers equipped with small and ineffective bombs.

Although desiring to remain neutral, the blustering Mussolini could not tolerate nonbelligerence and maintain Italy's status as a Great Power. He and his military experts knew that Italy's military was not prepared for war and that the Italian people could not sustain a long war. Thus, Mussolini opted for a policy of joining Germany, declaring war on France on 10 June 1940.

Defeats in Greece, Albania, and North Africa accompanied by Allied strikes on Italian industrial cities led to Mussolini's demise. King Victor Emmanuel III, along with army leaders and some fascist party members, had Mussolini arrested and imprisoned. After a daring rescue, the Germans, established him as their puppet head of the Italian Social Republic. Italian partisans executed Mussolini on 28 April 1945 while he was attempting to escape to Switzerland.

George M. Watson Jr.

References

Hibbert, Christopher. *Il Duce: The Life of Benito Mussolini.* Boston: Little and Brown, 1962.

Knox, Macgregor. *Mussolini Unleashed, 1939–1941: Politics and Strategy in Fascist Italy's Last War.* Cambridge, UK: Cambridge University Press, 1982.

Watson, George M. Jr. "British Press Reaction to Fascism in Italy, 1922–1929." Doctoral diss., Catholic University of America, Washington, DC, 1974.

Mutual Assured Destruction

A theory of nuclear deterrence—in sum, that nuclear war can be prevented by assuring that both sides would be destroyed in a nuclear exchange. To accomplish this, each nuclear power would need second-strike capability sufficient to destroy the enemy despite a surprise first strike. In such a situation, no one would have an incentive to initiate the use of nuclear weapons, and thus nuclear war would be averted.

The importance of deterrence was recognized at least as early as 1946 by the nuclear theorist Bernard Brodie. In the 1950s, U.S. officials stressed the ability of the United States to destroy the Soviet Union in retaliation for a Soviet initiation of war, a point generally understood as massive retaliation. In private, U.S. military officials further hoped that in the event of a war, the United States could preempt the Soviet Union by striking so hard in the war's first moments that few, if any, Soviet nuclear weapons would survive to reach the United States.

Thus, when Secretary of Defense Robert S. McNamara publicly stated in the mid-1960s that U.S. nuclear strategy was based on the principle of assured destruction, he was simply reemphasizing a long-standing aspect of U.S. nuclear policy. The key question was how much destruction would be sufficient. Eventually it was determined that 20–33 percent of the Soviet population and 50–75 percent of Soviet industrial capacity would have to be wiped out. Though in theory assured destruction was designed to deter the Soviet Union, in practice it was also used within the Department of Defense to curtail ever-growing demands in the U.S. military for more strategic nuclear forces. In this latter capacity it did enjoy some apparent success, as the numbers of U.S. ICBMs and SLBMs remained relatively constant from the mid-1960s through the end of the Cold War (at approximately 1,000 and 650, respectively). This numerical stability may also have represented a recognition of diminishing returns on nuclear targeting.

What disturbed critics of the new policy was not the assured destruction of the Soviet Union but the implicit abandonment of the prospect of preempting the Soviet Union. These advocates of damage limitation argued that it was morally and strategically wrong to allow, let alone embrace, the ability of the Soviet Union to destroy the United States in the case of nuclear war, and they derided the policy as mutual assured destruction (MAD). It nonetheless remained the basic philosophy underpinning U.S. nuclear strategy until the 1980s, when President Ronald Reagan's Strategic Defense Initiative challenged MAD by attempting to reduce the damage to the United States in the case of nuclear war.

This represented only the public side of U.S. nuclear strategy. The extent to which public debates affected actual plans remains a question shrouded in secrecy and continues to surround nuclear targeting policy to the present. In the post–Cold War world, public debate over U.S. nuclear strategy has largely subsided, replaced to some extent by a general emphasis on preventing the proliferation of nuclear weapons to so-called rogue states such as Iran, Iraq, and North Korea.

David Rezelman

See also

Antimissile Defense; Atomic Bomb; Cold War; Massive Retaliation; Missiles, Intercontinental Ballistic; Strategic Air Command

References

Bundy, McGeorge. *Danger and Survival: Choices About the Bomb in the First Fifty Years.* New York: Random House, 1988.

Carter, Ashton B., John D. Steinbruner, and Charles A. Zraket, eds. *Managing Nuclear Operations.* Washington, DC: Brookings Institute, 1987.

N

Nagasaki

Site of the second U.S. atomic attack against Japan. When no Japanese surrender was forthcoming after the atomic attack on Hiroshima on 6 August, the United States dropped a second atomic bomb, this time on the city of Nagasaki. On 9 August 1945, the B-29 *Bock's Car* under the command of Major Charles Sweeney took off from the island of Tinian to deliver the plutonium bomb (using Pu-239) code-named "Fat Man" to the primary target, Kokura. But the city was hidden by cloud cover, so the target was changed to Nagasaki, a port city on the southern island of Kyushu that had been placed on the target list very late by military planners. It was an industrial center that housed the Mitsubishi shipyards, a leading producer of aerial torpedoes.

At 11:02 A.M. the city was struck by a weapon that produced the equivalent of 20,000 tons of TNT. The bomb detonated at an altitude of 503 meters and killed approximately 70,000 people (out of 260,000 inhabitants). It wounded at least as many. There was less destruction than in Hiroshima because hills dividing the city in half deflected the blast. Nevertheless, a radius of 6.7 square kilometers and approximately 18,400 buildings were destroyed.

On the day of the Nagasaki bombing, the Soviet Union opened, as Joseph Stalin had promised at the Yalta Conference, a second front and attacked Manchuria. After bitter debates within the Japanese war council, the emperor finally moved toward surrender. On 14 August, Japan surrendered officially. In a radio address, the emperor made mention of the atomic attacks on Nagasaki and Hiroshima. He informed his subjects of the terrible power of the new weapon and warned that it might, should the war continue, lead not only to the destruction of Japan but of civilization itself.

The collective Japanese memory of the atomic bombing was heavily shaped by cultural expressions of victims once the strict censorship of the postwar occupation government was lifted. Most famous in the early years after the war was the best-selling novel *Nagasaki no kane* (The Bells of Nagasaki) by the Catholic doctor Nagai Takashi, who survived the atomic attack with his two children but lost his wife. He continued to live in the ruins and became a charismatic focal point of nuclear martyrdom. He died in 1951 of leukemia. His book and the resulting movie have strongly shaped memorial culture of the atomic bombing of Nagasaki.

Frank Schumacher

References

Hiroshima and Nagasaki City. *Hiroshima and Nagasaki: The Physical, Medical, and Social Effects of the Atomic Bombings.* New York: Basic Books, 1981.

Nagai, Takashi. *The Bells of Nagasaki.* Trans. William Johnston. New York: Harper and Row, 1984.

Nagumo, Chuichi (1886–1944)

Japanese admiral. Chuichi Nagumo was born in 1886 and graduated from the Japanese Naval Academy in 1908. He was a torpedo specialist and one of Japan's most experienced sailors at the outset of World War II. In 1941, Nagumo was placed in command of the Kido Butai, Japan's powerful carrier strike force that Fleet Admiral Isoroku Yamamoto planned to use to destroy the U.S. Pacific Fleet at Pearl Harbor. It was an ironic appointment, for Nagumo was an expert in surface, not aerial, operations, he and Yamamoto were not on good terms; and Nagumo opposed the Pearl Harbor operation.

Nagumo's failure to follow up his initial successes at Pearl Harbor and the fact that U.S. aircraft carriers were not pres-

The Nakajima B5N-2 "Kate" was an excellent torpedo plane for its time, and Japanese torpedoes were perhaps the best in the world. With special training, they worked well at Pearl Harbor. (U.S. Navy)

ent meant that the success was far short of what Japan needed or Yamamoto expected.

In spite of Yamamoto's disappointment in him, Nagumo's popularity left him in command of the Kido Butai. Over the next six months it roamed the Pacific, seemingly invincible. In April 1942, four of Nagumo's carriers made a successful air raid on British installations in Ceylon. Although the May engagement at Coral Sea halted the Japanese advance across the Pacific, plans went forward to attack the strategically vital U.S. base at Midway Island in June.

Nagumo survived the disaster of Midway and continued to command the remaining Japanese carrier forces during the August Battle of the Eastern Solomons and the 25–27 October Battle of Santa Cruz (part of the Guadalcanal campaign). Both were Japanese defeats, and by November Nagumo was relieved of his command.

Nagumo was eventually placed in charge of all naval forces in the Mariana Islands region. He was overall commander during the U.S. invasion of Saipan. When it became clear Saipan would fall, Nagumo, feeling responsible for the defeat, took his own life on 6 July 1944.

William Head

See also

Coral Sea, Battle of the; Guadalcanal; Midway, Battle of; Pearl Harbor

References

Belote, James H., and William M. Belote. *Titans of the Seas.* New York: Harper and Row, 1975.

Dupuy, Trevor N. *Understanding Defeat.* New York: Paragon House, 1990.

Fuchida, Mitsuo, and Masatake Okumiya. *Midway: The Battle That Doomed Japan.* Annapolis, MD: Naval Institute Press, 1955.

Reynolds, Clark G. *War in the Pacific.* New York: Archive, 1990.

Nakajima Aircraft

Japanese aircraft manufacturer. Nakajima was started in 1917 by retired naval engineer Chikuhei Nakajima and

Seibei Kawanishi as the Japan Aeroplane Manufacturing Work Co. Ltd. In 1920, after a disagreement between the two principals, it became Nakajima Aeroplane Co. Ltd.

In 1924, after several successful airframe designs, Nakajima began producing engines. The first engine produced was a French-licensed water-cooled Lorraine. The following year, Nakajima imported the British Bristol Jupiter. From this engine, Nakajima developed the Model VI.

During World War II, Nakajima was one of the few companies that controlled all aspects of its manufacturing. From airframes to engines to all subparts and assemblies, Nakajima produced each part in its own factory. This allowed Nakajima to produce more than 19,500 aircraft from 1941 to 1945. This made up 28 percent of all Japanese aircraft produced and 37 percent of all Japanese combat aircraft produced. Nakajima provided the Ki 43 Oscar, Ki 44 Tojo, Ki 84 Frank fighters and the Ki 49 Helen heavy bomber for the army. For the navy, it produced the B5N Kate and B6N Jill attack bombers and the J1N Irving twin-engine fighter.

In 1946, Nakajima was reorganized as Fuji Sangyo Co., Ltd. In 1950, Fuji Sangyo was divided into 12 smaller corporations. Between 1953 and 1955, four of those corporations again merged to become Fuji Heavy Industries, the name by which it is still known today.

David A. Pluth

References

Francillon, Rene J. *Japanese Aircraft of the Pacific War.* Annapolis, MD: Naval Institute Press, 1995.

National Advisory Committee for Aeronautics (NACA)

U.S. government agency for aeronautics and aeronautical research. The United States taught the world to fly, but Europe first exploited the "aeroplane." Secretary of the Smithsonian Institute, Dr. Charles D. Walcott, understood that the lack of coordinated aeronautical research in America had done much to impede aeronautical engineering and public support. In contrast, European governments and industries had worked together to shape a research agenda and had benefited in the form of advanced aircraft engineering and supporting infrastructure.

World War I underscored the differences in the state of aviation that existed between the United States and Europe. In 1914, Walcott began lobbying for the creation of a government agency whose purpose would be one of advancing the science of aeronautics and coordinating aeronautical research. President Woodrow Wilson, concerned that direct government involvement might be viewed as a violation of U.S. neutrality in World War I, opposed the idea. However, when the Navy appropriations bill containing a rider establishing the National Advisory Committee for Aeronautics appeared on his desk, he signed it. NACA was officially established on 3 March 1915.

The new law required the composition of NACA to be both military and civilian. President Wilson appointed NACA's first 12 members, including four representatives of the Army and Navy; seven scientists, such as Joseph S. Ames from Johns Hopkins University; and a nontechnical representative. Walcott, who became its first chair, represented the Smithsonian Institution.

The purpose of NACA, according to the enabling legislation, was to "direct" and "supervise" scientific aeronautical research. During the next 43 years, NACA was responsible for the advancement of aeronautical research, including the development of airfoil standards, engineering standards, research instrumentation, and enhanced wind-tunnel testing techniques.

The NACA also played an important role in the development of commercial aviation, greatly influencing legislation that ultimately defined commercial aviation, the Air Commerce Act of 1926. On 23 March 1921, Walcott wrote to Herbert Hoover, the secretary of commerce under President Warren Harding, outlining NACA's position for the advancement of commercial aviation. Under the NACA proposal, the Departments of War and Navy would retain control of their individual air arms, NACA would continue its mission as focal point for "aeronautical activities" and "direct continuous prosecution of scientific research in aeronautics," and a Bureau of Aeronautics would be created within the Department of Commerce. NACA considered commercial aviation to be the "backbone of military preparedness."

NACA continued its mission until 1958, when President Dwight Eisenhower signed into law the National Aeronautics and Space Act, transforming NACA into the National Aeronautics and Space Administration.

Randy Johnson

References

Bilstein, Roger E. *Orders of Magnitude: A History of the NACA and NASA, 1915–1990.* NASA SP-4406. Washington, DC: U.S. Government Printing Office, 1989.

National Aeronautics and Space Administration (NASA)

U.S. government agency that coordinates aeronautics, aerospace exploration, and related research. Deriving from the National Advisory Committee for Aeronautics (1915–1958),

NASA was officially established on 1 October 1958. Designed to explore scientific and technological experiments in human spaceflight, NASA's ongoing efforts contribute greatly to aerospace exploration, space science, and space applications. Experimentation by NASA has expanded our knowledge of the universe and the earth and has resulted in advances in airpower, computing, medicine, meteorology, communications, and applied science. Preparing astronauts for existence in space has advanced many fields of human activity.

In the mid–twentieth century, Project Mercury explored human survival in space. Project Gemini followed, with a spacecraft built for two astronauts, and Project Apollo set its sights on exploration of the moon. In 1969, astronaut Neil Armstrong was the first to walk on the lunar surface. Following Skylab and the Apollo-Soyuz Test Projects in the 1970s, NASA's human spaceflights resumed in 1981 with the Space Shuttle program. The International Space Station (under construction) links NASA and the United States with other nations in far-reaching and innovative global cooperation.

NASA's continuing interest in flight brought about joint ventures with the Department of Defense and United Kingdom in pioneering vertical-takeoff-and-landing aircraft and fostering the research and technology for an advanced short-takeoff-and-landing aircraft. NASA undertook flight research with the forward-swept-wing X-29 and with the development of low-speed propfan technology for fuel efficiency in subsonic airliners of the future.

Headquartered in Washington, D.C., NASA operates through the following field centers, each with areas of emphasis and expertise:

* Ames Research Center, Information Technology, Sunnyvale, CA
* Dryden Flight Research Center, Atmospheric Flight Ops, Edwards, CA
* Glenn Research Center, Turbomachinery, Cleveland, OH
* Goddard Space Flight Center, Scientific Research, Greenbelt, MD
* Independent Validation and Verification Facility, Software Systems, Fairmont, WV
* Jet Propulsion Laboratory, Deep Space Systems, Pasadena, CA
* Johnson Space Center, Human Operations in Space, Houston, TX
* Kennedy Space Center, Launch and Cargo Processing Systems, Titusville, FL
* Langley Research Center, Structures and Materials, Hampton, VA
* Marshall Space Flight Center, Space Propulsion, Huntsville, AL
* Moffett Federal Airfield, Shared Federal Facility, Sunnyvale, CA
* Stennis Space Center, Propulsion Testing Systems, Slidell, MS
* Wallops Flight Facility, Suborbital Research Programs, Wallops Island, VA
* White Sands Test Facility, Testing and Evaluating Hazardous Materials, Components, and Rocket Propulsion Systems, Las Cruces, NM.

NASA continues to blaze the path into space with the International Space Station, research vehicles that travel to the outer reaches of the solar system, as well as unmanned Mars landings and plans for a manned flight to Mars.

Ann Cooper and Charles Cooper

See also

National Advisory Committee for Aeronautics

References

Bilstein, Roger E. *Orders of Magnitude: A History of the NACA and NASA, 1915–1990.* NASA SP-4406. Washington, DC: U.S. Government Printing Office, 1989.

McCurdy, Howard E. *Inside NASA: High Technology and Organization Change in the U.S. Space Program.* Baltimore: Johns Hopkins University Press, 1994.

National Emergency Airborne Command Post (NEACP)

Beginning in 1965, specially modified Boeing EC-135Js based at Andrews Air Force Base, operated under Project Nightwatch as the National Emergency Airborne Command Post. These aircraft were flown by the 1st Airborne Command and Control Squadron (1st ACCS), reporting directly to Air Force Headquarters.

The E-4A (a version of the Boeing 747–200) was assigned to the 1st ACCS on 1 November 1975. An improved version, the E-4B, was introduced on 4 August 1976. On 1 November 1975, the 1st ACCS was reassigned to the 55th Strategic Reconnaissance Wing (55th SRW) and became part of Strategic Air Command. In addition to the flight crew, the E-4s carried a battle staff and a ground-security element from the 55th SRW Security Police Squadron.

The mission of NEACP airplanes is to provide an airborne haven for the president of the United States and his immediate staff in the event of a nuclear attack. From this aircraft, the president and his advisers—supported by the airborne battle staff—would be able to maintain command and control of U.S. forces.

Alwyn T. Lloyd

References

Lloyd, Alwyn T. "Versatility Unlimited—The Boeing KC-135 Story." *Air International,* part 2 (December 1980).

______. *A Cold War Legacy: A Tribute to Strategic Air Command, 1946–1992.* Missoula, MT: Pictorial Histories, 2000.

National Security Act of 1947

Legislation passed by the United States Congress that made sweeping changes to America's defense organization. After World War II, the Air Force Association of wartime veterans lobbied Congress for a separate air branch of the military. The United States Air Force was established on 17 September 1947 as a separate entity, coequal with the Army and Navy. General Carl A. "Tooey" Spaatz was named the first Air Force Chief of Staff.

The Departments of War, Army, and Navy were combined into the Department of Defense. James V. Forrestal, former secretary of the Navy, became the first secretary of defense. While the Joint Chiefs of Staff coordinated military activities, the National Security Council worked as the interface between the Department of Defense and the State Department and served as an adviser to the president. An outgrowth of the World War II Office of Special Services, the Central Intelligence Agency (a branch of the National Security Council) was tasked with correlating and evaluating all intelligence activities involving national security except internal security, which came under the purview of the Federal Bureau of Investigation. Rear Admiral Roscoe Hellenkoeter was made the first director of the CIA.

Alwyn T. Lloyd

References

Davis, Richard G. *Carl A. Spaatz and the Air War in Europe.* Washington, DC: Center for Air Force History, 1993.

Lloyd, Alwyn T. *A Cold War Legacy: A Tribute to Strategic Air Command, 1946–1992.* Missoula, MT: Pictorial Histories, 2000.

National Security Council (NSC)

Established by the National Security Act in 1947 to advise the U.S. president on domestic, foreign, and military policy related to national security. A later amendment placed the NSC within the Executive Office of the President (EOP). The NSC is the highest executive-branch entity reviewing and providing guidance for the conduct of national security policy.

The statutory members of the NSC are the president, vice president, secretary of defense, secretary of state, director of the Central Intelligence Agency, Chairman of the Joint Chiefs of Staff, and the national security advisor (NSA), who has primary responsibility for the daily management of the NSC and is the principle adviser to the president with respect to national security affairs.

Because the NSC is part of the EOP, it has traditionally been regarded as beyond congressional oversight. For this reason presidents have occasionally employed NSC staff in tasks and missions to avoid the risk of public disclosure that relying on other agencies of the government might entail. (Iran-Contra, the arms-for-hostages scandal during Ronald Reagan's presidency, is one example.)

Craig T. Cobane

See also

Central Intelligence Agency

References

Crabb, Cecil V., and Kevin V. Mulcahy. *American National Security.* Pacific Grove, CA: Brooks/Cole, 1991.

Lord, Carnes. *The Presidency and the Management of National Security.* London: Collier Macmillan, 1988.

Naval Aircraft Factory (NAF)

U.S. government-owned and -operated aircraft manufacturing facility (1917–1956) created in part as a progressive response to wartime profiteering at the start of U.S. involvement in World War I. The NAF was established to meet the Navy's needs for long-range flying boats. Construction began on 10 August 1917 at the Philadelphia Navy Yard, and the NAF's first assembly building was ready for occupancy on 28 November 1917; the first airplane, a Curtiss-designed H-16 twin-engine flying boat, flew on 27 March 1918.

To produce the large numbers of H-16 and F-5-L flying boats needed by the Navy, NAF turned to subcontractors for components, heralding a fundamental structural change in the U.S. aircraft industry that enabled it to expand output during both world wars. At the height of the conflict, NAF employed 3,640 workers, nearly a quarter of them women. After World War I, successive aircraft in the PN series of flying boats pioneered metal airframe construction in the navy.

The factory was also responsible for the fabrication of ZR-1 *Shenandoah,* the Navy's first rigid airship, in 1919–1923, the GB-1 Giant Boat, TS-1 shipboard fighters, record-breaking Navy racing aircraft, catapults and arresting gear, and pilotless aircraft and guided missiles. In addition, the NAF was at times the Navy's chief aviation overhaul and repair facility, and its supply department was the major disbursing agency for aircraft parts and equipment. As the nation's only government-owned and -operated aircraft manufacturing facility, the NAF became the center of a dispute with private industry over aircraft and engine procurement.

To guarantee an autonomous source of airplanes, naval officers argued for retention of the aircraft design and manufacturing capabilities of the NAF after World War I. This attitude coincided with that of political leaders and the general public, who castigated armsmakers for unconscionable profits in the sale of weapons and who considered the NAF and other government facilities vital to maintaining a competitive environment and as yardsticks in the accurate determination of the costs of privately supplied material. Moreover, as an integral unit within the Bureau of Aeronautics, the NAF provided a valuable opportunity for naval officers to learn firsthand how an airplane was designed and built, how to draw up specifications, and how to negotiate contracts. The NAF also provided technical verification of airplanes, engines, and components. Starved for orders after World War I, the civilian aviation industry regarded the NAF as anathema and demanded the elimination of the factory's design and production activities.

Rear Admiral William A. Moffett, chief of the Bureau of Aeronautics, arranged a compromise in 1922 whereby the NAF ceased series production in favor of designing and building limited numbers of airplanes and doing specialized work that did not appeal to most aircraft manufacturers. In 1934, as a result of the Vinson-Trammell Act, production returned to Philadelphia with the design and construction of the famous N3N series of biplane trainers, nearly 1,000 of which were completed by 1942. During World War II, the NAF produced variations of private designs, among them 300 OS2N-1 scout-observation airplanes (similar to the Vought OS2U Kingfisher) and 156 PBN-1 twin-engine flying boats (an improved version of the Consolidated PBY Catalina). By 1944, employment at the factory reached 13,400.

After World War II, the factory ended aircraft production and focused its activities on experimental projects and research and development. Laboratories specialized in testing material, structures, power plants, and instruments for the Navy. The Naval Air Material Center, created in 1942, provided administrative oversight for the factory, its labs, the Aviation Supply Office, the Aeronautical Engine Laboratory, and other engineering and experimental offshoots of the original factory. On 9 May 1956, the Navy redesignated the factory as the Naval Air Engineering Facility (Ship Installations), although many of its previous activities continued under successor organizations into the early 1990s.

William F. Trimble

References

Gordon, Robert A. "Naval Aircraft Factory Giant Boat." *W.W.I Aero: The Journal of the Early Aeroplane,* no. 98 (February 1984): 12–37.

Misa, Thomas, and Ed Todd. *History of the Naval Air Development Center.* Report No. NADC-82251-09. Warminster, PA: Naval Air Development Center, 1982.

National Aircraft Factory. *Cavalcade of Aircraft.* Philadelphia: Naval Air Material Center, 1948.

Swanborough, Gordon, and Peter M. Bowers. *United States Navy Aircraft Since 1911.* Rev. ed. Annapolis, MD: Naval Institute Press, 1976.

Trimble, William F. "The Naval Aircraft Factory, the American Aviation Industry, and Government Competition, 1919–1928." *Business History Review 60* (Summer 1986): 175–198.

______. *Wings for the Navy: A History of the Naval Aircraft Factory, 1917–1956.* Annapolis, MD: Naval Institute Press, 1990.

NAVSTAR Global Positioning System

For thousands of years, the ability to determine one's position and to move precisely from place to place has proved vital to the success of military and other ventures. Travelers devised various methods to plot their location and course: observing familiar landmarks (pilotage); noting the positions of the sun and stars (celestial navigation); assuming or estimating speed, time, and direction of movement (dead-reckoning); using extremely accurate instrumentation to measure acceleration in all directions and computers to integrate that data for calculation of velocity and position (inertial navigation); and employing electronic signals from ground- or space-based transmitters (radio navigation). Satellites were first used for radio navigation in a system called TRANSIT, which the Applied Physics Laboratory of Johns Hopkins University and the U.S. Navy developed during the early 1960s for the Navy's submarine ballistic missile system. Since it took several minutes to receive the TRANSIT signals needed to calculate one's position exactly, the system was practical only for slow-moving platforms. Given the further limitation that TRANSIT worked in only two dimensions, it could not fulfill the navigational requirements of high-speed aircraft, rail-mobile ICBM launch crews, and operators of other rapidly moving platforms.

To meet those requirements, the services sought to demonstrate the feasibility of a defense navigation satellite system. The Navy weighed in with TIMATION, a program for two-dimensional navigation and time transfer based on atomic clocks. In October 1963, the U.S. Air Force directed the Aerospace Corporation to pursue design of a highly accurate, three-dimensional capability officially designated System 621B (Satellite System for Precise Navigation). Phil Diamond, director of System 621B study at the Aerospace Corporation, unofficially dubbed the proposed capability the Global Positioning System (GPS), and in May 1974 the system officially became the Navigation Satellite Time and

Ranging (NAVSTAR) GPS. Much of the conceptual work essential to its success had been initiated during the late 1950s by Ivan Getting, then Raytheon Corporation's vice president for engineering and research and, subsequently, first president of the Aerospace Corporation. Nevertheless, several scientists at the U.S. Naval Research Laboratory also made important technical contributions, especially in design of highly accurate onboard cesium and rubidium clocks. A 17 April 1973 memorandum issued by Deputy Secretary of Defense William Clements designated the Air Force as the "executive service" to merge the various satellite navigation efforts into a single comprehensive system. The Air Force established a GPS joint program office in July 1973 and proceeded with the first phase of development—concept validation—in December 1973.

Engineers envisioned a system consisting of a 24-satellite constellation, utilizing six orbital planes at a 55-degree inclination, with a minimum of four satellites per plane. Orbiting at an altitude of 10,900 miles, the GPS satellites would transmit signals on two different L-band frequencies. Anyone, military or civilian, possessing a hand-held receiver about the size of a cellular telephone could process the signals and determine their position in three dimensions to an accuracy of about 50 feet, as well as the time at that location to within one-millionth of a second. Using an S-band signal, the Air Force could monitor all the satellites from five different stations—Kwajalein, Hawaii, Diego Garcia, Ascension Island, and Colorado—and command them from a master control station at Schriever Air Force Base near Colorado Springs.

Planners envisioned a multitude of military and civilian uses for GPS. It would guide infantry, armor, air, and sea forces to their desired destinations in a highly coordinated fashion. Furthermore, the system would enhance delivery of weapons, air-traffic control, rendezvous for air refueling, all-weather airdrops, photomapping, missile guidance system updating, minelaying and -sweeping, antisubmarine warfare, range instrumentation, search and rescue, and satellite navigation. Civil uses included managing global airspace, locating commercial fishing traps and gear, monitoring icebergs, navigation for motor vehicle operators, train control and collision avoidance, precision timing for computer networks, surveying and prospecting for natural resources, hiking and other recreational activities, ground mapping of ecosystems, law enforcement activities, and farming. Despite this broad range of dual uses, military and civil, nobody foresaw the phenomenal growth in worldwide demand for GPS services, which a 1995 report projected would exceed $31 billion annually by 2005.

With the end of concept validation in August 1979, full-scale development and system testing began using Block I satellites. That phase of the program continued into 1985, when production and deployment of the operational system commenced. In February 1989, the Air Force launched the first Block II GPS satellite from Cape Canaveral Air Station, Florida, atop a Delta II rocket. Although the full 24-satellite constellation would not be completed until 9 March 1994, GPS contributed mightily to the performance of Coalition land, sea, and air forces in the Persian Gulf region during Operation DESERT STORM in 1991. Troops carried more than 9,000 portable receivers, many of them commercial models due to a shortage of more accurate military models, and GPS was used strategically to ensure that sea- and air-launched cruise missiles reached their targets. Shortly after the conflict, Lieutenant General Thomas S. Moorman Jr., commander of Air Force Space Command, described GPS as "critical to the victory." Two years later, during Operation RESTORE HOPE, GPS proved essential to ensuring the successful air-dropping of food and supplies into remote areas of Somalia. Meanwhile, in 1992 the National Aeronautic Association awarded its prestigious Collier Trophy to the GPS team—the Aerospace Corporation, U.S. Air Force, U.S. Naval Research Laboratory, Rockwell International Corporation, and IBM Government Systems.

Rick W. Sturdevant

See also
Satellites

References
Alford, Dennis L. *History of the Navstar Global Positioning System (1963–1985).* ACSC Report Number 86-0050. Maxwell AFB, AL: Air Command and Staff College, Air University, 1986.
National Academy of Public Administration. *The Global Positioning System: Charting the Future—Full Report.* Washington, DC: National Academy Press, May 1995.
National Research Council. *The Global Positioning System: A Shared National Asset.* Washington, DC: National Academy Press, 1995.

Nesterov, Pyotr (1887–1914)

Pioneer aviator and Russian war hero. Pyotr Nikolaevich Nesterov was born February 27, 1887, in Nizhnyy Novgorod in a military family. As was customary for his social class at that time, he was educated in a cadet school, then attended a military academy. Commissioned into the artillery in 1906, his first assignment was as an observer in the balloon detachment at Vladivostok. He became obsessed with flying and began to study. In 1909, he designed his first airplane, an advanced concept utilizing a V-shaped tail, which was not accepted for building, and in 1911 he first flew in a glider of his own design.

In 1912, Nesterov was transferred to the aviation branch and trained as a pilot. He was often in trouble for his continuing experiments, including a steep banked turn then considered reckless. On 8 September 1913, Nesterov executed the world's first full vertical loop, for which he suffered 10 days' arrest. On 11 February 1914, he became commander of XI Corps Aviation Detachment, which later proved to be Russia's preeminent flying unit during World War I. On 25 August 1914, Nesterov completed possibly Russia's first bombing mission, when his observer dropped grenades on Austrian troops. Two days later, on 27 August, Nesterov went aloft to intercept an Austrian Albatros reconnaissance airplane that had been troubling the Russians. Determined to destroy the enemy at any cost, but having no gun, Nesterov dived on the Albatros and rammed its upper wing with his landing gear and propeller. Both machines crashed to earth, and Nesterov was killed. Because of the circumstances of his death, as well as his potential as an exemplar, Nesterov was one of the few czarist officers honored by the Soviets even during their early years, and he has remained one of the patron saints of Russian aviation.

George M. Mellinger

See also

Imperial Russian Air Service; Taran

References

Durkota, Alan, Thomas Darcey, and Viktor Kulikov. *The Imperial Russian Air Service: Famous Pilots and Aircraft of World War I.* Mountain View, CA: Flying Machines Press, 1995.

Netherlands East Indies (1942)

Site of early Japanese successes during World War II. In early 1942, the Japanese moved toward the Dutch East Indies in force. Dutch airpower on Java consisted of only a few obsolete Fokker fighters and U.S.-built Martin B-10 bombers. These were reinforced by several British Hawker Hurricanes flown in from HMS *Indomitable* and some U.S. Curtiss P-40s, as well as various survivors of the debacle in Malaya, such as RAF Lockheed Hudsons and Bristol Blenheims and Fleet Air Arm Vickers Vildebeest torpedo-bombers.

This polyglot Allied force (ABDA, for American, British, Dutch, Australian) was heavily outnumbered in the air by the Japanese 23d Naval Air Flotilla. The Japanese seized one lightly defended island after another: Tarakan off Borneo on 11 January, Celebes on 24 January, Amboina (Ambon) on 31 January, Bali on 19 February. Sumatra, with its important oil fields, was invaded on 14 February. In one of the few parachute drops of the Pacific War, Japanese airborne troops seized airfields on Sumatra.

Four Japanese carriers passed through the East Indies on their way to the Indian Ocean. Aircraft from this fleet attacked Port Darwin in Australia on 15 February, causing heavy damage.

The old U.S. carrier *Langley,* converted to an aircraft transport, sailed from Australia with a load 32 P-40E fighters and a freighter with 27 more crated P-40s. Japanese aircraft found these ships just south of Java, however, and sank *Langley.* The crated P-40s could not be unloaded after they reached Java and had to be thrown into the sea.

As a result, the Japanese invasion fleet approached Java virtually unhindered by Allied air threat. ABDA's surface naval force under Dutch Admiral Karel Doormann attempted to interfere but was defeated in the Battle of Java Sea. Japanese forces landed on Java on 1 March, and resistance ended on 9 March with almost 100,000 Allied troops taken captive. Throughout the campaign, the Japanese proved adept at quickly and effectively preparing newly seized advanced bases for air operations.

Frank E. Watson

See also

Curtiss P-40 Warhawk; Hawker Hurricane

References

Morison, Samuel Eliot. *History of United States Naval Operations in World War II, Volume 3: Rising Sun in the Pacific, 1931–April 1942.* Boston: Little, Brown, 1948.

Sakai, Saburo. *Samurai.* New York: Ballantine Books, 1957.

Neuve Chapelle, Battle of (1915)

The world's first real lesson in modern trench warfare. Throughout World War I, the fighting subsided during winter while the armies geared up for the following spring. Following the initial war of movement in 1914, soldiers had settled into the trenches. Their first significant emergence during 1915 was at the Battle of Neuve Chapelle, which began on 10 March.

During the winter lull, experiments in aerial photography had been conducted, and just before fighting renewed, a series of vertical shots was taken by the Royal Flying Corps (RFC). For the first time, such photos were assembled like a jigsaw puzzle, and from the resulting panorama a set of maps of the German trenches was made. Consequently, when British troops went over the top at the opening of the battle, they went equipped with an accurate description of German positions. The photos and maps had also been used by the artillery in making plans for the destruction of enemy assets.

The effective use of photography was not the only first at Neuve Chapelle. Aircraft had been used for bombing since the opening days of the war, but in planning for Neuve Chapelle the British command for the first time assigned specific targets to the RFC, expecting aircraft to be responsible for objectives beyond the reach of the artillery.

Since no World War I battle can be accurately assessed without considering the artillery, it needs be said that following the initial artillery bombardment aircraft were expected to form an integral link in the regulation of counter-battery fire. This would be achieved for the first time by wireless, each RFC squadron having been equipped with transmitters (they could still not receive) in order to send corrections to the batteries.

The battle was not a complete aerial success. Although command was beginning to appreciate the potential of the third dimension, its use was not yet fully understood. The military eye had not yet been completely trained, and though it knew something important was being seen, the accurate interpretation of aerial photos still lay in the future. Enemy strength was underestimated, and the hoped-for results were not achieved. The proper exploitation of aerial reconnaissance during a battle—for example, the use of contact patrols to locate the front line—also lay ahead. But a foundation had been laid, and a glimpse of the potential of airpower had been seen.

James Streckfuss

See also

Royal Flying Corps/Royal Naval Air Service/Royal Air Force; World War I Aviation

References

Henshaw, Trevor. *The Sky Their Battlefield.* London: Grub Street, 1995.

Raleigh, Sir Walter, and H. A. Jones. *The War in the Air: Being the Story of the Part Played in the Great War by the Royal Air Force.* 6 vols. Oxford: Clarendon Press, 1922–1937.

Nguyen Cao Ky (1930–)

South Vietnamese aviator and political leader. Nguyen Cao Ky was born on 8 September 1930 in Son Tay Province, northwest of Hanoi, the only son of a schoolteacher father. In 1951, he was drafted into the Vietnamese National Army, later being commissioned an infantry lieutenant. He volunteered for pilot training, spending three years in Morocco, France, and Algeria learning to fly combat and transport aircraft.

He returned home as a rated pilot in 1954 as the French withdrew from Indochina. He joined the Republic of Vietnam Air Force (RVNAF) in South Vietnam. By 1960, Major Ky commanded Tan Son Nhut Air Base near Saigon. He also flew agents into North Vietnam for William Colby, Saigon station chief for the Central Intelligence Agency.

In November 1963, Ky played a role in the coup against Ngo Dinh Diem by securing RVNAF support. Coup leader General Duong Van "Big" Minh promoted Ky to brigadier general and RVNAF commander. Soon members of the new Military Revolutionary Council (MRC) began to plot against each other. In January 1964, Ky supported Major General Nguyen Khanh's coup against Minh. Khanh became premier and appointed Ky air vice marshal.

On 21 July 1964, Ky garnered international attention when he publicly disclosed his work for the CIA and advocated the systematic bombing of the North. In December, part of a military faction known as the Young Turks, which included Major General Nguyen Van Thieu, replaced the older officers in the MRC, creating the Armed Forces Council (AFC) in January 1965.

By February 1965, Ky, alarmed by rumors that Khanh was secretly seeking negotiations with the National Liberation Front and supported by U.S. Generals Maxwell Taylor and William Westmoreland, sought to remove Khanh. On 24 February, Khanh left South Vietnam for the last time, as a "roving ambassador."

Earlier, on 8 February, the swashbuckling Ky again captured worldwide attention by leading RVNAF air strikes during Operation FLAMING DART I, President Lyndon Johnson's reprisal attacks against the Dong Hoi military barracks north of the Demilitarized Zone.

On 12 June, Ky, Thieu, and General Nguyen Huu Co replaced the AFC with the 10-member National Leadership Committee (NLC). Ky became chief executive (premier), running the daily business of government, and Thieu became chief of state. Ky tried to institute what he called "social justice." He strengthened the military, instituted needed land reforms, initiated school and hospital construction, and facilitated economic reforms such as price controls. He also tried to purge corruption from his government.

Unfortunately, there was a dark side to Ky. He took repressive measures against the media and violated individual civil liberties. Between April and June 1966, supported by the United States, he used troops and heavy weapons to suppress Buddhist dissidents, accusing them of communist sympathies.

In February 1966, Ky met with President Johnson for two days in Hawaii. The meeting enhanced his credibility, and it led to democratic reforms in the South. Between May 1966 and May 1967, a new constitution was created calling for a powerful president, premier, and cabinet responsible to a two-chamber legislature.

As the September presidential elections approached, tensions between Ky and Thieu rose. Many South Vietnamese leaders feared hostilities. Instead, the NLC forced Ky and Thieu onto a joint ticket, with the older Thieu as the presidential candidate and Ky as the vice presidential candidate.

Thieu and Ky defeated 10 other tickets, receiving 34.8 percent of the vote. Although some have questioned the process, it seems that it was a fair-enough election to suggest that Thieu and Ky should have won. Over the next four years, Ky's influence faded. In 1971, Thieu passed a law to block Ky and others from running for president. Although the Vietnamese Supreme Court overturned the law, Ky did not run. Thieu won, but his high-handed style damaged the new government's status.

Ky left the government but remained publicly active. In 1975, South Vietnam was faced with the communists' Ho Chi Minh Offensive. Ky's later writings and public statements criticize Thieu's tactical withdrawal of Army of the Republic of Vietnam (ARVN) forces from the Central Highlands. He believed this led to the disintegration of ARVN resistance.

In early April, Ky participated in a public demonstration in front of the U.S. Embassy, where he and hundreds of officers vowed to stay and fight. On 29 April, he flew a helicopter to USS *Midway* and left Vietnam. He emigrated to Los Angeles and opened a liquor store. He seemed to do well, but in 1985 he declared bankruptcy, citing a $20,000 gambling debt.

Since then, Ky has maintained a low profile, rarely making public appearances. It has been said that, unlike many U.S. leaders of the time, Ky "remains thoroughly unrepentant." Many would argue that he has little for which to repent.

William Head

References

Bui Diem, with David Chanoff. *In the Jaws of History.* Boston: Houghton Mifflin, 1987.

Nguyen Cao Ky. *Twenty Years and Twenty Days.* New York: Stein and Day, 1976.

Karnow, Stanley. *Vietnam: A History.* New York: Viking Press, 1983.

NICKEL GRASS (1973)

Code name for 32-day airlift by U.S. Military Airlift Command (MAC) Lockheed C-141s and C-5s into the intense fighting of the Arab-Israeli Yom Kippur War. Neither as well known as the Berlin Airlift nor as large as DESERT STORM, Operation NICKEL GRASS airlifted thousands of tons of materiel and restored the balance of power, helping Israel survive the Soviet-backed assault from Egypt and Syria. It also solidified the U.S. Air Force's theory of global mobility while transforming the C-5 Galaxy's image from expensive lemon to potent symbol of U.S. airpower.

In 1967, the Israelis captured large areas of Egypt, Syria, and Jordan. Diplomatic efforts to persuade or even force the release of those lands had failed. By 1973, Egypt and Syria were carefully planning an offensive to bring about that goal, and on 6 October they attacked, catching Israel by complete surprise. The Egyptian Third Army pretended to conduct exercises until the Israelis began to ignore their machinations. Choosing the most holy day in the Jewish calendar, Yom Kippur, the Day of Atonement, in hopes of catching the Israelis off-guard, the Egyptians attacked across the Suez Canal. The Israeli army was overconfident and indecisive at the operational and strategic levels. Egyptian forces pressed

For many years a highly controversial aircraft, the Lockheed C-5 Galaxy proved itself beyond doubt in the Yom Kippur War, during Operation NICKEL GRASS. *(Walter J. Boyne)*

their advantage and quickly overwhelmed Israeli forces at the beginning of the war.

Israeli Prime Minister Golda Meir asked U.S. President Richard M. Nixon for help. Paralyzed by events at home—the end of the Vietnam War, Watergate, and the resignation of Vice President Spiro T. Agnew—Nixon was slow to respond. Moreover, coming to Israel's aid would require a balancing act: protecting the new détente that had been achieved with the North Vietnamese at the Paris peace talks while avoiding an Arab oil embargo against the West.

On 9 October, Nixon responded to Meir's request for the U.S. resupply of Israel. It took four more days to decide how that effort would take shape. It was Nixon who, on 12 October, made the decision that MAC aircraft would be used. The Air Force had been preparing for the contingency, and in nine days MAC's 268 C-141 Starlifters and 77 C-5s were ready—but not fast enough for Nixon.

The fear of an oil embargo caused some U.S. allies to deny landing and air access to the flights. Only Portugal agreed, allowing the airlift to use Lajes Field in the Azores. The average distance from the points of departure in the United States to Lajes was 3,297 miles, with another 3,163 miles from Lajes to Lod/Ben-Gurion Airport in Israel. The aircraft flew to Gibraltar in Spain, then along a narrow corridor across the Mediterranean on the Flight Information Region Boundary line that divided the airspace of hostile African states to the south and friendly European states to the north.

The U.S. Sixth Fleet provided protection for the transports until they were within 200 miles of Israel, at which time Israeli Defense Force fighters took over. Relieved Israelis greeted the MAC airplanes and developed a system to accelerate unloading procedures.

With the 4,000-ton airlift requirement growing daily, the USAF sent four C-5s and 12 C-141s. By 21 October, six C-5s and 17 C-141s moved in and out daily, a level maintained until 30 October, when requirements began to decline.

Because of the continuous supply of war materiel from the United States, the Israelis did not need to conserve ammunition and other consumables. As a result, the Israelis could mount an offensive late in the war. In the north, they recovered lost ground and began to march on Damascus. In the Sinai, tank forces crossed the Suez Canal, encircled the Egyptian Third Army, and threatened Ismailia, Suez City, and Cairo. Egypt and Syria had previously refused to negotiate, but to prevent the destruction of the Egyptian Army, on 22 October they accepted a cease-fire brokered by Washington and Moscow.

Israel wanted to gain as much as possible before the cease-fire, so it was reluctant to comply. Moscow threatened unilateral action, and on 24 October the United States took its armed forces to DEFCON III alert to demonstrate its willingness to use whatever force necessary. After several fruitless attempts, the cease-fire began on 28 October.

The airlift officially ended on 14 November. The Air Force had delivered 22,395 tons of cargo during 145 C-5 and 422 C-141 sorties. The C-141s had carried more tonnage, but the C-5s had delivered outsized equipment that only they could carry—M-60 tanks, 155mm howitzers, ground radar systems, mobile tractor units, CH-53 helicopters, and A-4E components.

The airlift proved vital to Israel's victory. Moreover, the performance of the U.S. transports substantiated that they were both reliable and economical, with the C-5 about 81 percent reliable and the C-141 about 93 percent reliable. No accidents occurred, and less than 2 percent of scheduled flights had to be aborted.

In the lessons-learned column, Air Force officials placed the importance of Lajes as a forward staging area and the need for aerial refueling as a standard practice. Indeed, Operation NICKEL GRASS directly resulted in the modification of the C-141 for aerial refueling. Moreover, the realization that commercial airlines could not be expected to meet airlift requirements with volunteer manpower and machinery brought about the consolidation of airlift aircraft under MAC and its designation as a specified command on 1 February 1977. Finally, the C-5 proved its worth and that it was not the costly military mistake portrayed by the media.

Diane Truluck

References

Boyne, Walter. "NICKEL GRASS." *Air Force Magazine* 81, 12 (December 1998).

Head, William. "Reworking the Workhorse: C-141B Stretch Modification Program." Robins AFB, GA: USAF Monograph, WR-ALC Office of History, 1984.

Nieuport Aircraft

One of the major aircraft builders during World War I. The firm built both two-seat and single-seat designs, most of which were best known for their sesquiplane layout. The sesquiplane—literally, "one-and-a-half-wing"—had a full-size upper wing and a narrow-chord single-spar lower wing. The intent was to maximize the downward view.

Nieuports were light on the controls and maneuverable. Powered by rotary engines ranging in rating from 80 horsepower to an eventual 150 horsepower, armament was generally provided either by a Lewis machine gun on an elevated mount to allow fire over the propeller or a synchronized Vickers firing through the arc. Occasionally, both types of guns were carried, but the extra weight of the second gun was usually too much for the aircraft. Le Prieur rockets, intended for use against balloons, were sometimes fitted on the struts.

The first of the single-seat "V-strutters"—the little Nieuport 11—may also have been the first aircraft to have worn the kind of bright colors that characterized fighter aircraft in the later years of the war when French ace Jean Navarre painted the fuselage of his aircraft bright red.

The Nieuport Type 11, nicknamed Bébé (Baby), was the first successful French single-seat fighter. The Bébé was powered by the 80-hp LeRhone rotary engine and mounted an elevated Lewis machine gun. The Nieuport 11 earned its fame in the fight against the Fokker Eindecker, which it was generally able to outmaneuver.

A succession of improved and enlarged versions of sesquiplane Nieuports followed. Despite the inherent structural problem of the V-strut, they were used with great success. The most handsome of the line, the Nieuport 28, returned to a conventional biplane layout and was powered by the large 160-hp Gnôme rotary engine. Armament was also upgraded from earlier practice, with twin Vickers machine guns being carried in lieu of the single Vickers or Lewis that had generally supplied the muscle of the earlier types.

Refused by the French for their own air force, the Nieuport 28 was plagued with inflight fires and structural failures, including the separation of the upper wing's leading edge in a dive. Nonetheless, it served well in U.S. units, to which the French handed it off.

The earlier V-strut models did not vanish from the scene completely. They continued to serve as advanced trainers in French schools as well as at the U.S. Third Aviation Instruction Center at Issoudun.

Identification of the individual Nieuport models in historical records is sometimes complicated by references to the square-meter area of the wings rather than official model numbers.

James Streckfuss

References

Davilla, James, and Arthur M. Soltan. *French Aircraft of the First World War.* Mountain View, CA: Flying Machines Press, 1997.

Rickenbacker, Edward V. *Fighting the Flying Circus.* New York: Doran, 1919.

Nieuport-Delage NiD-29

The immediate successor of the SPAD fighters in the French squadrons after World War I. Although slower than the Wibault 1, it was preferred by the French for its better control harmonization and efficiency.

An answer for a 1917 fighter program, the first of three prototypes flew in 1918. Production models of the NiD-29C1 reached operational units in 1922. Five years later, 620 had been delivered to the French air force, and a total of more than 700 were produced for France until 1928. Only three saw active service, used during one month in Morocco for bombing and strafing against rebels.

The NiD-29C1 was a great export success. Spain bought 30, Belgium 109, Italy 181 (including 175 produced under license), Sweden 10 (called J2), and Argentina and Siam unknown quantities. The most important customer was Japan, with no less than 608 built as the Ko 4 between 1924 and 1932. It was the front-line fighter of the Japanese army for several years and fought during the Japanese war against China. Some Ko 4s were still used for training when Japan entered World War II. The NiD-29C1 is one of the very few aircraft whose service life spanned both world wars. In its heyday in 1924, it was considered by U.S. General Billy Mitchell to be the best pursuit plane of the high-speed diving type in the world.

Stéphane Nicolaou

Night Witches (46th Guards Night Bomber Regiment)

The only all-woman aviation unit in history and one of the most distinguished Soviet air units in World War II. During autumn 1941, after intense urging by the famed female aviator Marina Raskova, Soviet dictator Joseph Stalin authorized the creation of three regiments of women aviators. One was the 588 NBAP (Night Bomber Aviation Regiment), established at Engels in December 1941. Although the other women's regiments later acquired some male members, the 588th remained totally female. Committed to battle in May 1942, the regiment flew the Polikarpov Po-2 biplane trainer, equipped as a night-bomber. Their bombing deprived the German troops of sleep and frequently caused serious damage to German supply depots and headquarters. When the Germans discovered that some of the crews were women, they named them the Night Witches. Flying up to 15 sorties a night, many crews flew 700–1,000 missions. In recognition of its outstanding accomplishments, on 8 February 1943 the 588 NBAP was honored as the 46th Guards Regiment. During the war the 46th flew about 24,000 sorties, lost 30 airwomen, and saw 23 of its members awarded the Hero of the Soviet Union.

George M. Mellinger

See also

Polikarpov, Nikolai N.; Raskova, Marina Mikhaylovna

Some of the great architects of naval victory in World War II: from the left, Admiral Raymond A. Spruance, Fleet Admiral Ernest J. King, Fleet Admiral Chester W. Nimitz. With them is Brigadier General Sanderford Jarman. (U.S. Navy)

References

Cottam, Kazimiera J. *Women in Air War: The Eastern Front of World War II.* New Military, Nepean, Canada, 1997.

Noggle, Anne. *A Dance with Death: Soviet Airwomen in World War II.* College Station: Texas A&M University Press, 1994.

Nimitz, Chester William (1885–1966)

U.S. admiral and master of the operational art of war; commanded in the Pacific during World War II. Born in Fredericksburg, Texas, on 24 February 1885, Nimitz attended the U.S. Naval Academy, graduated in 1905, and served on and commanded surface ships and submarines. Other command assignments included submarine, cruiser, and battleship divisions. He served in no major aviation-related positions. Staff assignments culminated in promotion to rear admiral and assignment as chief of the Bureau of Navigation in 1939. Shortly after Pearl Harbor, Nimitz was selected to command the U.S. Pacific Fleet and, soon, all Allied forces in the Pacific.

Nimitz appreciated the offensive capabilities of naval aviation and was blessed with competent and aggressive subordinates on whom he relied. Nimitz risked defeat in carrier battles at Coral Sea (May 1942) and Midway (June 1942) to gain major victories that decimated Japanese carrier-based airpower and turned the war in the Pacific.

These battles also won back the Solomon Islands (February 1943) and set the stage for success in campaigns for the Gilbert Islands (November 1943), the Marshall Islands (February 1944), and the Mariana Islands (August 1944). Commanding from Hawaii, Nimitz oversaw major victories at Leyte Gulf (supporting the Philippines campaign), Guam, Iwo Jima, and Okinawa. Throughout, he used carriers offensively, taking the war to the enemy, while not ignoring air support for the amphibious operations necessary to reach Japan.

Nimitz took strategic guidance from Admiral Ernest King—his superior as Chief of Naval Operations (CNO) and commander in chief of the U.S. Fleet—and often left the tactical details to trusted subordinates like Admiral William "Bull" Halsey. Nimitz concentrated instead on the operational level of the U.S. war effort in the Pacific. A thorough campaign planner, Nimitz ensured solid logistical support for operating forces, utilized invaluable intelligence at critical junctures, and maneuvered his carrier forces boldly when victory required it.

Nimitz coordinated his movements with his neighboring Allied commander, General Douglas MacArthur, on his flank. Nimitz's ability to provide operational naval air support to MacArthur while conducting his own island-hopping campaign was masterful.

Nimitz was promoted to the five-star rank of fleet admiral in 1944 and represented the United States as signatory of the Japanese surrender document at war's end. He subsequently served as CNO and, upon retirement from the Navy in 1949, as United Nations commissioner appointed to resolve the dispute over Kashmir between Pakistan and India. Nimitz died in San Francisco on 20 February 1966.

Michael S. Casey

See also

Coral Sea, Battle of the; Gilbert Islands; Guadalcanal; Guam, Battles of; Halsey, William F.; Iwo Jima; King, Ernest J.; Leyte Gulf, Battle of; Midway, Battle of; Yamamoto, Isoroku

References

Brink, Randall. *Nimitz: The Man and His Wars.* New York: Penguin, 2000.

Driskill, Frank A. *Chester W. Nimitz: Admiral of the Hills.* Austin, TX: Eakin Press, 1983.

Potter, E. B. *Nimitz.* Annapolis, MD: Naval Institute Press, 1976.

Nishizawa, Hiroyoshi (1920–1944)

Imperial Japanese Navy warrant officer and leading ace. Hiroyoshi Nishizawa was born on 27 January 1920 in Nagano Prefecture. He joined the navy in June 1936 and completed flight training in March 1939.

Just before the outbreak of war, Nishizawa was transferred to the Chitose Air Group in the Marshall Islands. When that group was moved to Rabaul in February 1942, Nishizawa was transferred to the 4th Air Group, also on Rabaul, and got his first victory on 3 February 1942 with that group.

In April 1942, the Tainan Air Group, which included aces such as Saburo Sakai and Toshio Ota, was transferred to Rabaul, and Nishizawa was transferred to the 2d Squadron of that air group. From April to November, Nishizawa recorded 30 air victories with as many as six victories in a single battle.

On 25 October, Nishizawa's aircraft was damaged in battle and he was forced to land on Cebu Island. He boarded a transport on 26 October for the return to Luzon, where he was based. The transport was intercepted over Mindoro Island and shot down, killing all aboard.

Nishizawa was Japan's leading ace of World War II, with estimated total kills ranging from 86 to more than 150 aircraft.

David A. Pluth

References

Sakaida, Henry. *Imperial Japanese Navy Aces, 1937–1945.* London: Osprey, 1998.

Hata, Ikuhiko, and Yasuho Izawa. *Japanese Naval Aces and Fighter Units in World War II.* Annapolis, MD: Naval Institute Press, 1989.

Nonlethal Weapons

A class of weaponry that incapacitates personnel and materiel while minimizing fatalities, permanent injury to personnel, and undesired damage to property and the environment. Unlike conventional weapons, nonlethal weapons do not rely upon blast, fragmentation, and penetration for their effects but instead utilize other means to stop their target from functioning. These weapons range from mechanical and kinetic devices to chemical compounds, biological organisms, and various forms of directed energy. From an airpower perspective, the more exotic of these weapons offer strategic-paralysis and mass-disruption capabilities. In the Vietnam War, emulsifying agents were thought to be air-dispersed over the Ho Chi Minh Trail by the United States in an attempt to degrade the logistical lifeline of Vietcong forces. Low-energy lasers were reportedly used by British naval forces in a counteroptical role against Argentine aircraft during the Falkland Islands War. During the Gulf War, carbon fiber–filled cruise missiles were said to be used by the United States against Iraqi power plants that resulted in their temporary shutdown.

Robert J. Bunker

References

Alexander, John B. *Future War: Non-Lethal Weapons in Twenty-First-Century Warfare.* New York: St. Martin's, 1999.

Klaaren, Jonathan W., and Ronald S. Mitchell. "Nonlethal Technology and Airpower: A Winning Combination for Strategic Paralysis." *Airpower Journal.* Special Edition (1995): 42–51.

Robert J. Bunker, ed. *Non-Lethal Weapons: Terms and References.* Occasional Paper no. 15. Colorado Springs, CO: USAF Academy: Institute for National Security Studies, July 1997.

Normandie-Niemen Regiment

Free French fighter unit during World War II. The Normandie Squadron was organized in Syria in September 1942 from Free French pilots impatient to fight the Germans. After training in Russia, they entered combat under the command of Jean Tuslane on the Western Front on 22 March 1943 and were assigned to the 303 IAD (Fighter Aviation). They flew for the rest of the war in Russia and expanded to an overstrength regiment. In June 1944, the Soviet government awarded them the honorific title Niemen for distinguished combat at that river. Initially equipped with the Yak-1 fighter, they later received the Yak-9 and in 1944 the Yak-3. Their last commander was Louis Delfino. They flew 4,534 combat hours and fought 869 air combats, scoring 273 victories in exchange for 42 pilots killed or missing. Fourteen pilots scored 10 or more victories, and the top ace was Marcel Albert, who scored 22 victories in Russia and one in France in 1940. The French and Russian governments each retain an air unit perpetuating the lineage and traditions of the Normandie-Niemen Regiment.

George M. Mellinger

References

Ketley, Barry. *French Aces of World War 2.* London: Osprey, 1999.

Normandy, Task Force

Coalition force that spearheaded the Gulf War's major offensive. At approximately 11:38 P.M. Greenwich Mean Time on 16 January 1991, eight U.S. AH-64A Apache attack helicopters from the 1st Battalion, 101st Aviation Regiment, 101st Airborne Division, fired the first shots of the war, a salvo of Hellfire missiles onto two radar facilities in south-central Iraq north of the Saudi Arabian border. This element—Task Force Normandy, named in honor of the men from the 101st Airborne Division who led the Allied invasion of France on D-Day five decades earlier—was under the direct command of Lieutenant Colonel Richard A. "Dick" Cody, an innovative U.S. Army aviator. The attack's purpose was to silence the radar facilities, denying the Iraqis early detection of U.S. aircraft penetrating Iraqi airspace en route to strategic targets in and around Baghdad.

The Apaches used on the raid were configured in such a way as to make the mission feasible and achievable. Remote ground-refueling operations were necessary because of the long distances involved. Lieutenant Colonel Cody proposed using the AH-64A in a slightly modified configuration. In place of one rocket pod capable of carrying 19 2.75-inch folding-fin aerial rockets, each of the eight aircraft selected for the mission carried one 230-gallon auxiliary fuel tank. Remaining armament included 19 rockets, eight Hellfire missiles, and approximately 1,000 rounds of 30mm high-explosive rounds. In this configuration, the Apaches were set up to fly the mission without an intermediate refueling requirement and deliver sufficient ordnance on the targets to ensure their destruction.

On 17 January 1991 at approximately 12:01 A.M. in Saudi Arabia, Task Force Normandy departed Al Jouf, crossed the border into Iraq, and proceeded along northerly routes as two separate teams in the direction of the radar sites, which were separated by about 40 miles of open desert. At precisely 10 seconds prior to the prescribed engagement time, the mission commander gave the signal to the other aircraft to stand by for missile launch, breaking radio silence for the first time since before departing Al Jouf. At 2:38 A.M. local time in Saudi Arabia, eight missiles—four per radar site—impacted their targets. In all, several dozen missiles were fired, first at the power-generating equipment, then immediately on the radar dishes, command-and-control vans, and antennae simultaneously. After a distant engagement using missiles, the aircraft proceeded to within a half-mile of their targets, engaging all the way with rockets and 30mm rounds. The radar facilities had been immediately disabled and, within only a few moments, completely destroyed.

By midafternoon on 17 January, all but one mission aircraft had returned safely to their home base at King Fahd International Airport. The eighth Apache, along with the logistics aircraft, had remained at Al Jouf to address some main rotor damage caused by flying debris or small-arms rounds from Iraqi sentries. Within 24 hours, however, those aircraft also returned to King Fahd International Airport, ready to continue with the task of fighting a war that was now well under way.

The success of Task Force Normandy redefined the U.S. Army's use of attack helicopters and reshaped the battlefield. Apache unit commanders across the Kuwaiti theater began equipping their aircraft with one auxiliary fuel tank on a regular basis as dictated by mission requirements.

Rafael J. Garcia Jr.

References

Garcia, Rafael J. Jr. *Paladin Zero Six: A Desert Storm Memoir by a 101st Airborne Attack Helicopter Company Commander.* Jefferson, NC: McFarland, 1994.

Taylor, Thomas. *Lightning in the Storm: The 101st Air Assault Division in the Gulf War.* New York: Hippocrene Books, 1995.

Norstad, Lauris (1907–1988)

U.S. Air Force General Lauris "Larry" Norstad was a fighter pilot, planner, and staff officer. During World War II he served in North Africa, the Mediterranean, and Washington.

After the war, Norstad worked on the Air Staff in Washington until 1950, when he was made commander of United States Air Forces in Europe. Two years later, he was awarded his fourth star—at age 46 the second-youngest American to achieve that rank.

In April 1956, Norstad was chosen as Supreme Allied Commander Europe—the first airman to hold that position. A strategic airpower advocate, he suited the Eisenhower administration, which propounded a strategy of massive retaliation. Over the next six years, he led NATO through a series of major events, including the Berlin Crisis of 1961. More notably, he guided the debate regarding the control and use of nuclear weapons in NATO. Seeing himself as an "international general" more than an American commander, he was out of step with the Kennedy administration that took office in 1961. Relations deteriorated, and in 1963 Norstad was forced into retirement. He served as CEO of Owens-Corning Fiberglass Corporation for a number of years before retiring again in 1973.

Phillip S. Meilinger

See also

North Atlantic Treaty Organization; U.S. Air Forces in Europe

References

Belote, Howard D. *Once in a Blue Moon: Airmen in Theater Command.* Maxwell AFB, AL: Air University Press, 2000.

Jordan, Robert S. *Norstad: Cold War NATO Supreme Commander.* London: Macmillan, 2000.

———. *Generals in International Politics: NATO's Supreme Allied Commander, Europe.* Lexington: University Press of Kentucky, 1987.

North African Campaign

Although Benito Mussolini's Regia Aeronautica attacked the British bastion of Malta in early June 1940, the aerial war in North Africa took a long time to develop, despite skirmishing with Royal Air Force planes flying from bases in Egypt. Initially the small Italian air force in North Africa included only 84 modern bombers, including the Savoia-Marchetti SM 79 Sparviero. It also possessed 144 obsolescent fighter aircraft, such as the durable Fiat CR 42 Falcon biplane. A miscellany of approximately 100 other aircraft rounded out the force.

What subsequently became the RAF's Western Desert Air Force was, if anything, weaker still. It constituted a scratch force of castoffs from imperial service augmented by a few machines just being sent out from the home islands. The latter included, in late 1940 and early 1941, the first arrivals of Hawker Hurricanes (Mk.Is and, later, Mk.IIs). They complemented the few Westland Lysander liaison/reconnaissance aircraft, Bristol Blenheim twin-engine bombers, and venerable Gloster Gladiator biplane fighters with which the RAF defended the Nile Delta.

The arrival of the German Afrika Korps in North Africa in early 1941 altered matters. Accompanying the German ground forces were Luftwaffe units equipped with Messerschmitt Bf 109 single-engine and Bf 110 twin-engine fighters and fighter-bombers. The ground attack role was ably filled by the veteran Junkers Ju 87 Stuka dive-bomber. Italy also reinforced its squadrons with small numbers of agile (and elegant) Macchi-Castoldi MC.202 Folgore single-engine fighters. These aircraft helped carry Italo-German forces to a string of successes in 1941. In mid-1942, they played a positively decisive role in the Axis victories at Bir Hakim and Tobruk.

In the fall of that year, however, factors beyond North Africa's shores began to impede reinforcement of Italo-German forces in the theater. Axis armies and air forces in Egypt were at the end of their logistical network, and precious little fuel, replacement aircraft, and spare parts reached them. By contrast, British armies and Allied air forces in Egypt went from strength to strength, particularly with the activation of the U.S. Army Middle East Air Force's Desert Air Task Force (DATF), consisting of RAF and USAAF fighter and light and medium bombardment groups. Operating, among others, Curtiss P-40 Warhawks ("Tomahawks" and "Kittyhawks" in British and imperial service), and North American B-25 Mitchell and Douglas DB-7 Boston twin-engine bombers, these formations supplied critical air support in defeating the last-ditch Axis effort at Alam el Halfa (31 August–6 September).

At El Alamein as well (24 October–4 November), the DATF helped break the back of Axis resistance to the British Eighth Army's offensive. The early simultaneous landings of Operation TORCH (7 November) brought into northwest Africa what would become the U.S. Twelfth Air Force. Axis forces were now caught in a strategic vise.

From December 1942 to May 1943, Allied airpower grew in strength. Nevertheless, Axis air forces fought on grimly in the struggles of the Tunisian bridgehead. Using all-weather airfields around Tunis and Bizerte, they contested Allied advances as much as their increasingly limited logistics would permit and were especially effective at the turn of the year when Allied planes were either too far from the front or operated from inadequate bases.

The weight of numbers told, however. By early spring 1943, the Luftwaffe and Regia Aeronautica existed as mere remnants in Tunisia. Furthermore, they suffered appalling losses of transports and aircrews to marauding Allied fighters and light bombers in a desperate attempt at aerial reinforcement. The remaining Axis air and ground forces surrendered on 13 May 1943.

D. R. Dorondo

See also
Alam el Halfa, Battle of; El Alamein, Air Battles of; Malta, Siege of; Regia Aeronautica (World War II); TORCH

References
Craven, Wesley F., and James L. Cate, eds. *The Army Air Forces in World War II, Volume 2: Europe: TORCH to POINTBLANK, August 1942 to December 1943.* Washington, DC: Office of Air Force History, 1983.
Gilbert, Adrian, ed. *The Imperial War Museum Book of the Desert War.* London: Motorbooks International, 1995.
Heckmann, Wolf. *Rommel's War in Africa.* Trans. Stephen Seago. Garden City, NY: Doubleday, 1981.

North American Aerospace Defense Command (NORAD)

Joint U.S.-Canadian command responsible for the air and space defense of North America. Defense cooperation had been close between these two neighbors since the August 1940 formation of the Permanent Joint Board on Defense. In 1951, Royal Canadian Air Force liaison officers were first formally assigned to Air Defense Command's headquarters in Colorado Springs, Colorado, and by the mid-1950s procedures for joint air defense operations in an emergency were well established. Relevant military forces from both nations were now under the operational control of the commander of NORAD, a general from the United States, with a Canadian general as his deputy, a pattern that has continued to the present day.

Virtually simultaneous with the creation of NORAD was the dawn of the ICBM age, signified by the October 1957 Soviet launch of an earth satellite. Though Sputnik foreshadowed NORAD's eventual emphasis on space operations, defense against bomber attack remained a critical mission for years to come. In 1959, the United States approved construction of the hardened underground Combat Operations Center for NORAD, designed to withstand attacks by multimegaton nuclear weapons at least long enough to raise the alert of an attack and, hopefully, long enough to manage the defense against the first wave of bombers that would likely follow an ICBM first strike. Completed in 1965, this structure is buried beneath 1,500 feet of granite deep within Cheyenne Mountain. Defenses against a bomber attack on North America peaked in size in the early 1960s and declined thereafter, as the emphasis gradually shifted to providing early warning of Soviet missile attacks; in 1981 the "Air" in NORAD's name was changed to "Aerospace" in recognition of the increased importance of space operations.

Despite the end of the Cold War, as well as numerous reorganizations of U.S. Air Force commands beneath it, NORAD remains in existence entering the twenty-first century. Its mission has, if anything, expanded (it has become increasingly involved in the U.S. war on drugs), and it promises to play a major role in any future national missile defense system.

David Rezelman

See also
Air Defense Command; Antimissile Defense; Ballistic Missile Early Warning System; Canadian Air Force; Cold War; Continental Air Command; Distant Early Warning; SAGE Defense System; Soviet Aircraft Development and Production; Sputnik; Strategic Air Command; Tactical Air Command

References
Crosby, Ann Denholm. *Dilemmas in Defence Decision-Making: Constructing Canada's Role in NORAD, 1958–1996.* New York: St. Martin's, 1998.
Holman, D. Fraser. *NORAD in the Next Millenium.* Toronto: Irwin, 2000.
Jockel, Joseph T. *No Boundaries Upstairs: Canada, the United States, and the Origins of North American Air Defence, 1945–1958.* Vancouver: University of British Columbia Press, 1987.

North American Aviation

Major U.S. aircraft manufacturer and defense contractor. North American Aviation was incorporated in Delaware on 6 December 1928 and was listed on the New York Stock Exchange for the first time in March 1930. The legendary James H. "Dutch" Kindelberger moved the company to Southern California in 1934, occupying a 159,000-square-foot facility that cost $600 a year to rent. With him came two key designers from Douglas Aircraft: Lee Atwood and J. S. "Stan" Smithson.

The company's first aircraft was the NA-16 single-engine trainer that evolved into the BT-9; the first combat aircraft was the BC-1, a derivative of the same airframe. With a world war looming, North American designed and produced such notable aircraft as the T-6 Texan, B-25 Mitchell, and P-51 Mustang. During the five years of wartime production, North American built 41,000 aircraft; in fact, between 1935 and 1967 manufactured more military aircraft than any other U.S. contractor. At the end of the war, North American employed more than 91,000 people; within months the workforce dropped below 5,000 as war contracts were cancelled and the nation demobilized.

After the war, North American built the AJ Savage bomber for the Navy and the first U.S. jet-powered bomber, the B-45 Tornado, for the Air Force. More important, North American developed the F-86 Sabre, the first operational U.S. swept-wing fighter that went on to great fame in the skies over Korea. Other postwar aircraft included the F-82 Twin Mustang and F-100 Super Sabre for the Air Force, the

Designed as an air superiority fighter, the North American F-100 Super Sabre would prove itself as a close support and reconnaissance aircraft in Vietnam. (U.S. Air Force)

A-5 Vigilante for the Navy, the experimental XB-70 Mach 3 bomber prototypes, and the rocket-powered X-15 research airplane.

In the late 1940s, North American formed a missiles division that experimented with ballistic and guided missiles, eventually producing the X-10 demonstrators, SM-64 Navaho prototypes, and GAM-77 Hound Dog cruise missile used on the B-52. North American's Space and Information Systems Division built the Apollo spacecraft that took men to the moon, and it eventually won the contract to build the Space Shuttle orbiters.

Dennis R. Jenkins

North American B-25 Mitchell

One of the best medium bombers of World War II. The B-25, though close to the company's NA-40 and NA-62 of the previous year, was ordered into production in 1939 without a prototype. The Mitchell was a shoulder-wing twin-engine aircraft with a twin rudder and could carry about 3,000 pounds of bombs. The first flew on 19 August 1940—a year and a week after the order—and 25 had been delivered by the end of 1940. Sixteen B-25Bs took part in the famous April 1942 raid led by Jimmy Doolittle against Japanese cities, taking off from a Navy aircraft carrier 800 miles out in the Pacific. As with most wartime models, constant improvements were introduced: A models added armor, the B powered turrets, the C an autopilot and uprated engines, the G a 75mm cannon for antishipping missions, and the H even heavier firepower. The B-25J was the most numerous, with nearly 4,400 of the 9,800 total B-25s when production stopped in August 1945. In July 1945, a B-25 crashed into New York City's Empire State Building in heavy fog. The Mitchell remained operational in subsidiary roles with the U.S. Air Force until 1960 and for much longer in many other nations.

Christopher H. Sterling

See also

Doolittle, James H.; Mitchell, William; North American Aviation

References

Avery, Norman L. *B-25 Mitchell: The Magnificent Medium.* St. Paul: Phalanx, 1992.

Johnsen, Frederick A. *North American B-25 Mitchell.* WarbirdTech Series Volume 12. North Branch, MN: Specialty Press, 1997.

Scutts, Jerry. *B-25 Mitchell at War.* London: Ian Allen, 1983.

North American B-45 Tornado

The first production all-jet bomber in the United States Air Force. Design development began in 1944, and the first prototype flew in March 1947. The Tornado was a straight-wing design with four jet engines, two in a single nacelle under each wing. The crew of four included the pilot and copilot in tandem under the canopy, a navigator-bombardier in the lower nose, and a tailgunner.

In November 1948, the USAF accepted initial delivery to an operational unit, the 47th Bombardment Group, Barksdale Air Force Base, Louisiana. Subsequently, the 47th Bombardment Wing was assigned to Langley AFB, Virginia, and then Royal Air Force Station Sculthorpe in May 1952. The 47th Bombardment Wing with its B-45As provided the first tactical nuclear delivery capability for the theater commander in Europe. The B-45 was modified for delivery of atomic weapons under the Backbreaker program. The Air Force procured 96 B-45As and 10 B-45Cs, which were improved by the addition of wing tanks and aerial refueling for extended range.

The last production version of the Tornado was the reconnaissance variant, the RB-45C. The RB-45C was assigned to strategic and tactical reconnaissance units, conducting combat operations during the Korean War and flying reconnaissance missions over Soviet and other communist countries during the early 1950s.

The USAF retired the B-45 from operational service in 1958. The B-45A had a maximum speed of 496 knots, a combat radius of 463 nautical miles, and a maximum payload of 22,000 pounds.

Jerome V. Martin

References

Knaack, Marcelle Size. *Post–World War II Bombers, 1945–1973.* Washington, DC: U.S. Government Printing Office, 1988.

Wagner, Ray. *American Combat Planes.* 3rd ed. Garden City, NY: Doubleday, 1982.

North American B-70 Valkyrie

Experimental high-speed bomber developed for the U.S. Air Force. In 1954, Strategic Air Command commander General Curtis E. LeMay put forth a requirement for an advanced bomber with the highest speed and altitude possible. Both Boeing and North American were awarded development contracts for what was then known only as Weapon System 110. After a hard-fought competition between the two firms, in late 1957 North American got the nod to proceed on the

The first operational jet bomber of the U.S. Air Force was the North American B-45. It served well in the reconnaissance role. (Walter J. Boyne)

WS-110 program. After this, the WS-110 air vehicle was designated B-70 and named Valkyrie.

The Valkyrie was to be a very-high-speed, very-high-altitude bomber intended first to supplement and then to replace the Boeing B-52 Stratofortress during the 1965–1975 period. It was to cruise at speeds exceeding 2,000 mph (Mach 3) at heights above 80,000 feet.

During the B-70's development, on 1 May 1960, Francis Gary Powers's Lockheed U-2C was shot down while overflying Russia. That action, in addition to the advent of operational ICBMs, began to change U.S. defense policy for manned bomber aircraft missions. It had become obvious that Russian defenses could meet and defeat high-flying aircraft. Thus, instead of flying high and fast, it was decided to fly low and slow.

In 1962, the B-70 was canceled as a weapons system. Only two examples were built, as research aircraft for the U.S. Supersonic Transport program and designated XB-70A.

The first XB-70A made its maiden flight on 21 September 1964; the second flew for the first time on 17 July 1965. Both aircraft achieved their maximum performance goals of Mach 3 on their seventeenth flights (respectively, on 14 October 1965 and 3 January 1966). The highest speed and altitude reached: 3.08 Mach and 74,000 feet.

On its forty-sixth flight on 8 June 1966, XB-70A number-two was lost in a midair collision with a NASA F-104 chase plane. Both the copilot of the XB-70A, Major Carl S. Cross, and the pilot of the F-104, Joseph A. Walker, died in the mishap.

The last remaining XB-70A flew on until flight number 83 on 4 February 1969, during which it was ferried to the U.S. Air Force Museum at Wright-Patterson AFB, Ohio.

In all, the two XB-70A Valkyrie aircraft flew 229 times. They remain the largest and heaviest aircraft to have flown at such heights and speeds.

Steve Pace

References

Pace, Steve. *North American XB-70A Valkyrie.* New York: McGraw-Hill, 1990.

North American F-86 Sabre

The first production U.S. aircraft to take full advantage of German World War II research into swept wings. The original design for the new high-speed pursuit plane had been approved with straight wings, but on 1 November 1945 the Air Force approved a plan to incorporate a wing and empennage swept back 35 degrees. The XP-86 made its maiden flight at Muroc, California, on 1 October 1947; the first production aircraft followed on 20 May 1948. Extensive testing was conducted before the new fighter was declared operational, and shortly thereafter the aircraft entered combat in the skies over Korea.

The actual aerial combat statistics for the F-86 have been revised several times as additional information has been declassified, and although the current numbers are not as great as originally believed, the F-86 went on to establish an outstanding reputation as an air superiority fighter. The top ace of the conflict, Captain Joseph McConnell Jr., had 16 victories in the F-86, followed by Captain James Jabara with 15. Other models were optimized for interception duties and even ground attack (including tactical nuclear strike), but most people remember the simple F-86 day-fighter.

No less than 26 countries eventually used the F-86, and Australia, Canada, and Japan set up production lines to produce the aircraft. Both the Australian and Canadian aircraft used indigenously produced engines instead of the General Electric engines that powered most other Sabres. Taiwan used F-86s, including some reconnaissance models, during the 1958 dispute with Mainland China over several islands; this combat resulted in the first operational use of the AIM-9 Sidewinder missile on 24 September 1958. The last F-86 rolled off a production line in Japan in February 1961. And the type served front-line units of several air forces until the late 1960s and second-line units well into the 1970s.

Dennis R. Jenkins

References

Curtis, Duncan. *North American F-86 Sabre.* Wiltshire, UK: Crowood, July 2000.

Dranem, Walter, and Chris Hughes. *North American F-86 Sabrejet Day Fighters.* WarbirdTech Series Volume 3. North Branch, MN: Specialty Press, 1997.

North American OV-10 Bronco

Twin-engine high-wing square-tailed aircraft that saw extensive combat with the United States Air Force, Navy, and Marines in the Vietnam War. Built by North American Aviation at its Columbus, Ohio, plant in the 1960s, the OV-10 was the result of a study done by the Marines that proposed an observation aircraft able to "live" in the field with the troops it was to support and optimized for light strike and forward air control (FAC) duties. Seeking a new aircraft for counterinsurgency as well as FAC duties, the Air Force also backed the concept.

As designed and delivered beginning in late 1967, the OV-10 was powered by two Garrett Air Research turboprop engines. It was equipped with ejection seats for two crewmembers in a long tandem cockpit with bubble canopies that afforded excellent visibility. Onboard radios

The XP-86 was a combination of North American's traditional engineering and design excellence, sweetened by the swept-wing fruits of captured German aeronautical knowledge. (U.S. Air Force)

were totally compatible with all services, and the aircraft was capable of carrying a wide range of ordnance.

In 1968, the aircraft was delivered to U.S. units in Southeast Asia. Eventually, several dozen saw combat duty while assigned to U.S. Marine Observation Squadrons VMO-1, VMO-2, and VMO-6. These three units provided direct support to the 1st and 3d Marine Divisions in northern South Vietnam. New aircraft were also delivered to the U.S. Air Force 504th Tactical Air Support Group and its subordinate squadrons. These aircraft ranged over the breadth and depth if Southeast Asia, from the Plain of Jars and Ho Chi Minh Trail in Laos, to the battlefields of South Vietnam, to the coasts of southern Cambodia.

In 1971, 15 aircraft were specially modified to carry laser designators for the precision placement of laser-guided bombs (Pave Nails), the forefront of the precision-weapons revolution. One OV-10 forward air controller, Captain Steven Bennett, was posthumously awarded the Medal of Honor for his actions near Quang Tri, South Vietnam, on 29 June 1972. The U.S. Navy also had a squadron of OV-10s in South Vietnam (VAL-4, the "Black Ponies"). They specifically worked with riverine and special forces units in the Mekong Delta.

With the cessation of U.S. involvement in Southeast Asia, most OV-10 units were disbanded and the aircraft transferred to other units in Korea, Europe, and the United States. The U.S. Marines deployed OV-10s to combat once again during Operation DESERT STORM. In that conflict, two were shot down; the four crewmen either captured or killed. Subsequently, all remaining OV-10s were removed from active service.

Although no longer used by U.S. military forces, OV-10s are still actively used by the air forces of Thailand, Colombia, and Venezuela.

Darrel Whitcomb

North American P-51 Mustang

One of the best-performing fighters of World War II. The P-51 began as an attempt to meet an April 1940 British Purchasing Mission specification. Though it was rapidly built—the prototype was completed 117 days after the go-ahead—power plant problems delayed the first flight until 26

One of the most famous photos of one of the world's most famous fighters, the North American P-51 Mustang. (U.S. Air Force)

October 1940. The first production models (the NA-73) arrived for British squadrons in 1941. Restricted to tactical work by limitations in the Allison engine, the Mustang (as the British named it) still resulted in more than 600 orders. Many were used in photoreconnaissance.

With installation of the Merlin engine, however, the Mustang reached 440 mph at nearly 30,000 feet; mass production for the U.S. Army Air Forces resulted in nearly 4,000 of the B and C models alone. The D model introduced the bubble canopy; nearly 8,000 were built. More than 500 of the H model and 1,500 of the K model followed, for a total of nearly 15,400 Mustangs built before V-J Day. The fighter was employed in virtually every theater of the war, generally outclassing whatever the enemy could put up against it. The type remained in service with some Latin American air forces into the 1960s. A number also became postwar racing aircraft.

Several hundred of the closely related P-82 (later F-82) Twin Mustangs were built late in and after the war as night-fighters and long-range escorts; some were among the first U.S. aircraft involved in the Korean War in 1950. A tandem-seat version of the aircraft was offered for use in 1967 as a counterinsurgency aircraft.

Christopher H. Sterling

See also
North American Aviation

References

Davis, Larry. *North American P-51 Mustang: A Photo Chronicle.* West Chester, PA: Schiffer Military History, 1992.

Gruenhagen, Robert W. *Mustang: The Story of the P-51 Fighter.* Rev. ed. New York: Arco, 1976.

North American T-6 Texan

Two-place piston-engined transition trainer; bridged the gap for new pilots between basic trainers and higher-performance first-line tactical aircraft.

An evolution of North American Aviation's BC-1 basic trainer, the AT-6 (later designated T-6) first flew in 1939. It featured retractable landing gear, an enclosed cockpit, a variable-pitch propeller, and strong aerobatic performance. It performed all manner of training, at times carrying fixed forward-firing machine guns, flexibly mounted armament in the rear cockpit, and bombs or rockets under the wing. With such diversity, the T-6 provided sound tactical training in both air-to-air and air-to-ground environments while having lower operating and maintenance costs than a front-line fighter.

In spite of having been designed as a trainer, the T-6 was pressed into front-line combat service as a forward air control platform in Korea. The Texan had a much longer loiter capability than the early jets and, once outfitted with an adequate tactical communications system, proved ideal in this role as well.

Eventually operated by 34 nations around the world, the T-6 acquired various names, including Texan (U.S. Army Air Forces), SNJ (U.S. Navy), and Harvard (Royal Air Force). Although retired from active military service, many T-6s still fly at the hands of civilian pilots. The famous Reno Air Races feature a competition dedicated exclusively to the type.

Braxton Eisel

References

Green, William, and Gerald Pollinger. *The Aircraft of the World.* New York: Hanover House, 1956.
Ohlrich, Walt, and Jeff Ethell. *Pilot Maker: The Incredible T-6.* North Branch, MN: Specialty Press, 1983.

North American X-15

Rocket-powered research aircraft. The X-15 provided hypersonic data on stability and control during atmosphere exit and reentry, aircraft performance, shock interaction, materials, skin friction, aerodynamic heating, pilot physiology, and energy management. Twelve research pilots from NASA, North American Aviation, the Air Force, and the Navy flew three different X-15 aircraft from 1959 to 1968.

Although the number-two aircraft was later modified, the basic X-15 was a single-seat, midwing monoplane designed to explore the areas of high aerodynamic heating rates and other problems relating to hypersonic flight (above Mach 5). It was powered by rocket engine (initially two XLR-11s, then an XLR-99).

North American's Scott Crossfield, who had helped with the design of the aircraft, made the first unpowered flight on 8 June 1959 and the first powered flight on 29 September 1959. On 22 August 1963, NASA pilot Joseph A. Walker achieved an unofficial world altitude record of 354,200 feet (67 miles) in X-15 No. 3. Air Force Major William J. Knight followed this up with an unofficial world speed record of Mach 6.7 (4,520 mph) on 3 October 1967 in X-15A-2 (modified from the original No. 2 aircraft). NASA's William H. Dana was the pilot for the final flight in the program on 24 October 1968. All of these flights took place within what was called the "High Range" surrounding Edwards Air Force Base, California, and NASA's Flight Research Center (later called the NASA Dryden Flight Research Center).

More important than the records were the more than 765 research reports from the program and the data they contributed to the nation's space program, the Space Shuttle, and any future hypersonic aircraft that may emerge. More intangible but no less important, the X-15 project led to the acquisition of new knowledge about manned aerospace flight by many government and industry teams. They had to learn to work together, face unprecedented problems, come up with solutions, and make this first manned aerospace project work. These teams constituted a critical national asset in the ensuing space programs.

J. D. Hunley

See also

Research Aircraft

References

Jenkins, Dennis R. *Hypersonics Before the Shuttle: A Concise History of the X-15 Research Airplane.* NASA SP-2000–4518 Washington, DC: NASA/U.S. Government Printing Office, 2000.
Thompson, Milton O. *At the Edge of Space: The X-15 Flight Program.* Washington, DC: Smithsonian Institution Press, 1992.

North Atlantic Treaty Organization (NATO)

Mutual defense alliance currently containing 19 members from Western Europe and North America formed after World War II to offset the substantial military advantage possessed by the Soviet Union. The new organization was intended to be a military alliance capable of deterring the threat posed by the Soviet military.

The original members of NATO, founded on 4 April 1949, were: Belgium, Canada, Denmark, France, Iceland, Italy, Luxembourg, the Netherlands, Norway, Portugal, the United Kingdom, and the United States. Over the next 50 years, NATO expanded to include Greece and Turkey (1952), West Germany (1955), Spain (1982), and the Czech Republic, Hungary, and Poland (1999).

Although NATO forces were always assumed to be better-equipped and -trained, the huge numerical advantage possessed by the Soviet Union and Warsaw Pact militaries meant that Western European security rested partly on the deterrent effect of U.S. nuclear retaliation. Additionally, another important element in the NATO defense of Western Europe was the superiority of Western airpower.

The collapse of the Soviet Union in 1989 opened a new chapter in NATO's history when for the first time it authorized military action outside of its mandate. In April 1993, NATO warplanes began patrolling the skies over Bosnia and later began air strikes against Serbian military targets.

In 1998, the Serbian province of Kosovo, with its Albanian majority, threatened secession, leading to widespread Serbian persecution of civilians. NATO responded with a controversial 78-day bombing campaign, forcing Serbian leaders to capitulate. For supporters of airpower this event was touted as an example of the potential for precision air strikes.

Craig T. Cobane

See also

Warsaw Pact Aviation

References

Naslund, Willard E. *NATO Airpower: Organizing for Uncertainty.* Santa Monica, CA: RAND, 1993.

Ripley, Tim. *Air War Bosnia: UN and NATO Airpower.* Osceola, WI: Motorbooks International, 1996.

Northrop Aircraft

Major U.S. aircraft manufacturer and defense contractor that completed a merger with Grumman in the mid-1990s. John Knudson "Jack" Northrop (1895–1981) joined the Loughead (later Lockheed) brothers in 1916, then, after brief wartime service, joined Douglas in the 1920s. He returned to Lockheed in 1926 and designed the Vega monoplane. He set up his own firm (Avion) in 1928 and, though it was soon taken over by United Aircraft, served as chief designer. Northrop created the Alpha all-metal seven-passenger monoplane, of which 17 were built. A new Northrop firm was formed as a subsidiary of Douglas in the early 1930s (and was absorbed in 1937). Products included the high-speed Gamma passenger monoplane, of which more than 30 were built.

Yet a third Northrop firm was created in 1939. Its products included the twin-engine P-61 Black Widow, designed as a radar-fitted night-fighter; more than 700 were manufactured. This third firm focused on Northrop's fascination with flying wings (he had built his first in 1929). Several N-9 models laid the groundwork for the piston-engine YB-35 that first flew in 1946. The jet-powered version, the YB-49, flew a year later but, amid great controversy, was canceled in favor of the Convair B-36. The XP-56 took the flying-wing idea into fighters, but only two were built in 1943. The F-89 Scorpion fighter was built to replace the P-61 and first flew in 1948. The F-89D model alone achieved nearly 700 examples manufactured.

Nearly 1,200 T-38 Talon trainers were built between 1959 and 1972. The similar F-5 Freedom Fighter entered service in 1964, and more than 2,600 had been built when produc-

Two of the great men in aviation: John K. Northrop greets General Henry H. "Hap" Arnold. (U.S. Air Force)

A Northrop P-61 Black Widow, a highly successful night fighter, flies chase on the radical Northrop XB-35 Flying Wing. (U.S. Air Force)

tion ended in 1987. An advanced version became the F-20 Tigershark, but the program was canceled short of mass production. The B-2 stealth bomber—the ultimate version of the flying wing concept—first flew in 1989 and 19 of the $1 billion aircraft were placed into service. Northrop was merged into Grumman in 1994.

Christopher H. Sterling

See also

Douglas Aircraft; Lockheed Aircraft; Northrop Flying Wings; Northrop Grumman B-2 Spirit; Northrop T-38 Talon, F-5 Freedom Fighter, and Tiger II

References

Anderson, Fred. *Northrop: An Aeronautical History.* Los Angeles: Northrop, 1976.

Pape, Gary, and John M. Campbell. *The Flying Wings of Jack Northrop: A Photo Chronicle.* Atglen, PA: Schiffer, 1994.

Northrop Flying Wings

One of the most innovative of the early aviation designs. John Knudson "Jack" Northrop believed that an aircraft should be reduced to its most essential configuration—a flying wing. Early trials began as early as 1929. By July 1940, Northrop had flown the N-1M flying wing, demonstrating that it was possible for an aircraft to dispense with the normal fuselage and empennage. In theory this would allow a significant savings in weight and drag.

Northrop entered a flying-wing design in a U.S. Army Air Corps bomber competition and, on 22 November 1941, was awarded a contract for the prototype XB-35. Four 30-percent scale N-9M models were constructed to test the configuration, and the first XB-35 eventually flew on 25 June 1946. Flight-test results of the two propeller-driven bombers were mixed, but in June 1945 the Army Air Forces directed Northrop to finish subsequent aircraft as YB-49s with eight jet engines. The first YB-49 flew on 21 October 1947, but unfortunately the second aircraft crashed on 5 June 1948, killing Captain Glen W. Edwards (the Muroc test location was renamed Edwards Air Force Base in his honor).

The flying wing continued to demonstrate serious stability and control problems because of its unique configuration and the limitations of the stability-augmentation systems of the era. Although various production contracts were issued for the type, only one more flying-wing bomber would fly—the single YRB-49A reconnaissance prototype. In 1951, the Air Force officially terminated the program in favor of the Convair B-36 and ordered all the remaining airframes destroyed. Proposals for large commercial airliners and cargo aircraft based on the flying-wing concept quietly faded from the scene following the Air Force's decision to cancel the bomber program.

Northrop also proposed flying-wing fighters during World War II, and the small MX-324 and MX-334 were used to validate the basic aerodynamics of the concept. The first of the fighters, the XP-56 Black Bullet, actually used a very small fuselage but did not have horizontal stabilizers and resembled a wing shape more than a traditional aircraft. First flown on 6 September 1943, the aircraft crashed a few weeks later. A second example flew six months later but could not compete with the P-47s and P-51s that were already in production; it quickly faded from sight. Subsequently, three true flying wings (the XP-79) were ordered, although the failure to develop a suitable rocket engine to power them led to the first two being cancelled before they were completed. The third, designated XP-79B, was completed with two jet engines. The aircraft made its first and only flight on 12 September 1945, crashing and killing test pilot Harry Crosby.

By far the most successful Northrop flying wing would come along 30 years later. Begun as a highly classified project during the early 1980s, the first B-2 Spirit stealth bomber made its maiden flight on 17 July 1989. A true flying wing—with no fuselage or empennage—the B-2 is exactly what Jack Northrop tired to create with the XB-35/49. The primary difference is that by the 1980s computers allowed the creation of stability-augmentation systems that could successfully control the unstable shape. Unfortunately, the B-2 proved to be enormously expensive, and production was capped at 21 aircraft, providing the U.S. Air Force with only a single squadron of stealth bombers.

The B-2 bomber has a crew of two pilots—an aircraft commander and mission commander—and flies at about 650 mph. The B-2 has 136 onboard computers, with far more computer power than the Space Shuttle. The B-2 relies on its computers to evade enemy radar defenses, for flight stability, and for many other functions.

Each B-2 can carry nuclear bombs, 40,000 pounds of regular munitions, or a payload of 2,000-pound satellite-guided bombs. Once over the target, these "almost-smart" bombs can hit within several yards of a target.

In the 11 weeks of the air war in Kosovo, six B-2 Spirits flew 45 missions and dropped more than 600 bombs. They were never seen by the enemy or hit by enemy fire.

Dennis R. Jenkins and Henry M. Holden

See also

Northrop Aircraft

References

Pace, Steve. *B-2 Spirit: The Most Capable War Machine on the Planet.* New York: McGraw Hill, 1999.

Wagner, Ray. *American Combat Planes.* 3rd ed. Garden City, NY: Doubleday, 1982.

Northrop Grumman B-2 Spirit

The world's first stealth bomber. It is made mostly of a carbon graphite material, which is stronger than steel and lighter than aluminum. This material also absorbs most of the radar energy directed at it. Each one of these four-engine bombers costs about $2 billion to construct.

The B-2 has a crew of two pilots—an aircraft commander and mission commander—and flies at about 650 mph. The B-2 bomber has 136 onboard computers, with far

The Northrop B-2A Spirit stealth bomber has proved itself to be a remarkable long-range weapon in the war on terrorism. (U.S. Air Force)

more computer power than the Space Shuttle. The B-2 relies on its computers to evade enemy radar defenses, for flight stability, and for many other functions.

Each B-2 bomber can carry nuclear bombs, 40,000 pounds of regular munitions, or a payload of 2,000-pound satellite-guided bombs. Once over the target, these semi-smart bombs can hit within several yards of a target.

During the 11 weeks of the air war in Kosovo, six B-2 Spirits flew 45 missions and dropped more than 600 bombs. They were never seen by the enemy or hit by enemy fire. They also distinguished themselves in the action in Afghanistan.

Henry M. Holden

References

Wall, Robert. "Pentagon Details Flaws in Kosovo Weapons." *Aviation Week and Space Technology* (21 February 2000): 43.

Northrop T-38 Talon, F-5 Freedom Fighter, and Tiger II

During the mid-1950s, the U.S. Air Force required a trainer with higher performance than the Lockheed T-33 to better prepare student pilots for the latest tactical aircraft that were then coming into service. The aircraft chosen was the T-38A, which offered high performance with low maintenance and operating costs. The T-38A became the Air Force's first supersonic trainer. The T-38A prototype first flew on 10 April 1959, and production continued until 1972. A total of 1,189 T-38As were built, and a small number were later modified into AT-38Bs with external armament for weapons training. Jacqueline Cochran set eight performance records in the fall of 1961 flying a production T-38A, and in February 1962 a T-38A set four international time-to-climb records. The Air Force Thunderbirds aerobatic team used T-38As from 1974 to 1982 because of their economic operation and high performance. Other users of the T-38A have included the U.S. Navy in their Top Gun program and NASA as astronaut-proficiency trainers. Approximately 562 remain in service throughout the Air Force. An ongoing program called Pacer Classic, the structural life extension program for the T-38, is integrating 10 modifications, including major structural renewal, into one process. As a result, the service life of T-38s should extend to 2010.

Based on the development of the T-38, Northrop management decided to use company funds to construct a light fighter variant aimed primarily at the foreign sales market. The development of the resulting N156 continued as a private venture until the Department of Defense issued a contract for three prototypes in May 1958. The first aircraft made its maiden flight on 20 July 1959, but internal disagreements within the defense community delayed a production contract until 22 October 1962. The first production single-seat F-5A flew in October 1963, the first two-seat F-5B on 24 February 1964. The slightly larger and more powerful F-5E and F-5F were introduced in late 1972. In 1979, Northrop decided to use company funds to create a further upgraded model, initial designated F-5G and later F-20 Tiger II. This was a major redesign that replaced the two General Electric J85 engines used by earlier models with a single General Electric F404 turbofan. Although a significant advancement, the F-20 found itself competing with the General Dynamics F-16, and none were sold.

Although it did not have the performance of some of its more costly contemporaries, the F-5 Freedom Fighter was reliable, easy to maintain, and inexpensive. It served only in relatively small numbers with the United States armed forces, first as a trial with the U.S. Air Force in Vietnam, later as an adversary aircraft with all three U.S. military air arms. However, the F-5 was widely exported, with no fewer than 27 countries operating the type, often on a second- or third-hand basis. A total of 1,871 F-5s were built by Northrop, and a further 776 were built under license in Canada, Spain, Switzerland, South Korea, and Taiwan. The F-5 is still an important part of many foreign air forces.

Dennis R. Jenkins

References

Logan, Don. *T-38 Talon.* Atglen, PA: Schiffer, 1995.
Wagner, Ray. *American Combat Planes.* 3rd ed. Garden City, NY: Doubleday, 1982.

Norwegian Air Campaign (1940)

Germany invaded Norway on 9 April 1940, after having struck Denmark and seized its two major airfields. The Luftwaffe used the bases to ferry troops and supplies into Norway—the first major airlift of the war. The major port cities of Norway were attacked simultaneously, as was the airfield at Stavanger. These attacks employed approximately 1,000 aircraft—including virtually entire airlift capacity of the Luftwaffe. By the end of the first day all objectives had been accomplished.

In an attempt to liberate Norway, the Allies landed at Trondheim and Narvik. Trondheim, however, was within range of Luftwaffe aircraft, and after two days the Allies realized that without air superiority they would have to evacuate. With its nearest air base more than 600 miles distant, the

RAF could not intervene, and the Fleet Air Arm—equipped with obsolete aircraft such as the Swordfish and Skua—was outmatched. Even if the Allies had been able to recapture Trondheim, they could not have held it in the face of the Luftwaffe. Within a fortnight the Allies evacuated.

The situation at Narvik was not quite as dismal for the Allies because it was so far north even the Luftwaffe had difficulty getting there. The RAF carved three airstrips out of the snow and deployed some aircraft. As a result, Allied ground forces were able to make headway. Unfortunately, on 11 May 1940 the Battle for France began, and before the Allies had even retaken Narvik they were planning its evacuation. It fell on 25 May, but the Allies departed two weeks later. The Germans soon reoccupied it.

The key observation of the campaign was the necessity for air superiority. The Allies hoped that command of the sea would allow them to seize or establish air bases for defense of a lodgment. This was impossible because the Luftwaffe had already achieved air superiority over the littoral. Control of the air determined who would control the surface beneath it.

Phillip S. Meilinger

See also

Fleet Air Arm; Royal Flying Corps/Royal Naval Air Service/Royal Air Force

References

Kersaudy, Francois. *Norway, 1940.* New York: St. Martin's, 1991.

Maier, Klaus, et al. *Germany and the Second World War, Volume 2: Germany's Initial Conquests in Europe.* Oxford: Clarendon Press, 1991.

Moulton, J. L. *A Study of Warfare in Three Dimensions: The Norwegian Campaign of 1940.* Athens: Ohio University Press, 1967.

Novikov, Aleksandr Aleksandrovich (1900–1976)

Soviet air force commander during World War II. Aleksandr Aleksandrovich Novikov was born on 19 November 1900 in the Kostroma region of Russia. He fought in the civil war and was trained as one of the new Red Commanders. In 1933, he transferred to the air service. He participated in the Finnish Winter War as Air Chief of Staff, Northwestern Front. In 1940, he was appointed commander of the air forces of the Leningrad Military District, designated the Northwestern Front in June 1941. During the first months Novikov again distinguished himself in defending Leningrad, managing the air bridge that helped the city survive the first winter's blockade.

On 11 April 1942, he was promoted to lieutenant general and appointed commander of the air forces. Novikov's most notable reform involved removing the dispersed air assets from the direct control of ground-forces commanders, reorganizing them into air divisions based on tactical function and concentrating them in newly organized air armies under a commander responsible for coordinating all air activities for the front. He also reformed the training and deployment of replacements. Other tactical and operational reforms included the air blockade of Stalingrad, as well as a more aggressive use of tactical airpower. Six decades later, Novikov's organizational reforms are still almost intact in the Russian air forces.

On 17 March 1943, Novikov was promoted to marshal of aviation and, in February 1944, to chief marshal of aviation. He was awarded his first Hero of the Soviet Union on 17 April 1945 and received a second for his leadership in the Japanese war on 8 September 1945. In February 1946, he was arrested and imprisoned until June 1953, when he was rehabilitated and appointed commander of long-range aviation. He was removed by Nikita Khrushchev in March 1955 as part of the policy favoring missiles over bombers. Novikov died on 3 February 1976.

George M. Mellinger

References

Erickson, John. "Novikov." In *Stalin's Generals,* edited by Howard Shukman. New York: Grove Press, 1993.

Fetzer, Leland, trans., and Ray Wagner, ed. *The Soviet Air Force in World War II: The Official History.* Garden City, NY: Doubleday, 1973.

Nowotny, Walter (1920–1944)

One of the most successful German fighter pilots who entered service after the start of World War II. Nowotny joined a front-line fighter unit, Jagdgeschwader 54 (JG 54; 54th Fighter Wing) in February 1941 and took part in Operation BARBAROSSA, the German invasion of the Soviet Union, that June. He remained with JG 54 on the northern sector of the Eastern Front until he was grounded in November 1943, after his 256th air victory, for which he became the eighth member of the Wehrmacht to receive the Oak Leaves with Swords and Diamonds to the Knight's Cross of the Iron Cross. After a period in a training wing, he was chosen by Adolf Galland to command the unit that would introduce the Me 262 jet fighter to combat. The success of this unit was crucial if the Me 262 was to play the role that Galland envisioned for it in the air defense of Germany. Nowotny scored two victories while flying the jet but was apparently not an especially skillful unit commander, having received no training for this role. Galland was compelled to visit Nowotny's Achmer base to evaluate his performance and, while there on 8 November 1944, witnessed Nowotny crash to his death on the edge of the airfield after a battle with P-51s.

Donald Caldwell

See also

German Air Force (Luftwaffe)

References

Obermeier, E. *Die Ritterkreuztraeger der Luftwaffe, 1939–1945, Band 1: Jagdflieger* [Recipients of the Knight's Cross]. Mainz: Verlag Dieter Hoffmann, 1989.

O

O'Grady, Scott

Downed F-16C pilot who eluded capture by Serbian forces during NATO operations in the former Yugoslavia. On 2 June 1995, Captain Scott O'Grady, assigned to the 555th Fighter Squadron at Aviano AB, Italy, took off as the wingman in a flight of two aircraft. He and his leader, Captain Bob Wright, were on a mission over Bosnia as part of DENY FLIGHT, a huge NATO operation designed to enforce a UN-mandated no-fly zone over northern Bosnia. O'Grady's call sign was "Basher 52."

While on orbit at 26,000 feet just south of the city of Banja Luka, his aircraft was hit and destroyed by a Serbian SA-6 surface-to-air missile. Ejecting, he floated down into an area occupied by Serbian forces and civilians. He quickly hid in a forested area as the enemy personnel furiously searched for him.

For the next five days, NATO aircraft and personnel frantically searched as rescue forces stood by to attempt a recovery. In the early morning hours of 8 June, a fellow F-16 pilot from Aviano made radio contact with O'Grady and initiated a rescue effort.

At the direction of Admiral Leighton Smith, the commander of NATO's southern forces, a rescue task force from the 24th Marine Expeditionary Unit, afloat in the Adriatic Sea aboard the USS *Kearsarge* and other ships, took off to make the pickup.

The task force consisted of a platoon of Marines aboard two CH-53 helicopters, two AH-1W Cobra gunships, two AV-8 Harriers, and almost 40 other support aircraft of all types. This large formation entered Bosnian airspace just as the sun was beginning to rise.

Arriving near O'Grady's location, one of the Cobra pilots made radio contact with him and then spotted his location. The pilot then directed the landing of the two CH-53s. As the lumbering aircraft touched down, the Marines on board quickly disembarked and established a defensive perimeter. O'Grady made a dash for one of the CH-53s. He was quickly pulled aboard, and the security team was recalled. With every Marine onboard, the task force departed.

Now alerted to the action of the NATO forces, Serbian units along the egress route began to react. Numerous enemy troops began firing at the aircraft. Several of the helicopters were hit—all without serious damage to aircraft or injury to personnel. And at one point, several heat-seeking missiles were also fired at the task force. But the Marine pilots were able to successfully evade all of them.

The recovery aboard the USS *Kearsarge* was uneventful. Captain O'Grady was returned to his unit, and the mission was recorded as a complete success.

Darrel Whitcomb

Ohain, Hans Joachim Pabst von (1911–1998)

Recognized as an independent coinventor of the jet engine. Hans von Ohain was born in Dessau, Germany, on 14 December 1911, grew up in Berlin, and received his doctorate in physics from the University of Goettingen in 1935. While a student, he was attracted to problems surrounding aircraft propulsion efficiency and formulated his early concepts concerning gas turbine or jet engines. In 1934, with the help of his dissertation adviser, R. W. Pohl, he began experimental work to explore those theories. Two years later, in 1936, again with help from Pohl, von Ohain found himself working for aviation industrialist Ernst Heinkel. With Heinkel's backing, work on the jet engine proceeded quickly, and on 27 August 1939 the first turbojet-powered aircraft flight was made with von Ohain's HeS.3B propelling Heinkel's He 178 test aircraft into the sky. Von Ohain continued to work for Heinkel throughout World War II.

Following the war, von Ohain was invited to the U.S. under Project Paperclip and was assigned to Wright Field. He remained there for the next 32 years, retiring in 1979 as chief scientist of the Aero Propulsion Laboratory of the Air Force Wright Aeronautical Laboratories. He then entered academia as a professor at the University of Dayton Research Institute, Ohio, and as a visiting professor at the University of Florida.

Stanley W. Kandebo

See also

Heinkel Aircraft; Wittle, Frank

References

Boyne, Walter J., and Donald S. Lopez, eds. *The Jet Age.* Washington, DC: Smithsonian Institution Press, 1979.

Wagner, Wolfgang. *The First Jet Aircraft.* Atglen, PA: Schiffer, 1998.

O'Hare, Edward H. (1914–1943)

U.S. Navy fighter ace. Born 13 March 1914 in St. Louis, Edward "Butch" O'Hare was a section leader in Fighting Squadron 3 flying from the carrier *Lexington* when that ship, approaching Rabaul in a raid on 20 February 1942, was sighted by the Japanese. In the first clash between U.S. and Japanese carrier aircraft, O'Hare attacked repeatedly one Japanese formation of nine Nakajima B5N "Kate" torpedo-bombers. Flying a Grumman F4F Wildcat fighter, he made the most of his limited ammunition, shooting down five of the bombers (one of which tried to crash into the *Lexington*) and damaging a sixth. For this gallant and effective action, O'Hare received the Medal of Honor from President Franklin D. Roosevelt.

In the fall of 1943, O'Hare commanded Air Group Six, which was tapped by Rear Admiral Arthur W. Radford for experimental work, code-named BLACK PANTHER, in night-fighter tactics. Flying from the *Enterprise* during Operation GALVANIC, O'Hare on 26 November led two F6F Hellcat fighters and one radar-equipped TBF Avenger torpedo-plane in a risky intercept operation against two Mitsubishi G4M "Betty" bombers. Although the Japanese planes were both downed, so was O'Hare, possibly by friendly fire. Despite an intensive search, no trace of him was ever found. He had, nonetheless, pioneered the way for effective night intercept operations from carriers.

Recommended for a second Medal of Honor, he was awarded the Navy Cross. Among his other honors is the perpetuation of his name by Chicago's O'Hare International Airport.

Malcolm Muir Jr.

See also

GALVANIC; Gilbert Islands; Grumman F4F Wildcat; United States Navy, and Aviation

References

Ewing, Steve, and John B. Lundstrom. *Fateful Rendezvous: The Life of Butch O'Hare.* Annapolis, MD: Naval Institute Press, 1997.

Kernan, Alvin. *Crossing the Line: A Bluejacket's World War II Odyssey.* Annapolis, MD: Naval Institute Press, 1994.

Morison, Samuel Eliot. *History of United States Naval Operations in World War II, Volume 3: The Rising Sun in the Pacific, 1931–April 1942.* Boston: Little, Brown, 1963.

Okinawa

Springboard for an invasion of the Japanese home islands that never occurred. The U.S. Joint Chiefs of Staff, on 25 October 1944, determined to undertake the invasion of Okinawa. By 1944, the Japanese had constructed four major airfields on Okinawa and another on nearby Ie Shima. Okinawa was within striking distance for aircraft operating from Kyushu on the mainland.

When Allied operations commenced, airfields on Iwo Jima were not yet available to provide support. B-29s alone could strike from land bases, but General Henry H. "Hap" Arnold released them from strategic bombing operations only for two preinvasion missions—bombing Kyushu airfields and laying mines. Consequently, naval aviation had to fulfill almost all airpower needs in the operation's early stages.

Task Force 58 raided Japan on 18–21 March. Although the task force inflicted heavy losses on Japanese forces, three of the carriers were forced to withdraw, crippled by kamikazes. The carriers, joined by the British Pacific Fleet, then launched concentrated bombardments of Okinawa and nearby bases to prepare for the invasion. Task Force 58 deployed 11 fleet and six light carriers while BPF had four armored fleet carriers. In total, the carriers operated over 1,400 combat aircraft.

Losses from the Kyushu strikes and a misapprehension of U.S. objectives initially minimized Japanese aerial reaction to the invasion. Nevertheless, Admiral Toyoda contrived a partial concentration of forces in Kyushu and Formosa and initiated Operation TEN-GO on 6–7 April. Almost 700 aircraft (355 kamikazes) attacked the invasion fleet, sinking or damaging 22 vessels. The surface fleet launched its own assault, sending the battleship *Yamato,* escorted by a cruiser and eight destroyers but without any air cover. Task Force 58 intercepted this force on 7 April as it approached. U.S. aircraft attacked almost continuously for more than an hour, sinking *Yamato,* the cruiser, and four destroyers.

It would be nice to think that General Billy Mitchell and Admiral William Moffett were looking down on this scene—the death of the giant battleship Yamato, *on 7 April 1945. It was on a kamikaze mission to Okinawa when it was sunk by naval air power. (U.S. Navy)*

Despite heavy losses, Japanese forces launched nine mass attacks against U.S. forces off Okinawa in addition to less concentrated assaults. A total of 1,465 kamikaze aircraft took part in these mass assaults; a further 450 made smaller attacks. The Japanese navy and army also sent some 3,500 conventional sorties against the invasion fleet. Japanese air attacks sank or damaged no less than 125 U.S. warships, from carriers to landing craft, and hit all the British carriers, plus several smaller vessels, although no Allied carriers were sunk.

As U.S. forces advanced on Okinawa, airfield development became the priority. Marine Corps artillery observation aircraft began operations on 2 April, and Corsairs came ashore five days later. From then on, the Marine Corps aircraft took an expanding role in local air defense and close air support. Army P-47s arrived on 14 May, the first of many AAF units.

The fast carriers departed on 13 June, and air operations became largely the domain of land-based forces, both on Iwo Jima and in the Ryukus. The Okinawa campaign officially ended on 2 July 1945.

Paul E. Fontenoy

See also

British Pacific Fleet; Iwo Jima; Japan, Air Operations Against; Kamikaze Attacks; McCain, John S.; Mitscher, Marc Andrew; Spruance, Raymond A.; Task Force 38/58; Vian, Philip L.

References

Craven, Wesley F., and James L. Cate, eds. *The Army Air Forces in World War II, Volume 5: Pacific: Matterhorn to Nagasaki, June 1944–August 1945.* Washington, DC: Office of Air Force History, 1953.

Frank, Richard B. *Downfall: The End of the Imperial Japanese Empire.* New York: Random House, 1999.

Olympic Arena/Guardian Challenge

The names of the annual competition for USAF ICBM and space operations units. The competition has several goals, the chief of which is to use competition to enhance crew performance. Secondary goals include encouraging innovation during competition preparation, enhancing esprit de corps, providing a venue to recognize top performers in the command, and enhancing public relations.

Strategic Air Command (SAC) began the competition in 1967 under the name Curtain Raiser. SAC cancelled the competition in 1968 due to its commitments to the Vietnam War, but the competition recommenced in 1969 as Olympic Arena. In 1993, Air Combat Command gained control of USAF ICBMs and hosted the final Olympic Arena.

In 1994, ICBM forces moved to Air Force Space Command, and Olympic Arena was renamed Guardian Challenge. The change reflected that command's motto—"Guardians of the High Frontier"—and the inclusion of space units in four mission areas: space operations, spacelift, space warning, and satellite operations. Over time, the number of participants and mission areas represented at Olympic Arena and Guardian Challenge expanded from the competition's initial focus on operations to include several different types of missile and support equipment maintenance, space equipment maintenance, security forces, helicopter operations, and food-service personnel.

Grant Weller

See also

Missiles, Intercontinental Ballistic; Strategic Air Command; United States Air Force, Organizational History

Onishi, Takijiro (1891–1945)

Japanese vice admiral; early advocate of naval airpower. Unlike many contemporaries, he almost exclusively held aviation billets throughout his career, where he significantly advanced development and deployment of the navy's air arm.

Onishi graduated from the Naval Academy in 1911, served with the navy's first air units during World War I, and studied wartime air combat experience in Britain. Upon returning, he held increasingly important line and staff aviation positions. He forcefully condemned new battleship construction, urging instead carrier primacy and long-range shore-based bomber development.

In 1939, Rear Admiral Onishi became Chief of Staff, Eleventh Air Fleet. He assisted planning of the Pearl Harbor attack and coordinated the devastating air assault on the Philippines. Promoted vice admiral in 1943, he returned to Tokyo, then went to the Philippines in October 1944, commanding the First Air Fleet. There he developed aerial suicide attack concepts and directed the first such operations.

Onishi became vice chief of the navy General Staff in May 1945. He committed ritual suicide on 15 August 1945.

Paul E. Fontenoy

See also

Iwo Jima; Japanese Naval Air Force, Imperial; Kamikaze Attacks; Leyte Gulf, battle of; Netherlands East Indies; Pearl Harbor; Philippines; Yamamoto, Isoroku

References

Evans, David C., and Mark R. Peattie. *Kaigun: Strategy, Tactics, and Technology in the Imperial Japanese Navy, 1887–1941.* Annapolis, MD: Naval Institute Press, 1997.
Millot, Bernard. *Divine Thunder: The Life and Death of the Kamikazes.* New York: McCall, 1971.
Naito, Hatsuho. *Thunder Gods: The Kamikaze Pilots Tell Their Story.* Tokyo: Kodansha international, 1989.
Willmott, H. P. *Empires in the Balance: Japanese and Allied Pacific Strategies to April 1942.* Annapolis, MD: Naval Institute Press, 1982.

Operations, Military

All military operations are arranged according to their code names (e.g., ALLIED FORCE).

Osirak Nuclear Reactor

Iraqi facility attacked by Israel in the early 1980s to thwart Iraq's acquisition of weapons-grade uranium. Nuclear proliferation in the Middle East has been a steady source of concern for Israel, Arab states, and their superpower supporters. By the late 1960s, most Arab nations took for granted an Israeli nuclear capability and worked to establish their own. With French duplicity, Iraq appeared to have completed this goal by 1980. The Tammuz I reactor at the Osirak nuclear reactor facility at Tuwaitha, near Baghdad, would begin producing weapons-grade plutonium between July and September 1981.

Israel was not the only potential atomic target, as Iraq had been at war with the Islamic Republic of Iran since 1980. Western hostility toward revolutionary Iran meant a blind eye to Iraq's nuclear efforts. Amid seeming indifference from the West, Israel alone viewed the imminent Iraqi nuclear capability as a threat to be eliminated. Consequently,

Israeli Prime Minister Menachem Begin decided to act unilaterally to destroy the reactor.

In a spectacular aerial operation on 7 June 1981, the Israeli Air Force launched Operation BABYLON. Eight General Dynamics F-16s and six McDonnell Douglas F-15s flew undetected some 600 miles at altitudes around 100 feet above Saudi Arabia and Iraq. At approximately 4:30 P.M. with the setting sun behind them, the F-15s climbed to 25,000 feet to provide aerial cover for the F-16s as they dropped pairs of conventional 2,000-pound bombs on the complex. Unchallenged by MiGs, the aircraft turned west and returned to Israel without loss. Despite claims otherwise, the F-16s were not refueled during the flight, completing the 1,000-plus mile mission well in excess of the manufacturer's design limits on range. The Iraqi reactor facility was badly damaged. By some assessments, the attack delayed its operation by five years but did not halt it altogether. This proved nettlesome to the West, as fear of potential Iraqi nuclear weapons affected Coalition planning during the 1991 Gulf War.

Robert S. Hopkins

See also

DESERT SHIELD; DESERT STORM; Iraqi Air Force; Israeli Air Force; Israeli-Arab Conflicts; Lockheed Martin F-16 Fighting Falcon

References

Halperin, Merav, and Aharon Lapidot. *G-Suit.* London: Sphere Books, 1990.

Hersh, Seymour. *The Sampson Option.* New York: Random House, 1991.

McKinnon, Dan. *Bullseye One Reactor.* San Diego: House of Hits, 1987.

Nakdimon, Shlomo. *First Strike.* New York: Summit, 1987.

Ozawa, Jisaburo (1886–1966)

Japanese vice admiral; Japan's principal carrier force commander from 1944 onward. Ozawa graduated from the Naval Academy in 1909 and served in surface vessels until 1937, when he became Chief of Staff of the Combined Fleet. In 1940, he took command of the 1st Carrier Division, then, as a vice admiral, led the Southern Expeditionary Fleet in support of the successful Japanese assault on Malaya and the Dutch East Indies.

Ozawa commanded Japan's main carrier forces, the First Mobile and Third Fleets, at the Battle of the Philippine Sea in June 1944, during which he was outmatched and outfought by Admiral Raymond Spruance and Task Force 58. He then led the remaining Japanese carriers to their destruction as decoys at Cape Engano during the Leyte campaign in October.

Paul E. Fontenoy

See also

Cape Engano, Battle of; Japanese Naval Air Force, Imperial; Leyte Gulf, battle of; Netherlands East Indies; Philippines; Task Force 38/58

References

Dull, Paul S. *A Battle History of the Imperial Japanese Navy, 1941–1945.* Annapolis, MD: Naval Institute Press, 1978.

Evans, David C., ed. *The Japanese Navy in World War II in the Words of Former Japanese Naval Officers.* Annapolis, MD: Naval Institute Press, 1986.

Evans, David C., and Mark R. Peattie. *Kaigun: Strategy, Tactics, and Technology in the Imperial Japanese Navy, 1887–1941.* Annapolis, MD: Naval Institute Press, 1997.

Willmott, H. P. *Empires in the Balance: Japanese and Allied Pacific Strategies to April 1942.* Annapolis, MD: Naval Institute Press, 1982.

P

Pacific Air Forces

The USAF major command controlling combat forces in the Pacific region and serving as the air component for U.S. Pacific Command (PACOM). Far East Air Forces (FEAF) became Pacific Air Forces (PACAF) in July 1957 when the Joint Chiefs of Staff (JCS) modified the U.S. Unified Command Plan and Far East Command was merged into PACOM. In April 1954, the JCS created a small command element titled Pacific Air Force (note singular) to serve as the air component staff for PACOM, specifically to enhance USAF support in contingency planning and emergency operations. Pacific Air Force was subordinate to Far East Air Forces, and it was briefly redesignated Pacific Air Force/FEAF (Rear) during the transfer of FEAF Headquarters from Japan to Hawaii in 1956 and 1957. Headquarters PACAF was established on Hickam Air Force Base in Hawaii, with primary operational units in Japan, Okinawa, Korea, and the Philippines, as well as two major subordinate organizations: Thirteenth Air Force, headquartered in the Philippines, and Fifth Air Force in Japan.

During the Vietnam War, PACAF was the senior USAF major command in the Pacific region. The initial formal USAF command element in Vietnam was the 2d Air Division (AD) Advanced Echelon (ADVON), activated in November 1961. The 2d AD ADVON was a subordinate organization of PACAF's Thirteenth Air Force, with responsibility for controlling Air Force assets supporting the U.S. Military Assistance Advisory Group Vietnam (MAAG). When MAAG became the U.S. Military Assistance Command Vietnam (MACV), a subunified command under PACOM, in 1962, 2d AD became the air component. The 2d AD controlled USAF operations within South Vietnam; USAF operations outside South Vietnam remained under the control of Thirteenth Air Force and PACAF. To better support expanded operations in Southeast Asia, in March 1966 2d AD was replaced by Seventh Air Force, which reported to MACV for operations in South Vietnam and to Headquarters PACAF for operations in the rest of Southeast Asia in collaboration with Thirteenth Air Force. This command structure remained in effect until the end of the war, with the modification in March 1973 of MACV transforming into the U.S. Support Activities Group and transferring to Nakhon Phanom Royal Thai Air Base, Thailand, along with its air component, Seventh Air Force. Seventh Air Force was deactivated in June 1975. Command relationships were complex throughout the Vietnam War, and the USAF and PACAF continuously sought a centralized control system for all airpower, but the Navy and Marines maintained considerable independence under the direction of PACOM. Even within the USAF, efforts were not centralized, as the Strategic Air Command (SAC) maintained control of its resources operating in Southeast Asia.

In the post–Cold War period, the USAF modified the PACAF structure. The JCS assigned the Alaskan area to PACOM in 1990, and PACAF assumed responsibility for USAF units in Alaska by taking command of Eleventh Air Force, formerly the Alaskan Air Command. In 1991, Thirteenth Air Force left Clark Air Force Base in the Philippines and moved to Anderson AFB on Guam as PACAF assumed responsibility for that base from SAC. The other subordinate numbered air forces in PACAF were Fifth Air Force in Japan and Seventh Air Force in Korea (reestablished in September 1986). PACAF units deployed to Southwest Asia and fought under U.S. Central Command direction during Operation DESERT STORM. Under the USAF expeditionary aerospace force concept in the late 1990s, PACAF provided units on rotation to participate in U.S. Central Command and U.S. European Command security and peacekeeping operations in Southwest Asia and the Balkans.

Jerome V. Martin

See also
Far East Air Forces; Vietnam War

References

Futrell, Robert F. *The Advisory Years in Southeast Asia, to 1965.* United States Air Force in Southeast Asia Series. Washington, DC: U.S. Government Printing Office, 1981.

Momyer, William W. *Airpower in Three Wars.* Washington, DC: U.S. Government Printing Office, 1982.

Schlight, John. *The War in South Vietnam: The Years of the Offensive, 1965-1968.* United States Air Force in Southeast Asia Series. Washington, DC: U.S. Government Printing Office, 1988.

Pakistan Air Force

The Dominion of Pakistan initiated its constitution on July 1947 after the partitioning of India. The Pakistan Air Force (PAF) began on 15 August 1947, taking more than 50 aircraft transferred from the Indian Air Force as a part of the partitioning. Among these aircraft were British Austers, Harvards, Tempests, and Tiger Moths and Douglas Dakotas, most in need of major maintenance. With these aircraft came 44 pilots, 2,000 airmen, and 200 British-trained officers. Some sources suggest that initially the PAF's officers were British RAF officers. Certainly PAF's structure resembled the RAF in the organization of its squadrons and training facilities. Shortly after the establishment, a training facility was created at Risalpur along the lines of Britain's military training ground at Cranwell. Pilots trained on British de Havilland Tiger Moths and North American Harvards from the United States. Pilots and ground crews trained at Risalpur, Australia, Germany, the United States, and Britain.

Currently, the PAF utilizes aircraft from around the world—fighters, transports, trainers, and reconnaissance aircraft, with an emphasis on interceptor/ground attack aircraft. The PAF maintains 30 air bases across Pakistan. The PAF maintains at least two pilots to every aircraft, though often it is much more. These well-trained pilots maintain their skills by fighting with their Arab allies in conflicts in the Middle East. Pakistan flies aircraft built in the United States, France, and China, with principal reliance placed on the Lockheed Martin (formerly General Dynamics) F-16 Fighting Falcon.

Wendy Coble

References

Green, William, and John Fricker. *The Air Forces of the World: Their History, Development, and Present Strength.* New York: Hanover House, 1958.

Palau, Battle of (1944)

Air operations in preparation for and support of U.S. Marine amphibious invasion during World War II. The Palau Islands served as stepping-stones toward the Philippines. A general Allied air offensive throughout the area during the summer of 1944 cleared away most Japanese air opposition in the Palaus, Moluccas, and northwestern New Guinea. Ten escort carriers provided close support of the U.S. Marine and Army landings on 15 September. In spite of total dominance in the air, close support was largely ineffective in the ensuing battles because of the rugged nature of the key island of Peleliu and questionable techniques used by carrier pilots trained primarily in the attack of naval targets. As a result, casualties to the ground troops were high, with the 10,000 Japanese defenders exacting a cost 7,000 U.S. casualties before being overcome. Capture of the islands provided bases for the upcoming Allied landings on Leyte and a key fleet anchorage at Ulithi. The battle shows the limitations of air attacks in poor terrain and the importance of specific training relevant to the mission at hand—in this case, low-level attack.

Frank E. Watson

References

Craven, Wesley F., and James L. Cate, eds. *The Army Air Forces in World War II, Volume 5: Pacific: Matterhorn to Nagasaki, June 1944–August 1945.* Chicago: University of Chicago Press, 1953.

Palomares Nuclear Incident

Incident involving the destruction of four U.S. thermonuclear bombs as a result of a collision between a Strategic Air Command bomber and a tanker near the Mediterranean coast of Spain.

Late in the morning of 17 January 1966, a SAC B-52G Stratofortress and a KC-135 tanker collided during the course of a normal refueling operation. The bomber was on a routine strategic airborne alert as a part of Operation CHROME DOME and was carrying four Mk.28 (B28) free-fall parachute retarded thermonuclear bombs. The collision took place at 30,500 feet just offshore of Palomares on Spain's southeastern coast. The KC-135's load of jet fuel exploded, destroying both aircraft. All four of the tanker's crew were killed, as were three crewmembers aboard the B-52. Four of the bomber's crew parachuted to safety.

Three of the nuclear weapons fell with the wreckage and impacted the ground near Palomares. One Mk.28 was damaged but remained intact. The high-explosive components of the other two weapons partially detonated, resulting in the destruction of their nuclear components. No nuclear fission occurred in either case, and thus there was no nuclear yield to the accident. The nuclear components were partially pulverized, however, which led to the dispersion of a quantity of finely divided radioactive material beyond the accident perimeter.

The fourth weapon fell into the sea and was not immediately located. Trajectory analysis from Sandia Corporation and the eyewitness account of a Spanish fisherman narrowed the search zone, and a month after the accident three Navy submersibles began exploring the area. The weapon was finally located some 5 miles offshore by the crew of the Navy research vehicle *Alvin*. The bomb casing was damaged but intact, and there was no spread of contamination in the seabed. It was recovered successfully on 7 April.

The cleanup and decontamination operation on the land involved hundreds of U.S. personnel, assisted by Spanish personnel and the Guardia Civil. A large tent city, dubbed "Camp Wilson," was raised near the beach. Large numbers of journalists and visitors attracted by the publicity complicated the operation and made it difficult to control the spread of possible contamination. Eventually, some 1,400 tons of topsoil and vegetation were excavated and removed to the United States for disposal.

Although the accident did not result in a nuclear explosion, it was classified as a Broken Arrow (the USAF code name for an accident involving loss of or damage to a nuclear weapon) because of the nonnuclear detonation of the two weapons and the consequent spread of radioactive material.

Raymond L. Puffer

See also

Strategic Air Command

References

Brookings Institution. *Atomic Audit: The Costs and Consequences of U.S. Nuclear Weapons Since 1940.* Washington, DC: Brookings Institution, 1998.

Hansen, Chuck. *The Swords of Armageddon.* Vol 8. Sunnyvale, CA: Chucelea, 1995.

Szulc, Tad. *The Bombs of Palomares.* New York: Viking Press, 1967.

Panama Invasion (1989)

Operation JUST CAUSE; massive invasion of the Republic of Panama by U.S. forces to remove a corrupt military regime and protect the lives of U.S. citizens living there. General Manuel Noriega had been the virtual dictator of Panama since the death of General Omar Torrijos in 1981. In May 1989, Noriega, who had been indicted by the United States on drug-trafficking charges in 1988, nullified an election when unofficial counts indicated a clear victory by the opposition slate headed by Guillermo Endara. Noriega survived an aborted coup attempt on 3 October 1989.

U.S. General Maxwell R. Thurman, commander in chief of U.S. Southern Command, placed the command at a heightened state of readiness and updated contingency plans for combat operations in Panama. On 15 December 1989, the Panamanian National Assembly declared Noriega "maximum leader of national liberation." He subsequently declared that Panama was in a state of war with the United States. On 16 December 1989, USMC Lieutenant Robert Paz was killed at a Panama Defense Force roadblock. Shortly thereafter, a U.S. Navy officer and his wife were arrested, interrogated, and roughed up by the Panama Defense Forces.

These two incidents were the catalysts that caused President George Bush to order Noriega's apprehension and the neutralization of the Panama Defense Forces. Under Thurman's direction, Lieutenant General Carl Steiner, commanding general of XVIII Airborne Corps, formed and led a task force of 26,000 U.S. troops in a complex joint operation to do just that. Launched in the early-morning hours of 20 December 1989, the operation involved airborne and air assault troops airlifted from the United States linking up in the hours of darkness with on-the-ground mechanized, light infantry, and special operations units. More than 3,000 soldiers, including Army Rangers, parachuted in—the largest airborne operation since World War II.

The Air Force contingent numbered nearly 3,400, mostly units from the 830th Air Division. The operation included the first action undertaken by the F-117 stealth fighter.

The operation was a resounding success. Twenty-three targets were seized almost simultaneously, virtually decapitating the Panama Defense Forces. Guillermo Endara was installed as the duly elected president of Panama. Noriega sought refuge in the Vatican Embassy but gave himself up on 3 January 1990 to U.S. authorities, who escorted him to the United States to stand trial on drug charges. U.S. casualties in Operation JUST CAUSE included 23 killed and 324 injured.

James H. Willbanks

References

Donnelly, Thomas, Margaret Roth, and Caleb Baker. *Operation Just Cause.* New York: Lexington, 1991.

Woodward, Bob. *The Commanders.* New York: Simon and Schuster, 1881.

Panavia Tornado

Originally known as the Multi-Role Combat Aircraft; an excellent example of international cooperation. The primary

The SEPECAT Jaguar is the joint product of British Aerospace and Breguet Aviation (now part of Dassault) and, with the Panavia Tornado, greatly advanced international cooperation in warplane production. (Kev Darling)

Flown about five years later than the Jaguar, the Panavia Tornado featured cooperation among the United Kingdom, Italy, and Germany. (Kev Darling)

constituent partners are the United Kingdom, Italy, and Germany, each being responsible for the manufacture of certain parts of the airframe, engines, and avionics.

The birth of the Tornado can be traced to the turmoil within various European governments that concerned the next generation of combat aircraft. After nearly three years of individual development, the three participating governments finally signed the order to proceed for Panavia on 15 March 1973. A total of 809 aircraft were initially ordered, although this has fluctuated (the Tornado F.3, built for the RAF, was a long-range fighter).

On 14 August 1974, the first prototype made its maiden flight. This was to be the start of a very long development program that saw the airframe undergoing some changes.

The first Tornado deployed was the GR.1 and entered service at Cottesmore for the training of aircrews for all three nations. Throughout its life, the Tornado has undergone numerous upgrades. Some have been reworked to carry out reconnaissance using infrared linescan equipment; the majority of the fleet is being rebuilt to the GR.4 standard. The deployment of the Tornado to the Bundesluftwaffe, Marineflieger, and Aeronautica Militar Italiano began in February 1984 (to Germany; Italy began to operate the Tornado from August 1982).

Overseas sales of the Tornado have been limited to Saudi Arabia, which purchased a mixed package of GR and F.3 aircraft. Abortive attempts to sell the aircraft to Oman and Malaysia eventually failed due to economic reasons.

The RAF used the fighter version. The definitive version became the mainstay of the RAF's defensive effort and is 80 percent compatible with the attack variant. Italy now leases Tornado aircraft from the RAF.

Kev Darling

References

Richardson, Douglas. *Tornado.* London: Salamander Books, 1986.

Panay, USS

During the warlord years following the Chinese Revolution of 1911, Western powers assigned gunboats to patrol the Yangtze River to protect the lives and property of their nationals from bandit gangs and guerrilla forces. The USS *Panay* (PR-5) was one of five shallow-draft gunboats in China and was commissioned on 10 September 1928. Displacing 450 tons and capable of 15 knots, the ship had a company of 65 men and carried two 3-inch guns and 10 .30-caliber antiaircraft machine guns.

After war erupted between Japan and China on 7 July 1937, Japanese forces attacked Nanking in November, causing the U.S. ambassador, Nelson T. Johnson, to leave on 22 November; on 11 December the remaining U.S. officials and a number of civilians boarded the *Panay* to sail upriver, escorting three Standard Oil of New York (SOCONY) ships. Two British gunboats and several British craft joined this flotilla, which was peppered by Japanese shore batteries.

At 9:40 A.M. on Sunday, 12 December, the *Panay* was stopped by Japanese soldiers. Lieutenant Commander James J. Hughes, the captain of the *Panay,* allowed an armed Japanese party to board in violation of naval procedure. Hughes explained that he was heading upriver "to keep clear of artillery fire" and answered some routine questions but refused to allow a search of the ship; the Japanese disembarked, allowing the *Panay* to continue.

At 11:00 A.M., the *Panay* and the SOCONY ships anchored near Ho-sien, about 28 miles upstream of Nanking. *Panay* displayed a large American flag at the gaff and had 18- by 14-foot American flags painted on the awnings and topdecks; all were illuminated at night. Shortly after the noon meal, Japanese aircraft approached the ship at high altitude and descended to release bombs. This first attack scored a direct hit that wrecked the bridge and one 3-inch gun and seriously wounded Captain Hughes, his executive officer, and several others.

Several attacks, from as low as a few hundred feet altitude, crippled the ship. The crew responded with .30-caliber Lewis machine guns but the ship lost all power and propulsion. Captain Hughes reported that another storm of bombs fell both on the *Panay* and the SOCONY ships.

As the *Panay* began to sink, Hughes ordered the crew to abandon ship. All personnel made their way to a reed bank along the shore where they hid while Japanese aircraft continued to strafe the ship and the boats. The bombing ceased at 2:25 P.M.; a Japanese motorboat approached and machine-gunned the ship, then briefly put men on board to search it. At 3:54 P.M. the *Panay* sank bow first, its colors still flying. In the attack, two sailors and one civilian passenger died and 11 officers and men were seriously wounded. Chinese civilians assisted the survivors to rendezvous with the USS *Oahu* and the HMS *Ladybird* two days later.

Commander Masatake Okumiya declared that the fliers were not informed of the gunboat's presence in the area but were told the mission was to bomb Chinese troops escaping upriver. Japan declared the attack a "regrettable accident" resulting from miscommunication and young, inexperienced pilots that failed to clearly identify the ships.

A U.S. Naval Court of Inquiry held at Shanghai concluded that the sinking was deliberate. Washington, in the throes of isolationism and unprepared for a military conflict, accepted the Japanese explanation, an apology, and indemnity. The *Panay* was the first United States Navy ship to be sunk by hostile aerial bombardment and was a portentous event.

Richard C. DeAngelis with D. Y. Louie

References

Hughes, James J. *Commanding Officer, U.S.S. Panay, Report to the Secretary of the Navy via the Commander in Chief U.S. Asiatic Fleet.* Shanghai, China: General Records Navy Department, 1937.

Okumiya, Masatake, and R. Pineau. "How the *Panay* Was Sunk." *U.S. Naval Institute Proceedings* 78, 6 (1953).

Okumiya, Masatake. "Account of *Panay.*" Trans. D. Y. Louie.

Pantelleria

Italian island; site of Allied air operations during World War II. As the Allies pressed their way across North Africa, they also began bombing distant targets across the Mediterranean Sea in preparation for the invasion of Southern Europe. Of interest was the Italian island of Pantelleria, located 62 miles southwest of Sicily and some 100 miles east-southeast of Tunis, with a population of some 11,500 people. The island was in the shipping lanes between Tunisia and the larger island of Sicily.

Beginning on 8 May 1943, fighters and light bombers of the North African Tactical Air Forces initiated attacks on landing grounds on the small island. Subsequently, B-17s and B-24s bombed the island. Up until 3 July 1943, 40 air strikes were made against the island. These attacks battered Italian emplacements and demoralized the troops. When a surface assault was made on Pantelleria on 11 June 1943, the Allied forces marched ashore unopposed and were met with white flag–waving enemy forces. This marked the first time in history a complete surrender resulted solely from air attack without ground action. With the capture of Pantelleria and two neighboring islands, Lampedusa and Linosa, Allied seapower had complete control of the sealanes to Italy and Sicily. This marked the first Allied occupation of Italian territory during the war.

Alwyn T. Lloyd

References

Brereton, Lewis H. *The Brereton Diaries: 3 October 1941–8 May 1945.* New York: William Morrow, 1946.

Carter, Kit C. and Robert Muller. *The Army Air Forces in World War II: Combat Chronology, 1941–1945.* Maxwell AFB, AL: Office of Air Force History, 1973.

Pape, Robert A. (1960–)

Influential airpower theorist. Robert Anthony Pape was born in Erie, Pennsylvania, on 24 April 1960. He graduated from the University of Pittsburgh with two degrees in 1982; he received a doctorate from the University of Chicago in 1988. He taught conventional airpower strategy for the United States Air Force at the School of Advanced Airpower Studies, Maxwell AFB, Alabama from 1991 to 1994, and taught international relations in the Government Department at Dartmouth College from 1994 to 1999. In July 1999, he became associate professor of political science at the University of Chicago.

His 1996 book *Bombing to Win: Air Power and Coercion in War* offers a new theory of coercive airpower and tests it in all the major cases of strategic bombing from 1914 to 1991, including the use of airpower against Germany, Japan, Korea, Vietnam, and Iraq. He argued that strategic bombing has not worked in the past and that the strategic air campaign in Operation DESERT STORM was the least effective application of airpower.

His analysis of airpower theory, based on social-science research on the history of international disputes, has greatly influenced both civilian and military audiences.

John Andreas Olsen

See also

DESERT STORM; Warden, John A. III

References

Pape, Robert A. *Bombing to Win: Air Power and Coercion in War.* Ithaca: Cornell University Press, 1996.

Parachutes

Pilot safety device developed from ballooning. The concept of the parachute dates back to at least the seventeenth century, but it wasn't until 1797 that the first successful human jump was made. On 22 October of that year, Frenchman Andre Garnerin jumped from a balloon at an altitude of 2,000 feet; over the next few years, he made additional jumps in France and England. In 1808, the first emergency parachute jump was made when Polish balloonist Jordaki Kuparento was forced to exit the balloon he was piloting after it burst into flames. Kuparento was the first person to save his life with a parachute.

Experimentation with parachutes continued throughout the nineteenth and early twentieth centuries, and by the time World War I began, a successful jump from a powered aircraft had already been made. In addition, new technical advancements had been perfected, including the development of the apex hole to reduce oscillation, the pilot chute to aid in main chute deployment, and the static line for parachute activation.

World War I served to speed up the evolution of the art of parachuting—at least from lighter-than-air craft. The highly flammable hydrogen-filled observation balloons used on the Western Front during World War I made it necessary for observers to carry parachutes aloft. When attacked, observers wasted little time in exiting the wicker basket by way of parachute.

The use of parachutes in powered aircraft in World War I was limited, with few exceptions, to the Germans. Despite the fact that technical problems were unresolved, many German airmen, including second-ranking ace Ernst Udet, saved their lives by leaping to safety from their damaged aircraft.

Between the wars, parachutes became more and more practical, to the point of becoming standard safety equipment in military aircraft. Parachutes subsequently became so successful that an exclusive club, composed of airmen who had managed to save their lives by jumping from a stricken aircraft, was formed. The so-called Caterpillar Club—named in honor of the silkworm, which secreted the substance that early parachutes were made of—numbered 210 members by 1930. By 1955, the club's ranks had grown to over 40,000.

Other uses for the parachute were also developed during this period. During the barnstorming days of the 1920s and in the years afterward, parachuting developed into a popular form of entertainment for both jumpers and spectators. Parachutes were also used for dropping emergency supplies and for delivering smokejumpers quickly and accurately (smokejumpers are courageous firefighters who descend to fight forest fires from the air). In addition, with another world war looming, parachutes began to be used for tactical military purposes. Airborne assault units were deployed in one form or fashion by all the major powers during World War II.

Today, the use of parachutes is commonplace, and they perform many essential functions in the modern world. Skydiving is now a popular sport worldwide. Also, dragchutes are used to help slow high-performance aircraft after they have landed, and spacecraft routinely use parachutes while reentering the earth's atmosphere. Today, parachutes are as much a part of aviation safety as virtually any other device.

Steven A. Ruffin

References

Hearn, Peter. *Sky People: A History of Parachuting.* Shrewsbury, UK: Airlife, 1990.

Sellick, Bud. *Parachutes and Parachuting.* New Jersey: Prentice-Hall, 1971.

Paris Air Agreement

The 1926 agreement that opened the door to German rearmament following the World War I Armistice. From 1919, when Germany signed the Versailles Treaty, its air force was officially banned, forcing the country to use different methods to maintain knowledge and develop new air operational plans. The Paris Air Agreement, signed on 1 September 1926, did not change the ban on an air force, but it dissolved the Allied Aviation Guarantee Committee, which had overseen the enforcement of the treaty on German territory. The agreement also returned complete control of civil aviation to Germany, allowing it to expand commercial airlines and build transport dirigibles. In exchange, the German government agreed to stop funding gliding, which had been introduced as a means to train young pilots. However, in so doing, it shifted the assets of the Sports Flying Group and divided them among the Commercial Pilot Training School (DVS), the Academic Flying Group (Akaflieg—active among university students), and the Aviation Group, a generic name that served as a cover for military air activities on German soil.

The implications of the Paris Air Agreement for plans laid before 1926 by the Truppenamt—the code name under which the German army operated—made several operations easier, such as recruiting replacement fliers for the army's elite 180 pilots, almost half of whom were retiring or unable to fly by the mid-1920s. The new recruits were selected through a program implemented by the German Ministry of Transportation and then trained at schools near Berlin and Braunschweig. The program was classified secret, as was the fact that under German-Russian Treaty of Rapallo, a German base at Lipetsk, Russia, was set up to train fliers. There instructors, recruited from Lufthansa and the DVS, trained pilots. In addition, Lipetsk came to serve as a testing ground for German aircraft, such as the Heinkel 46, Junkers K 47, and Dornier Do 11. Such activities were reduced when the Great Depression hit Germany but did not stop until Adolf Hitler became chancellor in 1933.

In Germany, the Paris Air Agreement also allowed more leeway in how the army camouflaged its industrial activities. Contracts for the development of prototypes were run through dummy corporations, and the operation of several civilian aircraft types had to incorporate instructions concerning wing stresspoints in a way that would allow them to affix bombs and incorporate guns. So as not to anger civilian officials, the phrases used in correspondence stressed that all such aircraft (including Lufthansa machines), were for "defensive use"; nowhere did the word "bomber" appear. Manufacturers went along with the instructions, but the limited orders for each machine type frustrated industrialists involved in these projects. A greater concern was the development of new engines, hampered by the limits of the Versailles Treaty (the Benz aircraft-engine factory was in the Rhineland demilitarized zone, which was under French control until 1930), as well as limited funding.

The result was that by 1932 the German army had more than 200 aircraft ready for combat, including a majority of civilian planes. One study even projected the need for a new air force that would have close to 1,000 aircraft, many of them bombers. However, the poor economy and the fact that most aircraft manufacturers did not have the means to produce so many machines meant that the army would have to wait for improved economic conditions as well as a shift in budget priorities.

Overall, then, the Paris Air Agreement allowed for further maturation of the German army's air planning, from training to testing, operations, and projections. When Hitler came to power, his future chief of the Luftwaffe, Hermann Goering, took advantage of the prepared plans and made them the Third Reich's own, including the so-called 1,000-aircraft program of 1933.

Guillaume de Syon

See also

German Air Force (Luftwaffe); Versailles Treaty

References

Corum, James S. *The Luftwaffe: Creating the Operational Air War, 1918-1940.* Lawrence: University Press of Kansas, 1997.

Homze, Edward. *Arming the Luftwaffe: The Reich Air Ministry and the German Aircraft Industry, 1919–1939.* Lincoln: University of Nebraska Press, 1976.

Park, Keith Rodney (1892–1975)

Royal Air Force air chief marshal. Born in Thames, New Zealand, Park served in the artillery in Egypt and on Gallipoli, where he was commissioned in 1915, and then on the Western Front until wounded and hospitalized in England. Transferring to the Royal Flying Corps in December 1916, he received his wings and briefly instructed before joining No. 48 Squadron in France flying Bristol Fighters. Rising to command No. 48 Squadron by the Armistice, he had been shot down twice, was credited with five victories plus 14 aircraft driven down out of control, and was awarded the Military Cross and Bar plus the Croix de Guerre.

Postwar, Park held a number of successively senior positions in the RAF. By 1938, he was senior air staff officer to Air Chief Marshal Sir Hugh Dowding at Fighter Command, perfecting RAF plans for the defense of Britain. In April 1940, he was promoted air vice marshal, commanding No. 11 Group with responsibility for the fighter defense of London and southeastern England. From July to September 1940, his group provided the principal front-line fighter opposition to the Luftwaffe during the Dunkirk evacuation and the Battle of Britain.

Replaced somewhat controversially in December 1940, Park next commanded a training group, where he was instrumental in the creation of the Air Sea Rescue organization. Appointments as air officer commanding (AOC) Egypt and then Malta followed. Promoted to Air Marshal, he was AOC in chief to Egypt during 1944 and then air commander in chief, South-East Asia Command, during 1945–1946. He was confirmed as air chief marshal in 1946.

Postretirement, he worked for Hawker-Siddeley, returning to New Zealand as the Pacific representative of the Hawker-Siddeley Group. He died in Auckland on 6 February 1975.

Christopher J. Terry

See also

Britain, Battle of; Dowding, Hugh C.T.; Dunkirk; German Air Force (Luftwaffe); Leigh-Mallory, Trafford; Malta, Siege of; Mediterranean Theater of Operations; Radar; Royal Flying Corps/Royal Naval Air Service/Royal Air Force

References

James, John. *The Paladans.* London: McDonald, 1990.

Orange, Vincent. *Sir Keith Park.* London: Methuen, 1984.

Patrick, Mason Mathews (1863–1942)

U.S. Army major general. Mason Mathews Patrick was born in Lewisburg, West Virginia, on 13 December 1863. In June 1886, he graduated second in his class from the U.S. Military Academy at West Point. One of his classmates and friends was later General of the Army John J. "Black Jack" Pershing.

Patrick had a wide-ranging career as an engineer, and in 1901 Patrick became the assistant to the chief of the Air Service when the United States entered World War I in April 1917. The U.S. commander, General Pershing, assigned Patrick to the first U.S. contingents to go to France. In September, he was named chief engineer of lines of communication and director of construction and forestry for the American Expeditionary Forces.

The various U.S. aviation units in Europe were uncoordinated and often in competition over resources and missions. Pershing also had two headstrong aviation officers, Brigadier Generals William B. "Billy" Mitchell and Benjamin D. "Benny" Foulois, who separately led operational and supply/administrative aspects of Army aviation. Their rivalry over the use and structure of the Air Service led Pershing, in

May 1918, to place Patrick over all Air Service units and promote him to temporary major general.

After the war, Patrick returned home as an engineering officer. In 1921, Pershing became the Army Chief of Staff. On 5 October, he appointed Patrick chief of the newly reformed Army Air Service. Promoted to permanent major general, Patrick declared that "airmen should be led by an airman!" In 1923, at the age of 60, he had Major (later Major General) Herbert A. Dargue teach him to fly.

Patrick was a visionary who privately agreed with Mitchell that airpower would eventually become an essential part of national defense. However, Patrick believed in gathering overwhelming evidence that proved military aviation's potential and just how far behind U.S. aviation was at the time.

Even though Patrick tried to channel Mitchell's passion for airpower and sent him on long "inspection" tours of European and Pacific installations, he could not keep him out of trouble with Army and civilian leadership. By the fall of 1925, Mitchell, while right in most ways, had clearly been insubordinate. Between 28 October and 17 December 1925, Patrick sat through Mitchell's bitter court-martial and predictable conviction. He was left to save the Air Service's reputation, which he did.

Patrick seized opportunities to garner positive publicity for the Air Service. Under Patrick's steady leadership, Army airmen set many aviation records. He also facilitated the creation of flight laboratories and experimental flying facilities at Wright Field, all of which became part of the Materiel Division (1927–1942) and today's Air Force Materiel Command.

In 1926, Patrick played a key role in the formulation and passage of legislation that created the Army Air Corps—a major step toward organizational independence. The Air Corps's formation led to the creation of the position of assistant secretary of war for air, a powerful new subcabinet post.

Patrick retired on 12 December 1927, living the remaining years of life as a revered aviation expert and grand old man of the air force. He died at Walter Reed Hospital on 29 January 1942, at age 78, and was buried at Arlington National Cemetery. On 26 August 1950, the Air Force's long-range proving ground near Cocoa Beach, Florida, was named Patrick AFB in his honor.

William Head

See also

Dargue, Herbert A.; Foulois, Benjamin D.; Mitchell, William

References

Head, William P. *Every Inch a Soldier: Augustine Warner Robins and the Building of U.S. Airpower.* College Station: Texas A&M University Press, 1995.

Patrick, Mason M. *Military Aircraft and Their Use in Warfare.* Philadelphia: Franklin Institute, 1923.

Patterson, Robert Porter (1891–1952)

Post–World War II secretary of war; instrumental in desegregating the Army and creating the Department of Defense. Born in Glens Falls, New York, on 12 February 1891, Patterson was educated at Union College and Harvard Law School, where he was president of the *Harvard Law Review.* He practiced law in New York City from 1915. In World War I, he earned two citations for gallant and meritorious service "in utter disregard of personal danger." He was awarded the Distinguished Service Cross and won a Purple Heart for wounds received in an action on 16 August 1918. He returned to the United States in April 1919, mustered out of the Army as a major, and resumed his law practice in New York.

In 1940, he became assistant secretary of war. Then he became the first undersecretary of war. In that position, he was responsible for procurement of more than $100 billion worth of supplies and equipment, the largest amount of business ever carried out by one organization to that time. He was also largely responsible for the desegregation of the Army.

After World War II ended, he served as secretary of war. As the Cold War set in, Patterson advised President Harry S. Truman on China, Greece, Turkey, and other troublespots in the lead-up to the Truman Doctrine. Patterson's tenure (1945–1947) was one of rapid demobilization, but it was also a time for rethinking the structure of U.S. military forces. Patterson played an important role in the negotiations, politicking, and maneuvering that eventuated in the unification of the armed forces, the establishment of an independent Air Force, and the creation of the Department of Defense. He elected to return to private business rather than become the first secretary of defense.

He died in a commercial airliner crash on 22 January 1952 and was buried in Section 30 of Arlington National Cemetery. His wife, Margaret T. Winchester Patterson, died on 28 May 1988 and rests beside him.

John Barnhill

References

Boettcher, Thomas D. *First Call: The Making of the Modern U.S. Military, 1945–1953.* Boston: Little, Brown, 1992.

Pattle, Marmaduke Thomas St. John (1914–1941)

South Africa's ace of aces; perhaps the best fighter pilot in the Royal Air Force/Commonwealth Air Forces during World War II. He was a squadron leader in the RAF, with 34-plus victories in the Middle East and Greece. He was awarded the Distinguished Flying Cross and Bar.

Pattle was born on 23 July 1914 in Butterworth, Cape Province, South Africa. In 1936, he became a cadet in the Special Service Battalion. When Pattle was assigned to No. 80 Squadron, flying Gloster Gladiators, he was evaluated as "exceptional"—a highly skilled marksman and an above-average flier.

When Italy entered World War II in June 1940, the Egypt-based No. 80 Squadron got its first taste of combat. Pattle mostly flew the Gladiator, although the squadron also had a small number of Hurricanes. On 4 August 1940, Pattle's flight of four Gladiators engaged 27 Italian aircraft; he scored two kills. He was shot down over Libya that day but made it back to the British lines after a two-day walk.

November 1940 saw Pattle's No. 80 Squadron transferred to Greece. He scored two Fiat CR.42 kills on his first sortie. Upon taking command of the squadron on 25 November 1940, Pattle was presented with the Distinguished Flying Cross (DFC). On 12 March 1941, he took command of the Hurricane-equipped No. 33 Squadron with promotion to squadron leader. By this point, he had 20 kills and several unconfirmed. Eleven days later her earned the Bar for his DFC by getting one air victory, several unconfirmed, and three ground kills.

On 6 April 1941 the Germans attacked Greece, and Pat Pattle began a regular pattern of German kills, many of which were never recorded due to the desperate Allied situation. Pattle grew very ill around this time, a combination of fatigue and influenza, but continued to fly even after the medical officer grounded him except in the case of air raids.

On 20 April, in grave physical condition, Pattle and the combined No. 80 and No. 33 Squadrons intercepted more than 100 German aircraft. He was killed over Eleusis Bay after saving another Hurricane and shooting down several German fighters.

Some estimates of his enemy kills exceed 60, but many of official records were destroyed, so the actual number is unknown. This man—small in stature but large in courage and ability—was one of South Africa's great air heroes of the conflict.

Scott R. DiMarco

References

Baker, E.C.R. *Ace of Aces: M. St. J. Pattle: Top Scoring Allied Fighter Pilot of World War II.* Rivonia, South Africa: Ashanti, 1965.

Tidy, D. P. "South African Air Aces, 1939–1945." *South African Military History Society—Military History Journal* 1, 3.

Pave Nail

Early code name for laser-guided munitions, or smart bombs. In the late 1960s, the U.S. Air Force began using laser-guided bombs in the Vietnam War. A tremendous advancement in aerial delivery of ordnance, they allowed aircraft to destroy precise targets with one or two bombs instead of dozens or even hundreds of unguided dumb bombs.

Laser beams generated by guidance pods carried by aircraft guided the munitions to the targets. The first Pave Nail planes were 15 OV-10 Broncos assigned to the 23d Tactical Air Support Squadron stationed at Nakhon Phanom Air Base in northeastern Thailand. These aircraft were modified in 1971 to carry a Pave Spot guidance pod and a LORAN long-range navigation system. This gave them all-weather precision-guidance capability. The crew consisted of a forward air controller/pilot in the front seat and a forward air navigator who sat in the back seat and operated the Pave Spot system.

Seventh Air Force used this system very effectively in the COMMANDO HUNT operations along the Ho Chi Minh Trail, against the invading North Vietnamese Army in the Easter Offensive of 1972, in the last operations over Cambodia in 1973, and in search-and-rescue operations throughout. Two of the aircraft were downed by enemy ground fire, and one was downed by an SA-2 surface-to-air missile during the rescue operation for Bat 21 Bravo in April 1972. In 1974, the Pave Spot pods were removed and the program was terminated.

Darrel Whitcomb

See also

BAT 21

References

Project CHECO: COMMAND HUNT VII. Washington, DC: Office of Air Force History, 1975.

Whitcomb, Darrel. *The Rescue of Bat 21.* Annapolis, MD: Naval Institute Press, 1998.

Pearl Harbor

Surprise Japanese attack on U.S. Pacific Fleet in the Hawaiian port of Pearl Harbor on 7 December 1941; resulted in the United States entering World War II. The first strike occurred at 7:52 A.M. local time followed by a second strike at 8:55 A.M. that lasted about an hour. Casualties from the attacks included 2,335 dead servicemen, 1,104 of whom perished aboard the USS *Arizona* when a direct hit to the magazine resulted in an explosion that ripped the ship apart; 1,178 wounded; and 68 civilians dead. Capital damage included the destruction of 188 planes and eight battleships. In addition, three light cruisers, three destroyers, and three smaller vessels sustained irreparable damage.

Japanese pilots, under the command of Admiral Nagumo Chuichi, took off from six aircraft carriers located 274 miles

The Japanese-eye view of the attack on Pearl Harbor, showing a torpedo hit on the USS West Virginia. *(U.S. Navy)*

off the coast of Oahu on the morning of 7 December. The first wave of 183 planes—assigned to target specific airfields and "Battleship Row," where the majority of the U.S. Pacific Fleet remained moored—headed for Hawaii at 6:00 A.M. At 7:02 A.M. two Army radar operators stationed at Opana Radar Station detected the approach of the planes, but a junior officer failed to relay the information, believing that the planes were B-17s scheduled to arrive from the West Coast.

At 7:15 A.M. the second wave of fighters headed for Hawaii. By 7:53 A.M. the first group of Japanese planes, which included 51 Val dive-bombers, 40 Kate torpedo-bombers, 50 high-level bombers, and 43 Zero fighters under the command of Mitsuo Fuchida, commenced their attack. The Wheeler, Kaneohe, Ford Island, Hickam, Bellows, and Ewa airfields sustained damage during the first wave of attack. The battleships hit included the *Arizona, Oklahoma, West Virginia, Pennsylvania, Tennessee, Maryland, Nevada,* and *California.* The USS *Lexington, Saratoga,* and *Enterprise,* out of port at the time of attack, remained undamaged and played a role in the destruction of Japanese submarines.

Japanese losses included 27 aircraft and five midget submarines dispatched into the harbor with orders to torpedo any undamaged ships. Following their victory at Pearl Harbor, the Japanese attacked numerous islands throughout the Pacific with impunity for six months before the U.S. Fleet regrouped and started winning major naval battles, eventually turning the tide with the victory at Midway Island, where U.S. forces destroyed four Japanese battleships.

Investigations into defense preparations on the island occurred after the attack. Admiral Husband E. Kimmel and Army Lieutenant General Walter C. Short were relieved of duty for failing to implement appropriate defense measures. Admiral Chester W. Nimitz assumed command of the Pacific Fleet. By attacking the United States, the Japanese created a sense of urgency among officials that extended past the surrender of Germany and Italy.

Cynthia Clark Northrup

See also

Fuchida, Mitsuo; Nagumo, Chuichi; Nimitz, Chester William

References

Hamer, David J. *Bombers Versus Battleships: The Struggle Between*

One of the most famous photos of the damage resulting from the Japanese raid on Pearl Harbor, 7 December 1941. (U. S. Navy)

Ships and Aircraft for the Control of the Surface of the Sea. Annapolis, MD: Naval Institute Press, 1998.

Sweetman, Jack, ed. *Great American Naval Battles.* Annapolis, MD: Naval Institute Press, 1998.

PEDESTAL (1942)

Code name for convoy operation that suffered heavy losses while bringing desperately needed supplies to British Malta in the central Mediterranean. By August 1942, Malta was short of almost all supplies, and rations had been cut substantially. The British Admiralty planned a massive convoy moving east from Gibraltar to bring in enough supplies to end the danger of Malta being starved into submission. Four aircraft carriers and two battleships escorted 14 merchantmen.

From the beginning, Italian reconnaissance aircraft tracked the convoy. A U-boat sank the carrier *Eagle,* and Axis bombers heavily damaged the carrier *Indomitable.* Two Italian fighters, with silhouettes similar to that of the British Sea Hurricane, entered the carrier *Victorious*'s landing pattern in a daring attack and dropped two 1,000-pound bombs. One hit the bow and scattered fragments over the antiaircraft gun crews, and the other hit the deck and broke up without exploding. Nine of the merchantmen were sunk and three damaged by a combination of U-boats, E-boats, torpedo bombers, and dive-bombers, but the convoy delivered 55,000 tons of supplies.

The supplies enabled Malta to resume offensive operations against Axis supply lines to Africa. By the time another supply convoy was necessary, the Allies had gained the advantage in the Mediterranean and the convoy was only lightly opposed.

Grant Weller

See also
German Air Force (Luftwaffe); Hawker Hurricane; Malta, Siege of; Mediterranean Theater of Operations; Regia Aeronautica (World War II)

References
Cameron, Ian. *Red Duster, White Ensign.* New York: Doubleday, 1960.

Peenemünde

Site of German special-weapons research and subsequent Allied attacks. As the Allies became aware of German special-weapons development during World War II, and of the important developmental role of the Peenemünde site on the Baltic coast, extensive monitoring of the area by aerial reconnaissance and photography was undertaken. Ultraintelligence contributed to a growing picture of an extensive missile program. CROSSBOW, the overall code name for the Allied response to what became the German V-1 and V-2 programs, determined that the missiles were in advanced testing and that they—as well as key German scientific personnel—had to be destroyed as soon as possible.

On the evening of 17–18 August 1943, three waves of 560 RAF bombers—Halifaxes, Stirlings, and Lancasters—were sent on Operation HYDRA against Peenemünde targets. At the same time, a small force of eight RAF bombers were sent to Berlin to act as decoys to confuse the Luftwaffe's response to the main raid.

Over Peenemünde, Pathfinders led the first wave of 227 bombers to obliterate the site's worker housing estate (18 of 30 huts destroyed), though the specific aim of this wave was the scientific and technical personnel who were housed nearby. The second wave was 113 Lancasters aimed at the V-2 production works located at Peenemünde South. And the third wave of 180 bombers was sent to attack the experimental development works of Peenemünde East and hit 50 of 80 buildings. In all, 1,600 tons of high-explosive and 250 tons of incendiary bombs were dropped in the three waves, which accomplished their attacks on a moonlit night between 1 A.M. and 2 A.M.

The Luftwaffe was successfully decoyed over Berlin and did not attack the Peenemünde force until the third wave, shooting down 40 bombers, or about 7 percent of the RAF aircraft. But while that aspect of the British attack was successful, and more than 730 were killed, Operation HYDRA accomplished only some of its aims. Most of those killed were prisoners and foreign workers, as the bombs were misdirected and thus killed few of the important scientific and technical people. And while the attack delayed V-1 and V-2 implementation for 4–8 weeks, several vital facilities were only partially damaged or not damaged at all. These included the vital control building, liquid oxygen manufacturing site, wind tunnel, and the airfield where V-1 experiments were taking place. The large Test Stand VII used for launching test-model V-2s was only slightly damaged.

Ironically, the attack may have aided the Germans. As basic missile and rocket development work at Peenemünde had been completed, the chief effect of the attack was to alert the Germans to disperse V-1 and V-2 mass production to protected sites underground. Further, as Peenemünde remained under constant monitoring, the Germans left much of the damage in place to persuade the Allies that all work had stopped.

After V-1s began to drop on Britain, a later U.S. Army Air Forces daylight precision raid by more than 375 B-17s on 18 July 1944 was followed up with missions on 4 and 25 August 1944. All told, more than 800 bombers dropped 1,900 tons of bombs on the three raids. By the time the Russians occupied the site in May 1945, Peenemünde was but a shadow of its developmental days with only a skeleton garrison.

Christopher H. Sterling

See also
German Rocket Development; Ultra; V-1 Missile and V-2 Rocket

References
Middlebrook, Martin. *The Peenemunde Raid: The Night of 17–18 August 1943.* London: Allen Lane, 1982.

Peltz, Dietrich (1914–)

German major general; one of the most controversial commanders in the Luftwaffe. Peltz joined the German Army in 1934, transferred to the Luftwaffe in 1935, and was in command of a *staffel* (squadron) of Ju 87 dive-bombers during the Polish and French campaigns. He transferred to Ju 88 medium bombers during the Battle of Britain and won the Knight's Cross of the Iron Cross for his bravery and skill. After leading bomber units on all fronts, he was promoted to colonel and named general of the bomber arm, a staff position within the Luftwaffe High Command, but returned to combat duty in March 1943 as *Angriffsfuehrer* England (Attack Leader England). The bombing campaign he led, called the "Baby Blitz" by the English, was ordered by Hitler in revenge for Allied air attacks on Germany. It was finally called off in early 1944 owing to its ineffectiveness and high German losses, but Peltz was held blameless; he was awarded the Oak Leaves with Swords to the Knight's Cross of the Iron Cross and promoted at age 29 to brigadier general.

Peltz's career took a startling turn in October 1944, when he was named commander of II Jagdkorps (Fighter Corps), which contained all of the fighters on the Western Front. Peltz had no experience in fighters, and morale among the fighter-unit commanders plummeted. German fighter losses over the Ardennes were extremely high, and on 1 January 1945 Operation BASEPLATE (*UNTERNEHMEN BODENPLATTE*), which Peltz had planned, cost the Luftwaffe 214 fighter pilots, including 19 formation leaders, and destroyed the fighter force beyond any hope of rebuilding.

Peltz was next given command of IX Fliegerkorps (Jagd) (Air Corps [Fighters]), which contained all of the Luftwaffe's Me 262 fighters and, in March 1945, was promoted to command the Reichsluftverteidigung (Air Defense of Germany), the position he held at war's end. Postwar, his management skills were in great demand, and he had a very successful career in German industry.

Donald Caldwell

See also
German Air Force (Luftwaffe)

References

Obermeier, E. *Die Ritterkreuztraeger der Luftwaffe, 1939–1945, Band 2: Stuka und Schlachtflieger* [Recipients of the Knight's Cross]. Mainz: Verlag Dieter Hoffmann, 1976.

Pepelyaev, Evgenii Georgievich (1918–)

Soviet fighter ace during the Korean War. Evgenii Georgievich Pepelyaev was born on 18 March 1918 in Bodaibo, Siberia. He joined the army in 1936 and completed flight school in 1938. He spent World War II in the Far East and flew only 42 combat missions. In 1950, he became commander of the 196 IAP (Fighter Air Regiment), and in April 1951 he led this regiment to Antung, Manchuria, for combat over Korea. When the regiment stood down in February 1952, it had claimed 104 victories for the loss of 25 aircraft and five pilots. Pepelyaev flew 108 missions over Korea and fought 38 air combats. He was officially credited with 20 victories, including 16 F-86s, and gave three more victories to his wingman. He was never shot down. Pepelyaev was awarded the Hero of the Soviet Union on 22 April 1952. He retired in 1973.

George M. Mellinger

See also
Fighter Air Corps; Soviet Air Force

References

Gordon, Yefim, and Vladimir Rigmant. *MiG-15: Design, Development, and Korean War Combat History.* Osceola, WI: Motorbooks International, 1993.
Seidl, Hans D. *Stalin's Eagles: An Illustrated Study of the Soviet Aces of World War II and Korea.* Atglen, PA: Schiffer, 1998.

Pershing, John Joseph (1860–1948)

General of the Army; commanded the American Expeditionary Forces in France during World War I and became the most influential U.S. military officer in the years after the war. Born in Laclede, Missouri, "Black Jack" Pershing graduated from the U.S. Military Academy in 1886. He served in the cavalry on the frontier and in Cuba, but he made his reputation in the Moro Wars (1903–1913). That reputation and his marriage to the daughter of the chairman of the Senate Military Affairs Committee gained his promotion from captain to brigadier general in 1906.

Pershing's first extensive exposure to aircraft came in 1916. He commanded the Punitive Expedition dispatched by the Woodrow Wilson administration to pursue the Mexican revolutionary and bandit Pancho Villa, who had raided into the United States. The Signal Corps's 1st Aero Squadron, commanded by Captain Benjamin D. Foulois, accompanied the expedition, composed largely of horse cavalry units. Pershing anticipated that Foulois's aircraft would provide reconnaissance, flank protection, and communications between his dispersed mounted columns. Initially, the 1st Aero Squadron was able to fulfill these expectations, but the aircraft soon broke down due to a combination of mountainous terrain, desert climate, and continuous operations, forcing the unit to withdraw to the United States for refitting. The trucks and automobiles of the squadron's ground section proved more valuable than the aircraft. They provided the nucleus of the motorized supply line that Pershing improvised when President Venustiano Carranza denied the Punitive Expedition access to the Mexican national railways.

Although Pershing was disappointed, this unpromising beginning did not prejudice him against military aviation. When assigned to command the American Expeditionary Forces in 1917, Pershing made aviation in France completely independent of the Signal Corps. Generally, Pershing followed the advice of experts in this as well as other technical areas. During operations he gave his aviation commanders considerable freedom to innovate, in contrast to the control he exercised over his corps commanders.

When a destructive feud developed between Foulois, now a brigadier general, and Colonel William Mitchell, Pershing assigned Foulois to the support base, gave Mitchell an operational command, and brought in his West Point classmate, Brigadier General Mason M. Patrick, to head aviation in the American Expeditionary Forces.

In the postwar congressional hearings on reorganizing the War Department, Pershing took a progressive stance on aviation's role in the Army (in contrast to his position on armor). He called for a separate department of aviation that would fund research and development, procurement of equipment, and personnel but would assign military and naval aircraft (and their pilots and ground crews) to the control of the War and Navy Departments. When Congress did not adopt these recommendations, Pershing supported the creation of the Army Air Service. Although he continued to recognize the need for further development of the aerial arm, he was not willing to advocate it at the expense of the other arms and services of the Army.

Secretary of War John W. Weeks blocked Pershing's attempt to present his concerns about lack of funds in the Army's budget directly to President Warren G. Harding. Pershing, although he disagreed with this decision, accepted it as a legitimate exercise of civilian control.

Although Pershing agreed with Mitchell, now a brigadier general, that something was wrong with the postwar Air Service, he regarded Mitchell's methods of appealing directly to the public as too "Bolshevik."

Pershing, because of his command of the American Expeditionary Forces, came to symbolize the Army in the 1920s. As Chief of Staff he was also head of the General Staff. Mitchell and his followers attacked the General Staff as wrongheaded and reactionary in its supervision of military aviation, the cause of all the Air Service's problems. The General Staff, however, was simply enforcing the programs of the Harding and Calvin Coolidge administrations.

But Mitchell could not attack the president of the United States by name: To do so would have been an attack on the principle of civilian control. Pershing saw military aviation as an important adjunct of the ground forces. In his view, aviation could not act independently and decisively in war. Thus, there were real differences between Pershing and Mitchell on aviation policy. Pershing was much more concerned with what aircraft could do in the present and the immediate future while Mitchell was more focused on their long-term potential.

Edgar F. Raines Jr.

References

Futrell, Robert F. *Ideas, Concepts, Doctrine: Basic Thinking in the United States Air Force, 1907–1984.* 2 vols. Maxwell AFB, AL: Air University Press, 1989.

Hurley, Alfred E. *Billy Mitchell: Crusader for Air Power.* Bloomington: Indiana University Press, 1975 [1964].

Meilinger, Phillip S., ed. *The Paths of Heaven: The Evolution of Airpower Theory.* Maxwell AFB, AL: Air University Press, 1997.

Smythe, Donald. *Guerrilla Warrior: The Early Life of John J. Pershing.* New York: Charles Scribner's Sons, 1973.

______. *Pershing: General of the Armies.* Bloomington: Indiana University Press, 1986.

Peru-Ecuador Boundary Conflict

A series of local wars during the twentieth century. The independence of Latin America, with the division of the Spanish regions into many republics, left a legacy of disputed boundaries, particularly between Ecuador and Peru. Airpower became a factor during local boundary wars.

Peru, the larger and somewhat more stable nation, achieved important aviation progress during the 1920s. Important connections with U.S. aircraft manufacturers developed. Much less aviation effort was undertaken in Ecuador.

Peruvian officers had observed U.S. Marine Corps aviation in Nicaragua (1931). In July 1941, the conclusion of a Peruvian offensive was likened to a blitzkrieg, for their modern North American (NA-50) and Douglas (DB-8A) monoplanes and twin-engine Italian Capronis met no opposition from Ecuador.

World War II led to the true development of an Ecuadorian air force, which became separate from the army in 1944. U.S. Lend-Lease aid was generous to repay use of Ecuadorian bases to protect a flank of the Panama Canal. A military flying school was definitively organized in March 1942; Ecuadorian pilots also trained in Texas. After World War II, the powerful Republic P-47 Thunderbolts required additional preparation in the United States for Ecuadorian pilots.

Both countries continued to modernize their air forces, and conflicts were frequent. In early 1981, Peru attacked Paquisha, an outpost in the disputed region. Unlike 40 years earlier, Ecuadorian airpower was able to patrol the national territory and limit Peruvian effectiveness during the few days of combat. On 28 January 1981, aerial combat between Cessna A-37B ground attack aircraft of both sides produced slight damage. In the aftermath of Paquisha, significant improvements were made by Ecuador. Weapons upgrades for the Dassault Mirage F.1 and the Israeli Kfir C.2, plus a radar system enabling these interceptors to be effectively deployed, evened the airpower balance.

When the dispute again erupted in 1995 (the War of the Condor, or Upper Cenepa War), several Peruvian aircraft were shot down or damaged. Fortunately, the localized war soon ended, and an acceptable boundary agreement was achieved by 1998.

Airpower played an important role in projecting armed force into a remote region. Evolving tactics and equipment proved crucial, even above unexplored mountains and jungle. The boundary dispute helped develop Peruvian and especially Ecuadorian military aviation. These air services are capable today of important logistical and emergency operations, now that peace has come to the defined frontier.

Gary Kuhn

References

Zook, David H. Jr. *Zarumilla-Maranon: The Ecuador-Peru Dispute.* No publ. available, 1964.

Petersen, Frank E. (1932–)

Three-star general; the first African American pilot in the U.S. Marines. Born in Topeka, Kansas, Frank Petersen learned electronics in his father's shop. When he joined the Navy in 1950, he attended electronics school after a debate with the recruiter over whether or not he cheated. He qualified for Navy pilot training after Jesse L. Brown, the first black Navy pilot, died in Korea. The Navy had two other black fliers. Petersen opted for the Marines, survived training and racism, and earned his wings, becoming the first African American Marine pilot (between 1950 and 1953, black Marines increased from 2 percent to 6 percent of the Corps).

Not wanting a southern U.S. assignment, Petersen received orders to El Toro, California. He flew in Korea as a Marine Corps Reserve second lieutenant, finishing 64 missions and earning the Distinguished Flying Cross. Promoted to first lieutenant and made regular in 1954, he served in El Toro until 1960, at which time he went to Hawaii, then to Iwakuni, Japan. At Iwakuni, Major Petersen made his first investigation of racial conditions in the Marines.

At Quantico's Amphibious Warfare School in 1964, his staff study was on racism in the Marines. He continued to rise, finishing college and making lieutenant colonel in 1967. In Vietnam he became the first black fighter-squadron commander in the Marines; as commander of the Black Knights he won a Purple Heart, and the squadron was considered the best in the Marines. He continued his controversial investigation of military racism as special assistant to the commandant in the late 1960s and early 1970s.

In the 1970s, he completed studies at the National War College. He was promoted to colonel in 1975 and to brigadier general in 1979. He attained three-star rank in 1986. He retired in 1988 from command at Quantico. Petersen is the first black Marine general and highest-ranking black Marine to date.

John Barnhill

References

Petersen, Frank E., with J. Alfred Phelps. *Into the Tiger's Jaw: America's First Black Marine Aviator.* Novato, CA: Presidio Press, 1998.

Petlyakov Aircraft

World War II bomber aircraft designed by V. M. Petlyakov. Vladimir Mikhailovich Petlyakov was born on 27 July 1891 and studied aerodynamics with Nikolai Zhukovsky, the father of Russian aviation. During the 1920s, he became one of the leading deputies of Andrei Tupolev, specializing in wing design. From October 1931, he was chief of the heavy aircraft design brigade, playing a central role in the design of the Maxim Gorky and the TB-3. In July 1937, Petlyakov, like many Soviet designers, was arrested and sent to a design prison (*sharaga*), officially for excessive delay in completing the ANT-42 heavy bomber, designated TB-7 by the air force, and later redesignated Pe-8 in his honor. While in prison he also designed the Pe-2, which became the standard wartime Soviet tactical bomber. After his release in 1940, Petlyakov was appointed director of his own design bureau in Kazan but was killed in a flying accident in January 1942.

The Pe-8, the only heavy bomber used by the Soviets during World War II, had four engines on the wings and a fifth mounted in the fuselage to power a compressor. It was not very successful, and only 91 were built. The Pe-8 conducted a number of raids on Berlin, Königsberg, and Danzig during 1941 but flew few missions during the rest of the war. Its most famous flight, on 19 May 1942, brought Foreign Minister V. M. Molotov and his staff to Britain.

Far more significant was the Pe-2, the standard twin-engine dive-bomber, with 11,467 examples built, including 365 fighter variants. Its speed and maneuverability made it difficult to intercept. After the war, many examples were handed down to Eastern European countries.

George M. Mellinger

See also

Tupolev Aircraft

References

Gordon, Yefim, and Dmitrii Khazanov. *Soviet Combat Aircraft in the Second World War.* Vol. 2. Leicester, UK: Midland Counties, 1999.

Gunston, Bill. *The Encyclopedia of Russian Aircraft, 1875–1995.* Osceola, WI: Motorbooks International, 1995.

Kerber, L. L. *Stalin's Aviation Gulag.* Washington, DC: Smithsonian Institution Press, 1996.

Pfalz Aircraft

Bavarian aircraft manufacturer. The Pfalz Flugzeug Werke opened operations in the summer of 1913 with financial help from the government of Bavaria. The political demands of the confederation of kingdoms, principalities, duchies, and free cities that made up the German Empire during World War I required the maintenance of separate military units for the larger ones. Bavaria was the first of the non-Prussian kingdoms to establish its own aviation units, and its government was naturally just as interested in a having a reliable, non-Prussian source of supply as it was in having its own soldiers. The company was managed by the Eversbusch brothers: Alfred, Ernst and Walter. Prior to the war, the brothers obtained a license to produce Morane-Saulnier aircraft.

The Eversbusch brothers (minus Walter, who had been killed testing a company design in 1916) also became known as aggressive marketers, and there are many photographs of them socializing with, or showing off company products to, the leading German pilots of the day. After having contributed a monoplane fighter that bore a strong resemblance to the Fokker Eindecker, Pfalz produced another single-seater, the D.III, in 1917.

The Pfalz D.III, like its Albatros D.III counterpart, had a sesquiplane layout, the lower wing being narrower than the upper. The lines of the Pfalz were much cleaner than the Albatros, however, giving it one of the sleekest appearances of any World War I fighter.

Armament was the conventional arrangement of two LMG.108 (Spandau) machine guns firing through the propeller, the guns being buried under the engine cowling. This proved a maintenance problem, and in the refined D.IIIa they were moved to an exposed position. Slower than the Albatros, the Pfalz did not replace it but did serve as a supplement to it in several *jagdstaffeln* (fighter squadrons).

The last wartime Pfalz design to see significant production was the D.XII. A single-seat fighter with two-bay wings and the same "N" struts that characterized its contemporary, the Fokker D.VII, the Pfalz made its first appearance at the second German fighter trials in June 1918. The trial's winner was the Fokker D.VIII monoplane, but the Pfalz made a sufficient impression that it was ordered into production.

Although it utilized the same engines as the Fokker D.VII (the Mercedes or the BMW) and fit its same general description, the D.XII was not initially as popular as the Fokker, either with the pilots who flew it or the crews who had to maintain its more complex rigging. Reports indicate, however, that once they had grown used to it, pilot opinion changed. Late in 1918, the D.XII served with Jagdgeschwader III, a half-dozen other *jagdstaffeln,* and a few home-defense units.

James Streckfuss

References

Gray, Peter, and Owen Thetford. *German Aircraft of the First World War.* London: Putnam, 1962.

Philippines (1941, 1944)

Key archipelago in the Pacific Theater; site of U.S. occupation, Japanese conquest, and eventual Allied liberation.

1941 Air Operations

In August 1941, ground forces from the United States Army Forces Far East (USAFFE) were supplemented by air assets (composed of the 4th Composite Group, 19th Bombardment Group, 24th Pursuit Group, 27th Bombardment Group, and the 2d Observation Squadron) already stationed on the islands. These units were redesignated the USAFFE Air Force. In reality, this "air force" consisted of only 210 aircraft, less than half considered modern. The rest of the force consisted of obsolete Boeing P-26A and Seversky P-35A fighters, Martin B-10 and Douglas B-18 bombers, and various reconnaissance and cargo aircraft. Throughout the fall, the 24th Pursuit was strengthened by the arrival of additional Curtiss P-40E fighters and the 19th Bombardment Group by new Boeing B-17C and B-17D bombers, bringing the total number of aircraft to more than 250. The bombers were gathered at the only two fields that could handle them, Clark and Del Monte. The fighters were based at various airfields on Luzon. Patrol Wing 10 made up the USAFFE naval air assets in Manila and consisted of 28 Catalina PBY amphibious planes, one observation plane, four utility planes, and four seaplane tenders. Because the 27th Bombardment Group's planes never arrived, their pilots flew from Luzon to Australia after 7 December.

On 8 December, after Japanese army bombers bombed military installations near Baguio, 108 twin-engine Japanese naval bombers, escorted by 84 Zero fighters, headed for the Clark and Iba airfields. The U.S. forces armed and fueled their bombers for a raid on Japanese airfields on Formosa while fighters from the 3d, 17th, and 21st Pursuit Squadrons were sent aloft to deter any Japanese attacks. For reasons still disputed to this day, the Japanese Eleventh Air Fleet caught the USAFFE Air Force planes at Clark and Iba off-guard, destroying most of them on the ground. P-40s from the 3d returning to Iba managed to drive off strafing Zeros, but the P-35s from nearby Del Carmen were able to shoot down only three Zeros over Clark. The attack left the USAFFE with only 17 B-17s, 54 P-40s, and 49 P-35s intact; the installations at Clark and Iba were heavily damaged. Patrol Wing 10, based at Cavite and Olongapo, was not damaged. The Japanese struck again on 10 December, hitting Cavite and Clark, Del Carmen, Iba, and Nichols airfields. This attack and subsequent ones on 12 and 13 December left the USAFFE with 16 operational bombers, 22 P-40s, about a half-dozen P-35s, and a few P-26s. On 12 December, Patrol Wing 10 lost seven of its PBYs to Zeros that followed them back to Olongapo. Several more PBYs were lost the following day. To keep from losing all their bombers, the 19th's B-17s were moved on 15 December from Del Monte to Darwin, Australia.

Before the B-17s evacuated Luzon, Japanese forces landed at Appari and Gonzaga. In an effort to drive off the landing forces, two B-17s from Clark attacked the transports. Although their attack resulted in little damage to the invasion force, it did provide the USAFFE and America its first World War II hero, Captain Colin P. Kelly, who posthumously earned the Distinguished Service Cross for this action and subsequent saving of his crew when they were attacked by Zeros. USAFFE sent small groups of P-35s, P-40s, and B-17s to disrupt the Japanese landings at Vigan and Legaspi. The attacks resulted in only a few transports sunk at Vigan and a few enemy fighters shot down at Legaspi.

After the destruction of Clark Field and other airbases around Manila, USAFFE was left at the mercy of Japanese bombers. Although some aircraft of the 24th Pursuit were able to keep flying, lack of spare parts and replacements spelled the end of U.S. airpower and the eventual capture of U.S. strongholds at Bataan and Corregidor by the Japanese. Those air units that were still intact, such as the U.S. Navy's Patrol Wing 10, abandoned the Philippines in mid-December and its Dutch East Indies bases of operation in the winter of 1942 for the safer and more secure Australian shoreline near Perth.

1944 Air Operations

The year 1944 saw the return of U.S. forces to the Philippines as Task Force 38, lead by Vice Admiral Marc A. Mitscher, sent carrier aircraft to bomb and strafe Japanese airfields on northern Luzon (11 and 14 October), Formosa (12–14 October), and the area around Manila (15 October), destroying more than 800 enemy aircraft, with more than half shot down by U.S. carrier planes. These attacks achieved their goal of clearing possible reinforcement areas and paved the way for the landing of U.S. Army troops on Leyte on 20 October. Besides carrier-based support from Task Force 38, the escort carriers (CVEs) of Task Force 77.4, lead by Rear Admiral Thomas L. Sprague, added their aircraft to operation on 18–23 October.

The Japanese fleet, intent on stopping the invasion, converged on the islands as a three-pronged force, but carrier aircraft from the U.S. forces attacked the southern and central Japanese forces in the Sulu and Sibuyan Seas. They sank the Japanese battleship *Musashi* and a destroyer, and Japanese air attacks claimed the CVE *Princeton.* The Japanese southern prong was defeated by elements of the U.S. Seventh Fleet in the Surigao Strait, losing two battleships and three destroyers. The central prong was able to gain passage through the San Bernardino Strait and bombarded Task Force 77.4's CVEs and escorts, sinking *Gambier Bay* and a destroyer escort, while carrier aircraft sank three Japanese heavy cruisers. Almost simultaneously, Task Force 38 found the northern prong of the Japanese force off Cape Engano, sinking the Japanese carrier *Zuikaku* and light carriers *Chiyoda, Zuiho,* and *Chitose.* In the Leyte Gulf, Japanese kamikazes made their first appearance, sinking the CVE *St. Lô* and damaging the CVEs *Sangamon, Suwannee, Santee, White Plains, Kalinin Bay,* and *Kitkun Bay.*

As the battered Japanese forces retired homeward on 26–27 October, U.S. carrier aircraft struck a final time, sinking a light cruiser and four destroyers. On the last day of the naval battle, carrier aircraft struck Japanese airfields in the Visayas. The outcome of this battle, which gutted the Imperial Japanese Navy, allowed the U.S. invasion of Leyte to continue unmolested.

In response to these raids, the Japanese launched kamikaze attacks beginning on 29 October and continuing through 25 November. Carriers damaged by these actions included *Intrepid, Franklin, Belleau Wood, Lexington, Essex,* and *Hancock* and the CVE *Cabot.* To blunt U.S. airpower on occupied Leyte, the Japanese also conceived a suicide mission involving paratroop drops on airfields near San Pablo and Buri. Although the paratroops succeeded in taking the airfield at San Pablo, it was a short-lived victory, and overwhelming U.S. forces eventually retook the field. U.S. forces undertook amphibious, airborne, and glider operations to secure Luzon and, by April 1945, had isolated the three Japanese armies, occupying the Philippine archipelago.

Brian B. Carpenter

References

Bartsch, William H. *Doomed at the Start: American Pursuit Pilots in the Philippines, 1941–1942.* Foreword by Herbert Ellis. College Station: Texas A&M University Press, 1992.

Morton, Lewis. *Fall of the Philippines.* Vol. 4. United States Army in World War II: The War in the Pacific series. Washington, DC: U.S. Government Printing Office, 1953.

Piaggio Aircraft

Italian aircraft and engine manufacturer. Founded in 1884 as a sawmill by Rinaldo Piaggio (1864–1938), it soon extended its activity to naval furnishings and rolling stock. In World War I, Piaggio repaired seaplanes and manufactured spare parts. It joined the great Caproni Ca.5 program but only produced a few floatplane conversions.

Acting in a personal capacity, Senator Piaggio in 1921 helped found CMASA, which built Dornier Wal seaplanes in circumvention of the Versailles Treaty; a number were eventually assembled by Piaggio and used by SANA, an airline created in 1924 with Piaggio participation. In 1923, Piaggio took over the Pegna-Bonmartini firm, hiring its chief designer, Giovanni Pegna (1888–1961). A number of advanced prototypes were built to Pegna designs, including the PC.7 hydrofoil seaplane racer (1927), but the factory subsisted largely on license production of SIAI Marchetti seaplanes, including an all-metal S.55 variant designed by Giuseppe Gabrielli (1903–1987), who in 1931 left for Fiat. In 1930, Piaggio started building variable-pitch propellers from the patents of Corradino D'Ascanio (1891–1981), who also designed the PD.2 and PD.3 experimental helicopters.

Piaggio entered the engine field in 1924 with a license for the Bristol Jupiter, to which it later added the Gnôme-Rhône 14K. In 1937–1939, Piaggio engines set 21 records, including a 17,083-meter world altitude record in the Caproni Ca.161 *bis,* but during World War II the vital high-powered engines were plagued by reliability problems.

In 1936, Pegna was replaced by Giovanni Casiraghi (1904–1984), whose experience in U.S. industry helped introduce the modern concepts epitomized in the P.108B (1939), the only four-engine bomber used by the Axis. Its effectiveness was constrained by the lack of a strategic doctrine and even more by production limited to 24 aircraft plus a dozen transport models. Other Casiraghi designs were mere technology demonstrators, so production relied mainly on licenses for Cant and other aircraft.

Postwar, Piaggio thrived on the revolutionary Vespa scooter (1946), designed by D'Ascanio using aviation technology and components. The first new aircraft was the P.136 amphibian (1948), followed by the P.148 and P.149 trainers (1951–53), the latter also built under license in Germany, and the P.166 (1957) twin-engine utility transport. In 1963, separate companies were formed for the motorcycle and aero businesses, the latter introducing the PD.808 business jet (1964) designed in association with Douglas. All these aircraft found limited use outside Italian armed forces or government agencies. The radical P.180 twin-turboprop business aircraft (1986) suffered an uncertain fate due to the early withdrawal of U.S. partner Gates Learjet in addition to a financial crisis that led the company to bankruptcy. Resurrected under new ownership as Piaggio Aero Industries, it continues to build the P.180 and participates in a number of engine programs.

Gregory Alegi

See also

Alenia; Cant Aircraft; Caproni Aircraft; Fiat; Italian Aircraft Development; Regia Aeronautica (Pre–World War II); Regia Aeronautica (World War II); SIAI Marchetti

References

Donald, David, and Jon Lake, eds. *Encyclopedia of World Military Aircraft.* London: Aerospace, 1996.

Garello, Giancarlo. "Piaggio P.108." Turin: *La Bancarella Aeronautica* series, 2000.

Stevens, James Hay. "The Piaggio Story." *Air Pictorial* (August-September 1968).

Piasecki Helicopters

U.S. firm that helped pioneer practical use of the helicopter. It was formed in Pennsylvania in 1946 by Frank Nicholas Piasecki (1919–) to design and produce tandem-rotor helicopters.

In 1943, Frank Piasecki's P-V Engineering Forum invented and flew the second successful helicopter in the United States. Securing a Navy contract for a transport helicopter in 1944, Piasecki developed and flew the tandem-rotor XHRP-X in 1945. Needing capital to develop the helicopter, Piasecki incorporated the Piasecki Helicopter Company and attracted Rockefeller and DuPont money, which had controlling interest in the company.

The new company produced a succession of tandem-rotor helicopters, noted for their stability as loads were shifted to different points between the rotors. The Navy HRP-1 Rescuer, first delivered in 1947, was used in antisubmarine warfare tests, minesweeping tests, Marine tests of amphibious assaults, and the first long-distance rescue at sea.

From 1952 to 1954, Piasecki delivered 339 HUP-2s to the Navy. This helicopter also had tandem rotors, but the rear rotor was mounted on a high pylon to lessen the danger of the rotors clashing. This same type was procured by the Army as the H-25A Mule. The H-21 first flew in 1952. The H-16, appearing in 1953, was the largest U.S. helicopter then flying, but it was underpowered and never found military use.

In 1954, all H-21s were grounded because of design and production flaws, which led to the reorganization of the company. Needing the H-21s to service its distant early warning radar network in the Arctic, the Air Force brought pressure on the company to solve its problems. In 1950, the Rockefeller and DuPont interests that controlled the company had Frank Piasecki removed as president and made chairman of the board and head of research and development. They appointed a weak president at first, but in 1955 they appointed Don Berlin as president, and he and Piasecki clashed. Unhappy in his association with Berlin, Piasecki formed Piasecki Aircraft Company (for research) in 1956. To avoid confusion, Berlin changed the name of the original helicopter company to Vertol.

Seeing a great market in military helicopters, Vertol used its own funds to develop the new tandem-rotor Model 107. This model had a rear ramp and armor and used the dynamic components of the H-21. Needing capital to produce the 107, Vertol merged with Boeing in 1960 to form Boeing Vertol. Insisting on reliability, redundant systems, and safety, Boeing engineers also designed an efficient production line. The Model 107 became the Navy's CH-46 Sea Knight, produced from 1964 to 1971 largely for Marine troop transport.

The Army liked the CH-46 design but desired a larger helicopter. The result was the Model 114 (very similar to the CH-46), which became the CH-47 Chinook medium-lift helicopter. The Chinook was first used in Vietnam in 1965, and it made possible the Army's practice of large-scale air assaults. A very successful helicopter, the CH-47 was modernized in the 1980s, and variants continued in production in the 1990s.

Failing in the 1970s to win design competitions for the Army's UH-1 Huey follow-on or the Navy's LAMPS helicopter, Boeing Vertol changed its name in 1988 to Boeing Helicopter Company. It has focused on composite materials production for the aircraft industry and played a role in the development of the V-22 Osprey tilt-rotor and the Comanche helicopter.

John L. Bell

See also

Piasecki Helicopters

References

Polmar, Norman, and Floyd D. Kennedy Jr. *Military Helicopters of the World.* Annapolis, MD: Naval Institute Press, 1981.

Pilatus

Aircraft company established in 1939 in Stans, Luzern, Switzerland; represented an attempt to further develop the Swiss aircraft industry to manufacture training aircraft and supply the military. World War II slowed down any hope the company had of swift production, yet by 1944 the model SB-2, a high-wing single-engine transport, was completed, although it did not sell well. The P2, a two-seat cantilever low-wing trainer, flew successfully in 1945, at which point Pilatus was able to convince the Swiss air force of the machine's value. Following modifications, the Swiss air force took delivery of 26 P2-05s (built in part with spares from Swiss Bf 109s). In 1947, a second series of 26 machines, the P2-06, was built for use as armed trainers by the Swiss air force and served until 1981.

Though the P2 rendered great service, its capacities as a trainer could not fully prepare student pilots for the transition to jets. In response to a Swiss air force call for proposals, Pilatus went back to the drawing board, and a team came up with the P3. Although there were serious flat-spin problems that required installation of a central keel, some 73 P3s served with the Swiss air force; the Brazilian navy also ordered several machines.

The PC-6 Porter and its Turboporter variant are arguably the most successful aircraft Pilatus has produced in its own factory. First flown in 1959,the PC-6 saw service with Air America, the CIA-funded operation that operated during the Vietnam War. Still in production in 1999, more than 500 PC-6 have been built. Pilatus also produced over 320 B4 all-metal gliders in the 1970s.

Currently, Pilatus's production focuses on three products: the PC-7 Turbo Trainer, the PC-9 Advanced Turboprop Trainer, and the PC-12 single-engine transport. More than 430 PC-7s had been produced by 2001, serving with air forces as well as civilian pilot training schools. The PC-9, extrapolated from the PC-7 (later productions of both models share a modular fuselage), first flew in 1984 and is far more powerful than its predecessor, to the point where it can replace jet trainers in several capacities. Successful in several international competitions, it is also produced in the United States under license by Raytheon for fulfillment of the T-6 Texan II contract.

Finally, the PC-12's introduction in the early 1990s reflected Pilatus's goal of diversifying its production and entering the market of single-large-single engine aircraft by offering both business and cargo options. A surveillance version, the Eagle, began production in 1995.

As a means to diversify its holdings, Pilatus in 1978 purchased the British firm Britten-Norman, producer of the highly successful Islander twin-engine transport. Twenty years later, however, it sold the firm. It did, however, establish subsidiaries in the United States and Australia. As for Pilatus, the company has remained in Swiss hands but changed owners several times, from the Oerlikon-Buehrle industrial concern, then to Unaxis Holdings, and as of 2001 to a group of Swiss investors.

Guillaume de Syon

See also

Swiss Air Force; Swiss Aircraft Industry

References

Gunti, Peter. "A Far from Lame Duck: Pilatus P-3, Sire to a Training Dynasty." *Air Enthusiast* 60 (November-December 1995): 29–34.

Urech, Jakob. *The Aircraft of the Swiss Air Force Since 1914.* Stäfa, Switzerland: Gut, 1975.

Wyler, Ernst. *Chronik der schweizer Militäraviatik* (Chronicle of Swiss Military Aircraft). Frauenfeld, Switzerland: Huber, 1990.

Piper Aircraft

U.S.-based light-aircraft manufacturer. William T. "Bill" Piper founded the Piper Aircraft Corporation in 1936, taking over the assets of the defunct Taylor Aircraft Company. The Piper Cub was Walter Jamouneau's development of R. G. Taylor's original design and was marketed with far more success, coming to dominate the light aircraft field. More than 14,000 Cubs were produced; some 5,700 saw military service as trainer and liaison aircraft.

After the war, Piper developed the basic Cub into more sophisticated variants, including the Super Cub, and then launched a long series of modern aircraft that gained widespread acceptance. These included single-engine all-metal light planes such as the Comanche and Cherokee and twin-engine aircraft such as the Apache, Aztec, Twin Comanche, and Navajo. Piper also built agricultural aircraft, such as the Pawnee and Pawnee Brave. Piper aircraft were license-built in Argentina, Brazil, and Poland.

During the early 1980s, the upsurge in product liability litigation, which hampered the activity of all light-plane manufacturers, coincided with a series of changes in Piper ownership, resulting in the shutdown of production after building more than 100,000 Piper aircraft. In 1995, the New Piper Aircraft Company was formed with the intent to revive the Piper name with a line of new aircraft, including the very advanced Malibu Mirage and Malibu Meridian.

Walter J. Boyne

References

Gunston, Bill. *World Encyclopedia of Aircraft Manufacturers.* Sparkford, UK: Patrick Stephens, 1993.

Platz, Reinhold (1886–1986)

Fokker's chief welder and production manager. At the start of World War I, Martin Kreutzer was chief designer for Fokker. Kreutzer was responsible for the successful Eindecker series and the lackluster early biplanes that followed it. Following Kreutzer's death, Fokker designs had a new look. Years later A. R. Weyl, in his 1965 book *Fokker: The Creative Years,* led the world to believe that the real talent behind the later Fokker successes—the triplane, D.VII, and D.VII fighters—was Reinhold Platz. Evidence of the trust Fokker placed in Platz was seen in his being left in charge of the German operation when Fokker returned to Holland following the war.

More recent research by aviation historian Peter Grosz has established, however, that Platz's role was limited to the initiation of engineering shortcuts intended to speed up the production process, perhaps the design of small parts, and his primary interest—welding.

The value of these skills should not be diminished, considering the need for ease and reliable rapid-production techniques in the German wartime aircraft industry, but they did not make Platz a designer. Unfortunately, the identity of the team responsible for the triplane, the D.VII, and the D.VIII remains unknown.

James Streckfuss

See also

Fokker Aircraft (Early Years)

References

Grosz, Peter: "Reinhold Platz and the Fokker Company." *Over the Front* 5, 3 (1990): 213–222.

Weyl, Alfred R. *Fokker: The Creative Years.* London: Putnam, 1965.

Ploesti Oil Refineries

Eight massive oil refineries surrounding Ploesti, Romania, that were bombed and destroyed by the Allies during World War II. The refineries supplied more than a third of the fuel needs for the Luftwaffe and Panzer corps. The first raids on Ploesti's refineries in 1941 and 1942 by Soviet and U.S. bombers were unsuccessful. After the raids, Ploesti, once an easy target, was strengthened with flak batteries, barrage balloons, and heavy fighter defenses.

On 1 August 1943, a new series of raids took place with 177 bombers launched. Crossing the Albanian coast, they ran into a large formation of cumulus clouds that split the bomb groups. When they dropped to 500 feet for their final run, German radar lost them. However, the lead element's navigator misidentified the second of three checkpoints, and other units right behind turned toward Bucharest. The trailing planes saw the error and called a warning to no avail.

Lieutenant Colonel Addison Baker, commander of the 93d Bomb Group, and copilot Major John Jersted saw Ploesti and decided on their own authority to attack. Coming in from a different direction, their new flight path brought them over the heaviest flak corridor. Fifty-two fighters attacked the bombers as they began their bombing runs. Baker's plane was hit but continued, dropped its bombs, and crashed. The two pilots received the Medal of Honor. The group reformed and found that only 15 of the original 39 planes were in the air; they had destroyed 40 percent of the plant's capacity. The most successful attack came when Lieutenant Colonel James Posey and 21 B-24s totally destroyed the Creditul Minier refinery, losing two planes.

The survivors were attacked while departing the area. Some detoured to RAF bases on Cyprus or bases in Turkey. Some ditched and were rescued. Of the 92 planes that returned, four crash-landed. Of the remaining 88, only 33 were still fit to fly. Altogether, 446 airmen were killed or captured and 106 were wounded.

Bombing reduced refinery production to 42 percent. The high loss rate meant that a follow-up mission was not practical. Although the targets were severely damaged, the plants were soon operating at premission capacity.

In the summer of 1944, B-24s, B-17s, and RAF Lancasters, now based in Italy, returned to Ploesti. After 19 missions, production capacity was cut by 80 percent. The USAAF lost 286 bombers and 2,829 crewmembers, the RAF 38 bombers and 200 crewmembers.

William Head

References

Hill, Michael. *Black Sunday: Ploesti!* Westchester, PA: Schiffer, 1994.

Wolff, Leon. *Low Level Mission.* "Introduction," by John R. Kane. Rpt. Alexandria, VA: Time Life Books, 1991.

POINTBLANK (1942–1945)

Allied code name for the Combined Bomber Offensive against Germany. U.S. and British air doctrine prior to the war had called for such an offensive, directed at the industrial potential of an enemy nation. This doctrine, formulated at the Air Corps Tactical School and the RAF Staff College, posited that a large long-range bomber force could disrupt and destroy an enemy's warmaking potential using high altitude daylight precision formation tactics.

POINTBLANK was ordered by the Combined Chiefs of Staff on 10 June 1943, and its top priority was the destruction of the German aviation industry so as to achieve air superiority over the continent. Simultaneously, the bombers were to strike key industries such as oil, chemicals, and ball bearings.

It was quickly realized, however, that fighter escort was necessary to protect the bombers on deep strikes into Germany. RAF Bomber Command moved to night operations. For the United States, this realization became painfully obvious in fall 1943 when unescorted U.S. bombers suffered heavy losses on missions against Schweinfurt and Regensburg.

Long-range escort fighters—the P-47 Thunderbolt and P-51 Mustang—soon arrived in theater and made their presence felt. During Operation ARGUMENT in February 1944—unofficially known as BIG WEEK—Allied bombers struck aircraft and engine factories while escort fighters severely mauled German air defenders. Air superiority was finally achieved and then maintained for the remainder of the war. The bomber offensive in turn grew in size and power and by early 1945 had destroyed much of Germany's industrial potential.

Phillip S. Meilinger

See also

Air Superiority; ARGUMENT; AWPD/1 and AWPD-42; Casablanca Conference; Combined Bomber Offensive; Doolittle, James H.; Eaker, Ira C.; Schweinfurt-Regensburg Raids

References

Craven, Wesley F., and James L. Cate, eds. *The Army Air Forces in World War II*. 7 vols. Chicago: University of Chicago Press, 1948–1958.

Hansell, Haywood S. Jr. *The Air Plan That Defeated Hitler*. Atlanta: Higgins-McArthur, 1972.

Pokryshkin, Aleksandr (1913–1985)

Russian fighter ace during World War II. Aleksandr Ivanovich Pokryshkin was born on 6 March 1913 in Novosibirsk. He joined the military in 1932 and served as a mechanic until graduating from flight school in 1939. In June 1941, he was a senior lieutenant assigned to the 55 IAP (later 16 GIAP). By the end of the war he was a colonel commanding the 9th Guards Fighter Division. He flew the P-39 Airacobra over the northern Caucasus, Kuban, and Berlin. He flew more than 650 missions, engaged in 156 air combats, was shot down four times, and scored 59 individual victories to become the second-ranking Allied ace after Ivan Kozhedub. In addition, Pokryshkin claimed a further 13 victories that could not be confirmed because he scored them during missions in the German rear.

Pokryshkin was also a tactical innovator and teacher. He was one of the earliest Soviet pilots to switch from the three- to the four-aircraft formation and taught the formula *height-speed-maneuver-fire*. In 1943, he introduced the Kuban Ladder formation of fighters in stepped echelon, still used successfully by the Vietnamese three decades later, and he pioneered aggressive free-hunt missions. He received his first Hero of the Soviet Union on 24 May 1943 and his second five months later; on 18 August 1944 he became the first person to be awarded a third. After the war he held a number of responsible positions and was promoted to marshal in 1972, retiring in 1981. Pokryshkin died on 13 November 1985.

George M. Mellinger

See also

Kuban Air Battles

References

Hardesty, Von. *Red Phoenix: The Rise of Soviet Air Power, 1941–1945*. Washington, DC: Smithsonian Institution Press, 1982.

Seidl, Hans D. *Stalin's Eagles: An Illustrated Study of the Soviet Aces of World War II and Korea*. Atglen, PA: Schiffer, 1998.

Poland, Aircraft Development and Production

Until 1927, the Polish air force was equipped entirely with aircraft designed in other nations and, for the most part, built elsewhere. However, two Polish factories, Samolot in Poznan and Podlaska Wytwornia Samolotow (PWS) in Biala Podalska, constructed aircraft from designs of other nations. These included Hanriot H.D. 14 trainers, as well as Potez 15A2 and 27A2 reconnaissance planes. French engineers were on hand to supervise the work and train personnel. These were built in fairly large numbers, with about 750 being constructed between 1924 and 1926.

The first indigenous combat aircraft to be designed and built in Poland was the Zalewski WZX, a conventional biplane that clearly showed its French heritage and first flew in August 1926. PWS produced a large number of designs, including trainers, transports, and fighters and was a major factor until about 1934, when it began building licensed designs and slowly faded from the scene.

At about this time, the Polish air force was reorganized and the concept of combat brigades was introduced, a system not unlike the modern USAF Air Expeditionary Force. The combat brigades were to have fighter and bomber regiments and report directly to the commander in chief of the Polish armed forces. By 1926, Poland's large and well-equipped air force was second only to France in Europe.

By 1927, another aircraft manufacturer, Lublin, was contributing new designs, and another, Bartel, began manufacturing the M.4a primary and M.5a intermediate trainers. Poland also began its own aircraft engine industry with the establishment in 1927 of the Polish Skoda Works, where both the Lorraine Dietrich and Jupiter radial engines were manufactured.

It was also in 1927 that a new organization came into place—PZL (Panstwowe Zaklady Lotnicze, or National Aviation Establishments). PZL was to specialize in metal aircraft construction and soon began producing some of the most exciting aircraft of the time.

In 1928, Zygmunt Pulawski laid down the basic outline of the P-1, an all-metal fighter. Pulawski was a graduate of the Warsaw Technical University and a first-rate engineer. It was not until 1931, however, that the first of his Jupiter-powered P.7a monoplane fighters entered production. By 1933, Poland was the first country in the world to be armed entirely with all-metal monoplanes. The P.7 was immensely popular with its pilots and received attention all around the world; it replaced the PWS 10 in service.

The P.7 was developed successively into the P.11 and then an export version, the P.24. These PZL fighters were comparable to any in the world at the time of their introduction but were still in service when the Germans attacked in 1939. PZL also built a light bomber, the P.23 Karas, and a twin-engine bomber, the P.37A Los. It also had other, more advanced designs in work when the war began.

Tragically for Poland, its air force was now obsolete and unable to cope with the invaders. Many members of the Polish air force escaped to France and England, where they distinguished themselves with skill and bravery.

After the war Poland became a Soviet satellite and its air force was equipped with Soviet aircraft. In time, however, indigenous Polish designs began to emerge, including the LWD Junak, a primary trainer. Polish factories were reconstituted to build Soviet designs, including the MiG-15 fighter (as the LiM-2). The largest plant was WSK-Mielec, which has produced almost 20,000 aircraft since 1948, the great majority of them Antonov An-2 biplanes. The WSK-Swidnik plant concentrated its efforts on building helicopters of Soviet design.

PZL returned to active manufacturing in 1955 and produced a series of influential aircraft, particularly in the agricultural field. It also built the first Polish jet, the TS-11 Iskra trainer, powered by an indigenous 2,200-pound/thrust SO-1 turbojet engine and first flown in February 1960.

The Polish aviation industry has survived World War II and 46 years as a Soviet satellite; it is well positioned to meet the challenges of the future.

Walter J. Boyne

See also
PZL Aircraft

References

Cynk, Jerzy B. *History of the Polish Air Force, 1918–1968.* Reading, UK: Osprey, 1972.

Donald, David, gen. ed. *The Complete Encyclopedia of World Aircraft.* New York, Barnes and Noble, 1997.

Gunston, Bill. *World Encyclopedia of Aircraft Manufacturers.* Sparkford, UK: Patrick Stephens, 1993.

Polikarpov, Nikolai N. (1892–1944)

Leading Russian aircraft designer during the 1920s and 1930s. Nikolai Nikolaevich Polikarpov was born on 8 March 1892 and worked as a junior designer before the revolution. After the Russian civil war, his first major task was the manufacture of the R-1 biplane, a copy of the de Havilland D.H. 9. This was the first mass-produced aircraft in the Soviet Union, about 3,000 of which were produced from 1920 to 1932. The R-1 was also the first Soviet aircraft exported to the Third World, several examples going to Persia and Afghanistan during the 1920s. Polikarpov became one of two leading designers in the Soviet Union, specializing in production of single-engine aircraft; Tupolev concentrated on large airplanes. In 1929, he was arrested on trumped-up charges and while confined in a special prison designed the I-5 fighter. In 1933, Polikarpov was released and made director of his own design bureau. He gained Stalin's patronage and continued to work until dying at his desk on 30 July 1944. In addition to the R-1, five of his designs became famous during the 1930s.

The U-2 (Uchebnyi trainer) was a biplane trainer capable of about 90 mph, redesignated Po-2 in honor Polikarpov after his death. It was so successful that more than 33,000 had been built in 59 different versions when production ceased in 1952. During the desperate days after the German invasion of World War II, it was used as an emergency night-bomber but proved so successful that it remained in service in large numbers throughout the war, equipping more than 100 regiments, the most famous of which was the women's 46 GvNBAP (Guards Night Bomber Aviation Regiment). It was again used in this role during the Korean War.

Almost as successful was the R-5 single-engine biplane bomber-reconnaissance aircraft, which entered production in 1930. By 1937, when production ceased, 6,727 had been built, including civilian versions and other variants heavily modified as armored ground attack and torpedo aircraft. It saw significant use as a day-bomber in Spain and China and was again used as a light bomber after 1941 until replaced by the even older and slower U-2.

The I-15 biplane fighter was designed with a gull wing, and several hundred were produced from 1934 to 1936 before Polikarpov reverted to a conventional straight wing for the I-15 *bis* (also I-152) version, produced in 2,408 copies from 1937 to 1939. About 155 I-15s were sent to Republican Spain, which also produced some local examples, together with a few of the later I-15 *bis*. In Spain the I-15 was called the "Chato" (Flat-nose) by the Republicans and "Curtiss" by the Nationalists, who incorrectly believed the design must have been copied by Soviet engineers incapable of such work themselves. About 270 I-15 *bis* were sent to China during the late 1930s. They were badly mauled over Khalkin Gol and Finland, and by 1941 they were of use for little more than ground attack; the few survivors were retired from service. The I-153 was essentially a derivative of the basic family, reverting to the original gull wing but adding the innovation of retractable landing gear. It entered service in 1939 and, contrary to some claims, never flew over Spain. It first saw action over Khalkin Gol. It was modestly successful at first, chiefly due to surprise, but as soon as the Japanese learned to recognize it they proved that the concept was outdated, a lesson taught again by the Finns and then the Germans. Still, 3,437 examples were produced, and it remained in service until 1943.

The I-16 entered service in 1934 alongside the I-15 and remained in service until 1942, with 10,292 produced. Its appearance in Spain (217 sent) surprised everyone, and it was the most effective fighter until the Bf 109B arrived. It was called the "Mosca" (Fly) by the Republicans and the "Boeing" or the "Rata" (Rat) by the Nationalists. It appeared in large numbers over China, then fought over Khalkin Gol and Finland. At the time of the German invasion, it provided more than half the Soviet fighter strength, and most Soviet aces flew it at some time in their careers. It remained in service on secondary fronts until 1944.

George M. Mellinger

See also

Khalkin Gol Air Battles; Night Witches; Soviet Volunteer Pilots

References

Gordon, Yefim, and Dmitrii Khazanov. *Soviet Combat Aircraft of the Second World War.* Vols. 1 and 2. Leicester, UK: Midland Counties, 1988 and 1999.

Gunston, Bill. *The Encyclopedia of Russian Aircraft, 1875–1995.* Osceola, WI: Motorbooks International, 1995.

Polish Air Force

During World War I, many Poles were drafted into Russian, Austrian, and German aviation units. The conclusion of World War I marked the beginning of many independent air forces around the world, including Poland. Poland's air force was created from the Polish army under General Józef Haller. In 1916, the German and Austro-Hungarian governments granted a constitution similar to the duchy of Warsaw to the territory of Poland under their control. Because of this constitution, Poles fought against Russia until the Russian Revolution when, on 3 March 1917, Polish leader Józef Pilsudski formed several legions of his own and fought to recover Polish provinces in foreign hands. Despite being thrown into prison for refusing to order his troops to fight with the Germans, Pilsudski and his troops prevailed after the Brest-Litovsk Treaty, when Austrian/German domination collapsed and Russia renounced their hold on the Polish territories. The Riga Treaty ended warfare on 18 March 1921.

The Polish army corps had an aviation squadron in 1917 filled with pilots who had trained and served in the Russian, German, and Austrian air forces. The squadron was part of General Jozef Haller's XI Corps. Two of these pilots were the first Poles to obtain a license. General Haller also sent pilots for training in Dijon, France, in the summer of 1918. By 23 March 1919, there were 88 Polish pilots, three observers, two technical officers, and 110 airframe and engine mechanics. They had acquired a total of 60 aircraft by this time. (Poland's first aircraft factory and school had been founded in Warsaw in 1910 and a year later had produced 12 airplanes, but whether the factory and school were still functioning by the end of World War I is not known.) Six months later, on 29 September 1919, General Haller inaugurated Poland's separate air force. With this force, Poland fought against Russia.

After World War II, many Poles fled the now communist-occupied territory. The former Polish flying units were assembled into Soviet units. In 1956, all Soviet personnel were removed and the new Air Defense Force, a missile-based independent air arm, was created. By 1990, these two forces merged into a single force: the Polska Wojska Lotnicze I Obrony Powietrznej (Polish Air Force and Air Defense Force).

In 1999, a decade after the fall of the Soviet Union, Poland became a member of NATO. It still flies equipment derived from Soviet and Russian sources.

Wendy Coble

References

Cynk, Jerzy B. *Polish Aircraft.* London: Putnam, 1971.

Glass, Andrze. *Polish Wings.* Trans. Emma Harris. Warsaw: Interpress, 1985.

Polish Auxiliary Women's Air Force Service (1943–1945) and [British] Air Transport Auxiliary (1941–1945)

The Pomonicza Lotnicza S-UBA Kobiet (PLSK; the Auxiliary Women's Air Force Service), founded by order of the minister of defense of the Polish government-in-exile on the model of British Women's Auxiliary Air Force to replace Polish servicemen in support roles on Polish air bases in the United Kingdom.

Initially, 36 women candidates were sent in May 1943 for basic training to Falkirk, Scotland. The group qualified as instructors, of whom 12 became officers and were awarded both Polish and British ranks in October 1943. General recruitment to PLSK began in November 1943, including Polish women from Canada, the United States, France, Argentina, Switzerland, China, and Japan. Many volunteers came from Polish units evacuated from the Soviet Union to the Middle East.

Serving in 26 units of the Polish air force, personnel were trained in 45 specialties. One Polish source estimates the total strength of PLSK at 1,436, constituting 10 percent of Polish air force strength in the West and including 52 officers and 110 NCOs (an earlier source cites a total of 1,653, including 52 officers and 163 NCOs).

In addition, three Polish women served with the British Air Transport Auxiliary (ATA): Anna Leska-Daab, Jadwiga Pilsudzka, and Barbara Vojtulanis. RAF Flight Lieutenant Leska-Daab was the sole woman flying with ATA (1941–1945) to receive the Royal Medal. She became flight leader in the spring of 1943 and was placed in charge of eight women ferry pilots—five British and one each from the United States, Chile, and Argentina. Stationed at Hatfield and Hamble, she ferried 93 types of aircraft and amphibia and logged 1,241 hours in the air.

Kazimiera J. Cottam

See also

Lewandowska, Janina; Sosnowska-Karpik, Irena

References

Leska-Daab, Anna. "Leska-Daab's War Reminiscences" (in Polish). *Skrzydlata Polska,* no. 20 (18 May 1980): 14.

Malinowski, Tadeusz. "From Aircraft to Aircraft" (in Polish). *Skrzydlata Polska,* no. 10 (8 March 1981): 3,5.

Portal, Charles (1893–1971)

RAF air chief marshal, British military leader during World War II, one of the main architects of the Allied victory in the air war in Europe. He was a devoted champion of Anglo-American strategic interdependence and cooperation. Charles "Peter" Portal was born on 21 May 1893 at Eddington House near Hungerford. He was educated in Winchester and Christ Church, Oxford.

During World War I, Portal served in the Royal Engineers and Royal Flying Corps (since 1915). He participated in more than 900 operational sorties and finished the war with military decorations as lieutenant colonel.

Portal's distinguished career in the RAF since its creation in 1919 won him numerous decorations and honors as well as promotion to all ranks, as high as acting air chief marshal (1940), and Marshal of the RAF (1944). During the interwar period, he spent some years training and took staff positions at the RAF Cadet College and Imperial Defense College. Portal commanded a bomber squadron (1927–1939) and British forces in Aden (1934–1935), where he succeeded in air-policing of hostile tribes.

In 1931–1933 and 1937–1939, Portal took various positions at the Air Ministry, handling RAF organization, expansion, and improvement of its combat effectiveness.

As a head of Bomber Command (1940) and Chief of Air Staff (1940–1945), Portal revolutionized RAF technology, strategy, and tactics including area- and night-bombing of Germany. He also presided over the spectacular RAF victory in the Battle of Britain, as well as the course of war in Europe.

Charles Portal coordinated the Combined Bomber Offensive against Germany with dramatic success, although his compromise with the U.S.-promoted precision air strikes on German targets brought him into conflict with Arthur Harris, who strongly favored sustained area-bombing. Widely admired for his tremendous cooperation skills, Portal also contributed greatly to common strategic decisions at the Allied conferences in Casablanca, Washington, and Quebec.

Portal retried from the RAF in 1945 and took a number of civilian positions, including chairman of British Aircraft Corporation (1960–1968). Portal, First Viscount of Hungerford, died of cancer at West Ashing House on 22 April 1971.

Peter Rainow

See also

Britain, Battle of; Casablanca Conference; Combined Bomber Offensive; Radar; Royal Flying Corps/Royal Naval Air Service/Royal Air Force; Ruhr Bombing Campaign; Strategic Bombing; World War I Aviation; World War II Aviation

References

Andrews, Allen. *The Air Marshals: The Air War in Western Europe,* New York: William Morrow, 1970.

Boyne, Walter J. *Clash of Wings: Air Power in World War II.* New York: Simon and Shuster, 1994.

Richards, Dennis. *Portal of Hungerford: The life of Marshal of the Royal Air Force, Viscont Portal of Hugerford, KG, GCB, OM, DSO, MC.* London: Heinemann, 1977.

Porte, John C. (1884–1919)

British pilot; helped develop the early flying boats. Born on 26 February 1884 in Bandon, County Cork, Ireland, Porte entered service with the HMS *Britannia* in 1898 and, after initial training, joined the submarine service, receiving his first command in 1908. In 1911, Commander Porte was diagnosed with pulmonary tuberculosis and invalided out of the Royal Navy.

Porte became interested in aviation in 1910. After retiring, he obtained his pilot's license. He became technical director and test pilot for the newly formed British Deperdussin Company and also won acclaim in racing and display flying. After the company, failed he worked for the White and Thompson Company as a test pilot.

In April 1914, Porte joined Curtiss as a pilot. He helped redesign *America,* the Curtiss flying boat designed to win the *Daily Mail*'s £10,000 prize for the first transatlantic flight. When war came in August, he offered his services, despite his tuberculosis, and took command of the Royal Naval Air Service training school at Hendon. He also brought *America* to Captain Murray Sueter's attention, leading to substantial British Admiralty orders for the type.

Porte became commander of Felixstowe Naval Air Station in 1915. He conducted many experiments with the early Curtiss boats to improve their performance. He successfully combined engineering design with combat flying, giving him instant operational feedback. His development work generated later larger Curtiss products and the famous Felixstowe type that was the ancestor of most flying boats developed in Britain, Japan, and the United States.

Porte died in 1919 from his tuberculosis.

Paul E. Fontenoy

See also

Flying Boats; Royal Flying Corps/Royal Naval Air Service/Royal Air Force; Sueter, Murray

References

Goodall, Michael H. *The Norman Thompson File.* Tunbridge Wells, UK: Air-Britain (Historians), 1995.

King, Brad. *Royal Naval Air Service, 1912–1918.* Aldershot, UK: Hikoki, 1997.

Roskill, Stephen W. *Documents Relating to the Royal Naval Air Service, Volume 1: 1908–1918.* London: Navy Records Society, 1989.

Snowden Gamble, H. F. *The Story of a North Sea Air Station.* London: Neville Spearman, 1967.

Potez 25

French single-seat aircraft of high performance. Few visitors to the ninth Paris Air Show in 1924 paid any heed to the single-engine biplane Potez 25 A2 on display, preferring instead to focus on the Breguet 19, which had earned several endurance records. Yet the Potez, although smaller, had already surpassed the Breguet.

Built of wood and metal, this two-seater could be powered by any number of 400–500-hp engines. Tough and easy to maintain, the aircraft was ideal to undertake a variety of civilian and military tasks. Sponsoring a series of advertising long-distance flights, the Potez firm eventually received orders from some 15 air forces, including a total of over 2,400 machines for the French air force, delivered from 1926 to 1934. The machine was manufactured in four French factories, and production licenses were also granted to Poland, Portugal, Romania, and Yugoslavia.

The versatility of the aircraft led to multiple records, including the 1926 distance record of 4,305 kilometers. Its altitude capacity (the only single-engine aircraft of its kind to be able to reach over 21,000 feet) prompted the French airline Aéropostale to purchase several for its Andes postal link. Overall, some 3,500 machines in 87 different variants were built. Although technically obsolete by the 1930s, some saw service in the Spanish civil war. The longest-serving aircraft were stationed in French Indochina until 1945.

Guillaume de Syon

See also

Potez Aircraft

References

Cortet, Pierre. *Le Potez 25.* Series Histoire de l'aviation #1. Boulognes-sur-Mer: LELA Presse, 1996.

Potez 63

In October 1934, the French air force issued a requirement for a three-seat aircraft for use as a command, reconnaissance, and interception fighter that would be equipped with two 20mm cannons. Potez's entry, Model 63 #1, first flew on 25 April 1936. Built entirely of light alloys, its performance prompted the air force to give the go-ahead for a series of 10 prototypes intended to help define further the operational envelope and purpose of the plane. Several of these became two-seaters, including the prototype versions of ground attack, bombing, and night-fighter versions. Total production of the 63 reached 1,684, including construction of the Model 630, of which 84 were built, and the Model 631.

The Potez 631 constitutes the first dedicated night-fighter, which was used according to interception protocols adopted in 1934 and still in effect at the beginning of World War II. During the so-called Phony War that lasted through May 1940, Potez 631 crews underwent nighttime training.

Intending to match the Messerschmitt Bf 110, these aircraft nonetheless lacked sufficient engine power and armament. Several documented instances note that instead of two 20mm cannons, some aircraft only had one, while the second was replaced with a 7. mm machine gun. With the beginning of the German offensive, the Potez-equipped squadrons took off nightly to intercept German bombers. The first confirmed victory for the night-fighters came on 18 May, when a 631 downed a Heinkel He 111 bomber. Overall results of such sorties were disappointing, however, as the 631 showed its weakness in a lack of proper protection and insufficient armament. In addition, night-fighting operations lacked proper infrastructure and training for non-Potez crews. Consequently, both French antiaircraft defenses and non-Potez crews were prone to mistake the 631 for Messerschmitt Me 110s, thus leading to death by friendly fire. This prompted a change in the decoration of the planes to include a long white stripe on each side of the fuselage.

Meanwhile, under the conditions of the massive German attack into French territory, the 631-equipped squadrons were turned into daytime-fighters, and the planes received a further two machine guns under each wing. This, however, affected overall performance, which was already suffering from limited engine performance, and many planes were lost. By the time the armistice went into effect on 25 June 1940, some 400 Potez 63s had been destroyed. After the cease-fire, several squadrons were incorporated into the Vichy air force, but by 1943 these squadrons had switched to other aircraft.

Guillaume de Syon

See also

Potez Aircraft; Vichy French Air Force

References

Facon, Patrick, *L'armée de l'air dans la tourmente.* Paris: Economica, 1997.

Potez Aircraft

French aircraft manufacturer. Born in 1891, Henri Potez graduated in 1911 from the French aeronautical engineering school. During World War I, Potez worked with Marcel Bloch (later Dassault) on standardizing production of the Caudron G.3 and on the design of a new propeller. Together, along with engineer Louis Corroler, they then founded SEA, an aeronautical design company that obtained a contract for the development and production of a trainer. The end of World War I blocked further development, but Potez offered aircraft out of his own factory, founded in 1919. The Potez works produced several highly popular machines, including the Potez 25 and Potez 36.

Potez also built the notorious Model 54 (540) in 1933, a bomber that also existed as a 14-passenger civil version. It also built several civil aircraft, some of which established performance records. As of 1936, Potez controlled five aircraft factories, which were nationalized and formed the northern group of government factories. Potez agreed to preside over them. By the time World War II started, Potez's works had produced 40 prototypes and 7,000 aircraft, including some 1,300 commercial and civil machines. The most important of these was the Potez 63 twin-engine aircraft. Potez resigned from the directorship in 1940 but continued to administer the group until his arrest and brief detention by German authorities in 1942. After the war, his engine division began work immediately, but Potez did not return to aircraft design until 1952.

That year, convinced that he needed to offer an aircraft capable of ground attack to support ground troops, Potez ordered the development of the Model 75. This heavily armored single-engine pusher proved remarkably capable when it was first tested in 1953, but it failed to sell and was cancelled five years later.

In the postwar years, the Potez group was able to survive through diversification that included a series of joint productions and subcontracts. These included the acquisition in 1957 of the Air Fouga firm, which produced the highly successful CM-170 Magister jet trainer.

Henri Potez attempted to market the Potez 840 beginning in 1960. This four-engined turboprop was intended for short-haul links from regional airports. First flown in April 1961, the firm reportedly obtained an order for 120 machines from a U.S. company, Turboflight. In fact, the contract was not fulfilled, even though Henri Potez went so far as to set up a factory in Ireland to produce the machine. Consequently, only four such aircraft were built beyond the two prototypes.

One of the last Potez projects was a cooperative venture with the Heinkel firm in Germany to produce the CM-191, a four-seat VIP version of the CM-170 Magister. The project failed, and only two prototypes were built. Disappointed with the shortcomings of his last projects (the Model 75 and Model 840 in particular), Potez met with representatives of Sud-Aviation (later Aérospatiale-Toulouse) on 3 April 1967 and signed a contract that transferred the Potez holdings to the state company. Potez then spent the rest of his life in quiet retirement until his death on 9 November 1981.

Guillaume de Syon

See also

Potez 25

References

Castello, Christian. *Planeurs et avions.* Toulouse: Le Lézard, 1993.

Noetinger, Jacques. *Histoire de l'aéronautique française.* 3 vols. Paris: France-Empire, 1978.

Powers, Francis Gary (1929–1977)

U.S. reconnaissance pilot shot down while flying a CIA U-2 over the Soviet Union, Francis Powers; the incident became one of the enduring symbols of the Cold War.

Powers was born in Burdine, Kentucky, on 17 August 1929, the second of six children born to Oliver and Ida Powers. Although the Powers family was usually poor, young Francis worked hard to get an education and graduated from Milligan College in 1950. Enlisting in the Air Force that October, Gary Powers (as he was known at the time) was trained as a photo technician.

Powers was accepted as an aviation cadet in November 1951, and he received his commission and wings 13 months later. He was assigned to Turner AFB, Georgia, where he flew the Republic F-84. He was highly regarded as a pilot and considered one of the best gunners in the wing. While in the Air Force he married Barbara Gay Moore.

Powers left the Air Force for the CIA in 1956 and began training at a secret base in the Southwest, learning to fly the Lockheed U-2. He went on to fly 27 missions, including several overflights of the Soviet Union, before his last fateful flight.

On 1 May 1960, Powers took off from Peshawar, Pakistan, for a planned overflight of several high-priority targets in the Soviet Union. Near Sverdlovsk, where he was flying at 70,000 feet, Soviet air defenses scrambled interceptors and fired a salvo of 14 SA-2 missiles at the U-2. Shockwaves from a nearby missile explosion blew the tail off the aircraft, and Powers parachuted onto a collective farm, where he was immediately captured.

Charged with espionage and subjected to a show trial in Moscow, Powers was sentenced to 10 years in prison. He passed the time in jail by keeping a diary, writing home, and knitting rugs. On 10 February 1962, he was exchanged for Rudolf Abel, a KGB colonel who had been arrested and imprisoned in the United States.

Powers took a desk job with the CIA upon his return, but office work bored him and he soon accepted an offer from the Lockheed Skunk Works. There he test-flew U-2s that had returned to Lockheed for maintenance or modification.

His marriage to Barbara ended in divorce soon after his return from the Soviet Union, and he married Claudia "Sue" Downey in October 1963. The following August he adopted Claudia Dee, Sue's daughter by a previous marriage, and in June 1965 Francis Gary Powers Jr. was born.

His job with Lockheed ended in October 1969, and he eventually found work as a traffic reporter for a Los Angeles radio station. Moving on to television in 1976, he learned to fly helicopters and covered weather, fires, and police chases from a Bell Jet Ranger.

During a flight on 1 August 1977, his engine failed due to fuel exhaustion. He attempted an emergency landing, but he swerved to avoid a group of children on the ground and the helicopter crashed, killing him instantly. Francis Gary Powers was buried at Arlington Cemetery.

Mark E. Wise

See also

Lockheed U-2; Republic F-84 Thunderjet/Thunderstreak

References

Beschloss, Michael R. *Mayday: Eisenhower, Khrushchev, and the U-2 Affair.* New York: Harper and Row, 1986.

Powers, Francis Gary, with Curt Gentry. *Operation Overflight: The U-2 Spy Pilot Tells His Story for the First Time.* New York: Holt, Rinehart, and Winston, 1970.

Precision-Guided Munitions

Highly accurate aerial weapons. Precision-guided munitions (PGMs) are any of a variety of accurate firepower systems that use midcourse guidance to hit targets with single-round efficiency. Although guidance techniques vary, most PGMs fit into one of three categories. *Correlation guidance* involves the map-reading and terrain-matching capabilities typical of long-range cruise missiles. *Precision-fixing weapons* use synchronized beacons from ground stations or navigational satellites to steer to a target. And *seeker guidance,* including laser designation and electro-optical television guidance, allows a projectile to home in on natural or induced electromagnetic signatures.

Efforts to develop PGMs began as early as 1917. However, for the next 50 years attempts at precision—including the use of gyroscopic guidance in World War I and radio control in both World War II and Korea—met with very limited success, and these primitive guided weapons saw little action. During the early bombing campaign in Vietnam, in 1965, it quickly became obvious that greater bombing precision was still needed, and military authorities commissioned a variety of projects intended to make bombing more effective and less costly in terms of both lives and dollars. Incorporating newly developed technologies, including lasers and large-scale integrated circuitry, the Air Force's Paveway Task Force developed an effective class of terminal-guided munitions, using laser and electro-optical seeker technology. When tested in Southeast Asia in 1968, Paveway PGMs recorded an unprecedented circular error probability of just 20 feet, with fully one in four bombs scoring direct hits. Used extensively during the LINEBACKER air campaigns of 1972, PGMs produced unprecedented results. For example, on 13 May 1972, F-4 aircraft armed with laser-guided bombs destroyed the infamous Thanh Hoa Bridge, accomplishing in a single mission what seven years and 869 nonprecision bombing sorties had failed to achieve.

Since their full capabilities were first demonstrated in Vietnam, so-called smart weapons have worked a virtual revolution in warfare. U.S. policymakers have come to rely on PGMs, with their promise of reduced collateral damage and danger of escalation, as a humane military option applicable in a wide variety of crises. The 1991 Gulf War, with its vivid TV news coverage of precision air strikes, clearly demonstrated the benefits of single-bomb target destruction. The result has been a trend toward increased reliance upon precision weapons. Thus, whereas only 8 percent of the total bombs dropped during the Gulf War were precision-guided, fully 98 percent of those used by the U.S. military in the Balkans, DELIBERATE FORCE in 1995, and ALLIED FORCE in 1999 were PGMs. The newest generation of precision weapons intertwines seeker guidance with precision-fixing Global Positioning System satellite links to give virtually every U.S. warplane in the inventory precision capability.

The U.S. airstrikes in Afghanistan in the war against terrorism unleashed the entire menu of PGMs against a range of targets.

Paul G. Gillespie

See also

Aircraft Armament; Gulf War; Missiles, Air-to-Surface; Vietnam War

References

Keaney, Thomas A., and Eliot A. Cohen. *Revolution in Warfare?: Air Power in the Persian Gulf.* Annapolis, Md.: Naval Institute Press, 1995.

Preddy, George E., Jr. (1919–1944)

World War II fighter ace. Major George Preddy was the third-ranking U.S. fighter ace in the European Theater of Operations (ETO) and the highest-scoring U.S. ace in Europe to lose his life in action. Born in Greensboro, North Carolina, Preddy graduated from flight training in December 1941. His first assignment was with the 49th Fighter Group stationed in Australia. After flying a number of missions, he was seriously injured in a midair collision and returned to the United States to recuperate.

In December 1942, he joined the 352d Fighter Group of the Eighth Air Force, flying with the 487th Fighter Squadron, commanded by future ace John C. Meyer. Flying the Republic P-47 Thunderbolt, Preddy flew his first mission in the ETO in September 1943. Three months later, he scored his first aerial victory, a Messerschmitt Bf 109.

In April 1944, the 352d traded in its Thunderbolts for the new P-51 Mustang long-range fighter. Soon afterward, Preddy achieved his fifth confirmed victory. Within a few months, he had become one of the leading aces in the ETO. He completed his 200-hour combat tour, and then four successive 50-hour extensions, as his victory tally mounted. On 6 August 1944, flying his distinctive Mustang *Cripes A' Mighty,* Preddy shot down six Bf 109s in a single mission—the first U.S. fighter pilot to accomplish that feat.

In November 1944, after taking leave in the States, Preddy rejoined the 352d Fighter Group, but this time as commander of the 328th Fighter Squadron. On Christmas day, flying out of Asche, Belgium, Preddy downed two enemy aircraft, bringing his score to 26.83 victories. Sighting a Focke-Wulf Fw 190 trying to escape far below, Preddy dove to the deck after him. Skimming over U.S. ground troops in hot pursuit of the enemy aircraft, *Cripes A' Mighty* was mistakenly hit by friendly fire and Preddy was instantly killed in the ensuing crash.

As the leading active ace in Europe at the time of his death, it is likely that if not for this tragic error Preddy would have soon become the ETO ace of aces. Instead, he died the sixth-ranking U.S. Army Air Forces ace of World War II and the eighth-ranking U.S. fighter ace of all time. His brother William, also a Mustang pilot with the Eighth Air Force, was killed in action only a few months later. George Preddy's decorations included the Distinguished Service Cross and the Silver Star with one Oak Leaf Cluster.

Steven A. Ruffin

References

Beaman, John R. Jr. "The Unknown Ace." *American Aviation Historical Society Journal* (Winter 1969): 242.

Bright, Charles D., ed. *Historical Dictionary of the U.S. Air Force.* New York: Greenwood Press, 1992.

Scuts, Jerry. *Mustang Aces of the Eighth Air Force.* London: Osprey, 1995.

Presidential Aircraft

Famous among civilians today as Air Force One; 12 U.S. presidents have flown aboard these specially modified airplanes.

Transports

The first aircraft outfitted specifically for use by a president was a C-87A Liberator Express, an adaptation of the B-24 Liberator bomber.

The C-87A was a VIP transport version of the no-frills C-87. Designed for passenger comfort, it was fitted with 16 Pullman-type upholstered seats that could be converted into five berths. It had a maximum speed of 220 mph and a cruising speed of 188 mph. Its range was 3,300 miles with a service ceiling of 28,000 feet.

Six C-87As were built. Serial number 41-24159 was designated as the presidential aircraft, underwent additional modification, and was renamed the *Guess Where 2.* Eleanor Roosevelt used it for a trip to Central and South America (however, the president was never aboard). In 1945, the *Guess Where 2* was scraped.

Since the Douglas C-54 Skymaster had proved to be one of the world's safest and most reliable aircraft, the U.S. Army contacted Douglas for a special version for the president. The VC 54-C serial number 42-107451 provided for President Franklin Roosevelt had a cruising speed of 250 mph, a range of 3,900 miles, and a service ceiling of 22,300 feet. It carried a crew of seven and could accommodate 15 passengers. A conference room was provided with a large desk and an elevator behind the cockpit to lift the president in and out of the aircraft.

Roosevelt preferred travel by ship or train and made only one round-trip aboard *Sacred Cow,* as it was nicknamed, to attend a conference in Yalta with Churchill and Stalin. Roosevelt traveled to Malta aboard the cruiser USS *Quincy.* From there on 3 February 1945 Roosevelt flew aboard *Sacred Cow* to Saki (near Yalta). On 12 February *Sacred Cow* returned the president to the USS *Quincy* at Cairo.

President Harry Truman loved to fly and would keep the crew of *Sacred Cow* busy. Truman did not reserve *Sacred Cow* for his use only. Among those who used the aircraft were General George C. Marshall, Secretary of State James F. Byrnes, Winston Churchill, former President Herbert Hoover, China's Mme. Chiang Kai-shek, and others. At Truman's urging, General Dwight Eisenhower used *Sacred Cow* when returning from Europe to a hero's welcome.

On 26 July 1947, Truman signed the National Security Act of 1947 while aboard *Sacred Cow.* This act established the Defense Department and created the U.S. Air Force as an independent service. Later that month, *Sacred Cow* was retired as the primary presidential aircraft. On 4 December 1961, ownership was transferred to the Smithsonian Institution, and it is now on display at the Air Force Museum in Dayton, Ohio. In 1946, the Air Force purchased a Douglas DC-6 with the military designation VC-118 to replace *Sacred Cow.* The aircraft was named *Independence,* in honor of Truman's Missouri hometown.

The next presidential aircraft was a Lockheed Constellation, which Air Force officials mistakenly thought would be used by the expected winner of the presidential election, Thomas E. Dewey. Lockheed modified one of the Constellations on the production line and gave it special features suitable for a president. Air Force serial number 48-608 with the unofficial name *Dewdrop* was delivered to the embarrassed Air Force. Truman was aware of the blunder, and when the aircraft was offered he refused it. Someone had given Truman a mustache cup (Governor Dewey wore a mustache). Truman gave the cup to the Air Force and ordered that it be displayed in the cockpit of *Dewdrop. Dewdrop* never would fly as Air Force One, however, it did make several flights as backup to *Independence.*

A Boeing 707 was selected next, succeeded by a Boeing 747. Two identical 747s are used today as presidential transports. When the president is aboard either aircraft (or any Air Force aircraft), the radio call sign is "Air Force One." When the vice president travels on one, the call sign is "Air Force Two."

The "Air Force One" call sign was first used in 1959 after confusion arose between an Eastern Airlines flight and the president's aircraft. The president's aircraft could have had a serious accident, so from then on any aircraft the president was flying in became known as Air Force One.

The current Air Force One, a 231-foot-long Boeing 747-200B, was delivered in 1990 to President George H.W. Bush. It has an office for the president, a conference room that is as large as the one in the White House, a dining room, and sleeping quarters for the president and first lady. The president's bedroom has twin beds and a bathroom with a shower. Guests, senior staff, Secret Service personnel, and the news media have separate accommodations. Air Force One has leather seats, wood-grain furniture, and paneling similar to what is found in the White House. Next to the president's office is a medical room, complete with an operating table and equipment to treat medical emergencies.

Air Force One can fly 9,600 miles without refueling. It has almost as much communications equipment as is in the White House. There are 85 telephones, 57 antennas, 19 television monitors, 11 videocassette players, and several computers that communicate with computers on the ground. There are more than 230 miles of electrical wiring, more than twice the amount in a normal 747. The communications equipment permits the president to get information from satellites and communicate with submarine commanders. Air Force One has two galleys that can provide up to 100 meals at one sitting. Freezers hold enough food for a week. In an emergency, with aerial refueling, the president could live on the aircraft for seven days.

Air Force One also carries top-secret military equipment. It has electronic equipment that can jam enemy radar and other communications. The crew can release flares to lure heat-seeking missiles away from the aircraft and release "chaff" to help hide the aircraft from radar.

Helicopters

In 1957, President Eisenhower asked his military aides about using helicopters for short trips. The Air Force and

Army aides expressed concern about the safety of helicopters. The Secret Service concluded that helicopter travel was most likely as safe for travel as the traditional motorcade. The Air Force purchased two Bell UH-13J helicopters for use by the White House.

The Bell UH-13J is the military designation for the Bell 47-J Sioux. First manufactured in 1945, the Sioux carried two passengers, had a cruising speed of 90 mph, and a range of 250 miles.

On 12 July 1957, Eisenhower flew from the White House to Camp David aboard a Bell UH-13J and became the first chief executive to travel via helicopter. This started almost weekly flights to either Camp David or to Eisenhower's Gettysburg farm.

After their White House assignment, the two UH-13Js were used to transport high-ranking Department of Defense personnel. In July 1967, both were transferred to the Smithsonian Institution. The craft that Eisenhower used to make the first helicopter flight is at the Paul E. Garber facility; the other is on loan to the Air Force Museum in Dayton.

On 1 January 1958, the U.S. Army Executive Flight Detachment, Fort Belvoir, Virginia, was activated. Along with Marine Helicopter Squadron One (HMX-1), U.S. Marine Corps Air Station, Quantico, Virginia, it was given the primary mission of the emergency evacuation of the president, his family, and other key government officials as well as providing routine helicopter transportation. When the president is aboard, the helicopter's call sign is "Marine One."

In January 1958, both the Executive Flight Detachment and HMX-1 were using the Sikorsky H-34C as the primary helicopter. The H-34C was used to transport the president while Sikorsky built the first of the VH-34Ds. The "V" designation stands for "VIP" and means that an aircraft has been modified with customized interiors and other special equipment suitable for a VIP. This designation was first used during Truman's presidency and continued until President Jimmy Carter ordered the VIP designation be dropped. However, President Ronald Reagan allowed the designation to be restored.

The VH-34D is the military transport version of the Sikorsky S-58. It was designed specifically for the U.S. Navy as an antisubmarine attack helicopter. The VH-34 carried a crew of four and could transport up to 10 passengers. It had a cruising speed of 130 mph and a range of 270 miles.

In 1961, the VH-3D Sea King began to replace the VH-34D as the primary executive transport. Developed for the Navy as a carrier-based all-weather antisubmarine helicopter, with extensive interior modifications it became the favored VIP transport. In addition to the interior improvements, many protective measures were utilized. Light armor protects the crew and passengers from small-arms fire and medium-explosive projectiles. Special protection is provided for the electrical system and flight controls. Self-sealing and crash-resistant fuel tanks, along with energy-absorbing landing gear and seating, improve crash survivability.

In 1962, President John F. Kennedy requested that the VIP aircraft have distinctive markings. The aircraft were to have a green color scheme, with "United States of America" painted on both sides of the fuselage, and the American flag on both sides of the tail. The presidential seal appears on both sides of the nose.

The VH-60N is the VIP transport version of the Sikorsky UH-60 Black Hawk first developed for the Army as a troop and cargo-lift transport. The UH-60 first flew in 1974. The VIP version has energy-absorbing landing gear and seating in an effort to increase crash survivability. It has self-sealing puncture-resistant fuel tanks with an armor-protected control system and seats. Protective armor on the Black Hawk can withstand 23mm shells. The unique interior design of the passenger cabin incorporates several conveniences that help make the flight comfortable and enjoyable. Design features include a quiet interior, large windows, special communications equipment, a refreshment galley, and a restroom.

The history of presidential aircraft does not stretch as far back as the earliest days of aviation. However, Air Force One and Marine One will continue to serve important functions during times of peace and war.

Henry M. Holden

Pressurized Cabins and Cockpits

Life-support for pilots, crews, and passengers. The need for cabin pressurization arose from the increasingly high altitudes aircraft were able to attain in the years leading up to World War II. Although crewmen in high-flying unpressurized aircraft could function by breathing supplemental oxygen, wearing oxygen masks was not always practical. Moreover, at altitudes surpassing 40,000 feet, the nearly nonexistent atmospheric pressure was found to be incompatible with life, even with supplemental oxygen. The solution to both of these problems was cabin pressurization. This would allow aircraft occupants to breathe normally at any altitude in an environment similar to that near sea level.

The first attempt at cabin pressurization—ultimately unsuccessful—was in 1920 at McCook Field, Dayton, Ohio. And though the first successful design appeared in 1928 in Germany, the true predecessor of modern pressurized aircraft was the Lockheed XC-35. This modified 10E Electra won the 1938 Collier Trophy for the Army Air Corps. During World

War II, some British and German aircraft were pressurized; the first mass-produced pressurized aircraft in the United States was the Boeing B-29. Since the war, virtually all aircraft capable of high-altitude flight have been pressurized.

Steven A. Ruffin

References

Robinson, Douglas. *The Dangerous Sky: A History of Aviation Medicine.* Seattle: University of Washington Press, 1973.

van Patten, Robert. *A History of Developments in Aircrew Life Support Equipment, 1910–1994.* Bellbrook, OH: Privately printed, 1994.

Prisoners of War

Although combatants were captured and made prisoners long before the development of airpower, the advent of the airplane opened a new dimension in captivity. Aircrew POWs differ from ground or naval POWs in two respects. First, ground or naval POWs are most commonly, though not always, captured in a group, generally the same group with which they had been fighting prior to their capture. Aircrews parachuting from disabled aircraft often arrive on the ground and evade or are captured alone. This is the case even in multiplace aircraft, where aircrew members are likely to be scattered in the act of bailing out. Second, as airplanes often operate well behind the traditional front lines, troops, reserves, local police, and even armed—and often angry—civilians can capture aircrews. Their isolated nature makes aircrew POWs the most likely to be mistreated or killed, as often they are the only ones accessible to the angry populace. Such mistreatment is most likely for those who unfortunately bail out over or near their targets.

The first aircrew POWs were captured in World War I. In contrast to the mud and anonymity that characterized the front lines for ground troops, aircrews were often treated as something different—chivalric knights of the air. A captured pilot, if not injured, often enjoyed a meal in the mess of an enemy flying squadron, sometimes breaking bread with the man who shot him down before being moved to a POW camp.

In World War II, the majority of aircrew POWs went down far from the front lines and faced immediate capture in the enemy's heartland or a long and dangerous period of evasion. In contrast to World War I's chivalric code, Allied aircrews in Europe were characterized by the Nazi leadership as "terror-bombers" or "luft-gangsters." There is no way to tell how many were murdered by vengeful civilians, but accounts from POWs of being protected from such mobs by German military forces are common. Allied aircrews who fell into the hands of Nazi functionaries such as the SS or Gestapo were in for a rough time, but Hermann Goering, head of the Luftwaffe and a World War I fighter ace, clung to the notion of chivalry and did much to ensure the safety and comfort of his fellow airmen. These conditions, however, do not match those portrayed in popular movies and TV shows. Allied aircrews captured by the Japanese faced immediate execution or a life of slave labor until death or liberation. Axis aircrews who fell into Allied hands generally met humane treatment in accordance with the Geneva Convention of 1929. Soviets in German hands and Germans in Soviet hands faced barbaric treatment, no matter their service.

Following World War II, a new philosophy regarding POWs emerged. Socialist revolutionaries believed POWs were tools for furthering the revolution. They could be converted to the socialist cause or exploited for propaganda. Attempts at the former predominated in Korea, where aircrew prisoners were generally not differentiated from prisoners from other services. Attempts at the latter predominated in Vietnam, where aircrew prisoners were labeled "air pirates." The name is reminiscent of Nazi Germany, but conditions for POWs more resembled those in Japan or Korea. In the Gulf War, all Coalition POWs were mistreated, regardless of service, but the war ended relatively quickly, resulting in a short captivity.

Since World War II, search-and-rescue techniques and technology have drastically improved. The efforts of such personnel have often been able to prevent the capture of downed aircrews. These search-and-rescue efforts have taken on increasing importance, as airpower has been the first choice for military action since the Gulf War and Western political leaders have been increasingly reluctant to risk the capture and exploitation of POWs.

Grant Weller

See also

BAT 21; Combat Search and Rescue; Ejection Seats; German Air Force (Luftwaffe); Germany, and World War II Air Battles; Japan, Air Operations Against; Korean War; Powers, Francis Gary; Risner, Robinson; USS Pueblo; Vietnam War; World War I Aviation

References

Doyle, Robert C. *A Prisoner's Duty.* Annapolis, MD: Naval Institute Press, 1997.

______. *Voices from Captivity.* Lawrence: University Press of Kansas, 1994.

Durand, Arthur. *Stalag Luft III: The Secret Story.* Baton Rouge: Louisiana State University Press, 1988.

Propellers

Aeronautical propulsion technology. The propeller, used in conjunction with the reciprocating internal combustion piston engine, was the main form of aerial propulsion for the first 50 years of heavier-than-air flight.

Propellers are essentially a series of twisted airfoils, or blades, connected to a central hub that convert through helical motion the energy supplied by its power source. The blades strike the air at a certain angle (pitch) and generate thrust by creating an area of high pressure behind the propeller, which pushes the airplane forward. The continued refinement of the propeller exhibited the strong interrelationship between technology and airpower doctrine.

The development of the propeller is firmly connected to the development of airpower. When the airplane emerged as an important military weapon during World War I, fixed-pitch propellers were simple in operation, efficient for one operating regime, and gave adequate performance for aircraft that operated at low altitudes. For propellers to be efficient enough to contribute to the overall performance and military mission of the airplane, engineers needed to develop a variable-pitch propeller, which allowed the pitch at which each propeller blade rotated through the air to vary according to different flight conditions.

Military aeronautical research facilities in Europe and North America fostered this development during the war and on into the interwar period. In the United States, where the first practical variable-pitch propellers were introduced in 1932, the Army employed leading propeller engineers, built the required testing facilities, determined the engineering standards, and issued the production contracts that supported a growing U.S. industry.

By the outbreak of World War II, engineers had introduced the constant-speed propeller, which changed blade pitch automatically according to varying flight conditions while the engine speed remained the same. These propellers provided more responsive control of pitch variation. They facilitated multiengine synchronization for bombers and transports and removed the risk of fighter aircraft "overspeeding" the engine while diving. Another major feature was its ability to "feather," which positioned the blades to prevent propeller windmilling after engine failure. As a result, constant-speed propellers played a key role in the aerial campaigns of World War II.

The Allies manufactured approximately 1 million high-performance propellers for the war effort with more than 75 percent of that total being propellers designed by the Hamilton Standard Company of East Hartford, Connecticut.

The advent of jet technology during World War II meant the propeller would play a lesser role in the postwar period, but the propeller-driven airplane would remain valuable in transport, observation, and tactical operations. The combination of the variable-pitch propeller with the gas turbine resulted in the turboprop, which increased propulsive efficiency, fuel economy, and generated less noise. The highly successful turboprops Lockheed C-130 Hercules and P-3 Orion began military operations in the mid-1950s.

Jeremy R. Kinney

See also

United Aircraft Corporation; Wright-Patterson Air Force Base

References

Miller, Ronald, and David Sawers. *The Technical Development of Modern Aviation.* London: Routledge and Keegan Paul, 1968.

Rosen, George. *Thrusting Forward: A History of the Propeller.* Windsor Locks, CT: United Technologies Corporation, 1984.

Pueblo, USS

U.S. surface vessel that was attacked by North Korea in 1968. Some seven months after the Israeli attack on the USS *Liberty,* another U.S. intelligence-gathering ship came under hostile fire. On 23 January 1968, USS *Pueblo* was conducting electronic-intelligence and oceanographic operations in international waters approximately 15 miles off the coast of the Democratic Republic of Korea. North Korean naval vessels approached the *Pueblo* with intent to board her. When *Pueblo* refused, the North Korean vessels opened fire, ultimately killing one crewmember. *Pueblo* finally surrendered to the North Korean vessels and proceeded to the harbor at Wonson, where the crew was interned. As with the *Liberty,* the *Pueblo* did not benefit from the prompt protective cover of U.S. naval or aerial forces, which some critics argue was an inherent betrayal of all U.S. intelligence-gathering forces. Indeed, some extremist views hold that *Pueblo* was intentionally compromised in an elaborate U.S. scheme, although such claims are wholly unproven. Although the Korean attack was an isolated instance of aggression, U.S. policymakers feared it was a harbinger of a broader communist expansion in Asia, concurrent with the surprise Tet Offensive in Vietnam. As such, the United States quickly strengthened its military presence in Korea with the PORT BOW and COMBAT FOX deployment of Boeing B-52s and numerous tactical aircraft for potential operations (including nuclear) against North Korea and the People's Republic of China.

Robert S. Hopkins

See also

Ferrets; *Liberty,* USS

References

Brandt, Ed. *The Last Voyage of the U.S.S. Pueblo.* New York: Norton, 1969.

Bucher, Lloyd M. *My Story.* New York: Doubleday, 1970.

Liston, Robert. *The Pueblo Surrender.* New York: Evans, 1988.

The Polish air force was one of the most modern in Europe in the early 1930s, when the PZL series of fighters became operational. Unfortunately, they were still in service and obsolete when Germany attacked on 1 September 1939. (Walter J. Boyne)

PZL Aircraft (Panstwowe Zaklady Lotnicze)

Polish aircraft manufacturer; founded in 1928 as the Polish National Aircraft Establishment, it was chartered to manufacture both airframes and engines. Its airframes were PZL-designed, but most of its engines were license-built Bristol designs. Several PZL (Polish Skoda) engine designs were run, but it is not known that any were put into production.

The chief designer of PZL airframes, Zygmunt Pulawski, produced a series of fighters from 1929 to 1936 that were world-class in their early years, partly because they were high-wing monoplanes when much of the world's air forces still used biplanes. Designated P.1 through P.24—the P.1 being the first fighter of indigenous Polish design—they featured gull wings and all-metal construction. The P.24 was the first with an enclosed cockpit. Pulawski continued to refine the aerodynamics of his aircraft, but these fixed-gear fighters were not competitive with the new generation of German fighters they faced in 1939.

The P.1 first flew on 29 September 1929, the P.6 in August 1930, the P.7 in October 1930, the P.11 in August 1931, and the P.24 in May 1933. The P.24F had a 297 mph maximum speed at 13,945 feet and was the last of the series.

The differences between them were minor except that each made use of the most powerful engine then available, the largest being the Gnome-Rhone 14N 07 of 970 shp. Armament was two small-bore machine guns throughout production until the P.24, which added two 20mm cannons in the wings. The P.7 was still in service with the Polish air force when the Germans invaded in 1939. Other users were the Romanian (license-built by IAR), Albanian, Bulgarian, Greek, and Turkish air forces. Total production of the fighter series comprised approximately 500, about 200 for foreign customers.

The P.38 Wilk, a twin-engine low-wing two-place multirole fighter powered by inverted air-cooled V-8 engines of PZL manufacture, first flew in May 1938 with the Ranger

SGV-770B engine and in January 1939 with the intended PZL engines. Maximum speed was 289 mph.

PZL built several advanced prototypes, including the P.43, a single-engine low-wing all-metal three-place reconnaissance and attack fixed-gear monoplane; the P.27, a twin-engine midwing all-metal three-place bomber; and the P.44, a twin-engine low-wing all-metal 14-passenger transport with a twin-fin tail, designed to replace the DC-2 and Lockheed 10 and 14 airliners in Polish service.

Douglas G. Culy

References

Green, W., and G. Swanborough. *The Complete Book of Fighters.* London: Salamander, 1994.

Q

Quesada, Elwood R. (1904–1993)

Aviation pioneer; USAF lieutenant general. Born in Washington, D.C., in 1904, Quesada's military career spanned aviation history from post–World War I biplanes to supersonic jets.

Quesada started his military career during a period of intense experiment and development in aviation, entering the Army Air Service as a flying cadet in 1924. Having only a reserve commission, he returned to civilian life, playing baseball for the St. Louis Cardinals. In 1927, he returned to active service, reporting to Bolling AFB, where he joined Major Carl "Tooey" Spaatz and Captain Ira Eaker in developing air-to-air refueling techniques.

In the years before World War II, Quesada concentrated on the tactical application of airpower and became one of the prime developers of the concept of close air support. When the war started, he got an opportunity to put his ideas to work. In December 1942, he was promoted to brigadier general and sent to North Africa to command the XII Fighter Command. The techniques that he perfected there were incorporated into *Command and Employment of Air Power*, Army Air Forces field regulations published in July 1943.

In October 1943, Quesada went to England to assume command of IX Fighter Command in preparation for the Normandy invasion. During this period, Quesada pioneered many of the techniques that mark modern air-ground cooperation. He placed forward air observers with divisions on the ground where they could call for and control close air support. He mounted radios in tanks so ground commanders could contact pilots directly. He developed the use of radar to vector planes during attacks, which was particularly critical during the Battle of the Bulge in December 1944 when bad weather hid many German targets.

After the war, Quesada was the first commander of the Tactical Air Command. He moved the headquarters from Tampa, Florida, to Langley AFB, Virginia, so he could be close to the headquarters of the Army Ground Forces.

Lieutenant General Quesada retired from the Air Force in 1951. He served as the first head of the Federal Aviation Administration and held numerous positions in several private firms. Quesada died in Washington in 1993.

James H. Willbanks

See also

Close Air Support; Tactical Air Command

References

Hughes, Thomas Alexander. *Overlord: General Pete Quesada and the Triumph of Air Power in World War II.* New York: Free Press, 1995.

Question Mark

Pioneering aerial-refueling aircraft. *Question Mark* was not the first aircraft to be refueled in midair, as the U.S. Army Air Service first demonstrated inflight refueling as early as 1923. However, the much-publicized flight of *Question Mark*, beginning on New Year's Day 1929, demonstrated aerial refueling's tremendous military potential and galvanized interest in this new airpower role.

This Fokker C-2A trimotor monoplane took its name from the large white question marks painted on the fuselage, as well as the underlying question of how long it could remain airborne. Its crew of five included future Air Force leaders Carl Spaatz, Ira Eaker, and Elwood Quesada. After taking off from Van Nuys, California, *Question Mark* flew continuously for 150 hours and 40 minutes until a faltering engine forced it to land on 7 January. During this historic mission, 43 tanker sorties delivered 5,660 gallons of fuel, plus oil and supplies, to *Question Mark.*

Paul G. Gillespie

The flight of the Question Mark *demonstrated that aerial refueling would be important in the future, but it did not come into extensive use until well after World War II. (U.S. Air Force)*

See also

Aerial Refueling; Eaker, Ira C.; Quesada, Elwood R.; Spaatz, Carl Andrew

References

Frisbee, John L. *Makers of the United States Air Force.* Washington, DC: Office of Air Force History, 1987.

R

Rabaul

Captured on 23 January 1942, becoming the cornerstone of Japan's position in the Southwest Pacific. The action allied one of the best natural harbors in the region with a complex of four major and one minor airfields, supporting 200–300 aircraft and heavy antiaircraft defenses. After Guadalcanal fell to the Allies, Rabaul's importance increased. Allied planners, however, determined to neutralize the base through aerial bombardment.

General George C. Kenney's Fifth Air Force opened the offensive on 12 October 1943. The first attack, by 349 aircraft, was the precursor of a series of raids through 2 November that wrecked many installations, causing the Japanese to excavate replacement underground facilities. The offensive also led Admiral Koga Minechi to reinforce Rabaul with the Combined Fleet's air groups (175 aircraft), which arrived 1 November, and Vice Admiral Kurita Takeo's heavy cruiser force.

Koga's reinforcement prompted a swift reaction. Rear Admiral Frederick C. Sherman's Task Force 38 (*Saratoga* and *Princeton*) struck Rabaul on 5 November, heavily damaging four heavy and two light cruisers. Task Force 38, joined by Pacific Fleet carriers *Essex, Bunker Hill,* and *Independence,* attacked again on 11 November, damaging most remaining warships. The carriers beat back a Japanese counterattack, inflicting such losses that Koga withdrew his battered carrier air groups from Rabaul.

Air Solomons Command, almost 500 aircraft, constructed new airstrips at Torokina on Bougainville, 210 miles from Rabaul, initially supporting only fighters. Fighters swept over Rabaul on 17 December; heavier raids followed through 28 December, but the Japanese made good their losses. Allied attacks recommenced on 5 January, more effectively once Torokina accommodated bombers from 21 January. Two light and one medium or heavy bomber missions struck Rabaul almost daily, accompanied by strong fighter escorts. Fighter opposition remained strong. Reinforcements were flown in from Truk, but attrition took its toll. Few replacements arrived after 1 February, and surface vessels were barred from the area.

The tempo of Allied operations intensified in February. Close to 3,000 sorties were flown over Rabaul to 19 February, almost equaling the total between October and January. A major assault that day, with almost 200 aircraft in two waves, devastated the harbor and airfields and destroyed a quarter of the defending interceptors. Coming two days after the Pacific Fleet struck Truk, it induced the Japanese to withdraw their remaining serviceable fighters. Unescorted Allied bombers assailed Rabaul daily to 15 May, dropping 7,410 tons of bombs on the town and harbor, airfields, and supply dumps. Rabaul was neutralized, despite its garrison of 100,000 troops.

Paul E. Fontenoy

See also

Bismarck Sea, Air Battle of; Boyington, Gregory; Cactus Air Force; Kenney, George C.

References

Brown, J. David. *Carrier Operations in World War II: The Pacific Navies.* London: Ian Allan, 1974.

Craven, Wesley F., and James L. Cate, eds. *The Army Air Forces in World War II, Volume 4: The Pacific: Guadalcanal to Saipan, August 1942–July 1944.* Chicago: University of Chicago Press, 1958.

Morison, Samuel E. *Breaking the Bismarck's Barrier.* Boston: Little, Brown, 1954.

Radar and How It Works

Originally, the acronym for "radio detecting and ranging." Radar equipment was developed to a high level of performance during World War II for the detection of enemy aircraft and surface vessels. It was of crucial importance during the Battle of Britain and, subsequently, in the Combined Bomber Offensive against Germany. The Allies generally were able to stay ahead of the Axis nations, particularly in the Pacific, where United States radar equipment completely surpassed that of the Japanese.

Immediately after the war, radar became widely used in commercial applications, including monitoring weather and controlling air traffic. Early radar systems were heavy and cumbersome and included many separate units. Today, radar units use solid-state devices and microelectronics in compact systems.

Radar systems operate on the echo principle: High-energy radio waves in pulse form are directed in a beam toward a reflecting target. The beam of pulses is like a stream of bullets from a machine gun, with a relatively long space between each pulse of energy. When a pulse of energy strikes a target, which may be a mountain, rain clouds, or an airplane, a portion of the pulse is reflected back to the receiving section of the radar system. A portion of the pulse is reflected and returns toward the airplane. When the reflected pulse reaches the airplane, a second, smaller "pip" appears on the radar screen. The time between the two pips indicates the distance from the airplane to the target. The time between the two pips is shown as microseconds, which represents distance. A typical radar signal may consist of a carrier wave of 8,000 megahertz (MHz) broken into pulses with a duration of 1 microsecond and spaced at intervals of 1/400 second or 2,500 microseconds. This yields a ratio of roughly 2,500:1 for the time of no signal to the time of signal. The ratio of the length of a pulse to the time of no signal varies considerably with the frequency, which ranges from 1,000 to 26,500 MHz.

The length of the pulses of a radar signal may vary from 0.25 to 50 microseconds, depending on the requirements of the system. The pulse repetition frequency also varies according to the distance over which the signals must travel. For very long distances, the pulse rate must be slow enough so that the return signal will be received before another pulse is transmitted. If this were not accomplished, it would be difficult to tell whether the pulse shown on the viewing screen (CRT) was the one transmitted or the one received. The use of the pulse system in radar makes it possible to transmit very powerful pulses. In effect, all the power is concentrated in the very short bursts. If the average power output of a transmitter is 10 watts, the pulse power may be as high as 25,000 watts.

In early types of radar systems, the display on the CRT was a horizontal scale and was called an "A scan." The time between the transmitted pulse and the received pulse indicated the distance of the target from the transmitter. With this type of scan, the direction of the target could not be determined except by noting the direction in which the antenna was pointed. To enable the radar to provide direction information, the P scan was developed. This type of radarscope is also called "plan position indicator" (PPI), since it indicates both the distance and direction (azimuth) of the target. On the face of the PPI, the time-trace starts at the same time that a pulse is transmitted from the radar antenna, and the reflected pulses cause bright spots along the trace line. The trace line is adjusted so that its intensity is very light or almost invisible except at the point where a target signal is received. The pulses are generated at such a frequency that the trace lines scan the entire face of the scope as the antenna makes a complete revolution; hence, as reflected signals appear on the screen, a picture appears in shape similar to that of the object that reflects the signal. The fluorescent coating inside the face of the CRT is of a type that retains a fluorescent glow for several seconds after being activated by the electron beam. Thus, the picture remains on the screen and is reactivated each time that the time trace makes a complete circle.

Albert Atkins

References

Eisminn, Thomas K. *Aircraft Electricity and Avionics.* New York: Macmillan/McGraw-Hill, 1999.

Radar, and the Battle of Britain

In Britain late 1934, a government committee under Sir Henry Tizzard asked Robert Watson-Watt, a scientist at the National Physical Laboratory, to conduct experiments on the use of radiated radio waves in the detection of aircraft. In reply, Watson-Watt expressed the possibility of using radio telecommunications for intercepting enemy aircraft.

By 1936, future Air Chief Marshal Sir Hugh Dowding met and conferred with Watson-Watt about the possibilities and advantages of using radio detection in the event of war. Dowding, impressed with the scientist's views, gave it his full support. When Henry Tizzard gave the approval to Watson-Watt, the government proposed expenditure on the construction of four radio detection stations. This was further extended to include the construction of 20 stations around the eastern and southern coasts by August 1937. The range of these stations, located at 20-mile intervals, was 83 miles (132 km) and a height of 13,000 feet (3,939 m); 50 miles (80 km) 5,000 feet (1,515 m); 35 miles (56 km) 2,000 feet (606 m); and 25 miles (40 km) 1,000 feet (303 m), respectively. The masts of these stations were no less than 50 feet (15 m) above sea level and had a minimum height of 200 feet (60 m).

The radio stations, called Chain Home, did have one big disadvantage: Detection of aircraft below 5,000 feet was unreliable. To solve this, the more complicated Chain Home Low was installed. Using a frequency of 200 megahertz (MHz), a power output of only 150 kilowatts, and with a range of only 50 miles (80 km), it could only read straight ahead. But it covered the gap between the lower edge of the Chain Home beam and the surface of the sea, allowing the system to detect aircraft crossing the English Channel at low levels.

With no point more than 20 minutes from the coast, Britain's biggest problem was detecting enemy planes in time to intercept them. Radar enabled the RAF to stay on the ground until the Luftwaffe was known to be approaching, thereby offsetting to some extent the numerical superiority of the enemy.

British planes were first equipped with radar sets of limited range in 1939. In July 1940, a radar-equipped plane shot down the first enemy plane. In August of that year, the RAF began to receive its first Beaufighters equipped with improved radar sets, a combination that was to prove highly effective.

The use of radar by the British provided enough of an edge to meet the Luftwaffe threat and postpone the planned Nazi invasion of Great Britain.

Andy Blackburn

References

Gurney, Gene. *The War in the Air: A Pictorial History of World War II Air Forces in Combat.* New York: Crown Publishers, 1964.

Rall, Guenther (1918–)

The third-highest scoring fighter pilot of all time. Rall joined the German army in 1936 and transferred to the Luftwaffe in 1938. He was assigned to Jagdgeschwader 52 (JG 52; 52d Fighter Wing) in August 1939 and remained in this most successful of all fighter units for the next four years. He scored steadily against the Red Air Force, received the Oak Leaves with Swords to the Knight's Cross of the Iron Cross, and on 28 November 1943, became the second Luftwaffe pilot after Walter Nowotny to claim 250 victories.

On 19 April 1944, Rall was summoned to Germany to take command of the 2d Gruppe (Group) of JG 11, a fighter unit in the Reichsluftverteidigung (Air Defense of Germany). Like many pilots who transferred from the Eastern Front, Rall quickly became a casualty—on 12 May 1944, after scoring his 275th and last victory, he was shot down by a P-47 and lost a thumb. After his hospital stay he was given a school posting and then, in February 1945, took command of JG 300, another Reichsluftverteidigung fighter wing. However, the fuel shortage and chaos accompanying the war's final days prevented Rall from achieving any success with his new command.

Rall joined the Bundesluftwaffe, West Germany's postwar air force, in 1956 and rose to command it from 1970 to 1974. His final rank was major general.

Donald Caldwell

See also

German Air Force (Luftwaffe)

References

Heaton, C. and G. Rall. "Guenther Rall Remembers." Available online at The History Net Website, http://www.thehistorynet.com/WorldWarII/articles/1997/0297_text.htm.

Obermeier, E. *Die Ritterkreuztraeger der Luftwaffe, 1939–1945, Band 1: Jagdflieger* [Recipients of the Knight's Cross]. Mainz: Verlag Dieter Hoffmann, 1989.

Raskova (née Malinina), Marina Mikhaylovna (1912–1943)

Soviet major; commanding officer of the 587th Dive-Bomber Regiment (renamed 125th "M.M. Raskova" *Borisov* Guards Dive-Bomber Regiment). She formed three women's combat wings in Engels, near Stalingrad, in 1941–1942. Earlier, she was a navigator of an ANT-37 named *Rodina* (Homeland)—pilot Valentina Grizodubova, copilot Polina Osipenko—on a pioneering nonstop flight from Moscow to the Pacific (6,450 kilometers) on 24–25 September 1938. Raskova was awarded the Hero of the Soviet Union for this feat, becoming one of the first three Soviet women to be thus honoured.

She acquired specialized knowledge of navigation while employed at the Zhukovsky Air Force Engineering Academy. Raskova was the first Soviet woman to earn the diploma of professional air navigator and became an instructor at the academy. She received flight training at the academy's expense.

A senior navigator in Moscow's May Day air shows, she participated in important flights from 1935, including the *Rodina* flight. On this occasion, her pilot—short of fuel—had no choice but to land immediately. Fearful of nosing over, he ordered Raskova, who was positioned in the forward cabin, to bail out. As a result, she spent 10 days wandering in the taiga, a difficult ordeal to survive.

When Raskova's bold proposal to form a women's air group was finally accepted in 1941, she was faced with the difficulty of transforming civilians into disciplined military personnel. After she died in a crash during a heavy snowstorm on 4 January 1943, her subordinates pledged to become worthy of bearing her name and qualify as Guards regiment, which they did in 1943. In the same spirit, her No. 2 Squadron's tactics, as applied in the air battle of 4 June 1943, became a model for Soviet bomber aviation.

A pupil of famous navigators A. Belyakov and I. Spirin, she cultivated the best qualities in everyone. Raskova was a talented organizer and a bold dreamer, with a personality that endeared her to subordinates. This was the key to her success. Her ashes were placed in the Kremlin Wall beside those of Osipenko.

Kazimiera J. Cottam

See also
Grizodubova, Valentina; Soviet Women's Combat Wings

References

Cottam, Kazimiera J. *Women in War and Resistance.* Nepean, Canada: New Military, 1998.

Markova, Galina. *Takeoff: Hero of the Soviet Union M. M. Raskova* (in Russian). Moscow: Izdatel'stvo Politicheskoy Literatury, 1986.

Ravens (1966–1974)

Experienced volunteer USAF forward air controllers (FACs) during the Vietnam War; served directly with the armed services of Laos to stop invading North Vietnamese forces. These FACs were initially introduced in mid-1966 under a program called "Steve Canyon." This was part of Project 404, a Joint Chiefs of Staff–directed initiative to covertly assign U.S. military personnel to Laos. Flying out of austere forward airfields in small O-1, U-17, and T-28 aircraft, the Ravens directed U.S. Air Force, Navy, Marine, and allied aerial forces in direct support of Laotian ground units and to interdict North Vietnamese supply columns. With the end of hostilities in February 1973, the Ravens were transferred to Udorn Air Base in northern Thailand. There, they trained FACs for the Royal Cambodian Air Force until deactivated in 1974. Less than 200 USAF officers served as Ravens. Thirty-one were killed in the conflict, and none were ever listed as prisoners or released by the North Vietnamese or Laotian communists at the end of the conflict.

Darrel Whitcomb

References

Robbins, Christopher. *The Ravens.* New York: Crown, 1987.

Read, Albert C. (1887–1967)

U.S. Navy rear admiral. Born on 28 March 1887 in Lyme, New Hampshire, Read graduated from the U.S. Naval Academy in 1906. He served at sea until 1913, at the Naval Torpedo Station for two years, and then completed flight training in 1916. After further sea service, he commanded naval air stations in the eastern United States during World War I.

Lieutenant Commander Read in March 1919 assumed command of the flying boat NC-4, one of four aircraft selected to undertake a transatlantic flight led by Commander John H. Towers. In the event, NC-4 and its crew completed the first aerial transatlantic crossing (17–27 May) from Trepassey Bay, Newfoundland, to Lisbon, with a stop in the Azores.

Between 1920 and 1929, Read commanded various naval air squadrons and stations and attended the Naval War College. He then served at the Bureau of Aeronautics until 1938, with a two-year stint commanding USS *Wright,* before returning to sea as captain of the carrier *Saratoga* until 1940. Read, promoted rear admiral in 1941, next commanded Naval Air Station Pensacola until 1942, when he became chief of air technical training. His final assignments were as commander, Fleet Air, Atlantic Fleet, 1944–1945, and in the office of the deputy Chief of Naval Operations (Air) until September 1946, when he retired. Read died in Miami, Florida, on 10 October 1967.

Paul E. Fontenoy

See also
Curtiss Aircraft; Towers, John H.

References

Smith, Richard K. *First Across: The U.S. Navy's Transatlantic Flight of 1919.* Annapolis, MD: Naval Institute Press, 1973.

Reber, Samuel (1864–1933)

U.S. Army colonel. Born in St. Louis, Missouri, Reber was the grandnephew of General William T. Sherman. He belonged to the West Point class of 1886 that also included John J. Pershing, Mason M. Patrick, and Charles T. Menoher. Upon graduation, Reber joined the cavalry. After studying electrical engineering at Johns Hopkins University, Reber transferred to the Signal Corps in 1894. During the Spanish-American War, he served in Puerto Rico under General Nelson A. Miles. In 1900, he married Miles's daughter, Cecelia.

Reber, an accomplished balloonist, was among those Army officers who early on recognized aviation's military potential. He became head of the Signal Corps's Aeronautical Division in 1913 and a year later became the first chief of the new Aviation Section. He subsequently expressed to Congress his concerns regarding the nation's unpreparedness for aerial combat and the lack of reliable information about events overseas. Reber and Chief Signal Officer George P. Scriven served as the Army's initial representatives to the National Advisory Committee for Aeronautics formed in 1915.

A highly intelligent and energetic officer, Reber's promising career was cut short amid controversy. In 1914, the inspector general had issued an unfavorable report about conditions at the Signal Corps Aviation School in San Diego, successor to the original facility at College Park, Maryland. Accidents were frequent and often fatal, and a serious rift had developed between aviators and their administrators.

For reasons unknown, Reber suppressed the report and failed to fully implement its recommendations to improve safety. The Signal Corps replaced pusher planes with tractors, but the underlying institutional problems remained. The situation at San Diego fed the growing sentiment to withdraw aviation from the Signal Corps. Secretary of War Newton D. Baker censured both Scriven and Reber. After further investigation, Baker removed Reber as chief of the Aviation Section in May 1916. Although Reber remained in uniform until 1919, his official aviation duties had ended.

After retirement, Reber enjoyed a successful second career with the Radio Corporation of America. He is buried in the Miles family mausoleum at Arlington National Cemetery.

Rebecca Robbins Raines

References

Cameron, Rebecca Hancock. *Training to Fly: Military Flight Training, 1907–1945.* Washington, DC: U.S. Government Printing Office, 1999.

Raines, Rebecca Robbins. *Getting the Message Through: A Branch History of the U.S. Army Signal Corps.* Washington, DC: U.S. Government Printing Office, 1996.

Reeves, Joseph M. (1872–1948)

U.S. Navy admiral; the father of carrier warfare. Joseph Mason Reeves was born in Tampico, Illinois, on 20 November 1872. After graduating from the U.S. Naval Academy, Reeves was commissioned as an assistant Engineer in the Engineering Corps. In 1898, Reeves won commendations for his performance on the USS *Oregon* during its epic voyage around Cape Horn and spectacular performance at the Battle of Santiago (Spanish-American War). After transferring to the line in 1899, Reeves became one of the leading gunnery officers in the Navy.

In 1913, Reeves was ordered to duty in command of USS *Jupiter,* the first turboelectric-powered ship in the Navy. When Reeves returned to the ship in 1925 as commander, Aircraft Squadrons, Battle Fleet, *Jupiter* had been transformed into the Navy's first aircraft carrier and renamed USS *Langley.* During the next four years, Reeves transformed the Navy's nascent air force from a small auxiliary command whose primary mission was to support the battle force into a powerful strike force that could attack inland or far at sea in advance of the battle line.

Admiral Reeves was the first qualified aviation officer in the U.S. Navy to achieve flag rank. He was the first to bear the title "carrier commander" and holds the distinction of being the first aviation officer in the Navy to serve as commander in chief, United States Fleet.

Thomas Wildenberg

References

Melhorn, Charles M. *Two-Block Fox.* Annapolis, MD: Naval Institute Press, 1974.

Wildenberg, Thomas. *Destined for Glory: Dive Bombing, Midway, and the Evolution of Carrier Airpower.* Annapolis, MD: Naval Institute Press, 1998.

Regia Aeronautica (Pre-World War II)

The Regia Aeronautica (Royal Air Force, RA) was created on 28 March 1923, merging the Italian army and navy air services to fulfill fliers' aspirations for independence. Nominally comprising all the military air forces of the kingdom and of its colonies, the RA consisted in fact of the Armata Aerea (Armera, the air army tasked with air war missions, including air defense); and the Aviazione per il Regio Esercito and Aviazione per la Regia Marina (Esercitavia and Marinavia, respectively the army and navy auxiliary air services)—the last two under the operational control of the army and navy, which also issued technical specifications. The basic air unit was the *squadriglia* (squadron, normally nine aircraft under a captain); the largest were the territorial air zones (ZATs) and commands (e.g., the Aeronautica dell'Egeo). In wartime, each ZAT generated a *squadra aerea* (air force) comprising divisions and brigades, which in turn controlled *stormi* (wings).

The RA reported to the Commissariat for Aeronautics, formed on 24 January 1923 and upgraded to Air Ministry on 30 August 1925, which controlled all aeronautical activities, including procurement, research and development, and civil aviation. From 1923 to 1929, the post of high commissar/minister was held by Benito Mussolini, whose multiple other positions ensured that aviation was run by the deputy commissars and undersecretaries like Aldo Finzi (1923–1924), General Alberto Bonzani (1924–1926), and Italo Balbo (1926–1929). Balbo became minister in 1929, but Mussolini returned to the position from 1933 to 1943 and called on Chief of Staff General Giuseppe Valle to double as undersecretary (1933–1939). Compounded by his lack of an independent power base, this created a damaging short-circuit between policy, procurement, and operations.

The new unified organization was symbolized by the Air Ministry building, inaugurated in 1931 to bring together offices dispersed in 12 locations; between 1926 and 1932 airfields grew from 105 to 180, and a comprehensive test center was built at Guidonia, near Rome. Few regular and virtually no senior officers transferred to the RA, so leadership was another challenge. The Air Academy was formed in 1923, followed by the Air War School in 1934, but up to World War II many generals were former air observers or came from the airship branch (disbanded in 1928); units remained staffed largely by NCO and short-term commissioned pilots.

Aviation pioneer Giulio Douhet never held any RA position, and his command-of-the-air doctrine was more a justification for independence than a blueprint for expansion; indeed, his outspoken critic Amedeo Mecozzi was allowed to organize a fighter-bomber "assault brigade," crippled only by inadequate aircraft. Both agreed on the use of poison gas and discounted targeting and intelligence. The large exercises held in 1927 and 1931 helped bridge the gap between theory and practice, but the RA developed as a tactical force geared to army and navy needs: Although the 1937–1939 expansion plan called for up to 1,043 bombers, the strategic component never exceeded 12 aircraft.

Considerable efforts were channeled into propaganda to increase domestic air-mindedness but also to display the progress made by Italy under Mussolini. The RA successfully vied for world records for speed, altitude, distance, and endurance, and in 1939 it still held one-fourth of all records recognized by the International Aeronautical Federation. Aircraft exports and aeronautical missions in countries ranging from the Soviet Union to China became valuable foreign-policy tools. German aircrews were trained secretly during 1933–1934.

Fascist rhetoric and some historians link aviation and the regime, but actually the RA remained the junior service. More important, its modest budget (roughly 15 percent of all Italian military expenditures) had to provide for both the Esercitavia and Marinavia. Because it threatened to circumvent RA independence, this arrangement created interservice tension, and the air force fought successfully to gradually reduce its external commitments; in return, it undertook to make Armera assets available when necessary. The RA kept its word in Ethiopia and Spain, emerging with great prestige as a modern, if not advanced, air force. Its crews had gained considerable combat experience, partially offsetting their inadequate training. Unfortunately, the prolonged war effort delayed the much-needed renewal of front-line aircraft, and on the eve of World War II the RA was on the verge of obsolescence.

Gregory Alegi

See also

Balbo, Italo; Ethiopian War; Italian Aircraft Development; Regia Aeronautica (World War II); Spanish Civil War

References

Alegi, Gregory. *L'aile brisée* (The Broken Wing). Paris: Lariviere, 2000.

Catalanotto, Baldassare, and Hugo Pratt. *Once Upon a Sky: 70 Years of Italian Air Force.* Rome: Lizard, 1993.

Regia Aeronautica (World War II)

Interwar and World War II Italian air force, created on 28 March 1923 by merging the Italian army and navy air services to fulfill fliers' aspirations for independence. When the Nazis invaded Poland, Italian dictator Benito Mussolini committed Italy to "nonbelligerence"; on 31 October 1939, he appointed General Francesco Pricolo (1891–1980) as undersecretary and Chief of Staff. Pricolo set out to rebuild the Regia Aeronautica (RA), drained by its efforts in Ethiopia and Spain. Believing that the design competitions of 1938–1939 would soon produce modern types, he began by eliminating obsolete aircraft. But Mussolini, fearing that a victorious Hitler would dictate the future of Europe, rushed Italy into war to gain a seat at the peace table. This led to the paradox of the so-called parallel war, in which Italy competed with its German ally rather than combine forces.

On 10 June 1940, the RA had 84,000 men and 1,795 operational aircraft (3,300 total), distributed among 23 landplane and two seaplane bomber wings, the equivalent of 10 fighter wings, an "assault" wing, and two heavy fighter groups. These reported to three *squadre aeree* (air forces), raised to five by the end of the year, and four geographical commands (Sardinia, Albania, the Aegean, and East Africa); in addition, large auxiliary air services came under direct army and navy control.

An operational HQ—Superaereo—was formed, but air assets came under theater commanders—invariably army generals, who also dominated the Supreme Command. The resulting ignorance of airpower translated in the lack of an air campaign against strategic targets such as Malta; instead, medium bombers were employed against unsuitable tactical targets like French forts in the Alps or Greek strongpoints on the Epirus. This fundamental misconception was compounded by internal shortcomings. Training, still patterned upon World War I practice, was inadequate. Pilots reached operational units with 150 hours experience, gained in more than a year, with much emphasis on aerobatics and formation flying but little on navigation, gunnery, and tactics. Operational training and, at first, conversion, occurred largely in combat units, increasing losses among newly assigned aircrews. The limited industrial resources were severely mismanaged, with political influence allowing dominating manufacturers to continue producing obsolete aircraft like the Fiat CR.42. Furthermore, while the RA sought to improve performance by introducing new types rather than developing existing ones, its blend of perfectionism and design interference delayed until 1943 the service entry of designs already flying in 1939, like the Cant Z.1018. As a result, up to September 1943 Italy built 11,500 aircraft, supplemented by 400 received from Germany and 97 French war prizes.

These considerations largely explain why the RA could not win the war as prophesied by Giulio Douhet. Still the RA fought bravely on every front, with some tactical success, and the fragmentary evidence available confirms that it did not shirk. In 1940–1945, the RA flew some 280,000 sorties for 560,000 hours, claiming 2,533 air-to-air victories plus 474 aircraft destroyed on the ground, and 144 pilots were credited with five or more kills; aggregate losses to all causes came to 6,805 aircraft and 22,805 personnel (including 25 percent aircrews).

An unremarkable campaign was flown against France just before its surrender to Germany. The next theater was East Africa, so isolated from Italy that its fate was sealed from the beginning. After unsuccessful attacks on Aden, the RA conducted tactical operations until resistance ended on 27 November 1941. From October 1940 to January 1941, the RA also participated in the Battle of Britain with two bomber wings and a fighter wing. Because of limited navigation skills, different radios, and language problems, operations with the Luftwaffe proved difficult and little was achieved. On 28 October 1940, Italy attacked Greece and the RA was called to provide ground support against bitter resistance. In April 1941, the war extended to Yugoslavia, where rugged army observation biplanes, lacking aerial opposition, were used effectively against partisans in an unsung campaign that dragged on until the Italian armistice. The harsh winters were the chief enemy of the fighter group and the observation group deployed to Russia in 1941–1943.

North Africa was the main RA theater of war, and the local 5th Squadra received the best units and equipment. Unfortunately, they were used mostly to counter mobile British land units and compensate for army immobility. The arrival of modern aircraft, including Macchi fighters and Stuka dive-bombers, allowed temporary air superiority, and large-scale fighter sweeps confirmed the principle of mass, but they remained very rare. In the interior, the colonial air units created before the war against Libyan rebels proved equally adept against British intruders.

Postwar navy literature makes much of the alleged RA veto on carrier construction, but actually the RA played a crucial role in the Mediterranean, showing both limitations and virtues. When hundreds of medium bombers attacked British ships at Punta Stilo (8–15 July 1940), their light bombs proved inaccurate and ineffective. Pricolo reacted swiftly, and already on 15 August the first S.79 torpedo-bombers struck ships in Alexandria Harbor. The new branch expanded rapidly, peaking in 1943 at 12 groups and three operational training units, staffed by combat veterans. Their hard-won successes included 18 warships (including eight cruisers and a battleship) sunk or requiring up to 48 months to repair; their own losses were correspondingly heavy. Significant air assets were also absorbed by convoy escorts and maritime reconnaissance. Malta was the subject of constant attacks, most effective when carried out with the Luftwaffe. Unfortunately, the German X Fliegerkorps was withdrawn in summer 1942 when the island was about to capitulate.

Pricolo was relieved on 15 November 1941, ostensibly for having postponed dispatching to Libya the first Macchi C.202 wing but also because of clashes with the Supreme Command. His replacement was the pragmatic General Rino Corso Fougier (1894–1963), a World War I ace who put into production the Macchi C.205 against considerable Fiat resistance. In November 1942, the Axis defeat at El Alamein triggered the final African retreat, which ended with the fall of Tunisia in May 1943. For six months, the army was supplied and evacuated largely by air. Initially formed by requisitioned airliners, the Comando Servizi Aerei Speciali (Special Air Services Command, CSAS) grew to comprise numerous wings. In the face of grievous losses, CSAS performed sterling work and peaked at 100 sorties per day.

When the Allies used North Africa to launch an air campaign against Italian cities, the RA proved inadequate. Daylight fighters were largely obsolete and night-fighters were in their infancy; there was neither centralized fighter control nor coordination with antiaircraft artillery, which was an army responsibility; attacks on airfields and factories compromised mobility and depleted resources. Although its personnel had grown to 180,000, by summer 1943 the RA fielded only 400 combat aircraft. The loss of Sicily and the U.S. bombing of Rome (19 July 1943) signaled defeat.

On 25 July, the fascist Grand Council voted against the dictator, allowing the king to name Marshal Pietro Badoglio prime minister. Badoglio appointed General Pietro Sandalli air minister and negotiated with the Allies the armistice that was announced on 8 September 1943. The king and military leadership repaired to Brindisi, in the south, leaving the country in chaos. The Germans interned more than 600,000 men and killed thousands who resisted. On 13 October 1943, Italy declared war against Germany and was recognized as "cobelligerent" by the Allies. Reduced to 20,000 personnel and less than 500 aircraft, the RA became part of the Balkan Air Force. Fighters were assigned tactical roles, and bombers dropped supplies to Italian troops and partisans in Yugoslavia; air/sea rescue (occasionally behind German lines), target-towing, and other support duties were carried out for the Allies. With Allied mistrust finally overcome, limited quantities of P-39s, Spitfire Vs, and Baltimores arrived in June 1944; simultaneously, Sandalli was replaced by General Pietro Piacentini, succeeded by political undersecretaries after only six months. Despite the difficulties generated by conflicting U.S. and British perspectives for the Mediterranean, RA activities during 1943–1945 helped lay the foundation for a postwar recovery in the Western camp.

Gregory Alegi

See also

Aeronautica Nazionale Repubblicana; Britain, Battle of; CRUSADER; Greece; HUSKY; Italian Aircraft Development; Italian Campaign; Mareth Line; Mediterranean Theater of Operations; North African Campaign; Pantelleria; PEDESTAL; Regia Aeronautica (Pre–World War II); Salerno, Battle of; Somalia; Taranto Air Attack; TORCH; Ultra

References

Alegi, Gregory, and Baldassare Catalanotto, eds. *Wings of Italy.* Milan: GAE, 1996.

Apostolo, Giorgio and Giovanni Massimello. *Italian Aces of World War 2.* London: Osprey, 2000.

MacGregor, Knox. *Hitler's Italian Allies.* Cambridge, UK: Cambridge University Press, 2000.

Reitsch, Hanna (1912–1979)

The most celebrated female aviator of Nazi Germany. She won world fame as a glider pilot before the war. Reitsch worked as a test pilot for the Luftwaffe, performing demonstrations for Charles Lindbergh and making a famous indoor flight of the Focke autogiro/helicopter in 1938. An ardent Nazi, she was the second woman recipient of the Iron Cross Second Class, being decorated by Hitler personally in 1941. She was the only woman to win the Iron Cross First Class, after being injured testing the Messerschmitt 163 rocket fighter in 1942. Her most legendary flight was landing a damaged Fieseler Storch near the Brandenburg Gate at the height of the Battle of Berlin (April 1945). Ordered by Hitler to leave the Führerbunker before the Russians assaulted it, she took off from the Tiergarten in central Berlin between artillery barrages. Her flight fed rumors of Hitler's possible escape. Jailed by the Allies for more than a year, she continued competitive gliding after the war.

Christopher Simer

See also

Fieseler Fi 156 Storch

References

Reitsch, Hanna: *Flying Is My Life.* New York: Putnam's, 1954.

Republic Aircraft

U.S. aircraft manufacturer. In 1935, the USAAC began a series of design competitions in order to obtain an advanced monoplane fighter. The Seversky Aircraft Corporation won the competition and received an order for 77 examples, designated the P-35. In 1939, Founder Alexander Seversky then lost control of the company, which changed its name to Republic Aviation.

Republic produced an export version of the P-35 that had a more powerful engine and two additional machine guns. One hundred twenty of these were sold to Sweden, but 60 were subsequently diverted to U.S. stocks and served in the Philippine Islands.

After Republic had finished the production run of the P-35A, it set out to develop a more advanced version. Two different projects resulted—the XP-41 and the P-43. Both had more powerful engines than the P-35A, as well as a redesigned airframe, but retained the characteristic wing shape that was designer Alexander Kartveli's signature note. Testing of these prototypes resulted in a USAAC service test contract for 13 YP-43s in March 1939, followed by production orders for 54 P-43s, 80 P-43As, and 125 P-43A-1 fighters for China.

The next Republic aircraft to reach production was the P-47 Thunderbolt. While the first P-47B was testing, Republic was hard at work at getting production under way in the new plant building just completed at Farmingdale on Long Island, New York. In addition to this, the first of three new paved runways was completed. Ultimately, expansion of this facility would quadruple the size of the factory floorspace. Even so, all this new construction was inadequate to meet the future contract demands for the Thunderbolt.

In November 1942, the War Production Board authorized a new plant to be constructed adjacent to the Evansville, Indiana, airport. This would provide the critical production volume that would enable the P-47 to become the most-produced U.S. fighter of World War II. Production would ramp up slowly, largely a result of the extensive testing involved.

The F-105 was the first aircraft developed specifically as a single-seat Mach 2 nuclear fighter-bomber and gained its fame in the skies over Southeast Asia. (Walter J. Boyne)

In the post–World War II period, Republic resumed production of attack aircraft, including the F-84 and F-105. It attempted to build civilian aircraft (the Seabee amphibian) but was not successful. It was purchased by Fairchild Hiller in 1965 and became Fairchild Republic in 1971, building the A-10 Warthog.

Albert Atkins

See also

Fairchild A-10 Thunderbolt II; Republic F-105 Thunderchief Republic F-84 Thunderjet/Thunderstreak; Republic P-47 Thunderbolt; Seversky Aircraft

References

Wagner, Ray. *American Combat Planes.* 3rd ed. Garden City, NY: Doubleday, 1982.

Republic F-105 Thunderchief

The first aircraft developed specifically as a single-seat Mach 2 nuclear fighter-bomber. Alexander Kartveli began designing the aircraft in 1952, and the first flight of the YF-105A was made on 22 October 1955. The results were disappointing—the aircraft was underpowered and had more drag than expected. The incorporation of the area-rule principle and a new Pratt and Whitney J75 engine solved these problems, and 78 F-105Bs were produced. Their MA-8 fire-control system never lived up to expectations, and the aircraft were quickly relegated to Air National Guard and Air Force Reserve service. An improved ASG-19 Thunderstick fire-control system was incorporated into 610 F-105Ds and 143 two-seat F-105Fs produced between 1959 and 1965. The F-105 gained its fame in the skies over Southeast Asia—carrying weapons it was not designed to use in a war it was not supposed to fight. More than 20,000 combat missions were flown by Thunderchiefs in Southeast Asia, resulting in the loss of 336 aircraft. Many F-105Fs were adapted as the first successful Wild Weasel defense suppression aircraft, with 65 being redesignated F-105G. The last Thunderchiefs were retired in 1983.

Dennis R. Jenkins

See also

ROLLING THUNDER; Wild Weasel

References

Jenkins, Dennis R. *F-105 Thunderchief: Workhorse of the Vietnam Era.* New York: McGraw Hill, 2000.

Wagner, Ray. *American Combat Planes.* 3rd ed. Garden City, NY: Doubleday, 1982.

Republic F-84 Thunderjet, Thunderstreak, and Thunderflash

The first jet fighter designed in the United States after World War II; at least three distinctive variants of the Republic F-84 had long careers. The first production F-84s began appearing in June 1947, and 1,414 of these straight-wing Thunderjets were produced.

Republic incorporated a swept wing into the F-84F Thunderstreak, which ran into significant development problems. This led to the production of another straight-wing variant, the F-84G Thunderjet, the first fighter equipped for boom-style aerial refueling and the first Air Force fighter capable of delivering tactical nuclear weapons. Straight-wing F-84s began arriving in Korea during the summer of 1950, scoring their first MiG kill on 21 January 1951. As an air-to-air fighter, however, the F-84 was a disappointment—only nine enemy aircraft were downed for a loss of 18 Thunderjets. Therefore, most of the 86,400 F-84E/G sorties were used to deliver 55,987 tons of bombs.

Production of the F-84G totaled 3,025 aircraft, and 2,236 of these equipped the air forces of Belgium, Denmark, France, Greece, Iran, Italy, the Netherlands, Norway, Portugal, Taiwan, Thailand, Turkey, and Yugoslavia.

Although the swept-wing F-84F had flown as early as November 1952, it was not until January 1954 that production aircraft began to be delivered. By August 1957, however, 1,711 had been built. These swept-wing fighters were so different than the earlier F-84s that it is regrettable that their original F-96 designation was not retained. NATO received 1,301 F-84Fs for Belgium, France, Greece, Italy, and Turkey. The Thunderstreak was also the first modern fighter to equip the West German Bundesluftwaffe.

A reconnaissance variant that moved the air intake from the nose to the wing roots was also produced. These RF-84F Thunderflashes, with 715 built, served with Belgium, Denmark, France, Germany, Greece, Italy, the Netherlands, Norway, Turkey, and Nationalist China in addition to the United States. A few special RF-84K FICON (fighter-conveyor) versions were modified to be carried semisubmerged in the bomb bay of GRB-36F bombers.

Dennis R. Jenkins

References

Jacobsen, Meyers K., et al. *Convair B-36: A Comprehensive History of America's Big Stick.* Atglen, PA: Schiffer, 1999.

Jenkins, Dennis R. *Convair B-36 "Peacemaker."* WarbirdTech Series Volume 24. North Branch, MN: Specialty Press, 1999.

Republic P-47 Thunderbolt

The high-altitude Republic P-47 Thunderbolt fighter was the evolutionary culmination of warplanes designed and built by Alexander Seversky. In 1933, Michael Gregor, a Seversky engineer, demonstrated the semielliptical wing planform with high-speed airfoil and metal cantilever construction that would lay the foundation of P-47 performance.

In 1940, when the USAAC required a heavily armed high-altitude fighter, Alexander Kartveli and the Republic firm, the successor to Seversky, offered an aircraft featuring a 2,000-hp radial turbosupercharged engine and armed with eight wing-mounted .50-caliber machine guns.

Based in England, Thunderbolt units went into action in April 1943. In November 1943, P-47s entered the fray in the

The Republic P-47 was beloved by its pilots, many of whom survived combat and accidents solely because of the great strength and power of the Thunderbolt. (U.S. Air Force)

The radical and unsuccessful Northrop XP-56 Black Bullet was one of several exotic responses to the Request for Data R40C. (Walter J. Boyne)

Mediterranean. Thunderbolt formations commenced fighting in the Southwest Pacific in June 1943 and in China by April 1944.

The P-47 was hampered by a poor turn radius, a low rate of climb, and a range that prevented escort of U.S. bombers over Germany. But these aspects were offset by high speed—428 mph at 30,000 feet—rapid roll rate, dive speed, and subsequent zoom climb. A number of German pilots, accustomed to fighting against Spitfires, often made the fatal mistake of diving away from pursuing Thunderbolts. A combat loss rate of less than 0.7 percent testified to the Thunderbolt's exceptionally strong construction. The P-47 also proved to be a devastating fighter-bomber and wrought havoc on enemy ground forces, railroads, and air bases.

Many improvements were incorporated in the P-47. Modified propeller blades greatly increased climb rate. Range was extended through the use of external fuel tanks. A bubble canopy enhanced pilot visibility.

More Thunderbolts, 15,683, were built for the USAAF than any other fighter. Together with the North American P-51, the formidable P-47 won the struggle for control of the skies over Europe in World War II.

Sherwood S. Cordier

See also

Engine Technology; Republic Aircraft; Seversky Aircraft

References

Bodie, Warren M. *Republic's P-47 Thunderbolt: From Seversky to Victory.* Hiawassee, GA: Widewing, 1994.

Johnson, Robert S., with Martin Caidin. *Thunderbolt!* New York: Ballantine Books, 1958.

Request for Data R-40C: The XP-54, XP-55, and XP-56 Fighter Programs

U.S. Army Air Corps fighter program based on a Request for Data rather than the usual Circular (Request for) Proposal just prior to World War II. In mid-1939, the USAAC realized that U.S. fighter aircraft such as the Lockheed P-38, Bell P-39, and Curtiss P-40 might not be competitive with the Messerschmitt Bf 109 and Supermarine Spitfires already in service. They believed that continued improvement in foreign aircraft would outpace the rate of improvement in the United States. The USAAC's goal was to accelerate the development of faster aircraft (specified: 425 mph, desired: 525 mph). To assist in this, in addition to the 1,250-shp Allison V-1710, two new "Hyper" engines would be available—the 1,700-shp Continental IV-1430 and the 1,850-shp Pratt and Whitney X-1800.

The solicitation by means of a Request for Data deviated from the usual Circular (Request for) Proposal procurement method and specified a three-phase program: 30-day preliminary design data generation, building and testing wind-tunnel models, and design and fabrication of prototypes, with first delivery by 30 June 1941.

Twenty-three proposals were received from seven manufacturers, including two divisions of Curtiss-Wright. These were grouped into three categories: I—those that were mere modifications of existing production designs; II—those advanced designs capable of production by 1942; and III—those designs needing an advanced engine, whether or not the airframe design was advanced.

Three designs were selected from Category II: the Vultee

The Bell X-2 suspended below a Boeing B-50D carrier plane. (Walter J. Boyne)

Model 70-2, the Curtiss Model P-249C, and the Northrop Model N-2B; all were pushers, a configuration selected for higher aerodynamic efficiency. Each was contracted for the first phase of development in June 1940.

The proposed Vultee Model 70-2 had a single seat, single X-1800 engine, twin fuselage booms, twin tail, a 40-foot inverted gull wing, and tricycle landing gear. Changing USAAC requirements and cancellation of the X-1800 engine program resulted in the Model 78 (XP-54) with the Lycoming XH-2470 engine. It first flew in January 1943, 18 months late. Two were built, and maximum speed was 381 mph.

The proposed Curtiss Model P-249C was the result of studies that predated the R40-C invitation by a year and was so radical (a swept-wing with a canard-type free-floating elevator at the nose of the airframe) that after wind-tunnel tests the AAC cancelled the program as being too risky. Curtiss-Wright saw promise in the test results and decided to fund a proof-of-concept demonstrator, the CW24-B, which flew in December 1941. Flight tests validated the concept, and the XP-55 contract was reinstated in July 1942. Initially, three engine alternatives were proposed: the V-1710, the IV-1430, and the Wright R-2160. The IV-1430 was initially selected, but when the XP-55 started construction the IV-1430 and the R-2160 were not ready, so the V-1710 was selected, and the first flight of the XP-55 was in July 1943, two years late. The XP-55 had a maximum speed of 390 mph.

The Northrop N-2 was proposed with four engine alternatives: the R-2800, the X-1800, the V-1710, and the R-1830. The X-1800 had been selected, but cancellation of the X-1800 program resulted in selection of the R-2800 driving counter-rotating propellers. The N-2 (XP-56) was a flying wing with a stubby fuselage and made extensive use of magnesium in the structure and skin. Two were built, with engine and airframe problems delaying the first flight to September 1943, more than two years late. Maximum speed was 340 mph.

Although all three of the R40-C airplanes showed promise, each missed performance goals, further development was required, and it was realized that they would not be available in time to affect the war. Also, by early mid-1944, the promise of the jet fighter was being realized, and the three programs were cancelled in May. The XP-54 had 63 flying hours, the XP-55 had about 60, and the XP-56 had about 15. One each of the XP-55 and XP-56 prototypes crashed during flight-testing, but flight evaluation of these programs continued after cancellation. The two XP-54 prototypes were scrapped shortly after cancellation.

Douglas G. Culy

References

Balzer, Gerald H. "Request for Data R40-C." *American Aviation Historical Society Journal* 40, 4; 41, nos. 1-4; 42, 1 (Winter 1995–Spring 1997).

Research Aircraft

Vehicles that provide design data for military aircraft and spacecraft. Research aircraft can be any airplane used for flight research, that is, gathering data to better understand some aspect of flight. The primitive airplane the Wrights flew in 1903 at Kitty Hawk was the first research aircraft; its successors have included an enormous variety of airplanes, from gliders and subscale research vehicles to the latest X-plane.

Most people probably think of research aircraft as X-planes, with several dozen having been developed to date. In the United States, this series of research aircraft (as distinguished from prototypes) began in the 1940s to gather data supersonic flight. Pursuit aircraft like the P-38 Lightning were approaching this speed in dives—with often disastrous results. Aerodynamicists lacked accurate wind-tunnel data for the speed range Mach 0.95 to Mach 1.2 until a slotted-throat wind tunnel became available at midcentury. Since then, design and performance of research aircraft have greatly advanced, offering valuable data on atmospheric and space flight.

J. D. Hunley

See also

Bell X-1; Douglas D-558; Lockheed P-38 Lightning; North American X-15; Wright, Orville; Wright, Wilbur

References

Hallion, Richard P. *On the Frontier: Flight Research at Dryden, 1946–1981.* NASA SP-4303. Washington, DC: NASA SP-4303, 1984.

Wallace, Lane E. *Flights of Discovery: 50 Years at the NASA Dryden Flight Research Center.* NASA SP-4309. Washington, DC: NASA SP-4309, 1996.

The famous Red Baron, Captain Manfred Richthofen, seen here with his younger brother, Lothar. He rose quickly through the ranks and was shot down 21 April 1918, nobody can say for sure by whom. (Smithsonian Institution)

Richthofen, Manfred von (1892–1918)

The legendary Red Baron of World War I. Manfred von Richthofen was the eldest son of a Prussian officer. As a boy he attended a military academy where, apart from sports, he was considered average. When World War I began he was with the cavalry. But during the summer of 1914 movement had come to a standstill and the armies dug into the trenches. Bored, Richthofen sought a transfer to aviation.

After duty first as an observer, then as a bomber pilot, Richthofen met and impressed the ranking German ace, Oswald Boelcke, who invited him to join Jasta 2, which was just forming for the Battle of the Somme.

Under Boelcke, Richthofen quickly developed into a deadly tactician. By the time of his mentor's death, his score stood at seven and was rising fast. His sixteenth brought him Prussia's highest award, the Pour le Mérite, and a command of his own Jasta 11.

Painting his Albatros red so his pilots would see him in combat, Richthofen acquired the nickname by which he has been immortalized. Over the next months his legend grew with his scores, awards, ranks, and responsibilities. By early summer he was a *rittmeister* (cavalry captain, a reference to his original unit affiliation) in command of a *jagdgeschwader* (fighter wing) with 56 victories when he suffered a head wound. His wound slowed the scoring pace, and his number stood at 63 when the German offensive opened in March 1918.

Regaining his stride, Richthofen drove his victories to 80 by 20 April, the day before his death. On 21 April, he took off flying the red Fokker triplane with which he's perpetually linked. Leading two flights of Jasta 11, his group encountered a similar number of Sopwith Camels from RAF No. 209 Squadron. Richthofen began chasing Lieutenant Wilfred May over the Somme River Valley. May's plight attracted the attention of Captain Roy Brown, who dove after the red triplane. As the trio came over the Morlancourt Ridge, several Australian ground gunners began firing. Richthofen fell, opening the debate "who killed the Red Baron?"—a question that still perplexes World War I aviation historians.

James Streckfuss

See also

Albatros Aircraft; Boelcke, Oswald; Fokker Aircraft (Early Years); German Air Service; Voss, Werner

References

Ferko, A. E. *Richthofen.* London: Albatros, 1995.

Kilduff, Peter. *Richthofen: Beyond the Legend of the Red Baron.* London: Arms and Armour, 1993.

Richthofen, Manfred von. *Der Rote Kampflieger* (The Red Battle Flyer). Berlin: Ullestein A.G., 1933

Richthofen, Wolfram Freiherr von (1895–1945)

One of the most influential Luftwaffe commanders. Von Richthofen joined the German cavalry in 1913, took flight training in 1917, and was assigned to the fighter unit commanded by his more famous cousin, Manfred (the Red Baron). He left military service after World War I and obtained a doctorate in mechanical engineering before joining the Reichswehr, the interwar army, in 1923. His unique technical education brought him a wide range of assignments in the newly formed Luftwaffe. He served two tours with the Kondor Legion in Spain: the first as Chief of Staff, the second as commander with the rank of brigadier general. While in Spain he originated and codified the doctrine of air-ground support that the Wehrmacht later used so successfully and became known as the father of the ground attack arm. From 1939 to 1942 he led the VIII Fliegerkorps (Air Corps), a specialized ground attack command, on all fronts, and then commanded Luftflottes 4 and 2 (Fourth and Second Air Forces). Von Richthofen's high intelligence and energetic leadership gained him the respect of the faction-riddled Luftwaffe High Command. He was promoted to field marshal in 1943, the youngest member of the Wehrmacht to hold that rank, but a brain tumor forced him to take medical leave in 1944. He never returned to active service and died on 12 July 1945 in a U.S. military hospital in Europe.

Donald Caldwell

See also

Blitzkrieg; German Air Force (Luftwaffe); Spanish Civil War

References

Corum, J. *The Luftwaffe: Creating the Operational Air War, 1918–1940.* Lawrence: University Press of Kansas, 1997.

Muller, R. *The German Air War in Russia.* Baltimore: Nautical and Aviation, 1992.

Rickenbacker, Edward Vernon (1890–1973)

One of history's greatest combat pilots, a pioneer airline executive, and an American hero whose name was once a household word among millions of admirers. He was born in Columbus, Ohio, on 8 October 1890. He anglicized his original surname, Rickenbacher, for professional purposes during his early career as an automobile racing driver but retained the Germanic spelling until 1918, when he was flying with the 94th Pursuit Squadron in World War I.

Working at the Oscar Lear Company, which made automobiles, Rickenbacker impressed his boss, Lee Frayer, by spending his lunch hours studying a mail-order course in automobile technology that he had bought on credit with his meager earnings. Taking Rickenbacker under his wing, Frayer taught him automotive engineering and took him to the 1906 Vanderbilt Cup Race as his riding mechanic. Thus began a career that would see Rickenbacker become a nationally famous race-car driver, winning $60,000 in 1916.

On a business trip to England, Rickenbacker resolved to become a combat pilot and emulate the exploits of U.S. volunteers who were fighting in the famed Lafayette Escadrille. After returning to the United States, he recruited a group of racers who hoped to become fliers and go to France under his leadership, but the Signal Corps rejected the idea. Its tradition-bound officials felt that Rickenbacker and his friends lacked the upper-class status and educational credentials that would make them officer material. This attitude would haunt—and inspire—Rickenbacker.

In late May 1917, while Rickenbacker was in Cincinnati getting ready for a Memorial Day race, an admirer, Major Lewis Burgess, telephoned him from Washington asking if he wanted to become a driver for General John Pershing and his staff, who were about to sail to Europe. Rickenbacker jumped at the offer and caught an overnight train to New York, where he enlisted the next day as a sergeant in the American Expeditionary Force. By evening he was aboard the *Baltic,* the oceanliner that took Pershing and his entourage across the Atlantic.

Whether Rickenbacker actually drove for Pershing himself is not clear. Lieutenant Colonel William "Billy" Mitchell, chief of the Zone of Advance, became aware of his mechanical ability and commandeered his services. Driving for Mitchell, Rickenbacker showed his mechanical genius by repairing his staff car in emergencies and gained his admiration. Rickenbacker was determined to escape being a driver as soon as possible and be transferred to the infant Air Service for flight training.

Rickenbacker took preliminary flight instruction at Tours, then at Issoudun. While doing his primary duty as an engineering officer, he became increasingly proficient in flying and persuaded Major Carl "Tooey" Spaatz (née Spatz), to post him for aerial gunnery training at Cazaux.

At both Issoudun and Cazaux, Rickenbacker was ostracized by pilot trainees with superior social backgrounds. Reed Chambers, a former National Guard pilot with modest origins, became an outcast for befriending Rickenbacker, beginning a lifelong comradeship between the two men. After completing gunnery school at Cazeau, Rickenbacker was sent for advanced combat-pilot training to an aerodrome at Villeneuve-les-Vertus and assigned to the 94th Pursuit Squadron.

Rickenbacker arrived at Villeneuve before his squadron had been equipped with French-built Nieuport 28s, a highly maneuverable plane that turned out to have serious structural defects. Major Raoul Lufbery, a phenomenal fighter pilot, was sent to the 94th as flight instructor. Lufbery saw Rickenbacker's enormous potential, became his mentor, provided him superb training, and paid him the honor of choosing him to fly in the first armed U.S. patrol across enemy lines on 28 February 1917.

After the onset of a major German offensive, the 94th was sent briefly to Epiez and then transferred to the Toul sector, a relatively inactive combat zone, to be seasoned for future operations against stronger German units. Rickenbacker grew increasingly adept in air-to-air combat. He scored his first victory in a sortie with James Hall on 29 April and won several more in May. Credit for one of these kills was denied him because Hall, its sole witness, was shot down behind enemy lines and became a German POW. As a result, Douglas Campbell, Rickenbacker's main rival, beat him out in winning the five official victories required to become the first U.S. ace. A more serious loss to Rickenbacker was the death of his mentor, Lufbery, on 19 May in an action over Maron, a village near Nancy.

Rickenbacker gained increasing esteem among his comrades as his valor and effectiveness in combat became more and more apparent. After Hall was taken prisoner, Rickenbacker became a flight leader in the squadron. He was also decorated with medals, including the Croix de Guerre. But flying at high altitude and executing dives and other sudden maneuvers took a toll on his ears. He also had a terrifying experience when he pulled out of a dive too sharply and began to lose fabric from his upper right wing. His Nieuport spun out of control and plummeted toward the ground until he finally managed to raise the nose of the plane, attain a horizontal position, and limp back to base.

By early June, as the Nieuports were replaced with more rugged SPAD XIIIs, Rickenbacker was sent to a hospital in Paris with an abscessed ear. After arriving in the city he learned that he had been credited with his fifth official victory and was now an ace. He returned to action for a short time but was soon prostrated by a mastoid infection and sent back to the hospital, where he languished for most of the summer while his unit—now facing the best planes and fliers the Germans had to offer—was suffering mounting casualties. Determined to return to the front, he spent his time thinking deeply about what he had already learned from his experiences and how he could correct his faults. By the time he went back into action, he had gained a maturity of purpose that transformed him from a mere ace into a supremely fearsome air warrior.

The SPAD XIII, which could dive at high velocity into a dogfight and exit with a speed that few airplanes could match, was well-suited to his fighting style. Like the cars he had raced before the war, it had the horsepower and structural integrity he craved. Throughout September and October, his hit-and-run tactics became a scourge to his opponents, and he ended the war with 25 official victories (21 against enemy airplanes, four against balloons). In time, the early kill he had scored during the mission with Hall was also credited to him, bringing his total to 26.

In late September, Rickenbacker also became commander of his unit and was promoted to captain. Determined to set the best possible example for his men, he went aloft the next day and took on seven German aircraft single-handedly, bringing down two and scattering the rest. For his gallantry in this action he was belatedly awarded the Medal of Honor in 1930. He came out of the war as America's ace of aces, with the Distinguished Service Cross and nine Oak Leaf Clusters and the French Croix de Guerre with three Palms. Soon after the war, he became a chevalier of the Legion of Honor. The 94th, acknowledged to be the best U.S. air unit of the war, received the honor of accompanying Pershing's army of occupation to Coblenz, Germany.

Rickenbacker returned home to a hero's welcome in February 1919. He continued to promote aviation and had a checkered career in the automobile industry, through no fault of his own. He became a successful executive with General Motors. In April 1938, he was able to purchase Eastern Airlines and build it into a highly successful company.

In February 1941, however, he was badly mangled when a Douglas DST crashed near the Atlanta airport. Initially given up for dead, he endured an agonizing recovery from multiple injuries, including a crushed hip socket, a broken pelvis, and a fractured knee. He was still recuperating when the Japanese attacked Pearl Harbor on 7 December 1941 and thereby plunged the United States into World War II. Despite his shattered condition, he volunteered for special missions for General Henry H. "Hap" Arnold, Chief of Army Air Forces, starting with an inspection tour of domestic military bases in March and April 1942. He went on another mission in September to inspect bases in England and reported on how to improve U.S. planes. He rejected appointment as a two-star general to preserve his independence on such tours.

On 21 October 1942, a Boeing B-17 carrying Rickenbacker from Hawaii to Canton Island, a refueling stop, had to be ditched in the ocean because of a navigational error that led it off-course. For three weeks Rickenbacker and seven companions, one of whom died at sea, drifted through shark-infested waters on three tiny rubber rafts and suffered from hunger, thirst, and exposure to the elements. His survival and rescue gave the American public a huge boost in morale at a major turning point in the war.

Rickenbacker's World War II experiences reinforced his heroic stature in the eyes of his fellow citizens. Returning to Eastern from his wartime missions, Rickenbacker presided for a time over the nation's most profitable airline but began making a series of decisions that adversely affected its interests. In 1958, he was shoved upstairs to chairman of the board and forced into unwilling retirement in 1963.

Rickenbacker fell ill with pneumonia and died in his sleep on 23 July 1973, a tragic hero yet considered by many to be a great man and a great American.

W. David Lewis

References

Lewis, W. D. *American Hero: A Life of Eddie Rickenbacker.* Baltimore: John Hopkins University Press, forthcoming 2002.

Lewis, W. D., ed. "A Man Born out of Season: Edward V. Rickenbacker, Eastern Air Lines, and the Civil Aeronautics Board." In *Airline Executives and Federal Regulation: Case Studies in American Enterprise from the Airmail Era to the Dawn of the Jet Age.* Columbus: Ohio State University Press, 2000.

Ridgway, Matthew Bunker (1895–1993)

U. S. Army general; pioneered airborne warfare in World War II and took the offensive against Chinese–North Korean forces in the Korean War.

As Army Chief of Staff (1953–1955), Ridgway criticized Air Force support of Army missions. Although he supported massive nuclear retaliation as a protective shield for the nation, he felt that the Air Force was putting too many resources into strategic bombers.

Believing that massive retaliation would not prevent limited wars, Ridgway wanted more aviation assets devoted to the Army. He wanted better close air support from low- and slow-flying aircraft, but the Air Force was developing jets that flew higher and faster. Ridgway also desired transports to deliver troops and supplies to unimproved fields in the combat zone, something C-123s and C-130s could not do. He believed that flying trucks and jeeps that could hop and skip about the battlefield would enhance mobility. Because the Air Force was not interested in giving greater support to these needs, Ridgway supported increased development of Army aircraft, especially helicopters.

Ridgway was thus not opposed to airpower; to the contrary, he wanted more airpower for the Army.

John L. Bell

Risner, Robinson (1925–)

U.S. Air Force brigadier general. James Robinson "Robbie" Risner was born in Mammoth Spring, Arkansas, on 16 January 1925. When he joined the Army Air Corps on his eighteenth birthday, an omission on his birth certificate forced him to enlist as "Robinson," whereupon he abandoned his boyhood name. He received his pilot wings in May 1944 and spent the remainder of World War II flying P-38 and P-39 aircraft in Panama.

Following the war, Risner served with the Oklahoma Air National Guard until recalled to active duty and assigned to Korea in May 1952. Flying the F-86 Sabre, he completed 109 combat missions, destroyed eight enemy aircraft, and became the twentieth jet ace of the Korean War. He subsequently commanded fighter squadrons in Germany and California and achieved fame by flying the Charles A. Lindbergh Commemoration Flight from New York to Paris on 20 May 1957, the thirtieth anniversary of Lindbergh's historic solo flight. Flying his F-100F *Spirit of St. Louis II,* Risner set an official transatlantic speed record of 6 hours, 37 minutes.

In August 1964, Risner accepted command of an F-105 Thunderchief squadron in Okinawa, Japan. His squadron deployed to Thailand in 1965, where he flew combat missions over North Vietnam and became the first recipient of the Air Force Cross. On 16 September, he was shot down and captured by the North Vietnamese. During his seven years in captivity, Risner served first as the senior-ranking U.S. officer, then as vice commander of the allied POW wing. After being repatriated in February 1973, he was promoted to brigadier general and continued to fly fighter aircraft as a wing and air division commander, then as vice commander of the USAF Fighter Weapons Center (Top Gun) in Nevada. Since retiring from the Air Force in July 1976, Risner has served as executive director of the Texans' War on Drugs and as a delegate to the United Nations General Assembly.

Paul G. Gillespie

See also
Prisoners of War

References
Frisbee, John L., ed. *Makers of the United States Air Force.* Washington, DC: Office of Air Force History, 1987.
Risner, Robinson. *The Passing of the Night: My Seven Years as a Prisoner of the North Vietnamese.* New York: Ballantine Books, 1973.

Ritchie, Richard S. "Steve" (1942–)

U.S. Air Force brigadier general. Richard S. "Steve" Ritchie was born on 25 June 1942 in Reidsville, North Carolina. He was a star halfback at the United States Air Force Academy, leading the Falcons to the Gator Bowl in 1963. He graduated in June 1964 and, a year later, finished first in his flight-training class at Laredo AFB, Texas.

Ritchie's first assignment was with Flight Test Operations at Eglin AFB, Florida. In 1967, he transferred to Homestead AFB, Florida, for combat-crew training in the F-4 Phantom II. A year later, he was assigned to Da Nang Air Base, in South Vietnam, and flew the first F-4 forward air controller (FAC) missions in Southeast Asia.

In 1969, he returned home to the Fighter Weapons Center (Top Gun) at Nellis AFB, Nevada. Again he graduated tops in his class and soon became the youngest instructor in the school's history. In late 1971, Ritchie volunteered for a second tour in Southeast Asia. In January 1972, he joined the 432d Tactical Fighter Reconnaissance Wing, serving as wing weapons officer.

Between 10 May and 28 August, Captain Ritchie shot down five MiG-21s, becoming one of five U.S. aces (three Air Force, two Navy) during the Vietnam War and the only U.S. pilot ever to shoot down five MiG-21s. Ritchie downed two MiGs on 8 July in a classic low-altitude dogfight in which he outmaneuvered both enemy pilots. Since F-4D Weapon System Officers, or "backseaters," were given full credit for victories during Vietnam, it is worth noting that four of Ritchie's kills came with Captain Charles B. DeBellevue, the top U.S. ace in Vietnam with six victories.

Ritchie returned to the United States in late 1972 and retired from active duty in April 1974, later reaching the rank of reserve brigadier general. In recent years, he has flown a restored McDonnell F-4 at air shows to promote the USAF.

Among many awards, he received the Air Force Cross, four Silver Stars, 10 Distinguished Flying Crosses, 25 Air Medals, Air Force Meritorious Service Medal, Air Force Commendation Medal, 1972 MacKay Trophy, 1973 VFW Armed Forces Award, and 1973 Outstanding Young Man of America Award. He retired from the reserves on 29 January 1999 after more than three decades of service.

William Head

References
Futrell, R. Frank. *Aces and Aerial Victories: The United States Air Force in Southeast Asia, 1965–1973.* Washington, DC: Office of Air Force History, 1976.
Haulman, Daniel L., and William C. Stancik. *Air Force Victory Credits: World War I, World War II, Korea, and Vietnam.* Maxwell AFB, AL: U.S. Historical Research Center, 1988.

Rocket Research in Germany (World War II)

Rockets had been used on both sides during World War I. Afterward, the Allied victors lost interest, focusing research efforts on tanks, planes, and other somewhat successful weapons from the war. Germany, however, continued to pursue rocket research. The Verein fur Raumschiffahrt (Society for Space Travel) was established in 1927 in Breslau. The first successful rocket test took place in 1930, with other tests following, but by 1934 the amateur society was defunct. The German army took over rocket-testing, consistent with its practice from the 1920s of working illegally with Russia on weapons research. The army sought a better artillery weapon, so the research was in the ordnance department.

In 1932, Wernher von Braun joined army rocket research at Kummersdorf. The first test of a 650-pound/thrust motor fueled with alcohol and liquid oxygen fed into the combustion chamber by nitrogen failed when the engine blew up. Undaunted, von Braun and staff designed the Aggregate 1 (A-1) rocket.

The A-1 was approximately 4.5 feet long with a 1-foot diameter and a takeoff weight of 330 pounds. The engine developed 650 pounds of thrust for 16 seconds. Stabilization was built in as a design factor. The nose of the rocket spun, serving as a gyroscope; before launch, an electric motor revved it to 9,000 rpm, and it ran down during flight. The first three A-1 tests at Kummersdorf failed.

Even before the first A-1 test, the A-2 was designed with the same 650-pound/thrust engine but separate fuel and liquid oxygen tanks with a gyroscope in the middle close to the rocket's center of gravity. A-2 tests relocated from Kummersdorf to preserve secrecy (by this time the Nazis were in power and suppressing information and amateurs). Von Braun's 1934 Ph.D. thesis referred to his work as "combustion experiments."

In December 1934, two A-2s were launched successfully at Borkum (and were named *Max* and *Moritz,* the Katzenjammer Kids) from a 40-foot launch platform. They attained 1.4 miles of altitude and landed, with a parachute assist, approximately 800 meters from the launchpoint. When the army asked him about the weapon potential of the A-2, von Braun noted that conventional artillery had the same capability.

In March 1935, Hitler repudiated the Versailles Treaty, and the buildup was on. Kummersdorf was renamed Experimental Station West. The A-3 was on the drawing board, and the Army Ordnance Office began a cooperative effort with the Luftwaffe that eventuated in the special-weapons development center at Peenemünde.

Peenemünde was in northern Usedom. Its conversion to a test center began in 1936. By 1937, the Kummersdorf contingent could relocate all their work, except for engines, which remained at Kummersdorf until 1940. Peenemünde provided a clear, 300-kilometer firing range, harbors, and all other required facilities. Most noteworthy was its supersonic wind tunnel, which initially was smaller than the one at Aachen that tested up to Mach 3.3. By 1942, the capability of the wind tunnel at Peenemünde exceeded Mach 4.4, the best in the world until after the war. Peenemünde also had a rocket production facility.

The A-3 was 21 feet, 8 inches long, 2 feet, 4 inches in diameter; its takeoff weigh was 1,650 pounds. Inside the nose was a telemetry package to measure heat and pressure during flight. There was a guidance system to control attitude, a liquid oxygen tank and nitrogen reservoir, and a parachute container. In the rear was the 6-foot-long motor, encased in the alcohol tank, with 1.5 tons of thrust. The rocket had four fins and jet vanes in the nozzle for better early-flight control and in the thin upper atmosphere, where fins were ineffective.

The A-3 took nearly two years to build because of difficulties developing a guidance system. A combination of four gyroscopes spinning at 20,000 rpm to control yaw and pitch helped keep the rocket level. The 1937 test on the island of Greifswalder Oie failed because the gyro system couldn't control beyond 30 degrees and couldn't correct the A-3's tendency to turn into the wind. Because the A-3 hadn't burned or exploded, the group felt confident enough to develop a small A-5 to refine the new technologies. The A-4 was the designation for the military rocket that became the V-2. The V-2 became the experimental vehicle for both the United States and the Soviet Union. Von Braun led the U.S. space effort for many years.

John Barnhill

References

Johnson, David. *V-1, V-2: Hitler's Vengeance on London.* New York: Stein and Day, 1981.

King, Benjamin, and Timothy J. Kutta. *Impact: The History of Germany's V-Weapons in World War II.* Rockville Centre, NY: Sarpedon, 1998.

Rockwell International

Major U.S. defense contractor. The Rockwell Standard Company was started in 1919 as an autoparts factory in Wisconsin and evolved into one of the largest manufacturers of defense and aerospace products in the world. In 1966, Rockwell and North American Aviation merged to form North American Rockwell Corporation. The new company continued contracts for the Apollo lunar spacecraft, as well as various engines for the Saturn, Thor, and Atlas rockets and the Sidewinder and Sparrow air-to-air missiles. By 1973, the Rocketdyne Division had built more than 8,900 large rocket engines. The Atomics International Division had built prototype liquid-sodium nuclear reactors and was working on the first large-scale demonstrator of a breeder reactor. Autonetics was producing guidance systems for a variety of aircraft, missiles, and ships. What was not being produced, in any great number, were aircraft.

In 1973, North American Rockwell acquired Collins Radio, a leading producer of aircraft avionics, commercial telecommunications, and communications systems, and the company changed its name to Rockwell International. This expansion into electronics was subsequently increased with the purchase of Milwaukee-based Allen-Bradley in 1985 and, a decade later, the acquisition of Reliance Electric, an industrial motor, drive, and transmission company.

While under the Rockwell name, very few aircraft were produced. The six Space Shuttle orbiters, four B-1A prototypes, and 100 production B-1B bombers were the most notable, although the two X-31 high-alpha demonstrators were also manufactured.

On 6 December 1997, Rockwell International announced that it was selling its aerospace and defense divisions to Boeing, which attempted to preserve some of the heritage by naming its new division Boeing North American. The Boeing North American operation performs modifications to operational B-1B bombers, has participated in the Lockheed

X-33 program, and assisted building the two X-32 Joint Strike Fighter demonstrators.

Dennis R. Jenkins

ROLLING THUNDER (1965–1968)

U.S. code name for bombing of North Vietnam from 2 March 1965 to 31 October 1968—the longest bombing campaign ever conducted by the U.S. Air Force. It was also one of the least decisive, most costly, and intensely controversial bombing campaigns in U.S. history.

ROLLING THUNDER had two objectives. It began as an attempt at strategic persuasion: forcing Hanoi to stop supporting the Vietcong and negotiate and end to the conflict. In July 1965, when the United States committed the Army and Marine Corps to the ground war and large numbers of U.S. servicemen and women were sent to South Vietnam, ROLLING THUNDER switched its primary objective from strategic persuasion to interdiction in an attempt to reduce the flow of troops and supplies moving from the North into the South. From July 1965 through October 1968, ROLLING THUNDER remained primarily an interdiction campaign, although elements of strategic persuasion operated concurrently.

To accomplish the campaign's objectives, the Air Force, Navy, and Marine Corps bombed military installations to include radar sites, barracks areas, and some airfields. Petroleum storage facilities (North Vietnam had no refineries), railyards, rail and highway bridges, and ammunition depots were struck. The bombing began modestly, constrained to the southern panhandle of North Vietnam, and moved steadily northward, increasing in scope and intensity through the spring and summer of 1965. Generally, the Air Force struck targets in the northern and western parts of North Vietnam and in the southern panhandle while Navy and Marine aviators, flying from aircraft carriers on Yankee Station in the Gulf of Tonkin, hit targets in the western part of the country and along the coastal plain. The Air Force relied on the Republic F-105 Thunderchief, or "Thud," and the McDonnell F-4 Phantom II to carry the brunt of its bombing to the North Vietnamese heartland. The Navy and Marine Corps flew fighter-bombers like the F-4 Phantom, A-4 Skyhawk, all-weather A-6 Intruder, F-8U Crusader, and A3D Skywarrior twin-engine bomber. Over the course of the campaign, the Air Force flew some 2,360 B-52 sorties against targets in the southern panhandle.

North Vietnam's air defenses increased in sophistication when the Soviet Union and the People's Republic of China provided what became one of the world's most potent air defense systems. It included SA-2 surface-to-air missiles (SAMs) that forced U.S. aircraft to approach their targets at altitudes as low as 500 feet and along a gauntlet of antiaircraft fire from 23mm, 37mm, and 57mm guns, many of which were radar-controlled. The North Vietnamese incorporated their population into air defense so that hundreds of thousands of people were given rifles and machine guns to blaze away at the hated Yankee air pirates.

As if SAMs, antiaircraft guns, and an aroused populace were not enough, the North Vietnamese possessed a healthy stable of interceptors. Planes like the MiG-17, MiG-19, and MiG-21 all proved to be highly maneuverable and somewhat more capable than many U.S. airmen originally thought. Air-to-air action was the exception rather than the rule, but it did take place, with the United States losing 67 planes in dogfights while downing 137 aircraft for a kill ratio of about 2.2:1 in the U.S. favor.

During ROLLING THUNDER, the Air Force, Navy, and Marines flew nearly 1 million sorties against North Vietnam, some 600,000 of which were strike sorties. Estimates are that airpower destroyed 77 percent of all ammunition depots and 65 percent of the enemy's petroleum storage facilities. Bombing degraded electric-power generating capabilities by more than 50 percent and brought down 55 percent of North Vietnam's bridges.

But ROLLING THUNDER failed to achieve its strategic objectives in that the North Vietnamese did not agree to negotiate until the United States agreed to stop the bombing; the flow of troops and supplies moving from North to South doubled each year from 1965 through 1968.

ROLLING THUNDER was a strategic failure in the classic sense because conventional airpower was used against the North in an attempt to affect an unconventional war in South Vietnam. There are three reasons. First, North Vietnam was a preindustrial agricultural power not susceptible to the kind of bombing that helped defeat Japan and Germany in World War II, but airpower leaders never understood that. Second, Washington exercised far too much control over the targeting process, which was convoluted, inefficient, and ineffective. Third, North Vietnam proved to be much more determined than was the United States.

Estimates are that it ultimately cost the United States $6 for every $1 in damage inflicted on the North. It also cost about 770 Air Force, Navy, and Marine aircraft and more than 600 aircrewmen killed, captured, or missing in action. In the end, ROLLING THUNDER is best described with a line from Shakespeare's *Macbeth:* "Full of sound and fury, signifying nothing."

Earl H. Tilford Jr.

References

Clodfelter, Mark. *The Limits of Air Power: The American Bombing of North Vietnam.* New York: Free Press, 1989.

Morroco, John. *The Vietnam Experience: Thunder From Above: The Air War, 1941–1968.* Boston: Boston Publishing Company, 1984.

Tilford, Earl H. Jr. *Crosswinds: The Air Force's Setup in Vietnam.* College Station: Texas A&M University Press, 1993.

Rosendahl, Charles E. (1892–1977)

U.S. Navy vice admiral. Charles Emery Rosendahl was born in Chicago on 15 May 1892. Attending public schools in Kansas and Texas, he was appointed to the U.S. Naval Academy and graduated with the class of 1914.

Rosendahl held duty aboard various surface units, notably destroyers, and a postwar tour as instructor at Annapolis. In April 1923, he reported to the Naval Air Station in Lakehurst, New Jersey, for training in lighter-than-air craft. Designated naval aviator (airship) on 22 November 1923, Rosendahl was detailed to duty in the rigid airship USS *Shenandoah* (ZR-1). The lieutenant was navigator and senior survivor when the ship was torn apart by severe atmospheric instability near Ava, Ohio, in September 1925. Following the inquiry, which made the young officer a public figure, Rosendahl was ordered to duty as executive officer of USS *Los Angeles* (ZR-3), the U.S. Navy's most successful rigid. In May 1926, he assumed command, serving aggressively as skipper for three years. Relieved temporarily, "Rosie" accompanied the first westward crossing of the North Atlantic in *Graf Zeppelin* in October 1928 and, in 1929, was guest aboard the peripatetic Zeppelin during its round-the-world flight.

After service in the Plans Division of the Bureau of Aeronautics, he assembled the nucleus crew of USS *Akron* (ZRS-4) and had charge of fitting out that fleet airship—a strategic aerial scout that carried airplanes. He flew ship's trials and assumed command when ZRS-4 was placed in commission in October 1931, retaining command until relieved for line duty in mid-1932. From June 1934 through August 1938, Rosendahl was back as commanding officer of the Lakehurst Naval Air Station. During that tour, the lieutenant commander (and fellow naval airmen) served as U.S. naval observer aboard *Hindenburg* as it plied the North and South Atlantic and was on the landing field when *Hindenburg* took fire on 6 May 1937.

The years 1938–1940 saw further sea duty, this time as executive officer of USS *Milwaukee.* Then came duty in Washington in the office of the secretary of the Navy, the office of the Chief of Naval Operations, and the Bureau of Aeronautics, assignments in which he pressed for and planned the expansion of naval lighter-than-air aircraft to help fight World War II. The primary mission of the nonrigid airship, or blimp, was antisubmarine warfare.

In September 1942, Rosendahl assumed command of USS *Minneapolis.* The cruiser lost its bow to Japanese torpedoes off Guadalcanal but continued its engagement with the enemy before withdrawing for major repairs. The incident earned its commander a Navy Cross. From *Minneapolis,* Rosendahl was ordered to the States, promoted from captain to rear admiral, and assigned duty as chief of naval airship training and experimentation at Lakehurst, a new billet inspired by the contributions of Lighter-than-air (LTA) operations in the Atlantic and Pacific Fleets, including the Caribbean, South American, and western Mediterranean Theaters. In addition to this, the admiral was special assistant for LTA to the deputy Chief of Naval Operations (Air).

Charles E. Rosendahl was transferred to the retired list of the Navy in November 1946, with the rank of vice admiral. By sheer force of personality, his commands and tireless advocacy, the Rosendahl name is virtually synonymous with lighter-than-air aeronautics.

William Althoff

References

Althoff, William F. *Sky Ships: A History of the Airship in the United States Navy.* New York: Orion Books, 1990.

Royal Aircraft Factory

One of the five original components of the Royal Flying Corps; originally intended to act as a repair station for damaged aircraft. In its two years of peacetime operation, however, the definition of "repair" was so liberally interpreted that by the outbreak of war (the name was changed in 1918 to Royal Aircraft Establishment to avoid confusion over the acronym assumed by the Royal Air Force) it had clearly become a research and design facility as well.

Before and during the war years, it turned out original designs in several categories, all with the common word "experimental" in their title, a nod to the research role the factory had assumed. Thus are seen the "BE" (some accounts say the "B" stands for "Blériot," others for "Bombing"), the "FE" (Fighter Experimental), "RE" (Reconnaissance Experimental), and "SE" (Scouting Experimental). The lines frequently became blurred, resulting in considerable functional overlap between the BE and RE types and the FE and SE types.

The activities of Royal Aircraft eventually threatened private manufacturers, who were highly critical of what they

Perhaps the finest of the designs of the Royal Aircraft Factory, the SE 5a fought well on the Western Front and was used in limited numbers in the postwar years by the U.S. Army Air Service. (U.S. Air Force)

saw as a Royal Flying Corps manufacturing preference for its own types. Many were driven as a result into closer business relationships with the Royal Naval Air Service (RNAS) and the British Admiralty. This became a factor in the interservice rivalry that developed between the RFC and the RNAS and was of more than casual importance in the decision to merge the two into the Royal Air Force.

Royal Aircraft designs spanned the quality scale from the distinctly inferior BE 2, through the slightly better RE 8, to the truly outstanding SE 5/5a fighter.

The SE 5a was the aircraft to which any British neophyte fighter pilot would want to be assigned. It was fast, strong, easy to fly, well-armed (with a synchronized Vickers and a wing-mounted Lewis), and lacked the fatal habits that characterized its contemporary, the Sopwith Camel.

Built around the Wolsley Viper engine, a British copy of the direct-drive Hispano Suiza, the SE 5a was designed for high-altitude fighter patrols. In the hands of pilots like James McCudden, who scored 50 of his 57 victories on the type, the SE was a truly dangerous fighter, every bit the equal of the Camel or any of its German rivals.

James Streckfuss

References

Bruce, J. M. *British Aeroplanes 1914–1918.* London: Putnam, 1959

Royal Australian Air Force (RAAF)

The Royal Australian Air Force had its humble beginnings in September 1912 as the Australian Flying Corps when a flight of four aircraft was authorized for the army. In 1913, its first two pilots went to England and returned with five aircraft and number of maintenance personnel. A total of 2,275 RAAF personnel served with British aviation forces during World War I.

Starting in January 1929, brushfire-spotting became a new mission for the RAAF. This was followed a year later by dusting for pest control.

With World War II looming, two major training expansions were instituted in 1938 and 1939. Plans were made for 32 squadrons with 360 aircraft in June 1940, but this was increased to 73 squadrons in May 1941. The RAAF began combat operations during World War II in the Southwest Pacific alongside U.S. forces. Eventually, the RAAF had squadrons fighting in almost every theater of the war. By the end of World War II, the RAAF comprised 3,187 first-line aircraft dispersed in 52 squadrons. Their missions included fighter, bomber, reconnaissance, antisubmarine, clandestine operations, and transport.

The first jets to enter RAAF service were de Havilland Vampires in May 1946. These were followed by Gloster Meteors and North American Sabres. The RAAF was part of the UN operation in Korea, employing its Meteors.

When the South Vietnamese government asked for assistance through the Southeast Asia Treaty Organization, the Australians joined the anticommunist efforts. During the Vietnam War, RAAF Bell Iroquois helicopters supported Australian ground forces. An RAAF English Electric Canberra squadron served alongside a USAF Martin B-57 Canberra wing for more than four years. Another RAAF squadron provided airlift support operations with de Havilland Caribous between 1964 and 1971.

Maritime patrol operations began in World War II with Avro Lancasters and Consolidated Liberators. Subsequently Avro Lincolns were employed along with a number of large flying boats. This mission was then performed by Lockheed Neptunes and, later, Lockheed Orions.

During the early 1970s, the RAAF leased 24 USAF McDonnell F-4E Phantom IIs until they were replaced by the General Dynamics F-111C. The Lockheed Hercules entered the RAAF inventory in 1958 and has since became the mainstay of RAAF transport units.

Wherever and whenever called upon, the RAAF has served Australia, the British Empire, and the United Nations. A staunch supporter of U.S. interests, RAAF personnel bring professionalism to every operation they undertake.

Alwyn T. Lloyd

References

Green, William, and John Fricker. *The Air Forces of the World.* New York: Hanover House, 1958.

Parnell, Neville, and Trevor Boughton. *Flypast: A Record of Aviation in Australia.* A Civil Aviation Authority bicentennial project. Canberra: Australian Government Publishing Service, 1988.

Royal Bulgarian Air Force

Bulgaria had originally been among the pioneers in the use of airpower, a Bulgarian Blériot XI dropping grenades on the Turkish fortress of Odrin. Yet for most of its existence, the air force of Bulgaria has never been among the largest, or even most important, of the world,

After World War I, Bulgaria built aircraft in the national airplane factory Dazhavna Aeroplanna Rapotilnitsa and purchased others from abroad for use in civilian roles. At the same time, a secret air component of the army, the Vozdushni Voiski, was established.

The expansion of the air component of the army began in 1935, when the first air wing, comprising one fighter, one training, and two reconnaissance squadrons, was established. The air force was reformed illegally in 1936, with the aim of forming four wings during 1937–1939. In July 1938, when the constraints imposed upon Bulgaria by the post–World War I peace were lifted, Bulgaria was finally able to reveal the existence of the air force to the public.

Although the first actual combat aircraft to arrive were Polish PZL P.24B fighters and P.43A light bombers, the largest group of planes represented remnants of the Czechoslovakian air force that Germany had seized when occupying the remaining parts of Czechia in March 1939. Thus, Bulgaria received 78 Avia B.534 fighters, 24 Avia B.71 medium bombers, 62 Letov S.328 army cooperation planes, and 12 Aero MB.200 bombers; the air force expanded to five air battalions (or squadrons). But with this sudden expansion came an urgent need for trained pilots, and 160 Bulgarian pilots received training in Italy, Hungary, and Germany.

During 1940 and 1941 expansion continued, a number of additional air battalions were formed, and Bulgaria received 11 modern Dornier Do 17Ms. Furthermore, the air battalions were now organized into four air regiments. In all, these contained 561 machines, with 411 operationally ready.

During the Axis invasion of Yugoslavia (for which Bulgaria provided bases), a number of attacks by Yugoslav and British bombers were experienced. When the Allies bombed the Ploesti oil fields later in the war, Bulgarian aircraft attacked with former Czech aircraft and some German Messerschmitt Bf 109s. Bulgaria also received 96 former Vichy French Dewoitine D.520s and some additional Dornier Do 17s.

On 10 January 1944, 180 B17s with heavy fighter escort attacked the Bulgarian capital of Sofia. Some 70 Bulgarian and 30 German fighters rose in its defense, but the destruction wrought upon the capital was severe, with 4,100 buildings reduced to rubble.

Although Allied bombings of Bulgaria remained few in number, their impact was heavy. The Soviet invasion and subsequent coup on 10 August 1944 brought about the inevitable, and Bulgaria declared war on Germany on 5 September.

The following two months saw the Royal Bulgarian Air Force flying 4,400 missions against Axis forces in Macedonia, Serbia, and Kosovo, losing 23 aircraft. The air force received 120 Yakovlev Yak-9 fighters and 120 Ilyushin Il-2 ground attack planes but continued to use German Messerschmitt Bf 109Gs and Junker Ju 87Ds (the famous Stuka) against its former ally. After World War II Bulgaria became part of the Soviet bloc, and the Bulgarian Air Force flew Soviet equipment.

Henrik Krog

References

Neulen, Hans Werner. *In the Skies of Europe.* Ramsbury, Marlborough, UK: Crowood, 2000.

Thomas, N., and K. Mikulan. *Axis Forces in Yugoslavia, 1941–1945.* Oxford, UK: Osprey, 1998.

Royal Canadian Air Force

See Canadian Air Force

Royal Flying Corps (RFC)/Royal Naval Air Service (RNAS)/Royal Air Force (RAF)

British military aviation has its roots in the Royal Engineers, which established a balloon corps in 1908. In May 1912, the Royal Flying Corps was established with a military wing, which worked for the army; a naval wing for operations with the fleet; the Central Flying School for instructional purposes; a repair depot called the Royal Aircraft Factory; and a reserve.

A form of interservice rivalry developed almost at once between the military and naval wings, and shortly before the declaration of war, in the summer of 1914, the naval wing broke away to become the Royal Naval Air Service.

When war was declared, the RFC deployed with the British Expeditionary Force; an aircraft park and four squadrons (Nos. 2, 3, 4, and 5), each equipped with the entire mixed bag of aircraft then in the British inventory. After a series of moves necessitated by the initial British retreat, headquarters in France was established at Saint Omer, where it remained for most of the war. The first field commander of the RFC was Brigadier General David Henderson. Henderson would shortly return to England, though, leaving command in the field to Hugh Montague "Boom" Trenchard.

Initially, each RFC unit acted as something of a self-contained air force, performing the complete range of activities, which at the time consisted primarily of reconnaissance duties with the occasional bombing mission. As the war progressed, the force grew in number, and by 1916 squadrons began to specialize either as fighter, bombing, or reconnaissance units, the latter role being further divided into photographic and artillery functions. As a consequence of specialization, the practice of units having a multiplicity of types was abandoned, and squadrons started to become known not only by their role but also by what type of equipment they possessed. Balloon companies using tethered observation balloons as artillery spotters began appearing in British service in 1915 and remained a fixture on the Western Front throughout the war.

Technological advances were rapid during the war, and keeping up with the enemy in the design and deployment of new types was a constant problem. The British sometimes suffered severely as a result. When the Germans were first to develop an interrupter gear—allowing a machine gun to fire through the propeller arc—the RFC found itself on the receiving end of the "Fokker scourge." During the spring of 1917 the problem reached a crisis. During the Battle of the Somme, the previous autumn, the Luftstreitkräfte (Air Service) had organized its single-seat fighter force into heterogeneous *jagdstaffeln* (fighter squadrons) and reequipped with the Albatros D.I and D.II. The type had been refined over the winter into the D.III.

The RFC, however, had lagged in the introduction of new types and went into the spring with the same complement of tired aircraft, mostly BE 2s that had been in use for the last two years. It paid a high price—the highest number of casualties in a single month it would suffer during its existence—a month that went down in history as "bloody April."

Technological advantage was not the only factor in these losses; doctrine also played a part. Throughout the war, Trenchard followed an offensive policy. This action has attracted its share of criticism, but faced with German occupation of the high ground and the insatiable intelligence needs of the army, often only satisfied by aerial reconnaissance, the RFC seems to have had little choice but to press on with what it had.

The situation improved over the summer of 1917 with the introduction of the Sopwith Camel, the SE 5/5a, the de Havilland D.H. 4, and the Bristol Fighter; the SE 5/5a was the best design to emerge from the Royal Aircraft Factory during the war, the other three, of course, being the products of private firms. From that point on, technology remained fairly balanced, and casualties returned to a manageable level until spiking again in September 1918 following the German introduction of the BMW-powered Fokker D.VII.

The Royal Flying Corps did not operate exclusively on the Western Front, however. After some initial jurisdictional feuding with the RNAS, the RFC had assumed responsibility for the aerial home defense of Great Britain, thereafter regularly scrambling a hodgepodge of mostly second-line equipment in response to Zeppelin and Gotha attacks.

Outside of England and France, units also served in Egypt and Palestine, Mesopotamia, and Russia, providing support to British army operations in those theaters.

The Royal Naval Air Service mission was primarily, if not exclusively, the support of British maritime endeavors. This covered a wide range of activities, from antisubmarine patrols and general reconnaissance duties in connection with the fleet, to bombing missions against submarine pens and Zeppelin bases. To fulfill these missions, the RNAS developed a varied inventory that included floatplanes, flying boats, the first experimental torpedo-bombers, and lighter-than-air airships. Ships were also adapted to work with aircraft, leading to the balloon ship (which extended the effective range of vision of the group to which the balloon vessel was attached), the crane-equipped seaplane carrier, and, eventually, to the first flight-deck aircraft carriers.

In addition to new equipment, innovative techniques were also developed for work over the water, one of the most useful to the prosecution of the war being the so-called spider web. The spider web was an invisible grid over the English Channel and North Sea that provided an organized method for aircraft to use in searching for underwater mines and U-boats. Provision for aerial escort as part of the convoy scheme also contributed to the safety of Allied shipping as it crossed the Atlantic to and from North America.

As mentioned, the RNAS did not operate exclusively over the water. Throughout the war, naval units were deployed for land-based operations on the Western Front. And among the Allied forces, the RNAS could take credit for the first tentative attempts at strategic bombing. In the summer of 1916, the RNAS organized No. 3 Wing and equipped the unit with Sopwith 11/2 Strutters and Breguet bombers with the aim of attacking targets inside Germany. The group was stationed at Luxeuil, near Nancy, putting it within reach of manufacturing plants in the Saar River Valley. Bad weather—the perpetual enemy of aerial operations—kept No. 3 Wing grounded throughout much of its life, but its first—and most memorable—raid took place on 12 October 1916 when it attacked the Mauser Works at Oberndorf. The raid was a truly international operation involving not only the British naval unit but also French bombers and an escort of Nieuport fighters provided by the U.S. volunteers of the Lafayette Escadrille. By spring, however, the lackluster results achieved led to the breakup of the group and the reassignment of its crews to other units, many going to the navy's single-seat squadrons up near the channel coast. There, some pilots, such as Canadian ace Raymond Collishaw, would go on to great success flying the Sopwith Pup, Triplane, and later the immortal Camel, supplementing the RFC in support of army operations.

Relations between the two British aviation services were always somewhat tense, accusations of various intrigues going in both directions. The rivalry heightened to the point that a government committee merged the RFC and RNAS into the Royal Air Force on 1 April 1918.

Trenchard was ordered to run the Independent Force and General John Salmond became the RAF's first field commander. There is little evidence to indicate that a true merger of the two services really took place prior to the Armistice, however. There was a new "RAF blue" uniform issued, but not many people are seen wearing it in wartime photos, most clinging not only to the old uniform but also to the practices and brief traditions of their earlier branch. Previously, naval squadrons were renumbered, each having "200" added to its original designation (e.g., Naval Eight became No. 208 Squadron, RAF), and a few swaps of personnel were effected, probably the most notable being the transfer of RNAS ace Roderick Dallas to the command of No. 40 Squadron, an old RFC fighter unit. But these changes were largely cosmetic, and the real birth of the Royal Air Force is more likely found in the postwar struggles to remain funded and stay alive, all taking place under the stewardship of Trenchard. The fruits of his labor became apparent in 1940 when the RAF rose to the Nazi threat and achieved its finest hour during the Battle of Britain.

James Streckfuss

See also
World War I Aviation
References

Penrose, Harald. *British Aviation: The Great War and Armistice.* New York: Funk and Wagnalls, 1969.

Royal Norwegian Air Force (RNAF)

Independent air service formed by Norway in November 1944. Its principal tasks today are to ensure the territorial integrity of the country, ensure the safe reception of allied forces sent in support of Norway, and contribute to NATO operations. The RNAF is part of the Norwegian Total Defense Concept, with an emphasis on defending its territory; the combat-aircraft element is focused on air defense.

The RNAF holds 58 updated F-16s as its most important weapons system within the air defense role, but together with four updated P-3C Orions it also plays an important part in maritime operations. In addition, the RNAF works closely with other NATO countries in the Air Command and Control System (ACCS) program. The ACCS integrates the command-and-control system in order to meet the requirements of identifying and destroying hostile sorties.

Under the two principal subordinate commands, COMNON and COMSONOR, the RNAF organization consists of various air bases and radar sites. The air defense is organized as a network where the most important air bases are defended by NASAMS, the Norwegian advanced surface-to-air missile system, integrated with RB 70 missiles and, in the event of mobilization, L 70 guns.

The RNAF is in the process of reorganization, and its current peacetime organization consists of 5,800 officers and civilians and 2,700 conscripts. The RNAF participated in

Operation ALLIED FORCE with F-16s, conducting combat air patrol. Although the organization has a history of international engagements, including the use of C-130s and helicopters, it is increasingly adapting to participation in future peacekeeping and peace-enforcement operations. As such, the RNAF has a national as well as an international edge through its Immediate Reaction Force, located at the main air base in Orland.

John Andreas Olsen

Royal Thai Air Force (RTAF)

Military aviation in Thailand (Siam until June 1939) began in February 1912 when the Ministry of War sent three officers to France for pilot training. When they returned with eight French-built aircraft in November 1913, they were formed into the Army Aviation Section. On 27 March 1915, shortly after the airmen moved into their permanent home at a newly constructed airfield at Don Muang, outside Bangkok, the Ministry of War reorganized the Aviation Section into the Army Flying Battalion, under the command of French-trained Lieutenant Colonel Phraya Chalerm Akas.

King Vijiravudh was an enthusiastic supporter of the country's growing air force. The monarch believed that aviation promoted national unity, fostered a spirit of modernity, and enhanced prestige in the world community. Army Chief of Staff Field Marshal Prince Chakrabonse Bhuvanart also led the way in promoting aeronautical development. In 1983, in grateful memory of his assistance during its formative years, the air force placed a statue of the prince in front of headquarters, inscribed "The Father of the Royal Thai Air Force."

The government sent an aviation contingent to France in June 1918, but the war ended before the Siamese pilots entered combat. Nonetheless, the decision to assist the French not only increased the kingdom's prestige but also allowed the air force to gain valuable experience. On 19 March 1919, the Flying Battalion became the Aeronautical Department of the Army, with three operational flying units (pursuit, observation, bombardment). A further reorganization took place on 1 December 1921 when the air component was renamed the Department of Aeronautical Service (more familiarly, the Royal Aeronautical Service). At the same time, the air force was designated as a special service with a separate budget, although it remained under the direct control of the commander in chief of the army.

The air force achieved complete independence on 9 April 1937 as the Royal Siamese (soon Thai) Air Force within the Ministry of Defense. The airmen adopted the blue uniforms and rank designations of the Royal Air Force. Group Captain Phra Vechayan Rangsarit became the service's first commander.

By 1940, the RTAF boasted five fighter squadrons and six bomber squadrons, equipped with Curtiss Hawks, Vought Corsairs, and Martin 139 WSs. This force fought a border war with French Indochina in the winter of 1940–1941, claiming five French planes shot down at a cost of three Thai losses.

The RTAF flew briefly against the Japanese in early December 1941. The government then concluded a military alliance with Tokyo. The air force operated, without great enthusiasm, under Japanese direction until it shifted to support Thai resistance in the later stages of World War II. By war's end, the RTAF had reached its nadir, with less the 50 percent of its aircraft in serviceable condition.

A new era dawned on 17 October 1950 when Thailand and the United States signed a mutual defense assistance agreement. The RTAF was reorganized along U.S. lines and reequipped with U.S. aircraft. It subsequently sent transport contingents to assist the United States during the Korean and Vietnam Wars. By 2000, the RTAF's inventory consisted of 153 combat aircraft, including one squadron of F-5 A/Bs and two squadrons of F-16 A/Bs. Although not the largest air force in Southeast Asia, the well-trained RTAF stood ready to protect its country's borders, as it had since its inception.

William M. Leary

References

Young, Edward M. *Aerial Nationalism: A History of Aviation in Thailand.* Washington, DC: Smithsonian Institution Press, 1995.

Royal Yugoslav Air Force (RYAF)

The history of Yugoslavia's air force started in 1923, when the army spun off its air units to a separate arm. They had seen their first post–World War I combat four years earlier when Austrian and Slovenian planes battled each other in the skies over the region of Karinthia.

Equipped with French remnants after World War I, the air force was expanded to two air regiments, one at Novi Sad and one at Mostar, of six squadrons each. Indigenous aircraft manufacture began in the 1920s with Rogozarski, Ikarus, Zmaj, and DFA, which began producing large numbers of primarily French but also German planes under license.

As Germany and Italy undertook expansionist policies, the need for a larger air force was obvious. Yugoslavia faced the Nazi invasion on 6 April with a highly diverse mix of aircraft that were not yet familiar to all pilots. Among the 487 airworthy planes of the air force (including the marine air element) were British Hurricane, German Messerschmitt Bf 109, and Yugoslav Ikarus IK-2 fighters, as well as British Bristol Blenheim, German Dornier Do17, and Italian Savoia-Marchetti SM.79 bombers. These were organized for the most part into four air brigades and some miscellaneous units.

The German attack opened with a thorough bombing of the capital of Belgrade, lasting two days and totally overwhelming the Yugoslav defenses. The odds against the RYAF were simply too great. When an armistice was signed on 17 April, only 11 days after the initial attack, the force was essentially crushed. Only 44 planes managed to make it out of the country to the Greek airfield at Ioannina but were subject to a German attack there. Only six bombers and 10 seaplanes escaped to Egypt. There, they were formed into Nos. 1 and 2 Yugoslav Squadrons, but they were progressively weakened by losses of planes; by 1942 both had disbanded, the pilots going to other RAF units. Some elements of the RYAF, for a very short time, became part of the partisan movement.

Major expansion came in 1944, when an agreement was made between the Partisans and the royal government-in-exile. As a result, new air units were formed in the Middle East from former RYAF aviators and pilots flown out from occupied Yugoslavia. Two squadrons were formed in the Middle East. The 1st and 2d Yugoslav Fighter Squadrons became the 352d and 351st Yugoslav Squadrons RAF on 22 April and 1 July and, after intensive training, transferred to Italy, then to the island of Vis in the Adriatic Sea, and finally to Skabrnje airfield near Zadar on the Yugoslav mainland. When World War II ended, the two squadrons were organized into the 1st Fighter Regiment before being disbanded as RAF units on 15 June 1945, the equipment being transferred to Yugoslavia's air force.

At the same time, the Partisans requested help from the Soviets (who had entered Yugoslav territory in the fall of 1944) in forming air units. Group Vitruk, a Soviet air corps consisting of the 10th Guards Assault Air Division and the 236th Fighter Air Division, was transferred to Yugoslavia and took on Yugoslav personnel as extras, trained to do the same tasks as the Soviets. Then in December 1944, they formed three fighter and three air assault regiments with mixed Soviet-Yugoslav crews, who were later subordinated to the new Yugoslav 11th Fighter Air Division and 42d Assault Air Division.

Combat was first joined by Yugoslav pilots on 17 January 1945 on the Syrmian Front, and the two air divisions were taken over by a Yugoslav HQ in March 1945, when the Group of Air Divisions of the (Yugoslav) Army was formed. On 1 April the first independent Yugoslav unit was formed at Klenak airfield from the 112th Fighter and 422d Assault Regiments, which had been transferred there on 29 March. This Air Group South was to support the final offensive of the Yugoslav army. On 12 April 1945, they undertook the largest Yugoslav air offensive of World War II, when 180 planes launched simultaneous attacks on Axis installations in preparation for the final Yugoslav offensive. Yugoslav planes flew primarily harassing missions until the war ended on 7 May 1945.

Yugoslav planes did not cease operations, however, and continued flying missions until 25 May 1945 against its own citizens—Croat, Serbian, and Slovene nationalists refusing to give up in the face of the communist-dominated Partisans.

Henrik Krog

References

Tarnstrom, Ronald. *Balkan Battles.* Lindsborg, KS: Trogen Books, 1998.

Thomas, Nigel, and Simon McCouaig. *Foreign Volunteers of the Allied Forces, 1939–1945.* London: Osprey, 1998.

Rudel, Hans-Ulrich (1916–1982)

Luftwaffe colonel; by any standard the most successful military aviator in history. He joined the Luftwaffe in 1936 as an officer candidate and, after completing flight training in 1938, was assigned to a unit equipped with the Junkers Ju 87 "Stuka" dive-bomber. He was apparently a slow starter and lost his pilot status temporarily. He participated in the Polish campaign as an observer in a reconnaissance unit and did not rejoin the Stuka force until he had received additional training.

Rudel's star began to rise with the German invasion of Russia in June 1941. He first came to the attention of the German public that September, when he dive-bombed and sank the Soviet battleship *Marat.* He continued to fly ground support missions on the Eastern Front for the rest of the war, taking only brief respites to recover from injuries. In late 1944, Rudel was promoted to colonel and given command of the last day unit still flying the Ju 87, Schlachtgeschwader 2 (SG 2; 2d Ground Attack Wing). He was awarded successively higher decorations, in the German custom, and on 1 January 1945 was summoned to Hitler's headquarters to receive a new supreme award, the Golden Oak Leaves with Swords and Diamonds to the Knight's Cross of the Iron Cross, of which he was the only recipient.

Rudel flew a total of 2,530 combat missions and was credited with the destruction of 519 tanks, one battleship, one cruiser, one destroyer, 70 landing ships, 150 gun emplacements, 800 combat vehicles of various types, and seven airplanes. He was shot down 30 times and was wounded five times. In February 1945, his most serious injury necessitated the amputation of his lower right leg. He continued to fly missions despite orders grounding him; the Soviet vehicles he destroyed thereafter were credited to the "*geschwader* account" (i.e., to the overall unit).

On 8 May 1945, Rudel led the remaining aircraft of his unit to a U.S. airfield, where he performed a perfect ground loop on landing, shearing off his Stuka's fixed landing gear. The Americans, obviously impressed with this feat and the well-dressed girlfriends some of his pilots were carrying as passengers, did not return Rudel to the Soviets—despite a 100,000-ruble bounty on his head—but kept him in a POW camp until April 1946.

After his release Rudel joined the Focke-Wulf firm and traveled to Argentina as its representative. While in Latin America he wrote his memoirs, which had great success worldwide; he became friends with dictator Juan Perón and developed into a skilled mountain climber. He returned to Germany in the 1960s, but his right-wing associations and outspoken defense of the Third Reich made him unwelcome in the armed forces and aviation industry; he eventually became a ski instructor, despite his artificial leg. He died in 1982 of a brain hemorrhage.

Donald Caldwell

See also

German Air Force (Luftwaffe)

References

Obermeier, E. *Die Ritterkreuztraeger der Luftwaffe, 1939–1945, Band II: Stuka und Schlachtflieger* [Recipients of the Knight's Cross]. Mainz: Verlag Dieter Hoffmann, 1976.

Rudel, H. *Stuka Pilot.* New York: Ballantine, 1958.

Rudenko, S. I. (1904–1990)

World War II Soviet air commander. Sergei Ignatevich Rudenko was born on 20 October 1904 in Ukraine and joined the Red Air Force in 1924. In June 1941, he commanded the 31st Air Division and was one of few commanders to distinguish himself during the early months of the war, particularly during the defense of Moscow. From September 1942 until the end of the war, he commanded the 16th Air Army, which took part in the major operations of the war, including the Battles of Stalingrad and Kursk, and the capture of Berlin. Rudenko was promoted to colonel general in May 1944 and was awarded the Hero of the Soviet Union on 19 August 1944. In December 1948, he was appointed commander of airborne troops and in August 1950 was appointed commander of long-range aviation. In 1955, he was promoted to marshal of aviation, and in 1958 he was made first deputy commander in chief of the air force. Beginning in 1968 he was chief of the air force academy, retiring in 1973. He died in July 1990.

George M. Mellinger

See also

Kursk, Battle of; Stalingrad, Battle of

References

United States Air Force. *The Command and Staff of the Soviet Army Air Force in the Great Patriotic War, 1941–1945: A Soviet View.* Trans. and publ. United States Air Force, 1978.

Woff, Richard. "Rudenko." In Harold Shukman, ed., *Stalin's Generals.* New York: Grove Press, 1993.

Ruhr Bombing Campaign

Allied destruction of the German industrial heartland during World War II. At the onset of war, RAF Wellington, Whitley, and Hampden bombers could carry their bombloads about 400 miles, a range that included the Ruhr River Valley. This was the location of fully 75–80 percent of German war targets. The first British raid on 15–16 May 1940 involved 93 heavy bombers. By 18 June, Britain had raided 1,666 times with six or more bombers. Included were several low-level attacks against the aqueducts of the Dortmund-Ems Canal, the sole water link between the Ruhr and eastern Germany and the North Sea and Baltic outlets. The British suffered heavy losses to the superior numbers and quality of German planes.

With the loss of France and the threat of Operation SEALION, the German code name for the planed invasion of England, raids diminished as the RAF shifted priorities to marshalling yards and barges. In December 1940, Britain shifted to nighttime bombing for two raids against Gelsenkirchen; 296 planes claimed hits, but postraid photos showed no significant damage and only a handful of craters where reports indicated there should be around 1,000.

An 8–9 March raid on Essen, the Ruhr's largest industrial city, featured the first use of Gee. Under the Gee system, three radio beams from British locations allowed navigators to pinpoint their location over the target to within one-tenth of a mile. An August 1941 report by the British Air Ministry stated that fewer than 20 percent of bombers dropped their payloads within 5 miles of their target, and a 7 November raid cost 10 percent of the 400 planes. Raids over Germany stopped until Sir Charles Portal's RAF could get the 4,000 planes, with state-of-the-art navigational and bombing aids, that Churchill promised.

Air Chief Marshal Arthur Harris assumed command of

Along with other aircraft, the Mosquito played an important role in the Allied bombing of Ruhr, Germany. (U.S. Air Force)

Bomber Command in February 1942. He switched from precision bombing to area raids using 2- and 4-ton bombs, clustered incendiaries, and marker bombs. Four-engine bombers entered the inventory, including the Short Stirling, Handley Page Halifax, and Avro Lancaster.

During the night of 6–7 March, Harris attacked Essen, the largest industrial center in the Ruhr, with 442 bombers. The bombing device called "Oboe" was used. Pathfinding Mosquito bombers dropped red and green markers for the bombers to follow. The raid set fire to an area 2 miles in diameter, with only 14 aircraft being lost. Five more attacks through July destroyed Essen and the Krupps works (locomotives, shells, fuses, guns). Raids near the Ruhr targeted Cologne and Dusseldorf. Bomber Command now had the simple H2S radar, with superior range but less reliability than Oboe. The RAF also had Mk.XIV bombsights and clustered 4-pound incendiaries.

In June 1943, the Combined Bomber Offensive began, with the RAF bombing by night and the Americans by day. A 16 May raid against the Ruhr dams at Möhne, Eder, and Sorpe cost 10 of 19 Lancasters but drowned 1,284, including Russian and German POWs and slaves. The Germans diverted hundreds of antiaircraft weapons and rebuilt the Möhne Dam, a major provider of electricity. There was no follow-up raid.

The Eighth Air Force's first major Ruhr raid was against the synthetic rubber plant at Huls on 22 June. Cost: 186 dead and more than 1,000 wounded. I. G. Farben reopened the plant within a month, and the next raid against Huls was not until March 1944. That spring, raids against petroleum targets damaged production of synthetic rubber. The offensive halted in the fall of 1943 while the Allies awaited long-range fighter support and prepared the groundwork for Operation OVERLORD by destroying the Luftwaffe and German communications that made it so effective. In February 1944, BIG WEEK defeated the Luftwaffe, and the Combined Bomber Offensive resumed against a defeated enemy air arm.

In 1944, raids continued against dams and the industrial web in the Ruhr as the Germans retreated and concentrated forces. Although the focus of the Combined Bomber Offensive was all of Germany, the Ruhr still received extensive attention. As German defenses crumbled, the Ruhr was the backup target in case of bad weather. The Allies bombed the Ruhr because it was so heavily industrialized that there was little chance of missing some valuable target or another.

Although the results of the bombing were not as dramatic as desired, they did put a cap on German production and eventually caused it to decline. In the meantime, the Germans were forced to assign a huge amount of resources in the form of personnel, radar equipment, and guns that might have been better used on the Eastern Front against the Soviet Union.

John Barnhill

See also

Avro Lancaster; Handley Page Halifax; Harris, Arthur T.

References

Morrison, Wilbur H. *Fortress Without a Roof.* New York: St. Martin's, 1982.

Murray, Williamson. *Strategy for Defeat: The Luftwaffe. 1933–1945.* Maxwell AFB, AL: Air University Press, 1983.

Rumpler Aircraft

German aviation company noted for aircraft capable of high-altitude photographic reconnaissance work. German observation units used the Rumpler aircraft to great advantage throughout the last two years of World War I. Allied combat reports did not often mention the Rumpler, for the common practice among Rumpler crews was to climb to altitude over their own side of the lines before dashing over to take pictures and quickly return to safety. Most Allied pilots never encountered one.

The exception to the rule was James McCudden, the No. 56 Squadron flight commander whose 57 victories put him at the top of the Allied aces list during the first part of 1918. McCudden made a specialty of lying in wait at high altitudes to pounce on the German reconnaissance planes, and his score included several captured on the Allied side of the lines.

Rumpler's three principal products were the C.I, a general utility aircraft; the C.IV, the high-flier that established its reputation; and the C.VII, an improved version of the C.IV.

The C.VII used a Maybach MB IV six-cylinder inline 240-hp engine designed with high-altitude operations in mind, an improvement over the Mercedes used in the earlier C.IV. In consideration of their duties, Rumpler crews also served as human guinea pigs in the development of protective clothing and breathing apparatuses for aircrews, who were venturing to heights never before reached by man.

Armament for the Rumpler consisted of a synchronized Spandau gun for the pilot and a Parabellum gun mounted on a pivoting ring for the observer. Occasionally, a small bombload was also carried on external racks. So generally secure was the Rumpler from attack, however, that the pilot's gun was omitted from the Rubild, a revised version of the C.VII.

James Streckfuss

References

Gray, Peter, and Owen Thetford. *German Aircraft of the First World War.* London: Putnam, 1962.

McCudden, James. *Five Years in the Royal Flying Corps.* Bath, UK: Cedric Chivers, 1965.

Russian Air Force (Post-Soviet)

The Russian Air Force changed dramatically after 1991 due to the end of the Cold War and national penury. Some 6,200 Soviet combat aircraft threatened NATO in 1990, but Russia now has only 2,000 aircraft barely able to suppress Chechen guerrillas.

The air force and air defense troops merged in 1998. This created an integrated automatic command-and-control system that linked all air, air defense, antimissile, and space-defense assets and reduced staff, maintenance, and logistical burdens. All told, 580 units were disbanded, with equipment distributed among other units, and 123,500 positions were eliminated. Currently, two air armies comprising heavy bombers and transport aircraft are subordinated to the armed forces High Command. Six combined air/air defense armies, organized regionally, are subordinated to the military district commanders in Moscow, Rostov-on-Don, St. Petersburg, Yekaterinburg, Novosibirsk, and Khabarovsk.

The Russian aviation industry today struggles for survival, and long-term prospects are grim. About half of Russia's excellent aviation scientists and engineers quit in the 1990s, and few young people replaced them. Poverty forced Russia to forego new acquisitions, focusing instead on modernization, research, and marketing abroad.

Fighter modernization seeks to create multifunctional aircraft from older single-purpose designs. Mig-29, Su-27, and MiG-31 interceptors will gain new avionics, radars, and night/all-weather/inflight refueling capabilities. Armament will include new air-to-air missiles with a range of 300 kilometers, electro-optically–guided bombs, and antiradiation missiles. Modernized bombers will carry a new stealthy conventional cruise missile, reportedly with a 5,000-kilometer range.

Five fighter research programs are under way. All are multifunction aircraft, featuring thrust-vectoring engines, stealth, and supersonic cruising speeds. Two single-engine programs provide less-expensive alternatives to the two twin-engine heavy programs. The fifth program is a larger,

The name Ryan always meant quality and never more so than with the Firebee drones being carried on the versatile Lockheed C-130 transport. (U.S. Air Force)

modernized version of the MiG-29. Research has also commenced on a stealth bomber and a multirole spaceplane.

Russia was the second-largest supplier of arms to developing countries after 1991. Exports emphasized Asia, although the 1998 financial crisis limited sales. Iran, China, and India accounted for about 90 percent of revenue. Russia sold MiG-29s and Su-27s to India, Malaysia, Bangladesh, and Vietnam, Su-30s to China and India, and licensed the production of 120 Su-30s in India and 200 Su-27s in China. China bought A-50 AWACs aircraft, significantly increasing its capabilities.

Russian aircraft are rapidly aging: 48 percent are more than 15 years old, 51 percent are 5–15 years old, and 1 percent are less than 5 years old. Production dropped from 430 fighters, 40 bombers, and 120 transports in 1990 to a four-year *total* of 130 fighters, five bombers, and 12 transports from 1994 to 1997 (most were exported—Russia acquired only eight new combat aircraft in these years).

From 1991, then, overall readiness had been very poor. Lack of spare parts—particularly engines—grounded 50–70 percent of the inventory. Lack of fuel and poor serviceability prevented normal training. Pilots flew an average of 21 hours per year, compared to 200-plus hours per year in Western countries. Russia has few simulators to facilitate training, and poor flying skills caused several fatal crashes per year in recent years. Exercises emphasized long-range deployment (8,500 kilometers) of tactical aviation to troublespots, and bombers recently simulated nuclear cruise-missile attacks on North America.

Russia's near-total air superiority in Chechnya could not ensure victory and revealed seriously deficient training, equipment, logistics, and tactics. All-weather operations and air-ground coordination were particular problems. In 1994–1996, Russia flew 9,000 fixed-wing sorties, including 5,300 ground attack missions. Su-24/25s dropping unguided bombs generally failed to hit mobile Chechen units, instead causing heavy civilian casualties. Russia's second intervention in 1999 similarly emphasized Su-24/25 ground attack missions primarily with unguided bombs and fuel-air explosives.

James D. Perry

References

Butowski, Piotr. "Russia's New Air Force Enters a Tight Manoeuvre." *Jane's Intelligence Review* (1 May 1999).

______. "New Weapons, Old Wings: Russian Aviation's Way." *Jane's Intelligence Review* (27 August 1998).

Ryan Aircraft

U.S. aircraft manufacturer. Tubal Claude Ryan (1898–1982), fresh from flying for the Army, began a small airline and flying school in San Diego in 1922. Facilities were also used to rebuild and convert aircraft. The first original design was the M-1 high-wing monoplane (1926), of which 16 were built. The similar M-2 saw seven examples built, but by then Ryan had split with the firm and sold his portion of the airline and manufacturing firm to partner B. F. Mahoney. Shortly thereafter came the order from Charles Lindbergh for what became the Ryan NAP (New York to Paris) *Spirit of St. Louis* for his legendary transatlantic flight in May 1927.

Publicity from that flight led to the sale of some 240 Ryan Broughams. Continuing to operate his flying school, Ryan formed a second manufacturing firm in 1934, also based in San Diego. Its successful initial product was the Ryan ST (Sports Trainer) of 1934. Small orders led to the more widely produced PT-20/22 primary trainer aircraft series, of which more than 1,000 were built for use throughout World War II. The FR-1 Fireball for the Navy resulted from a 1942 specification for an aircraft with both a piston and a jet engine. The hybrid first flew in 1944, and more than 60 were built and used through 1947. This was the first U.S. Navy aircraft to have a flush-riveted fuselage exterior and metal (rather than cloth) control surfaces. One unit was rebuilt to use the first turboprop engine designed and built in the United States, but the resulting XF2R-1 Flying Shark did not enter production.

Postwar production included the Nation private business aircraft, rights to which had been purchased in 1947 and more than 1,000 of which were built. Remaining Ryan work centered on vertical-flight research aircraft, including two examples of the X-13 Vertijet that could take off straight up from a mobile trailer-launcher. Several other VTOL/STOL experimental aircraft followed, as did some 4,500 Firebee target drones. Ryan eventually retired; his firm was purchased by Teledyne in 1969.

Christopher H. Sterling

References

Wagner, William. *Ryan the Aviator: Being the Adventures and Ventures of Pioneer Airman and Businessman T. Claude Ryan.* New York: McGraw-Hill, 1971.

S

Saab Aircraft

Swedish aircraft manufacturer. The 1936 call by the Swedish parliament for a more robust air force put considerable demands on the country's small and fragmented aircraft industry. One major consequence was the 2 April 1937 incorporation of Trollhattan-based Svenska Aeroplan Aktiebolaget AB. The company was restructured in March 1939 as Svenska Aeroplan Aktiebolaget Saab, becoming Sweden's primary airframe manufacturer. Although Saab designed a number of indigenous aircraft, the outbreak of World War II made it extremely difficult to produce them. Saab was not completely dormant, however, as it built a fair number of foreign aircraft under license, including those from North American, Northrop, Hawker, Gloster, and Junkers. These airplanes not only served in the Swedish air force but also were exported to Finland, where they saw combat against the Soviet Union.

By the end of World War II, Saab was committed to progressive aircraft development, especially commercial aircraft and jet fighters. The 90 Scandia was an excellent twin-engine transport, capable of carrying some 30 passengers. After the successful large-scale production of the J29 Tunnan, Saab undertook the development of a series of innovative fighter aircraft, beginning with the J32 Lansen in 1952. Like aircraft manufacturers around the world, Saab struggled with jet-engine development, and the J32 was eventually equipped with a British Avon. Still, Saab engineers were not afraid to take design risks and produced the J35 Draken, which entered service in 1959 with export versions to follow. The unique double-delta planform of the J35 established a reputation for Saab as daring, creative, innovative, and unorthodox—descriptors that apply quite well to the subsequent J37 Viggen and J39 Gripen. The 1960s and 1970s saw considerable corporate reorganization, and through mergers and acquisitions Saab now builds not only airplanes but trucks and cars. Saab's legacy is a consistent string of world-class aircraft from a neutral nation on the fringes of the Cold War.

Robert S. Hopkins

See also

Finland, and Air Operations During the "Continuation War"; Saab J-35 Draken; Swedish Air Force

References

Andersson, Hans G. *Saab Aircraft Since 1937.* Washington, DC: Smithsonian Institution Press, 1989.

Saab J-29 Tunnan

In the years immediately after World War II, aircraft development substantially relied upon two key German advances: jet power and swept wings. Surprisingly, Western Europe's first such fighter came from neutral Sweden in the form of the J-29. Arguably little more than an engine with wings, its shape gave rise to its nickname—"Flygande Tunnan" (Flying Barrel). Proposed, planned, and approved between 1945 and 1947, the airplane reached early production during 1948, with its first flight on 1 September 1948. Initial operational deliveries went to F13 Wing in May 1951.

The airplane was quite capable and set a number of speed records. It handled well but was a challenge for pilots unaccustomed to flying a swept-wing aircraft, especially during landing. There were five variants of the J-29, including the S-29 reconnaissance version and the J-29F, equipped with afterburner, for a total of 665 aircraft. The Tunnan acquitted itself well in combat while participating in the United Nations Peacekeeping Force in the Congo from 1960 to 1963. From 1962 to 1972, the Austrian air force operated 30 former Swedish J-29s, half with photoreconnaissance capability. In May 1967, the J-29 ended its combat service with the Swedish air force but remained in use as a target tow and countermeasures trainer until August 1976.

Robert S. Hopkins

See also
Saab Aircraft; Swedish Air Force

References

Andersson, Hans G. *Saab Aircraft Since 1937.* Washington, DC: Smithsonian Institution Press, 1989.
Widfeldt, Bo. *The Saab J-29.* London: Profile #36, 1965.

Saab J-35 Draken

One of the most unusual fighters of the 1950s. It featured a license-built Rolls-Royce Avon complete with reheat units installed in a double-delta airframe. This gave the fighter excellent handling characteristics throughout all flight regimes. In the extreme of the nose is installed a radar-tracking unit developed by Ericsson Electronics. This in turn provided guidance for a variety of air-defense missiles that included the U.S.-made Falcon and Sidewinder.

The airframe was eventually equipped with a total of nine pylons capable of carrying missiles, rockets, bombs, or, on the center-line pylons, a selection of fuel tanks. Another innovation built into the aircraft from the outset was the ability to operate from Swedish motorways.

After completing flight-testing and undergoing the usual refinements, the Draken was cleared for use by the Royal Swedish Air Force. Saab sold Draken aircraft to both Denmark and Finland. Variants included in all of these packages included fighter-bombers, trainers, and reconnaissance aircraft. Although age is slowly creeping up on the fleet, a few aircraft are still operated by Finland and Austria, which gained some second-hand examples in the 1990s.

Kev Darling

See also
Saab Aircraft; Saab J-29 Tunnan; Saab J-37 Viggen; Saab JAS-39 Gripen

Saab J-37 Viggen

Sweden's primary air defense cover for many years. Its replacement is another innovative Saab creation, the JAS-39 Gripen.

With the J-35 Draken already in service, Saab had turned its attention to the replacement that would inevitably follow. Design work had begun in 1954 with the first prototype, a canard double-delta powered by a license-built reheated Rolls-Royce Spey engine rolled out in December 1962. From the outset the Viggen was designed for operation from the country's motorways as well as normal airfields. Further innovation resulted in an aircraft that could be maintained by newly trained conscripts.

The Viggen was intended as a multirole aircraft. Weapons capability extends to missiles for air defense and antishipping roles plus bombs, rockets, and other munitions intended for ground support missions. Deliveries to the Royal Swedish Air Force—the only operator—began in the early 1970s with the interceptor version entering service first. This was followed by variants that covered training, reconnaissance, and antishipping. To cover all these vital tasks, a total of 329 machines were delivered, far less than the original projected total of more than 800.

Since the Saab Gripen entered service, the Viggen has slowly been leaving front-line service, although it should be many years yet before this most unique of shapes in the sky finally disappears.

Kev Darling

See also
Saab Aircraft; Saab J-29 Tunnan; Saab JAS-39 Gripen

Saab JAS-39 Gripen

In March 2000, four squadrons of the Saab Gripen fighter were in service with the Royal Swedish Air Force; this should reach eight squadrons (25 aircraft each) by 2004. British Aerospace and Saab collaborated to sell export models of the Gripen, which fills a niche between the Hawk 200 and the Eurofighter Typhoon.

A sophisticated swing-role single-engine lightweight fighter, the Gripen performs air superiority, attack, and reconnaissance missions. To fit the Swedish strategy of dispersed operations from highways, the Gripen takes off and lands within 800 meters. In 10 minutes a Gripen is rearmed and refueled by one technician and five conscripts.

Flying canard foreplanes and a delta wing, controlled by an electronic system, furnish excellent STOL capability, climb, and instantaneous turning rate. At low level, Gripen attains Mach 1.1 from Mach 0.5 in 30 seconds. The JAS 39 employs a reliable, low-maintenance General Electric F404-400 turbofan engine modified by Volvo to offer swift startup and high thrust. Pilot workload is minimized by an excellent display array, highly automated radar and weapons controls, and a self-contained navigation and precision-landing system.

Through an advanced datalink, Gripen shares information with other aircraft, ground forces, and ships. Real-time intelligence is immediately portrayed on the cockpit displays.

Sherwood S. Cordier

See also

Saab Aircraft; Swedish Air Force

References

English, Malcolm. "Gripen." *Air International* (July 2000): i–xvi.

Griffiths, Dan. "AFM evaluates the Gripen." *Air Forces Monthly* (March 2000): 18–24.

Hewson, Robert. "Saab JAS 39 Gripen." *World Air Power Journal* (Autumn 2000): 60–102.

Safonov, Boris (1915–1942)

Soviet fighter ace. Boris Feoktistovich Safonov was born on 26 August 1915 in Sinyavino, Russia. He joined the military and completed flight school in 1934. In 1940, he was transferred to naval aviation and was assigned to a regiment flying the Polikarpov I-16 in defense of Murmansk and the Arctic convoys. During the first days of the war, Safonov was one of the few successful Soviet pilots, and by September 1941 he had scored 11 victories, being awarded the Hero of the Soviet Union (HSU) on September 16. During the winter he flew with the British pilots who brought Hawker Hurricanes to Murmansk and was awarded the British Distinguished Flying Cross. After flying the Hurricane, he converted to the Curtiss P-40 Kittyhawk.

On 30 May 1942, he was lost in action flying over convoy PQ-16. It is uncertain whether the motor of his P-40 failed or he was shot down. Though some sources credit him with as many as 34 victories, Safonov's logbook claims 20 individual and six group air victories. He was awarded a second HSU posthumously in June 1942 and became a major focus of Soviet publicity.

George M. Mellinger

References

Seidl, Hans D. *Stalin's Eagles: An Illustrated Study of the Soviet Aces of World War II and Korea.* Atglen, PA: Schiffer, 1998.

SAGE (Semiautomated Ground Environment) Defense System

Pioneering air defense computer system. In the early 1950s, the USAF still relied on manual equipment and voice communications to direct its interception of incoming aircraft. After intense competition among contractors, in 1953 the USAF placed its sole support behind the system being developed around the new Whirlwind digital computer at the Massachusetts Institute of Technology's Lincoln Laboratories.

This Lincoln Transition System, renamed SAGE in 1954, would integrate search and height-finding radars, along with other sources of information such as picket ships, early warning aircraft, and even ground observers. All of this would be processed by a central computer, which could then display on a cathode-ray tube target information to ground controllers and relay that information to other air defense facilities around the country. Air battles would be directed from eight combat operations centers and 32 interconnected SAGE direction centers distributed throughout North America. Each direction center was a massive above-ground concrete shock-resistant windowless monolith capable of supporting up to 100 individual ground controllers. In times of emergency a SAGE center could also partially assume the duties of another, presumably destroyed, center, even remotely launching surface-to-air missiles from hundreds of miles away. This was an extremely ambitious program, pushing 1950s technology to its very limit, but extensive and successful testing in 1954 dissipated much of the skepticism within the USAF surrounding the program.

Even before the first SAGE installation could become operational, however, it was threatened with obsolescence by the first Soviet ICBM tests of 1957. Though the Soviet bomber force would presumably remain a problem for years to come, missiles were obviously the threat of the future, and SAGE was solely an antiaircraft system. The program did proceed, however, and the first SAGE air defense sector became operational around New York in the summer of 1958. The following year the scale of the planned SAGE deployment was reduced, and as a result only 23 direction centers of the 32 envisioned reached operational capability (one in Canada, the rest in the United States). The SAGE system was fully operational by 1963, and it did perform as designed, vastly increasing the air defense capabilities of the continental United States. Succeeding years saw improvements such as the incorporation of direct datalinks with interceptor aircraft and a secondary system of Backup Interceptor Control stations. Still, as the 1960s progressed it became increasingly clear that the threat from Soviet bombers had largely failed to materialize and that SAGE centers were unlikely to survive an initial Soviet ICBM attack. In the early 1980s, SAGE was replaced by new Joint Surveillance System, and in 1983 the last SAGE center went offline.

Though in retrospect its mission was disappearing even as it was being deployed, the SAGE defense system left a lasting military and technological legacy. It was the first large-scale real-time computerized command-and-control system in the world, and it clearly advanced the state of the art in digital computers in the 1950s. In a less tangible but probably even more important role, SAGE also provided invaluable experience in the very new fields of large-scale hardware and especially software development. It therefore played a role in U.S. history in the twentieth century in much the same way the Erie Canal did in the nineteenth century—as the training ground for an entire generation of engineers.

David Rezelman

See also

Air Defense Command; Cold War; Distant Early Warning; North American Air Defense Command; Radar; Strategic Air Command

References

Edwards, Paul N. *The Closed World: Computers and the Politics of Discourse in Cold War America.* Cambridge: MIT Press, 1996.

Schaffel, Kenneth. *The Emerging Shield: The Air Force and the Evolution of Continental Air Defense, 1945–1960.* Washington, DC: United States Air Force, Office of Air Force History, 1991.

Saint Mihiel, Battle of (1918)

Largest Allied air operation of World War I. General John J. Pershing planned to eliminate the Saint Mihiel salient in early September to secure the rear of the U.S. Army for its participation in a general Allied offensive later in the month to end the war. The salient was a German bulge in the French lines that had existed since 1915, measuring 24 miles across the base and 14 miles deep. Aerial photographs revealed a series of defensive lines with wire and obstacles in three belts.

Pershing's First Army conducted a converging attack on both sides of the salient to pinch off enemy forces while a French corps made a supporting attack against the salient's nose.

The first Army chief of air service, Colonel William Mitchell, coordinated the largest aggregation of air forces in a single operation during World War I to support the attack. The French, British, and Italian air forces provided units to reinforce the U.S. Air Service's 28 squadrons. The greatest contribution came from the French—a total of 58 squadrons, mostly pursuit and bombardment. Major General Hugh Trenchard's Independent Force of the Royal Air Force provided eight nighttime bombardment squadrons in support of Mitchell, but not under his direct command. The Italians provided three more nighttime bombardment squadrons for a total of 701 pursuit, 366 observation, 323 daylight bombers, and 91 nighttime bombers—adding up to 1,481 airplanes, 12 balloons, and some 30,000 men. The Germans were outnumbered in pursuit aircraft by a factor of 10.

Allied pursuit aircraft engaged the enemy over its own airfields and strafed and bombed enemy road traffic. Pilots such as Frank Luke, the famed "Arizona balloon-buster," attacked enemy balloons. Bombers attacked major road and rail junctions. Poor weather inhibited Mitchell's aerial offensive, but his strategy overwhelmed the opposing German air forces and maintained Allied air supremacy throughout the battle, contributing to its success.

Bert Frandsen

See also

Independent Bombing Force; Luke, Frank Jr.; Mitchell, William; Trenchard, Hugh

References

Cooke, James J. *The U.S. Air Service in the Great War, 1917–1919.* Westport, CT: Praeger, 1996.

Nalty, Bernard C., ed. *Winged Shield, Winged Sword: A History of the United States Air Force.* Vol. 1. Washington, DC: Air Force History and Museum Program, 1997.

Saint-Exupéry, Antoine de (1900–1944)

French writer and aviator. Antoine de Saint-Exupéry brought the adventure of aviation to millions. His works tell of aviation's pioneering days and swept up readers depicting men flying vast distances in brutal weather over uninhabited terrain. One of the best is *Wind, Sand, and Stars* in which Saint-Exupéry tells of his crash in the Sahara Desert and the Spanish civil war.

Drawing from these experiences he wrote the children's story *The Little Prince.* Here, a young prince arrives on earth and meets a crashed pilot, plying him with questions concerning life, happiness, adventure, and humanity. In May 1940, Saint-Exupéry, who had worked energetically to get a combat assignment, flew useless reconnaissance missions during the blitzkrieg. *Flight to Arras* tells of fighting for France's life while comprehending the fruitlessness of his efforts. Nevertheless, he risked his life to show that France remained alive. Exiled in New York, he exhorted Frenchmen to cease fighting among themselves and drive out the Germans. *Wartime Writings* related his disgust about France's divisive politics.

Once back in combat, he was shot down by the Luftwaffe on 31 July 1944. In 1998, a fisherman discovered his P-38 and ID bracelet off France's southern coast. France inscribed his name in the Pantheon and put his likeness on French currency; he remains an enduring aviation and literary legend.

Benjamin F. Jones

References

Cate, Curtis. *Antoine de Saint-Exupery: His Life and Times.* New York: Paragon House, 1970.

Schiff, Stacy. *Saint Exupéry: A Biography.* New York: Da Capo, 1997.

Sakai, Saburo (1916–2000)

Ensign in the Imperial Japanese Navy; one of the empire's great aces. Saburo Sakai was born in the small farming village of Nishiyoka Mura in Saga Prefecture on 26 August 1916. Sakai enlisted in the navy at Sasebo naval base in May 1933. Sakai graduated and was assigned to the battleship *Kirishima.*

In June 1936, Sakai was accepted into flight training after twice flunking the entrance exam. Sakai graduated first in his flight-training class in November 1937. Sakai was then sent to China, where on his first combat mission (5 October 1938) he achieved his first aerial victory.

In October 1941, Sakai was transferred to the Tainan Air Group. As a member of that group, he participated in the Philippines and Dutch East Indies campaigns. In April 1942, Sakai's group was transferred to Rabaul, then to Lae, New Guinea. On 7 June 1942, Sakai was severely wounded by a .30-caliber bullet fired by a U.S. SBD Dauntless. Sakai made it back to his base on Rabaul but would spend a good deal of time recovering.

Upon his recovery, Sakai was transferred to the Omura Air Group and then the Yokosuka Air Group. Sakai's last mission was in June 1944, when he participated in an intercept action over Iwo Jima. Sakai's failing eyesight forced him into an instructor's role with the Yokosuka Air Group and Air Group 343.

Sakai finished the war having flown more than 200 missions, never losing a wingman and scoring 64 air victories.

David A. Pluth

References

Sakaida, Henry. *Imperial Japanese Navy Aces, 1937–1945.* London: Osprey, 1998.

Hata, Ikuhiko, and Yasuho Izawa. *Japanese Naval Aces and Fighter Units in World War II.* Annapolis, MD: Naval Institute Press, 1989.

Salerno, Battle of (1943)

Air operations in support of amphibious invasion of Italy. On 9 September 1943, the U.S. Fifth Army landed at Salerno, south of Naples, in Operation AVALANCHE. The operation was supported by aircraft flying from Sicily and from four escort carriers offshore. The landing was preceded by a devastating attack on the Axis airborne complex at Foggia by U.S. heavy bombers and strafing Lockheed P-38 fighters. German forces in the area reacted quickly and launched armored counterthrusts against the beachhead that were not overcome until September 15. Much of the fighting centered around the control of the airfields of Paestum and Monte Corvino.

The Luftwaffe struck repeatedly against offshore shipping, and the battle is notable for the first use of new FX 1400 and Hs 293 glider bombs in attacks that damaged the cruisers USS *Savannah* and HMS *Uganda* and the battleship HMS *Warspite.*

As in Sicily, Allied air forces were less successful in providing close support of ground forces, and the final defeat of the German counterattacks can probably be attributed more to the effect of naval gunfire than to Allied airpower.

The invasion site of Salerno—at the limit of Allied land-based fighter cover from Sicily—shows the importance Allied planners placed on land-based air cover for amphibious operations. A landing farther north would have been more desirable for both political and military reasons had fighter cover been available.

Frank E. Watson

See also

Italian Campaign

References

Craven, Wesley, and James L. Cate. *The Army Air Forces in World War II, Volume 2: Europe: Torch to Pointblank, August 1942 to December 1943.* Washington, DC: U.S. Government Printing Office, 1949.

Hickey, Des, and Gus Smith. *Operation Avalanche: The Salerno Landings, 1943.* New York: McGraw-Hill, 1984.

Salmond, John M. (1881–1968)

Marshal of the Royal Air Force. After graduating from Sandhurst and serving as an infantry office for a number of years, "Jack" Salmond transferred to the Royal Flying Corps and won his wings in 1912. He rose rapidly in rank and by the end of World War I was a major general in command of all RAF units in France.

For the decade following the war, he proved an excellent administrator and especially distinguished himself as commander of the British forces in Iraq in 1922, when he dealt with a Turkish invasion and Kurdish uprising.

In 1929, Salmond was named Chief of Air Staff at a most difficult time. The Depression, as well as the Geneva disarmament conference that opened 1932, led the British government to seek deep cuts in the defense budget, especially the RAF. Thanks largely to the intransigence of Germany and France, the talks collapsed and the RAF was spared.

Salmond retired in 1933 but remained active in air matters, both military and commercial, for the remainder of his life.

Phillip S. Meilinger

See also

Royal Flying Corps/Royal Naval Air Service/Royal Air Force; "Ten-Year Rule"; Trenchard, Hugh

References

Laffin, John. *Swifter Than Eagles: A Biography of Marshal of the Royal Air Force Sir John Salmond.* Edinburgh, UK: William Blackwell, 1964.

Probert, Henry. *High Commanders of the Royal Air Force.* London: HMSO, 1991.

Salmson Aircraft

Early French engine and aircraft manufacturer. The Société des Moteurs Salmson, like many other World War I engine manufacturers, elected to also try its hand at the design and production of aircraft to accompany its engines. In 1916, its first attempt—the Salmson Moineau—was built around a design by the prewar French aviator Raymond Moineau.

Its most successful product, however, was the famous Salmson 2A2, which equipped some 55 French reconnaissance escadrilles and, in the summer of 1918, another 11 squadrons of the U.S. Air Service. Examples were also used by faraway air services like Russia's and Japan's.

Powered by the 230-hp Salmson 9Za nine-cylinder rotary, the aircraft was a two-bay biplane with equal-span wings and a single Vickers .303-caliber machine gun equipped with an interrupter gear to allow firing through the propeller arc. Strong and fast, the 2A2 could climb to 5,000 meters in less than half an hour and cruise at that altitude at 168 kph. There was no finer Allied reconnaissance aircraft produced during World War I.

Further variants numbering through the Salmson 7 were attempted, but only 20 examples of the last numbered version were built, and the rest seem to have not made it beyond the prototype stage. In the postwar years Salmson introduced only a few new designs and became part of CFA in 1936.

James Streckfuss

References

Davilla, James, and Arthur M. Soltan. *French Aircraft of the First World War.* Mountain View, CA: Flying Machines Press, 1997.

Salyut

The world's first space station. In 1971, the Soviet Union launched Salyut in honor of the tenth anniversary of Yuri Gagarin's historic spaceflight. Launched by a Proton rocket, the 45-foot, 40,000-pound Salyut consisted of four different cylinders containing equipment, experiments, and a propulsion system. After the Soyuz arrived at Salyut 's front docking port, the crew transferred through a hatch into the station's three work compartments: a small work compartment, the frustum, and a large work compartment. Seven workstations controlled Salyut, and designers took advantage of three dimensions by installing the scientific equipment on all compartments' surfaces that were different colors for crew orientation. Other amenities included a dining table and sleeping bags. A hygiene station, encased in washable material to retard bacteria growth, was located at the back of the large compartment.

The first three successful cosmonauts on Soyuz 11 completed 24 days of experiments and public television programs, then deorbited only to be killed by an open valve that depressurized the spacecraft. Next, the Soviet military began a space station program, but its first craft, Salyut 2, failed. The Salyut 3 and Salyut 5 crews successfully occupied the stations that were smaller than their civilian counterparts, had rear docking ports, used encrypted communications, and flew much closer to the earth. Attached to the front of the station was a film-return capsule. A civilian craft, Salyut 4, had three steerable solar arrays, a hatch with an extravehicular activity airlock, and many new experiments. Two crews successfully occupied the station for 92 days.

Two docking ports enabled Salyut 6 crews to use an unmanned space freighter, Progress, to resupply the station with food, water, and fuel. Additions to the large work compartment included a telescope, a gamma radiation detector, and the new docking port that permitted fuel transfer from the Progress to a modified propulsion system. Eighteen crews accomplished missions on Salyut 6, and 12 Progress spacecraft automatically docked. Salyut 7 incorporated electric stoves, hot water, refrigerators, experimental furnaces, and improved medical facilities while two new portholes allowed limited ultraviolet radiation to kill microorganisms and mold. In February 1985, Soviet mission controllers lost control of Salyut 7, and a repair crew was launched to the tumbling vehicle. The cosmonauts docked, reactivated the frozen systems, and revived the station. Twelve crews and 12 Progress spacecraft successfully occupied Salyut 7 until May 1986, when Mir began spaceflight missions, thus terminating the Salyut program.

John F. Graham

References

Clark, Phillip. *The Soviet Manned Space Program.* New York: Orion Books, 1988.

Samson, Charles R. (1883–1931)

Royal Air Force air commodore. Samson, born on 8 July 1883 in Manchester, entered service on HMS *Britannia* in 1896. In 1911, Samson was among four naval officers selected for flying training. He undertook the navy's first experimental flights from ships, flying off the anchored battleship *Africa* on 10 January 1912 and *Hibernia* on 9 May while it steamed at full speed. When the Royal Flying Corps formed in 1912, he took command of the naval wing and led development of aerial wireless communication, bomb- and torpedo-dropping, navigation, and night-flying.

When war came in 1914, Samson took the Eastchurch Squadron to France. It supported Allied ground forces along the coast with aircraft and improvised armored vehicles and conducted several successful attacks on German Zeppelin sheds. The unit transferred to the Dardanelles in March 1915 to provide air cover during the unsuccessful Gallipoli campaign, after which it disbanded. Samson then commanded a seaplane carrier squadron that ranged throughout the eastern Mediterranean, reconnoitering and attacking Turkish positions.

From March 1917 until the end of hostilities, Samson commanded the Great Yarmouth Air Station, which controlled North Sea antisubmarine and anti-Zeppelin air operations.

Samson resigned his naval commission in August 1919, becoming a group captain in the new Royal Air Force. He was appointed air officer commanding (Mediterranean) in 1921 and then commanded the Kenley fighter group (1922–1926). As chief staff officer, Middle East Command, until August 1927, he organized and led the first bomber formation flight from Cairo to Capetown.

Samson resigned his commission in 1929 and died at Cholderton, Wiltshire, on 5 February 1931.

Paul E. Fontenoy

See also

Fleet Air Arm; Royal Flying Corps/Royal Naval Air Service/Royal Air Force; Sueter, Murray

References

Cronin, Dick. *Royal Naval Shipboard Aircraft Developments, 1912–1931.* Tonbridge, UK: Air-Britain (Historians), 1990.
King, Brad. *Royal Naval Air Service, 1912–1918.* Aldershot, UK: Hikoki, 1997.
Roskill, Stephen W. *Documents Relating to the Royal Naval Air Service, Volume 1: 1908–1918.* London: Navy Records Society, 1989.

Santa Cruz, Battle of (1942)

Air operations in support of carrier engagement during the Guadalcanal campaign. Covering a land offensive on Guadalcanal, the Japanese Combined Fleet sortied east of the Solomons with the carriers *Shokaku, Zuikaku,* and *Junyo* and the light carrier *Zuiho.* A U.S. task force based on carriers *Enterprise* and *Hornet* engaged.

On the morning of 26 October, scout planes from *Enterprise* located and damaged the light carrier *Zuiho.* Both sides soon detected each other's main force and launched major strikes that passed each other on the way to their targets. The U.S. strike badly damaged the carrier *Shokaku* and cruiser *Chikuma* while the Japanese strike was setting *Hornet* afire. *Hornet* was abandoned, then sunk by Japanese destroyers shortly after.

The battle continued the attrition of naval aircraft and pilots, which the Japanese could ill afford after the cumulative losses of this and previous battles. The Japanese carrier force would not seriously oppose U.S. moves until the invasion of the Marianas, more than a year and a half later.

Santa Cruz provides the best example of the simultaneous strike of two offensive air groups against each other's base. Tactically, the valuable defensive performance of *South Dakota* against Japanese air attacks proved the worth of the newly installed heavy antiaircraft armament on U.S. battleships.

Frank E. Watson

See also

Guadalcanal

References

Hoffman, Carl W. *Carrier Strike: The Battle of the Santa Cruz Islands.* Pacifica, CA: Pacifica Press, 1999.

Saro Aircraft

British aircraft manufacturer. More properly known as Saunders Roe, the Saro firm came into existence in 1928 when Alliott Verdon Roe moved over from the Avro firm. Joining with John Lord, they acquired the small firm of S. E. Saunders, which had already built a series of small amphibians.

The new Saro firm produced some amphibians for the civilian market before building the London sea-biplane for the RAF, followed by the Lerwick seaplane for Coastal Command, both operating in the patrol role.

During the early years of the jet age, the company created the Saro SR.AI1 jet fighter and the enormous Princess flying boat that featured coupled turbines as its power plants.

A switch to the production of small helicopters began in 1951 with the Skeeter for the British army. Its last venture was the Saro PSI, which eventually became the Wasp after the company was taken over by Westland.

Kev Darling

References

London, Peter. *Saunders and SARO Aircraft Since 1917.* London: Putnam, 1981.

Satellite Command and Control

Without satellite command and control, there would have been no verifiable space firsts. Beginning with the earliest satellite developments, engineers understood the need for a satellite command-and-control segment to monitor and gather data from their satellites. The U.S. government selected the Vanguard program for the first civilian space project in part because it included plans for a space-to-ground communications segment. The earliest military satellite programs also included a ground segment that was not at all related to the civilian program.

Artificial satellites are orbited for many reasons. Some are used as very-high-altitude reflectors, passive or active, of signals sent from the earth and received again on earth. Others spend time in space and then are recovered, dropping back to earth with information, instruments, or a crew that has accomplished a space mission. In many other cases, information that is collected, either about space itself or the earth, which a satellite is observing, is transmitted back for use on earth. These radio connections between earth and space are the primary reasons for orbiting satellites into their lonely paths, hundreds or thousands of miles above the earth.

Communications, command and control, as well as the satellites themselves are basic elements in a complete space system. The satellite may send back data obtained from its sensors, information regarding the "health" of its subsystems, or responses to questions sent from earth. An earth station can receive the data transmitted, give commands (such as transfer to a redundant subsystem), change velocity vector, determine the satellite orbit, and ask questions. Ground tracking stations and an integrated command-and-control system are essential for any space mission. The tracking stations can control and obtain information from the satellites only while they are within sight of the ground antennas.

One element of the CORONA program, America's first spy satellite, was designed to demonstrate U.S. Air Force capabilities for the launch, stabilization, control, and recovery of instrumented capsules from orbit. Ground tracking stations and an integrated command-and-control system were essential for such a program. By the end of 1958, these stations were installed and checked out, ready for the first CORONA launch in early 1959. During May and June 1959, CORONA was divided into three distinct satellite programs, and the command-and-control function was separately identified. This function consisted of a control center, called the Satellite Test Center (STC), a number of Remote Tracking Stations, and all the equipment and software required to track and control satellites during ascent, on-orbit, and recovery from space operations. The STC was located near the Lockheed facility in Sunnyvale, California. NASA satellites are largely controlled from the Goddard Space Flight Center in Greenbelt, Maryland, using the Deep Space Network.

Fundamentally, any satellite control network is a service organization, providing critical contact between humans on the ground and robots hurtling through space. A satellite control network controls, in real time, multisatellite on-orbit space vehicle operations, 24 hours a day, 7 days a week.

David C. Arnold

See also

National Aeronautics and Space Administration; Satellites; SENTRY (Samos) Reconnaissance System; Space Shuttle, and Military Use

References

Gavaghan, Helen. *Something New Under the Sun: Satellites and the Beginning of the Space Age.* Washington, DC: Copernicus, 1998.

Satellites

Man-made objects orbiting the earth or other celestial bodies. The theoretical and experimental groundwork for building, launching, and employing satellites began during the late nineteenth century and continued well into the twentieth century. Three individuals, all inspired by the science fiction of Jules Verne (1828–1905) and H. G. Wells (1866–1946), were especially prominent in developing scientific theories of space flight: Konstantin Tsiolkovsky (1857–1935) in Russia; Robert Goddard (1882–1945) in the United States; and Hermann Oberth (1894–1989) in Germany. Inspired by these theories, such prominent engineers as Sergei Korolyov (1906–1966) in Russia, Wernher von Braun (1912–1977) in Germany and the United States, and Hsue-shen Tsien (1911–) in the United States and China spearheaded creation of the launch vehicles and space programs needed to make satellites possible. On 25 May 1945, Arthur C. Clarke (author of *2001: A Space Odyssey*) presented to the British Interplanetary Society a memorandum detailing the principles of communications satellites in geostationary orbit 22,300 miles above the earth. This—the first serious proposal for a satellite application—reached a wider audience through publication in the October 1945 issue of *Wireless World* magazine.

During the decade following the end of World War II, several studies sponsored by defense organizations pointed to the feasibility of launching satellites for various purposes. The U.S. Navy's Bureau of Aeronautics issued a report in November 1945 that said a "space ship" orbiting above the earth might enhance our knowledge of science, communications, and meteorology. With or without humans aboard, it could perform reconnaissance of enemy positions, deliver explosive charges, or intercept and combat enemy craft of a similar type. Not long thereafter, in May 1946, engineers from Douglas Aircraft Company's Project RAND presented the U.S. Army Air Forces with a 250-page report titled "Preliminary Design of an Experimental World-Circling Spaceship." According to that report, the United States could construct and launch a "satellite vehicle" in approximately 5 years at a cost of $150 million. It pointed to such uses as reconnaissance, weapons delivery, meteorology, scientific research, and communications, as well as journeys beyond earth orbit.

In the Soviet Union, as early as 1947 Mikhail Tikhonravov began contemplating the use of multistage rockets to launch satellites. He formally presented a seminal paper on the potential uses of satellites to a special session of the Soviet Union's Academy of Artillery Sciences on 15 March 1950. Finally, in March 1954 James Lipp and Robert Salter completed RAND's two-volume *Project Feed Back Summary Report* for the USAF. Although focused primarily on high-resolution reconnaissance from space, their assessment added navigation to the list of previously identified satellite applications.

Even as the United States and Soviet Union secretly proceeded with plans to develop satellites for reconnaissance and other defense-related applications, civilian experts openly proposed using them for peaceful scientific research during the upcoming international geophysical year (July 1957–December 1958).

At the fourth Congress of the International Astronautical Federation in Zurich, Switzerland, in 1953, University of Maryland physicist S. Fred Singer drew from an earlier study by several BIS members and proposed the Minimum Orbital Unmanned Satellite of the Earth (going by the acronym MOUSE). The following year, von Braun's team from the U.S. Army's Redstone Arsenal and members of the Office of Naval Research (ONR) joined ranks to propose Orbiter, a small scientific satellite. On 15 July 1955, President Dwight Eisenhower announced that the United States planned to launch an Orbiter-type satellite using a modified military Jupiter-C rocket. Shortly thereafter, it was decided that America's first satellite attempt would be made using a civilian launcher under Project Vanguard.

Meanwhile, the Soviet Union's Korolev and Tikhonravov pressed their government to support ongoing efforts to beat the United States into space. On 4 October 1957, the Soviet Union launched the world's first satellite—Sputnik 1—carrying only a simple radio transmitter. The Soviet Union launched a second satellite, which carried a canine passenger, the following month. After failing in its initial attempt to launch a Vanguard satellite in December 1957, the United States successfully sent Explorer 1 into orbit on 31 January 1958 and, using onboard instrumentation, discovered the Van Allen radiation belts.

Meanwhile, the U.S. defense establishment proceeded with plans for military satellites. On 27 November 1954, the USAF Air Research and Development Command issued the first formal requirement for a reconnaissance satellite. Actual development of the advanced satellite system, designated Weapon System (WS)-117L, commenced in October 1956 with the award of a contract, under the project name Pied Piper, to Lockheed Aircraft Corporation. Sometime between early December 1957 and the end of March 1958, it was decided that the photographic subsystem offering the best prospect for early success—recoverable film capsules—would be split off from WS-117L, placed under joint CIA-USAF management, and designated Project CORONA. To defuse widespread public speculation about spy satellites and to conceal CORONA's real purpose, a press release on 3 December 1958 announced the initiation of a technology-demonstration and biomedical-experimentation series called Discoverer. A second, more sophisticated photographic reconnaissance capability—direct read-out from space—was dubbed Sentry and, later, Samos. The original WS-117L program's remaining subsystem, which involved space-based detection of potentially hostile long-range missile launches, was renamed Midas—the Missile Defense Alarm System. Discoverer 1, launched from Vandenberg AFB, California, on 28 February 1959, became the world's first polar-orbiting satellite. The first recovery of an object from orbit occurred with the launch of Discoverer 13 on 10 August 1960 and the ejection of its capsule, which was snagged from the Pacific Ocean. Just a week later, the Discoverer 14 launch resulted in the first midair recovery of a space capsule—one containing film footage of Soviet military sites.

America's development of prototype and first-generation satellites for a variety of civil and military purposes—meteorology, navigation, communications, missile warning, and nuclear detection—flourished during the 1960s. NASA, which was established in 1958 to handle U.S. civil space activities, sent the world's first weather satellite—Tiros 1—into orbit on 1 April 1960. Unique requirements associated with Samos and certain other national security satellite operations led to the USAF launching, on 23 August 1962, of the world's first military satellite for weather observation—forerunner to the Defense Meteorological Satellite Program (DMSP). On 13 April 1960, the U.S. Navy's Transit 1B became the world's first navigation satellite. That service's GRAB 1—the world's first electronic intelligence (ELINT) satellite, known originally as Solrad 1—hitched a ride into space with the third Transit on 22 June. With the launches of NASA's Echo 1 on 12 August 1960 and the Army's Courier 1B on 4 October 1960, the U.S. fielded, respectively, the first passive and active-repeater communications satellites. Syncom 2, another NASA communications satellite, became the world's first geosynchronous satellite on 26 July 1963. A dedicated military capability emerged on 16 June 1966 when the USAF launched a cluster of seven satellites in what later became the Initial Defense Satellite Communications System (IDSCS).

Midas satellites during the 1960s paved the way for the fully operational Defense Support Program (DSP) missile-warning satellites of the 1970s. The first pair of Vela nuclear detection satellites on 17 October 1963 gave the United States oversight of Soviet compliance with the Limited Nuclear Test Ban Treaty. By 1970, the United States led the rest of the world in satellite applications.

If the United States outdistanced the Soviet Union in the realm of satellite types, the Soviet Union assumed an overwhelming lead in terms of the sheer number of satellites launched and did not lag far behind in developing an equally diverse range of applications. The Soviets began their space-based photographic reconnaissance missions in 1962 and meteorological satellite program in 1964. With the launch of Meteor 1 on 26 March 1969, the Soviet Union initiated a single integrated space-based network to meet both civil and military needs. That, incidentally, was something the United States did not attempt until 1998, when the USAF transferred DMSP to the National Oceanic and Atmospheric Administration. The Molniya 1-1 launch on 23 April 1965 gave the Soviet Union its first communications satellite. Kosmos 192, patterned after the U.S. Transit network and launched on 23 November 1967, became that nation's prototype navigation satellite. The Soviets also achieved a space-based ELINT capability in 1967. Not until Kosmos 520 in September 1972 did they have a space-based missile-warning capability. By the turn of the century, Russia had launched more than twice as many satellites as the United States and all other countries combined.

Several nations sought to join the United States and Russia by independently launching their own satellites. France became the world's third space power with its launch of Asterix in 1965. It established a high-resolution imaging capability with SPOT 1 in 1986 and an ELINT capacity with Helios 1A in 1995. Australia entered the ranks in 1967 with its launch of the Weapons Research Establishment Satellite (Wresat 1), as did the United Kingdom with Prospero in 1971, but these were the only successful independent launch attempts by those nations. China and Japan became space powers in 1970 with their launches, respectively, of Dong Fang Hong-1 and Osumi. China subsequently deployed its own recoverable photographic reconnaissance satellite system (1975), a geosynchronous communications satellite (1984), an experimental meteorological satellite (1988), and a navigation positioning satellite (2000). Japan also put up its first experimental communications satellite (1975), a meteorological spacecraft (1977), and geodetic payload (1986). Established officially in 1975 with 11 member nations, the European Space Agency succeeded in using its Ariane 1 booster to launch test equipment in 1981 and telecommunications satellites in 1984. India launched its first domestically produced satellite—Rohini 1—in 1980 using a Russian booster and became a full-fledged space power in 1997 with the launch of an earth-imaging satellite atop its own domestically produced launch vehicle. Not to be excluded, Israel used its Shavit rocket to launch its own Offeq-1 experimental satellite in 1988. Others developed their own satellites but relied on the space powers for launch services.

Although satellites obviously performed numerous peaceful functions and provided the military superpowers with unprecedented strategic capabilities during the Cold War, reliance on space-based platforms during actual hostilities was slow to develop. In October 1962, weather pictures of the Caribbean returned by the first DMSP satellite enhanced the effectiveness of aerial reconnaissance missions over suspected Soviet missile batteries in Cuba. Use of DMSP satellites during the Vietnam War (1963–1975) allowed cancellation of tactical weather reconnaissance flights and thereby kept American pilots out of harm's way. The USAF also used two NASA Syncom satellites, as well as its own IDSCS constellation, for voice communications and transmission of digitized photographic intelligence from Southeast Asia back to the United States. The latter permitted more timely analysis and, consequently, quicker decisionmaking with respect to war plans. During the Yom Kippur War of 1973, U.S. satellites verified Egyptian noncompliance with the cease-fire agreement. U.S. DSP satellites detected missile exchanges during the Iran-Iraq War (1980–1988). Communications satellites played a major role in British operations during the Falkland Islands War of 1982, America's Operation URGENT FURY in Granada in 1983, and Operation JUST CAUSE in Panama during 1989–1990. Field commanders of all services gradually began to acknowledge that space-based systems provided significant strategic, tactical, and operational advantages on the battlefields of the late twentieth century.

Not until Operations DESERT SHIELD/DESERT STORM (1990–1991) in the Persian Gulf, however, did the United States apply the full range of space-based capabilities in theater operations. Allied forces used more than 60 military satellites, plus others from the civil and commercial sectors. More than 90 percent of all communications to and from the area passed over satellite links, with daily traffic at the height of operations climbing to 700,000 voice calls and 152,000 digital messages. Full-time television usage of satellite channels increased from two to 22, with short-time usage peaking at more than 400 channels one day in January 1991. Imaging satellites, such as America's multispectral Landsat and France's extremely high-resolution SPOT, facilitated the preparation and timely updating of detailed battlefield maps. Data from DMSP and civil meteorological satellites helped optimize the application of airpower by allowing planners to shift targets, types of aircraft, and kinds of weapons quickly in response to harsh, rapidly changing weather conditions.

Although the full 24-satellite NAVSTAR Global Positioning System (GPS) would not be completed until 1994, the existing 16-satellite constellation greatly assisted Coalition forces in determining their position and coordinating troop movements across the trackless desert. The value of GPS in precision bombing also became evident. Finally, DSP satellites detected Iraqi SCUD missile launches against Israel, Saudi Arabia, and Kuwait, thereby allowing command centers in Colorado Springs, Colorado, to alert forces halfway around the globe. All of this led then USAF Chief of Staff General Merrill McPeak to label it "the first space war" and Lieutenant General Thomas S. Moorman Jr., then commander of Air Force Space Command, to describe it as "a glimpse into the future" of warfare.

At the turn of the century, U.S. military forces contemplated even greater reliance on satellite systems. The USAF established the Space Warfare Center in 1993 and the Space Battlelab in 1997 to generate improved support to war fighters. In 1994, the USAF launched the most secure, survivable satellite ever built—Milstar 1—and even before controllers had completed on-orbit checkout, the military used it for critical communications during operations in Haiti. Planners looked toward purchasing additional communications capacity from commercial providers and buying 1m-resolution imagery from a Colorado company flying the Ikonos satellite. To improve missile warning and, potentially, play a crucial role in ballistic missile defense, the United States undertook procurement of the extremely complex Space-Based Infrared System to augment and, eventually, replace DSP. The USAF sponsored development of the Space Maneuver Vehicle, which would make it easier to position payloads over specific hot spots at specific times, and it advocated fielding a space-based radar system to track and identify targets in all operating media—space, air, land, and water. Cognizant of shrinking budgets and the adage that there is strength in numbers, the military services and intelligence organizations began studying less-expensive microsatellites that would allow broader coverage of the earth, greater survivability, and easier replacement if damaged or attacked. Given the presence of some 2,700-plus satellites in earth orbit, any thoughtful observer could clearly see the growing importance of space to the well-being of all humankind.

Rick W. Sturdevant

See also

Defense Support Program, and Missile Detection; NAVSTAR Global Positioning System

References

Day, Dwayne A., John M. Logsdon, and Brian Latell, eds. *Eye in the Sky: The Story of the CORONA Spy Satellites.* Washington, DC: Smithsonian Institution Press, 1999.

Gavaghan, Helen. *Something New Under the Sun: Satellites and the Beginning of the Space Age.* Washington, DC: Copernicus, 1998.

Launius, Roger D., John M. Logsdon, and Robert W. Smith, eds. *Reconsidering Sputnik: Forty Years since the Soviet Satellite.* Newark, NJ: Harwood Academic, 2000.

Mack, Pamela Etter. *Viewing the Earth: The Social Construction of the Landsat Satellite System.* Cambridge: MIT Press, 1990.

Spires, David N. *Beyond Horizons: A Half Century of Air Force Space Leadership.* Rev. ed. Maxwell AFB, Alabama: Air University Press, 1998.

Schmid, Josef (1901–1956)

An officer of the Luftwaffe General Staff; known today for his miscalculations as head of Abteilung 5 (No. 5 Intelligence Section) in 1940. His consistent underestimation of the combat strength of RAF Fighter Command and failure to identify profitable targets were two of the principal reasons the Luftwaffe lost the Battle of Britain.

In 1935, "Beppo" Schmid transferred from the German army into the Luftwaffe. Unlike many promising staff officers who made this move, Schmid never became a pilot. After a number of staff postings in Berlin, he was given command of the Hermann Goering (Luftwaffe) Armored

Division in Tunisia, where he won the Knight's Cross of the Iron Cross. He was evacuated before the May 1943 Axis surrender in North Africa and replaced J. Kammhuber as commander of the XII Fliegerkorps (Air Corps), which contained all of the night-fighters defending Germany.

He proved to be a quick study and immediately took the measures necessary to restore his command's effectiveness. The XII Fliegerkorps was later renamed the I Jagdkorps (Fighter Corps) and was expanded to include all of the day and night-fighters of the Reichsluftverteidigung (Air Defense of Germany). Schmid's pleas to the Luftwaffe High Command to strengthen and reorganize the Luftwaffe fighter arm led to a strong and lasting relationship with Adolf Galland, a man with whom he otherwise had little in common. In December 1944, he was given command of Luftwaffenkommando West (Air Force Command West), which comprised the air units supporting the army on the Western Front. He ended the war in this post, with the rank of major general. After the war he was a principal author of the USAF historical studies on the German air force.

Donald Caldwell

See also

German Air Force (Luftwaffe); Germany, and World War II Air Battles

References

Obermeier, E. *Die Ritterkreuztraeger der Luftwaffe, 1939–1945, Band 1: Jagdflieger* [Recipients of the Knight's Cross]. Mainz: Verlag Dieter Hoffmann, 1989.

Murray, Williamson. *Luftwaffe*. Baltimore: Nautical and Aviation, 1985.

Schnaufer, Heinz-Wolfgang (1922–1950)

Luftwaffe major; the world's highest-scoring night-fighter pilot. Schnaufer joined the Luftwaffe as an officer candidate in late 1939 and completed flight training in 1941. While training in the Bf 110 he teamed up with an aircrewman, Fritz Rumpelhardt, who remained with him as his radio and radar operator until the end of the war. The pair volunteered to join the new night-fighter force and were posted in November 1941 to Nachtjagdgeschwader 1 (NJG 1; 1st Night-Fighter Wing). Schnaufer and Rumpelhardt began shooting down RAF night bombers with regularity from mid-1942. Their score increased steadily. In late 1944, Hitler awarded Schnaufer the Oak Leaves with Swords and Diamonds to the Knight's Cross of the Iron Cross for his 100 nighttime victories. At year's end Schnaufer was promoted to major and given command of NJG 4. His greatest success came on the night of 21–22 February 1945, when he shot down nine bombers in two missions. By V-E Day Schnaufer's score stood at 121.

Schnaufer took over his family's successful wine business after the war, and in 1950 he was in France on a wine-purchasing trip when his convertible sportscar collided with a truck. Gas cylinders fell off the truck and struck Schnaufer, killing him.

See also

German Air Force (Luftwaffe); Germany, and World War II Air Battles

References

Obermeier, E. *Die Ritterkreuztraeger der Luftwaffe, 1939–1945, Band 1: Jagdflieger* [Recipients of the Knight's Cross]. Mainz: Verlag Dieter Hoffmann, 1989.

Schriever, Bernard A. "Bennie" (1910–)

The father of the USAF ballistic missiles program; managed a technical and industrial revolution of enormous scale and scope with unprecedented success.

The difficulties in creating an ICBM ranged from building a rocket able to carry the huge warheads then thought to be required, along with such problems as guidance and control, engine staging, reentry, and so on. Early estimates indicated that the Atlas rocket being designed by Convair would have to weigh 440,000 pounds to be able to carry a thermonuclear warhead.

A breakthrough occurred in 1953, when Edward Teller and John von Neumann independently concluded that a thermonuclear warhead weighing only 1,500 pounds was feasible. A high-level board of scientists (the so-called Teapot Committee) recommended that the Atlas rocket be developed to carry the new lightweight high-yield warhead, and Brigadier General Bernard Schriever was picked to head the Western Development Division (WDD), the office charged with its development.

Schriever was the right man at the right time, for he possessed rapport with the scientific, military, and industrial communities and was able to weld them into an efficient team. The ICBM was given top priority within the Air Force, and Schriever began an entirely new management style, using the WDD as a military integrating facility for the combined efforts of science and industry.

The organization Schriever headed eclipsed the Manhattan Project in terms of scientific difficulty, budget, and, most important, urgency. Had the Manhattan Project failed, the outcome of the war against Japan would have been the same. There was no chance that Japan could have developed an atomic bomb and delivered it on the United States. In stark

One of the most important leaders in U.S. Air Force history, Benny Schriever was responsible for fielding the U.S. intercontinental ballistic missile fleet and in doing so laid the foundation for U.S. efforts in space. (U.S. Air Force)

contrast, the Soviet Union was more advanced than the United States in rocketry, and it had developed atomic as well as hydrogen bombs. If Schriever and his team had failed, the United States would have been at the mercy of a nuclear ICBM–equipped adversary.

Fortunately, Schriever elicited almost miraculous achievements from the military-scientific-industrial organization, fielding no less than three operational ICBM systems and one IRBM system in less than eight years. These included the Atlas, Titan, and Minuteman ICBMs and the Thor IRBM. And as Schriever often stated at the time, the ICBM experience paved the way to the exploitation of space. The modern network of intelligence, meteorological, communications, and navigation satellites owes its existence to the brilliant work of Schriever and his team.

Walter J. Boyne

See also
Missiles, Intercontinental Ballistic

References

Boyne, Walter J. *Beyond the Wild Blue: A History of the United States Air Force, 1947–1997.* New York: St. Martin's, 1997.

Schütte, Johann (1873–1940)

Born near Oldenburg to a royal administrator, Johann Heinrich Karl Schütte first studied ship engineering at the technical institute in Berlin-Charlottenburg, after which he went to work for the northern German Lloyd shipping firm. There he tested optimal hydrodynamic shapes, developing a degree of knowledge that made him famous in ship design. He was promptly offered a chair in ship design at a newly opened technical institute in Danzig in 1904. There, he began expanding his interest in other technologies. The heavy media coverage of the crash of Count Zeppelin's LZ-4 airship in August 1908 prompted Schütte to analyze the causes of the failure. Schütte wrote Zeppelin's engineering department and offered suggestions for improvement, which included strengthening the keel, improving the vertical and horizontal stabilizers, and better placement of the engines and propellers. He got no response.

Schütte then sought to build his own airship project and obtained the assistance of industrialist Karl Lanz (1873–1921). Together, they established the Schütte-Lanz (SL) airship factory at Rheinau in 1909, where the first project, SL-1, flew in 1911. It was delivered to the German army late the following year but was destroyed by a storm while anchored at mast in July 1913. Meanwhile, Schütte went about improving his designs for airship orders by the army and navy. Both services saw advantages in his solution, and the German navy used his improvements to put pressure on the Zeppelin firm to do the same with its own machines.

Schütte, for example, had devised enclosed cabins to protect the crew, placed engines in the center of the ship rather than on the side, and designed cruciform rudders, based on shipbuilding experience, that turned out to be the ideal solution for proper steering. The disadvantage of Schütte's solution involved the use of wood in the rigid structure of his ships. Initially, wood helped take care of many stress problems, as its material dynamics were better known than those of aluminum, which Zeppelin was using.

As the size of airships grew, however, and their intended functions increased, wood showed its limits, not least because of how humidity affected its tensile strength. Nonetheless, the patents that Schütte had acquired were of such importance that the German army actually requisitioned and transferred them to the Zeppelin firm for application in its war dirigibles starting in 1914. The twenty-second and last SL airship, with a capacity of 56,300 cubic meters and more than 600 feet long, was delivered in 1913 to the German navy.

Several SL dirigibles saw service during the war, by which time the general public simply referred to any airship as a "Zeppelin." When asked about this, Schütte stated that he bore no grudge. After the war, however, hoping to restart his operations, he sued Zeppelin in court over the patents and lost. Projects he had kept handy for a transatlantic airship as well as one to fly to the Arctic led nowhere, as Schütte failed to find financial support in the United States for his ideas.

Out of luck and out of funds, the SL firm closed in 1925. Although Johann Schütte deserves high praise for his initial designs, credit also goes to several SL engineers who put such ideas into practice. After the end of SL, Schütte remained active in aeronautics, teaching in Berlin and heading the German Aeronautical Science Society until its dissolution on orders of the Nazis in 1935. Schütte retired from teaching three years later.

Guillaume de Syon

See also

Airships; Zeppelin, Ferdinand von

References

Meyer, Henry Cord. *Airshipmen, Businessmen, and Politics, 1890–1940.* Washington, DC: Smithsonian Institution Press, 1991.

Schütte, Johann, ed. *Der Luftschiffbau Schütte-Lanz, 1909–1925* (The Airships of Schütte-Lanz, 1909–1925). Munich: Oldenbourg, 1926 (reprinted in facsimile, 1984).

de Syon, Guillaume. *Zeppelin! Germany and the Airship, 1900–1939.* Baltimore: Johns Hopkins Univerity Press, 2001.

Schwarzkopf, H. Norman (1934–)

Overall commander of U.S., British, and French military forces in the Kuwaiti Theater of Operations during the Gulf War.

Born in Trenton, New Jersey, Schwarzkopf graduated from the U.S. Military Academy in 1956. A much-decorated veteran of numerous military assignments, including two tours of duty in Vietnam, he first attained the rank of general in 1978 and in October 1983 was deputy commander of U.S. forces in the invasion of Grenada.

In 1988, he was appointed to head U.S. Central Command. After Iraq invaded Kuwait in August 1990, he was responsible for planning and executing Operations DESERT SHIELD/DESERT STORM. Along with Saudi Arabian Lieutenant General Khalid Bin Sultan, the commander of the Arab/Islamic Joint Forces Command, with whom he established a combined headquarters, Schwarzkopf was responsible for the conduct of air, land, and sea campaign against Iraqi military forces. After extensive air and naval operations that set the stage, Schwarzkopf directed a turning movement by the U.S. VII and XVIII Corps that enveloped the Iraqi defenses. In 100 hours, the ground operation was over, the Coalition's objective of forcing the Iraqis from Kuwait achieved.

Schwarzkopf relinquished command of Central Command on 9 August 1991 and retired from active duty on 31 August of that year. He remains active in public affairs as a noted speaker.

James H. Willbanks

See also

AirLand Battle; DESERT SHIELD; DESERT STORM; Horner, Charles A.; Jointness

References

Cohen, Roger, and Claudio Gatti. *In the Eye of the Storm: The Life of General H. Norman Schwarzkopf.* New York: Farrar, Straus, and Giroux, 1991.

Schwarzkopf, H. Norman. *It Doesn't Take a Hero.* New York: Bantam, 1992.

Schweinfurt-Regensburg Raids

Part of the Combined Bomber Offensive initiated by a 10 June 1943 Combined Chiefs of Staff directive. On 17 August, the first anniversary of the U.S. Eighth Air Force's initial raid at Rouen, Major General Ira Eaker sent his bombers on their deepest penetration raid. The 3d Bombardment Division was to attack Regensburg and the 1st Bombardment Division Schweinfurt. Regensburg was 500 miles from England, Schweinfurt 400 miles. Such distances allowed the Luftwaffe to deploy all its defenses.

Plans called for the 1st Bombardment Division to hit Schweinfurt 10 minutes after the 3d Bombardment Division hit Regensburg, with the 3d returning over the Alps to Tunisia and the 1st returning the way it came. Fighter support extended less than halfway to the targets, as most escorts did not have long-range drop tanks.

Early-morning fog on 17 August forced a change in plans. While the 3d departed at about 6:30 A.M., the 1st was delayed 5 hours. German coastal monitoring stations picked up the formations at 17,000 feet. The first fighters attacked over Belgium. Of the 3d's 146 B-17s, 122 reached the target and dropped 250 tons of bombs.

The 1st's delay allowed German fighters time to refuel and hit them hard. The 1st struck four hours after the 3d, returning through a gauntlet of fighters. Only 184 of the original 230 bombers dropped 380 tons on Schweinfurt. Ten were forced to abort due to mechanical problems. Of the total of 376 B-17s, 60 (24 over Regensburg and 36 over Schweinfurt) were lost to enemy action. Of the 306 that returned from the mission, more than 25 percent were heavily damaged. They lost 601 airmen killed, wounded, or captured. The Regensburg loss rate was 16.4 percent, Schweinfurt 15.7 percent. The Germans acknowledged 25 fighters lost; U.S. crews claimed more than 100.

Although bombing accuracy was excellent and most primary buildings were damaged at Regensburg, few of the machine tools were destroyed, and they were back in production in four weeks. According to the German armaments minister, Albert Speer, the Regensburg raid sped up German plans to disperse parts production to hard-to-bomb shops in nearby villages and towns. Initial German estimates put August-September fighter production losses at 800. Unknown, however, was the fact that the raid destroyed new fuselage jigs for the Me 262 jet fighter. German managers later speculated that this delayed jet production by a critical four months. At Schweinfurt, ball-bearing production suffered a 38 percent decline. However, by October overall production had actually increased.

In spite of criticism of U.S. tactics, the mixed success of the raids had less to do with flaws in strategic bombing doctrine and more to do with the inability of the 500- and 1,000-pound bombs to fully destroy the machine tools.

On 14 October, with ball-bearing production restored, a second Schweinfurt raid was attempted. Black Thursday, as it became known to history, cost the USAAF 60 of 291 aircraft and more than 600 men. The raid cut production 67 percent. After the war, Speer expressed surprise that the Allies had not sent follow-up raids he believed might have destroyed ball-bearing production entirely. The cost would have been high; AAF leaders were not able to pay the price, and the RAF was unwilling to try. The second raid left 133 planes so badly damaged that it took four months to bring the Eighth Air Force back to anything approaching full strength. Deep-penetration raids were suspended until long-range fighters became available in 1944.

In retrospect, the raids proved that with better fighter escort AAF bombers could play a decisive role in the war. The raids also had a greater effect on the enemy than anyone at the time realized, especially in regard to jet production. They forced Germany's already depleted industrial resources to focus on defensive fighter production and not offensive aircraft that could have made a difference elsewhere.

William Head

References

Coffey, Thomas. *Decision over Schweinfurt: The U.S. 8th Air Force Battle for Daylight Bombing.* New York: David McKay, 1977.

Craven, Wesley F., and James L. Cate, eds. *The Army Air Forces in World War II, Volume 2: Europe: Torch to Pointblank, February 1942 to December 1943.* Rpt. Washington, DC: Office of Air Force History, 1983.

SENTRY (Samos) Reconnaissance System

One of two technological approaches to satellite photography pursued by the first U.S. photoreconnaissance satellite program, Project WS-117L. CORONA satellites returned their film to earth via capsule for development. SENTRY (Samos) satellites developed the film onboard, scanned the film, converted the data into electrical signals, and transmitted the data to earth, where the data were reconverted into photographs. Ultimately, CORONA proved more successful, and only two Samos satellites reached orbit before the program was cancelled in 1962.

Project WS-117L commenced in March 1955 when the U.S. Air Force requested studies of a satellite system. In late 1957, after the Soviet Union launched Sputnik 1, President Eisenhower approved a major increase in funding for satellite programs. Both SENTRY and CORONA proceeded in parallel to ensure that at least one program would succeed. Samos 1 was launched on 11 October 1960, but failed to reach orbit. Samos 2 went aloft on 31 January 1962 and transmitted photographs for nearly a month. Samos 3 and Samos 4 (9 September and 22 November 1961) failed to achieve orbit. The final launch (22 December 1961) orbited until 14 August 1962.

Samos satellites were 22 feet long, weighed about 4,100 pounds without fuel, and were launched on Atlas Agena boosters from Vandenberg AFB. Samos ground resolution was about 20 feet, and an electronic intelligence package intercepted Soviet radar signals. Most sources contend that Samos produced no useful imagery. One source, however, claims that imagery from Samos 2 contributed to the demise of the so-called missile gap in late 1961.

James D. Perry

References

Day, Dwayne A., et al., eds. *Eye in the Sky.* Washington, DC: Smithsonian Institution Press, 1998.

Peebles, Curtis. *Guardians.* Novato, CA: Presidio Press, 1987.

Richelson, Jeffrey. *America's Secret Eyes in Space.* New York: Harper and Row, 1990.

Seversky, Alexander P. de (1894–1974)

Russian national and veteran of World War I; emigrated to the United States and began a aircraft-manufacturing firm. Seversky flew with the Imperial Naval Air Service and lost a leg when he was shot down in 1915. Unfazed, he convinced his commanders to allow him to fly with his artificial leg. Ultimately, Seversky was credited with shooting down 13 German aircraft before the Russian government reached an armistice with Kaiser Wilhelm in 1917.

In early 1918, Seversky received a commission to study aircraft design and manufacturing in the United States. While Seversky was in the United States, the Bolshevik revolution in his homeland made it exceptionally dangerous to return. Seversky heard of the mass executions of his fellow officers and promptly applied for U.S. citizenship.

During his early years in America, Seversky gained a position as a test pilot and consultant with the fledgling U.S. Army Air Service. Seversky's brilliance was quickly recognized, and he was assigned as an assistant to General William "Billy" Mitchell. During the next 8 years, Seversky applied for no less than 360 U.S. patents, including a gyrostabilized bombsight purchased by the Army Air Corps. In addition, Seversky managed to obtain a commission in the Army Air Corps Reserve.

Major Seversky formed a company registered as Seversky Aero Corporation. Unfortunately, the small firm did not survive the stock market crash of 1929. Undaunted, Seversky attracted enough investors to form a new firm. In February 1931, elected president of the new Seversky Aircraft Corporation, Seversky quickly surrounded himself with several expatriate Russian engineers, including Michael Gregor and the man who would ultimately head the P-47 design team, Alexander Kartveli. The Russian connection quickly produced results. Edo Aircraft Corporation of College Point, Long Island, New York, manufactured the first design under contract. Designed as a low-wing monoplane, the SEV-3 was a floatplane. Edo, being the leading manufacturer of aircraft floats, was an ideal choice considering that Seversky had no manufacturing facilities. Even with Edo's expertise, however, construction took two years, largely due to lack of capital funds. Finally, in June 1933 the SEV-3 took off from Long Island waters with Seversky at the controls. Painted in a stunning bronze, the SEV-3 was one of the more advanced aircraft in the world. Several months later and fitted with a more powerful engine, the SEV-3 set a new world speed record for amphibians. One major contributor to the excellent speed of the plane was its broad, semielliptical wing. This distinctive wing was used for the P-47 a decade later.

Economic and political difficulties forced the Seversky Aircraft Corporation out of business, its assets taken over by Republic Aviation. Seversky continued to write and was an advocate of airpower, his principal work being *Victory Through Airpower.*

Albert Atkins

References

Bodie, Warren M. *Republic P-47 Thunderbolt.* Hiwassee, GA: Widewing, 1994.

Seversky Aircraft

U.S. aircraft manufacturer founded by Alexander de Seversky, a Russian immigrant and aviation pioneer. The firm was founded by Seversky in February 1931. Design work on its first aircraft, the all-metal three-place SEV-3 executive aircraft, began that year, and it flew in June 1933 (license X-2106), powered by a Wright R-975 350-shp engine that was soon upgraded to 420 shp. Its initial configuration was as a twin-float amphibian with the floats hydraulically adjustable to optimize their angle of incidence for landing on water or land; retractable wheels were buried in the floats.

In October, the SEV-3 set a world speed record for amphibians (180 mph), and the Columbian air force ordered three in 1934. The wing was a semielliptical planform with a very thin airfoil and was used with very little change on all Seversky aircraft through the P-47 Thunderbolt. As the SEV-3L, the plane was revised to a fixed, spatted, wheeled landing-gear configuration and entered in the 1934 Army trainer competition. During this competition, the SEV was reworked as the SEV-3XAR and won the competition for 30 trainers, being designated the BT-8 and powered by a Pratt and Whitney R-985. The first production BT-8 was delivered in February 1936, and the last was delivered before the end of that year. In the summer of 1935, the SEV-3 was converted back to float configuration, reengined with an R-1820 of 750 shp, and entered the Thompson Trophy race, taking fifth place. Shortly thereafter it set another speed record at 230 mph.

The second Seversky prototype, the SEV-3M, also an SEV-3 design (license X-18Y), was built as a two-place landplane with fixed spatted landing gear, almost identical to the first prototype, and initially powered by a Wright XR-1670 twin-row engine of 775 shp. Variations of the design won the 1935 Army pursuit competition, Seversky receiving an order in June 1936 for 77 SEV-1XPs as the P-35, with Pratt and Whitney R-1830 850-shp engines. The first production P-35 flew in April 1937. The penultimate P-35 was delivered in August 1937. The last P-35 was retained and modified with lengthened fuselage, a 1,200-shp R-1830, and flush-retracting gear as the XP-41.

Sixty fighters ordered by Sweden as EP-1-106s were requisitioned by the U.S. government and designated P-35A. They featured a lengthened fuselage and the 1,050-shp R-1830 but were identified as Republic aircraft. The third Seversky prototype, the SEV-X-BT (license N-189M), started design early in 1936 as an improved BT-8, with an R-1340 engine of 550 shp and retracting landing gear. Reequipped with an R-1820 engine of 875 shp, it was designated 2PA Convoy Fighter and flew in July 1937. Twenty were sold to Russia as 2PA-Ls with 1,000-shp Cyclones, being delivered in late 1937 and early 1938, and 20 were sold to Japan as 2PA-B3s with 1,000-shp R-1830s.

In 1938, Seversky built the AP-7 (NX-1384), which flew in May, with a 20-inch fuselage extension to test as a remedy for ground-looping problems with the P-35. The AP-7 set a transcontinental speed record in August 1938 and won the Bendix Trophy race in September. In 1941 it was sold to Ecuador.

Sweden bought 120 EP1s as single-seat fighters and 52 2PAs as two-seat dive bombers. The U.S. government sequestered 50 of the 2PA dive-bombers, redesignating them as AT-12 Guardsmen advanced trainers.

The AP-4 (NX-2597) was designed with a turbocharger mounted in the baggage space behind the cockpit of the P-35/AP-1. It was built in parallel with the XP-41, had flush-riveted skin, and flew in January 1939. Thirteen of the turbocharged AP-4 with the R-1830 were ordered as the YP-43 and 154 as Republic P-43s.

After building other prototypes, in September 1939 Seversky was ousted from the corporation bearing his name. The firm was renamed Republic Aviation Corporation.

Douglas G. Culy

References

Bodie, Warren M. *Republic's P-47 Thunderbolt.* Hiawassee, GA: Widewing, 1994.

Green, William, and Gordon Swanborough. *The Complete Book of Fighters.* London: Salamander, 1994.

Shenyang J-6 and J-8

Supersonic jet fighters built by the Shenyang Aircraft Corporation in Manchuria, formerly a Japanese aircraft assembly facility. These advanced airplanes began serving the newly formed People's Republic of China (PRC) in 1949. Initially, Soviet-built MiG-15 and MiG-15 *bis* jet fighters were assembled at the facility after being shipped by rail from the Soviet Union. The Shenyang facility became the focal point for the construction of a modern Chinese air force in 1953 and today still produces fighter aircraft as well as civilian aircraft and other products. Although the MiG-15 provided the People's Liberation Army Air Force (PLAAF) with an effective interceptor for the still poorly trained Chinese pilots to use against the USAF and Taiwanese pilots during the early 1950s, it was not built by the Chinese themselves.

Mao Tse-tung and the Chinese communist leadership wanted to demonstrate that the PRC was ready to take its place among the Great Powers. In order to do so, the Chinese needed to produce modern weapons. The Sino-Soviet alliance lasted long enough for the Chinese to receive enough aid to begin building their own aircraft.

The first supersonic jet aircraft built in the PRC was the Jianjiji-6 (J-6; Fighter Aircraft-6). The J-6 was a license-built version of the Soviet MiG-19 and began service with the PLAAF in 1958. Although the MiG-19 was phased out of production in the Soviet Union by the 1960s, the J-6 served into the 1990s in the PRC. Although the J-6 was a qualitative step forward for Chinese military aviation, it was still a foreign design, and its length of service revealed the inherent weakness of Chinese technology.

The Jianjiji-8 was the first jet fighter designed by the Chinese. Although derived in part from the Soviet MiG-21 (J-7 in Chinese service), the J-8 was developed by the Chinese beginning in 1964. In the case of the twin-engine Mach 2 J-8, it was not Chinese technology that delayed production but rather Chinese politics. The massive dislocations of Mao's Great Leap Forward and Cultural Revolution kept the F-8 on the drawing board until 1979. By then the aircraft was several generations behind U.S. and Soviet frontline fighters.

The April 2001 collision between a PLAAF F-8IIM and a U.S. Navy EC-121 spyplane revealed that the F-8 was still serving, albeit in upgraded versions, as a modern interceptor. The PRC has returned to its Russian partner to begin upgrading its air forces with Su-27 and Su-30 aircraft. China has yet to solve the problem of domestically producing high-tech weapons systems and aircraft. The development of the Shenyang J-6 and J-8 are excellent illustrations of China's struggle to be a world-class power.

Mark A. O'Neill

References

Taylor, Michael J.H., ed. *Jane's Encyclopedia of Aviation.* New York: Portland House, 1989.

Short Aircraft (Early Years and World War I)

The Short Brothers firm was one of the pioneers in British aviation, starting in the days when all aircraft more or less resembled the box-kite format first employed successfully by Wilbur and Orville Wright in 1903. In 1911, they began a relationship with the British Admiralty as the result of the loan of a Short aircraft by Francis McClean, who intended to help naval officers learn to fly.

In the years that followed, Short played on that relationship by specializing in seaplanes and the development of all things having to do with naval aviation. These latter devices included such peripheral items as floats, wheel float attachments, airbags used as floats to keep wings out of the water, folding wings that enabled aircraft to be stored more efficiently aboard ship, wing attachments for lifting aircraft out of the water with shipboard cranes, experimental armament arrangements for naval aircraft, and the airborne launching of torpedoes.

The Short 184 was the large seaplane workhorse of World

War I. Spanning more than 63 feet, it had a 40-foot fuselage and stood more than 13 feet tall. Power could be provided by a variety of 225–275-hp Sunbeam engines, a 240-hp Renault, or the 250-hp Rolls-Royce Eagle. Armament consisted of a single Lewis machine gun and any combination of bombs totaling 500 pounds, these being carried on a straight-line external rack slung under the fuselage.

More than 650 Short 184s were built, and nearly 300 of those were still in service with the Royal Air Force at the time of the Armistice. The Short 184 was used at RNAS stations throughout the British Isles as well as in France, Italy, and throughout the Mediterranean. One Short 184 was flown by the immortal "Rutland of Jutland"—Lieutenant F. J. Rutland, who spotted German ships at Jutland on 31 May 1916. It also saw service on the *Ben-my-Chree, Raven II, Anne, Campania, Empress, Engadine, Furious, Nairana, Pegasus, Riveria, Vindex, City of Oxford, Auethusa,* and *Aurora.* One Short 184 went to Japan.

Of the more than 20 Short types produced, most were intended for use on the water. One exception was the Short Bomber, a landplane conversion of the famous Short 184 seaplane. The bomber was fitted with wings of unequal span, the upper wing being considerably longer than the lower, its overhang being braced by wires running from the bottom of the interplane struts on the lower wing out near the tips and then up to tall kingposts. Ailerons were fitted to the upper wing only. Of course, the undercarriage was also different, consisting of four wheels connected to the fuselage by a maze of struts and the customary tailskid. Power was provided either by a 225-hp Sunbeam or the 250-hp Rolls-Royce Eagle. Defensive armament was on the light side, only a single Lewis gun being carried, but for offensive purposes the Short could carry four 230-pound bombs or eight 112-pounders. Only limited use was made of the Short, the decision having been made to concentrate on other types, notably the Handley Page.

James Streckfuss

References

Bruce, J. M. *British Aeroplanes, 1914–1918.* London: Putnam, 1957.

______. *The Aeroplanes of the Royal Flying Corps (Military Wing).* London: Putnam, 1982.

Short Aircraft (Post–World War I)

Great Britain's Short Brothers firm added to its successful World War I aircraft with the introduction of the all-metal Silver Streak biplane in 1920, which foreshadowed the use of aluminum alloy in their later projects.

Short was best known for its large multiengine flying boats, which included such biplane types as the Singapore, Calcutta, Sarafand, and Kent. Both France and Japan built Short aircraft under license. The biplane formula carried over to a series of stately landplanes used for air transport by Imperial Airways. The company led the world with the introduction of a line of cantilever monoplane flying boats that included the Empire series and led to the classic Sunderland of World War II. Another Short contribution to World War II was the four-engine Stirling heavy bomber.

In the postwar period, Shorts (as it became known) produced a whole series of prototypes, some of very advanced design ranging from high-speed research aircraft to VTOLs to jet transports. It had small production runs of the Seamew antisubmarine aircraft and the very large four-turboprop-engine Belfast. However, the firm survived primarily by subcontracting parts or producing the designs of other companies. It reentered moderately large scale production with the introduction of the Skyvan series of light utility transports. These were transformed over time from the very boxy look of the first aircraft to quite sleek 32-passenger airliners. The Skyvans have been sold worldwide. Shorts was purchased by Bombardier in 1989.

Walter J. Boyne

See also

Short Stirling; Short Sunderland

References

Barnes, C. H. *Shorts Aircraft Since 1900.* London: Putnam, 1967.

Short Stirling

Unique in RAF history as the first four-engine monoplane bomber designed from the outset as such. The specification issued in 1936 also placed a restriction on the wingspan to match the available 100-foot hangar width. This resulted in the aircraft receiving a very-low-aspect ratio wing.

This design limitation meant the Stirling suffered from a lack of service ceiling; the wing spar and fuselage design meant that the bomb bay was restricted in the size of bombs that could be carried. The first prototype first flew on 14 May 1939, although it was destroyed upon landing. Service deliveries began to No. 7 Squadron in August 1940, operations beginning soon afterward. The first operation of note was against the German capital ships *Scharnhorst* and the *Gneisenau* in Brest Harbor.

Further notable actions took place during the 1,000-bomber raids, interspersed with daylight raids across occupied Europe. On one raid against Turin, the first Victoria Cross for the RAF was awarded to Flight Sergeant R. H. Middleton.

When more Lancaster and Halifax bombers became available, the Stirling was relegated to less arduous roles, such as minelaying, and special duties involving radio and radar countermeasures. As the war progressed, duties changed to target-towing, for which purpose the nose was modified and towing equipment fitted in the rear fuselage. The last version of the Stirling was built purely from the outset as a transport and lasted in RAF service until replaced by the Avro York beginning in 1946.

Kev Darling

References

Falconer, J. *Stirling Wings: The Short Stirling Goes to War.* London: PSL, 1997

Short Sunderland

British flying boat based on a 1933 Air Ministry order. Short Brothers began development of what would become the S.25 Sunderland naval four-engine flying boat. The first prototype flew on 14 October 1937, though the wing and power plants were already being improved. The first squadron equipped was in Singapore in 1938, by which time British home squadrons were also being equipped as aircraft came off the production line. Steady improvements through Mks.I–V improved the aircraft's performance in the air, though at some disadvantage in water handling.

With a speed of 165 mph and a payload of just under 10,000 pounds, the aircraft had a range of about 1,000 miles. The aircraft was primarily used in long (10–12-hour) patrol and reconnaissance missions, including convoy protection and U-boat searches, as well as some search and rescue. Sunderland production stopped with 749 built (456 were Mk.III) by the end of World War II, though the type would remain in service in Britain to 1957 and elsewhere through 1967. An improved model, the S.45 Seaford, was designed, but only a handful were built. Three dozen copies of both models were converted for postwar civil use.

Christopher H. Sterling

See also

Flying Boats

References

Barnes, C. H. *Shorts Aircraft Since 1900.* 2nd ed. Annapolis, MD: Naval Institute Press, 1989.

Bowyer, Chaz. *The Short Sunderland.* Bourne End, UK: Aston, 1989.

Short, Michael C. (1944–)

USAF lieutenant general. Michael C. Short was born in Princeton, New Jersey, on 24 February 1944. He earned a bachelor of science degree from the USAF Academy in 1965 and a master's degree from the University of Southern California in 1974. He was a distinguished graduate at the Air Command and Staff College in 1977 and attended the Industrial College of the Armed Forces in 1985.

General Short has commanded several of the fourth-generation squadrons (334th Tactical Fighter Squadron, 4450th Tactical Group, 335th Tactical Training Wing, 67th Tactical Reconnaissance Wing, and the 4404th Composite Wing). He is a command pilot with more than 4,600 flying hours in fighter aircraft, including 276 combat missions in Southeast Asia. He has flown the F-102, F-106, F-4C/D/E, RF-4C, A-10, A-7, F-117, F-15E, and F-16C.

In July 1995, General Short became Chief of Staff for the Allied Air Forces Southern Europe (Naples) and then director of operations at USAF Headquarters Europe (Ramstein). In June 1999, he was commander for Allied Air Forces Southern Europe, Stabilization Forces Air Component and Kosovo Forces Air Component (NATO), and Sixteenth Air Force, U.S. Air Forces Europe (Naples).

He was the air commander during Operation ALLIED FORCE and has since lectured and spoken extensively about the chosen airpower strategy. In brief, General Short argues that the execution of the air operations was compromised for political reasons and that the preferred strategy would have been to engage in an intense strategic air campaign directly against the sources of Slobodan Milosevic's power base. General Short retired from the USAF on 1 July 2000 with many decorations, including the Defense Distinguished Service Medal, Distinguished Service Medal, Distinguished Flying Cross, Meritorious Service Medal, and the Air Medal. He is currently an independent consultant, specializing in training for joint and coalition operations and advising on defense and national security matters in general.

John Andreas Olsen

See also

ALLIED FORCE

SIAI Marchetti

Italian aircraft manufacturer formed on 12 August 1915 as Società Idrovolanti Alta Italia (SIAI) to build flying boats at Sesto Calende. Its founders were Luigi Capè, owner of an industrial sawmill, and Domenico Lorenzo Santoni, who held the Franco-British Aviation license and a patent to brand his aircraft "Savoia" in honor of the Italian royal family. During World War I SIAI also operated a flying school and gradually introduced new seaplanes designed by Raffaele Conflenti, including the S.12, which won the 1920 Schneider Trophy, and the S.16 used by Francesco de Pinedo for his 1925 flight to Australia. This spawned the S.59 (1925), S.62 (1926), and S.78 (1932) that equipped Italian naval aviation.

When Santoni and Conflenti left for France in 1920, Capè recruited Alessandro Marchetti (1884–1966), who also acquired a shareholding and in 1937 added his name to the company—which, confusingly, still referred to aircraft as "Savoia." Starting from the S.51 racer (1922), Marchetti launched a series of new designs, the most famous of which was the twin-hulled S.55 flying boat (1924) used to cross the Atlantic in formation in 1930–1931 and 1933. Almost overnight, SIAI became the leading Italian airframe manufacturer. The twin-boom layout was successfully replicated on the S.66 trimotor passenger seaplane (1931) and S.64 long-distance record landplane (1928) but failed on the S.65 Schneider Trophy racer. Finally, by mating the wooden outer wings of the S.55 to a steel-tube fuselage and fixed landing gear, Marchetti created the S.73 trimotor airliner (1934). Its S.81 bomber derivative saw extensive use in Ethiopia and Spain; transport variants were still in production in 1943.

In 1934, the S.79 introduced a completely new wing and advanced features including retracting landing gear, variable-pitch propellers, flaps, and slats. Conceived as a racer, the sleek trimotor was adopted as a medium bomber but found permanent fame beginning in 1940 as a torpedo-bomber across the Mediterranean. Production ceased in 1943 after more than 1,200 had been built by SIAI and licensees; derivatives included the S.83 airliner and twin-fin S.84. Although larger, the S.75 airliner (1937) and S.82 military transport (1940) were essentially similar, including the wooden wing and steel-tube fuselage. Now firmly established as an airplane manufacturer, SIAI in 1938 built a new factory and airfield at Vergiate. Several prototypes were flown in the following years, but all attempts to diversify production failed. Worse, SIAI failed to master the complexities of all-metal construction, creating a technological gap that proved impossible to bridge.

Unsurprisingly, postwar SIAI survived on overhauls and subcontracts, adding small batches of the SM.95 airliner (1945), SM.102 general-purpose twin (1949), and FN.333 amphibian (1952). Marchetti retired in 1960, and SIAI was acquired by the Protto family, whose business plan focused on a family of light aircraft that included the S.205 (1965) and S.208 (1967) four-seaters, S.210 six-seat twin (1970), and S.202 basic trainer (1969). Although about 800 were built over 15 years, these in-house designs were eclipsed by the success of the SF.260 sportplane and trainer (1964) conceived by Stelio Frati (1919–), still in production in 2001 with more than 900 exported to 26 countries.

SIAI also built the SM.1019 observation plane (1969), in essence a turbine-powered Cessna L-19, but was acquired by Agusta in 1973, and helicopter subcontracts soon represented 65 percent of its workload. Unsuccessful attempts to renew the product line centered around the SF.600 utility twin-turboprop (1978) and the S.211 jet trainer (1981), entered in the U.S. J-PATS competition under the Grumman banner. The SIAI story ended in late 1996, when Agusta sold its fixed-wing business to Aermacchi, which transferred production and support to Venegono. Agusta retained Vergiate, but the historic Sesto Calende factory was torn down.

Gregory Alegi

See also

Aermacchi; Agusta; Balbo, Italo; Italian Aircraft Development; Regia Aeronautica (Pre–World War II); Regia Aeronautica (World War II)

References

Catalanotto, Baldassare. *SIAI Marchetti SM.82.* Turin: La Bancarella Aeronautica, 2000.

Donald, David, and Jon Lake, eds. *Encyclopedia of World Military Aircraft.* London: Aerospace, 1996.

Gentilli, Roberto, and Giorgio Bignozzi. *Aeroplani SIA,I 1915–1935.* Florence: EDAI, 1982.

Gori, Cesare. *SIAI S.79.* 2 vols. Turin: La Bancarella Aeronautica, 1998–1999.

Signals Intelligence (SIGINT)

Intelligence that derives from the interception and decryption of enemy signals traffic. SIGINT can be further broken down into several categories of intelligence, specifically communications, electronics, radar, laser, and nonimaging infrared intelligence. SIGINT has traditionally been considered one of the most important and sensitive forms of intelligence. Indeed, it has been suggested that the British decryption of German radio signals during World War II shortened the war by two years. The ease with which signals can be intercepted and understood by the enemy depends on the method of transmission, the frequencies employed, and the encryption system used to conceal the content of the signal from unauthorized personnel.

SIGINT can provide data on a nation's diplomatic, scientific, and economic plans or events, as well as the characteristics, capabilities, and often intentions of its armed forces. For example, during the North African campaigns during World War II, the British had virtually unlimited access to Italian codes and ciphers with beneficial results in what has been described as a perfect (if rather miniature) example of the cryptographers' war.

Brad Gladman

References

Hinsley, F. H. *British Intelligence in the Second World War.* London: HMSO, 1993.

Gladman, Brad. "Air Power and Intelligence in the Western Desert Campaign, 1940–1943." *Intelligence and National Security* 13, 4 (Winter 1998).

Sikorsky, Igor I. (1889–1972)

Pioneer aviator and innovative designer of fixed-wing and rotary-wing aircraft. The son of a pre-Freudian psychiatrist in Kiev in imperial Russia, Igor I. Sikorsky studied math and engineering at the Russian Naval Academy in St. Petersburg and the Polytechnic Institute of Kiev. Science fiction by Jules Verne and European flight demonstrations by Wilbur Wright sparked his interest in an aviation career.

Sikorsky traveled to Paris in 1909 and learned aeronautical principles from French pioneers such as Louis Blériot. Returning to Kiev, he made two unsuccessful attempts to build helicopters before designing the first of his Winged-S airplanes. The S-6, a tractor biplane, won prizes as well as the Russian military competition of 1912. His triumph led to financial rewards and a contract with the Russo-Baltic Wagon Company, which subsidized his design (1912–1913) of a four-engine behemoth, the Grand. Its successor, the "Ilya Muromets," broke world records and flew in the summer of 1914 on a 1,500-mile round-trip between St. Petersburg and Kiev. The outbreak of World War I overshadowed the spectacular cross-country flight. Nevertheless, Russia's military appreciated Sikorsky's accomplishment and ordered the "Ilya Muromets" into production as the world's first four-engine bomber-reconnaissance aircraft.

The 1917 Russian Revolution interrupted Sikorsky's career as well as Russia's participation in the war. Bolshevik ascension to power during the revolution's second phase prompted Sikorsky to flee Soviet Russia and travel first to France (1918) and then to the United States (1919).

Employed briefly by the U.S. Army Air Service at McCook Field (later Wright-Patterson) in Dayton, Ohio, Sikorsky designed a U.S. bomber that went unfunded. He then journeyed to New York City, where he taught math at an institute and contacted members of the Russian émigré community. These contacts enabled him to finance in 1923 the Sikorsky Aero Engineering Corporation.

The company's most successful multiengine product, the S-38 amphibian, gained national attention for Sikorsky and 111 sales contracts to various buyers such as Pan American Airways. Moving from Long Island, New York, to a new facility in Stratford, Connecticut, Sikorsky in 1929 merged his firm with United Aircraft and Transport Corporation (later United Technologies). Although the originator of luxurious flying boats, Sikorsky faced a small market filled in the 1930s with stiff competition from Boeing and Martin. Moreover, he lost out to Consolidated in his bid to secure a U.S. Navy contract. As a result, United Aircraft turned over a major portion of the Sikorsky plant to another subsidiary, Chance-Vought Aircraft.

Meanwhile, Sikorsky returned to his first love—helicopters. In the early 1930s, he applied for a U.S. patent for a single-rotor helicopter, then built and tested in 1939 the VS-300. The military version, the R-4 and variants R-5 and R-6, entered serial production during World War II. By war's end, a total of 425 Sikorsky helicopters flew for the U.S. Navy, Coast Guard, and Army Air Forces. Conceived initially as a tactical reconnaissance vehicle, it also proved its worth in air rescue and transport missions, roles reconfirmed during the Korean War.

Sikorsky retired from the Sikorsky Division of United Technologies in 1957. He then devoted time to revising his memoirs and preparing mystical tracts entitled *Message of the Lord's Prayer* and *The Invisible Encounter.* He received numerous awards, including the prestigious Collier Trophy for his life's work in aviation in 1951.

James K. Libbey

See also

Air Rescue; Boeing Company; Consolidated Aircraft Corporation; Martin Aircraft; Sikorsky, Igor I.; U.S. Army Air Forces; U.S. Army Air Service; U.S. Coast Guard Aviation; United Aircraft Corporation; United States Navy, and Aviation; Wright, Wilbur

References

Delear, Frank J. *Igor Sikorsky: His Three Careers in Aviation.* New York: Dodd, Mead, 1976.

Finne, K. N. *Igor Sikorsky: The Russian Years.* Trans. Von Hardesty. Washington, DC: Smithsonian Institution Press, 1987.

Sikorsky, Igor I. *The Story of the Winged-S.* New York: Dodd, Mead, 1967.

Sikorsky S-55/H-19 Chickasaw

Utility, troop transport, antisubmarine warfare, and search-and-rescue helicopter used by all U.S. military services and many other nations. Military use of the S-55 began in 1950. The U.S. Army and Air Force designated it the H-19, the Army calling it the "Chickasaw." The Marines designated it the HRS and the Navy the HO4S. Sikorsky and foreign licensees produced more than 1,800 S-55s in many different models.

The S-55 was bulky in appearance, with a cabin seating 10–12, a three-blade rotor, a high tailboom, and a tailrotor. The radial engine was mounted in the nose at a 45-degree angle to the rotor mast, and the two pilots sat atop the cabin and engine. The Soviet Mi-4 Hound closely resembled the S-55.

The S-55 saw service during the 1950s in the Korean War, British counterinsurgency operations in Malaya, the Algerian War, and the British-French attack on Suez.

John L. Bell

References

Polmar, Norman, and Floyd D. Kennedy Jr. *Military Helicopters of the World.* Annapolis, MD: Naval Institute Press, 1981.

Sikorsky S-61R/CH-3/HH-3 Jolly Green Giant

Transport helicopter. In June 1967, two Sikorsky HH-3Es completed the first nonstop helicopter crossing of the Atlantic Ocean. Supported by nine aerial refuelings, they flew from New York to the Paris Air Show in 30 hours, 46 minutes. At the time, the HH-3E, equipped with two General Electric T58-GE-5 1,500-shp turboshaft engines and designed for the combat rescue mission, was the latest variant of the Sikorsky S-61 series. Earlier versions had been developed for the U.S. Navy in rescue and antisubmarine roles.

The U.S. Air Force first used S-61 series helicopters in 1962 when borrowed Navy aircraft supported the offshore radar-operating Texas Towers. The S-61R, with its rear loading ramp and retractable undercarriage, first flew in 1963 and was used by the USAF as the CH-3E and HH-3E and by the Coast Guard as the HH-3F. Redesignated from SH-3As to CH-3A/Bs, good long-range performance resulted in an Air Force order of 75 CH-3Cs equipped with a new rear fuselage design with cargo ramps that enabled straight-in loading and T58-GE-1 engines.

In 1966, the CH-3E was introduced for combat and special operations and equipped with the uprated 1,500-shp GE-5 engines and pod-mounted turrets, with NATO 7.62mm miniguns, on each sponson. HH-3Es, with GE-5 engines, armor, self-sealing fuel tanks, rescue hoist, and a retractable aerial-refueling probe were designated for combat rescue. They became known as "Jolly Green Giants" during their Vietnam service.

The U.S. Coast Guard version of the S-61R, designated the HH-3F, began manufacture in 1968. Advanced electronics were added for the search-and-rescue mission. Combat-related features were removed.

Charles Cooper and Ann Cooper

References

Taylor, John W.R. *Jane's All the World's Aircraft, 1969–1970.* London: Jane's Yearbooks, 1969.

Sikorsky S-64 Skycrane/CH-54 Tarhe

U.S. heavy-lift helicopter. The enormous and versatile Skycrane transported construction equipment and armored vehicles, carried downed aircraft to safety, and even dropped bombs on a few occasions. Some of the records Skycranes set decades ago stand today.

The first six aircraft, Model YCH-54A, were built in 1962 and 1963. After testing and evaluation at Fort Benning, Georgia, 54 CH-54As were built, first entering Army service in late 1964. The Skycrane (almost never referred to as "Tarhe") was equipped with a six-blade main rotor powered by two Pratt and Whitney T73 engines for a total of 9,000 shaft horsepower. Seventy feet, 7 inches long, with a rotor diameter of 72 feet, the CH-54 weighed 19,234 pounds empty, could take off at a gross weight of 42,000 pounds, and achieve a top speed of 126 mph. It was flown by a crew of three, with the third pilot facing aft and operating the 15,000-pound-capacity hoist. Thirty-seven additional CH-54Bs, with uprated engines and twin-wheeled landing gear, were built in the late 1960s.

When not using the hoist, the Skycrane carried interchangeable universal military pods, also built by Sikorsky. Pods could be fitted out as troop transports, field hospitals, mobile command posts, or communications centers.

The CH-54 served in Vietnam with the 478th Aviation Company, also known as the 478th Heavy Helicopter Company, supporting the 1st Cavalry. In addition to hauling bulldozers and graders, Skycranes had retrieved more than 380 damaged aircraft by the end of 1969. The 478th also dropped 10,000-pound bombs from a Skycrane in 1968, near the demilitarized zone. The bomb was released from 6,000 feet and fused to explode 4 feet above the ground, creating an instant landing zone. Only one crew was lost to enemy fire in Vietnam. Several other Skycranes were shot down, but the crews survived.

After Vietnam, CH-54s in military service were transferred to the Army National Guard. Retired from National Guard service in the early 1990s, most Skycranes are now in civilian use, still providing heavy-lift service. Many have been modified for firefighting use as waterbombers (redesignated S-54E).

Among the many world records set by the CH-54B are maximum altitude in horizontal flight (36,122 feet), maximum altitude with a 15,000-kilogram payload (10,850 feet), time to climb to 3,000 meters (1 minute, 29.9 seconds), and time to climb to 9,000 meters (5 minutes, 57.7 seconds).

Mark E. Wise

See also

Helicopter Operations, U.S. Army; Helicopters, Military Use; Sikorsky, Igor I.; U.S. Army Aviation (Operations)

References
Gunston, Bill, ed. *Chronicle of Aviation.* Liberty, MO: JL International, 1992.
Holmes, Tony. *Jane's Historic Military Aircraft.* London: HarperCollins, 1998.
Taylor, John W.R. *Jane's All the World's Aircraft, 1969–1970.* London: Jane's Yearbooks, 1969.

Sikorsky S-65/CH-53 Sea Stallion

A two- or three-engine helicopter with wide field applications. The first S-65 flew on 14 October 1964 and went in production as the CH-53A "Sea Stallion" for the USMC. The Sea Stallion was involved in the Vietnam War, Grenada, Panama, Lebanon, and the Gulf War.

The S-65 was also designated MH-53A and used as a minesweeper. The CH-53D was the more powerful version of CH-53A. The MH-53J Pave Low was used by Special Forces. The HH-53B became the "Super Jolly" as a transport for USAF. It had more powerful engines and additional fuel tanks. The HH-53C was an improved HH-53B with better engines and seating for 44 troops; the RH-53A was a minesweeper; and the S-65C was a passenger helicopter. The YCH-53E a three-engine prototype, first flown on 8 December 1975.

Henry M. Holden

References
Reed Chris. *H-53 Sea Stallion in Action.* Atglen, PA: Schiffer,
Ripley, Tim. *Jane's Pocket Guide Modern Military Helicopters.* New York: HarperCollins, 1999.

Sikorsky S-70

Twin-engine helicopter designed to replace the Huey UH-1. The Sikorsky prototype competed against the Boeing-Vertol YUH-61A and won. The S-70 first flew on 17 October 1974 and went into production in 1978. A number of modifications to the S-70 were undertaken, including the UH-60A Black Hawk—utility helicopter for the U.S. Army; EH-60A—electronic countermeasures; HH-60A Jayhawk—rescue helicopter; SH-60B Seahawk—also known as S-70L, naval antisubmarine and patrol helicopter; SH-60C—fitted with CV-HELO sonar; MH-60 Pave Hawk—special forces helicopter; and S-76—passenger version. All U.S. military branches and the U.S. Customs service currently use it.

Henry M. Holden

References
Ripley, Tim. *Jane's Pocket Guide Modern Military Helicopters.* New York: HarperCollins, 1999.

Sikorsky UH-60 Black Hawk

Light transport helicopter first flown in October 1974; used for air assault, air cavalry, and aeromedical evacuation units. The UH-60A was developed as result of the Utility Tactical Transport Aircraft System program. The Black Hawk is the primary division-level transport helicopter, providing dramatic improvements in troop capacity and cargo-lift capability compared to the Huey UH-1 series it replaces. The UH-60A, with a crew of three, can lift an entire 11-man fully equipped infantry squad in most weather conditions. It can be configured to carry four litters, by removing eight troop seats, in the medevac role. Both the pilot and copilot are provided with armor-protected seats; protective armor can withstand hits from 23mm shells. The Black Hawk has a cargo hook for external lift missions, provides for a door mounting for two M60D 7.62mm machine guns on the M144 armament subsystem, and can disperse chaff and infrared jamming flares using the M130 general-purpose dispenser. It has a composite titanium and fiberglass four-blade main rotor, is powered by two General Electric T700-GE-700 1,622-shp turboshaft engines, and has a maximum cruising speed of 184 mph.

The UH-60 is the Army's first true squad assault helicopter to transport troops and equipment into combat, resupply medevac troops while in combat, reposition reserves, and perform command-and-control functions. It can transport a lightweight 105mm howitzer with crew and ammunition, with the range, endurance, and maneuverability required of a highly effective tactical assault vehicle.

The Army has two series in the fielded fleet. Delivery of the UH-60A began in 1978 and continued through September 1989, with a total of 980 delivered. In October 1989, with an improved durability main gearbox and an updated engine, the UH-60L series was introduced. Survivability characteristics include low-reflective paint; invisible engine smoke and flame; crashworthy armored crew seats; redundant flight controls, hydraulic systems, and electrical systems; crashworthy self-sealing fuel system; engine and auxiliary power unit fire-detector and -extinguisher system; wire cutters; and the Hover Infrared Suppression System to reduce the infrared signature of the engine exhaust.

Dennis R. Jenkins

Developed in 1974 as result of the Utility Tactical Transport Aircraft System (UTTAS) program, the Sikorsky H-60 offers dramatic improvements in troop capacity and cargo lift capability over earlier helicopters. (Walter J. Boyne)

See also
Combat Search and Rescue

References

Allen, Patrick. *The Helicopter: An Illustrated History of Rotary-Winged Aircraft.* Shrewsbury, UK: Airlife, 1996.

Single Integrated Operation Plan (SIOP)

Framework for U.S. war planning; articulates U.S. nuclear doctrine. Strategic warfare in the Cold War quickly became defined in terms of nuclear weapons and the destruction of an opponent's leadership, industry, military, and infrastructure. Planning for such a contingency began piecemeal, with each military service developing a separate plan, replete with excessive target redundancies plotted by other services. Moreover, the war plan was an absolute: peace or all-out nuclear conflagration, something economist Herman Kahn called "wargasm."

In August 1960, President Dwight D. Eisenhower authorized the Joint Strategic Target Planning Staff, responsible for producing a National Strategic Target List and the SIOP. The first of these was SIOP-62, which took effect on 15 January 1961 and provided for massive strikes against the Soviet Union and the People's Republic of China. The only option in SIOP-62 was its status as a preemptive attack or a retaliatory attack.

The following year SIOP-63, at the behest of Secretary of Defense Robert S. McNamara, allowed considerable selectivity. Major Attack Options, for example, enabled the president to launch a handful or hundreds of weapons at precise targets. In 1982, China was dropped from the SIOP, but Chinese targets were retained for Strategic Reserve Force strikes. SIOP-6F in 1989 saw a shift in emphasis to leadership and mobile targets, especially Soviet SS-25 ICBMs, as well as the development of adaptive target planning.

With the collapse of the Soviet Union and the end of the Cold War, SIOP refocused on Third World countries pursuing weapons of mass destruction. During 1997, President Bill Clinton issued Presidential Directive PD-60 on guidelines for atomic weapons, which reaffirmed this shift toward targeting so-called rogue states—nations with threatening nuclear, biological, and/or chemical capabilities. As such, by 1999 China was once again included in the SIOP. Aside from providing a sense of order to U.S. warplans, SIOP articulated U.S. nuclear doctrine from global holocaust to mutual assured destruction to a "winnable" nuclear war to strategic warfare with Third World.

Robert S. Hopkins

See also
Atomic Bomb; Cold War; Massive Retaliation; Mutually Assured

Destruction; Strategic Air Command; Strategic Triad Concept; U.S. Air Force Doctrine

References

Ball, Desmond, and Jeffrey Richelson. *Strategic Nuclear Targeting.* Ithaca: Cornell University Press, 1986.
Pringle, Peter, and William Arkin. *SIOP.* New York: Norton, 1983.
Ross, Steven T. *American War Plans, 1945–1950.* London: Frank Cass, 1996.

Six Day War

Few events in the history of airpower compare with the decisive aerial operations of the June 1967 Six Day War. Working from the idea of an overwhelming preemptive attack, Israeli Air Force (IAF) planners decided to destroy the bulk of the Arab air forces on the ground, thereby eliminating their vast numerical advantage. The plan—code-named MOKED—was developed by IAF pilot Jacob Nevo and proved a spectacular success. Some 400 Arab aircraft, the bulk of them Egyptian (including 30 Tupolev Tu-16 bombers), were destroyed in their ground revetments, while attempting to take off, or in the few aerial battles that did manage to develop.

With the Arab air forces eliminated, the IAF then devoted its attention to supporting Israeli ground forces, which captured the Sinai Peninsula, the Golan Heights, and the whole of Jerusalem. The Israeli victory solidified the reputation of the IAF as nearly invincible, contributing to a mystique of a flawless and impeccable fighting force. One dark moment for the IAF, however, was the intentional attack on the USS *Liberty,* a U.S. intelligence-gathering vessel off the coast of Egypt.

Robert S. Hopkins

See also

Dassault Mirage III; Israeli Air Force; Israel–Middle East Conflicts; Israel–Middle East Wars; USS *Liberty*

References

Dupuy, Trevor N. *Elusive Victory.* New York: Harper and Row, 1978.
Halperin, Merav, and Aharon Lapidot. *G-Suit.* London: Sphere Books, 1990.
Nordeen, Lon. *Fighters over Israel.* New York: Orion Books, 1990.

Slessor, John C. (1897–1979)

Marshal of the Royal Air Force. Although highly regarded as an able operational commander and a premier staff officer, RAF Marshal John C. Slessor may be remembered best as one of the great conceptual thinkers of airpower. Born in 1897, Slessor volunteered for the Royal Flying Corps in 1915 when his childhood polio prevented army service. He flew pursuit aircraft in the Sinai and Sudan, as well as home defense against Zeppelins.

During the interwar years, Slessor commanded No. 4 Squadron (Army Co-Operation) from 1925 to 1928 and No. 3 (Indian) Wing from 1936 to 1937, but he was best known as a talented writer. Noticed by legendary Chief of the Air Staff Hugh Trenchard in the 1920s, Slessor served as the chief's ghostwriter for policy papers, speeches, and articles. He articulated and honed the RAF's interwar air doctrine. Ironically, although a devoted "bomber man," Slessor's 1936 *Air Power and Armies* represented the best book on air-land warfare before World War II. He examined mechanization and airpower's impact on history and emphasized air superiority and interdiction in close cooperation with ground forces.

During World War II, Slessor served as deputy, then as director, of plans, Air Ministry (1937–1941). He commanded No. 5 Group (Bomber Command) during 1941–1942. In January 1943, his draft charted the Combined Bomber Offensive at the Casablanca Conference that largely reconciled Anglo-American doctrinal differences. The same year, Slessor played a role in defeating the U-boat menace as commander in chief (CinC) of Coastal Command.

In 1944, he replaced Air Chief Marshal Arthur Tedder as CinC RAF Mediterranean and Middle East and deputy air CinC Mediterranean Allied Air Forces. As air member for personnel, Air Council, in 1945–1946, Slessor struggled to reduce RAF numbers and create the postwar air force. In 1950, he became Chief of Air Staff and developed the V-bomber force. Upon retirement in 1952, he continued to write and speak effectively; his book *The Central Blue* confirmed his reputation as one of the RAF's great thinkers.

John Farquhar

References

Black, Adam, and Charles Black, eds. *Who Was Who, 1971–1980.* Vol. 7. New York: St. Martin's, 1981.
Probert, Henry. *High Commanders of the Royal Air Force.* London: HMSO, 1991.
Meilinger, Phillip S. "Trenchard, Slessor, and Royal Air Force Doctrine Before World War II." In *The Paths of Heaven: The Evolution of Airpower Theory.* Maxwell AFB, AL: Air University Press, 1997.

Smushkevich, Yakov "General Douglas" (1902–1941)

Soviet air commander during World War II. Yakov Vladimirovich Smushkevich was born on 14 April 1902 in

Lithuania. After fighting in the civil war he transferred to aviation. In September 1936 he was sent to Spain, where he commanded the Soviet air units under the pseudonym "General Douglas." His accomplishments included the air defense of Madrid and the routing by air attack of the Italian Littorio Division at Guadalajara, which became the model for ground attack operations in World War II. He was awarded the Hero of the Soviet Union (HSU) in June 1937. During the summer of 1939, he commanded the Soviet air units engaged over Khalkin Gol, reversing their initially poor performance. He was awarded a second HSU in November 1939 and became chief of the Red Army Air Force. Smushkevich was one of those arrested and blamed for the Soviet catastrophe when the Germans invaded on 22 June 1941 and was shot on 28 October. He was rehabilitated posthumously in December 1954.

George M. Mellinger

See also

Soviet Volunteer Pilots; Spanish Civil War

References

Hardesty, Von. *Red Phoenix: The Rise of Soviet Air Power, 1941–1945.* Washington, DC: Smithsonian Institution Press, 1982.

Howson, Gerald. *Aircraft of the Spanish Civil War.* Washington, DC: Smithsonian Institution Press, 1990.

SNCASO 4050 Vautour

French attack aircraft conceived in 1951 by Jean Charles Parot. The SNCASO 4050 Vautour (Vulture) was a successful multirole twin-jet transonic aircraft. The first of three prototypes flew on 16 October 1952. In June 1953, it reached over Mach 1 in a dive and on 29 December 1953, 60-year-old Louis Christiaens became the very first "supersonic minister" aboard the same plane.

Two single-seaters and four two-seaters were produced as preseries models. The first of 140 standard Vautour IIs achieved its first flight on 30 April 1956. Only 29 Vautour IIA attack single-seaters were built, plus 40 Vautour IIBs and 70 Vautour IIN night-fighters. A single Vautour IIBR was produced. Carrying a load up to 5,300 pounds, these Armée de l'Air bombers were used from 1958 to 1979. The night-fighters soldiered on from 1957 to 1973. They were equipped with four 30mm cannons and 208 unguided rockets packed internally. Many Vautour IIs flew special missions through atomic clouds and other tests until 1990.

The SO 4050 was selected in 1955 by Israel, which obtained 19 Vautour IIAs, four IIBs, and eight IINs. The night-fighters of Squadron 119 never had a kill and were transferred in 1963 to Squadron 110 for daylight bombing. Vautour attacks were very efficient during the Six Day War (June 1967), destroying many Egyptian, Syrian, and Iraqi planes on the ground. The following war of attrition, in which Egypt and Israel battled for two years, demonstrated again the capacities of the Vautours. They were replaced by much more modern Douglas Skyhawks in 1973.

Stéphane Nicolaou

References

Crosnier, Alain. *Le Vautour.* Boulogne-sur-Mer: Lalle Press, 1995.

Sokolovsky, Vasily Danilovich (1897–1968)

Soviet army marshal and writer on military theory and doctrine. Sokolovsky enlisted in the Red Army in 1918, participated in the Russian civil war, and subsequently graduated from the Voroshilov General Staff Academy and the Frunze Military Academy. He was deputy chief of the General Staff at the start of World War II and was a successful senior field commander in the campaigns against the German army, directing operations that were characterized by close cooperation between the Red Army and Frontal Aviation forces.

Sokolovsky was commander of the Soviet Group of Forces and head of the Soviet Military Administration in East Germany after World War II and was in command at the start of the Berlin blockade in 1948. He was reassigned to Moscow shortly before the blockade was lifted in the face of the successful Berlin Airlift. Marshal Sokolovsky served as Chief of Staff of the Soviet armed forces from 1953 to 1960 and was the senior editor of the influential statement of Soviet military thought, *Military Strategy* (three editions between 1962 and 1968). *Military Strategy* addressed the integration of missiles and nuclear weapons into the Soviet military, with emphasis on how wars would could be fought and won in the nuclear age.

Jerome V. Martin

See also

Berlin Airlift; Frontal Aviation; Soviet Air Force

References

Sokolovskiy, V. D., ed. *Soviet Military Strategy.* 3rd ed. American ed. Harriet Fast Scott. New York: Crane, Russak, 1977.

Somalia

During the afternoon of 3 October 1993, a U.S. Special Forces team (Task Force Ranger) was sent into downtown Mogadishu, Somalia, to capture two lieutenants of the local warlord Mohamed Farrah Aidid. This operation became known as the Battle of the Black Sea, or *Ma-alinti Rangers* (The Day of the Rangers) to the Somalis. It took place during the UN peacekeeping effort RESTORE HOPE. Two MH-60 Black Hawk helicopters were shot down in the city by Russian rocket-propelled grenades, and two more crash-landed back at the base. Desperate close-quarter fighting took place in confined urban terrain throughout the night at the assault and crash sites and along the avenue of approach of the relief convoys. Aidid's warriors were intermingled with the local populace, the Special Forces team did not have night-vision equipment, and a convoy got lost, which added to the overall confusion of the operation. During the assault and ensuing rescue mission, 18 Delta Force and Army Rangers were killed and dozens more injured. Somali causalities were more than 500 killed and 1,000 wounded. The connection to terrorist Osama bin Laden was discovered later.

Robert J. Bunker

References

Bolger, Daniel P. *Savage Peace: Americans at War in the 1990s.* Novato, CA: Presidio Press, 1995.
Bowden, Mark. *Black Hawk Down.* New York: Atlantic Monthly, 1999.

Somerville, James F. (1882–1949)

Royal Navy vice admiral. Born on 17 July 1882 in Weybridge, Surrey, Somerville entered service aboard HMS *Britannia* in 1897. He served afloat with distinction until April 1938, when tuberculosis invalided him home from command of the East Indies station. He retired as a vice admiral.

When war came in September 1939, Somerville volunteered his services. He distinguished himself in developing radar and then as Vice Admiral Bertram Ramsay's subordinate during the Dunkirk evacuation.

The Royal Navy established a covering force at Gibraltar after France fell with Somerville in command. To neutralize the French fleet, Force H launched successive attacks on Oran and Dakar with aircraft and gunfire. The carrier *Ark Royal*'s aircraft then struck Italian bases at Genoa, Livorno, and on Sardinia and Sicily while Force H covered multiple convoys to Malta from August 1940 to March 1942. Somerville's force also played a decisive role in the *Bismarck* chase in May 1941.

In March 1942, Somerville took command of the Eastern Fleet, conducting holding operations against Vice Admiral Nagumo Chuichi's First Air Fleet Indian Ocean offensive. His carriers covered the Diego Suarez and Madagascar operations in May and September 1942 before withdrawing to serve elsewhere. Somerville's Eastern Fleet carriers recommenced offensive operations in 1944 until he relinquished command in August; he was reinstated an admiral on the active list after five years war service at sea.

Somerville went to Washington, D.C., in October to head the British naval delegation. He became Admiral of the Fleet in May 1945 and retired permanently the next year. Somerville died on 19 May 1949 in Wells, Somerset.

Paul E. Fontenoy

See also

Bismarck, Air Operations Against; Burma; Malaya, Battles of; Malta, Siege of; Mediterranean Theater of Operations

References

Brown, J. David. *Carrier Operations in World War II: The Royal Navy.* London: Ian Allan, 1968.
Brown, J. David, ed. *The British Pacific and East Indies Fleets.* Liverpool, UK: Brodie, 1995.
Macintyre, Donald. *Fighting Admiral: The Life and Battles of Admiral of the Fleet Sir James Somerville.* London: Evans Bros., 1961.

Somme, Battle of the (1916)

The costliest engagement in British military history; proved significant to the use of airpower and its coordination with the work of the army. The battle opened on 1 July 1916 with the British Army striving to break the deadlock on the Western Front. It lasted until mid-November and cost 600,000 German and 700,000 Allied casualties without any significant results.

During World War I, the fighting brought home the importance of tight relations between the artillery battery and the airplane observer regulating its fire. General Henry Rawlinson, commanding Fourth Army, was prompted to suggest that control of all artillery aircraft actually be moved from the Royal Flying Corps to the artillery, a proposal echoed by H. S. Horne, commander of First Army. RFC Commander Hugh Trenchard was able to argue successfully against these attempts to encroach on his command, pointing out that the work of the RFC squadrons did not merely include artillery-spotting but contact patrol, trench reconnaissance, and trench photography work. The point was made: The days when ground commanders shunned the airplane as a useless toy were over; it was now regarded as an integral part of effective army operations.

It was agreed, though, that observation balloons were a particular concern to the artillery, and arrangements were made for refinements in the structure of balloon organization, including the incorporation of artillery officers as balloon observers. As is discussed elsewhere, by 1918 this approach was being taken by balloon services in other

Touted as the premier allied dogfighter of World War I, the Sopwith Camel replaced the successful Pup in 1917. (Walter J. Boyne)

countries as well, the roster of the U.S. Air Service Balloon Section being split nearly 50-50 between aviation and artillery officers.

Problems with transmission of wireless signals from RFC aircraft to artillery batteries during the battle prompted a close look at the whole system and many changes. Improvements in wireless equipment subsequent to the Somme allowed for a doubling of the number of artillery aircraft. This prompted an increase in the number of aircraft in RFC squadrons from 18 to 24.

Further advances included revision of the way in which zone calls were made and the institution of a special intelligence section within the RFC for better coordination and dissemination of information collected by airplane.

Finally, the level and quality of enemy fighter opposition had increased so significantly during the battle as a result of the German reorganization into *jagdstaffeln* (fighter squadrons) that the lone patrol was no longer possible. It was noted that experienced airmen would thereafter be able to work perhaps in pairs but that in most cases larger formations would be necessary.

James Streckfuss

See also

Royal Flying Corps/Royal Naval Air Service/Royal Air Force

References

Cruttwell, C.R.M.F. *A History of the Great War, 1914–1918.* 2nd ed. Chicago: Academy Chicago, 1991.

Raleigh, Sir Walter, and H. A. Jones. *The War in the Air: Being the Story of the Part Played in the Great War by the Royal Air Force.* 6 vols. Oxford: Clarendon Press, 1922–1937.

Sopwith Aircraft

British aircraft manufacturer. In 1912, yachtsman and pioneer pilot Thomas Sopwith established Sopwith Aviation, Ltd., in Kingston-upon-Thames and set out to build aircraft. Although products included both landplanes and seaplanes, its first success was the Bat Boat, a small flying boat.

The company's first major contributions to the war effort came in 1916 with the two-seat 11/2 Strutter and a small single-seater that the government would call the Scout but the rest of the world came to know as the Sopwith Pup.

The 11/2 Strutter, so named because the long arm of its "W" shaped center-section strut appeared to be half the length of its interplane struts, served in a general-utility role. From its introduction to the front, the Strutter flew all sorts of missions, from reconnaissance to bombing to fighter escort. Originally designed as a two-seater, the Strutter was the first British aircraft to sport a synchronized machine gun for the pilot in addition to the Lewis gun for the observer. In No. 3 Wing, Royal Naval Air Service—the first Allied attempt at a strategic bombing unit—the two-seat Sopwith operated alongside a single-seat version intended for use as a bomber. The two-seaters escorted the bombers to and from targets.

Appearing at about the same time as the two-seater, the Pup established a reputation of being delightful to fly. Its 80-hp LeRhone engine and easy-to-handle control surfaces made it a pilot's dream. The Pup played a prominent role in the RNAS, not only with the units operating in Flanders but also in early experiments leading to the development of the aircraft carrier. Even though the German Albatross was a superior aircraft, the Pup was still able to hold its own in a turning contest and hung on until 1917, when it was replaced by the Sopwith Camel.

The Sopwith Tripe triplane was an unusual design when it appeared in RNAS units at the end of 1916, when the biplane was the standard configuration. The layout allowed an increase in lifting area with no additional wingspan and produced an airplane with an impressive rate of climb. This was a tremendous asset in a fighter, and if imitation is the sincerest form of flattery, then the Tripe must have been highly regarded, as it set off a three-wing fad that affected nearly every aircraft manufacturer of the day—British, French, and German. Armed with a single Vickers gun, the triplane could outclimb anything then on the Western Front. This quality, plus its quick maneuverability, made it a deadly mount in the hands of skilled pilots.

The next Sopwith design was the Camel, the work of designers Herbert Smith and Fred Sigrist. Camel flight characteristics have sometimes been compared to riding a polo pony, a quality that contributed to its reputation as one of the war's ultimate dogfighters. The Camel is affectionately regarded—many decades after the fact—as the premier Allied dogfighter of World War I. Highly maneuverable, its tight turning radius made it a challenging opponent for most German fighter pilots. Although praised by those who lived to master its quirky behavior, it was approached with terror by the neophyte.

The Camel's weight was concentrated in its first 7 feet. This mass combined with its rotary engine to create a gyroscopic effect that made right turns potentially lethal. It is said that the Camel killed more in training accidents than it achieved victories, a significant claim considering it is credited with more kills than any other fighter of the war. (The total of these claims varies, according to source, from 1,294 to more than 3,000.)

The final wartime offering from Sopwith was the Snipe, an attempt to improve on the Camel by retaining its good qualities while designing out the control problems that made it difficult. The Snipe featured a more rounded fuselage, wings with dihedral in both upper and lower surfaces, balanced control surfaces, and a more powerful engine, the Bentley BR 2. Intended for use at high altitudes, the Snipe did not see service long enough to build a real reputation for itself. In one exceptional action, however, it distinguished itself highly in the hands of Canadian ace William George Barker.

The Snipe stayed on in the postwar RAF stable. The Sopwith name passed from the scene in 1920, but many workers remained in a new firm named for Sopwith test pilot Harry Hawker.

James Streckfuss

See also

Barker, William George; Sopwith, Thomas O.M.

References

Robertson, Bruce. *Sopwith: The Man and His Aircraft.* Letchworth, UK: Harleyford, 1956.

King, Horace F. *Sopwith Aircraft, 1912–1920.* London: Putnam, 1960.

Sopwith, Thomas O.M. (1888–1989)

Aviation pioneer and industrialist. Born in London on 18 January 1888, Sopwith received a thorough engineering training. A private income allowed him to pursue his interests in motoring, sailing, and aviation. After learning to fly in 1910, he won several substantial prizes for record flights, enabling him to establish the Sopwith School of Flying and the Sopwith Aviation Company in 1912.

Before and during World War I, Sopwith supplied both British air services with aircraft, particularly a successful series of single-seat scouts whose pinnacle was the Camel. Nevertheless, the postwar contraction hit hard, and he liquidated the company in 1920.

In November 1920, Sopwith's new firm, the H. G. Hawker Engineering Company, began operations. The name was taken from the famous Sopwith test pilot Harry Hawker. Small orders kept it afloat when in 1928 Sydney Camm's spectacularly successful Hart brought substantial contracts, making Hawker the RAF's principal supplier during the next decade. The firm's strength allowed Sopwith to put Camm's next design, the Hurricane, into production three months before receiving a government contract.

Hawker's commanding position enabled Sopwith to create the Hawker-Siddeley Group between 1935 and 1938, combining the Armstrong-Whitworth, Avro, Gloster, and Hawker firms with the Armstrong-Siddeley aero-engine and automobile firm. Postwar, Sopwith took over de Havilland (1959) and Blackburn (1963). That year he retired from his position as chairman, although he remained a member of Hawker-Siddeley's board until 1978, soon after the British government nationalized the firm as British Aerospace.

Sopwith died at his home, Compton Manor, in Hampshire on 27 January 1989.

Paul E. Fontenoy

See also

Armstrong Whitworth Aircraft; Avro Aircraft; Blackburn Aircraft; British Aerospace; Camm, Sydney; De Havilland Aircraft; Gloster Aircraft; Hawker Aircraft; Sopwith Aircraft

References

Bramson, Alan. *Pure Luck: The Authorized Biography of Sir Thomas Sopwith.* Wellingborough, UK: Patrick Stephens, 1990.

King, Horace F. *Sopwith Aircraft, 1912–1920.* London: Putnam, 1981.

Sosnowska-Karpik, Irena (1922–1990)

Colonel in the Polish air and air defense forces. She was a meritorious pilot-instructor and served as deputy wing commander, Officer Flying School, in Deblin, Poland. Sosnowska-Karpik was a World War II veteran who served with the Polish armed forces formed in the Soviet Union (the Union of Polish Patriots, a predecessor of the communist government in postwar Poland). Sosnowska-Karpik became an outstanding flying instructor after the war.

While serving with the Higher Officer Flying School after the war as pilot-instructor, she trained almost 1,000 new pilots. Upon transferring to the reserves, she had approximately 4,300 flying hours to her credit aboard both fixed-wing aircraft and helicopters.

Sosnowska-Karpik was decorated with the Knight's Cross of the Order of Rebirth of Poland and the Gold and Silver Crosses of Merit, as well as various Polish air force medals and badges.

Kazimiera J. Cottam

See also

Lewandowska, Janina; Polish Auxiliary Women's Air Force Service

References

Cottam, Kazimiera J. "Veterans of Polish Women's Combat Battalion Hold a Reunion." *Minerva* 4, 4 (Winter 1986): 1–7.

Lukaszewski, Stanislaw. "Time to Serve, Time to Remember" (in Polish). *Zolnierz Wolnisci* (13 October 1986): 1, 3. Also: obituary (in Polish), *Zolnierz Wolnisci* (14 March 1990): 6; and obituary (in Polish), *Zolnierz Wolnisci* (15 March 1990): 6.

South Atlantic/Trans-Africa Air Route

The principle aerial lifeline for the Allies during the early days of World War II.

As war loomed, the airplane had evolved into an efficient and reliable long-range transport. Germans, British, and Americans were all able to modify existing civilian aircraft designs, resulting in new military versions capable of conducting long-range airlift support for military forces. For the Allies, this capability became absolutely critical as the British homeland came under effective blockade by the Axis powers.

By early 1941, the British were facing daunting demands to support their military forces on battlefields across Europe, the Middle East, North Africa, and Asia. In June 1941, as German U-boats were destroying increasing numbers of surface ships in the North and South Atlantic and as the Mediterranean became more difficult to transit due to Axis air and sea patrols, Prime Minister Winston Churchill turned to the United States for help. Churchill consulted with Juan Trippe of Pan American Airways and U.S. President Franklin Roosevelt about how to move aircraft and supplies to Cairo, Egypt. After negotiations, five separate contracts were signed, and in less that 60 days Pan Am's newly formed subsidiary, Pan American Airways–Africa Limited (PAA-Africa) was organized, personnel were hired and sent to Africa, and the first scheduled flight operations across the South Atlantic and Africa commenced.

The route started in Miami, with planned stops in Port of Spain, Trinidad, and Belem and Natal, Brazil. From Natal, Boeing 314 flying boats and B-24s crossed the South Atlantic, landing at marine terminals in Liberia or airfields in the Gold Coast Colony (modern-day Ghana). In Africa, PAA-Africa built upon a rudimentary route (known as the Takoradi Route) established by the British in the late 1930s. Facilities were established or improved at Fisherman's Lake, Benson Field, and Roberts Field in Liberia; Accra and Takoradi in the Gold Coast; Lagos, Kano, and Maiduguri in Nigeria; Fort Lamy in Chad; El Geneina, El Fasher, and Khartoum in the Sudan; and Luxor and Cairo in Egypt. The Trans-Africa Route eventually extended through the Middle East, then India, and terminated in China. By June 1942, construction was completed at two new airfields, Ascension Island, located in the South Atlantic, and Roberts Field, located in Liberia. Thus, shorter-range aircraft could use the route.

The U.S. Army Air Corps, Pan Am (using several subsidiaries), RAF Ferry Command, Trans World Airlines, and the Free French air forces were all major users of this route. Users facilitated delivery of more than 11,300 Lend-Lease aircraft and vital military supplies to the front lines. Additionally, significant amounts of cargo critical to the war effort was shipped back to the United States over the route (for example, captured military equipment and large quantities of raw materials including platinum, uranium, raw rubber, and mica).

Presidents, kings, generals, and other VIPs used this secure route to travel to and from combat zones and warplanning conferences. For example, Colonel Jimmy Doolittle returned to the United States as a passenger over this route after his historic 1942 air raid on Japan. With Allied victories in North Africa, Europe, and the Pacific, alternate air routes became available, diminishing the Allies' reliance on this vital lifeline.

Thomas M. Culbert

References

Christie, Carl A. *Ocean Bridge: The History of RAF Ferry Command.* Toronto: University of Toronto Press, 1995.

Culbert, Tom, and Andy Dawson. *PanAfrica: Across the Sahara in 1941 with Pan Am.* McLean, VA: Paladwr, 1998.

Davies, R.E.G. *Pan Am: An Airline and Its Aircraft.* New York: Paladwr, 1992.

Southeast Asia Air War (1965–1972)

Air operations conducted over Southeast Asia during the Vietnam War. The air war consisted of three basic elements: attacks against North Vietnam, interdiction of communist supply lines in Laos and Cambodia, and support for ground forces in South Vietnam. Each element saw tactical successes and technological innovation but ultimate strategic defeat.

The theater air effort lacked unity of command. In 1965, Southeast Asian air assets were under Thirteenth Air Force, subordinate to Commander, Pacific Air Forces. The 2d Air Division in Saigon controlled operations in South Vietnam and reported to Commander, U.S. Military Assistance Command, Vietnam (COMUSMACV). The Seventh Fleet's Task Force 77—subordinate to Commander in Chief, Pacific Fleet (CINCPAC)—controlled carriers in the Tonkin Gulf. In 1966, the 2d Air Division became the Seventh Air Force, whose commander chaired the Air Coordinating Committee that allocated targets and radio frequencies. CINCPAC divided North Vietnam into seven areas, or "route packages," in which the USAF and Navy conducted relatively separate, uncoordinated campaigns.

The air war depended critically on aerial refueling. B-52s required "tanking" on 12-hour flights from Guam, and tactical aircraft demanded pre- and poststrike refueling. Tankers frequently flew into North Vietnam to refuel desperate aircraft; none were ever lost to enemy action. Boeing KC-135 numbers rose from 55 in 1965 to 94 in 1969, with 172 in-theater for the 1972 LINEBACKER operations. In nine years, Strategic Air Command KC-135s flew 194,687 sorties and made 813,878 refuelings.

The war over North Vietnam consisted of several operations: ROLLING THUNDER (March 1965–November 1968), LINEBACKER (March–October 1972) and LINEBACKER II (18–29 December 1972). ROLLING THUNDER began in reprisal for Viet Cong attacks on U.S. airbases in South Vietnam. Strict Rules of Engagement (ROE) governed operations, though ROE gradually loosened as the war progressed. ROE defined areas near Hanoi, Haiphong, and the Chinese border as "sanctuaries"—where North Vietnam naturally built airbases and surface-to-air missile (SAM) sites. U.S. President Lyndon Johnson tightly controlled target selection. His insistence on graduated escalation and clear weather missions made U.S. attacks predictable and increased losses. ROE prohibited attacks on certain targets, such as North Vietnam's irrigation system. MiGs could not be attacked without visual identification, which negated U.S. long-range air-to-air missile advantages and allowed MiGs to hide in clouds.

The USAF relied heavily on older aircraft (the North American F-100D/F, Lockheed F-104C/D, Republic F-105D/F, and Convair F-102A), the Navy on Douglas A-4s. Improved North Vietnamese defenses, including SAM batteries, eventually required employment of newer aircraft (McDonnell F-4C/D/Es and Grumman A-6s) on missions over the North, and many support aircraft, such as RF-4Cs, Douglas EB-66B/Cs, McDonnell RF-101Cs, and Lockheed EC-121s, participated in each mission.

Hanoi's air defenses consisted of radars, antiaircraft (AA) guns, SAMs, and MiGs. In 1965, Hanoi had about 1,500 AA guns; the number rose to 8,050 in 1968. Many were radar-controlled and fired proximity shells. AA accounted for 85 percent of aircraft downed in ROLLING THUNDER. By 1968, Hanoi had several hundred SA-2 SAM batteries that forced aircraft down into AA gun range and required Americans to fly jamming and suppression missions. Hanoi had about 30 fighters in 1965 and 75 in 1968. By 1972, Hanoi had 93 MiG-21s, 33 MiG-19s, and 120 MiG-17s. Under rigid ground control, these small, highly maneuverable fighters armed with cannons and (on MiG-21s) two to four Atoll heat-seeking missiles intercepted U.S. strike missions. MiGs used hit-and-run tactics, attacking at supersonic speeds through U.S. formations and firing a missile before escaping. U.S. aircraft were often forced to jettison their bombs, after which they could rarely catch the nimble MiGs.

ROLLING THUNDER focused on interdiction. Nearly 90 percent of the bombs struck transportation targets (roads, rail lines, and bridges). In 1966, emphasis briefly shifted to POL (petroleum, oil, lubricants), and 65 percent of Hanoi's storage sites were destroyed. In late 1966 and early 1967, industries, power stations, and military airfields were attacked. In 1968, air commanders requested intensified attacks in response to the Tet Offensive, but antiwar clamor at home forced Johnson to cancel attacks on North Vietnam on 31 March. In total, the United States dropped 643,000 tons of bombs but failed to hinder significantly Hanoi's war effort. Communist supply needs in South Vietnam were minimal, and North Vietnam required only negligible amounts of POL and electric power. China and the Soviet Union supplied ample weapons and equipment, and Johnson refused to close these supply routes. In short, U.S. planners overestimated airpower's ability to win the war and underestimated Hanoi's will to fight.

LINEBACKER I sought to halt Hanoi's 1972 invasion of South Vietnam. Air reinforcement of Southeast Asia commenced in February. Hanoi's invasion began on 30 March, and B-52s hammered enemy troop concentrations. F-4Es, F-105Gs, RF-4s, and EB-66s reinforced Southeast Asia from Korea, Japan, and the United States, and six carriers deployed in the Gulf of Tonkin. By June, the USAF alone had some 752 aircraft in-theater, including 393 F-4s, 172 KC-135s, and 138 B-52s. In May, President Richard Nixon authorized air attacks throughout North Vietnam and the mining of harbors.

B-52s smashed North Vietnamese airfields below the 20th Parallel, and F-4s suppressed SAMs. F-4s struck interdiction targets around the clock, and the use of laser-guided bombs freed more aircraft to fly escort. MiGs were effective until the USAF created the Teaball Weapons Control Center in August to provide pilots with combined radar and intelligence information. USAF kill ratios then climbed from 1:1 to 4:1. During LINEBACKER, 155,548 tons of bombs hit North Vietnam. Bridges, oil storage sites, docks, and power facilities were wrecked, and imports substantially declined. North Vietnam could not attack the South again until 1975.

In December, Nixon punished North Vietnam for its diplomatic intransigence. LINEBACKER II involved 729 night sorties against 34 targets with 206 B-52D/Gs. An additional 613 tactical strike and 2,066 support sorties were flown: EB-66s, EA-6s, and EA-3s jammed enemy radars, F-111s and A-7s struck airfields, F-4s and F-105s attacked SAMs, C-130s and HH-53s conducted search and rescue, and F-4s escorted, flew combat air patrol, and laid chaff. Hanoi's MiGs withdrew to China, but SAMs remained a threat. In total, 1,240 SA-2s were fired, downing 15 bombers (12 aircraft were lost to other causes). Rail traffic stopped, electric power generation fell 75 percent, and POL supplies fell 25 percent. More than 15,000 tons of bombs were dropped, but civilian casualties were minimal. Since Hanoi accepted Nixon's demands, LINEBACKER II was a clear victory.

The air campaign in Laos principally sought to interdict the Ho Chi Minh Trail, the primary targets being the thousands of trucks that used it. Roads, mountain passes, river fords, supply caches, AA sites, and troop concentrations were also hit. In 1965–1966, forward air controllers in O-1 observation planes located targets for tactical aircraft to strike. The enemy could soon move only at night and in bad weather yet still met the minimal needs of forces in South Vietnam. Attacks on roads were relatively easily repaired, although road maintenance eventually required 300,000–500,000 troops. Hanoi deployed some 700 AA guns to defend the Ho Chi Minh Trail.

The ineffectiveness of interdiction prompted installation of the Igloo White anti-infiltration system in 1967. Acoustic and seismic sensors in Laos beamed data to orbiting aircraft, which retransmitted the data to an assessment center in Thailand. The analyzed data enabled a C-130 airborne command center to direct gunships and fighters against targets around the clock. Unfortunately supplies still got through, and the Soviets quickly replaced destroyed trucks.

After operations over North Vietnam halted in March 1968, interdiction efforts in the Laotian panhandle intensified. Operation COMMANDO HUNT (November 1968–March 1972) dropped some 3 million tons of bombs on Laos, including massive B-52 strikes on the four mountain passes between North Vietnam and Laos. The USAF claimed large numbers of truck kills (9,012 in 1969, 12,368 in 1970), but the CIA argued that Hanoi had only 6,000 trucks total. Hanoi's ability to attack South Vietnam in 1972 demonstrated that COMMANDO HUNT failed.

In northern Laos, U.S. airpower supported the Laotian army and Hmoung guerrillas against communist forces, and the USAF established navigation sites on remote mountaintops. COMUSMACV controlled interdiction operations in southern Laos, but operations in northern Laos required coordination between the CIA, HQ Seventh/Thirteenth Air Force, and the air attaché in Vientiane. Ambassador William Sullivan micromanaged the effort through the attaché's office, and he frequently imposed absurd limits on air operations.

Nixon ordered strikes on six communist bases in Cambodia from March 1969 to May 1970. The Operation MENU bombings entailed 3,875 B-52 sorties that dropped 108,823 tons of bombs. The secret missions used strikes on South Vietnam as bureaucratic cover. The bombing significantly reduced enemy activity, but ground forces had to invade Cambodia in April 1970 to destroy the enemy bases completely.

When U.S. ground forces arrived in Vietnam in 1965, COMUSMACV ordered the USAF to give close air support (CAS) top priority. The 2d Air Division (later Seventh Air Force) Tactical Air Control Center (TACC) planned and coordinated the tactical air effort. The TACC allocated sorties to the Direct Air Support Center (DASC) in each corps area, and the DASC responded to CAS requests from units in the field. A combination of preplanned and dedicated alert sorties ensured that CAS was always quite plentiful. On an average day, 40 aircraft were on alert, and Seventh Air Force flew 300 sorties, 1st Marine Air Wing 200 sorties, and the South Vietnamese 100 sorties. Tactical aircraft based in South Vietnam and Thailand usually arrived on target within 35–40 minutes or within 15 minutes if diverted from elsewhere. Furthermore, COMUSMACV selected targets for B-52s that flew 1,800 sorties per month in South Vietnam. Nearly 4 million tons of bombs fell on South Vietnam from 1965 to 1972.

Two examples demonstrate the tremendous impact of CAS. During the 1968 siege of Khe Sanh, 24,000 fighter-bomber and 2,700 B-52 sorties delivered 110,000 tons of bombs. This smashed the North Vietnamese Army (NVA) and inflicted more than 10,000 casualties. In 1972, Hanoi attacked South Vietnam with more than 14 divisions and 600 tanks. One hundred thirty-eight B-52s and 247 tactical aircraft were immediately available, and hundreds of aircraft reinforced from around the world. Operational tempo was impressive: B-52 sorties rose from 689 in March to 2,223 in May, fighter sorties from 4,237 in March to 18,444 in May.

This enabled the shaky South Vietnamese Army to defeat the NVA and inflict 75,000–120,000 casualties.

James D. Perry

References

Clodfelter, Mark. *The Limits of Air Power.* New York: Free Press, 1989.
Cooling, Benjamin Franklin, ed. *Case Studies in the Achievement of Air Superiority.* Washington, DC: Center for Air Force History, 1994, chap. 10, "Southeast Asia."
Futrell, Robert F. *Ideas, Concepts, Doctrine: Basic Thinking in the United States Air Force, 1907–1984.* Vol. 2. Maxwell AFB, AL: Air University Press, 1989.
Tilford, Earl H. Jr. *Setup: What the Air Force Did in Vietnam and Why.* Maxwell AFB, AL: Air University Press, June 1991.

Soviet Air Force

In Western countries, typically known as the Red Air Force—one of the largest and most powerful air forces of the twentieth century. The rise and fall of the Soviet air force (1918–1991) reflected Soviet military might yet contributed enormously to the history of airpower.

The huge continental landmass and open areas of the Soviet Union, as well as the primacy of the ground forces in the structure of its military machine, defined air defense and ground support as the primary missions of aviation. The air force necessarily interacted with other independent airpower branches (air defense aviation and naval aviation) and undertook wider interservice coordination. Rapid expansion of the air force was driven mainly by the strategic ambitions and mobilization abilities of the communist regime and was supported by virtually unlimited resources. The air force accumulated broad experience, which greatly enhanced its operation, from the 1917 Russian Revolution through the Cold War.

The Bolshevik government inherited a shattered czarist air force. The progress of the civil war, which lasted from 1918 to 1920 and resulted in Lenin's rise to the pinnacle of power, as well as the Allies' intervention in Russia, forced the Bolsheviks to organize the Red Army, including an air arm. On 24 May 1918, the Chief Administration (Directorate) of the Workers' and Peasants' Red Air Fleet was organized. Simultaneously, regular Red Army air units were formed. Red Navy aviation existed in 1918–1920 as a separate service.

The rapidly changing pattern of the civil war, as well as the need to employ aircraft throughout diverse climatic and terrain conditions, posed daunting operational problems. Moreover, the air force suffered from extremely poor maintenance, logistics, and critical shortages in fuel, trained personnel, and spare parts (about 60 percent of the planes were of Western origin—Morane, Nieuport 17C.I, SPAD S.VII).

Although the air force conducted 17,377 combat sorties during the war and confronted some 635–770 enemy planes (White Russian, Allied, Ukrainian Nationalist, and Polish), air-to-air combat was somewhat rare, with only 131 engagements and 20 victory claims. Most of the effort was in ground support, bombing, and reconnaissance.

During World War I, the air force acquired significant operational and organizational experience that influenced its development. These included the value of highly centralized command and control, the use of airpower in mass, the value of interservice coordination in combined and joint operations, and some tactical innovations such as air assault on large cavalry formations and the use of aircraft in propaganda.

While previously relying on Western designs, the Soviets began building their own, such as the MK-21 Rybka naval fighter and I-1 and I-2 monoplane fighters. During the 1920s, two main design bureaus, led by Nikolai Polikarpov and Andrei Tupolev, emerged. The Soviets also benefited from the joint Soviet-German air training base in Lipetsk and particularly from Junkers production of all-metal monoplanes in Russia.

The first Five-Year Plans triggered a massive buildup of Soviet aviation, including many airplanes of indigenous design. Among them were maneuverable fighter biplanes, such as the Polikarpov I-15 and I-15 *bis;* the first cantilever monoplane with retractable landing gear to enter squadron service, the Polikarpov I-16; and a variety of bombers, including the Tupolev TB-7, SB-2/SB-3, and DB-3. Yet the Soviets failed to develop a reliable long-range bomber force. The established Soviet concept of air warfare envisioned the use of airpower predominantly in close support missions and under operational control of the ground forces command.

The Red Army Air Force under the command of Yakov Alksnis during 1931–1937 developed into a semi-independent military service with a combat potential, good training, and a logistics infrastructure spreading from European Russia into Central Asia and the Far East. Still, the Red Army Air Force exhibited marked deficiencies in several local conflicts (e.g., against the Chinese in 1929 and in the Spanish civil war, 1936–1939). In contrast, during the 1937–1939 air conflicts with Japan (China, Lake Khasan, Khalkin Gol) the Soviets effectively challenged the Japanese air domination and provided decisive close air support in the campaigns on Soviet and Mongolian borders. During the Winter War with Finland (1939–1940), however, the Red Air Force suffered heavy losses due to inflexibility of organization, its command-and-control structure, poor training of personnel, and deficiency of equipment.

The failures in Soviet airpower were reinforced by the terror of Stalinist purges. About 75 percent of the senior officers were imprisoned or executed, and some 40 percent of the officer corps was purged. The result was the critical decline of experience, initiative, and responsibility within the command of the air force and its combat personnel.

This decline was manifested in the initial phase of World War II. During the first six days of the German invasion in June 1941, the Luftwaffe wiped out 3,800 Soviet aircraft (most of them on the ground) and gained almost unrestricted air supremacy. The sporadic Soviet retaliatory strikes were poorly coordinated and led to devastating losses in aircraft and combat personnel.

But the highly centralized Soviet aircraft industry was relocated eastward. By the end of 1943, it resumed output of new types of aircraft to challenge the Germans. During the war, the Soviets produced about 137,000 aircraft. Among the new types were the MiG-3, LaG-3, and La-5 fighters and the Petlyakov Pe-2 bomber. Most important of all was the famous tank-killer—the Ilyushin Il-2 ground support aircraft, which Stalin said the Soviet soldier needed more than "bread and air."

The United States and Britain also supplied about 20,000 aircraft. Allied aid was of particular importance in 1942–1943, when Soviet aircraft production grew slowly. Some U.S. and British models influenced the work of Soviet designers.

In 1942 under General Aleksandr Novikov, the whole command-and-control system of the Red Army Air Force was radically centralized. The air units were withdrawn from direct operational control of the ground forces command and grouped into 17 air armies. These were attached temporarily to the fronts as well as to Long-Range Aviation Command and strategic air reserve.

These innovations enhanced the ground support role of Soviet military aviation, allowing it to mass airpower rapidly and decisively during all major operations on the Eastern Front. Additionally, it gave more flexibility to the air force command to conduct independent air operations. During the war, the Red Army Air Force performed some 3.125 million sorties and claimed 57,000 enemy planes shot down. Naval aviation claimed to have sunk 2 million tons of enemy shipping.

The professional skills of Soviet pilots as well as the combat and technical characteristics of the aircraft improved. Lieutenant Colonel Ivan Kozhedub had the final score of 62 aerial victories, which qualified him as the most successful Allied pilot of World War II. The contribution of Soviet airwomen was unprecedented in history (with three all-female air regiments). Junior Lieutenant Lydia Litvyak, with 12 confirmed victories, became the most successful woman fighter pilot in the world.

Despite Soviet air dominance during the last years of the war, there was nothing resembling the Anglo-American strategic bombing campaign in Europe. Small-scale strategic raids performed by long-range aviation on Berlin, Budapest, Constanta, Ploesti, Danzig, Königsberg, and other Axis targets revealed the lack of experience of Soviet pilots and problems in navigation.

The strategic and technological realities of the postwar world (the growing confrontation with the West, the invention of the atomic bomb, and the introduction of jet engines) shaped the development of the air force, which was reconstituted in 1946 as a fully independent armed service. Additionally, the Soviet concerns about the Anglo-American strategic air preponderance impelled the development of Soviet Air Defense (1954) into an independent service with a formidable air arm.

The study of German jet engines helped the Soviets develop their first jet fighters (in 1946, the MiG-9 and Yak-15 were introduced). At the same time, Soviet designers benefited from the wartime acquisition of several U.S. B-29 bombers. The strategic bomber force was reorganized in 1946 within the Soviet Air Force, equipped with Tu-4 heavy bombers (based on the B-29 design) and Il-28 medium bombers.

During the Korean War (1950–1953) the Soviets sent one air corps with three divisions, one separate night-fighter regiment, and a naval aviation regiment as well as the air defense and support units to fight the UN air force in Korea and on the Manchurian border. The Soviets performed 60,894 sorties and lost 335 aircraft and 120 pilots. While the air force and air defense units effectively forced UN bombers to suspend daytime raids, in pure air-to-air combat the Soviet MiG-15s were outgunned and outmaneuvered by the U.S. North American F-86 Sabre fighters.

The Korean experience led the Soviets to emphasize maneuverability and interception capability in their jet fighters. In 1955, the first Soviet supersonic fighter, the MiG-19, was introduced. Since 1950, the first helicopters appeared within the transport aviation. Also in the 1950s, the Soviet Air Force advanced its bomber development. Since 1956, the Tu-20/95 Bear turboprop bomber became the mainstay of the Soviet strategic bomber force.

The progress of the Cold War since the 1960s, the development of nuclear, thermonuclear, and missile weaponry, as well as the development of entirely new technologies, prompted significant changes in the Soviet Air Force. The political and military leadership needed a world-class airpower to back up rising global ambitions and be able to participate in any number of contingencies—nuclear and conventional. At the same time, the greater emphasis on ICBMs in the development of strategic power allowed the Soviets to reduce a number of obsolete aircraft without lowering the combat capability of its air force.

From the 1960 to the 1980s, the Soviets modernized their

fleet of strategic bombers and introduced the supersonic Tu-22 bomber (1963). Beginning in 1987, the Tu-160 strategic bomber entered service. This bomber force was an integral (although the smallest) part of the Soviet strategic triad. Additionally, air-to-surface cruise missiles enhanced the strategic function of these aircraft. The cruise missiles, as well as the introduction of the Tu-26 longer-range bomber, in 1974 gave the Soviet Air Force the ability to carry out deep strikes across Western Europe, the North Atlantic, and North America.

As for Soviet tactical aviation, an increasing number of attack aircraft (MiG-21/-23s; Sukhoi Su-7/-9/-11s, and others) were introduced, strengthening the traditional interceptor/fighter-bomber priorities. During the 1970s, the Soviets put in service multipurpose aircraft (MiG-27s, Su-17/-24/-25s) with enhanced ground support and strike capabilities to fight in Europe and the Far East. One major innovation was the 1973 introduction of the Mi-24 attack helicopter—flying tanks—which became an increasingly important component of tactical aviation.

Transport aviation expanded its airborne and long-range airlift capabilities with the new Antonov An-22, An-24, and An-26 and the Il-76. In the late 1980s, the heavy-lift An-124 entered service. The development of the Soviet blue-water navy, including the first aircraft carriers, led to the introduction of the V/STOL MiG-21, the Yak-36, as well as Kamov Ka-25 helicopters with antisubmarine warfare capabilities. Additionally, the air force expanded its contributions to the Soviet space program.

In 1980, a major reorganization of the air force's two main combat components—Long-Range Aviation and Frontal Aviation—took place. Five Strategic Air Armies comprising long-range, longer-range, and medium-range bombers were created, deployed in the European Soviet Union (three armies), Poland (one), and Siberia (one). The Strategic Air Armies, subordinated to the Soviet Supreme High Command, were to provide nuclear and conventional support for theater strategic operations. Additionally, the Moscow Air Army had the broader responsibility of oceanic and intercontinental operations.

The Frontal Aviation forces and the combat helicopter force (Army Aviation) organized into divisions, and independent units were assigned to the military districts in the Soviet Union and Soviet forces in Eastern Europe, Mongolia, and Afghanistan. The number of foreign interventions grew as well: Cuba during the Cuban Missile Crisis (1962), Egypt (1970–1972), and large-scale employment in Afghanistan (1979–1988). Additionally, Soviet pilots and instructors contributed to local air defense and participated in combat during wars in Vietnam (1965–1972), Angola (1975–1990), and Ethiopia (1977–1979). Although such interventions demonstrated the global projection capabilities of the Soviet Air Force and gained it ground support experience, they also revealed inadequacies in equipment, logistics, and organization, particularly in dealing with insurgencies.

By the mid-1980s, the air force had achieved its pinnacle of power. The strategic bomber force had about 670 aircraft. The tactical aviation had 6,000 ground attack, air combat, and reconnaissance aircraft and some 3,500 helicopters. The transport aviation had 650 aircraft. Additionally, there were some 1,300 interceptors in the air defense air arm. Soviet naval aviation added 1,100 aircraft and helicopters.

The development of the Soviet Air Force, particularly its enormous modernization during the 1960–1980s period, could not change the weakness and fundamental disadvantage of the underlying Soviet system. Generally, Soviet military philosophy envisaged a heavy reliance on numbers rather than on training, technology, flexibility, and innovation. The emphasis on a highly centralized command-and-control structure was sometimes effective, but it also limited pilot initiative, especially as to air warfare, one of the most individualized arts in the military.

Despite modernization efforts, most of the Soviet Air Force lagged behind NATO airpower in electronics, navigation systems, precision munitions, maneuvering, fighter-escort abilities, and other key aspects of air warfare. By 1985, some 35 percent of Soviet combat aircraft were obsolete. Moreover, long-standing weaknesses in logistics, maintenance, and repair meant that Soviet aircraft became obsolete faster than did their Western counterparts. Additionally, the failure to fulfill the potential of aerial refueling for the Long-Range Aviation forces weakened maneuverability and strategic strike capability. Maneuverability of airpower was also hampered by slow development of the Soviet aircraft carrier.

Although the Soviet Air Force has traditionally been strong in the ground support and interception abilities, its overreliance on ground command and control inevitably limited the combat flexibility of air units, as well as initiative among pilots.

Moscow's Cold War strategy forced the Soviet Air Force to enter a hopeless competition with the strongest, ablest, and the most dynamic airpower the world had ever known. As the Soviet Union fell into the dustbin of history during 1991–1992, so too did the Soviet Air Force.

Peter Rainow

See also

Chkalov, Valeriy Pavlovich; Commonwealth of Independent States; Finland, and Air Operations During the "Continuation War"; Gagarin, Yuri; Imperial Russian Air Service; Khalkin Gol Air Battles; Khomyakova, Valerya; Khryukin, Timofei T.; Korean War; Kozhedub, Ivan; Kuban Air Battles; Kursk, Battle of; Kutakhov, Pavel; Litvyak, Lydia; Novikov, Alexander Aleksandrovich; Pokryshkin, Alexandr; Rudenko, S. I.; Safonov, Boris; Smushkevich, Yakov "General Douglas"; Sokolovsky, Vasily Danilovich; Soviet Volunteer Pilots; Soviet Women's Combat

Wings; Stalingrad, Battle of; Sutyagin, Nikolai; TsAGI; Warsaw Pact Aviation; Winter War

References

Boyd, Alexander. *The Soviet Air Force Since 1918.* New York: Stein and Day, 1977.

Kilmarx, Robert. *A History of Soviet Air Power.* New York: Praeger, 1962.

Murphy, Paul J., ed. *The Soviet Air Forces.* Jefferson, NC: McFarland, 1984.

Whiting, Kenneth. *Soviet Air Power.* Boulder: Westview, 1986.

Soviet Aircraft Development and Production

Long shrouded in government secrecy, the Soviet aviation industry and its output became better known in the 1990s as historical records and existing aircraft became available to Westerners. The rapid ascension of Soviet aviation—despite the many roadblocks it faced—is simply an amazing story.

The Russian aviation industry first emerged in 1910–1912, with many small plants producing a handful of aircraft. Virtually all of wood construction, about 270 aircraft were produced in the final year before World War I (1913). Some plants built French types under license; virtually all aircraft engines were imported or assembled from imported parts, as the country lacked the necessary metallurgical skills.

Despite the small number of aircraft manufactured, some degree of specialization was already evident, including reconnaissance aircraft, fighters, and bombers. The most famous early Russian designer was Igor Sikorsky, whose trend-setting work with large aircraft gained worldwide attention. When the war began, there were about 250 operational aircraft on hand. During the war, Russian plants produced about 5,500 aircraft, mainly Western models built under license.

Following the November 1917 Bolshevik takeover in Russia, the aviation industry was nationalized (mid-1918), though many of its best people fled during the resulting civil war (1918–1921). The revolution had devastated industry installations, and manufacturing virtually disappeared. By the early 1920s, the country's leadership faced many priorities: reestablishing industry, training personnel to manufacture and to fly, and, biggest of all, how to make sufficient aero engines. The Soviet Union's science and industry needed to develop as it made use of imported aircraft as well as abandoned leftovers from the Allies' ill-fated 1918–1920 intervention.

The first mass-produced Russian aircraft was the R-1 (Reconnaissance), of which some 2,800 had been manufactured by the time construction stopped in 1931. This was also the first Russian aircraft to be exported (to countries in the Middle East). The U-1 (Utility) was based on the Avro 504 and used for training—some 700 had been made by the early 1930s. The first domestic fighter aircraft, the I-2 (Grigorovich), was serving with the air force by 1925.

At this point, aviation became part of the larger industrialization trend in successive Five-Year Plans. The first (1928–1932) and second (1933–1937) helped to organize the industry, weeding out some weak performers. The third (beginning in 1938) saw more of a focus on modernizing aviation, based on the poor performance of Soviet aircraft in the Spanish civil war. Although many new aircraft were designed, not many actually entered production. Part of the problem was the sweep of the Stalinist political purges of 1938–1940, which detained many of the key designers (Konstantin Kalinin was killed).

Most of the famous Soviet design bureaus first appeared during the interwar period (though many designers had been active earlier), including Beriev (1932), which focused on flying boats; Ilyushin (around 1937); Kalinin (1925–1940, focusing on transports); the MiG team (1939); Polikarpov (1937), who focused on fighters (his I-15 biplane began series production and some 3,000 of all models made in 1934–1939); and Sukhoi (1939). Perhaps the most famous, Tupolev, began in 1922—his output, according to some sources, included more types of diverse aircraft than any other designer in history. Early Tupolev aircraft included the ANT-4, the world's first all-metal two-engine monoplane bomber produced from 1929 to 1932 and in service until 1936 (one flew from Moscow to New York by means of the Far East in 1929), the huge four-engine ANT-6, which first flew in 1930 and entered production as the TB-3 with more than 800 made. Many consider this heavy bomber to be the first Soviet aircraft to surpass the rest of the world. Yakovlev's bureau began in 1934.

World War II caught Soviet aviation unawares—more than 1,200 aircraft were lost on the first day of the Nazis' June 1941 invasion. For the next 6–8 months, aircraft and other factories were shifted eastward to the Urals and Siberia, a huge undertaking largely completed by early 1942. Relocation made transport of finished aircraft to the fronts more difficult, but by late 1942 and in 1943 Soviet aircraft began to appear in huge numbers. Germany's output was exceeded in 1943. Fighters such as the Yak-3 and Yak-9 (more than 16,000 of the latter), Lavochkin La-5 (10,000), and La-7 (nearly 6,000) began to take a toll on German air strength. The Ilyushin Il-2 attack plane was the most-produced plane in the war (1,000 made every month after 1942 for total of over 36,000), and the later Il-10 reached production numbers of 5,000.

The Soviets also copied major U.S. designs such as the DC-3 transport (Li-2) and B-29 bomber (Tu-4). The latter was accomplished by reverse-engineering some 105,000 pieces from U.S. aircraft that landed in the Soviet Union in mid-1944. About 900 had been produced by 1951. The Antonov design bureau appeared in 1945.

Postwar production was dominated by Cold War concerns and focused on a quick conversion to jet fighters. The first Soviet types appeared in 1946 (Yak-15 and MiG-9), and the twin-engine Tu-14 and Il-28 jet bombers were flown by 1947–1948. The MiG-15 was the first Soviet jet to see combat, in Korea. The MiG-19 (1954) was the first mass-produced Soviet supersonic aircraft. Through the 1980s, several Soviet design bureaus produced ever-more effective supersonic fighters and bombers at the cutting edges of technology. Late-model MiG and Sukhoi fighters serve in many countries' air forces today.

During the Khrushchev era (1957–1964), the Soviets focused on missiles and air defense rather than strategic and tactical aircraft. Tactical aircraft saw a resurgence only in the late 1960s and included new work on helicopters. Based on prototypes dating to 1940, Soviet helicopters rapidly progressed. The Mil (1947) and Kamov (1948) bureaus focused on helicopters, though Yakovlev and other designers also participated. Beginning in the late 1960s, production runs of some models rose into the thousands given Soviet and Warsaw Pact needs.

Many Soviet aircraft served both military and civil masters. The archaic-looking but widely produced single-engine propeller An-2 biplane transport (perhaps 20,000 produced) first appeared in 1947 and was still in use at the turn of the century. The Soviets' pioneering jet transport, the Tu-104, appeared in 1956 and was based on the earlier Tu-16 bomber; likewise the huge Tu-114 turboprop transport of 1957 was based on the Tu-95 bomber. Yakovlev and Ilyushin joined Tupolev in the transport market, producing a variety of propeller and jet airliners. The long-running Russian theory that bigger is better continued with the production of nearly 100 copies of the 1982 An-124 Ruslan, the largest aircraft in quantity production, and its unique larger sister, the 1988 six-engine An-225 Myiya, the world's largest aircraft. The Soviet Tu-144 supersonic transport was the world's first to fly in 1968, two months before the Concorde, although this Tupolev craft served only briefly with Aeroflot.

Today the former member states of the Soviet Union are in economic disarray, which inhibits production of new types. Research continues, albeit at a limited level.

Christopher H. Sterling

References

Andersson, Lennart. *Soviet Aircraft and Aviation, 1917–1941.* London: Putnam, 1994.

Bratukhin, A. G., ed. *Russian Aircraft.* Moscow: Mashinostroenie, 1995.

Davies, R.E.G., and Mike Machat. *Aeroflot: An Airline and Its Aircraft.* McLean, VA: Paladwr, 1992.

Everett-Heath, John. *Soviet Helicopters: Design, Development, and Tactics.* London: Jane's Information Group, 1983.

Gunston, Bill. *The Encyclopedia of Russian Aircraft, 1875–1995.* London: Osprey, 1995.

Yakolev, A. S. *Fifty Years of Soviet Aircraft Construction.* Jerusalem: Israel Program for Scientific Translations, 1970 [orig. ed. Moscow, 1968].

Soviet Volunteer Pilots

Soviet pilots often participated in foreign military conflicts without official government involvement. The dispatch of volunteer Soviet airmen to assist allies and revolutionary forces was a regular practice from the beginning of the Soviet state. It allowed the Soviets to intervene on a limited scale without risking a wider conflict and provided the chance for practical tests of new tactics and equipment.

Soviet airmen were first sent to assist the Mongolian communists in their war against the Whites in June 1921 when Lenin sent a unit of four aircraft and crews that operated for several months before returning home. In October 1936, the first of several hundred Soviet volunteer aviators arrived in Republican Spain with the dual task of combating the Nationalist air forces and training the Republicans to fly Soviet aircraft.

Soviet pilots nominally camouflaged their presence by wearing Spanish uniforms and using noms-de-guerre, such as Pablo Palancar, Captain Jose, and General Douglas and generally stayed for about six months. The Soviets flew in squadrons integrated with Spanish and international volunteer pilots as quickly as they could be prepared to handle the modern Soviet equipment. Even before the Soviet withdrawal in October 1938 in the face of Republican defeat, Spanish pilots were being phased into command of the squadrons.

In October 1937, the Soviets again dispatched volunteer pilots, this time to assist the Chinese government against the Japanese, four fighter and two bomber squadrons initially being sent. Soviet pilots flew in China until 1939, and a few advisers remained through 1941. Though the number of aircrews dispatched is unknown, 1,250 aircraft were sent for use by Soviet volunteers and Chinese pilots, and during 1938 they provided the core of Chinese air defense.

From November 1950 to July 1953, Soviet pilots "performed their international duty" over North Korea. Their presence was officially denied, and the pilots wore Chinese uniforms. They flew about three-quarters of the communist air sorties and scored an even larger proportion of the air victories.

During the Cold War Soviet pilots occasionally participated in foreign air wars, including a clash with the Israeli air force over Egypt in 1970. During the Vietnam War, Soviet pilots were sent to North Vietnam as advisers and instructors and, on a number of occasions, unofficially flew combat missions, scoring victories that were credited to Vietnamese units.

George M. Mellinger

See also

Fighter Air Corps; Pepelyaev, Evgenii Georgievich; Smushkevich, Yakov "General Douglas"; Spanish Civil War; Sutyagin, Nikolai

References

Bruning, John R. *Crimson Sky: The Air Battle for Korea.* Dulles, VA: Brassey's, 1999.

Sarin, Oleg, and Lev Dvoretsky. *Alien Wars: The Soviet Union's Aggressions Against the World, 1919 to 1989.* Novato, CA: Presidio Press, 1996.

Soviet Women Pilots

Soviet airwomen achieved a historic record in service to their country.

Tamara Fedorovna Konstantinova was a senior lieutenant and deputy commanding officer, 999th Ground Attack Regiment/277th Ground Attack Division/First Air Army/3d Baltic Front. She was awarded the Hero of the Soviet Union on 29 June 1945.

Konstantinova was born in the Tver' region in 1919 and eventually became an instructor at the Kalinin Flying Club (Tver') in 1939. After war began, she was rejected for service at the front due to an alleged shortage of aircraft. She initially risked her life as a truck driver delivering ammunition. She then secured transfer to a communications subunit, where she flew the Po-2 and distinguished herself by evading German fighters. Upon joining the 566th Ground Attack Regiment in March 1944, she acquired a brand-new Ilyushin Il-2. She and her air gunner, Aleksandra Mukoseyeva, formed a cohesive and effective team.

In December 1944, she became deputy squadron leader after transferring to 999th Ground Attack Regiment. In West Prussia alone Konstantinova flew at least twice as many missions as other pilots did in a comparable period, maintaining she was fighting for two: her late husband and herself. By March 1945, Konstantinova had flown 66 operational missions and earned many decorations. After the war she flew light passenger aircraft out of Voronezh. In 1948, she was seriously injured during an emergency landing and permanently grounded.

Anna Aleksandrovna Timofeyeva (née Yegorova) was senior lieutenant and chief navigator, 805th Ground Attack Regiment/197th Ground Attack Division/Sixteenth Air Army/1st Belorussian Front. She was awarded the Hero of the Soviet Union on 6 May 1965.

Timofeyeva was born in the Tver' region in 1916. Upon graduating from the Kherson Flying School, she became instructor at Kalinin Flying Club (Tver'). At the beginning of the she war flew with 130th Independent Communication Squadron of the Southern Front. After a Messerschmitt set her unarmed machine afire, Timofeyeva became determined to fly combat aircraft.

She checked out in the Il-2 in early 1943 after flying only twice with an instructor, a difficult feat for such a complex aircraft. She received her baptism of fire over the Black and Azov Seas and soon became a skilled combat pilot and deputy squadron leader. She took part in fierce air battles over Taman' Peninsula and flew many missions in aid of Malaya Zemlya marines, attacking enemy tanks, ships, rail junctions, and airfields while coping with fatigue and heavy losses.

On 26 May 1943, she participated in voluntary laying of a smokescreen to enable ground troops to break through the enemy lines. Her daring was rewarded with decorations by the commander of Fourth Air Army himself.

After completing a two-month course for navigators in Stavropol, she received a new version of the Il-2. Dusya Nazarkina, formerly an armorer, became her gunner and rear set of eyes. When their wing reached the 1st Belorussian Front, Timofeyeva was appointed chief navigator. On 20 August 1944, during her 277th mission, she was shot down in flames east of Warsaw. In the Küstrin POW camp her life was saved by fellow inmates from both East and West. Upon release from the camp she was transferred to the reserves. Her 1965 Hero of the Soviet Union award was delayed by her internment in the POW camp.

Kazimiera J. Cottam

References

Cottam, Kazimiera J. *Women in War and Resistance.* Nepean, Canada: New Military, 1998.

Timofeyeva-Yegorova, A. A. *Hang in, Little Sister!* (in Russian). Moscow: Voyenizdat, 1983.

Soviet Women's Combat Wings (1942–1945)

Soviet Women combat wings were founded in Engels, near

Stalingrad, by Marina Raskova, when male pilots were not readily available. They were organized as follows:

46th Taman' Guards Bomber Regiment. Wing Commander: Yevdokiya Bershanskaya. A component of 4th Air Army, initially designated 588th Bomber Regiment. The unit remained all-female throughout the war, being equipped with U-2 biplanes (These were renamed Po-2 in 1944 in honor of their creator, N. Polikarpov). Originally a trainer, they were converted for short-range night bombing and flown by a two-woman crew.

The 46th was operational in May 1942 and by mid-1943 consisted of four squadrons, including a training unit. It operated in Ukraine, Caucasus, Crimea, Belarus', Poland, and Germany. The unit made more than 24,000 sorties and produced about 25 Heroes of the Soviet Union.

125th "M.M. Raskova" Borisov Guards Bomber Regiment. Wing commanders: Marina Raskova and Valentin Markov. The unit was subordinated to Fourth, Sixteenth, and Third Air Armies. It was initially designated 587th Bomber Regiment and comprised of two Petlyakov (Pe-2) dive bomber squadrons. The aircraft were equipped with five machine guns. The aircrews consisted of pilot, navigator-bombardier, and radio/operator-gunner (the last were mostly men, initially). Technical personnel also included men. The 125th went into action near Stalingrad then operated successfully over North Caucasus (hence honorific of "M.M. Raskova"), Orel-Bryansk sector, Smolensk, Belarus, the Baltic, and East Prussia. The 1134 medium-range sorties it delivered produced five Heroes of the Soviet Union.

586th Fighter Regiment. Wing commanders: Tamara Kazarinova and Aleksandr Gridnev. Using Yak-9 fighters, its personnel protected industrial centers, rail junctions and bridges in Saratov, Voronezh, Kastornaya, Kursk, Kyiv, Zhitomir, Budapest and Vienna. One squadron, including the future aces Lidya Litvyak and Yekaterina Budanova, was sent to Stalingrad. The unit included some male technicians and fighter pilots.

The 586th was not without problems. Aleksandr Gridnev alleged that Kazarinova had contributed to several unnecessary deaths of subordinates. In addition, after her transfer to Moscow's Air Defense HQ; he held her responsible, for the wing's apparent mistreatment by the authorities.

Kazimiera J. Cottam

See also

Litvyak, Lidya; Raskova, Marina Mikhaylovna

References

Cottam, Kazimiera J., ed. and trans. *Women in Air War.* Nepean, Canada: New Military, 1997.

Noggle, Anne. *A Dance with Death: Soviet Airwomen in World War II.* College Station: Texas A&M University Press, 1994.

Pennington, Reina. "Wings, Women, and War." Master's Thesis, University of South Carolina, 1993.

Soyuz Space Vehicle

Soviet space program; the third step toward putting a cosmonaut on the moon, it ended up as a standard orbital vehicle used to service Salyut and later Mir stations. Following automatic testing in 1966 as a Cosmos mission, the Soyuz 1 manned spacecraft orbited earth on 24 April 1967, with Vladimir Komarov onboard. Tragically, the parachutes slowing the capsule's descent to earth (the Soviets landed their craft on earth rather than water) tangled, and Komarov died on impact.

The program was halted for 18 months and resumed in October 1968 with a rendezvous (but no docking) between the automated Soyuz 2 and a single-manned Soyuz 3. Soyuz 4 and Soyuz 5 in January 1969 docked, and two of the three men in Soyuz 5 joined the Soyuz 4 pilot via extravehicular activity for return to earth. Meanwhile, five missions using the Soyuz spacecraft under the Zond program were used to gain experience about lunar orbit.

By then, the United States had won the moon race. While the United States concentrated further on the Apollo program, the Soyuz program was reworked into an orbital program and used to service first the Salyut space stations and later Mir. Another tragedy struck the Soyuz program, however. On 29 June 1971, Soyuz 11 returned from a record 24-day mission aboard station Salyut 1 when an improperly closed valve vented the capsule's oxygen, asphyxiating all three cosmonauts, who were not wearing their pressure suits due to space limitation. Consequently, Soyuz 12 was cancelled and Salyut 1 was abandoned in orbit. From then on, only two-man crews in full pressure gear were allowed to fly until the modified Soyuz T entered service in 1980. This also meant that Salyut mission times would be cut by more than 30 percent. Thus, the Soyuz 11 record would not be broken until 1975. Other Soyuz missions did fail, but not so spectacularly. Soyuz 18, for example, failed to achieve orbit and plunged back to earth, injuring its occupants. The Soyuz 18B had to be prepared in a hurry to service station Salyut 4, which needed supplies.

Meanwhile, following the 1972 U.S.-Soviet effort at détente, a modified mission, Soyuz 19, was prepared for orbital linkup with an Apollo command module. A modified capsule was thus launched in April 1975 for the symbolically important Apollo-Soyuz Test Project. Other modifications to the Soyuz program included the development of a simplified capsule, Progress, for resupply of a space station. Cosmonauts piled garbage into it and dispatched it into the atmosphere, where it burned up. The last original Soyuz design was Soyuz 40 and flew in 1981. It was then replaced by the improved Soyuz T, which routinely serviced Mir until the station was abandoned in 2001 and now serves as a shuttle alternative in reaching International Space Station Alpha.

Guillaume de Syon

See also

Apollo Space Program; Salyut

References

Harvey, Brian. *Race into Space: The Soviet Space Programme.* Chichester, UK: Ellis Horwood, 1988.

United States Congress. *Soviet Space Programs, 1981–1987.* Washington, DC: U.S. Government Printing Office, 1988.

Spaatz, Carl Andrew (1891–1974)

One of the major personalities behind the independent United States Air Force; the first USAF Chief of Staff. Carl A. Spaatz commanded Eighth Air Force and U.S. Strategic Air Forces Europe during World War II. As commander of Eighth Air Force, Spaatz supervised the massive B-17 and B-24 bombing campaign over Germany in 1942.

The results of that campaign, as well as a recommendation from close friend General Henry "Hap" Arnold, U.S. Army Air Forces commander, led to his selection by Dwight D. Eisenhower as air commander for Operation TORCH in 1942 and Operation OVERLORD in 1944. He was the only U.S. commander to be present at the surrenders of both Germany and Japan, having been transferred to the Pacific Theater to oversee air operations, including the atomic bombings at Hiroshima and Nagasaki.

On 2 February 1946, Spaatz succeeded Arnold as commander of U.S. Army Air Forces. He headed the U.S. Air Force as its first Chief of Staff from 26 September 1947 until his retirement on 30 April 1948. From 1948 until 1961, Spaatz contributed a military affairs column to *Newsweek* magazine and served as a member of the board of defense contractor Litton Industries. He died in Washington, D.C., and is buried at the U.S. Air Force Academy, Colorado Springs.

Spaatz was a vocal proponent of strategic daylight bombing tactics—doctrine developed by his fellow alumni at the Air Corps Tactical School. He advocated an independent air force and spoke as a witness at Brigadier General William "Billy" Mitchell's 1925 court-martial. Along with Mitchell and Arnold, Spaatz is considered one of the founding fathers of the United States Air Force.

Kevin Gould

See also

Arnold, Henry H. "Hap"; Mitchell, William; U.S. Army Air Corps

References

Davis, Richard G. *Carl A. Spaatz and the Air War in Europe.* Washington, DC: Center for Air Force History, 1993.

Wolk, Hermann S. *The Struggle for Air Force Independence, 1943–1947.* Washington, DC: Air Force History and Museum Program, 1997.

Zuckerman, Lord. *Six Men Out of the Ordinary.* London: Peter Owen, 1992.

Space Shuttle, Military Use of

During the development of the Space Shuttle, NASA realized that it was critical to have the military's support when asking for funds from Congress. Although the Air Force did not particularly see an immediate need for the capabilities offered by the Space Shuttle, it agreed to provide political support in addition to some minor funding of its own. During 1982–1983, the Department of Defense (DoD) paid NASA a total of $268 million for nine dedicated military Space Shuttle launches. In addition, the Air Force agreed to construct a launch site at Vandenberg AFB, California, that would be capable of letting the Space Shuttle reach polar orbits—something it was unable to do from the Kennedy Space Center, Florida, without dropping the external tank on inhabited landmasses.

The first dedicated DoD mission was STS-20 (51-C) on 24 January 1985 using the orbiter *Discovery.* Only one other DoD mission (STS-28/51-J) would be flown prior to the 1986 *Challenger* accident. The two missions were by far the shortest operational missions flown by the Space Shuttle prior to the standdown, although the Air Force never officially acknowledged what payloads were carried on these missions.

During the standdown caused by the *Challenger* accident, the Air Force decided to move back to using Atlas and Titan expendable launch vehicles and cancelled the construction of the SLC-6 shuttle site at Vandenberg. However, the Air Force had already paid for seven additional missions and saw no reason not to take advantage of them. When the shuttle returned to flight in 1988, the Air Force began to fly its remaining missions; STS-27R, STS-28R, STS-33R, STS-36, and STS-39 would be dedicated DoD missions conducted under a veil of secrecy. One further mission, STS-53, would be launched in 1992 and would carry a small DoD payload but would not be conducted in secrecy. All major national payloads are currently launched on expendable launch vehicles.

Dennis R. Jenkins

Every Space Shuttle launch is a tremendous challenge. Here is the Discovery, *bathed in the Cape Canaveral spotlights. (Walter J. Boyne)*

References

Harland, David M. *Space Shuttle: Roles, Missions, and Accomplishments.* West Sussex, UK: Praxis, 1998.

Jenkins, Dennis R. *Space Shuttle: The History of Developing the National Space Transportation System.* Cape Canaveral, FL: The Author, 1996.

Space Stations

Permanent platforms in space design for prolonged human living and scientific experiments. Space stations have been a fundamental part of space exploration and research since 1971 when the Soviet Union launched the first of seven Salyut space stations. The development of space stations was the direction that both superpowers took after NASA landed astronauts on the moon in 1969.

Originally, Salyut was intended as a military station. Cosmonauts would conduct military experiments and assess the feasibility of military outposts in space.

Claiming that the moon was never their goal, the Soviets took the lead in building and launching space stations and hold the record for the longest flight by an orbited platform. The Mir Space Station spent a remarkable 15 years in orbit—five times longer than intended. Unfortunately, its last years were plagued by fire and a series of accidents, including a collision with an unmanned supply ship. The station was brought out of orbit over the Pacific Ocean in March 2001.

Mir was launched before the Iron Curtain was lifted, and control of the station was transferred to the new government in Russia. Perhaps the most incredible aspect of Mir was that it helped bring NASA and the Russian Space Agency closer as U.S. Space Shuttles docked with the station and Americans spent time aboard the Soviet craft.

The United States had a space station of its own in the 1970s. Skylab was launched by a modified Saturn V rocket in 1973 and spent the next six years orbiting the earth and playing host to three crews. Each crew spent more time in space than the last; Americans spent 4,116 hours, 50 minutes in this station.

The Alpha International Space Station has been the focus of 16 countries' space endeavors since 1998. Crews have already been sent to the station and will continue to occupy it until completion, scheduled for 2003. The station will serve as a research facility and may aid in future journeys to Mars.

Erich Streckfuss

References

NASA. Official website. Available online at www.nasa.gov.

SPAD Aircraft

Early French aircraft. Originally the Société Provisoire des Aéroplanes Deperdussin (Deperdussin Airplane Company), the company's future was placed in doubt when founder Armand Deperdussin went to prison for fraud in 1913. New owners, including Louis Blériot, anxious to preserve the company's fortunes as well as its initials—which by that time had become very well known in aviation circles—changed the name to Société Anonyme pour l'Aviation et ses Derives (SPAD).

In the second half of World War I, SPAD aircraft equipped the air services of all the Allied powers, several thousand eventually being built. The SPAD VII represented the marriage of two outstanding designs: a Louis Bechareu airframe and Mark Birkigt's Hispano-Suiza eight-cylinder 180-hp V-8 engine.

The airframe combined a strong, wood-framed fuselage with single-bay biplane wings, the flying and landing wires braced at their intersection by an additional strut that gave the aircraft a two-bay appearance. Armament was a single Vickers gun.

The SPAD appeared in French escadrilles in 1916 and a pair of RFC squadrons the following year. The SPAD was the mount of the elite French unit, the four escadrilles that made up Les Cigognes (The Storks) of Combat Group 12. Enough were built that it fulfilled U.S. needs in 1918 as well. Though this model was not as well-armed as its successor, the SPAD XIII, the chronic engine troubles of the geared Hispano that powered the latter caused many to prefer the earlier model.

The SPAD XIII, which started appearing in September 1917, was essentially a scaled-up version of the SPAD VII, having a larger fuselage, tail surfaces, and wings, as well as a second gun and a more powerful engine. The different engine proved a problem for the Model XIII, however. The direct-drive 180-hp Hispano that had powered the Model VII was a reliable unit that caused few problems. The geared engine, though developing more horsepower, proved a maintenance nightmare. According to some reports, as many as 60 percent of SPAD XIIIs were out of commission due to engine problems at various times during the war. Had the war gone into 1919, it is likely the later-model SPAD would have been replaced.

In the summer of 1918, both single- and two-seat SPADs were sold to the United States Air Service, and on Armistice Day the SPAD XIII was the primary equipment of all but two U.S. fighter squadrons. On the morning of 12 September 1918, General William "Billy" Mitchell observed operation of the aerial armada he had assembled for the Battle of Saint Mihiel from the cockpit of the SPAD XVI that now hangs in the World War I gallery of the Unites States Air Force Museum.

James Streckfuss

The SPAD VII was a welcome replacement for the earlier Nieuport series of fighters, for while the Nieuports suffered from structural weakness, the SPAD was strongly built and capable of a good turn of speed. (U.S. Air Force)

See also
Birkigt, Mark

References

Davilla, James, and Arthur M. Soltan. *French Aircraft of the First World War.* Mountain View, CA: Flying Machines Press, 1997.

Spanish Air Force

The Spanish air force was only two years old when it first saw combat during the Spanish-American War (1898). The original branch of the air force consisted of captive balloons and was known as the Servicio Militar de Aerostacio. Fixed-wing aircraft were integrated into the air force in 1911 with the establishment of the Aeronautica Militar Espanola (AME).

The next milestone was the onset of the Spanish civil war in 1936. Pitting the Republicans (socialists) against the Nationalists (fascists), the Spanish civil war is seen by many as a dress rehearsal for World War II. The Republicans received aid from Great Britain, France, Russia, Canada, and the United States; the Germans and Italians eagerly provided aid to the Nationalists. From the outset, the AME was split into a Republican air force and a Nationalist air force. However, the key players in the air war would in fact be the third parties. The involved air forces were in the midst of their evolution from the biplanes of World War I to the sleek monoplanes that would fill the skies during World War II. Of particular note was the combat debut of the Messerschmitt Bf 109 and the Junkers Ju 87 Stuka; both played key roles in Germany's 1939 blitzkrieg.

The lessons learned during the Spanish civil war would shape not only air combat tactics but also the design of many of the aircraft. In its wake, the civil war left Spain in no mood for further conflict, and thus the newly formed Ejército del Aire (EDA; Army of the Air) would sit out World War II from a position of neutrality.

The involvement of third parties in the Spanish air force continued throughout most of the Cold War. A 1953 agreement between Spain and the United States established the exchange of military aid for U.S. military facilities within the country. Key among those were the now-closed U.S. facilities at the air bases of Rota and Torrejón. The presence of U.S. fighters on Spanish soil allowed the Spaniards to train with many of the premier aircraft of the time, and the F-4 Phantom eventually became Spain's front-line fighter.

A continuous upgrade program over the last 40 years has shaped the modern EDA. The current front-line fighter is the McDonnell Douglas E/F-18 Hornet. This modern combat plane is capable of effectively filling both the air-to-air and air-to-ground roles. In addition, the EDA maintains stockpiles of the Harm antiradar missile and the Harpoon antiship missile, further increasing the versatility of the E/F-18. The EDA also maintains approximately 60 Mirage F-1s in the fighter-bomber role and two squadrons of SF-5s (Spanish-assembled F-5s) in the tactical-reconnaissance and light-bomber roles. Additionally, one squadron of RF-4Cs has been retained solely for tactical reconnaissance.

The future of the EDA lies in the delivery of the Eurofighter Typhoon. Spain holds a 13 percent interest in the repeatedly delayed project and has ordered 87 aircraft. When these airframes are finally delivered, they will become the premiere fighters in the EDA and will most likely assume many of the missions now filled by the E/F-18.

Troy D. Hammon

See also

Blitzkrieg; Boeing F/A-18 Hornet; Junkers Ju 52/3m, Ju 87 Stuka, and Ju 88; Messerschmitt Bf 109; Spanish Civil War

References

"Spanish Air Force." *Scramble Magazine* Online [Dutch Aviation Society]. Available at http://www.scramble.nl/es.htm.

Taylor, Michael J.H. *Encyclopedia of the World's Air Forces.* New York: Facts on File, 1988.

Spanish Civil War

The 1936–1939 conflict in Spain between Republicans (socialists) and Nationalists (fascists); with the participation of several third parties, it became a proving ground for World War II air warfare.

Control of the air was one of the most important factors for the Nationalists in their victory. A week after the outbreak of rebellion on 18 July 1936, Nationalist emissaries approached German dictator Adolf Hitler in a desperate appeal for aircraft. Many of the best Nationalist troops were in Morocco, unable to get to Spain because the Republican government controlled the navy. The Nationalists wanted to purchase Ju 52 trimotor transports to ferry General Francisco Franco's troops to Spain. Hitler immediately loaned 10 Lufthansa Ju 52s and six Heinkel He 51 biplane fighters to provide protection. All had German aircrews. Beginning on 29 July, they flew 20,000 crack Spanish and Moroccan troops to Nationalist-controlled Seville in southern Spain. This was critical. Without it, the outcome of the war would have been different.

On 14 August, a Luftwaffe Ju 52 dropped two bombs on a Republican battleship, putting it out of action. Then in early November Hitler provided 10 Ju 52 bombers, and the German military presence in Spain grew steadily. Earlier aircraft were transferred to the Nationalist air force. The German presence was formalized in November 1936 as the Volunteer Corps, identified as Number 88 but popularly known as the Kondor Legion. It consisted of a bomber group, a fighter group, a reconnaissance group, a seaplane squadron, an antiaircraft group, and ground support elements. In all, its authorized strength was something less than 6,000 men and about 100 aircraft, but a total of 19,000 men and 300–400 planes served in Spain over the course of the war. These were not volunteers but regular German military units. A total of 298 members of the Kondor Legion died in Spain and 1,000 were wounded.

The best German bombers in Spain were two new twin-engine medium models: the Dornier Do 17 (the "Flying Pencil") and Heinkel He 111. In 1937, they replaced the Ju 52s, which were then turned over to the Nationalist air force. The Germans flew virtually all aircraft in the Luftwaffe inventory in Spain, including the Ju 87 Stuka dive-bomber. At first the main German fighter was the outdated He 51, but it was replaced beginning in 1937 by the Messerschmitt Bf 109, the best fighter in the war and one of the top fighters during World War II. Reconnaissance aircraft included the He 99 and He 70, He 59 and He 60 seaplanes, and one Ju 52 on floats.

The Germans used the conflict to the test these aircraft under combat conditions. Spain also provided a training school for the development of tactics, including the finger-four formation. This led to techniques like coordinating ground troops and tactical air assets that were to be devastatingly effective early in World War II. During the conflict, Kondor Legion pilots downed 380 Spanish Republican aircraft (56 to antiaircraft fire) against their own losses of 72 planes. An additional 160 German aircraft were lost to accidents.

Italy made a much greater commitment to the Nationalist side. As soon as dictator Benito Mussolini learned the Germans had sent aid, he sent a dozen transport aircraft. The world learned of the Italian intervention when, on 30 July 1936, two Savoia bombers on their way to Spain made a forced landing in Morocco and another crashed in Algeria. Mussolini ultimately sent 50,000 men and about a third of Italy's total armaments. The commitment was mostly in the form of ground units and nearly 2,000 artillery pieces, but it included 750 aircraft. Some 3,100 Italians died in the war (174 airmen). Despite its significant numbers, Italy's effort in Spain was nowhere nearly as effective as that of Germany.

The Spanish Republic's air force was quite small, but before London applied pressure on Paris, France had supplied the Republicans with 30 reconnaissance aircraft and bombers, 15 fighters, and 10 transport and training aircraft. Given the noninterventionist attitudes among major Western powers, Mexico and the Soviet Union became the principal suppliers of weapons to the Republicans. Soviet aid was purchased at market prices with 510 tons of Republican gold. Although no Soviet fighting units ever went to Spain, Soviet leader Joseph Stalin did send military equipment, including 731 tanks. In the air the Russians supplied some pilots, flying instructors, and 250 aircraft. This was clearly insufficient to save the Republican side.

German air cover and bombing was decisive in the outcome of the civil war. Kondor Legion units participated in all major Nationalist operations, and they were especially effective in blunting the last great Republic effort, the 1938 Ebro River Offensive. This and the terror-bombing of Spanish cities, especially Guernica, produced the false impression that airpower alone could win wars.

Spencer C. Tucker

See also

Dornier Do 17; Junkers Ju 52/3m, Ju 87 Stuka, and Ju 88; Messerschmitt Bf 109

References

Elstob, Peter. *Condor Legion.* New York: Ballantine Books, 1973.

Proctor, Raymond L. *Hitler's Luftwaffe in the Spanish Civil War.* Westport, CT: Greenwood Press, 1983.

Schliephake, Hanfried. *The Birth of the Luftwaffe.* Chicago: Henry Regnery, 1971.

Thomas, Hugh. *The Spanish Civil War.* New York: Harper and Brothers, 1961.

Special Operations

Special operations aviation has made strategic differences in warfare by providing the means to transport arms and create lines of communication to resistance groups, conduct precise attacks, and insert special operations forces. Misused by conventional-minded commanders, special operations airpower has often fallen short of the mark. Nevertheless, its successes demonstrate a remarkable capability for the cost.

The Royal Air Force first experimented with special operations in the form of air control, a plan to save money by policing the empire from the air. Air Marshal Hugh Trenchard argued the RAF could put down any revolt, and the first operational chance he got proved him correct in the eyes of the British government. Nine RAF de Havilland D.H. 9s working with the Camel Corps destroyed a rebel Somali force in 1919, paving the way for extensive further British use.

During World War II, the British advanced the concept following Prime Minister Winston Churchill's charge to "set Europe ablaze" with special operations. It was decided that the Resistance on the continent could be made into a viable force if they were dropped arms and given guidance. The U.S. Office of Strategic Services (OSS) joined British squadrons in late 1943 and, by mid-1944, supplied arms to resistance groups in Europe. "Carpetbagger" units flying from England and more OSS air units in North Africa and Italy helped armed resistance units to divert German forces. In the China-Burma-India Theater, U.S. Air Commandos took on the mission of long-range resupply to Allied forces. One such operation, Operation THURSDAY, infiltrated 9,000 men, 1,458 horses and mules, and 500,000 pounds of supplies more than 200 miles behind Japanese lines.

Despite this success, the United States virtually dismantled its own special-operations capability with the overall demobilization following World War II. By the time of the Korean War, it had to reinvent the wheel and labored under the constraints of conventional airpower thinkers.

Fighting the Vietnam War proved no less difficult and was often hampered by a lack of understanding and support from the U.S. Air Force, which was poised to fight a nuclear war with long-range bombers and faster and faster jets. Nevertheless, when energetically and imaginatively led, such forces made significant contributions by supporting friendly forces in Laos, Cambodia, and Vietnam against enemy forces. The units furthered psychological operations by dropping leaflets, using loudspeakers, and aiding in deceiving the enemy.

Again dismantling its special-operations capability, the United States found itself wanting during the 1980 Operation EAGLE CLAW and the Iran hostage rescue attempt. The result was the 1986 Goldwater-Nichols Act and the creation of United States Special Operations Command. The new command includes three service components: Air Force Special Operations Command (AFSOC); Army Special Operations Command (USASOC); and Naval Special Warfare Command (NAVSPECWARCOM). With a budget controlled by those who understand unconventional warfare, special operations aviation has matured into a significant force, providing surprise, speed, and purpose to unconventional warfare. When used in conjunction with conventional forces, it can achieve strategic indirection by maximizing resistance forces within the enemy's interior.

Benjamin F. Jones

References

Haas, Michael E. *Apollo's Warriors: United States Air Force Special Operations During the Cold War.* Maxwell AFB, AL: Air University Press, 1997.

Orr, Kelly. *From a Dark Sky: The Story of U.S. Air Force Special Operations.* Novato, CA: Presidio Press, 1996.

Towle, Phillip Anthony. *Pilots and Rebels: The Use of Aircraft in Unconventional Warfare, 1918–1988.* London: Brassey's, 1989.

Speer, Albert (1905–1981)

The organizational genius behind Germany's World War II manufacturing output, especially the manufacture of fighting aircraft.

The son and grandson of architects, Speer earned an engineering degree at the Technical University of Berlin and began a private architecture practice. He joined the Nazi Party in 1931 and became a member of the elite SS a year later. He designed the dramatic lighting effects and settings for the Nazis' annual Nuremberg rallies of the 1930s and thus came to the attention of Adolf Hitler, who appointed him general architectural inspector of the Reich in 1937 with orders to redesign the city of Berlin. He soon became a favorite of Hitler, who shared an interest in architecture. In 1942, Speer was named the new minister of armaments and war production following the death in a plane crash of Fritz Todt. A year later, all of Germany's war production came under his direction, making him the virtual dictator of the German war economy. Thanks to his organizing efforts, German industry continued to produce even as Allied bombing grew more severe. Some historians suggest he helped to prolong the war by holding German war production together for so long.

But in his ministerial role, he was directly involved in Germany's extensive use of slave labor to keep the plants operating. He was the only senior German official at the postwar Nuremberg trials to admit his guilt. He was sentenced to a 20-year term for his role in the slave-labor program, served 20 years at Spandau Prison, and was released in 1966. He had secretly begun to write his memoirs while in prison, and after revision they were published in 1969. Recent studies have called into question some of his more self-serving statements on his wartime role.

Christopher H. Sterling

References

van Der Vat, Dan. *The Good Nazi: The Life and Lies of Albert Speer.* Boston: Houghton Mifflin, 1997.

Sereny, Gita. *Albert Speer: His Battle With Truth.* New York: Knopf, 1995.

Speer, Albert. *Inside the Third Reich: The Memoirs of Albert Speer.* New York: Macmillan, 1970.

Sperrle, Hugo (1885–1953)

Luftwaffe field marshal. Sperrle enlisted in the German army in 1903 and was commissioned the following year. He attended the War Academy in 1914, transferred to the air arm in 1915, and spent the rest of World War I in a variety of staff and command positions. He remained in the armed forces after the war, transferring in 1934 into the still-secret Luftwaffe. In 1936, he was named to head the Kondor Legion in Spain and proved successful in a job that called for great political sensitivity; his blunt professionalism in combination with a willingness to listen to his coalition partners proved popular with Francisco Franco and the other Nationalist generals.

On his return to Germany in 1937, Sperrle was double-promoted to lieutenant general and given command of Luftflotte 3 (Third Air Force), which he led for the next six years. He was promoted to field marshal after the French campaign. After the end of the Battle of Britain, Luftflotte 3 remained in France while the rest of the Luftwaffe moved east for the Russian campaign. Sperrle made Paris his occupation headquarters and succumbed to the temptations of the good life. By mid-1944, the staff of Luftflotte 3 had apparently grown as bloated and indolent as their commander; their grossly inadequate airfield preparations ruined Berlin's carefully drafted plans for a massive reinforcement of Luftflotte 3 on D-Day. When the Luftwaffe retreated to the German border with the army in September 1944, Sperrle was relieved of his command and placed in the Führer Reserve. He never returned to active duty.

Donald Caldwell

See also

German Air Force (Luftwaffe); Spanish Civil War

References

Cooper, M. *The German Air Force, 1933–1945: An Anatomy of Failure.* London: Jane's Information Group, 1981.

Corum, J. *The Luftwaffe: Creating the Operational Air War, 1918–1940.* Lawrence: University Press of Kansas, 1997.

Spruance, Raymond A. (1886–1969)

U.S. admiral and fleet commander during World War II. Born in Baltimore on 3 July 1886, Spruance attended the U.S. Naval Academy, graduating in 1906. His initial assignments were on surface ships, including eventual command of destroyers and a battleship. Spruance was a student and an instructor at the Naval War College, where he learned the fundamentals of operational planning. In 1938, he was promoted to rear admiral and assigned to oversee naval preparedness throughout the Caribbean. When Pearl Harbor was attacked, Spruance, commanding Cruiser Division Five, led the escorts for Admiral William Halsey's invaluable aircraft carriers.

Escorting Halsey in his early raids against the Marshall Islands and Japan itself, Spruance later took command of the task force when Halsey became severely ill. At the Battle of Midway (June 1942), Spruance again stepped in when the USS *Yorktown,* Admiral Frank Fletcher's flagship, was knocked out of action. Assuming tactical control of the entire battle, Spruance masterfully employed the air wings from the carriers *Enterprise* and *Hornet.* Four Japanese carriers went to the bottom, and Midway became the turning point in the Pacific War as Japan was forced onto the defensive and the United States assumed the initiative.

Recognizing Spruance's extraordinary combat abilities, Admiral Chester Nimitz, commanding the Pacific Fleet, brought Spruance in as his deputy. Upon promotion to vice admiral, Spruance assumed command of Fifth Fleet, responsible for offensive operations throughout the Central Pacific. His forces, fighting hard against an entrenched, determined enemy, took the Gilbert Islands (1943) and the Marshall Islands (1944), then proceeded to the Mariana Islands for an eventual showdown with Japanese airpower in the Battle of the Philippine Sea (19–20 August 1944). In what became known as the "Marianas Turkey Shoot," Spruance's planes and ships shot down more than 400 Japanese aircraft and their irreplaceable pilots, eliminating Japanese naval airpower in the war effort.

Promoted to admiral in 1944, Spruance directed the naval element in the successful amphibious assaults on Iwo Jima (February 1945) and Okinawa (March-May 1945). He temporarily replaced Nimitz in command of Pacific Fleet at the conclusion of the war. Spruance rounded out his naval career by a tour as president of the Naval War College. He retired from the Navy in 1948 but went on to serve as U.S. ambassador to the Philippines (1952–1955). Spruance died in Pebble Beach, California, on 13 December 1969.

Not a naval aviator by training, Spruance nevertheless became a carrier-minded admiral and combat leader by dint of intellect and intuition. Always shunning the spotlight, unlike some of his peers, Spruance effectively employed U.S. carrier-based airpower in several of the most decisive battles of the war.

Michael S. Casey

See also

Gilbert Islands; Iwo Jima; Marshall Islands; Midway, Battle of; Okinawa; Tarawa, Battle of

References

Buell, Thomas B. *The Quiet Warrior: A Biography of Admiral Raymond A. Spruance.* Annapolis, MD: Naval Institute Press, 1987.

Forrestel, Emmet P. *Admiral Raymond A. Spruance.* Washington, DC: U.S. Government Printing Office, 1966.

Sputnik

The first manmade satellite to orbit in space; launched by the Soviets in 1957. During the mid-1950s, Cold War fervor and the prospect of nuclear war with the Soviet Union gripped America. By 1956, President Dwight D. Eisenhower assuaged concern over the so-called bomber gap, reassuring Americans that there was no Soviet superiority in strategic bombers and that the United States remained safe from nuclear attack. A bitter surprise took place on 4 October 1957, however, when the Soviet Union launched the first satellite into earth orbit. Named "Sputnik" (Fellow Traveller), the satellite weighed some 184 pounds and beeped as it orbited, enabling anyone with a radio to monitor its steady progress.

For Americans this was a shock. Defense pundits, especially congressional Democrats, warned that if the Soviets could launch a satellite they could launch nuclear weapons targeted at U.S. cities. Educational experts lamented that U.S. students were too busy learning about business and listening to rock and roll and not studying engineering and sciences, curricula that would enable America to maintain its lead over the Soviet Union. Americans planned backyard bomb shelters, fearful of a nuclear Pearl Harbor. U.S. rocket tests at the time were widely publicized failures, creating what Democrats then dubbed the "missile gap." Eisenhower and his closest advisers showed little concern over this perceived Soviet superiority in missiles, as top-secret U-2 overflights clearly demonstrated the real weaknesses in Soviet missile development.

Unwilling to share this knowledge with the American public, Eisenhower appeared weak on defense. The Soviets would subsequently launch a dog and, in the ultimate disgrace to American ingenuity and pride, a human, cosmonaut Yuri Gagarin, into orbit. The resulting U.S. attitude—hawkish on defense—contributed to Democrat John F. Kennedy's 1960 election as president, shortly after which new Secretary of Defense Robert S. McNamara inadvertently "revealed" that there never was a missile gap to begin with. Other than being the opening shot in the space race, Sputnik's legacy lies in the defense buildup and military policies of the Kennedy and Lyndon Johnson administrations.

Robert S. Hopkins

See also

Apollo Space Program; Cold War; Gagarin, Yuri; Mercury Space Program

References

Divine, Robert. *The Sputnik Challenge.* New York: Oxford University Press, 1993.

Roman, Peter J. *Eisenhower and the Missile Gap.* Ithaca: Cornell University Press, 1996.

Squier, George Owen (1865–1934)

U.S. Army major general and chief signal officer (1917–1923). A native of Dryden, Michigan, Squier graduated from the U.S. Military Academy in 1887. In 1893, he received a doctorate in electrical engineering from Johns Hopkins University, perhaps the first Army officer to do so. Originally assigned to artillery duty, he transferred to the Signal Corps in 1899. As a member of that branch, Squier played a pivotal role in the development of military aviation.

In 1905, Squier became head of the Signal School at Fort Leavenworth, Kansas. There he championed the use of balloons in military operations and required that students receive formal instruction in military aeronautics. He was aware of the Wright brothers' work and followed their progress. As assistant chief signal officer, Squier helped make aviation more prominent in the Signal Corps's mission. Squier recommended the formation of an aeronautical division in 1907 and prepared specifications for the Army's first aircraft. He supervised the flight trials at Fort Myer, Virginia, and even went aloft himself.

Serving as military attaché in London when World War I began, Squier secretly visited the front and observed airplanes in action. In 1916, he took charge of the Signal Corps Aviation Section. Appointed chief signal officer in 1917, Squier assumed responsibility for the Army's aviation and communications functions. Under his direction, the Army established two important research centers: Langley Field, Virginia, and the laboratories at Fort Monmouth, New Jersey. When the aviation program fell short of the nation's high expectations, President Woodrow Wilson removed it from Signal Corps control in May 1918. Squier continued, however, to push development of airborne radiotelephone equipment. He succeeded, but too late for combat service. After retiring in 1923, Squier continued his scientific pursuits. Holder of numerous patents, he is perhaps best known as the inventor of Muzak.

Though harshly criticized for his handling of the wartime aerial program, Squier's contributions to aviation far outweigh his administrative shortcomings. He was among the first Army officers to recognize military aviation's value and helped to lay the groundwork for today's Air Force.

Rebecca Robbins Raines

References

Clark, Paul W. "Major General George Owen Squier: Military Scientist." Ph.D. diss. Case Western Reserve University, 1974.

Raines, Rebecca Robbins. *Getting the Message Through: A Branch History of the U.S. Army Signal Corps.* Washington, DC: U.S. Government Printing Office, 1996.

Stalingrad, Battle of (1942–1943)

Air operations during the Battle of Stalingrad are divided into two phases: before and after 19 November 1942, the date that marks the start of the Soviet counteroffensive. Until this date, General Wolfram von Richthofen's Luftflotte 4 (Fourth Air Force) dominated the skies and supported the German ground forces, although the Soviet Eighth Air Army and 102 IAD-PVO (Fighter Aviation–Air Defense) Fighter Division provided an increasingly fierce defense of the city. From October, German bombers tried to isolate the battlefield by bombing the Volga crossings and the rear areas across the river. The Soviets' sunrise counteroffensive on 19 November utilized previously hidden reserves, adding three air armies and half of Long Range Aviation's resources to the Eighth Air Army and 102 IAD-PVO, for a total of 1,400 combat aircraft in 26 air divisions. Most of these aircraft were modern types, including the newest versions of the Il-2 Shturmovik and the new La-5 and Yak-9. Soviet pilots also showed aggressiveness and a willingness to operate in bad weather.

When the German Sixth Army was surrounded, the Luftwaffe promised to supply it by air, overconfident in their successes at Cholm and Demyansk the previous winter. The Sixth Army needed a minimum of 750 tons per day, requiring 375 flights, but the Luftwaffe proved unable to deliver more than 289 tons and averaged 85. In response, the Soviets introduced several new tactics, most notably the air blockade whereby the Soviets' first priority became interdicting German transport operations. Forward-based fighter units used standing patrols and free-hunt missions, as well as ground-to-air warning systems, to intercept transports in flight while bomber and ground attack aircraft targeted the airfields at Pitomnik, Gumrak, and Tatsinskaya. Shturmoviks were also used as air-to-air interceptors against the often unescorted German transport planes. As the airfields were captured and the flight distances grew longer, supply flights became impossible, and by mid-January Stalingrad was isolated.

The Soviets claimed 1,000 German aircraft destroyed in December and January, 80 percent of them transports. The Luftwaffe admitted the loss of 488 transports and 1,000 crewmen, a loss from which it never recovered. The Soviet air forces gained new confidence and made the air blockade a standard tactic for isolating the battlefield in future operations.

George M. Mellinger

See also

Airlift Operations, U.S.; Golovanov, Aleksandr; Ilyushin Il-2 Shturmovik; Junkers Ju-52; Khryukin, Timofei T.; Richthofen, Wolfram von; Rudenko, S. I.

References

Bekker, Cajus. *The Luftwaffe War Diaries.* New York: Ballantine Books, 1971.

Hardesty, Von. *Red Phoenix: The Rise of Soviet Air Power, 1941–1945.* Washington, DC: Smithsonian Institution Press, 1982.

Stapp, John Paul (1910–1999)

U.S. Army colonel. John Paul Stapp was born in Brazil to missionary parents. He always knew he wanted to help people, but as an adolescent his desire turned into absolute necessity after the accidental death of an infant cousin. After completing medical school at the University of Minnesota, he joined the U.S. Army and was soon transferred to the Army Air Corps.

As his interest in aviation medicine grew, he escaped the monotony of being a base doctor by developing life-support tests. Stapp served as his own test subject on many of these tests throughout the late 1940s and early 1950s.

Stapp's bravery was tested at the controls of a rocket sled in New Mexico. Stapp rode his rocket sled upward of 200 times and reached speeds beyond 600 mph, torturing his body with forces of up to 35 times the force of gravity. In one such test, after his sled stopped, Stapp undid his harness, stood, and set his own broken arm. That same test left the image of an X-1 rocket-plane permanently silhouetted in his right eye.

Stapp left an immeasurable impact on aerospace medicine. His work led to the development of better safety equipment for the pilot and better life-support systems for the aircraft. Ironically, his most significant contribution to safety on Air Force bases came on the ground, as it was Stapp's lobbying that made the wearing of seat belts in cars mandatory on all USAF bases.

Erich Streckfuss

References

Ryan, Craig. *The Pre-Astronauts.* Annapolis, MD: Naval Institute Press, 1995.

Stearman Aircraft Corporation

U.S. aircraft manufacturer. Lloyd C. Stearman was trained as an architect and was a naval aviator during World War I. Upon separation from the Navy, he became an airplane mechanic in Wichita, Kansas, eventually working his way up to chief engineer at the Swallow Airplane Company. He then joined with Walter Beech (founder of Beechcraft) and Clyde Cessna (owner of Cessna Aircraft). Together this trio formed their own company in 1925. Stearman left the group a year later and moved to Venice, California, to form Stearman Aircraft Company. Assisted by Mac Short, the company produced the C-1; originally powered by a 90-hp Curtiss OX-5, the aircraft carried two passengers side-by-side in the front cockpit. An improved C-2 powered by the surplus 240-hp French Salmson water-cooled radial engine evolved shortly thereafter and was followed by the C-3 with a Menasco air-cooled radial. Impressed with these designs, friends and investors invited Lloyd Stearman to bring his company to Wichita.

On 27 September 1927, the Stearman Aircraft Corporation of Wichita established a plant north of town. The new company's first product was a C-3MB mailplane for Varney Airlines. On 15 August 1929, the company became part of the colossal United Aircraft and Transport Corporation that included Boeing, Hamilton-Standard (propellers), Pratt and Whitney, Sikorsky, United Airlines, and Vought Aircraft. Lloyd Stearman became disenchanted with the large operation and departed the company in December 1930 to join Walter Varney with his airlines. In 1932, Stearman became president of Lockheed Aircraft Corporation of California.

In September 1934, the Air Mail Act forbade manufacturers of airplanes and engines from also operating airlines. Boeing withdrew from the giant United Aircraft and Transport Corporation, William E. Boeing (cofounder of the Boeing company) leaving under duress. The newly named Boeing Aircraft Company took Stearman as a wholly owned subsidiary.

In 1934, Stearman had negotiated a $300,000 military contract for the manufacture of 61 Model 73 biplane trainers (nicknamed "Kaydets"). Eventually, a total of 8,541 Kaydet trainers were built for the U.S. Army Air Corps, U.S. Navy, and Royal Air Force. The name "Stearman" has been indelibly identified with these aircraft even though they were produced while Stearman Aircraft was part of Boeing. The Kaydet has an even greater mystique about it than its stablemate, the North American T-6 Texan. Many of these aircraft went on to serve as cropdusters and are popular performers at air shows today.

Alwyn T. Lloyd

See also

North American T-6 Texan

References

Mayborn, Mitch, and Peter M. Bowers. *Stearman Guidebook.* Dallas: Flying Enterprises, 1972.

STEEL TIGER (1965–1968)

U.S. code name for Laotian complement to the ROLLING THUNDER air campaign over North Vietnam. Whereas ROLLING THUNDER operated as a dual attempt at interdiction and coercive strategic bombing, STEEL TIGER was purely an interdiction campaign.

From 3 April 1965 until November 1968, STEEL TIGER was the designation given for U.S. air operations over the southeastern portions of the Laotian panhandle from Mu Gia Pass south beyond the major transshipment point at Tchepone down to the triborder area where southern Laos, northern Cambodia, and western South Vietnam converge.

During the operation, Navy aircraft flying from carriers in the Gulf of Tonkin joined Air Force planes based in South Vietnam and Thailand to strike roads, pathways, storage areas, and repair facilities along the Ho Chi Minh Trail. Although fighter-bombers dominated the skies over Laos during the daylight, they proved too fast to spot and bomb trucks effectively and too vulnerable to antiaircraft fire. For their part, the North Vietnamese abandoned most daytime operations, opting for the cover of night. Meanwhile, day and night, B-52s struck storage areas and transshipment points throughout the operation.

The most effective aircraft were multiengine fixed-wing gunships: AC-47s, AC-119s, and AC-130s. Antiaircraft fire drove the AC-47s off the most of the trail by 1966, but AC-119s and AC-130s bore the brunt of the antiinfiltration effort, known as the war on trucks. In November 1968, after ROLLING THUNDER came to an end, STEEL TIGER was extended to cover the entire Ho Chi Minh Trail area and was subsumed into Operation COMMANDO HUNT.

Earl H. Tilford Jr.

References

Ballard, Jack S. *Development and Employment of Fixed-Wing Gunships, 1962–1972.* Washington, DC: Office of Air Force History, 1982.

Momyer, William. *Airpower in Three Wars: World War II, Korea, and Vietnam.* Washington, DC: U.S. Government Printing Office, 1978.

Tilford, Earl H. Jr. *Crosswinds: The Air Force's Setup in Vietnam.* College Station: Texas A&M University Press, 1993.

Van Staaveren, Jacob. *Interdiction in Southern Laos, 1960–1968.* Washington, DC: Center for Air Force History, 1993.

Steinhoff, Johannes (1913–1994)

A successful Luftwaffe fighter pilot, general, and combat commander on all fronts. "Macki" Steinhoff joined the German navy in 1934 as an officer cadet and transferred to the Luftwaffe in 1935. At the beginning of the war he was a pilot in the embryonic night-fighter force but preferred daylight fighting, and in mid-1940 he was able to transfer to Jagdgeschwader 52 (JG 52; 52d Fighter Wing) as a *staffelkapitaen* (squadron leader). After a long tour on the Eastern Front, he took command of Jagdgeschwader 77 in Tunisia just as the Western Allies were wresting air superiority from the Axis. His bitter experiences in Sicily formed the basis of his first book, *Die Strasse von Messina* (The Straits of Messina). In January 1945, after commanding several fighter units, he took an active role in the so-called fighter pilots' revolt in opposition to Hermann Goering and was sent on leave. He managed to join Adolf Galland's Jet Unit of the Aces and scored six victories in the Me 262, but on 18 April 1945 his heavily loaded fighter crashed on takeoff and burst into flames. He survived with severe burns that kept him in the hospital until 1947. Steinhoff was a recipient of the Oak Leaves with Swords to the Knight's Cross of the Iron Cross; his final victory total was 178.

Steinhoff had a very distinguished postwar career. In 1955, he left his job as an advertising salesman and joined the Bundesluftwaffe, the new West German Air Force. He rose swiftly through the ranks and became *inspekteur* (commander in chief) in 1966, just in time for the most serious crisis in the force's history. Its new fighter, the Mach 2 Starfighter, was falling from the skies in alarming numbers, provoking a crisis of confidence in the West German government. Steinhoff implemented drastic changes in training and maintenance and succeeded in cutting the Starfighter's accident rate in half in four years. After being promoted to full general, Steinhoff capped off his career with a tour as chairman of the NATO Military Committee (1971–1974).

Donald Caldwell

See also

German Air Force (Luftwaffe)

References

Obermeier, E. *Die Ritterkreuztraeger der Luftwaffe, 1939–1945, Band 1: Jagdflieger* [Recipients of the Knight's Cross]. Mainz: Verlag Dieter Hoffmann, 1989.

Steinhoff, J. *The Last Chance.* London: Arrow, 1979.

———. *The Straits of Messina.* London: Andre Deutsch, 1971.

———. *Voices from the Third Reich: An Oral History.* London: Da Capo, 1994.

STRANGLE (1951)

UN code name for operation during the Korean War. In late May 1951, as UN forces pushed the communists back toward the 38th Parallel, the Fifth Air Force was given responsibility for aerial interdiction of seven main transport and communication highways leading to the front. Named after an Allied aerial interdiction campaign conducted in Italy in 1944, STRANGLE unfolded as a joint campaign in which northern South Korea was divided into three target areas to be attacked by Air Force fighter-bombers, Task Force 77 Navy fighters, and 1st Marine Wing aircraft. Targets were mostly vehicular roads along with bridges, tunnels, and some rail lines.

Operations began on 31 May when F-51s postholed main roads with 500-pound bombs where repairs and bypasses were most difficult to effect; B-26s then dropped inert M-83 cluster bombs, which were detonated by enemy traffic; B-29s attacked bridges. As June unfolded and enemy forces retreated, Allied air raids turned toward airfields, rail marshalling yards, and logistics supply centers. At first, Operation STRANGLE was very successful, but as UN forces slowed their offensive in mid-June, the communists could resupply and regroup front-line troops at their own pace; Operation STRANGLE thus bore diminishing results.

Much as was the case 20 years later during COMMANDO HUNT operations in Vietnam, a key to the enemy's ability to thwart STRANGLE was the enormous number of labor troops deployed to quickly repair or bypass bomb damage. Repair materials such as rocks, timber, and churned up soil were always in ready supply.

Also, as would be repeated in Vietnam, the difficulty of destroying trucks, the ease of repairing vehicles, and the vast number of new trucks supplied to the North Koreans by the Soviet Union made interdiction almost impossible. UN air forces with limited resources, due to Cold War commitments in Europe and elsewhere, could not afford to maintain the initial pace of the campaign for very long.

By July, Far Eastern Air Force (FEAF) officials reported that Operation STRANGLE was not successful. In spite of this report, the campaign continued turning to new targets such as North Korean small-arms factories and Soviet and Chinese arms supplies coming in by rail.

Rail traffic and tracks seemed an inviting target, but both proved to be difficult to destroy. Even when stretches of track or rail bridges were destroyed, the enemy would simply transfer supplies from one train on one side to another on the other side. Here again, large labor crews usually repaired the damage very quickly. Worst of all, the communists placed very effective antiaircraft artillery batteries or MiG interceptor fields around regularly attacked targets, dramatically elevating the price for destroying the target.

By the end of July, USAF planners estimated that it would take six to eight months of a concentrated air campaign to interdict enemy rail or road supply efforts. Air Force leaders believed their resources allowed for no more than 90 days.

Plans for a new operation culminated on 18 August when a six-month operation, also named STRANGLE, began. To this day, there is controversy over whether this was STRANGLE II or simply Phase II of STRANGLE I. According to FEAF officials, STRANGLE II, which lasted until 23 December, was designed to cripple the communist logistics system to the extent that rapid redeployment of their forces and supplies in support of a sustained offensive was impossible.

The second operation focused on destroying 15- to 30-mile sections of track and rail bridges. It employed group gaggles of up to 64 fighter-bombers carrying 500-and 1,000-pound bombs to drop on the 56-inch-wide tracks. These raids were supported by B-29 missions against rail bridges and airfields. Only a direct hit did any real damage, and only 25 percent of the bombs hit their targets. Considering that similar attacks in World War II had only a 12.9 percent success rate, the FEAF did well.

By November, rail lines were being destroyed faster than the enemy could repair them. The UN's victory in the air battle against North Korea's railroads seemed imminent. An increase in MiG attacks and the effectiveness of new antiaircraft batteries raised the price of the campaign to alarming levels. Most missions had to be reduced and replanned. They didn't reach initial levels again until late November. By then, massive enemy repair efforts had reversed the tide of battle. In December, Fifth Air Force reports concluded that repairmen and bridge builders had broken the railroad blockade and won back the use of the key rail arteries.

Like most Korean air campaigns, STRANGLE I and II were full of good news and bad. On a positive note, senior North Korean prisoners captured later confirmed that enemy leaders had called off a major August offensive due to the destruction of 40,000 trucks. However, never in six months did the FEAF ever effectively stop enemy resupply of its combat forces.

As was the case with aerial interdiction efforts in Vietnam, in Korea airpower hobbled the enemy without totally destroying its capacity to resist.

William Head

References

Futrell, Robert F. *The United States in Korea, 1950–1953.* Washington, DC: Office of Air Force History, 1983.

Thompson, Wayne. "The Air War Over Korea." In Bernard C. Nalty, *Winged Shield, Winged Sword: A History of the United States Air Force.* Washington, DC: United States Air Force History and Museum Program, 1997, pp. 3–52.

Strategic Air Command

The strategic bombardment arm of the United States Air Force during the Cold War. By the end of World War II, the United States possessed the atomic bomb, a delivery system in the form of the Boeing B-29 Superfortress, radar for navigation and bombing, and electronic countermeasures for blinding enemy radar. Of even greater significance was the fact that the nation's atomic capabilities resided within a single numbered air force reporting directly to the Joint Chiefs of Staff.

A vast demobilization of U.S. military power had seen military units greatly reduced in size as servicemen became civilians once again. There were inevitably many reorganizations. One of these occurred on 21 March 1946, with the establishment of three new commands: Strategic Air Command, Air Defense Command, and Tactical Air Command. These three new commands joined the older Air Transport Command. As part of the reorganization, the Department of Defense and the United States Air Force were created on 18 September 1947 under the National Security Act.

SAC was headquartered at Bolling Field, in the District of Columbia, between 21 March and 20 October 1946, then moved to Andrews Field, Maryland, where it remained until 8 November 1948. In an effort to reduce traffic in the Washington area and to position SAC Headquarters out of harm's way, it was moved to Offutt AFB, Nebraska, where it remained for the balance of its existence.

The first commander of SAC was General George C. Kenney, who had commanded the Fifth Air Force and later Far East Air Forces in the Western Pacific under General Douglas C. MacArthur. General Kenney had served well as a theater commander with undoubtedly one of the largest areas of operations, the smallest number of assets, and at the end of a very long supply chain. While commanding SAC, General Kenney turned routine operations over to his deputy while Kenney promoted airpower to Congress, the media, and civil leaders. SAC, as with all military and naval commands during the early post–World War II era, was literally fighting for its existence, operating on shoestring budgets, and trying to maintain some semblance of military preparedness.

SAC needed to be energized and welded into a formidable force if the United States was to have any credibility during the early stages of the Cold War. Timing could not have been better for another senior officer with extensive strategic bombardment experience. Major General Curtis E. LeMay grew up with U.S. strategic airpower from its inception and commanded the nation's first nuclear force. General LeMay immediately began an extensive training program within SAC. He employed the old Army adage—"train easy, fight hard; train hard, fight easy." Missions were planned as if the United States was at war. Complex targets were selected, and the navigation legs simulated the vast distances that would be required to take the war to the enemy. From intensive individual aircrew training came more complex unit training. From this sprang a meaningful annual bombing and navigation competition that recognized the best of the best. Not only were the units recognized; outstanding crews were rewarded with spot promotions in which everyone was promoted one grade.

First and foremost, SAC was a long-range bombardment organization. These units took precedence in manning and budget. Next, SAC was a global reconnaissance organization. With inadequate intelligence, bomber crews could never effectively find and bomb their targets. Third, SAC had remembered its lessons from World War II and had its own fighter-escort units.

While trying to organize, develop, and train an effective nuclear strategic-bombing capability, SAC found itself knee-deep in the Korean War. SAC's fighter-escort units rotated to Korea for six-month tours throughout the war. Six SAC bombardment groups participated during the early stages but ran out of targets. Subsequently, only three B-29 Superfortress groups operated in the theater for the duration of the war.

Lessons from World War II led SAC leaders to believe that integral fighter-escort support would be essential for bombers to penetrate enemy air defenses en route to assigned targets. Seven SAC fighter wings made a total of 10 deployments between December 1950 and December 1954 in support of the Korean War. In January 1953, the units were redesignated Strategic Fighter Wings. SAC fighter pilots had to be proficient in air-to-air gunnery, air-to-ground gunnery, bombing, and nuclear-weapons delivery. Fighter wings were also part of SAC between 1947 and 1957.

SAC was innovative and took on challenges that would improve its warfighting capabilities. Finding the proper balance of payload versus range is the bane of mission planners—no airplane can fly its maximum load with a full fuel load. SAC found the answer in aerial refueling. Although the U.S. Army Air Corps and the British had dabbled in refueling since the 1920s, it took SAC in the late 1940s and 1950s to perfect the concept. SAC began by converting B-29s into hose and then boom tankers. Even better was the Boeing KC-97 Stratofreighter, which not only had a refueling boom but also a much greater fuel offload capability. To meet the all-jet requirements of the USAF, SAC ordered 720 KC-135s, followed by KC-10 Extenders. SAC was designated the single tanker task force manager for all U.S. military aircraft that might require aerial refueling.

Another major mission was aerial reconnaissance. When SAC was first activated, the 311th Reconnaissance Wing (Very Long Range) was assigned to the command. Although headquartered at Barksdale AFB, Louisiana, its units were distributed throughout the United States. Initially, RB-29s were the mainstay of the organization. These were strictly photoreconnaissance aircraft. Next came the Boeing RB-50s in three distinct series: The RB-50Es and RB-50Fs were employed solely for photo reconnaissance, whereas the RB-50G was equipped for electronic intelligence-gathering. Giant Convair RB-36 Peacemakers were equipped for both photographic and electronic reconnaissance missions.

The first jet reconnaissance aircraft in SAC's inventory was the North American RB-45C Tornado. This aircraft served well during the Korean War and from bases in Europe. During the Vietnam War, SAC pioneered the use of Lockheed DC-130 Hercules motherships coupled with Ryan Aeronautical AQM-34 Firebee drones. Next in the inventory came the Boeing RB-47 Stratojets, the most sophisticated being the RB-47H with a Brown Cradle belly pod housing three electronic countermeasures technicians. The Boeing B-52 Stratofortress was briefly employed in the reconnaissance role. The three most successful reconnaissance aircraft for SAC were the Boeing RC-135 Stratotankers and the Lockheed U-2 Dragon Lady and SR-71 Blackbird. SAC was restricted to peripheral reconnaissance of the Soviet Union—overflights were permitted only by direction from the president of the United States. Other overflights were strictly Central Intelligence Agency operations. Photoreconnaissance permitted detailed analysis of enemy installations and permitted development of accurate maps; electronic reconnaissance was used to gather data on enemy radar frequencies, radio frequencies, and command-and-control procedures.

In an effort to reduce the time to target, SAC began development of ICBMs. The first were powered by liquid-fueled rocket motors, making them extremely dangerous to handle. Early missiles were housed horizontally in buildings and erected to the vertical position for launch. Subsequently, ICBMs were placed in hardened underground silos for protection from any potential enemy first strike. The solid-fuel Martin Titan LGM-25 and Boeing Minuteman LGM-30 ICBMs were by far the most prolific and long-lived in SAC's inventory. Their biggest drawback was that they employed the so-called hot-shot launch method that literally destroyed the silos. It was not until the Boeing Peacekeeper LGM-118 missiles of the 1980s that U.S. ICBMs could employ a cold-shot method, thereby making the silo immediately reusable. By 1965, the number of ICBMs in SAC's arsenal exceeded that of bombers.

SAC was always innovative in its approach to its mission: deterrence. The command trained hard. It was flexible enough to recognize when changes were required. SAC adapted to the ever-changing threat and fielded new weapons systems to meet the challenges. Although some considered the manned bomber as obsolete, it is the only recallable weapons system. The time it takes to reach its target may be all that is required for policymakers and heads of state to come to a better conclusion. SAC was one of the main forces that brought the Cold War—and the Soviet Union—to an end. With these major international changes America reorganized its military forces; SAC was disestablished on 31 May 1992.

Alwyn T. Lloyd

See also

Boeing B-29 Superfortress; Boeing B-47 Stratojet; Boeing B-52 Stratofortress; Boeing KC-10 Extender; Boeing RC-135 Stratotanker; Consolidated B-36 Peacemaker; Lockheed SR-71 Blackbird; Lockheed U-2; North American B-45 Tornado; Strategic Air Command; Tactical Air Command

References

Lloyd, Alwyn T. *A Cold War Legacy: A Tribute to Strategic Air Command, 1946–1992.* Missoula, MT: Pictorial Histories, 2000.

Moody, Walton S. *Building a Strategic Air Force.* Washington, DC: Air Force History Office and Museum Program, 1996.

Strategic Arms Limitation Treaty (SALT)

The so-called SALT talks; originated in 1969 when the Soviet Union agreed to negotiate to prevent a further weapons buildup on both sides. Initially a U.S. proposal dating back to 1964, the SALT talks had been rejected for five years because the Soviet Union perceived a lack of parity in its weapons systems (1,054 U.S. ICBMS and 656 SLBMs in 1967 compared to 460 Soviet ICBMs and 130 SLBMs). The U.S. interest, by contrast, stemmed from concern over the Soviet Galosh system, an early antiballistic missile (ABM) that first appeared in public in 1964.

Other reasons for preventing the beginning of talks revolved around definitions of strategic defense and the Nuclear Non-Proliferation Treaty (NPT) then under negotiation. With the NPT signed in 1968 and the possibility—thanks to recent satellite technology—to ensure verification without resorting to physical inspection, the Soviet Union agreed to open talks, which began in Helsinki, Finland, in March 1969 and carried on alternately there and in Vienna.

Three years later, the SALT I treaty was signed. Focusing on strategic offensive forces (ICBMS, SLBMs, and ABMs), it established four agreements, known as (1) the Accident Measures Agreement; (2) the revised Hot Line Agreement; (3) the ABM Treaty; and (4) the Interim Offensive Forces Agreement. The most important of the four was the ABM Treaty, which limited each side to two ABM sites, one around the national capital and one around one ABM site. The treaty also prohibits the testing of any sea-, air-, space-, or land-based and mobile ABM systems. Unlimited in duration, the treaty is subject to review every five years and has recently become the source of some tension between the United States and Russia, inheritor of the Soviet treaties, over U.S. plans to build Ballistic Missile Defense, the so-called Star Wars system.

SALT I did not resolve the issue of forward-based systems, which included nuclear missiles based in Europe; the

Soviet Union wanted these counted, as they could reach the Soviet homeland. The U.S. side, however, rejected this view, stating that the tactical defense of Western Europe could not be counted in the negotiation process. In addition, SALT I never dealt with a new technology, multiple independently targeted reentry vehicles (MIRVs), which allow the affixing of several warheads to a single missile, ensuring greater potency for each missile launched.

SALT II sought to deal with the MIRV problem. In the meantime, the Vladivostok interim agreement of 1974 set up the aggregate limit of launchers and bombers on both sides at 2,400, with a sublimit of 1,320 MIRVed launchers. SALT II negotiations were long and arduous. Both sides made tactical mistakes, such as issuing public offers of reduction (which, if the other side accepted, would have been interpreted as a sign of weakness). Eventually, the Soviet Union agreed to keep the numbers set under the Vladivostok agreement and to allow each side to replace an ICBM type with a new model. In the case of the United States, it was the MX, a mobile system that would have shifted the missiles from one base to another by train to reduce vulnerability. The MX plan was so expensive that it was abandoned.

The range of cruise missiles was limited, and the Soviet Union separately promised to produce only limited numbers of its new bomber, the Tu-160 Blackjack. The treaty was signed in 1979, but when Senate Majority Leader Robert Byrd (D–W.V.) was about to put the treaty to a vote in December of that year, the Soviet Union invaded Afghanistan, and the treaty was withdrawn. Although never ratified by the Senate, both sides chose to observe the provisions beyond the 1985 expiration date.

Overall, then, SALT was a positive step, helping to stave off an arms race that went beyond the minimum amount of nuclear weaponry necessary to ensure effective deterrence. However, the accords failed to account for new technologies (with the possible exception of the broad terms of the ABM Treaty) but did lay the groundwork for a new round of negotiations that culminated in the Strategic Arms Reduction Talks.

Guillaume de Syon

See also

Missiles, Intercontinental Ballistic; Missiles, Intermediate-Range Ballistic; Strategic Arms Reduction Talks

References

Bennett, Paul R. *Russian Negotiating Strategy: Analytic Case Studies from SALT and START.* Commack, NY: Nova Science, 1997.

Blacker, Coit D., and Gloria Duffy. *International Arms Control.* Stanford: Stanford University Press, 1984.

Powaski, Ronald E. *Return to Armageddon: The United States and the Nuclear Arms Race, 1981–1999.* New York: Oxford University Press, 2000.

Strategic Arms Reduction Talks (START)

When President Ronald Reagan came into office in 1981, he declared that SALT—the previous negotiations with the Soviet Union over nuclear weapons—was flawed and needed to be replaced. Thus began the Strategic Arms Reduction Talks, which called for the further reduction of ICBMs and SLBMs, taking into account the number of warheads each missile could carry (a point of contention during the SALT talks).

The START Treaty was not signed until July 1991. It called for a phased reduction of offensive nuclear forces by 30 percent. However, the subsequent dissolution of the Soviet Union made the treaty's ratification and implementation even more complicated. Eventually, the United States proposed to recognize Ukraine, Russia, Belarus, and Kazakhstan as successor states to the Soviet Union. As of November 1992, three of the four new states had ratified the treaty, and only Ukraine delayed implementation of the treaty (agreeing to its provisions in 1993). Whereas START potentially left the United States with 9,500 warheads, proposals and counterproposals made by U.S. President George Bush and Russian President Boris Yeltsin in 1992 suggested levels of warheads equivalent to those that existed in the early 1970s. Following discussions, START II called for reducing the total numbers of warheads on each side to between 3,000 and 3,500 by 2003. However, no agreement was reached to modify the 1972 Anti-Ballistic Missile Treaty. Serious political infighting followed in the U.S. Senate, which did not ratify the treaty until January 1996. However, the Russian parliament has yet to ratify START II, due to a split in opinion among the centrist Russian parties.

As of 2001, plans for START III were floundering on several issues. Calls for bringing the nuclear warheads to less than 2,000 on each side conflicted with the current U.S. strategic war plan, known as the Single Integrated Operational Plan. Based on Presidential Decision Directive 60 (November 1997), SIOP includes an enormous list of potential targets in Russia and China, a list that has actually grown rather than diminished since START II was signed. Counting backups, multiple firing scenarios, and obsolescence factors, 2,500 warheads are currently deemed "essential" in SIOP. The START III floor may be lowered somewhat due to the dismantling of land-based silos in Russia as well as older missile scrapings. However, the second Bush administration's announcement of the resumption of research and development of Ballistic Missile Defense system may further complicate the next round of negotiations.

Guillaume de Syon

See also

Strategic Arms Limitation Treaty; Strategic Defense Initiative

The different configurations of aircraft require that much inflight refueling testing be done to ensure compatibility. A Boeing KC-135 refuels a YF-22 while an F-16 flies chase. (U.S. Air Force)

References

Cimbala, Stephen J., ed. *Strategic Arms Control after SALT.* Wilmington, DE: SR Books, 1989.

Mazarr, Michael J. *START and the Future of Deterrence.* New York: St. Martin's, 1991.

Powaski, Ronald E. *Return to Armageddon: The United States and the Nuclear Arms Race, 1981–1999.* New York: Oxford University Press, 2000.

Strategic Bombing

Using bombardment from the air as a means to achieve strategic goals. Even before the invention of the airplane, there were those who speculated on how aircraft would affect war. By the dawn of the twentieth century, Jules Verne and H. G. Wells were writing of air attacks carried out against major cities and their inhabitants, with events on the ground being determined by the war in the air.

Strategic bombing first occurred during World War I when belligerents on both sides used rigid airships and heavy aircraft to deliver bombs on enemy targets far behind the front lines. Given the technology of the time, air strikes were few in number, inaccurate, and had a minor military impact. The psychological impact, however, was disproportionately large. The reaction of the public and workforce was immediate, as evidenced by factory absentee rates, the numbers of people fleeing cities for the countryside, and the clamor for government action. This strong reaction was caused by the novelty of the air weapon, not by its accuracy or destructiveness.

This belief in the psychological effects of strategic bombing strongly affected the public, governments, and military leaders during the interwar period. The three leading air theorists of this era—Giulio Douhet (Italy), Hugh Trenchard (Britain), and William "Billy" Mitchell (United States)—all assumed such a psychological impact in their projections of future war. The irony of this belief was its implicit promise that the horrors of strategic bombing would be so great that resorting to war would be less likely. In short, early air theorists saw strategic bombing as a deterrent that would keep the peace.

If deterrence failed, however, airmen hoped that strategic bombing would offer an antidote to the trench-warfare carnage of World War I. Strategic bombing, so the argument went, could bypass the tactical battle and strike directly at the "vital centers" of an enemy country. Strategic bombing, in conjunction with surface operations, would quickly bring victory. The intended targets of the bomber offensive were the industrial, economic, transportation, and government centers of the enemy. Note that it was the objective that determined whether a target was strategic or tactical, not the aircraft or weapon being used. Douhet—but not Trenchard and Mitchell—also called for direct attack on the population in the belief that their morale would break and they would demand an end to the war.

Theory outran technology. Strategic bombing in World War II was not nearly as quick or decisive as air theorists had predicted. Populations were far more resilient than expected, as were modern economies. Rather than quick victory, the war again saw prolonged and bloody attrition as the battle raged—only this time overhead as well. The devastation and dislocation caused to the economies of the belligerents by strategic bombing was enormous, but this in turn raised questions of legality and morality. Hundreds of thousands of civilians were killed in the bombing. In response, airmen noted that as awful as these deaths were, they paled in comparison to the number of civilians killed by the traditional forms of war. More than 50 million people died in World War II, and the vast majority of these were not bombed; they were shot, shelled, or starved.

Paradoxically, the advent of the nuclear era in 1945 seemed to confirm the dominance of strategic bombing in modern warfare while also rendering it irrelevant. As nuclear war became increasingly unthinkable, strategic bombing seemed to have correspondingly less utility. In the limited conflicts of the post–World War II era, airpower still played a prominent part, but strategic bombing did not. In Korea and Vietnam, strategic bombing was not seriously attempted—the political restraints were too great. Thus, during the Korean War the centers of enemy power in China and the Soviet Union were off-limits. Similarly, in Vietnam strategic bombing was put under heavy limitations, and Operation ROLLING THUNDER—the bombing of North Vietnam between 1965 and 1968—was merely a half-hearted interdiction effort.

Technology once again changed theory. The introduction of stealth aircraft, precision-guided munitions, and electronic advances had a revolutionary impact on the 1991 Gulf War. The strategic bombing of Iraq was the most accurate in history. Moreover, it resulted in an extremely low loss rate for the attacking aircraft. This performance was repeated in the air war over Serbia in 1999. Once again, strategic bombing was proven accurate while at the same time incurring low casualties (both to the attacker and the attacked). It appeared that technology had finally caught up to theory.

The problem with such a conclusion is the same that has plagued airmen for decades: How does one measure strategic effects? Destroying targets quickly and easily does not equal victory. The only useful criteria for the efficacy of strategic bombing is whether or not it achieves the established political objectives. Attempting to sort out what factors caused a belligerent to yield is not a simple process. Until such a method is found, however, the utility of strategic bombing will remain hotly debated.

Phillip S. Meilinger

See also

AWPD/1 and AWPD-42; Berlin Air Battles; Combined Bomber Offensive; Dresden Bombing of 1945; LeMay, Curtis E.; LINEBACKER II; Tokyo Air Raids

References

Brodie, Bernard. *Strategy in the Missile Age.* Princeton: Princeton University Press, 1959.

Hall, R. Cargill. *Case Studies in Strategic Bombing.* Washington, DC: Air Force History and Museum Program, 1998.

Kennett, Lee. *A History of Strategic Bombing.* New York: Scribner's, 1982.

Meilinger, Phillip S., ed. *The Paths of Heaven: The Evolution of Airpower Theory.* Maxwell AFB, AL: Air University Press, 1997.

Strategic Defense Initiative (SDI, Star Wars)

The so-called Star Wars missile defense—President Ronald Reagan's plan to build a high-tech shield over the United States to protect against ballistic missile attacks. Reagan rejected the widely accepted doctrine of mutually assured destruction (MAD). Under MAD, both the United States and the Soviet Union maintained large enough nuclear arsenals to ensure that one would be able to destroy the other even after a surprise first strike. MAD formed the basis for nuclear deterrence during the Cold War. Reagan, however, believed that he had a responsibility to defend the American people, not simply avenge them, and launched SDI in 1982.

Many advisers and foreign leaders, including British Prime Minister Margaret Thatcher, tried to dissuade him, but he continued to pursue the goal of a missile shield. To Reagan, SDI was a legitimate means of defending the American people from a deliberate or accidental nuclear attack. To SDI's domestic opponents, it was an unworkable waste of money, a dangerous attempt to destabilize the tried-and-true doctrine of MAD. To the Soviets, Reagan's pursuit of SDI was an aggressive act that could leave the Soviet Union vulnerable to a U.S. attack without the means to strike back. Although SDI was finally abandoned, the United States continued to pursue a missile defense program on a more limited scale. Under the George W. Bush administration (2001), it came to be known as Ballistic Missile Defense.

Grant Weller

See also

Missiles, Intercontinental Ballistic; Strategic Arms Limitation Treat; Strategic Arms Reduction Talks; Strategic Triad Concept

References

Fischer, Beth. *The Reagan Reversal.* Springfield: University of Missouri Press, 1997.

Strategic Triad Concept

The deterrence formula used by the United States in the Cold War. The Triad consists of intercontinental ballistic missiles, submarine-launched ballistic missiles, and manned bombers, with each system offering advantages and disadvantages. ICBMs are the least expensive delivery system, can be deployed in large numbers, and are the fastest to arrive on target; but they are immobile and therefore vulnerable. SLBMs, carried aboard and launched from nuclear-powered submarines, are the most likely to survive an enemy strike but have a low availability rate due to submarine maintenance, are the most expensive weapons system to maintain, and are not capable of immediate response. Manned bombers are the most flexible deterrent system, capable of being recalled after launch, but they are vulnerable to enemy air defenses and are slow to reach their targets.

Although U.S. military leaders have made much of the Triad's three weapons systems' flexibility, it is probably not coincidental that the Triad had a role for both the Navy and the Air Force and ensured a continuing mission for aircraft pilots even during the missile age.

Grant Weller

See also

Missiles, Intercontinental Ballistic; Strategic Arms Limitation Treaty; Strategic Arms Reduction Talks; Strategic Defense Initiative

Student, Kurt (1890–1978)

The founder and principal commander of the German airborne forces. Student joined the Prussian infantry in 1910 and volunteered for air service as early as 1913. He spent World War I in various low-level air command and staff positions and remained in the service after the Armistice in the aviation testing department of the Reichswehr. In 1933, after some time in the infantry, he joined the still-secret Luftwaffe. In 1938, he began to raise the first Luftwaffe airborne division, the 7th, but it was not yet operational when war broke out. In May 1940, Student planned and led the operations of the 7th Division during the invasion of the Netherlands, during which he was accidentally shot in the head by a Waffen-SS soldier. After his recovery he planned a number of airborne attacks for the Mediterranean Theater, but the only one carried out—the invasion of Crete—was so costly that Hitler never again approved large-scale airborne assaults. Student was promoted to full general and spent a year devising plans for his gliders and paratroopers, but his men were fated to be employed as infantrymen. He was given command of the new First Airborne Army in Holland in 1944 and served briefly as commander of Army Group H at the northern end of the Western Front before being ordered into the Führer Reserve in early 1945. Plans to place him in command of a new northern army group came to naught.

Student was convicted of abetting war crimes in Crete and sentenced to five years in prison, but he was released after two. He died in West Germany in 1978 at the age of 88.

Donald Caldwell

See also

German Air Force (Luftwaffe)

References

Corum, J. *The Luftwaffe: Creating the Operational Air War, 1918–1940.* Lawrence: University Press of Kansas, 1997.

Way, G. "Lebenslauf Kurt Student." Available online at *Der Fallschirmjäger,* http://www.eagle19.freeserve.co.uk.

Stumpff, Hans-Juergen (1889–1968)

Prominent Luftwaffe commander. Stumpff joined the German Army in 1907 and was quickly judged to be qualified for a staff career. He attended the General Staff Course in 1917 and ended World War I on the staff of the German High Command. He remained in the service postwar, joined the still-secret Luftwaffe in 1933, and headed the Luftwaffe personnel office from 1933 to 1937.

He replaced Albert Kesselring as Chief of Staff in June 1937 and lasted 18 months; he had tired of the political squabbling in Berlin and asked for service in the field. He was promoted to full general and given command of Luftflotte 1 (First Air Force); then in April 1940 he took Luftflotte 5, the smallest of the air fleets, to Norway, where it played minor roles in the Battle of Britain and invasion of the Soviet Union. Stumpff remained in Norway until January 1944, when he returned to Germany to take command of Luftflotte Reich, a new air force with responsibility for the Reichsluftverteidigung (Air Defense of Germany)—the first time this effort had been centralized in a single command. He retained his position until V-E Day.

Donald Caldwell

See also

German Air Force (Luftwaffe)

References

Cooper, M. *The German Air Force, 1933–1945: An Anatomy of Failure.* London: Jane's Information Group, 1981.

Corum, J. *The Luftwaffe: Creating the Operational Air War, 1918–1940.* Lawrence: University Press of Kansas, 1997.

SUD Aviation

Originally the French SNCASO firm; created in 1936 after the merger of several private companies. The firm made several military models after World War II, but only the Vautour II reached production. Marcel Riffard (later, Lucien Servanty) conceived the SO 6000 Triton during the war. On 11 November 1946, it became the first French jet to fly. Five of this rotund design were built. The SO 8000 Narval was a strange twin-boom naval fighter powered by an Arsenal 12H-02 piston engine. It was rejected as a poor performer.

The first interceptor designed by Servanty, the SO 6020, flew on 12 November 1948, reaching a top speed of 600 mph. Four prototypes were produced as rocket-engine test-beds for the more ambitious Trident. The SO M2 was a mockup of the 28-ton SO 4000 bomber that achieved only a single flight in March 1951. A major effort was concentrated on the SO9000 Trident lightweight interceptor. Powered by two Marboré light turbojets, one at each wingtip, and an SEPR rocket engine in the fuselage, the Trident first flew on 2 March 1953. It reached Mach 1.63 and rolled at Mach 1.4. However, stability and control needed improvement. Unfortunately, the second prototype crashed during its first takeoff attempt, and two of the three improved SO 9050 Trident IIs were destroyed during the flight-testing program. Three operational-equipped preseries airplanes flew from 1957, reaching a top speed of Mach 1.96. They established two time-to-climb world records. On 2 May 1958, a Trident II reached 24,217 meters, an unofficial world record that occurred the day the program was cancelled in favor of the conventional Dassault Mirage III.

Later, Servanty became famous again, as one of the great designers of the Concorde. In the meantime, the SNCASO firm had became Sud Aviation.

Stephane Nicolaou

References

L'Industrie aéronautique et spatiale française. tome 3. Paris: GIFAS, 1984.

Sueter, Murray (1872–1960)

The Royal Navy's most important promoter of early aviation. As the Air Department's first commander, he firmly established the organizational and technological foundations of the naval aviation branch.

Sueter joined HMS *Britannia* in 1886. He evinced great interest in new naval technologies and, in 1896, became a torpedo specialist. Between 1902 and 1907, he served aboard the navy's first submarine depot ship and contributed to submarine development.

Sueter in 1909 became inspecting captain of airships prior to commanding the new Air Department in 1912. In July 1914, the Royal Naval Air Service separated from the Royal Flying Corps, largely at his urging. When war came a month later, Sueter oversaw the service's rapid expansion and much innovative technological development. He urged the design and rapid production of small nonrigid airships and strongly supported Commander John C. Porte's work on large flying boats. He pressed for effective torpedo-carrying aircraft that became operational during 1915. He initiated development of long-range heavy bombers that entered service in late 1916, laying the foundation for British strategic bombing.

Sueter left the Admiralty in December 1916 for an operational command in southern Italy. An intemperate campaign for greater recognition of his work on armored vehicles soon precipitated his dismissal. He remained on half-pay until 1920, when he retired as a rear admiral.

Sueter entered Parliament in 1921 and held his seat until 1945. There he pressed the development of airmail services, independent airpower, and tanks. He died in 1960.

Paul E. Fontenoy

See also

Fleet Air Arm; Porte, John C.; Royal Flying Corps/Royal Naval Air Service/Royal Air Force; Samson, Charles R.

References

Cronin, Dick. *Royal Naval Shipboard Aircraft Developments, 1912–1931.* Tonbridge, UK: Air-Britain (Historians), 1990.

King, Brad. *Royal Naval Air Service, 1912–1918.* Aldershot, UK: Hikoki, 1997.

Roskill, Stephen W. *Documents Relating to the Royal Naval Air Service, Volume 1: 1908–1918.* London: Navy Records Society, 1989.

Suez Crisis

Exploiting the rising fervor of revolutionary nationalism, Egypt's Gamal Abdul Nasser outraged France and Great Britain by nationalizing the Suez Canal on 26 July 1956. Moreover, Nasser blockaded the Strait of Tiran, closing access to the Israeli town of Eilat, something Israel declared to be an act of war. Despite a flurry of diplomatic efforts, a military operation soon became inevitable. On 29 October, Israel, in close coordination with Britain and France, dropped paratroops into key passes in the Sinai as part of Operation KADESH. Two days later, French and British forces attacked Egypt in Operation MUSKETEER despite British avowals to the United States that no such mission was planned. The war is notable for Israel's use of blitzkrieg tactics on the ground coupled with the first all-jet aerial battles in the Middle East. Israeli Dassault Ouragons and Mystere IVs engaged Egyptian MiG-15s and de Havilland Vampires, with the Israelis quickly establishing aerial superiority. Specially modified P-51 Mustangs cut Egyptian telephone lines, reflecting Israeli creativity to use older aircraft for niche missions.

British and French aircraft, including Canberras, were largely used for strategic bombing against targets in Cairo, especially Egyptian air bases. Interestingly, a U.S. Lockheed U-2 overflight actually photographed one such British bombing raid. Global political pressure, especially from the United States and Soviet Union, constrained British, French, and Israeli advances.

U.S. President Dwight D. Eisenhower found the affair particularly frustrating, as it shifted attention away from the concurrent Soviet invasion of Hungary, giving the Soviets added freedom to act without international restraint in their client state. For Israel, the war demonstrated the crucial relationship between airpower and ground operations, particularly during the Israeli capture of Sharm al-Sheikh. The Israeli Defense Force committed to building an all-jet combat air force, relying exclusively on France as a supplier of SUD Vautours and Dassault Mirage IIIs. Both Egypt and Syria increased their dependence on Soviet aircraft and advisers. Britain and France suffered considerable international opprobrium, arguably weakening Britain to a second-rate world power.

Robert S. Hopkins

See also

Close Air Support; Dassault Mystère; English Electric Canberra; French Air Force; Israel Aircraft Industries; Royal Flying Corps/Royal Naval Air Service/Royal Air Force; Six Day War

References

Dupuy, Trevor N. *Elusive Victory.* New York: Harper and Row, 1978.
Kingseed, Cole C. *Eisenhower and the Suez Crisis of 1956.* Baton Rouge: Louisiana University Press, 1995.
Nordeen, Lon. *Fighters over Israel.* New York: Orion Books, 1990.
Weizman, Ezer. *On Eagle's Wings.* New York: McMillan, 1976.
Yonay, Ehud. *No Margin for Error.* New York: Pantheon, 1993.

Sugita, Shoichi (1924–1945)

Imperial Japanese Navy (IJN) ensign. Shoichi Sugita was born in Niiagata Prefecture in 1924. At age 15, he withdrew from agricultural school to enter the IJN. In 1942, he graduated from Hei 3d Fighter Reserve Enlisted Trainee Class.

Sugita got his first victory on 1 December 1942 by shooting down a B-17 over Buin. Sugita participated in Midway but did not see air combat. As one of the flying escorts for Admiral Isoroku Yamamoto in 1943, Sugita shot down one Allied aircraft and damaged another but was unable to prevent a group of P-38s from downing the admiral's aircraft over harsh jungle terrain. This event would haunt Sugita for the rest of his life.

In December 1944, Sugita joined the 301st Squadron, an elite fighter group that was formed by Captain Minoru Genda (one of the masterminds of the Pearl Harbor attack). The group flew the newly commissioned Shiden-Kai (Allied code name "George"). On his first mission with the group, Sugita and his flight claimed three F6F Hellcats.

Sugita was killed on 15 April 1945 at Kanoya airfield when his aircraft was attacked while taking off and crashed. In a personal citation that was awarded posthumously, Sugita was credited with the destruction of 70 enemy aircraft and the joint destruction of 40 others as well as being given a double rank promotion to ensign.

David A. Pluth

References

Hata, Ikuhiko, and Yasuho Izawa. *Japanese Naval Aces and Fighter Units in World War II.* Annapolis, MD: Naval Institute Press, 1989.
Sakaida, Henry. *Imperial Japanese Navy Aces, 1937–1945.* London: Osprey, 1998.

Sukhoi Aircraft

Pavel Osipovich Sukhoi was born in July 1895. He studied engineering at Moscow University and the Moscow Higher Tech School before entering the Red Army in 1920. He came to the attention of Andrei Tupolev, who became his sponsor and mentor.

Sukhoi's designs emerged in the years just before World War II. His aircraft tended toward heavily armored, rugged designs best suited for ground support missions. The Su-2 single-engine two-place fighter-bomber was typical. His Su-8, a twin-engine monoplane bomber with eight wing-mounted machine guns, was a departure from his single-engine designs but typified the direction Sukhoi designs took: rugged and utilitarian in firepower delivery. Sukhoi fighter-bombers were well-suited to Soviet army doctrine as it emerged during World War II and carried over into the Cold War: firepower and maneuverability to exploit the effects of bombing.

After World War II, Sukhoi's first venture into jet design was the Su-9. This twin-engine fighter-bomber, with its underwing engine nacelles and all-dural airframe with flush rivets, bore a striking resemblance to the Germans' Me 262.

As was the case with the piston-engine designs, Sukhoi fighters in the postwar period were heavy and better suited to bombing and strafing than to aerial combat. Among these, the single-engine Su-7 was one of the most important design series. First produced in 1958, it remained in production for 20 years and was a mainstay in the Soviet air force, as well as the air forces of the Warsaw Pact countries, and was exported to Egypt and India.

With its variable-wing geometry, the Su-22 was an advanced variation on the theme established by the Su-7 series. Although designed with dual-role capabilities for both ground support and air-to-air combat, the Su-22 was not outstanding at either. In 1987, when two U.S. Navy F-14 Tomcats made quick work of a pair of Libyan Su-22s, the mismatch in capabilities between the two was apparent.

The Su-15 Flagon interceptor was a departure for the Sukhoi design bureau. The Flagon entered production in 1967, three years after the West first learned of its existence. With its delta wing and all-missile armament, it reflected Western design themes of the era apparent in the Convair F-102 and F-106 as well as the McDonnell F-4 Phantom series. The Flagon carried two giant AA-3 Anab missiles, with one being radar-guided and the other infrared-homing.

The Su-24 was Sukhoi's most successful swing-wing design. This two-seat multirole aircraft incorporated a 23mm twin-barrel cannon in the lower centerline and could accommodate a variety of air-to-air missiles and air-to-ground armaments. Although this design closely resembled that of the General Dynamics F-111, the code-named Fencer was thought by many to be more equivalent to the F-14 Tomcat.

The Su-24 represented a transition from clunker to competitor in Sukhoi aircraft. The Su-27, which first flew in 1981, is clearly in another class. Closely resembling the McDonnell-Douglas F-15 Eagle, the Su-27 is a world-class fighter. It is currently in production in Russia and will be built in China under license.

Earl H. Tilford Jr.

References

Bonds, Ray, ed. *The Soviet War Machine.* Seacaucus, NJ: Chartwell, 1976.

Gunston, Bill. *Aircraft of the Soviet Union.* London: Osprey, 1983.

Sukhoi Su-24

NATO code name "Fencer"; a two-seat variable-geometry multipurpose aircraft. First flown in July 1965, the Su-24 entered production in 1970, and by 1981 more than 900 had been produced. The Su-24 currently exists in several variants and is what the Russians call a "battlefield bomber." With a 2.5-ton bombload, the Fencer's range of 1,115 miles allows for interdiction missions deep into the enemy rear. Reconnaissance and electronic-countermeasures models also exist.

Powered by two afterburning Tumanskii R-29B engines rated at 27,500 pounds/thrust each, the Fencer can attain a maximum speed of Mach 2.4 with no external stores and Mach 1.4 (about 1,000 mph) with a combat load of 8 tons. At first derided in the West as an "F-one elevenski," the Fencer may be a much more flexible aircraft capable of both air-to-ground and air-to-air missions, the latter never being a capability of the F-111.

The Sukhoi design bureau has offered six distinct fleet modernization programs to keep the Su-24 competitive in its several variants to 2020 and beyond.

Earl H. Tilford Jr.

References

Bonds, Ray. *Illustrated Director of Modern Soviet Weapons.* New York: Prentice Hall, 1986.

Gunston, Bill. *Aircraft of the Soviet Union.* London: Osprey, 1983.

Jackson, Paul, ed. *Jane's All the World's Aircraft, 1999–2000.* Surrey, UK: Sentinel House, 2000.

Sukhoi Su-27

NATO code name "Flanker"; single-seat all-weather air superiority fighter variants and single-/twin-seat ground attack models. It is a mainstay of the Russian air force's fighter fleet. Beginning in 1969, Pavel Sukhoi led a design team charged with building an air superiority fighter with capabilities analogous to those of the F-14 and F-15 under development in the United States. The Su-27 first flew in 1977 and entered production two years later exclusively as an air superiority fighter. Two years later, ground attack models were observed.

A versatile aircraft, the Su-27, in addition to its internal GSh-301 30mm cannon with 150 rounds, can carry a wide range of ordnance on six underwing pylons and three fuselage stations. In 1993, a specially prepared Su-27 set 31 official world records, including a streak to 39,370 feet in 55.42 seconds.

China has received more than 50 Su-27s in recent years and has a license to build 200 at the Shenyang Aircraft Factory. Many of the former Soviet republics include Su-27s in their inventories, and models have been exported to Vietnam, Syria, and Ethiopia.

Earl H. Tilford Jr.

References

Jackson, Paul, ed. *Jane's All the World's Aircraft, 1999–2000.* Surrey, UK: Sentinel House, 2000.

Supermarine Aircraft

British manufacturer of classic warplanes. In 1913, the flamboyant British pioneer aviator Noel Pemberton Billing, obsessed with the idea of flying over the sea, created the firm that became Supermarine Aviation to design and manufacture flying boats. Supermarine joined the Vickers Group in 1928 and ceased independent operation in 1958.

The company's products fell into four basic categories. The first contained single-engine general-purpose flying boats and amphibians for both military and civilian use that began with the Baby in 1918 and terminated with the Seagull ASR.1 in 1948. Large multiengine flying boats, beginning with the Swan in 1924 and ending in 1934 with the Stranraer, formed the second group. There was also the highly specialized series of racing monoplane seaplanes built to compete for the Schneider Trophy between 1925 and 1931. Finally, between 1936 and 1958 the company produced a succession of single-seat landplane fighters from the Spitfire to the Scimitar.

The single-engine flying boats originated in Supermarine's cooperation with the Admiralty's Air Department during World War I. They mated conventional biplane flying surfaces with Linton Hope's innovative monocoque wooden hulls that combined light weight with great strength and flexibility. The firm developed the basic design, offering flying boats and amphibians ranging from the single-seat Sea Lion Schneider Trophy racers to the multiplace reconnaissance Seagulls and Scarabs. In the 1930s, Supermarine further developed this series into the metal-hulled Walrus and Sea Otter amphibians that saw widespread service in the reconnaissance and air-sea rescue roles.

The larger flying boats evolved from the earlier types. The first boats used wooden hulls, but the Southampton II introduced a lighter, stronger, all-metal design. Progressive refinements culminated in the Stranraer, some of which served as airliners into the 1960s.

The Schneider Trophy racers mated the smallest possible airframes with the most powerful available engines. The S.4 of 1925 was an all-wood cantilever-wing monocoque airframe using a special 700-hp Napier Lion engine. The S.5 adopted a duralumin monocoque fuselage and wing-surface radiators with the engine boosted to 750 horsepower, in which form it won the 1927 race. A new 1900-hp Rolls-Royce R engine powered the all-metal S.6, which won in 1929. In 1931, the S.6B, using an R engine developing 2,300 horsepower, won the Schneider Trophy in perpetuity for Great Britain.

Reginald Mitchell's Spitfire was among the most important and successful aircraft ever developed, but subsequent Supermarine single-seat fighters were far less successful. The Attacker and Swift were overshadowed by their rivals, Hawker's Sea Hawk and Hunter, and the Scimitar's performance failed to match either its elegance or its engines' sheer power. Vickers closed Supermarine's design office and terminated its independent existence in 1958 with the firm's fortunes at a low ebb.

Paul E. Fontenoy

See also

Mitchell, Reginald J.; Supermarine Spitfire

References

Andrews, C. F., and E. B. Morgan. *Supermarine Aircraft Since 1914.* London: Putnam Aeronautical, 1981.
Duval, G. R. *British Flying Boats and Amphibians, 1909–1952.* London: Putnam Aeronautical, 1966.
James, Derek N. *Schneider Trophy Aircraft, 1913–1931.* London: Putnam Aeronautical, 1972.

Supermarine Spitfire

Probably the most successful British fighter of World War II; placed in front-line service throughout the war. At least 22,759 Spitfire and Spitfire variants (photoreconnaissance aircraft and naval fighters) were built between March 1936 and March 1949 in 54 major marks (not counting variants in engine fit and prototypes).

The Spitfire was a pilot's airplane—a very responsive aircraft with superb control harmony that gave the pilot plenty of feedback as maneuver limits were approached. The ability of the Spitfire's airframe to accept progressively more powerful engines was a major factor in its continued success. Its only real fault was a relative lack of range on internal fuel (approximately 490 miles for a Mk.1, 660 miles for a Mk.VIII/IX with fuselage tank).

The Spitfire Mk.I was fitted with a Rolls-Royce Merlin III producing 990 bph using 87-octane fuel. It was armed with eight 0.303-inch Browning machine guns and played an important part in the Battle of Britain. A number of performance improvements were made during 1940, including the use of 100-octane fuel. From November 1940, all Spitfires were retrofitted with metal ailerons that increased the roll rate at high speed. The Mk.II was fitted with a 1,140-bhp Merlin XII. Tactical comparisons with a captured Messerschmitt Bf 109E showed that the Spitfire had a much better turning circle, was generally more maneuverable (particularly at high speed), and that the Bf 109 had a slightly better climb below 20,000 feet and was able to accelerate faster in a dive.

Photoreconnaissance Spitfires were stripped of non-essential equipment and received a highly polished paint finish. They carried two F.24 cameras and were 10–15 mph faster than standard Spitfires. Subsequent versions carried much more fuel, increasing range to a respectable 2,000 miles.

The Mk.V entered service in February 1941 and had a 1,450-bhp Merlin 45. It served in every theater during World War II and fought with distinction during the defense of Malta. Most Mk.Vs were armed with two 20mm Hispano cannons and four 0.303-inch Browning machine guns. The Mk.V was comparable to the Messerschmitt Bf 109F2, but it was severely disadvantaged by the Focke-Wulf Fw 190A, which outclassed the Spitfire V in every department except turning circle. The Spitfire LF Vb with a 1,580-bhp Merlin 50M redressed the performance balance at low altitude at the expense of performance above 12,000 feet, and a much higher rate of roll was achieved by removing the detachable wing tips.

Seafire Mk.Is, IIs, and IIIs were basically Spitfire V airframes with more powerful Merlins, local strengthening, arrestor hooks, and catapult spools on the later marks. The Seafire LIIc was equipped with a 1,640-bhp Merlin 32 and a four-bladed Rotol propeller and had an outstanding low-level performance (similar to the Spitfire LF Vb). Seafires required skill and precision to land on a carrier deck; their accident rate was high.

The Mk.IX appeared in June 1942 as an interim solution to the Fw 190 threat but eventually became the most numerous subvariant. It had a 1,565-bhp Merlin 61 with a two-stage supercharger that provided improved overall performance and large amounts of excess power at around 30,000 feet. Tactical comparisons of the Mk.IX with captured enemy aircraft showed that the Mk.IX was superior to the Messerschmitt Bf 109G6 in climb, turning circle, and roll and was mostly faster, although the Bf 109 was its equal around 16,000–20,000 feet and accelerated better in a dive. The Spitfire was also slightly faster than the Fw 190A, climbed better, and had a tighter turn although the Fw 190A had a much better roll rate and dive acceleration. The Mk.VII and Mk.VIII were similar to the Mk.IX but had a strengthened airframe and some detail aerodynamic improvements. The Spitfire XVI was the designation given to a Mk.IX with a Packard-built Merlin 66. Spitfire PR XIs were initially converted from Mk.IX airframes and carried two vertical cameras.

The Mk.XIV entered service in January 1944 and was equipped with 2,035-bhp Griffon 61. This engine gave a much better performance than the Mk.VIII and Mk.IX at all altitudes and a startling initial climb rate of more than 5,100 feet per minute, but the flight characteristics suffered slightly because of the huge amount of power that had to be absorbed by the relatively light airframe.

During 1944, Spitfires were fitted with Gyro gun sights, type E wings with two 20mm Hispano cannons and two 0.5-inch Brownings, a larger-area rudder, a bubble canopy, and additional fuel tanks in the rear fuselage.

The Spitfire Mk.XXI entered service in January 1945, and had a completely revised stronger wing with larger ailerons, and an armament of four 20 mm cannons. The Mk.XXII and Mk.XIV were externally identical to late-model Mk.XIs. The Seafire 47 was the last Spitfire version and had a contrarotating propeller to eliminate torque effects.

Andy Blackburn

See also

Aircraft Armament; Britain, Battle of; Focke Wulf Fw 190; Gun Sights; Malta, Siege of; Messerschmitt Bf 109; Mitchell, Reginald J.

References

Price, Alfred. *The Spitfire Story.* Oxford, UK: Arms and Armour, 1995.
Quill, Jeffrey. *Birth of a Legend: The Spitfire.* Quiller, 1987.

Suprun, Stepan (1907–1941)

Soviet test pilot and fighter ace. Stepan Pavlovich Suprun was born on 2 August 1907 in Ukraine but emigrated to Canada. In 1924, he returned to the Soviet Union and later trained as a pilot. He became a favorite of Stalin and received wide publicity. In 1939, he flew as a volunteer in China, scoring eight air victories. In June 1941, he formed a regiment of test pilots to fight at the front. Suprun scored another four victories before being shot down on 4 July 1941. He was twice awarded the Hero of the Soviet Union (20 May 1940 and posthumously on 22 July 1941).

George M. Mellinger

See also

Soviet Volunteer Pilots

References

Andersson, Lennart. *Soviet Aircraft and Aviation, 1917–1941.* London: Putnam, 1994.

Sutyagin, Nikolai (1923–1986)

Korean War Soviet fighter ace. Captain Nikolai Vasilevich Sutyagin was born on 5 May 1923 in Smagino, Russia. He entered the air force in 1941 and spent World War II in the

Far East, seeing brief combat against the Japanese in August 1945. From August 1951 to February 1952, he flew 150 missions over Korea with the 17 IAP (Fighter Air Regiment) and was credited with 22 individual and two group air victories, making him the top-scoring Korean War ace on either side. He was awarded the Hero of the Soviet Union on 10 October 1951. During the late 1960s, he was the chief air adviser to the North Vietnamese air force. In 1978, he retired with the rank of major general; he died on 12 November 1986.

George M. Mellinger

See also

Fighter Air Corps; Pepelyaev, Evgenii Georgievich

References

Gordon, Yefim, and Vladimir Rigmant. *MiG-15: Design, Development, and Korean War Combat History.* Osceola, WI: Motorbooks International, 1993.

Seidl, Hans D. *Stalin's Eagles: An Illustrated Study of the Soviet Aces of World War II and Korea.* Atglen, PA: Schiffer, 1998.

Swedish Air Force

In 1926, Swedish army and navy air units were combined to form an independent air force. But Swedish strategy was dominated by the navy and its fleet of coastal warships, including three new armored cruisers. Consequently, the air force was not considered equal to the other armed forces; its organization was rudimentary and its funding was neglected. The Defense Act of 1936 put the air force on an equal footing with the army and navy, expanded air force structure to include a staff, operations division, and college, and substantially increased funding.

In the course of the 1930s, 48 British Hawker Hart single-engine biplane light bombers, 42 of them license-built, were secured. In 1937, 55 Gloster Gladiator biplane fighters were ordered from England. Saab was founded to assemble and build 53 Junkers 86K twin-engine medium bombers. To replace the Hart, Sweden selected the U.S. Northrop 8A-1 single-engine attack monoplane, 102 of which were license-built in Sweden.

In 1938–1939, 46 U.S. engineers worked in Sweden. The Swedes learned the American way of working in teams. The impact of U.S. design and production techniques proved decisive for future Swedish aircraft production.

In 1939 and 1940, Sweden desperately needed modern fighters to replace the Gladiator. Sixty Seversky P-35s were delivered in June 1940. The Swedes secured 72 obsolete Fiat biplanes and 60 Reggiane 2000 monoplanes from Italy.

To keep up with the rapid pace of wartime technology, Sweden was compelled to greatly expand its warplane industry. Obstacles were many: shortages of engineers, machine tools, and duraluminium. Engines were the worst bottleneck. The radial Bristol Mercury of 980 horsepower was license-built. The Swedes copied and built the radial 1,065-hp Pratt and Whitney Twin Wasp. Protracted difficulties with the inline 1,475-hp Daimler-Benz delayed production until the end of the war.

Saab produced the first all-metal stressed-skin aircraft of Swedish design, a single-engine light bomber, 322 of which were built. In service, it was rugged, reliable, and possessed substantial payload and range. Since Saab needed all available duraluminum, the J-22 fighter was constructed of steel tubing and plywood. Some 500 companies outside of the aircraft industry were harnessed to produce 198 J-22s, which began to enter service in 1943. The compact fighter featured excellent handling and climb, but its speed was limited by the Twin Wasp engine.

Developed during the war but not in service until 1945, the Daimler-Benz–powered Saab 21A featured a rear-mounted engine with pusher propeller, a twin-boom tail unit, and tricycle landing gear. Fast, well-armed, and an excellent ground attack machine, 302 of these unconventional warplanes were manufactured.

The Swedish air force did successfully defend Swedish airspace in World War II. Many straying or damaged aircraft were escorted to Swedish airfields, including 126 German, 63 British, and 141 U.S. machines.

The Parliamentary Defense Act of 1948 emphasized airpower and jet fighters. Initially equipped with English de Havilland Vampires and, later, Hawker Hunters, the Swedish air force entered the jet age. Saab developed a series of outstanding jet fighters. Engines from Britain and the United States were license-built with power much enhanced by afterburners, a Swedish specialty. Weapons were secured from Britain and the United States and some were manufactured in Sweden. A sophisticated electronics industry emerged to meet military needs.

The J-29, aptly nicknamed the "Flying Barrel," entered service in 1951. A swept-wing design, the rotund fighter set a world speed record in 1954, averaging 607 mph over a 310-mile course. In 1963, J-29Fs were armed with U.S. Sidewinder air-to-air missiles. Saab factories were expanded to produce 661 of the de Havilland Ghost-powered Flying Barrels.

To meet the need for attack and night-interception missions, Saab designed the two-seat, large, swept-wing, Rolls-Royce Avon–engined J-32 Lansen (Lance). A search-and-attack radar was incorporated into the machine. The sleek Lansen could cover any section of the long Swedish coast in any weather, day or night, armed with a Swedish radar-homing antishipping missile. The night-fighter J-32B was well-armed with four 30mm British cannons and four U.S. Sidewinders. Between 1955 and 1960, 449 J-32s were manufactured.

By the mid-1950s, the Swedish air force numbered 1,000 jet fighters in 50 squadrons, all of them modern and most of Swedish design. From the 1960s, the Swedish air force has emphasized dispersed operations in wartime. Initially, such operations employed hardened sections of roads. These operations have been expanded to include networks of runways well concealed in the forests. Mobile support units service and repair the warplanes. Commando teams protect aircraft and crews. Consequently, Draken, Viggen, and Gripen fighters possess STOL capabilities. Designed to maintain a high and sustained sortie rate, these fighters can be refueled, rearmed, and serviced under wartime conditions by a ground crew of six.

By 2004, the Swedish air force will be reduced to eight fighter squadrons. But cutting-edge technology continues to be emphasized. Close cooperation with other nations is now a hallmark of Swedish policy. Sweden participates in the NATO Partnership for Peace program of exercises.

A compact and lightweight machine, the new Saab JAS-39 Gripen (Griffin) is a multipurpose fighter able to shift quickly from one role to another.

The history of the Swedish air force illustrates what effective leadership, close partnership between the armed forces, government, and industry, and a high level of education can achieve.

Sherwood S. Cordier

See also

Gloster Gladiator; Saab J-35 Draken; Saab J-37 Viggen; Saab JAS-39 Gripen

References

Andersson, Hans G. *Saab Aircraft Since 1937.* Washington, DC: Smithsonian Institution Press, 1989.

Böhme, Klaus-Richard. *The Growth of the Swedish Aircraft Industry, 1918–1945.* Manhattan, KS: Sunflower University Press, 1988.

Swiss Air Force

Although the Swiss army had decided as of 1911 that it might need aviation for observation purposes, no further action was taken in light of budgetary constraints. By 1914, however, under a 1912 fund drive, the Swiss air force came into being, but it was completely unprepared for World War I, as it was unable to take delivery of six German LVG machines it had ordered before the war started. Instead, Cavalry Captain Theodor Real, who commanded the Aviation Troops (later Flugwaffe, or Flight Weapon), was forced to rely on eight civilian machines and its mobilized owners. In addition, two balloon companies were assigned to border observation to maintain Swiss neutrality. By 1916, Real was encouraging a local aircraft industry.

By war's end, the Swiss air force included 112 pilots flying a mix of captured aircraft along with indigenous machines. However, it had seen little use, for it lacked a clearly defined legal status, and many in the army did not believe in the value of military aviation. The moment the war ended, pilot numbers fell to 30, with 234 machines spread among five squadrons.

Things began to change in 1925, when the federal government formally recognized the existence of an air force. Over the following 15 years, air force officers (lobbying through their association, AVIA), convinced the Swiss parliament to approve a budget to buy the necessary aircraft to renew the fleet. By 1933, 40 Fokker CVs and 65 Dewoitine D-27s were in service. The air force's strategy, however, remained focused on reconnaissance, thereby hindering the use of the new weapon as a guardian of Swiss neutrality. Thus, when Germany began sending troops and aircraft to Spain to fight in the civil war, no interceptions of the machines over Swiss airspace ever took place. No plans were made, however, to supply Switzerland with fighters until 1938, when the government acquired a license to manufacture Morane-Saulnier 406 aircraft. In addition, Messerschmitt Bf 109Ds and -Es were ordered.

In World War II, the Swiss air force used its meager resources to guard national airspace, intercepting and shooting down several German aircraft. However, Switzerland's awkward position of economic dependency on Nazi Germany led some Swiss officials to condemn these actions and to end air patrols against any incursions of fewer than three aircraft. Confrontations with Allied aircraft also occurred, leading to the interception and capture of lost bombers (more than 100 B-17s and B-24s).

After World War II, the Swiss air force entered the jet age by first acquiring British-built de Havilland Venom and Vampire jets. Failure to successfully develop an indigenous fighter led the government in the 1950s to order Hawker Hunters, which served as front-line interception machines, then as ground-attack types until retirement in 1994. Meanwhile, the Swiss air force entered the supersonic age with the Dassault Mirage III, first evaluated in 1961 but not delivered until 1970 due to a serious appropriations scandal that shook the air force leadership. The Mirage was completely retired at the end of 1999 and replaced by Northrop F-5s, in service since 1978, and some 34 Lockheed Martin F-18s ordered in the 1990s.

Unlike the other branches of the army, the air force is not

a formal army corps and functions autonomously. In peacetime, the Flugwaffe's aircraft are flown by a combination of militia personnel (the principle is similar to that of the U.S. National Guard) who serve a total of six weeks per year. There are also professional pilots who man the surveillance and interception squadron, but for legal reasons they are considered to be government employees whose desks happen to be cockpits.

Guillaume de Syon

See also
Pilatus; Swiss Aircraft Industry

References

Nicoli, Dott Ricardo. "Alpine Deltas: The Swiss Mirage Story." *Air Enthusiast* 88 (July-August 2000): 66–71.
de Syon, Guillaume. "Target Practice on a Swiss Balloon." *Over the Front* 9, 1 (Spring 1994): 81–82.
Urech, Jakob. *The Aircraft of the Swiss Air Force Since 1914.* Stäfa, Switzerland: Gut, 1975.

Swiss Aircraft Industry

The Swiss aircraft industry, like most Western European counterparts, experienced a golden infancy prior to and during World War I before facing economic and technical challenges associated with a small country's industrial potential.

Prior to World War I, pioneers Armand Dufaux and René Grandjean each sold aircraft they had designed to the army. During World War I, several engineers designed and produced local machines for use by the newly established air force. Robert Wild and August Häfeli each worked on new models, but regardless of progress in their respective designs the limited availability of suitable engines prevented a successful expansion of their businesses.

After the war, Häfeli continued to design aircraft at the Federal Construction Works in Thun, and the government-owned Swiss Locomotive Works in Winterthur began developing an aircraft engine. However, the Saurer firm offered a better engine by simply licensing a 150-hp model from Hispano-Suiza. This allowed the Swiss air force to order far more machines of the same series than ever before (in this case, the Häfeli DH-3 M IIIa) and gave a boost to aircraft manufacturing. As for private aircraft construction, it was dormant in 1918 as a result of the Swiss Locomotive and Machine Works (Schlieren) failing to successfully compete for a contract offered by the Swiss authorities for a training machine.

From then until 1925, all Swiss aircraft production was done under direct government supervision. In early 1926, however, the owner of an aircraft repair shop, Alfred Comte, set up his own company and sought to compete for military and civilian contracts. His AC-1 aircraft lost to the Dewoitine D-27, but the prototype was nonetheless acquired and served to train pilots in high-altitude flying until the late 1930s. Comte went on to design other projects, the most successful of which was the AC-4 Gentleman, a two-seat trainer that sold well enough to keep the company afloat.

The Great Depression, however, eventually forced Comte into bankruptcy, and several of its engineers transferred to the Pilatus factory, established in 1939. One exception was the Dornier factory in Altenrhein, on the Swiss bank of Lake Constance. Established in 1926, it manufactured the giant Dornier DO-X and dabbled in hydroplane projects throughout the interwar years. During World War II, the company was involved in studying various projects, such as a fighter based on the Morane-Saulnier 540. It later became known as FFA, focusing instead on training and light aircraft. Overall, then, limited orders and a lack of a clear appropriation process kept the Swiss aircraft industry limited to a few models. By the 1930s, it was clear that it was easier to purchase aircraft abroad than to begin new projects form scratch under limited funding.

One could, however, build under license. For example, the Federal Aircraft Factory in Emmen was involved manufacturing of Morane-Saulnier 406s under license.

After the war, with the advent of the jet age, the Swiss air force considered proposals for a combat jet from Swiss manufacturers. FFA's proposal was rejected in favor of the Federal Aircraft Factory's new delta combat aircraft proposal for four years, the N-20 Aiguilles. Engineers had relied on two 3:5-scale models, one flying as a glider, the other (the Arbalester, or Crossbow) with a small engine, to determine the best aerodynamics. Advanced though it was, the N-20 lacked power, as taxi trials showed that the four turbofan engines in the wings gave insufficient thrust. Following parliamentary refusal to allocate further funding for better engines, the project was abruptly cancelled in 1953, prompting many engineers to resign in disgust. The N-20 was a remarkable machine, and some of the knowledge acquired through its design helped in the preparation for another indigenous project, the P.16.

Although begun at approximately the same time as the N-20, the P.16 only flew two years after the Federal Aircraft Factory project shut down. Specifically tailored to Swiss climactic and geographic conditions, it was intended as a ground attack fighter. However, the first prototype crashed in the summer of 1955, after a fuel line failed (the pilot ejected safely). The second prototype, completed in 1956, was evaluated the following year and given moderate to good marks, and an order for 100 P.16 Mk.IIs was placed in 1958. The first preseries aircraft, however, also crashed during tests, and the project was suddenly dropped, even though FFA built two more planes at its own costs to no avail. The knowledge acquired was not entirely lost, however. At the time, the Swiss American Aircraft Corporation (SAAC) was formed with offices in Wilmington, Delaware, and Saint Gallen, Switzerland. Its founder, Bill Lear, capitalized on the P.16 wing and other features and used it on the SAAC 23, which became the first Learjet.

As a result of the N-20 and P.16 failures, the Swiss aircraft industry moved away from the full manufacture and design of front-line aircraft in favor of specialized machines (Pilatus and FFA offering trainers and light transports), as well as licensed production of planes the Swiss air force purchased (such as the F-5 in the 1970s and 1980s). Such assembly practices included preassembly of parts at the aircraft factories Federal Aircraft Factory in Emmen, FFA in Altenrhein, and Pilatus in Stans. In addition, other companies offered aircraft maintenance and spare storage, as in the case of the Farner firm. Engine manufacture has also taken place under license, for example, with production of the Mirage SNECMA ATAR 9C3 power plant by Sulzer in Winterthur. Thanks to licensing, technical know-how is maintained, and the Swiss economy benefits through the creation and maintenance of jobs at lower costs compared to full programs.

As is the case with the Israeli aircraft industry, the Swiss sought to improve equipment bought off-the-shelf, as with the Mirage III. Aside from costly modifications to match the support infrastructure, the plane benefited from improvements to the Hughes weapons-control system for the HM-55S Falcon AAM and later from the installment of canard winglets, developed independently from those found on the Israeli Kfir.

Today, the Swiss industry is involved in many aerospace projects for major manufacturers. Major Swiss consortiums as well as smaller companies work as subcontractors on projects such as radar electronics, helicopter composite parts, and rocket cones. As for the dreams of a major indigenous aircraft for defense purposes, they have been replaced with the reality of smaller civilian and trainer projects.

Guillaume de Syon

See also

Pilatus; Swiss Air Force

References

Bridel, Georg. *Schweizerische Strahlflugzeuge und Strahltriebwerke.* Luzern: Verkehrshaus, 1975.

Dollfus, Walter. *Early Days of Swiss Aviation.* Luzern: Verkehrshaus, 1975.

Urech, Jakob. *The Aircraft of the Swiss Air Force Since 1914.* Stäfa, Switzerland: Gut, 1975.

Syrian Air Force

Despite a history of many defeats, the Syrian air force remains one of the most potent in the Middle East. The air force was founded following the withdrawal of French forces in 1946. In the early 1950s, British-supplied fighters became the country's first combat aircraft. Strong ties with Egypt led to a transition to Soviet aircraft around 1955. The Israelis destroyed the majority of Syria's MiG-15s on the runways during 1956.

The largest buildup for the Syrian air force occurred following the election of Hafiz al-Assad (1930–2000) in March 1971. Shortly after being elected, President Assad, himself a pilot, began to build up the armed forces and foster strong ties with the Soviet Union that laid the foundation for the modern air force. The MiG-21 and MiG-23 air superiority fighters quickly became the backbone of the force, with some 400 eventually being delivered. In addition, Syria was one of a handful of countries to receive the MiG-25 high-speed interceptor. Its primary mission is to act as a force multiplier by engaging either AWACS or other high-value air assets. The fixed-wing ground attack role is filled primarily by Su-22s, Su-24s, and MiG-27s (the ground attack version of the MiG-23). The rotary ground attack role is filled by air force–operated Mi-25 and Gazelle attack helicopters.

The latest round of upgrades began in 1987 with the delivery of the advanced MiG-29 fighter. The upgrades came just in time, as very few of the MiG-21s and MiG-23s remained fully operational. Acquisition of the MiG-29 provides Syria an aircraft capable of battling Israeli F-16s for air supremacy.

Troy D. Hammon

See also

Mikoyan-Gurevich MIG-21; Mikoyan-Gurevich MIG-29; Six Day War; Sukhoi Su-24; Yom Kippur War

References

Jackson, Paul, ed. *Jane's All the World's Aircraft, 2000–2001.* London: Jane's Information Group, 2000.

Taylor, Michael J.H. *Encyclopedia of the World's Air Forces.* New York: Facts on File, 1988.

Systems Management

The set of managerial methods originally developed in the U.S. Air Force during the 1950s to develop large-scale weapons systems such as ICBMs. In 1965, these techniques became the standard for the Department of Defense. The essential elements of systems management are project organization, systems analysis, systems engineering, configuration management, and phased planning.

Project organization stems primarily from ideas gleaned from the Manhattan Project and implemented first through "project officers," assigned to each weapons system, who would coordinate the activities of contractors and government personnel. Systems analysis was developed by the RAND Corporation in the late 1940s and early 1950s as an implementation of mathematical techniques of operations research to proposed technologies and operations.

Systems engineering stemmed from government-industry interactions between the Massachusetts Institute of Technology, Bell Telephone Laboratories, and the Army during this same period and was instituted in the Air Force through the hiring of the Ramo-Wooldridge Corporation and, later, the creation of the Aerospace Corporation in 1960.

Configuration management was originally developed by Boeing in the late 1950s for aircraft manufacturing and came to the Air Force through Boeing's involvement as the integrating contractor on the Minuteman ICBM project. Phased planning was instituted by the Department of Defense in 1961 and 1962 during Robert McNamara's tenure as secretary of defense.

All of these ideas came together between 1954 and 1962 for ICBM development and, later, in Air Force Systems Command, led by General Bernard Schriever. While managing the ICBM program, Schriever circumvented the Air Force's usual processes and created new ones more suited to large, complex systems. These resulted in the AFR 375 series of regulations for systems management published between 1959 and 1961.

Stephen B. Johnson

See also

Missiles, Intercontinental Ballistic; Schriever, Bernard A. "Bennie"

References

Hughes, Thomas P. *Rescuing Prometheus.* New York: Pantheon, 1998.

Johnson, Stephen B. *The Secret of Apollo: Systems Management in American and European Space Programs.* Baltimore: Johns Hopkins University Press, forthcoming.

United States Air Force. *The United States Air Force and the Culture of Innovation, 1945–1965.* Washington, DC: United States Air Force, History Support Office, forthcoming.

T

TACAMO

An airborne communications system for use with submarines. The development of the fleet ballistic missile submarine brought a new challenge—how to communicate while submerged. The preferred answer was a land-based extremely-low-frequency system known as Sanguine. But this system required a long development effort, so the Navy began an interim project to place very-low-frequency (VLF) transmitters on aircraft. The unusual TACAMO acronym ("take charge and move out") was reportedly a challenge to the development team to get the interim system fielded as quickly as possible. With the passage of time, however, the acronym became synonymous with the mission itself.

The original TACAMO system was installed on a Lockheed C-130 during 1962 using a 25-kilowatt VLF transmitter radiating through a single 30,000-foot trailing wire antenna. As Sanguine became involved in increasingly heated debates over environmental and political issues, improved versions of TACAMO were fielded. By 1971, the TACAMO IV configuration used a 200-kilowatt transmitter and dual trailing wire antennas. Altogether, Rockwell Collins delivered 22 EC-130G and EC-130Q aircraft.

By the late 1970s, it was obvious that Sanguine would never be completed, but the EC-130s were becoming old and seriously overloaded with equipment. The Navy selected the E-3A AWACS airframe. This modified version of the venerable Boeing 707-320 was shielded against electromagnetic interference and had high-capacity electrical generating systems but opted for more powerful CFM56 engines. In April 1983, the Navy ordered 15 E-6As but, in order to save money, opted to transfer the communications equipment from the EC-130s as they were retired.

The age of the Air Force's Airborne Command Post EC-135s led to the incorporation of national command authority battlestaff positions and a specialized airborne launch-control system (ALCS) into the E-6B. The ALCS is capable of launching U.S. land-based ICBMs, in addition to the traditional TACAMO role of launching submarine-based missiles. The first E-6B was accepted in December 1997 and assumed its dual operational mission in October 1998. The E-6 fleet was scheduled to be completely modified to the E-6B configuration by 2003.

Dennis R. Jenkins

See also

National Emergency Airborne Command Post (NEACP)

References

U.S. Navy, Airborne Strategic Command, Control, and Communications (C3) Program. Available online at http://pma271.navair.navy.mil/history/history.html.

Tactical Air Command (TAC)

Established on 21 March 1946 as a major air command; disestablished in the early 1990s. TAC was responsible for all tactical air assets in the post–World War II era. On 1 December 1948, TAC was reduced from major command status and assigned to Continental Air Command as an operational command. During this period, TAC was principally involved in air reserve training programs and field exercises. TAC became an operational and administrative command under Continental Air Command on 20 September and returned to major air command status on 1 December 1950.

TAC's primary mission was to support Army ground forces, perform battlefield reconnaissance, and interdict railways and roads used to support the enemy's front-line forces. Equally important, TAC provided tactical airlift, primarily through troop-carrier operations. TAC developed the C-130 and numerous other tactical airlift aircraft and systems and was the first home of Air Force Special Operations aircraft and systems.

Initially, the principal aircraft were propeller-driven Republic F-47 Thunderbolts and North American F-51 Mustangs. Regarding jet-propelled fighters, the Lockheed P-80 Shooting Star entered operational service with TAC during the spring of 1946 on a limited basis. The Republic F-84 Thunderjet followed in December 1947. Both jets were considered as training aircraft for the fledgling pilots learning to cope with the different performance of jet aircraft.

When the Korean War erupted in June 1950, Far East Air Command fought a holding action using its heavy bomber and fighter units. TAC units were then deployed to the theater on a rotating basis throughout the conflict along with fighter units from the Air National Guard and Strategic Air Command. TAC also began rotating its units to bases in Europe primarily for training, as well as to augment existing forces stationed at Allied bases.

After the Korean War, two major international crises allowed TAC to flex its muscles and show U.S. resolve to protect peace around the world. First came the Taiwan Strait Crisis in 1955 when TAC deployed fighters and fighter-bombers to Taiwan. In 1958, TAC deployed a composite strike force to Lebanon. The show of force in both instances resulted in peaceable political solutions. The Nineteenth Air Force, better known as the "Suitcase NAF," lead the way in developing tactics, techniques, and procedures for deploying air forces during the Cold War.

The Cuban Missile Crisis occurred during the second half of 1960. Many of TAC's tactical units were deployed to bases in the southeastern United States in case they were needed. Both Strategic Air Command and TAC reconnaissance units performed admirably in gathering compelling data on the installation of Soviet ballistic missiles in Cuba. It was this data, coupled with U.S. political resolve, that convinced the Soviets to take their missiles home before an invasion of the island was necessary.

Larger aircraft used for tactical air support initially were the Douglas A-26 Invader, used effectively during World War II. The A-26 was also employed in Korea and again in special operations during the Vietnam War. Jet-powered light bombers came into the TAC inventory during the 1950s (the North American B-45 Tornado and Douglas B-66 Destroyer). Although the former was short-lived, the latter was converted into a jamming aircraft that flew support for tactical operations during Vietnam. Another tactical bomber employed by TAC was the British-designed Martin B-57 Intruder, which also served in Southeast Asia. For nighttime close air support, TAC developed and deployed three different gunships to Southeast Asia: the Douglas AC-47, Fairchild AC-119, and Lockheed AC-130.

TAC's principal airlift organization during the 1950s was the Troop Carrier Command. This mission was performed by TAC until the mission was transferred to Military Airlift Command in the 1970s.

The mid-1960s resulted in a reduction and final elimination of TAC's bomber force, which was replaced by an all-fighter force of larger, more capable aircraft such as the Republic F-105 Thunderchief and McDonnell F-4 Phantom II. Both of these aircraft performed a variety of missions during Vietnam, including the new Wild Weasel surface-to-air missile suppression role.

TAC pursued development of the LANTIRN system (Low Altitude Navigation and Targeting Infrared for Night) for installation on the F-15E and F-16C/D to significantly increase the combat effectiveness of these aircraft by allowing them to fly at low altitudes, at night, and under the weather to attack ground targets with a variety of precision-guided and unguided weapons. In April 1986, initial operational test and evaluation of the LANTIRN targeting pod proved that this precision-attack mission was indeed feasible. The Air Force approved low-rate initial production in June 1986. Introduction of the LANTIRN revolutionized night warfare by denying enemy forces the sanctuary of darkness and was combat-proven during Operation DESERT STORM.

TAC developed a number of electronic-warfare systems. In Southeast Asia, EB-66s provided navigation and electronic-countermeasures support for fighter organizations. With the Boeing E-3 Sentry in 1976 came an electronics package that permits the aircraft to serve as an airborne battle management command post. These aircraft also served in the secondary role of drug interdiction. Tethered Aerostat balloons were added to TAC's inventory in the 1980s. These balloons are permitted to rise to altitudes where their radar can see over the horizon and detect drug-trafficking operations.

When Air Defense Command was inactivated in 1979, the air defense mission was transferred to TAC but was mainly performed by the Air National Guard.

During the Gulf War, TAC assets were flown to the Middle East. The first unit to deploy was the 1st Fighter Wing from Langley AFB, Virginia. Not knowing what they would find, TAC sent the aircraft fully armed. Strategic Air Command aircraft provided tanker support from Barksdale AFB, Louisiana.

TAC's Tactical Air Warfare Center at Eglin AFB, Florida, was responsible for testing new weapons systems and developing tactical air warfare doctrine. TAC developed a large tactical air warfare training center at Nellis AFB, Nevada, known as the Red Flag Range. There students were taught aerial tactics and flew missions to hone their skills. At the Red Flag Range, TAC pilots and aircrews underwent rigorous classroom lectures and then put their lessons to the test, flying simulated combat missions over the range. A vast tracking system is part of the range and records all aircraft operations, which can then be debriefed in the classroom to show the students their effectiveness. The Red Flag Range was home for the Tactical Fighter Weapons Center, which was developed as a result of America's poor showing during the early years of the Vietnam War. During the 1980s, the range was opened to other USAF organizations flying bombers, tankers, and transports. The range still exists under the auspices of Air Combat Command.

Lessons learned in Southeast Asia resulted in the bare-base concept in which civil engineers are deployed to airfields that are useable by the tactical aircraft; prefabricated structures are brought in to serve all building requirements to conduct composite air strike operations.

Lessons learned since Vietnam permitted TAC to redefine its doctrine and tactics to meet the ever-changing threat. With the major reorganization of the Air Force in 1992, TAC, MAC, and SAC were disestablished. On 1 June 1992, Air Combat Command was established and gained all of the tactical fighter and support resources of TAC, the bombers, reconnaissance assets, and ICBMs from SAC, and parts of what had been MAC.

Alwyn T. Lloyd

See also

Air Defense Command; Air National Guard; Cuban Missile Crisis; DESERT STORM; Far East Air Forces; Korean War;

References

Nalty, Bernard C. *Winged Shield, Winged Sword: A History of the United States Air Force, Volume 2: 1950–1997.* Washington, DC: Air Force History and Museum Program, 1997.

Ravenstein, Charles A. *The Organization and Lineage of the United States Air Force.* USAF Warrior Studies. Washington, DC: Office of Air Force History, 1986.

Tactical Air Warfare

The use of airpower in combat operations within a theater of war. Tactical, or theater, air operations normally focus on the defeat of deployed enemy military forces in pursuit of national strategic objectives.

Historically, tactical air missions have primarily supported surface forces in joint multiple-service campaigns to defeat enemy surface forces and the supporting air arm. In comparison, strategic air operations are designed to directly accomplish national objectives, normally by attacking the enemy homeland. However, some theorists and the example of post–Cold War air operations (e.g., Operation DESERT STORM and Operation ALLIED FORCE) highlighted the potential of independent air operations and suggested redefining the concepts of tactical and strategic actions.

The core tactical air missions all emerged during World War I, with refinements during the interwar period and World War II. The primary combat missions in theater air warfare are reconnaissance, air superiority, close air support (CAS), and interdiction. Additionally, airpower provides important contributions to theater operations through a range of other roles, including airlift, aerial refueling, defense suppression, combat search and rescue, psychological operations, electronic warfare, airborne warning, and command and control.

At the beginning of World War I, the primary role for aircraft was reconnaissance/observation. Aircraft were used to extend the eyes of the ground commander and enhance his understanding of the situation facing his forces. The reconnaissance mission evolved during World War I to include photographs that could be more closely analyzed by specialists on the ground and provided more details than could be collected through visual observation.

During the interwar period and World War II, the art of reconnaissance developed rapidly, especially involving photographic missions. The Cold War saw continued development of reconnaissance techniques with improved sensors—including infrared, television, and radar—and platforms, especially satellites, combined with enhanced communications systems to allow the rapid use of the information by commanders and attack planners.

The value of reconnaissance led the air forces to develop aircraft designed to attack enemy reconnaissance aircraft, denying the use of the air to the enemy. These specialized aircraft—fighters—also protected friendly operations from enemy attack, ensuring access for all types of air operations. The fighter aircraft mission was to control the air, thereby gaining air superiority over the battlefield and, if possible, over the theater. Fighter operations could be defensive or offensive in nature. Defensive operations initially involved patrols of designated areas, a tactic that continued throughout the twentieth century. However, the effectiveness of defensive sorties was higher when the fighters were directed by a control system that warned of enemy air attacks and guided the defenders to the area of the threat. Aircraft specifically designed for the defensive reaction mission became known as interceptors, and their operations were complementary to ground-based antiaircraft systems.

During World War I and the interwar years, the warning and control systems for air defense operations relied on visual observation and listening posts to identify the location of threats. By World War II, the control of defensive fighters was enhanced by radar and radio control networks. After

World War II, computer-based control systems and new detection capabilities, such as airborne radar and control platforms, significantly improved the effectiveness of air defenses. Although defensive counter-air capabilities are required to combat enemy air attacks, offensive counter-air operations are considered the most effective means of gaining control of the air, or at least limiting the ability of the enemy to effectively use his airpower.

Fighters conduct several types of offensive counter-air missions, including sweeps over enemy territory, escort of friendly air missions, and attacks on enemy airfields and supporting facilities. During the Cold War, nuclear weapons provided a strong probability of success for planned airfield attacks. Late in the Cold War and during the post–Cold War period, precision-guided weapons allowed highly effective conventional attacks on airfields.

Although aircraft were used to attack ground targets in limited situations before World War I, the fighter pilots during that war began to use their machine guns to attack ground forces when opportunities developed. Fighter pilots and crews on observation aircraft also began to drop bombs on enemy targets. These informal ground attacks grew into formal missions, and aircraft were specifically designed for the role and generally identified as attack, fighter-bomber, or bomber aircraft. Operations involving direct support for ground forces in contact with the enemy became know as close air support. These missions were coordinated with artillery attacks and provided a flexible and responsive form of fire support for ground forces. During World War I, commanders also recognized the additional value of the extended range of aircraft and directed attack and bomber aircraft to strike enemy units and resources that were located far enough to the rear to be out of range of conventional artillery. These deep attacks became known as interdiction missions, designed to destroy, delay, and disrupt the movement of enemy forces and supplies before they could be committed to combat.

After World War I, ground attack capabilities grew significantly, especially in those nations that were developing mechanized ground forces. The speed, range, and flexibility of airpower made it a logical complement to fast-moving ground forces. In addition to specialized attack aircraft, operational concepts, doctrine, organizations, and command-and-control networks were necessary for the effective use of airpower in tactical operations. The German and Soviet militaries were very aggressive in the development of air-ground operational concepts. Other military forces involved in light military operations, such as the U.S. Marine Corps, also developed concepts for close coordination between attack aviation and ground forces. During World War II, the value of air-ground collaboration was validated in virtually all theaters, especially in the initial German Luftwaffe operations and then the successes of Soviet Frontal Aviation and British and U.S. tactical air forces. After air superiority was achieved, CAS and interdiction air attacks were a major factor in most successful theater campaigns.

Although ground forces personnel in all militaries tended to view CAS as the most important attack mission, senior theater commanders and air commanders tended to emphasize deeper missions as more effective in supporting theater-level plans (and strategic air advocates pushed for emphasis on so-called decisive targets). The inherent flexibility of airpower allowed commanders to shift aircraft from deep missions to CAS when the tactical situation required, as in defensive emergencies or during rapid offensive actions. After World War II, operational concepts, organizations, and command-and-control systems tended to build on the model of that war. During the Cold War period, ground-attack capabilities steadily improved with technological advances that enhanced communications and control systems, provided accurate and timely intelligence, reconnaissance, and targeting information, and allowed precision target identification and attack. In the post–Cold War period, the potential of deep attack based on quick target identification, survivable stealth aircraft, precision attack capabilities, and standoff precision weapons reinforced the orientation of air leaders and senior joint commanders toward the concept of independent, potentially decisive air operations.

In situations in which decisive operations were not possible or were not the focus of planning due to political or other factors, tactical airpower remained a critical component of theater operations. As in the early period of military aviation, the first priority remained securing the operating environment by achieving air superiority and then supporting the theater commander by providing clear information as well as focused firepower in CAS, interdiction, and strategic attack missions.

Jerome V. Martin

See also

Air Interdiction; Air Superiority; AirLand Battle; Close Air Support; Frontal Aviation; Tactical Air Command; U.S. Air Force Doctrine; World War I Aviation

References

Lambeth, Benjamin S. *The Transformation of American Air Power.* Ithaca: Cornell University Press, 2000.

Mason, R. A. *Air Power: An Overview of Roles.* Brassey's Air Power: Aircraft, Weapons Systems, and Technology Series. Vol. 1. New York: Brassey's Defence, 1986.

Mason, R. A., ed. *War in the Third Dimension: Essays in Contemporary Air Power.* New York: Brassey's Defence, 1987.

Momyer, William W. *Airpower in Three Wars.* Washington, DC: U.S. Government Printing Office, 1982.

Warden, John A. III. *The Air Campaign: Planning for Combat.* New York: Pergamon-Brassey's, 1989.

Tank, Kurt (1898–1983)

German aircraft designer. Kurt Waldemar Tank was born in Bromberg-Schwedenhohe, Germany, on 24 February 1898. He served in his father's cavalry regiment during World War I as a lieutenant and company commander, earning several medals and being wounded several times. His requests for transfer to the flying corps were denied because of his excellent soldiering. His idle time during the war was spent with a physics book, concentrating on fluid dynamics. After the war, he obtained an electrical engineering degree in Berlin in February 1924 with optional courses in mechanics, flight mechanics, and aerodynamics. Later, he was awarded an honorary doctorate and professorship. In his spare time while a student, he worked on sailplane construction and flying.

Upon graduation, his first job was with Rohrbach, where he expanded the design department. He made significant contributions to the design of all Rohrbach aircraft from then until he left. Tank at this time initiated his habit of test-flying his designs. In January 1930, Tank left Rohrbach to become director of the project department at the BFW firm in Augsburg, working for Willy Messerschmitt. Tank's philosophy of robust structural design was in conflict with Messerschmitt's ultralight design approach, and Tank left BFW in September 1931. He became director of the design and flight-test departments at Focke-Wulf two months later. Even as department manager, Tank continued to exercise significant influence on conceptual design. The Focke-Wulf Fw 190 is the most famous result of his work, the design of which was requested directly from Focke Wulf by the Technische Amt (Technical Office) in 1938 as a backup for the Bf 109 because of its high accident rate upon introduction into service. Another famous Tank design was the Fw 200 Condor airliner, conceived in March 1936 as a challenge to apply current technology to develop a transatlantic airliner, which was proven in several record-setting flights in 1938. Almost all of the designs he influenced were noteworthy, and this made his services in demand after Germany lost the war.

In 1947, Tank and about 60 colleagues from Focke-Wolf emigrated to Argentina to continue development of the Ta 183 jet fighter into the swept-wing FMA Pulqui II, which first flew June 1950, after which Tank did much flight-testing himself. In February 1956, Tank accepted design responsibility for the Indian HAL Marut fighter, first flown June 1961, and continued with HAL until the early 1980s. He then returned to Germany for a consultancy with the MBB firm. He suddenly took ill and died on 5 June 1983 in Munich.

Douglas G. Culy

References

Wagner, Wolfgang. *The History of German Aviation—Kurt Tank: Focke-Wulf's Designer and Test Pilot.* Atglen, PA: Schiffer, 1998.

Kurt Tank's influence on German aircraft design is obvious. The Fw 190 is the most famous result of his work, the design of which was requested to replace the Bf 109 because of its high accident rate. (Smithsonian Institution)

Taran (Ramming)

An unusual method of combat developed in World War II by Russian aviators involving deliberate aerial collision. Ideally, the attacking pilot either hit the enemy aircraft in a vital spot with his wing tip or used his propeller to chew up the enemy's tail surfaces. Although the tactic was frequently fatal for the attacker, with skill and luck a pilot could expect to survive, bailing out of his damaged aircraft or even returning to land at his airfield. The pilot's chances for survival distinguish this desperate tactic from the Japanese kamikaze attacks as well as Pyotr Nesterov's World War I suicide-ramming. During the early days of the war, pilots executed tarans when their old fighters ran out of ammunition. As the war progressed it became less common, but it was used until the end of the war in special circumstances. There may have been as many as 430 taran victories, N. D. Gulaev and B. I. Kovzan claiming four each and Aleksei Khlobystov actually conducting two successful tarans during one flight while flying a P-40. The taran does not seem to have been used in Korea, but on 28 November 1973 Captain G. N. Eliseev rammed an intruder over the Transcaucasus, winning a posthumous Hero of the Soviet Union.

George M. Mellinger

References

Quinlivan, J. T. *The Taran: Ramming in the Soviet Air Force.* RAND P-7192. Santa Monica: RAND, 1986.

Taranto Air Attack (1940)

The first carrier-based aircraft strike against a fleet of warships. Located on Italy's eastern coast, Taranto was the main Italian naval base in early World War II. The excellent natural

The sensational victory at Taranto was closely studied by the Japanese, who applied the methods at Pearl Harbor. (U.S. Navy)

harbor comprised two anchorages—Mare Grande and Mare Piccolo. When Italy entered the war on 10 June 1940, its sizeable Mediterranean fleet became a threat to the British, who were fighting alone following the fall of France that May.

The Axis envisioned this fleet controlling the Mediterranean shipping lanes and reducing supplies to British forces in North Africa. Concurrently, the Royal Navy sought to engage and destroy the Italian fleet to limit the resupply of Erwin Rommel and the Afrika Korps. To this end, Admiral Andrew B. Cunningham, commander in chief Mediterranean, sent British ships near the Italian coast to lure (without success) the Italians into a surface engagement.

British intelligence reported that increasing numbers of large ships were congregating at Taranto. Thus, Cunningham ordered his operational commander to plan an airborne carrier attack for 21 October 1940—Trafalgar Day.

Originally, the HMS *Eagle* and the new HMS *Illustrious* were to launch the attack. However, a fire aboard *Illustrious* delayed the operation until 11 November—Armistice Day. Additionally, *Eagle* suffered bomb damage and was removed from the operation. Some of its aircraft were transferred to *Illustrious.*

At 8:40 P.M. 11 November, *Illustrious* launched 12 old and slow Swordfish biplanes of the Nos. 813 and 815 Squadrons 170 miles southeast of Taranto. Fourteen Fulmer and four Sea Gladiator fighters of No. 806 Squadron flew air cover. Two Swordfish carried flares and four carried bombs. This first group arrived over the target at 11:00 P.M. and illuminated the harbor with the flares; the aircraft armed with bombs made a diversionary attack on the cruisers and destroyers.

The last six Swordfish in the first wave, armed with one torpedo each, attacked the six Italian battleships anchored at Mare Grande. A single torpedo put a hole in the *Conte di Cavour,* which began to sink. A second torpedo tore a hole in the *Caio Duilio,* which was run aground in shallow water. The first wave lost one plane; the crew survived.

Less than an hour later, as Italian crews were fighting fires and searching for shipmates, a second wave of nine Swordfish from Nos. 819 and 824 Squadrons struck. Five of the planes had torpedoes. This time the *Littorio* was heavily damaged and also run aground. A second torpedo hit the *Cavour,* sending it to the bottom in deep water. Numerous lesser ships were also damaged. The second wave lost one plane; both crew members were killed.

In one night, the British had taken a major step in wresting control of the Mediterranean from the Axis. The remainder of the Italian fleet soon withdrew to Naples on the western coast and out of range of British carrier planes. The *Cavour* took enormous resources to refloat and never returned to service. The other two were refloated in two months, but it took many more months to make them seaworthy. By that time the Italian navy was less of a factor. Cunningham noted that after Taranto the Italian fleet "was still a considerable force" but had been badly hurt.

Although some historians remain unconvinced, there is evidence that Britain's Taranto air attack inspired Japanese Admiral Isoroku Yamamoto to launch the 1941 carrier-based air attack on Pearl Harbor. Regardless, at Taranto a single British carrier and 21 antiquated biplanes crippled the Italian fleet in one nighttime raid, proving the vulnerability of surface vessels to aerial assault.

William Head

References

Lowry, Thomas P., and John W.G. Wellham. *The Attack on Taranto: Blueprint for Pearl Harbor.* Mechanicsburg, PA: Stackpole, 1995.

Schofield, Brian B. *The Attack on Taranto.* London: Allan, 1973.

Tarawa, Battle of (1943)

Part of Operation GALVANIC, the Allied assault on the Gilbert Islands during World War II. This was the opening round of the U.S. Navy's offensive in the Central Pacific and the baptism of fire for the Pacific Fleet's new Fast Carrier Task Force.

The GALVANIC air plan drew on three principal sources: General Willis H. Hale's VII Army Air Force (90 B-24s), Rear Admiral Charles A. Pownall's Task Force 50 (11 carriers with 702 aircraft), and eight escort carriers (embarking 228 aircraft) in two air support groups. Sixty-six land-based Navy patrol-bombers supplemented the Army B-24s, and some 100 Marine Corps aircraft provided base defense in the Ellice Islands.

Japanese air defenses against U.S. forces were far fewer. All but one of the Combined Fleet's carriers were in home waters, and their air groups were ashore at Rabaul. In early November, the imperial navy had also transferred most of its land-based aircraft from the Gilberts to reinforce Rabaul, leaving only 46 aircraft in the entire area when the assault began.

Preliminary U.S. offensive operations involved individual fast carrier task groups that raided Marcus Island, Tarawa and Makin, and Wake Island between 1 September and 6 October 1943. Although these raids inflicted significant damage, their real value lay in the operational training they provided to the new air groups. Furthermore, raiders brought back invaluable low-level photographic coverage of Tarawa's beaches, which was supplemented by Army and Navy land-based photoreconnaissance during October.

As D-Day approached, land-based air intensified its attacks on both Makin and Tarawa as well as airfields within supporting range. On 19 November, Task Force 50 aircraft provided ground support as Army troops landed on Makin. The following day, as the Marines went in at Tarawa, a major dawn air attack by Army and Navy forces formed part of the bombardment plan. Subsequently, Task Force 50 attack aircraft supplemented those of the escort carriers in providing dedicated ground support throughout the operation.

The first significant Japanese aerial counterattack occurred late on 20 November. Land-based torpedo-bombers seriously damaged the carrier USS *Independence,* which had to return to Pearl Harbor for major repairs. During GALVANIC, Task Force 50 fighters ensured that not one Japanese air attack disrupted unloading, and none of the several counterstrikes against the fleet caused further damage. During the operation on 25 November, Rear Admiral Arthur W. Radford's group also conducted the first carrier nighttime interceptions, defeating a torpedo attack during which Lieutenant Commander Edward O'Hare was shot down.

Paul E. Fontenoy

See also

O'Hare, Edward H.; Rabaul

References

Brown, J. David. *Carrier Operations in World War II: The Pacific Navies.* London: Ian Allan, 1974.

Craven, Wesley F., and James L. Cate, eds. *The Army Air Forces in World War II, Volume 4: The Pacific: Guadalcanal to Saipan, August 1942–July 1944.* Chicago: University of Chicago Press, 1958.

Morison, Samuel E. *Aleutians, Gilberts, and Marshalls.* Boston: Little, Brown, 1955.

Reynolds, Clark G. *The Fast Carriers: The Forging of an Air Navy.* New York: McGraw-Hill, 1968.

Task Force 38/58

The fast carriers of the U.S. Pacific Fleet during World War II. The Fast Carrier Task Force, initially designated Task Force 50, became Task Force 58 (TF58) on 6 January 1944. Thereafter it would be designated either TF58 or TF38, depending on whether Admiral Raymond F. Spruance or Admiral William F. Halsey was commanding the Fifth or Third Fleets, the matching designations of the Pacific Fleet. Throughout TF58's existence, Vice-Admiral Marc A. Mitscher commanded it; Vice Admiral John S. McCain alternated as commander of TF38 from October 1944.

TF58's first operation was the invasion of the Marshall Islands between 29 January and 11 February 1944. Its strikes won complete air control over the operational area. Only one significant Japanese air attack developed, and not one U.S. naval vessel was attacked.

Between 17 February and 1 April, a series of Pacific raids followed. Targets at Truk, Saipan and Tinian, and the Palau Islands were struck. The carriers' aircraft sank combatant vessels and merchant shipping and destroyed aircraft and shore facilities. They then supported landings at Hollandia, New Guinea, and struck Truk again as they withdrew.

TF58 next sailed in support of landings in the Marianas. The carriers launched heavy assaults on Saipan, Tinian, Guam, Iwo Jima, and Chichi Jima during 11–15 June, then provided cover for landings on Saipan itself. The Japanese Combined Fleet sortied to break up the U.S. attack. In the ensuing Battle of the Philippine Sea (19–20 June), TF58 fighters destroyed three-quarters of the Combined Fleet's entire strength on the first day with little loss. The long-range pursuit the next day, however, cost TF58 dearly. Its aircraft sank a carrier, and submarines two others, but 80 planes were lost on the return from the strike due to fuel shortage and the onset of darkness.

In October, TF38 played a key role in the Battle of Leyte Gulf, during which Japan lost four carriers, three battleships, nine cruisers, and other smaller vessels; American losses were one carrier, two escort carriers, and three smaller craft. The Leyte campaign also witnessed the introduction of Japanese suicide air attacks—the kamikazes.

TF58 next conducted a series of raids on Formosa and Japan to cover landings on Iwo Jima in February 1945. After further raids on Japan, the fast carriers struck Okinawa in preparation for landings that began on 1 April. They continued to support the operation through late May, pulling away only to crush a Japanese surface fleet sortie to attack the invasion force. TF58's aircraft sent *Yamato* to the bottom on 7 April amid a hail of torpedoes and bombs. No fast carriers were lost during this entire period of intense operations, but kamikazes heavily damaged three off Kyushu and a further three off Okinawa.

McCain's force next raided targets in the China Sea and then, from 10 July, commenced an almost continuous period of operations against the Japanese home islands that ended only with the formal surrender of Japan on 2 September 1945.

Paul E. Fontenoy

See also

British Pacific Fleet; Guam, Battles of; Iwo Jima; Japan, Air Operations Against; Kamikaze Attacks; Leyte Gulf, Battle of; Marshall Islands; Okinawa; Palau, Battle of; Philippines; Tokyo Air Raids

References

Brown, J. David. *Carrier Operations in World War II: The Pacific Navies.* London: Ian Allan, 1974.

Morison, Samuel E. *History of United States Naval Operations in World War II.* 15 vols. Boston: Little, Brown, 1947–1962.

Task Force 77

Formed in late June 1950, initially as an Anglo-American force built around carriers HMS *Triumph* and USS *Valley Forge*. *Triumph* departed on 31 July to join an all-British force as additional U.S. carriers arrived.

Offensive operations against North Korea commenced 3 July, but soon Task Force 77 (TF77) began providing essential close air support for the U.S. Eighth Army's retreat. After the situation stabilized, TF77 recommenced attacks on North Korean targets, preparing for landings at Inchon. The carriers provided defensive cover and close air support for this successful amphibious stroke and the advance northward.

When Chinese forces crossed the Yalu River, TF77's airpower again was crucial. It covered the second UN retreat, helped stabilize the front, provided close support through two long years of stalemate, and conducted offensive operations against North Korea in pursuit of the eventual cease-fire.

In 1964, as tension rose in Vietnam, TF77 was on station. On 2 August, when North Vietnamese torpedo boats attacked *Maddox*, carrier aircraft reacted. The retaliatory strikes against torpedo-boat bases that followed immediately marked the start of U.S. naval aviation's longest and most costly war.

ROLLING THUNDER, the full-scale strategic offensive against North Vietnam, began on 2 March 1965 and continued until 31 March 1968 with intermissions intended to induce North Vietnam to begin peace talks. TF77 contributed its striking power to this air campaign, taking responsibility for eastern areas. When ROLLING THUNDER ended, there were few indications that the campaign significantly impacted North Vietnam's will to fight, although naval air contributed greatly to halting the 1968 Tet Offensive.

In November 1968, President Lyndon Johnson ordered a halt in offensive operations over North Vietnam, which President Richard Nixon continued. TF77 operations interdicted Ho Chi Minh Trail traffic and supported ground forces in South Vietnam as needed.

The United States broke off stalemated peace talks on 23 March 1972; North Vietnam launched its expected offensive a week later. TF77 aircraft first supported South Vietnamese defenders and then struck northern targets. Operation LINEBACKER (10 May–22 October) intensified this campaign and incorporated a crippling mining campaign against harbors and waterways.

A halt did not hasten peace—North Vietnam hardened its position and broke off negotiations. During LINEBACKER II TF77 contributed 505 sorties in 11 days of intense operations that brought negotiators back to the table. Peace was signed on 23 January 1973. Nevertheless, operations continued over Laos and Cambodia until Congress ordered their complete cessation by 15 August.

Paul E. Fontenoy

See also

Close Air Support; Ho Chi Minh Trail; Indochina; Korean War; LINEBACKER II; ROLLING THUNDER; Vietnam War

References

Field, James A. *History of United States Naval Operations; Korea.* Washington, DC: U.S. Government Printing Office, 1962.

Francillon, René J. *Tonkin Gulf Yacht Club: U.S. Carrier Operations off Vietnam.* Annapolis, MD: Naval Institute Press, 1988.

Nichols, John B., and Barrett Tillman. *On Yankee Station: The Naval Air War over Vietnam.* Annapolis, MD: Naval Institute Press, 1987.

Taylor, Maxwell Davenport (1901–1987)

U.S. Army general. As Army Chief of Staff in the late 1950s, Taylor criticized the doctrine of massive nuclear retaliation. After retiring, he published *The Uncertain Trumpet* (1959), which argued for a new defense policy—flexible response. Taylor did not accept Giulio Douhet's theory that airpower alone could win or prevent wars. This was the theory upon which massive retaliation was based. Taylor offered the Korean War as an example of a limited war that nuclear superiority could not prevent or atomic bombs win. As the Soviet Union acquired nuclear weapons and ICBMs to deliver them, Taylor believed that mutual deterrence between the United States and Soviet Union had been achieved. Therefore, the Soviets could wage only limited wars using conventional means. Taylor thus argued for an increase in conventional forces with which to counter the Soviets in limited wars. At the same time, he supported the production of faster bombers and higher-yield nuclear weapons to deter the Soviets. His views found favor with President John F. Kennedy, who brought him out of retirement to serve as chairman of the Joint Chiefs of Staff.

John L. Bell

References

Taylor, John M. *General Maxwell Taylor: The Sword and the Pen.* New York: Doubleday, 1989.

Taylor, Maxwell D. *The Uncertain Trumpet.* New York: Harper and Brothers, 1959.

Tedder, Arthur W. (1890–1967)

Royal Air Force marshal. A diverse, spectacular career as a pilot, staff officer, operational commander, strategist, and diplomat marks Arthur W. Tedder as one of Britain's most influential airmen.

Born in 1890, Tedder entered the Royal Flying Corps after an injury prevented World War I service in the infantry. He flew in combat and commanded a squadron over the Somme before commanding a training wing in Egypt. After World War I, Tedder excelled in a variety of command and staff positions focused on training, including tours on the directing staff, RAF Staff College (1929–1931) and director of training, Air Ministry (1934–1936). He served as director-general of research and development (1938–1940) before earning fame as deputy, then air officer commanding in chief, RAF, and Middle East (1941–1943).

Partnered with Air Marshal Arthur Coningham, Tedder developed and executed forward air support links, the basis for a viable air-ground communications system. Equally important, Tedder worked effectively with Eighth Army commanders, including Claude J. E. Auchinleck and Bernard L. Montgomery, to gain air superiority and then form combined air, land, and sea campaign plans. As air commander in chief, Mediterranean Command (1943), and deputy supreme Allied commander (1943–1945), Tedder worked skillfully with General Dwight D. Eisenhower and played a major role in creating Allied strategy in Europe. He became known for the so-called Transportation Plan to isolate and immobilize German forces during the Normandy invasion and subsequent drive across France.

After World War II, Tedder succeeded Charles Portal as chief of the air staff (1946–1950). He shaped U.S.-U.K. early Cold War strategy as chairman of the British Joint Services Mission to Washington and as the U.K. representative to NATO's Military Committee (1950–1951). Capping his distinguished career, Tedder's books *Air Power in Modern War* and *With Prejudice,* as well as his Lee Knowles lectures at Cambridge, are classics of airpower theory. He died in 1967.

John Farquhar

References

Probert, Henry. *High Commanders of the Royal Air Force.* London: HMSO, 1991.

Tedder, Arthur. *With Prejudice: The War Memoirs of Marshal of the Royal Air Force Lord Tedder G.C.B.* London: Cassell, 1966.

Tereshkova, Valentina (1937–)

Textile worker and weekend parachutist who became the first woman in space. Valentina Tereshkova was the first woman to fly in space on 16 June 1963 aboard Vostok 6. She remained in orbit 70 hours, 50 minutes in order to eclipse the U.S. Mercury program's combined astronaut flight time of 54 hours. She was launched two days after Valeri Bykovsky, aboard Vostok 5, to make up the second Group Flight of the Vostok program to study the medical effects of spaceflight on more than one human body in space at the same time. She was married to fellow cosmonaut Andriyan Nikolayev and divorced him as soon as Nikita Khrushchev fell from power in 1964. Released from the Cosmonaut Corps in 1969, she served as a member of the Central Committee of the Communist Party and the Congress of Peoples' Deputies. She lives in Moscow.

John F. Graham

References

Congressional Research Service, Library of Congress. *Astronauts and Cosmonauts Biographical and Statistical Data.* Printed for the use of the Committee on Science, Space, and Technology, 103rd Cong., 2nd sess., 1994.

Terror Bombing

A bombardment concept that derives from strategic-bombing experiences begun in World War I and repeated during the Spanish civil war, World War II, and Vietnam. With strategic bombing defined as the destruction of a country's warmaking potential (as separate from its armed forces), the notion of terror-bombing becomes part of coercive airpower, demoralizing the individual element and thereby reducing national will to make war.

In his book *The Command of the Air* (1921), the Italian theorist Giulio Douhet began formalizing the notion of strategic bombing that would hit deep inside enemy territory. In the United States, proponents of strategic bombing and its terror dimension followed in the footsteps of General William "Billy" Mitchell and began to voice their opinions during the interwar years at Maxwell Field's Air Corps Tactical School, stressing the need to destroy vital centers on which modern life depended, thereby disrupting the social fabric of society.

In practice, however, the differentiation of targets within the strategic realm became difficult. Nighttime bombings of London during the Blitz and after (when no precision bombing was possible) killed almost 30,000 civilians yet failed to destroy the industrial potential as well as the morale of the population. When the types of targets were close together, or when the bombing of civilian targets was deemed an acceptable alternative to an industrial installation, attacks were carried out in massive waves. These yielded only limited results despite heavy loss of life.

Studies carried out at the end of World War II showed that even though support for one's leadership may have declined under terror-bombing, it did not imply a spiraling downward of the social system. Rather, civilians clung to elements of everyday life that indicated normality and turned their energy toward survival. Yet psychological investigation of air attacks suggested that a highly devastating initial attack, combined with repeated attacks increasing with time and targeting troops, may bring about some measure of success as a climate of fear builds in enemy areas. Consequently, despite arguable results, the notion of terror-bombing as part of coercive airpower has continued since World War II and was used during the Vietnam War and Gulf War.

Guillaume de Syon

See also

Dresden Bombing of 1945; Harris, Arthur T.

References

Lambert, A.P.N. *The Psychology of Air Power,* London: RUSI, 1994.

McIsaac, David. *Strategic Bombing in World War Two: The Story of the United States Strategic Bombing Survey.* New York: Garland, 1976.

Pape, Robert. *Bombing to Win.* Ithaca: Cornell University Press, 1996.

Terrorism

Throughout history, used as an instrument of political, military, and religious policy. It has been used by citizens in rebellion against an oppressive regime, by guerrilla troops against an invading enemy, and by the enemy against guerrilla troops. It was not until the latter part of the twentieth century that terrorism began to use airpower, primarily via the hijacking of civilian aircraft.

Initially, the objectives of hijacking were limited: gaining passage to another country or obtaining hostages, who were then used to negotiate ransoms or the release of prisoners. Then the acts of terror escalated as terrorists began to plant bombs aboard airliners, using the murder of innocent passengers as the instrument of their message.

The first hijacking of a U.S. aircraft occurred on 1 May 1961, when an airliner was forced to fly to Havana, Cuba. Over the years more aircraft were hijacked, one of the most spectacular being the 27 June 1976 seizure of an Air France airliner by the Baader-Meinhof Gang and Popular Front. The aircraft, with 258 passengers, was forced to land in Uganda. The passengers were rescued by Israeli commandos on 3 July in the famous Entebbe Raid. Terrorists also used bombs to bring down aircraft, including an Air India aircraft on 23 June 1985 and Pan Am Flight 103 on 21 December 1988. The latter aircraft was blown up over Lockerbie, Scotland; all 259 people aboard perished.

In addition to the successful Entebbe Raid, airpower has been used against terrorists, the most notable being Operation EL DORADO CANYON, which took place on 14–15 August 1986. U.S. Air Force and Navy planes struck targets in Libya. As a result, Libyan terrorist operations were substantially reduced for an extended period of time.

The 11 September 2001 hijacking of four U.S. airliners, three of which were then used to attack the World Trade Center and the Pentagon (the fourth crash-landed following the passengers' attempt to regain control, killing all aboard), was the beginning of a new and terrible chapter in world terror. The responsibility for the criminal acts rested with Osama bin Laden and the al-Qaeda terrorist group, although many other similar groups of Islamic orientation were implicated in the attacks.

Because of the shadowy nature of the terrorist organizations, as well as their use of Afghanistan and the Taliban government as a home base, airpower became the decisive weapon to counter terrorism. Rooting out the terrorist network, which was virtually inaccessible otherwise, was made possible only through the application of the most modern elements of airpower, including precision-guided munitions.

The air war in Afghanistan was conducted with skill and effectiveness, especially considering the difficulties of geography and terrain in Afghanistan, as well as U.S. determination to cause as few collateral casualties as possible. The war against terrorism in Afghanistan was also a signal that war would be conducted in a similar way against other terrorists and the states that support them.

The world is now more alert to the possibility of terrorists using airborne means to inflict damage upon innocent people to further their self-proclaimed jihad against the West, particularly the United States. These means might include the use of crop-dusting aircraft to dispense chemical or biological agents, as well as the use of private aircraft to crash into government or civilian facilities, including nuclear power plants. Traditional methods, such as hijacking or placing bombs on board airliners (including suicide bombers), remain a serious threat.

Although many Muslim leaders deny that Islam as a religion permits terrorist acts, others argue that it is in fact an Islamic duty to join the terrorists in their fight. Therefore, future battles in the fight against terrorists could take place on a worldwide basis, with attacks in Western states being met by counterattacks against states that sponsor terrorism all around the world. The official war on terrorism may have begun on 11 September 2001; it is impossible to say when it will end.

Walter J. Boyne

Thomsen, Hermann von der Lieth (1867–1942)

Key figure in creating the Luftstreitkräfte (German Air Service during World War I). Hermann von der Lieth-Thomsen was born in Flensburg, on the German-Danish border, in 1867. He served on the German General Staff (1901–1903, 1905–1914). Thomsen was awarded the Pour le Mérite on 8 April 1917 for his efforts in creating the German Air Service.

Assigned to oversee developments in military aviation in 1908, Thomsen championed airpower throughout World War I. In April 1915, he was named chief of field aviation. Displeased with the lack of strategic planning for aviation, he worked toward unification of all of the diverse agencies responsible for training, aircraft procurement, and deployment of flight troops into an independent branch of the service. In October 1916, the Luftstreitkräfte was established—as part of the Army—under the command of General Ernst von Hoeppner, with Thomsen as Chief of Staff.

After the Armistice, Thomsen served briefly and helped organize military air-courier lines between Weimar and other cities. He retired from the Army on 11 August with the rank of *oberst* (colonel), then spent five years in Moscow negotiating secret contracts between Germany and Russia. Blindness ended his career in 1928, and he died at his home on the island of Sylt in 1942.

Suzanne Hayes Fischer

Tibbets, Paul W. (1915–)

U.S. Air force brigadier general; piloted the B-29 that dropped the first atomic bomb on Japan. Born in Quincy, Illinois, Paul Warfield Tibbets moved to Florida in 1924. There he experienced his first plane flight with Douglas Davis (later a celebrated Eastern Airlines pilot) aboard a Waco 9. After pursuing a premed program in college, Tibbets applied to become a flying cadet in the Army Air Corps in December 1936.

Tibbets entered flying training Randolph Field, Texas, where he flew Consolidated PT-3 and North American BT-9 aircraft. In February 1938, Tibbets earned his wings at Kelly Field and was commissioned a second lieutenant at Fort Benning, Georgia. There he met and married his wife, Lucy Wingate, in June 1939. He later flew Martin B-10 bombers and, at Savannah, Douglas A-20 aircraft. In his spare time he hung out with his golfing partner, the future General George Patton.

In 1941, Tibbets was selected for training on the new Boeing B-17 bomber and later participated in Operation BOLERO, an aircraft-ferrying operation from the United States to the United Kingdom. As commander of the 340th Bombardment Squadron, 97th Bombardment Group, he participated in the first U.S. air raid in Europe on 17 August 1942, flying the B-17E *Butcher Shop.* By then, he had made major and begun to distinguish himself as an able commander. Although not above micromanaging his men, his meticulous checks on equipment actually helped train them better and may have saved their lives as they learned to fly according to his exacting standards.

In October 1942, Tibbets was promoted to lieutenant colonel and assigned to Operation TORCH, flying Lieutenant General Mark Clark to meet with French General Emmanuel Mast in Morocco. However, Tibbets's time in North Africa was cut short by his conflict with Major General Lauris Norstad. A disagreement over the risk Tibbets's men were being told to take in bombing at low altitude prompted the general to demand a court-martial for insubordination.

Tibbets's allies in the upper levels of command managed to transfer him back to the United States in March 1943, where he began familiarizing himself with a new bomber experiencing growing pains—the Boeing B-29 Superfortress. Tibbets eventually logged more than 400 hours with the plane, which made him one of the most experienced heavy bomber pilots in the Army Air Forces. By September 1944 Tibbets had been briefed on the Manhattan Project, the code name for the U.S. atomic bomb program, and was asked to prepare a special air unit that would be able to deliver such a weapon. He requisitioned 15 new B-29s and had them modified accordingly. His men came from the 393d Bombardment Squadron and were later incorporated into a new unit, the 509th Composite Group. Initially based in Utah, the group slowly moved out to Tinian Island in the Pacific, where on 5 August 1945 Tibbets received presidential clearance to use the first of two atomic devices that were ready.

On 6 August 1945, Tibbets piloted the B-29 *Enola Gay* (named after his mother) and flew to Hiroshima, where the uranium bomb code-named "Little Boy" detonated at 8:15 A.M. local time. Upon his return, Tibbets received the Distinguished Service Cross.

After the war, Tibbets remained in the service and participated in the Bikini Atoll atomic-bomb test. He then became involved in a variety of assignments, ranging from overseeing the acquisition of the Boeing B-47 Stratojet bomber (1950–1952) to serving at NATO headquarters in Paris. After his retirement from the U.S. Air Force in 1966 as brigadier general, Tibbets flew private jets in Geneva, Switzerland, then from 1970 to 1985 worked for Executive Jet Aviation in Columbus, Ohio, retiring as chairman of the board. When asked in interviews about his views on Hiroshima, Tibbets always expressed the opinion that he had done his duty and that his actions helped shorten the war.

In the 1995 controversy over the Smithsonian exhibition of the *Enola Gay,* Tibbets remained somewhat aloof of the passions generated by the proposed exhibit. He did call for the plane (which he had last flown to a storage area in Illinois) to be exhibited with a simple sign and no historical exhibits around it, similar to the display at the U.S. Air Force Museum in Dayton, Ohio, of the B-29 that bombed Nagasaki.

Guillaume de Syon

See also

Hiroshima; Nagasaki

References

Hogan, Paul. *Hiroshima in History and Memory.* New York: Cambridge University Press, 1998.

Tibbets, Paul W., Clair Stebbins, and Harry Franken. *The Tibbets Story.* New York: Stein and Day, 1978.

Tokugawa, Yoshitoshi (1882–1963)

Japan's premier aviator. Born in Tokyo on 23 July 1882, he became in 1908 the first person to make a balloon flight in Japan. As a student of the imperial military school, he was chosen along with several other students to travel abroad to study aviation. Japanese militarists quickly realized aviation's potential in warfare and decided to send students to Germany, the United States, and France, the three nations that were leaders in aviation at that time. In addition to learning to fly, students were authorized to purchase planes for the imperial forces.

Tokugawa went to France to learn aviation at the school near Paris established by the Farman brothers. Tokugawa purchased a Henry Farman biplane and successfully flew it sometime in mid-1910. Tokugawa obtained his international pilot's license on the Farman biplane on 8 November 1910, procuring one of the first 300 international licenses. This flight, although undoubtedly not his first, is his first documented solo flight and garnered him the distinction of the first Japanese heavier-than-air pilot.

Tokugawa returned to Japan in December 1910. In recognition for his achievement, the government honored him with the rank of captain of imperial exercises. He demonstrated the Farman biplane on 19 December over the field of Yoyogi in central Tokyo. During this flight, Tokugawa flew over the celebrated Temple of Meiji, obtaining a view that no one else had ever attained. His flight lasted nearly an hour and marked the first flight of a heavier-than-air machine in Japan.

Tokugawa became a career officer with the imperial forces and initially retired in 1939. His last post was commander of the Aero Corps of Exercises. At the age of 57, Tokugawa was not quite finished with his military service, however. During World War II, Japanese militarists requested he leave retirement and direct the official school of aviation. Under his direction, this school was the training ground for many of Japan's aggressive fighter pilots.

After the war, he retired a second time. Retirement this time was more peaceful, punctuated only by a fiftieth-anniversary celebration of his first 1910 flight. In 1959, a year before the celebration, the United States Air Force returned Tokugawa's original Henry Farman biplane from its temporary home in the U.S. Air Force Museum at Wright-Patterson Field in Ohio. U.S. forces had removed the Farman during the occupation of Japan after World War II. Yoshitoshi requested the plane be displayed in the Museum of Military Pilots in Yasukuni in memory of the victims of World War II in central Tokyo. A lifelong Japanese pioneer in aviation, Yoshitoshi Tokugawa died in 1963.

Wendy Coble

References

Kohri, Katsu, Ikuo Komori, and Ichiro Naito. *Aireview's The Fifty Years of Japanese Aviation, 1910–1960: A Picture History with 910 Photographs.* Tokyo: Kantosha, 1961.

Yoshitoshi Tokugawa. Biographical file CT-372000-01. National Air and Space Museum, Smithsonian Institution, Washington, DC.

Tokyo Air Raids

Two major raids against Japan's largest city. The 18 April 1942 raid was launched to improve sagging U.S. morale early during World War II, as the country had been shaken by a string of costly defeats. Army-Navy cooperation in planning was excellent. Lieutenant-Colonel James Doolittle acted as army coordinator and led the mission.

Because Japanese picket ships were stationed 500 miles off the home islands, the plan was to launch the attack at 550 miles. Although U.S. Army B-25B Mitchell bombers could take off from carriers, they would not be able to return to them; after striking Tokyo they would fly to China. Among the modifications to the B-25s, equipment was removed and collapsible fuel tanks were added to allow a flight of 2,000 miles. Each plane carried four 500-pound bombs.

The carrier USS *Hornet* sailed from San Francisco on 2 April with 16 B-15s on its flight deck. None of the pilots had actually flown a B-25 off a carrier. The *Hornet* was joined on 13 April by the carrier *Enterprise* to provide air cover. Task Force 16 consisted of the two carriers, four cruisers, eight destroyers, and two oilers.

The Japanese were aware from radio traffic that something was in the offing. Combined Fleet Headquarters ordered naval aircraft concentrated in the Tokyo area and alerted picket boats offshore. Early on 18 April, about 650 miles off the Japanese coast, one of these ships gave the alarm by radio, although it was promptly sunk; the original plan to launch the B-25s off on the afternoon of April 19 had to be scrapped. Task Force 16's commander, Vice Admiral William Halsey, ordered an immediate launch. Doolittle's B-25 was the first plane off, at 8:20 A.M.; all were away by 9:20 A.M. Task Force 16 then steamed away at flank speed.

The attack achieved total surprise because the Japanese assumed an attack range of 200 miles and hence a later launch. No bombers were downed over Japan, and only one was hit by ground fire, although all were subsequently lost because the Chinese airfields were not ready to receive them and the crews had to bail out or crash-land. One plane landed at Vladivostok and was interned. Three crewmen died of injuries, and eight were captured by the Japanese. The captured were subsequently tried on charges of bombing and strafing civilian targets. Three were executed; four others survived the war.

The raid inflicted little material damage. Doolittle was presented the Medal of Honor and jumped two ranks to brigadier general. The famed Doolittle Raid and other U.S. carrier attacks had far-reaching effects. A boost to American morale, they were an embarrassment to the Japanese, led to the shift of four fighter groups to defend Tokyo and other cities, and brought a Japanese army punitive expedition in China that killed perhaps 250,000 Chinese. It also increased support in Tokyo for pushing the outer defensive ring farther and drawing out the U.S. Fleet. This culminated in the June 1942 Battle of Midway.

Later in the war, the arrival of the new B-29 bombers in the Pacific brought the opportunity to strike Tokyo. Initially operating from India and China, with the July-August 1944 capture of Saipan, Guam, and Tinian, the B-29s moved there. On 25 November, the United States launched its first attack on the Japanese capital since the Doolittle Raid; 110 Superfortresses were sent against the Nakajima aircraft-engine manufacturing plant in the Tokyo suburbs, but only 24 of the planes bombed the primary target.

The B-29 was a superb aircraft, but to carry 3 tons of bombs 1,200 miles to Tokyo and back consumed 23 tons of gasoline. Precision bombing was impossible at 30,000 feet, and jet streams and crosswinds caused tremendous problems. It also had engine and other problems common to any new aircraft.

Although early B-29 raids affected worker morale and forced the Japanese to disperse industrial activity, the loss rate was running at an unacceptable 6 percent per mission, and General Henry W. "Hap" Arnold brought in Major General Curtis LeMay, who developed new tactics. These resulted from a successful 25 February 1945 raid on Tokyo involving 231 bombers with a mix of general-purpose and incendiary bombs that burned out a full square mile of the Japanese capital.

LeMay decided to send the B-29s in low at night, stripped of defensive armament save the tailgun. As most Japanese structures were of wood, he would use M-47 and M-69 firebombs rather than demolition bombs, and the planes would bomb at 5,000–8,000 feet. Removing machine guns, ammunition, and gunners more than doubled the bombload. His crews were astonished and believed they would be slaughtered. But the Japanese did not have radar and would have to locate the fast-flying B-29s with searchlights.

On the evening of 9 March, 334 B-29s carrying nearly 2,000 tons of bombs (average bombload, 6.6 tons) took off to bomb four designated aiming points in Tokyo. Some 325 B-29s reached the target in the early hours of 10 March. Forty-two were hit by antiaircraft fire and 14 were lost.

Firestorms exceeding 1,800 degrees Fahrenheit ("the flowers of Edo" was the poetic Japanese phrase for the events) burned out more than 15 square miles of the city. Official Japanese figures list 83,793 dead and 40,918 injured, but the actual total was probably higher. The destruction of 267,171 buildings left 1 million people homeless, and 18 percent of Tokyo's industry was gone. The firebombing of Tokyo was subsequently repeated over other Japanese cities. More than 60 were hit, destroying 3.1 million homes, killing 1 million people, and rendering 14 million more homeless.

The firebombing of Tokyo and other Japanese cities did not by itself bring the Japanese surrender that LeMay had sought, but the B-29s destroyed Japan's warmaking capacity, had a devastating effect on Japanese morale, and weighed heavily in the leadership's decision to sue for peace. After the Tokyo raid of 10 March, there could be no doubt that Japan had lost the war.

Spencer C. Tucker

See also

Boeing B-29 Superfortress; LeMay, Curtis E.

References

Coffey, Thomas M. *Iron Eagle: The Turbulent Life of General Curtis LeMay.* New York: Crown, 1986.

Kerr, E. Bartlett. *Flames over Tokyo: The U.S. Army Air Forces' Incendiary Campaign Against Japan, 1944–1945.* New York: Donald I. Fine, 1991.

Morison, Samuel Eliot. *United States Naval Operations in World War II, Volume 3: The Aleutians, Gilberts, and Marshalls.* Boston: Little, Brown, 1951.

Top Gun

During the Vietnam War, the U.S. Navy discovered that its fighter pilots had a 3:1 kill ratio. To improve this figure, the

Navy established an elite school for the top 1 percent of its pilots, its purpose to teach the art of aerial combat. The Navy calls it the Naval Strike and Air Warfare Center; pilots call it Top Gun.

Top Gun improves a pilot's sense of self-confidence and graduates the best fighter pilots in the world. This takes place through intensive training. By 1972, pilots trained at Top Gun were achieving a 13:1 kill ratio.

To qualify for Top Gun a pilot must have at least 500 flying hours, at least one tour on an aircraft carrier, and show high leadership skills. During the five weeks of school, the students attend classroom training and have about 100 flights against the "enemy." Upon graduating they return to aircraft carriers and train the other pilots in their squadron in advanced fighter tactics. During the flying exercises, instructor-pilots try to take advantage of the student's weaknesses. The students will learn that it takes teamwork to beat the enemy.

Every move the airplanes make is recorded and sent back to the Air Combat Management Range. When the pilots return to base they review the electronic records of their flights. They then analyze the whats, hows, and whys of their flights. In this way they learn how to improve performance for the next flight.

The highlight of the course is the Alpha Strike. This is a full-scale simulated battle between instructors and students. The students try to attack a land-based target, and the instructors try to intercept and eliminate the attackers before they can reach the target.

Henry M. Holden

References

Fallon Naval Air Station Website. Available online at http://fallon.navy.mil/nsawc.htm.

TORCH (1942)

Allied code name for operation to support the amphibious invasion of French North Africa. On 8 November 1942 Allied forces landed at Safi, Rabat, and Port Lyautey in Morocco, and at Algiers and Oran in Algeria. The British air base at Gibraltar, overflowing with aircraft, provided a base for Allied air cover from the RAF's Northwest Tactical Air Force and the USAAF's Twelfth Air Force. This was provided primarily by British Bristol Bisley (Blenheim V) and U.S. Boeing B-17, North American B-25, and Martin B-26 bombers. Twin-engined Lockheed P-38s and Bristol Beaufighters also proved particularly useful because of their long range.

These aircraft were supplemented by carrier-borne planes flying from the USS *Ranger* and five escort carriers off Morocco plus the British carriers *Victorious, Formidable, Argus,* and *Furious* and several auxiliary carriers off the Algerian coast. A German submarine sank the escort carrier HMS *Avenger.* This was one of the few direct uses of carrier aircraft in support of ground operations in the European theater.

French resistance was variable, but the Vichy air forces responded with interception of Allied aircraft with Dewoitine D.520 fighters and several strikes against the beaches and ships offshore. German and Italian aircraft from Sicily and Sardinia also attacked Allied invasion shipping.

Although Gibraltar was too far from the Algerian landing zones to allow for fighter cover, the base allowed for the staging of single-engine fighters to North African bases. Capture of the French airfields at Maison Blanc outside Algiers and La Senia and Tafaroui near Oran allowed fighter aircraft to ferry in from Gibraltar.

An attempt to fly U.S. paratroops from Britain across neutral Spain to land at captured airfields near Oran was not successful; poor navigation spread U.S. Douglas C-47 transports from Spanish Morocco to eastern Algeria, and very few men were delivered to the correct destinations.

French resistance soon ceased, but by then Axis air forces had begun transferring to Tunisia. Lack of advanced bases and poor weather hindered Allied air forces' support of attempts to take Tunisia. In early 1943, however, Allied air forces successfully shut down Axis naval resupply routes. The Axis resorted to aerial resupply attempts by Italian and Axis transports, including the huge six-engined Messerschmitt Me 323 "Gigants." Although partially successful for a time, these operations resulted in heavy losses in Axis transport aircraft and were ultimately doomed. The last Axis troops in Africa, cut off by Allied air and naval power, surrendered on 12 May 1943.

Frank E. Watson

References

Craven, Wesley, and James Cate. *Army Air Forces in World War II, Volume 2: Europe—Torch to Pointblank, August 1942 to December 1943.* Washington, DC: U.S. Government Printing Office, 1949.

Playfair, I.S.O., et al. *History of the Second World War: Med and Middle East, Volume 4: Destruction of Axis Forces in Africa.* London: HMSO, 1966.

Towers, John H. (1885–1955)

U.S. Navy admiral. Born on 30 January 1885 in Rome, Georgia, Towers graduated from the U.S. Naval Academy in 1906 and became naval aviator No. 3 in 1911. He spent 1914–1916 in London, surreptitiously saw combat on the Western Front, and returned to Washington to oversee naval aviation's wartime expansion.

Commander Towers achieved fame leading the Navy's

In wartime you do what you have to do—and for this Curtiss P-40 pilot it means taking off from a carrier to participate in the invasion of North Africa. (U.S. Air Force)

transatlantic flight, accomplished by Lieutenant Commander Albert C. Read, with NC-4 in May 1919. After shore service and further London attaché duty, he served on the Morrow Board and was successively executive officer and captain of the carrier USS *Langley* until 1928. Staff duty followed and he was promoted captain in 1930.

Towers commanded USS *Saratoga* (1937–1938) and then was assistant chief and, as rear admiral, chief of the Bureau of Aeronautics until 1942. Working with leaders in government and industry, he played a key role in crafting naval expansion, increasing U.S. and Allied airpower, and improving war mobilization.

In October 1942, Vice Admiral Towers became commander of the Air Force Pacific Fleet at Pearl Harbor with Admiral Chester W. Nimitz. A crucial member of Nimitz's inner circle, he overhauled and oversaw the strategic, doctrinal, and logistical requirements of the Navy's carrier-centric transpacific offensive against Japan. Symbolically, he took command of Task Force 38 the day before Japan signed surrender documents.

In October 1945, Towers was promoted to admiral, then became commander in chief of the Pacific in November. After further Washington service, he retired in December 1947 and became a member of the board of Pan American Airways. He retired in September 1953 and died in New York on 30 April 1955.

Paul E. Fontenoy

See also

Arnold, Henry H. "Hap"; Bureau of Naval Aeronautics; Halsey, William F.; McCain, John S.; Mitscher, Marc Andrew; Moffett, William Adger; Nimitz, Chester William; Spruance, Raymond A.; Task Force 38/58

References

Reynolds, Clark G. *The Fast Carriers: The Forging of an Air Navy.* New York: McGraw-Hill, 1968.

______. *Admiral John H. Towers: The Struggle for Naval Air Supremacy.* Annapolis, MD: Naval Institute Press, 1991.

Trenchard, Hugh (1873–1956)

Considered to be the father of the Royal Air Force.

Hugh Montague Trenchard (nicknamed "Boom" because of his deep voice) graduated from Sandhurst and entered army service in 1893, seeing active service during the Boer War (1899–1902), during which he was wounded. He became interested in aviation later in life, being taught to fly in 1912 by Thomas Sopwith at Brooklands in but 10 days, soloing just four days before his fortieth birthday. At that point his career began to move quickly. As a major, he was assistant commandant of the central flying school (Upavon, 1913–1914). A year later as a colonel, he was commandant of the administrative wing at Farnborough. From 1915 to 1917 as a general, he was in charge of all Royal Flying Corps activities on the Western Front. He was knighted in 1918.

Even though he did not learn to fly until almost 40 years of age, Hugh Trenchard is considered the father of the Royal Air Force. (U.S. Air Force)

On 1 April 1918, the Royal Flying Corps and Royal Naval Air Services were combined to create the Royal Air Force, with Trenchard as its Chief of Air Staff under Lord Rothermere as secretary of state. Just weeks later the two had a falling out and Trenchard resigned, returning to Europe as chief of the Inter-Allied Independent Air Force responsible for the bombing of Germany.

Trenchard was called back as chief of the RAF by Winston Churchill in February 1919. Both men agreed that military aviation needs had to take priority over civil developments. On 13 December 1919, Trenchard issued a white paper describing the future of the RAF—what Sir Samuel Hoare called "a constitution for a new fighting service"—with a major emphasis on training, rebuilding after postwar demobilization, developing research, establishing auxiliary (reserve) squadrons, and setting up training programs within universities. The paper became a blueprint for the RAF's formative years.

He promoted the use of military aviation as a means of patrolling British-controlled Iraq in 1920, calling it "control without occupation" to help cut costs. He established the air force college at Cranwell, as well as a permanent air staff, and pushed for large bombers and more squadrons. His RAF provided just enough contracts to British aircraft firms to keep key design teams intact, though few production contracts resulted. Trenchard became the first Air Marshal in 1919, Air Chief Marshal in 1922, and Marshal of the RAF in 1927. Upon his retirement in 1930, he was created a baron.

From 1931 to 1935, Trenchard served as commissioner of the London metropolitan police and helped to establish a training school at Hendon. There were complaints that he was militarizing the service.

He retired, was created a viscount in 1936, and until 1953 served as chairman of United Africa Company. He died in 1956 and is buried in Westminster Abbey.

Christopher H. Sterling

References

Allen, H. R. *The Legacy of Lord Trenchard.* London: Cassell, 1972.

Boyle, Andrew. *Trenchard: Man of Vision.* London: Collins, 1982.

Truman, Harry S.

Became U.S. president after the death of Franklin D. Roosevelt in 1945; made the decision to drop the atomic bomb and to defend Korea. He was reelected to a full term in 1948. In the years following World War II, Truman oversaw the dismantling of U.S. military forces on a spectacular scale. Although he would, to some extent, continue Roosevelt's "world policeman" policy, Truman recognized that large numbers of conventional forces spread around the globe would be too demanding on the U.S. economy. He believed that strategic airpower coupled with nuclear weapons would provide fiscally responsible military capability and serve as the foundation of national security policy (an idea that would later be developed more thoroughly into the "new look" under President Dwight D. Eisenhower).

As part of the National Security Act of 1947, Truman established the Air Force as a separate military service. Truman's blue-ribbon Finletter Commission confirmed the value of strategic airpower at the expense of tactical forces and dwindling expenditures for the other services. Throughout the postwar years, Truman sided with the Air Force during critical budget and policy battles. He tacitly approved the purchase of Convair B-36s and concurrent cancellation of the USS *United States* aircraft carrier as part of the interservice wrangling during the so-called revolt of the admirals.

Truman embraced the use of cargo aircraft rather than a troop convoy to support Berlin during the October 1948 crisis. Moreover, he rattled the nuclear saber by deploying "atomic-capable" Boeing B-29s to England (the airplanes had in fact not been converted to carry atomic weapons; neither were atomic weapons deployed—it is unclear if the Soviets were aware of this bluff). By 1949, Truman's commitment to strategic nuclear airpower increased with the loss of China to communists under Mao Tse-tung. Aware that conventional U.S. forces were ill-prepared and numerically incapable of fighting the Chinese in a land war, Truman reiterated his support for strategic airpower by approving an increased budget for the Strategic Air Command at the expense of other commands and armed services—another policy extrapolated under Eisenhower.

Two critical events altered Truman's view toward military spending but did not diminish his predilection toward airpower: the adoption of National Security Council Directive NSC-68 and the onset of the Korean War. NSC-68 warned of inadequate conventional and tactical military forces to protect U.S. global interests, a situation that could be remedied only by procuring more tanks, naval vessels, and troops. The June 1950 North Korean invasion of South Korea illuminated the limits of strategic nuclear airpower in the face of regional conflict. Consequently, Truman approved larger defense budgets for tactical weapons, including a much-needed boost in naval and Marine tactical air forces. Despite this, strategic airpower—and SAC in particular—remained the cornerstone of Truman's military power and national security policy.

Robert S. Hopkins

See also

Airlift Operations, U.S.; Atomic Bomb; Berlin Airlift; Consolidated B-36 Peacemaker; Finletter Commission; Korean War; Massive Retaliation; National Security Act of 1947; Strategic Air Command; United States Air Force, Organizational History; Vandenberg, Hoyt S.

References

Borowski, Harry. *A Hollow Threat.* Westport, CT: Greenwood Press, 1982.

Leffler, Mel. *A Preponderance of Power.* Stanford: Stanford University Press, 1990.

TsAGI

The Soviet Union's Central Institute for Aerodynamics and Hydrodynamics (Tsentral'nyi Aero-Gidrodinamicheskii Institut). Nikolai Yegorovich Zhukovsky, the acknowledged father of Russian aviation, founded TsAGI in December 1918. It formed the scientific foundation for Soviet aircraft designs throughout the twentieth century. Zhukovsky, born in 1847, had already distinguished himself as a mathematician and engineer. He worked with Otto Lilienthal and purchased several Lilienthal gliders to use in his work in the early 1900s. Zhukovsky remained in Russia after the 1917 revolution and established the Flight Laboratory at the Moscow Higher Technical School. It was the merger of the Flight Laboratory with Red Air Fleet aircraft designers that formed TsAGI. Andrei N. Tupolev, one of Zhukovsky's best students, was among those who helped coordinate Soviet aircraft production. In addition to testing aircraft from other designers, TsAGI scientists also conducted extensive wind-tunnel tests on their own aircraft designs and worked on all elements of flight and high-speed vehicles.

As aircraft speeds increased during the 1930s, TsAGI engineers found that their wind tunnels were inadequate to simulate the real stresses the new monoplane designs encountered. If it was to build more powerful tunnels, TsAGI had to move its facilities out of Moscow to a city specially constructed for aeronautical engineering. Originally named for the man who exceeded his coal-mining norm, Stakhanov, TsAGI's new city was renamed Zhukovsky after the institute's founder. Even as TsAGI itself expanded, it also spun off new research facilities manned by its former scientists.

The German invasion of Russian on 22 June 1941 meant that TsAGI staff had to focus on rapidly clearing new aircraft to defend the Soviet Union, but it continued its research mission all the same. This work continued despite the evacuation of the facilities to Kazan and Novosibirsk. When the German defeat allowed TsAGI to relocate back to the Moscow area, a new research institute was left in place back in Siberia.

After the war, TsAGI helped develop the jet engines and airframes that made the MiG-15 and MiG-21 such lethal foes in the Korean War and Vietnam War. In addition to advanced jet fighters, TsAGI personnel helped develop Soviet strategic bombers and rockets throughout the Cold War. Research into variable-geometry wings for the MiG-23 and Su-24 helped computerize the evaluation process to a greater degree. The excellent aerodynamics and maneuverability of the MiG-29 and Su-27 owe much to TsAGI facilities. TsAGI did not focus exclusively on military aircraft; it also tested passenger aircraft such as the Il-96 and Il-114.

The collapse of the Soviet Union left the Russian Federation short on the resources needed to keep TsAGI at the cutting edge of science and technology. Like the air force that it so successfully supported for more than 80 years, TsAGI's future is difficult and uncertain.

Mark A. O'Neill

References

Greenwood, John T. "The Aviation Industry, 1917–1997." In Robin Higham, John T. Greenwood, and Von Hardesty, eds., *Russian Aviation and Air Power in the Twentieth Century.* London: Frank Cass, 1998.

Pavlov, Nikolai. "The TsAGI Timeline." *Air Fleet: Russian Air Force, Aircraft, and Space Review* no. 4 (November/December 1998). Avialable online at http://www.airfleet.ru.

Tsiolkovsky, Konstantin Eduardovich (1857–1935)

Russian-born pioneer in rocketry. Konstantin Tsiolkovsky was born on 17 September 1857 in the town of Izhevskoye. At the age of 10, he almost lost his hearing completely. Isolated from his peers, he delved into reading and speculative thinking. This led to an interest in mechanical flight and aerostatics.

As a high school mathematics and physics teacher for 40 years, he conducted studies and experiments mostly at home with small grants from the Academy of Science and others.

In 1885 at age 28, he devoted his energies to aeronautics and the theoretical development of a metal dirigible. As a result, he published, "Maneuverable Metal Dirigibles" (1892) with the help of his brother and friends. A follow-up article comparing airplanes and dirigibles appeared two years later. In 1899, he examined air resistance in "Air Pressure Upon a Surface in an Artificial Flow of Air."

In 1903, his first article on rocketry, "Exploration of Space With Rocket Devices," appeared in *Scientific Review.* That same year, he drafted the design of his first reaction-thrust model rocket utilizing liquid hydrogen and liquid oxygen to reach the limits of space. Since a tremendous amount of fuel was required to reach escape velocity, he was convinced that multistage rockets were required. During the 1920s, he expanded on these theories in more than 60 works. In 1918, he was elected as a member of the Soviet Academy. He retired from teaching at age 64 to devote his remaining years to rocketry. Space pioneers Sergei Korolyov, Hermann Oberth, and Wernher von Braun have hailed him as a prophet and an influence.

Colin A. Fries

See also

Korolyov, Sergei; von Braun, Wernher

References

Blagonrarov, Anatolii Arkadevich, ed. *Transactions of the First Lectures Dedicated to the Development of the Scientific Heritage of K.E. Tsiolkovsky.* NASA technical translation TT F-544. Washington, DC: National Aeronautics and Space Administration, 1970 .

Kosmodemianskii, Arkadii Aleksandrovich. *Konstantin Tsiolkovsky: His Life and Work.* Trans. X. Danko. Moscow: Foreign Languages, 1956.

Tunner, William H. (1906–1983)

U.S. Air Force airlift specialist. William H. Tunner was born on 14 July 1906 in Elizabeth, New Jersey. He graduated from the United States Military Academy in 1928 and went on to complete Advanced Flying School the following year. In 1941, Tunner helped organize the Army Air Corps Ferry Command. Promoted to colonel in 1942, he became commanding officer of the Ferrying Division of the Army Air Forces Air Transport Command, where he was responsible for the safe delivery of thousands of aircraft per month to Allied air forces.

In September 1944, Brigadier General Tunner took over the India-China division of Air Transport Command. Under his driving leadership, tonnage flown over the treacherous Hump air route between India and China rose sharply. This wartime service established Tunner as the military's premier airlifter.

Tunner was called upon to direct the aerial supply of Berlin in 1948–1949 as head of the Combined Airlift Task Force. Emphasizing centralized command, standardized flying procedures, and strict crew discipline, he shaped the airlift into a model of efficiency. The tonnage that his airmen poured into the isolated city proved the key to victory over the Soviet Union in the first direct confrontation between the two superpowers during the Cold War.

Shortly after the outbreak of war in Korea in 1950, Tunner was assigned to the Far East Air Force as head of Combat Cargo Command. For a third time in his career, he applied his organizational skills to the creation of a massive airlift effort, this time in support of United Nations forces during the critical early months of the conflict.

Attaining the rank of lieutenant general in 1953, Tunner became commander in chief of United States Air Forces in Europe. Between 1958 and 1960, he served as head of the Military Air Transport Service, where he waged a largely unsuccessful battle for increased funding to enhance airlift capabilities. Only later would the wisdom of his advice be recognized.

William M. Leary

See also

Berlin Airlift; Combat Cargo Command; Hump Airlift

References

Haydock, Michael D. *City under Siege: The Berlin Blockade and Airlift, 1948–1949.* Washington, DC: Brassey's, 1999.

Leary, William M. *Anything, Anywhere, Any Time: Combat Cargo in the Korean War.* Washington, DC: Office of Air Force History, 2000.

Tunner, William H. *Over the Hump.* New York: Duell, Sloan, and Pearce, 1964.

Tupolev Aircraft

One of the most important and earliest Soviet aircraft design bureaus, specializing in multiengine aircraft. In addition to its own numerous creations, Tupolev also gave birth to many of the other major Soviet design teams, including Sukhoi, Arkhangelskii, Petlyakov, Myasishchev, and others, whose chiefs and designers began their careers working under Tupolev.

Origins and Early Models

Andrei Nikolaevich Tupolev was born on 10 September 1888, the son of a lawyer active in revolutionary politics, and was himself briefly arrested in 1911. Interested in engineering, Tupolev in 1908 began to study under Nikolai Zhukovsky, the father of Russian aviation, and by the time of the revolution had become his chief assistant. Both men, with leftish sympathies, cast their lots with the Bolsheviks, and together in 1918 they founded TsAGI (Central Institute for Aerodynamics and Hydrodynamics), which became the agency responsible for directing the work of all the aviation design teams in the Soviet Union and conducting all test-flying.

In 1922, Tupolev completed his own first aircraft design, the tiny ANT-1 metal monoplane with a 35-hp engine. In 1924, he completed his second design, the ANT-2, a single-motor small transport reminiscent of the Junkers K 16. In both designs Tupolev used a new material for construction, Kolchug, a derivative of duralumin. Corrugated Kolchug construction became a Tupolev trademark until the mid-1930s.

Tupolev's first series produced design was the ANT-3 (R-3) single-engine reconnaissance biplane designed in 1925. In 1926, one of the preproduction examples made a goodwill tour of the major European capitals, the first Soviet-designed aircraft seen by the outside world. Between 30 August and 2 September, it covered a circuit of 4,443 miles in 34 hours, 15 minutes of flying time. From 1927 to 1929, 100 R-3s were produced, and they became the first Soviet-designed aircraft to see combat, flying attack missions against the Basmachi in the Central Asian Soviet Republics. At about the same time, Tupolev designed his first multiengine aircraft, the TB-1, a twin-motor corrugated Kolchug bomber whose appearance foreshadowed its younger and larger brother, the TB-3.

The TB-1 first flew at the beginning of 1926; 217 were built, including 66 with float landing gear. Though the TB-1 never saw combat, some remained in second-line use as transports throughout World War II. About this same time, Tupolev designed the ANT-5, a sesquiplane fighter that went into service as the I-4. Thus, within five years of his first struggling design Tupolev had given the Red Air Force a tactical bomber, a fighter, and a heavy bomber—all accepted into series production.

From this time on, Tupolev became a specialist in multiengine designs while Polikarpov specialized in single-motor aircraft. Tupolev's next design made history, though it brought undeserved ridicule during the war. Design of the ANT-6 began at the start of 1926, and in February 1931 it made its first flight.

This aircraft, which went into production at the end of 1931, was the world's first four-engine all-metal heavy bomber. Four motors, huge fixed landing gear, and the classic Tupolev corrugation provided strength, a speed of about 180 mph, and a range of 620–840 miles, depending on the subtype. Its original purpose was to provide long-range air support to the proletarians of the western cities, whom communist strategists of the 1930s expected would revolt at the start of the anticipated next war. The occasion and circumstances of that war proved different, and when it came both the Axis and the Western Allies derided the TB-3's obsolete appearance and performance. Still, hundreds of TB-3s were in service before the first Boeing 299 flew, and production of 819 TB-3s had been completed before a single B-17 was accepted for service.

During the summer maneuvers of 1935, hundreds of TB-3s performed the world's first mass parachute drop near Kiev before German paratroops had even made a practice jump. The TB-3 flew bombing missions against the Japanese at Lake Khasan in 1938 and at Khalkin Gol in 1939, and in

1938 six were given to the Chinese, who used them mainly for transport. During the Winter War against Finland, the TB-3 flew a number of missions against Helsinki, mostly at night.

During the difficult days of June-July 1941 the TB-3 did fly unescorted low-level daylight bombing missions against the advancing German panzers, but this was in desperation; by late summer the survivors had returned to night operations. On other occasions in 1942, TB-3s were used in badly mishandled Soviet paratroop drops. For the rest of the war they continued in the valuable job of transport. Some were still in service in August 1945 and supported the brief war against Japan.

On the heels of the TB-3, Tupolev in 1934 designed the even bigger ANT-20, the Maxim Gorky, a monster with six engines mounted on the wings and two more mounted in tandem on a pylon above the fuselage. This aircraft was intended to be the center of a propaganda squadron, but further development was abandoned when it was destroyed in a midair collision with an escorting fighter during an air show. Advanced work was begun on an even more ambitious project, the ANT-26, which would have featured eight engines mounted on the wings and four engines mounted in two pylons over the wings. This project was never completed. Other important long-range projects designed by Tupolev were the ANT-25, a long-range single-engine aircraft that achieved fame during the 1930s for several world-record flights, including the first cross-polar flight to the United States. Another distance aircraft was the twin-engine ANT-37, originally designed as a bomber; one of the developmental examples was named *Rodina* and flown by Grizodubova, Osipenko, and Raskova on their historic distance flight of 24 September 1938.

After the TB-3, Tupolev's next military design to enter service was the ANT-40 (SB), generally but incorrectly known as the SB-2. This was a fast bomber (for which "SB" is the Russian abbreviation) introducing a number of new features for a Tupolev design: stressed-metal construction instead of corrugated, retractable landing gear, and enclosed crew stations. The SB entered service in early 1936 and a few months later saw its first combat over Spain.

Known to the Soviet and Republicans as "Katyuska," the Nationalists called it the "Martin," unable to accept that such a modern design could have originated with the backward Russians. Initially the SB could be overtaken by opposing fighters only if was caught unawares and they could dive from above before it accelerated. Only with the arrival of the Bf 109 was the SB at serious risk. It saw combat against the Japanese in China from 1937, flown by Soviet volunteers and in significant numbers by Chinese crews, as well as at the clashes over Lake Khasan and Khalkin Gol. It was the main bomber used over Finland in 1939, but by then the SB was starting to show its age. Unfortunately for the SB's reputation, it still constituted the overwhelming majority of Soviet bombers at the time of the German invasion and by then was outdated. Perhaps it could have managed with an effective fighter escort, but such was not to be had in 1941 and 1942, and the SBs were massacred until relegated to nighttime missions. By late 1942, almost all had been withdrawn from action against the Germans, though the Finns continued to fly a number of captured examples until their surrender in 1944. However, others continued in service in quiet areas, and even in August 1945 a few of the 6,831 SBs built remained in service to bomb the Japanese one last time.

During the 1930s, the Stalinist purges unjustly executed millions and jailed millions more, including thousands of the country's leading military, industrial, and scientific elites. Andrei Tupolev was no exception, but he did receive exceptional treatment. He was arrested on 21 October 1937 and charged with providing the Germans with plans for the Bf 110, incredible as that sounds. About the same time, most of his senior designers and assistants were also arrested. However, instead of being shot or sent to a death camp in northern Siberia like so many others, Tupolev and his engineers were treated relatively gently and confined to a special prison in Moscow where they continued their work designing combat aircraft.

The result of this labor was the Tu-2 twin-motor bomber. With the success of this design, Tupolev was freed in July 1941, followed by the other designers. In 1943, he was awarded the Stalin Prize for this design. The Tu-2 flew shortly before the German attack, but development was delayed by a lack of suitable engines and then by the industrial displacement of the war. The first small batch was accepted for service in February 1942, but production delays and training difficulties limited its use, and only by 1944 did the Tu-2 begin to reach the front in significant quantity. By the end of the war, 1,013 had been produced. postwar production continued until 1949, when the total had reached 2,527, plus a number of trainers. During the late 1940s, the Tu-2 was supplied to the air forces of several Warsaw Pact countries. From 1950, the Tu-2 was supplied to China and later to North Korea. These Tu-2s saw combat on a couple of occasions, being badly mauled by F-86s.

Post–World War II

During 1944, the Soviet Union acquired three B-29s that had been forced to land in the Far East after missions over Japan and kept them instead of returning them to the Americans. Stalin ordered that they were to be disassembled and that a reverse-engineered exact copy should be produced for the Soviet air force. Although Tupolev argued that it would be easier and better to use the information gained to produce a new and better original design, Stalin insisted that everything be copied except for substituting Soviet standard machine guns. The resulting aircraft was designated the Tu-4 (NATO code name "Bull") and entered service with Soviet Long Range Aviation in 1948. Between 1947 and 1951, 847 examples of the Tu-4 were produced, of which 24 were later provided to China. Incapable of reaching the United States, the Tu-4 did pose a threat to positions in Europe and the Far East and gave the Soviets their first experience of a genuine independent strategic bomber force and capability of carrying nuclear munitions. From the early 1950s, it was gradually replaced by Tupolev's original designs.

The first of these new Tupolev designs was the Tu-16 (NATO code name "Badger"), which entered production in 1953 and shocked the world when it appeared over Red Square in 1954. This was a twin-jet swept-wing bomber with the engines located in the wing roots and was capable of carrying nuclear or conventional weapons at a speed of about 650 mph over a range of 3,580 miles. Later variants were able to extend range through inflight refueling, and some Tu-16s were converted to aerial tankers to provide that capability. Modified versions were able to carry air-launched cruise missiles. From the beginning, the Tu-16 entered service with both Long Range Aviation and the naval air force, and production continued until 1965, when it was terminated on the order of Nikita Khrushchev, who wanted to shift emphasis to missiles. Production reached 1,511 Tu-16s, plus several hundred more manufactured in China as the B-6. During the 1970s, many Tu-16s were reengineered and updated to carry newer cruise missiles, to serve as electronic-warfare and reconnaissance aircraft, and to perform still other tasks.

In the early 1950s, a modification of the Tu-16 gave the Soviet Union its first civilian jet airliner. During the 1960s, large numbers of Tu-16s were exported to Soviet allies. In addition to pattern aircraft delivered to China in 1959, Indonesia received 26 Tu-16s, of both the bomb- and missile-carrying variants. Egypt received about 60 Tu-16s during its alliance with the Soviet Union, the first batch being wiped out on the ground in 1967, the others seeing action during the Continuation War and in 1973. Iraq received more than 20, and these flew some missions against Israel and then Iran. They were finally finished off during the 1991 Gulf War. In Soviet service, Tu-16s were active throughout the Cold War, patrolling near NATO borders, shadowing the U.S. fleets, and sometimes making dummy attacks on aircraft carriers. During the mid-1980s, they flew combat missions over Afghanistan; for this purpose, the missile carriers were retrofitted with conventional bomb racks. The Tu-16 remained in service until 1994.

Although the Tu-16 was intended as a theater bomber, the Tu-95, sometimes in the West mistakenly called the Tu-20, was a true intercontinental bomber. At a time when U.S. bombers had switched to swept wings and jet engines and had virtually abandoned defensive guns, the Tu-95 featured a unique combination: a swept wing, four huge turboprop engines with contrarotating propellers, and three gun turrets each with twin 23mm cannons. Western analysts immediately dismissed the plane (NATO code name "Bear") as an example of backward Russian technology. They felt much more threatened by the Myasishchev jet bomber (NATO code name "Bison"), which appeared a year earlier. In truth, they had it backward. Only 125 Bisons were produced between 1954 and 1962; the Bear, in 18 variants, remained in production until 1994, with about 400 airframes produced and many older airframes rebuilt and modernized, and it remains in useful service into the twenty-first century with no retirement date. The initial version of the Tu-95 carried free-fall nuclear bombs, but later versions were armed with a variety of nuclear and/or explosive cruise missiles. From 1960 to 1969, 53 Tu-95RTs (Bear D) were built for Soviet naval electronic reconnaissance, and their shape became even stranger with the addition of a huge bulbous pod under the belly. These aircraft became regular companions of U.S. carrier groups.

The last bombers, the Bear H, were built from 1980 to 1992, equipped with AS-16 cruise missiles. During the 1970s, another variant of the Bear appeared with a new designation—Tu-142 (Bear F). The Tu-142 was a major redesign and modernization of the original Tu-95, intended solely for the Soviet navy, which used it as a very-long-range antisubmarine-warfare aircraft, though during the 1980s a half-dozen were sold to the Indian navy; many of the 85 built for the Soviets remain in use. The very last version of the Bear was introduced into production only in 1989; 12 Tu-142MRs were built as strategic communications aircraft towing extremely-low-frequency cables to communicate with nuclear submarines on patrol. Although there were never as many Soviet bombers built or in service at one time as the West often feared, and though the Bear would have had trouble penetrating the NORAD system at its peak, it remains, alongside the B-52, one of the classic successes of Cold War aeronautics, loved by Russian pilots not even born when their bomber was built. An additional development of the Tu-95 must also be mentioned—the Tu-126. This was the Soviet Union's first AWACS aircraft; nine were built in the 1960s, serving until replaced by newer models in the 1980s.

During this period Tupolev designed more than just military aircraft. The Tu-16 was developed into the Tu-104, the first Soviet jet airliner, and the Tu-95 became the Tu-114, which gained fame transporting Khrushchev to New York in

1959. Together with a later series of jet airliners, the Tu-124, Tu-134, Tu-154 and Tu-204 have been built in big numbers—more than 2,300 aircraft, plus another 17 examples of the striking failure, the Tu-144 "Concordskii."

The intended successor of the Tu-16 was the Tupolev Tu-22 (NATO code name "Blinder"), a supersonic bomber with two engines mounted in pods above the rear fuselage. From 1960 to 1969, 311 were built, about half for the navy. The Tu-22 was built for free-fall bombing and as a missile carrier and also as an electronic-reconnaissance platform. During the 1970s, small numbers were provide to Iraq and Libya, the latter losing at least a couple during combat in Chad. A few Soviet Tu-22s, primarily the electronic-warfare versions, saw combat over Afghanistan, mainly in support of bombing missions by the Badger and Backfire. By the early 1990s, the type had been retired from service.

At the same time, Tupolev built one more fighter design, the Tu-128P (NATO code name "Fiddler"), a very-long-range missile-armed interceptor. Though an interceptor, it was large enough to be a Tupolev creation and bore a superficial resemblance to the Tu-22 Blinder. Between 1961 and 1966, 198 were built and then based at northern air bases with the mission of intercepting USAF cruise-missile carriers over the Arctic regions—long before they could get within launching distance of Soviet territory. The last of these aircraft were replaced during the late 1980s.

The next Tupolev bomber, known as the "Backfire" to NATO, again caused major controversies in the West. Even its designation has been controversial. Originally it was identified as the Tu-26, but Soviet sources insisted that it was the Tu-22M, a modified version of the Tu-22. However, Andrei Tupolev said that this was a deception strictly for political purposes. The Tu-22M Backfire has nothing in common with the Tu-22 Blinder beyond a design bureau. Backfire is a large transonic bomber with variable-sweep wings and is capable of carrying either conventional bombs or nuclear cruise missiles. When Backfire began entering service in small numbers in the mid-1970s, it caused near-panic in the West, and the United States alleged it was a new intercontinental bomber, pointing to its inflight refueling apparatus, and argued that even though the Backfire could not bomb the continental United States and return home, it could fly a one-way mission landing in Cuba or that the crews might be sent on one-way missions and sacrificed—not an implausible tactic in the event of a nuclear war. The Soviets dismissed these concerns as provocations and insisted that the Tu-22M was an intermediate-range bomber, a successor to the Tu-16 in the roles of European and Asian theater strike and naval cooperation. Finally, in the SALT II Treaty, the Soviets agreed to limit production of the Tu-22M to 30 per year and to remove the aerial-refueling apparatus. In the event, the Soviets did gain from the deception. The Tu-22M was produced until 1993, when about 500 had been completed, and it has seen combat of a sort unexpected by its designers (during the war in Afghanistan, subsequently against guerrillas in Tajikistan and Chechnya).

The final Tupolev bomber was the Tu-160 (NATO code name "Blackjack"), a variable-sweep supersonic bomber with intercontinental range. This bomber entered production only in 1989 as a replacement for the Tu-95 Bear, just as the Cold War Was ending. Although it is reported to handle and fly well, there have been persistent reports about incurable difficulties in its weapons, navigation, and electronic-warfare suites. Only 38 had been produced when the Soviet Union dissolved, and 20 were taken over by Ukraine, leading to a 10-year dispute over ownership between Ukraine and Russia. Eventually, lack of maintenance and the Tu-160's poor serviceability have defused the dispute.

During the postwar period, Andrei Tupolev remained active until almost the very end of his life. He died on 23 December 1972 and was succeeded by his son Aleksei as chief designer until 1992. With the end of the Cold War, Tupolev remains an active design bureau specializing in large aircraft but now concentrates on designing airliners.

George M. Mellinger

See also

Boeing B-29 Superfortress; Grizodubova, Valentina; Khalkin Gol Air Battles; Petlyakov Aircraft; Raskova, Marina Mikhaylovna; Spanish Civil War; Taran; Winter War

References

Gunston, Bill. *The Encyclopedia of Russian Aircraft, 1875–1995.* Osceola, WI: Motorbooks International, 1995.

______. *Tupolev Aircraft Since 1922.* London: Putnam, 1995.

Kerber, L. L. *Stalin's Aviation Gulag.* Washington, DC: Smithsonian Institution Press, 1996.

Tuskegee Airmen

A famous unit of African American combat pilots who served during World War II. Despite pressure from the black press and the National Association for the Advancement of Colored People, African Americans were prohibited from serving in the Army Air Corps throughout the 1930s. In 1939, African Americans were admitted to the government-sponsored Civilian Pilot Training Program (CPTP), but no black graduates were allowed to enlist in the Air Corps. Finally, in January 1941 the Air Corps announced the formation of its first black combat unit: the 99th Pursuit Squadron. Training was to commence at a new Air Corps field to be built in the vicinity of Tuskegee, Alabama.

Listening intently to the great "Chief," C. Alfred Anderson, these men are history in the making: the Tuskegee Airmen. Third from the left is Benjamin O. Davis Jr., who would lead the Tuskegee Airmen into combat. (U.S. Air Force)

This location meant that black trainees would have to live and work within the heart of the unreconstructed South. Many loathed the segregationist precedent, but officials, as well as the pilots themselves, saw an opportunity to prove their critics wrong. The "Tuskegee Airmen" quickly received a flood of national media attention, and it soon became apparent that much was riding on their success or failure. They would operate under intense public scrutiny for the entire war.

Training of enlisted support personnel soon began at the Air Corps Technical School at Chanute Field, Illinois, and in July 1941 the first class of pilots began military aviation training at Moton Field. All were previous CPTP graduates, with the exception of Captain Benjamin O. Davis Jr., son of the first black general in the history of the U.S. military. The younger Davis had endured four years at the U.S. Military Academy before graduating in 1936, and in 1941 the Davises were the only two nonchaplain black officers in the regular Army.

Captain Davis was rapidly promoted to lieutenant colonel and, in August 1942, assumed command of the 99th Fighter Squadron. An AAF inspecting general reported in October 1942 that the 99th was in excellent condition and ready for immediate departure overseas, but the unit was permitted only to continue training; by early 1943 morale had suffered considerably. Finally, in April 1943 the 99th Fighter Squadron shipped out for North Africa.

By June, the 99th was operating over the Mediterranean, but Allied aircraft already dominated the area, and contact with Germans was infrequent. In July, the squadron downed its first enemy aircraft, but a long dry spell followed throughout the rest of 1943. This was not surprising given the circumstances, but opponents of the "Tuskegee experiment" recommended, based upon the supposed poor performance of the 99th, that it be reassigned to noncombat duties. This recommendation was endorsed by officials throughout the chain of command, all the way up to the commanding general of the AAF, General Henry "Hap" Arnold.

In October 1943, Colonel Davis argued before the War Department's Advisory Committee on Negro Troop Policies that the 99th's combat record was comparable to similar white units and, further, that it had accomplished this despite the unique pressures it had to operate under. Further attacks from AAF leadership were undercut by the obvious success of the 99th following its transfer to the more active Italian Theater.

On 16 January 1944, during intense combat in the skies over the Anzio beachhead, the 99th Fighter Squadron downed a total of eight German Fw 190 fighters, suffering the loss of two Curtiss P-40s. The squadron continued to perform well in the combat that followed, but by mid-February German air activity had again tapered off and the 99th returned to ground support. Throughout February and March, the 99th was gradually joined in Italy by the all-black 332d Fighter Group, which when fully deployed eventually comprised the 99th, 100th, 301st, and 302d Fighter Squadrons, all now under the command of Colonel Davis. The new squadrons of the 332d first deployed with obsolete Bell P-39s, but beginning in April they began to receive very capable Republic P-47 Thunderbolt. In late June, the 332d began its conversion to the top Allied air superiority aircraft of the day, the North American P-51 Mustang, and by the end of the summer the Tuskegee Airmen had assumed as their primary mission the job of escorting friendly bombers, often deep into the heart of Germany.

Throughout the rest of 1944, the 332d earned a reputation as one of the better fighter groups in Europe. Bomber crews soon coveted the protection of the "Red Tails" (as they affectionately became known, due to their P-51s' distinctive paint jobs), and in fact by war's end the 332d had the unique distinction of being the only fighter group to have never lost a bomber to enemy aircraft. By late 1944, it was apparent that the Tuskegee Airmen had earned the respect of their fellow white units; although individual acts of discrimination did continue, their treatment by the chain of command was on the whole fairly good. They received widespread and very positive publicity within the United States and were even visited by numerous celebrities, including Lena Horne and Joe Louis. Their success continued into 1945: During one March escort mission to Berlin, pilots of the 100th Fighter Squadron downed three of the new German Messerschmitt Me 262 jet fighters; during another escort mission the following month, P-51s of the 332d downed 12 German aircraft for the loss of only three of their own. During its peak period of combat, from August 1944 through April 1945, the 332d destroyed approximately 500 enemy aircraft in the air and on the ground. Tuskegee Airmen received numerous decorations for bravery, including the Legion of Merit, Silver Star, 14 Bronze Stars, and more than 150 Distinguished Flying Crosses; in March 1945 the 332d Fighter Group received the Distinguished Unit Citation. These accomplishments did not come without a cost, however: Of the approximately 1,000 black pilots trained at Tuskegee, 66 were killed in action, 32 were taken prisoner, and some 80 pilots and support personnel were killed in training and other noncombat accidents through 1946.

The combat record of the Tuskegee Airmen is remarkable given the obstacles they had to overcome: racism in the service, segregation, lack of opportunity, and discrimination at home. Through it all Colonel Davis was their leader, the cornerstone of their success.

But the fate of the 477th Bombardment Group, many of whose pilots were also trained at Tuskegee, provides a different and instructive example. The unit was moved numerous times during 1944 and 1945 without seeing combat. In April 1945, approximately 60 black pilots from the 477th were arrested for entering a white-only officers club at Freeman Field, Indiana; later, 101 officers of the 477th were arrested when they refused a direct order to sign a document essentially acquiescing to the segregation of officers clubs. A subsequent investigation concluded that white-only facilities violated Army regulations. Due in part to the so-called Freeman Field mutiny, the 477th was never allowed into combat.

Following the end of the war, the 332d Fighter Group gradually returned to the United States, where most of its elements were disbanded as part of the general postwar demobilization; the rest were absorbed into what was now known as the 477th Composite Group. In 1946, the Army quietly closed Tuskegee Army Air Field. The influence of the Tuskegee Airmen, however, resonated for generations within the U.S. Air Force and American society in general. The 1948–1949 desegregation of the U.S. military owed much to the success of the 332d Fighter Group and the disgrace of the officers of the 477th Bombardment Group. Former Tuskegee Airmen continued to play important roles in the postwar Air Force, including most notably Benjamin O. Davis Jr., who retired as a three-star general, and Daniel "Chappie" James, who flew more than 60 combat missions during the Vietnam War and became the first African American to achieve four stars.

By the mid-1990s, African Americans represented more

than 5 percent of the officer corps and 17 percent of the enlisted personnel in the U.S. Air Force. Recent years have seen an explosion of interest in the Tuskegee Airmen, and in November 1998 President Bill Clinton approved a congressional resolution authorizing the creation of the Tuskegee Airmen National Historic Site at Moton Field in Tuskegee, Alabama.

David Rezelman

See also

Air Superiority; Bell P-39 Airacobra and P-63 Kingcobra; Curtiss P-40 Warhawk; Davis, Benjamin O. Jr.; James, Daniel "Chappie"; Mediterranean Theater of Operations; North African Campaign; North American P-51 Mustang; Republic P-47 Thunderbolt; STRANGLE; U.S. Army Air Forces; World War II Aviation

References

Davis, Benjamin O. Jr. *Benjamin O. Davis, Jr., American: An Autobiography.* Washington, DC: Smithsonian Institution Press, 1991.

Dryden, Charles W., with a Foreword by Benjamin O. Davis Jr. *A-Train: Memoirs of a Tuskegee Airman.* Tuscaloosa: University of Alabama Press, 1997.

MacGregor, Morris J. Jr. *Integration of the Armed Forces, 1940–1965.* Defense Studies Series. Washington, DC: Center of Military History.

Sandler, Stanley. *Segregated Skies: All-Black Combat Squadrons of World War II.* Washington, DC: Smithsonian Institution Press, 1992.

Scott, Lawrence P., and William M. Womack Sr. *Double V: The Civil Rights Struggle of the Tuskegee Airmen.* East Lansing: Michigan State University Press, 1994.

Twining, Nathan F. (1897–1983)

U.S. Air Force Chief of Staff; chairman of the Joint Chiefs of Staff at a time when massive nuclear retaliation developed into U.S. national strategy. Oddly, Twining was not being groomed for these weighty positions, as he planned to retire a lieutenant general in charge of the Alaskan command. It is to Twining's great credit that he adapted quickly and with considerable diplomacy to discharge these duties. Crucial among them was the balancing act necessary between the services as the Air Force, especially the Strategic Air Command, which received an increasing share of the budget and operational responsibilities. President Dwight Eisenhower's selection of Twining to chair the Joint Chiefs, effective 15 August 1957, reaffirmed the president's confidence in Twining to assuage interservice rivalries as well as limit defense demands on a budget that Eisenhower wanted to keep small.

Twining was the first Air Force Chief of Staff to visit the Soviet Union, where he attended a military parade intended to demonstrate Soviet military capability. General Twining retired on 30 September 1960.

Robert S. Hopkins

See also

ARC LIGHT; Cold War; Strategic Air Command

References

Bright, Charles D., ed. *Historical Dictionary of the U.S. Air Force.* New York: Greenwood Press, 1992.

U

Udet, Ernst (1896–1941)

Famous German fighter ace of World War I; chief of Luftwaffe supply and procurement and then head of the Luftwaffe technical office (1939–1941). Udet enlisted in the German army in 1914, learned to fly in 1915, and ended the war as a squadron leader in the fighter wing established by Manfred von Richthofen. His 62 aerial victories were second only to von Richthofen's total and won him the Pour le Mérite. Udet left the service after the Armistice, formed an aviation company, and became well known on both sides of the Atlantic as a stunt pilot and a genial bon vivant. He joined the Luftwaffe in 1935 at the urging of friend Hermann Goering. He was rapidly promoted to full general, but his performance as the head of the technical branch is widely considered to have been disastrous. On 17 November 1941, worn down by the carping of Goering and Milch, Udet put a pistol to his head and killed himself.

Donald Caldwell

See also

German Air Force (Luftwaffe)

References

Cooper, M. *The German Air Force, 1933–1945: An Anatomy of Failure.* London: Jane's Information Group, 1981.

Corum, J. *The Luftwaffe: Creating the Operational Air War, 1918–1940.* Lawrence: University Press of Kansas, 1997.

Ugaki, Matome (1890–1945)

Vice admiral in the Imperial Japanese Navy (IJN); a major force behind the attack on Pearl Harbor. Born on 15 February 1890 in Okayama Prefecture, Ugaki graduated from the naval academy in 1912. He served at sea, graduated from the staff college in 1923, and then joined the IJN general staff. He studied in Germany, commanded battleships, and was promoted to rear admiral in 1938.

In August 1941, Ugaki became Chief of Staff of Combined Fleet under Admiral Yamamoto Isoroku. He was involved in planning the Pearl Harbor attack and all other Combined Fleet operations until he and Yamamoto were shot down over Bougainville on 18 April 1943. Ugaki survived, seriously wounded, and returned to Tokyo to recuperate (Yamamoto did not survive).

Ugaki took command of the First Battleship Division on 25 February 1944 and fought at the Battle of the Philippine Sea and through the Leyte campaign.

Ugaki in February 1945 became commander of the Fifth Air Fleet, controlling remaining Japanese naval air forces on Kyushu, the front-line defense of the home islands. Emulating Rear Admiral Takijiro Onishi's example from the Philippines, he formed the Special Attack Corps (Tokkotai) to conduct kamikaze attacks on the U.S. Fleet. The Tokkotai was heavily engaged at Okinawa, using both standard production naval aircraft and specialized rocket-propelled suicide attackers launched from medium bombers.

After Okinawa's capture, Ugaki was engaged in refitting Fifth Air Fleet preparatory to repelling an invasion of Kyushu itself. On 15 August 1945, the Japanese emperor broadcast his decision to surrender. Ugaki, determined to die in the Tokkotai spirit, led an abortive suicide attack on the U.S. Fleet off Okinawa.

Paul E. Fontenoy

See also

Cape Engano, Battle of; Coral Sea, Battle of the; Eastern Solomons, Battle of; Guadalcanal; Japanese Naval Air Force, Imperial; Kamikaze Attacks; Leyte Gulf, battle of; Midway, Battle of; Okinawa; Pearl Harbor; Philippines; Santa Cruz, Battle of; Yamamoto, Isoroku

References

Dull, Paul S. *A Battle History of the Imperial Japanese Navy, 1941–1945.* Annapolis, MD: Naval Institute Press, 1978.

Evans, David C., and Mark R. Peattie. *Kaigun: Strategy, Tactics, and Technology in the Imperial Japanese Navy, 1887–1941.* Annapolis, MD: Naval Institute Press, 1997.

Goldstein, Donald M., and Katherine V. Dillon, eds. *Fading Victory: The Diary of Admiral Matome Ugaki.* Pittsburgh: University of Pittsburgh Press, 1991.

Ultra

The term applied to the successful breaking of the German Enigma (and later the Japanese Magic) machine codes during World War II. The German navy began using Enigma in 1926, the German army two years later, and the Luftwaffe only in 1935. The code was partially cracked by Polish intelligence in the 1930s, and work continued at England's Bletchley Park ("Station X"), with an emphasis on breaking German U-boat codes to protect Allied convoys.

In mid-1943, British and U.S. authorities agreed to cooperate on code-breaking activities, with the British concentrating on German and Italian codes, the Americans on Japanese codes. By the end of 1943, Bletchley code-breakers were providing more than 80,000 Enigma decrypts per month. As U.S. officers served as liaisons for U.S. forces, more air force–related intelligence resulted from Bletchley's "Hut 3" facility, considerably aided by poor Luftwaffe communications security. Even by 1943, however, Ultra was but one of many inputs into target selection for USAAF and RAF strategic bombing of Germany, as Enigma was not normally used to communicate industrial activity.

Ultra did provide insight into the impact of such bombing and offered details on Luftwaffe intent, organization, and, by 1944, declining operations. Ultra became the standard used to compare and evaluate other intelligence. Yet even by the end of the war, only 25–30 officers at the Eighth Air Force were cleared for Ultra intelligence along with a mere handful at Ninth Air Force headquarters. This was because security factors were uppermost in applying Ultra knowledge to military actions; thanks to such success, the Germans never learned their codes had been compromised. Enigma/Ultra intelligence remained highly classified until the early 1970s, partially because the British shared captured Enigma machines with other nations for decades after the war and could thus read their codes.

Christopher H. Sterling

See also

Air Technical Intelligence; Magic; Signals Intelligence; U.S. Army Signal Corps; Y-Service

References

Parrish, Thomas. *The Ultra Americans: The U.S. Role in Breaking the Nazi Codes.* Briarcliff Manor, NY: Stein and Day, 1986.

Putney, Diane T., ed. *ULTRA and the Army Air Forces in World War II.* USAF Warrier Studies. Washington, DC: U.S. Government Printing Office, 1987.

United Aircraft

U.S. aviation and aerospace corporation from 1934 to 1975; predecessor of the modern-day United Technologies. United Aircraft Corporation (UAC) exemplified the industrial foundation from which airpower is based. The design, development, and construction of sophisticated military aeronautical products required extensive investment in both facilities and personnel and a dependence on government contracts. Centered on a vast industrial complex near Hartford, Connecticut, UAC sustained itself as a primary contractor to the U.S. military for 40 years and provided the engineering and financial leadership that solidified its position in the ever-expanding U.S. military-industrial-research complex.

UAC has its origins in the Pratt and Whitney Company, founded in 1925 by Frederick B. Rentschler and other former Wright Aeronautical Corporation employees. They designed the Wasp radial engine, which was a key technology in the establishment of modern military and commercial aviation in the 1920s and 1930s. Rentschler envisioned the formation of a combine that represented a full-service approach to manufacturing, selling, and transportation within the entire aviation industry. Rentschler and airframe manufacturers William Boeing and Chance Vought organized the United Aircraft and Transport Corporation (UATC) in February 1929. The primary corporate members were Pratt and Whitney, Boeing, Vought, Sikorsky, the Hamilton Standard Propeller Company, and United Air Lines. UATC dominated the manufacturing and transportation segments of the U.S. aviation industry until airmail scandals and accusations of a UATC monopoly led to the division of the corporation in 1934.

The UAC, consisting of Pratt and Whitney, Vought, Sikorsky, and Hamilton Standard, persisted to remain the most successful U.S. aviation manufacturing combine of the 1930s. The corporation was a primary contractor to the U.S. government for airframes, engines, and propellers. During the aggressive world rearmament of the late 1930s, UAC also maintained a vigorous business through the licensing of its products to foreign nations, including France, Germany, Great Britain, and Japan.

During World War II, UAC was a primary military contractor. UAC manufactured an unprecedented quantity of airframes and propulsion systems for trainers, fighters, bombers, and transports. Hamilton Standard–designed propellers constituted more than 75 percent of all propellers used by Allied forces during the war. Pratt and Whitney produced 50 percent of the nation's total aerial horsepower in World War II. UAC achieved this through licensed production, which allowed nonaviation manufacturers to manufacture UAC products for the war effort. Sikorsky-built helicopters were the only U.S. types to see service in World War II.

UAC continued to be a leader in military aerospace technology after the war. The corporation's state-of-the-art research center employed many of the leading aerospace engineers of the twentieth century. Pratt and Whitney oversaw the introduction of the new jet-propulsion technology with the highly successful J-57 turbine, which powered early military turbojet aircraft such as the B-52, KC-135, and F-100. In the late 1950s, UAC began developing missiles, rockets, and spacecraft and acquired Norden, a manufacturer of advanced avionics. Military contracts dominated UAC's production and sales until the early 1970s. When the corporation began to diversify its product base into nonmilitary markets in 1975, UAC changed its name to United Technologies Corporation.

Jeremy R. Kinney

See also

Boeing Company; Civil Aviation, and Impact of Military Advances; Engine Technology; Propellers; Sikorsky, Igor I.; U.S. Aircraft Development and Production (World War I); Vought Aircraft

References

Fernandez, Ronald. *Excess Profits: The Rise of United Technologies.* Reading, MA: Addison-Wesley, 1983.

Horner, Horace M. *The United Aircraft Story.* New York: Newcomen Society of America, 1958.

Rae, John B. *Climb to Greatness: The American Aircraft industry, 1920–1960.* Cambridge: MIT Press, 1968.

United States Air Force: Organizational History

The National Security Act of 1947 established the Department of the Air Force on 18 September 1947. W. Stuart Symington, who had been serving as the assistant secretary of war for air, became the first Secretary of the Air Force, and General Carl A. Spaatz became the first Air Force Chief of Staff. Under law the civilian hierarchy was to have precedence over the military, but Symington considered the military the competent authority in training and readying forces for war. Symington envisioned his role as being the spokesman for the Air Force when pursuing its goals in Congress.

The newly created department authorized the Office of the Secretary of the Air Force, an undersecretary, and two assistant secretaries. More significant was the coequal status gained by the secretary and the USAF Chief of Staff with their counterparts in the Departments of the Army and Navy.

This status was not attained easily. It was the fruition of years of effort by advocates of airpower and a separate air arm. Army aviation activities ran the gamut: U.S. Army Signal Corps balloon observation in the Civil War and Spanish-American War; the foundation of the Signal Corps Aeronautical Division in 1907; the awarding of the first airplane contract (to the Wright brothers) in 1909; the establishment of the Signal Corps Aviation Section in 1914; and the valiant efforts of the 1st Aero Squadron during the Punitive Expedition against Pancho Villa in Mexico in 1916 and 1917.

On the eve of U.S. entry into World War I, the Army's air arm found itself ill-equipped and ill-prepared. It also failed to achieve its expansion goals by the spring of 1918. A reorganization seemed essential, and on 20 May 1918 President Woodrow Wilson ordered the War Department to establish the Air Service. This entity consisted of two agencies: one under a civilian head to deal with the manufacturers; the other under a military officer for training and organizing units. This structure was further streamlined in August 1918 when President Wilson appointed John D. Ryan as an aviation czar to strengthen the system.

The U.S. Army Air Service did enjoy some success in its brief World War I experience. With Major General Mason Patrick organizing the Air Service and Brigadier General William "Billy" Mitchell in charge of air combat, the air arm found immediate work flying reconnaissance missions, which proved valuable in locating enemy troop formations supporting U.S. ground forces. In air-to-air encounters, U.S. pilots made a good showing, with 71 American aces (those achieving five or more kills). Captain Eddie Rickenbacker led the way with 26 victories. During seven months of combat, U.S. air forces launched some 150 bombing missions and claimed 756 enemy aircraft and 76 balloons destroyed, losing 289 aircraft, 48 balloons, and 237 crewmen.

The achievements of World War I helped nurture a movement to establish an independent air force. But the U.S. Army's leaders viewed the airplane primarily as a support weapon for the infantry and relegated the Air Service to a status similar to the field artillery and engineers. In addition, between 1920 and 1926 attempts to legislate needed changes in the nation's air defense were blocked by a jurisdictional conflict with the Air Service on one side and the War Department and the Navy on the other.

During this period a series of boards and commissions studied and restudied the air organization issue, culminating in the Army Air Corps Act of 1926. Although the act did not grant independence or autonomy, it did establish the Army Air Corps, granting it more personnel, aircraft, and prestige than its predecessor. The act also called for Air Corps representation on the Army General Staff and reestablished a second assistant secretary (assistant secretary of war for air). F. Trubee Davison was the first to hold this position; he remained until 1932, when he ran for lieutenant governor of New York.

Despite opposition to a separate service and a paucity of funding (felt by all the services), the Air Corps managed significant achievements during the interwar period. In concert with record-breaking flights in speed, distance, and endurance accomplished by civilian and military fliers alike, an Air Corps doctrine of precision bombing of industrial targets by heavily armed long-range bombers began to emerge in the Air Corps Tactical School.

A major reorganization in March 1935 established the General Headquarters Air Force, which allowed the Air Corps to achieve unified command over its combat units. This command, headed by Brigadier General Frank M. Andrews, a bomber enthusiast and advocate of an independent air force, succeeded in removing combat air units from the control of local commanders by obtaining jurisdiction over all questions relating to the organization of units, maintenance of aircraft, as well as operation of technical equipment, maneuvers, and training.

Despite efforts by the Army General Staff to obtain larger appropriations for the air arm during the mid-1930s, the aircraft inventory in the Air Corps fell in 1936; Congress authorized it to purchase only a few of the new four-engine B-17s specifically designed for strategic bombing. As late as 1938, only 13 B-17s were in the inventory.

With the onset of World War II, the fortunes of airpower and its advocates changed as accounts from Europe in 1939 and 1940 presaged the dominant role of the airplane in war. On 20 June 1941, a further reorganization occurred when Major general Henry H. "Hap" Arnold, chief of the Air Corps, became chief of the Army Air Forces and assumed command of the Air Force Combat Command (as General Headquarters Air Force had been renamed). Less than a year later, in March 1942, Arnold became commanding general, AAF, which made him coequal with the commanders of the Army ground forces and services of supply. Arnold now reported directly to the Chief of Staff of the Army, General George C. Marshall, and both agreed that the AAF would have full autonomy within the War Department but that any move toward an independent Air Force would be postponed until the end of the war.

In the meantime, the civilian side of the Air Corps boosted its cause with the April 1941 appointment of Robert A. Lovett to assistant secretary of war for air, which had been vacant since Davison's departure. Lovett, an investment banker who had served in the naval Air Service during World War I, had retained a keen interest in aviation throughout the interwar years. Although not actually granted statutory power to direct procurement, Lovett was encouraged by Secretary of War Henry L. Stimson to promote aircraft production. While advising Stimson, Lovett worked closely with military leaders and was free to voice opinions on a variety of questions outside the formal chain of command.

From April 1940 until the end of World War II, Lovett was concerned that nothing should threaten industry's adherence to realistic aircraft production schedules. He attempted to settle labor disputes and at times intervened when the Office of Production Management and, subsequently, the War Production Board were at odds with AAF contractors, subcontractors, and suppliers. During the war, Lovett acted as a sounding board for industry complaints and requests. Henry L. Stimson had a clear conception of Lovett's role, telling him, "Whatever authority the Secretary of War has, you have."

Lovett and Arnold formed a partnership in fashioning the AAF into the world's most powerful air force. Indeed, beginning with 20,000 men and 2,400 aircraft in 1939, by war's end the AAF comprised 2.4 million personnel, and U.S. industry produced almost 160,000 aircraft, including the B-17 Flying Fortress, B-24 Liberator, and B-29 Superfortress—the workhorses of the European and the Pacific theaters; the P-47 Thunderbolt and the P-51 Mustang fighters; and the C-47 Skytrain transport. The tremendous increase in size necessitated a reorganization that replaced Air Force Combat Command with four air forces in the continental United States. This force was subsequently complemented with 12 additional overseas air forces.

After the war, the AAF and its newly appointed assistant secretary of war for air, Stuart Symington, worked toward independence. As the AAF demobilized, Symington sought to instill cost-control measures to coincide with an austerity-minded Congress and the public. He believed the AAF "had an unusual opportunity to look toward efficiency, no past heritages, no barnacled procedures to first overcome." He and General Carl A. Spaatz, the new AAF Chief of Staff, worked toward the goal of a 70-group postwar Air Force.

Independence was finally realized with the passage of the National Security Act in July 1947. The Air Force had previously created three major combat commands in the United States: Strategic Air Command, Tactical Air Command, and Air Defense Command. SAC, under Commanding General Curtis E. LeMay (1948–1957), became the dominant Air Force command. Even though the Military Air Transport

Service played the key role in airlifting supplies during the Berlin Airlift and tactical air forces were built up during the Korean War, SAC maintained first call on USAF resources. Leaving office in April 1950, Symington was disappointed at not attaining a 70-group Air Force. However, the Korean War provided a spurt in funding for a larger air force, new weapons systems, and more personnel, permitting Air Force Secretary Harold E. Talbott (1953–1955) to concentrate on other important issues such as military housing.

During the 1950s, three pieces of legislation diminished the authority of the secretary of the Air Force. The 1949 amendments gave more power to the secretary of defense by granting him an undersecretary and three assistant secretaries. The secretary of the Air Force, along with the other service secretaries, lost their seats on the National Security Council, where they had been coequal with the secretary of defense. The 1953 Reorganization Act further eroded the power of the service secretaries by adding six more assistant secretaries to Defense. Next, the 1958 Reorganization Act took the service secretaries out of the direct chain of operation (combat) command, which now ran from the president and secretary of defense through the Joint Chiefs of Staff to the unified and specified commands, making the service secretaries responsible for operations support such as training and logistics. Secretary of Defense Robert S. McNamara, appointed by President John F. Kennedy, took full advantage of the powers granted by this legislation.

In addition to the huge Korean War buildup of a 95-wing air force under the leadership of Air Force Secretary Thomas K. Finletter and Chief of Staff Hoyt S. Vandenberg, the 1950s also witnessed the advent of missile technology. The missile program was advocated by Trevor Gardner, an Air Force special assistant for research and development, and implemented by Brigadier General Bernard A. Schriever. Schriever founded the Space and Ballistic Missiles Organization and later became commander of Air Force Systems Command. Under Schriever, the Air Force developed the Atlas, Titan, and Minuteman long-range missiles and established the basis for the Air Force space program.

The retrenchment in personnel and equipment following the Korean War buildup was somewhat alleviated by the technological advancements in both missiles and satellites in response to advances by the Soviet Union, the country's Cold War nemesis. In 1957, spurred by the shock of Sputnik and fears of a missile gap, SAC began the process of complementing its bomber fleet with land-based missiles. By the end of the 1960s, more than 1,000 ICBMs were on alert as bomber numbers dwindled. Thus, the air force possessed two key legs—strategic bombers and land-based missiles—of the important "Triad" (the Navy fielded the third leg: submarine-launched ballistic missiles). In the meantime, TAC benefited from the Kennedy administration's emphasis on conventional forces that could respond to several protracted conventional conflicts under the sheltering nuclear umbrella.

In Southeast Asia, U.S. strategy was to hold off North Vietnam until South Vietnam became a viable nation able to defend itself. During the Vietnam War (1965–1973), the United States dropped three times the number of bombs that it did during World War II. During Operation ROLLING THUNDER (March 1965–October 1968), the air campaign against North Vietnam, the Air Force faced a formidable air defense system. Hampering its efforts were restrictive rules of engagement such as a 30-mile restricted area around Hanoi. ROLLING THUNDER caused about $2 billion in losses to the North Vietnamese economy at the expense of perhaps $2 billion in U.S. aircraft, but it failed in its purpose to thwart the communist efforts in the South.

Supplying and transporting troops was a major Air Force mission. This charge, as well as ensuring that service personnel were properly equipped, trained, and deployed, became, according to Air Force Secretary Eugene M. Zuckert, the role of the secretariat. Secretary of Defense McNamara took advantage of the legislation of the previous decade that had dampened the powers of the service secretaries to assert the centralized authority of his office. This was particularly troubling for Zuckert, who had witnessed the previous power of the secretariat as Symington's assistant secretary and also for the man who had constructed SAC, General Curtis E. LeMay. The Air Force Chief of Staff, who remained ultimately responsible for the day-to-day activities of the organization, also served on the Joint Chiefs of Staff. Thus, Air Force C-47 Skytrains, C-119 Boxcars, C-123 Providers, and C-130 Hercules maneuvered vast supplies about the jungle terrain while C-141 Starlifters and C-5 Galaxies, assisted by commercial airlines, moved troops and supplies from the United States to Vietnam. SAC B-52 bombers and tactical forces assisted the U.S. and South Vietnamese armies in South Vietnam and struck at North Vietnamese Army supply lines along the Ho Chi Minh Trail and in southern Laos, where their air strikes supported counterinsurgency efforts of the Laotian government. In addition, operations over Cambodia were designed to support the war in South Vietnam.

After the war, the Air Force had to adjust to tighter budgets and simultaneously build its strategic forces and maintain readiness in Europe, a theater that had been neglected during the conflict in Southeast Asia. In 1970, Secretary of Defense Melvin Laird popularized the term "Total Force" to describe the relationship between the active duty and reserve components.

John L. McLucas became Air Force secretary as the Vietnam War ended; he viewed his role as repairing the wreckage caused by equipment losses and dampened morale. He, along with his Chiefs of Staff, General George S. Brown and then General David C. Jones, sought to concentrate on newer weapons systems such as the B-1, F-15, and F-16 while in some cases selecting from rival prototypes to avoid the blunders experienced with the C-5A and FB-111 during the previous decade. In light of dwindling monies, General Jones professed a policy of "readiness," meaning streamlining headquarters organization and pursuing the development of high-tech weapons. Budgetary restraints had an effect throughout the force as training and flying-hour retrenchments led some to label the middle to late 1970s as the era of the "Hollow Force."

After taking office in January 1981, President Ronald Reagan announced an extensive effort to modernize the Air Force's strategic forces. The B-1B program, canceled in 1977, was revitalized, and the bomber reached initial operational capability in September 1986. The Air Force modified its B-52G and H models to carry air-launched cruise missiles, and it modernized its ICBM force by deploying Peacekeeper (formerly MX) missiles in Minuteman silos. Two stealth aircraft flew for the first time during the decade: the F-117A fighter-bomber (flying in June 1981) and the B-2A strategic bomber (1989).

The Reagan administration also devoted considerable attention to space. Air Force Space Command was activated on 1 September 1982, and the following March, Reagan introduced the Strategic Defense Initiative (SDI, or "Star Wars"), a wide-ranging effort to investigate technologies that could contribute to a missile shield. The Air Force transferred its SDI efforts to the Strategic Defense Initiative organization in 1994. Today it is more commonly known as Ballistic Missile Defense.

From the early to mid-1980s, Air Force budgets enjoyed five years of unprecedented double-digit growth, enabling Air Force Secretary Verne Orr (1981–1985) to concentrate on people-oriented issues such as housing and the advancement of women. The 1980s also witnessed a trend toward jointness among the services that was spurred by the Goldwater-Nichols Act. Both of Orr's chiefs of staff, General Charles A. Gabriel and then General Larry D. Welch, supported this effort even though this act reduced their power as well as that of the other service chiefs in favor of the chairman of the Joint Chiefs. Earlier, on 22 May 1984, General Gabriel and his Army counterpart, General John A. Wickham Jr., had signed a landmark agreement on 31 joint initiatives that the Army and Air Force had identified as essential to supporting affordable and effective air-land combat forces.

When Iraq invaded Kuwait in August 1990, President George Bush mobilized an international coalition and ordered U.S. military units to execute Operation DESERT SHIELD, an enormous deployment of forces to defend Saudi Arabia. Within six weeks Air Force cargo aircraft bought more tonnage (in terms of ton mileage) to Southwest Asia than they had carried during the entire 15-month Berlin Airlift. The DESERT SHIELD air transporters eventually moved 500,000 passengers and nearly 500,000 tons of dry cargo a third of the way around the world in about seven months.

On 17 January 1991 local time, the United States and its allies began Operation DESERT STORM to liberate Kuwait. The Gulf War that followed was remarkable for it brevity, relatively low Coalition casualties, and decisive results. The Air Force component of United States Central Command, United States Central Air Forces (CENTAF), provided the centerpiece of victory. The war lasted only 43 days, 39 of them devoted to a stunningly successful Coalition air campaign against targets throughout Iraq and the Kuwaiti Theater of Operations (southern Iraq and Kuwait). CENTAF aircraft destroyed Iraq's air defenses, crippled its electrical-source infrastructure, and leveled many of its nuclear, biological, and chemical warfare facilities. Coalition air attacks against Iraqi forces made possible the rapid success of the ground campaign that followed.

With the end of the Cold War, the Air Force entered another era of austerity: fiscal year 1992 and 1994 budgets showed -10.0 and -8.5 percentages of real decline. With a reduced force structure as well as a blurring of the distinction between strategic and tactical missions—which had been evident during the Gulf War—Air Force Undersecretary Donald Rice and Chief of Staff General Merrill McPeak began to reorganize several major commands. On 1 June 1992, the Air Force activated Air Combat Command, which combined all of Tactical Air Command assets with most of Strategic Air Command and a small portion of Military Airlift Command (MAC). On the same day, Air Mobility Command, which blended most of MAC's force structure with SAC's tankers, came into existence. Finally, Air Force Materiel Command, combining the resources of Air Force Systems Command and Air Force Logistics Command, was activated a month later. Although downsizing and retrenchment was part of the reorganization, the USAF adopted the expansive slogan "Global Reach—Global Power" and considered its future role as the guarantor of world stability.

Meanwhile, General McPeak responded to the downsizing mandated by Congress and the Clinton administration by setting out to reorganize the Air Force. In addition to major command restructuring, he experimented with different wing-level organization concepts, including the composite wing and the objective wing. McPeak stressed the heritage of the Air Force in determining which units would be retained and which ones would be cut.

McPeak's successors, Generals Roland R. Fogleman and Michael E. Ryan, fine-tuned this process: Fogleman supported a "Global Engagement" long-range plan and a "core values campaign"; General Ryan encouraged establishment of an Aerospace Expeditionary Force (AEF) capable of rapid deployment and ready to meet any global challenge. Ryan saw 10 AEFs each deployed for 90 days every 15 months with two AEFs on call at all times. Congress did not provide the sustained funding that his plan required, and at the turn of the century the Air Force was definitely a smaller force. Yet Congress—the engine for change—seemed to agree that the Air Force had been sufficiently downsized.

The beginning of the U.S. war on terrorism in the fall of 2001 changed the entire equation. The USAF was thrust into the front lines of an air campaign against an entrenched enemy in Afghanistan. The action carried significant implications for future military budgets and priorities.

George M. Watson Jr.

References

Davis, Richard G. *Carl A. Spaatz and the Air Force in Europe.* Washington, DC: Center for Air Force History, 1993.

Futrell, Robert F. *Ideas, Concepts, Doctrine: Basic Thinking in the United States Air Force, 1907–1984.* 2 vols. Maxwell AFB, AL: Air University Press, 1989.

Gropman, Alan L. *The Air Force Integrates, 1945–1964.* Washington, DC: Office of Air Force History, 1978.

Hallion, Richard P. *Storm Over Iraq: Air Power and the Gulf War.* Washington, DC: Smithsonian Institution Press, 1992.

Mark, Eduard. *Aerial Interdiction: Air Power and the Land Battle in Three American Wars.* Washington, DC: Center for Air Force History, 1994.

Maurer, Maurer. *Aviation in the U.S. Army, 1919–1939.* Washington, DC: Office of Air Force History, 1987.

______. *The U.S. Air Service in World War I.* Washington, DC: Office of Air Force History, 1978.

Nalty, Bernard C., ed. *Winged Shield, Winged Sword: A History of the United States Air Force, 1907–1997.* Vols. 1–2. Washington, DC: Air Force History and Museum Program, 1997.

Nalty, Bernard, John G. Shiner, and George Watson. *With Courage: The U.S. Army Air Forces in World War II.* Washington, DC: Air Force History and Museum Program, 1994.

Schaffel, Kenneth. *The Emerging Shield: The Air Force and the Evolution of Continental Air Defense, 1945–1960.* Washington, DC: Office of Air Force History, 1991.

Watson, George M. Jr. *The Office of the Secretary of the Air Force, 1947–1965.* Washington, DC: Center of Air Force History, 1993.

______. *Secretaries and Chiefs of Staff of the United States Air Force: Biographical Sketches and Portraits,* Washington, DC: Air Force History and Museum Program, 2001.

United States Air Forces in Europe (USAFE)

United States Air Forces in Europe has its origins in the Eighth Air Force from World War II. Established as the Eighth Air Force on 19 January 1942, activated on 28 January 1942, and designated Eighth Air Force on 18 September 1942; designated United States Strategic Air Forces in Europe on 22 February 1944. These organizations were responsible for planning and executing the U.S. strategic bombing plan against Nazi Germany from England as well as bases in the Mediterranean.

On 7 August 1945, the organization was designated United States Air Forces in Europe. Between 22 January 1951 and 1 July 1956, USAFE was identified as a specified command by the Joint Chiefs of Staff. USAFE was headquartered at Lindsey Air Station, Weisbaden, West Germany, until March 1973, when it moved to Ramstein AB, West Germany. USAFE headquarters is colocated with NATO's Allied Air Forces Central Europe (AIRCENT). The USAFE commander commanded both USAFE and AIRCENT.

The Berlin Airlift was the first real test of USAFE. Major General Curtis E. LeMay, USAFE commander, directed Major General William H. Tunner to establish an air bridge into Berlin. Subsequently, General Tunner developed and implemented the Air Logistics Service to provide scheduled deliveries of critical materiel throughout the European and Mediterranean areas.

With the formation of NATO, USAFE took on an even greater role in showing Western resolve against the ever-growing communist threat in the region. By the end of 1951, USAFE's responsibilities had expanded in Europe and eventually extended to French Morocco, Greece, Italy, Libya, Spain, Saudi Arabia, and Turkey. When Spain withdrew from NATO in 1967, all foreign troops were directed to leave their nation, resulting in a major restructuring of NATO.

When the Soviets began deploying mobile tactical nuclear weapons into Warsaw Pact nations adjacent to Western Europe, President Ronald Reagan called for a showdown. The USAF deployed ground-launched intermediate-range missiles to USAFE bases. This threat resulted in the Intermediate Range Nuclear Forces Treaty, ratified in 1988, that mandated the first-ever elimination of an entire class of weapons from U.S. and Soviet inventories. The Soviet missiles were withdrawn from their forward locations and dismantled, as were the U.S. weapons. By March 1991, the last of these missles were removed from Comiso Air Station, Italy.

During Operation DESERT SHIELD and Operation DESERT STORM, USAFE deployed more than 180 aircraft and 5,400 personnel; 100 aircraft and 2,600 personnel were deployed for Operation PROVEN PEACE staging out of Turkey. The command also established numerous aeromedical staging facilities in the event they were needed for combat in the Gulf region.

The Third Air Force, based in England, served as host for Strategic Air Command rotational forces during the 1950s through the 1980s. The Sixteenth Air Force, originally a SAC unit, was established at Torrejon AB, Spain, to support SAC operations in the region between 1956 and 1966.

During the Vietnam War, USAFE hosted Air National Guard (ANG) tanker units deploying to Europe to fulfill America's aerial refueling commitments for NATO while SAC tankers fought in the war. These ANG deployments were flown under Operation CREEK PARTY.

With the end of the Cold War, USAFE lost 67 percent of its operational bases; however, the organization continues to serve as a staging site for contingency operations and humanitarian relief missions throughout the region. Currently, USAFE controls two numbered air forces (Third Air Force at RAF Mildenhall, England; and Sixteenth Air Force, at Aviano). USAFE's main operating bases are RAF Lakenheath and RAF Mildenhall in England, Ramstein and Spangdahlem Air Bases in Germany, Aviano Air Base, Italy, and Incirlik Air Base, Turkey.

Alwyn T. Lloyd

See also

Air National Guard; DESERT SHIELD; DESERT STORM; LeMay, Curtis E.; North Atlantic Treaty Organization; STRATEGIC AIR COMMAND; Tunner, William H.

References

Lloyd, Alwyn T. *A Cold War Legacy: A Tribute to Strategic Air Command, 1946–1992.* Missoula, MT: Pictorial Histories, 2000.

Ravenstein, Charles A. *The Organization and Lineage of the United States Air Force.* USAF Warrior Studies. Washington, DC: Office of Air Force History, 1986.

United States Army Air Corps (USAAC)

Early aviation branch (1926–1941) of the U.S. Army. The U.S. Army Air Corps was established on 2 July 1926, as the Air Service had fallen into neglect during the years following World War I. By the mid-1920s, the Air Service had dwindled to the point of near nonexistence. Underfunded, undermanned, and underequipped, it had less than 1,000 officers and possessed only 60 pursuit and 169 observation aircraft. Most significantly, the Air Service had few bombers.

Because of the obvious need to improve and expand the air arm, President Calvin Coolidge in September 1925 appointed a board, headed by Dwight W. Morrow, to come up with a more efficient way to employ aircraft in the national defense. Although a congressional committee (the so-called Lampert Committee) had already proposed a unified air force independent of the Army and Navy, the report issued by the Morrow Board rejected that idea. Instead, it recommended that the Air Service be more prestigiously named and given representation on the U.S. Army General Staff. In addition, an assistant secretary of war for air affairs was to be appointed. The resulting Air Corps Act of 1926 officially put these recommendations into effect, creating the U.S. Army Air Corps.

Over the next few years, the sad state of the Air Corps improved somewhat, although the Depression significantly

The Boeing P-26 "Peashooter" was a transitional aircraft. The all-metal monoplane retained the open cockpit and fixed gear of its biplane predecessors. (U.S. Air Force)

slowed the planned expansion program. By 1931, a long-proposed flight center in San Antonio had been established, with the Air Corps Training Center located at the newly commissioned "West Point of the Air"—Randolph Field. A materiel division was also established at Wright Field, Dayton, Ohio, where technical and logistical experts began to set the stage for the future greatness of U.S. airpower. Other subordinate Air Corps agencies included technical, balloon/airship, and tactical schools. By 1939, the Air Corps roster had increased to 23,455 men and by 1941 to 150,000.

In terms of technical accomplishments, the USAAC also saw significant progress during the late 1920s and throughout the 1930s. Although the numbers of aircraft increased only nominally to 2,177 by 1939, numerous revolutionary advances were made. Aircraft engines improved in power-to-weight ratios, and wood-and-fabric open-cockpit biplanes gave way to sleek all-metal enclosed monoplanes. Other significant improvements included the variable-pitch propeller and retractable landing gear, as well as much-improved all-weather and nighttime navigational instrumentation. These changes collectively resulted in increased speeds, altitudes, and endurance, as well as greater load-carrying, bombing, and defensive capabilities.

With increased aircraft performance came an opportunity to demonstrate growing missions capability. Several record-setting flights were accomplished, including the 2,418-mile nonstop flight of the *Bird of Paradise* by Lester Maitland and Albert Hegenberger from California to Hawaii in 1927, the 151-hour endurance flight of the *Question Mark* by Carl Spaatz, Ira Eaker, and Elwood Quesada in 1929, and the 8,290-mile round-trip by a B-10 bomber formation flight from Washington, D.C., to Alaska and back, led by Lieutenant Colonel Henry "Hap" Arnold in 1934.

Even with such striking successes and technical improvements, the USAAC continued to lag behind many other countries—some of which were already preparing for the next world war—in airpower capability. This inadequacy was tragically emphasized by the airmail fiasco of 1934. When U.S. Postmaster James Farley cancelled government airmail contracts with commercial carriers in February of that year, the Air Corps was tasked to take over the overwhelming job of delivering the mail. USAAC pilots gamely took on the assigned mission without proper aircraft, equipment, training, experience, and organizational skills. By the time USAAC mail flights ended three months later, 12 Army fliers had been killed in 66 accidents, driving home the inadequacies of the Air Corps in the eyes of the American public. If there was a positive consequence, it was that Congress allocated funds for much-needed upgrades in Air Corps equipment and training.

Another important development of the mid-1930s was the creation—on the recommendation of a board chaired by a former secretary of war, Newton Baker—of the General Headquarters Air Force (GHQ AF) on 1 March 1936. The GHQ AF was made up of air combat units capable of operating independently or in cooperation with ground forces. Although it was viewed by some as a step toward an independent air mission and organization, it still kept the air arm under Army command—a sore point for many Air Corps leaders.

In the late 1930s, the most significant USAAC efforts centered around developing into a large, modern air force with global capabilities. Only this would ensure an airpower mission independent of surface forces. These efforts were boosted by the development of the new Boeing B-17 "Flying Fortress" heavy bomber. This revolutionary aircraft—destined to become the dominant symbol of American airpower—was heavily funded during this period, unavoidably at the expense of fighter development.

Unfortunately, some opposition was encountered by the U.S. Army General Staff, desperately in need of funds; consequently, critical funding for the mighty B-17, as well as other needed aircraft, was withheld until the rearmament process began just prior to World War II. Finally, in 1939 Congress authorized $300 million for the Air Corps to more than triple its existing paltry inventory of aircraft up to a total of 5,500; by 1940 this number was increased to almost 13,000. Likewise, pilot-training requirements were eventually increased a hundred-fold over previous levels.

As the USAAF rapidly expanded in the months leading up to World War II, its importance to national defense was realized. In November 1940, General Hap Arnold took on the dual role of acting deputy Chief of Staff for air, as well as chief of USAAC. By early 1941, U.S. Army Chief of Staff George Marshall wisely decided that the air arm needed more unity and authority, so he forcefully pushed forward a general reorganization. Army Regulation 95-5, issued on 20 June 1941, joined the USAAC with the newly named Air Force Combat Command (formerly GHQ AF) and other units to form the U.S. Army Air Forces. Although the Air Corps technically existed until the National Security Act of 1947, which established the U.S. Air Force, it was effectively superseded by the USAAF in 1941. The U.S. Army Air Corps had, however, over the preceding 15 years taken the air arm from near extinction to what would soon become the most formidable air force ever known.

Steven A. Ruffin

References

Goldberg, Alfred, ed. *A History of the United States Air Force.* New York: Arno, 1974.

Maurer, Maurer. *Aviation in the U.S. Army, 1919–1939.* Washington, DC: Office of Air Force History, 1987.

Nalty, Bernard C., ed. *Winged Shield, Winged Sword: A History of the United States Air Force.* Vol. 1. Washington, DC: Air Force History and Museum Program, 1997.
Shiner, John F. *Foulois and the U.S. Army Air Corps, 1931–1935.* Washington, DC: Office of Air Force History, 1983.

United States Army Air Forces

The World War II–era American air forces (1941–1947); replaced by the independent U.S. Air Force in 1947.

On 1 August 1907, the U.S. Army tackled the issue of airpower in military operations by assigning the Signal Corps oversight of ballooning, air machines, and all kindred subjects. At the time, the Signal Corps Aviation Section boasted four members; it took two years to receive its first aircraft. In March 1913, Signal Corps created the first air squadron in Texas City, Texas. The commander of that squadron was Major Benjamin Foulois; the squadron flew 540 courier and reconnaissance missions.

Shortly after the United States entered World War I in April 1917, President Woodrow Wilson signed the Aviation Act, which apportioned more money to military aviation. In August 1918, President Wilson created the U.S. Army Air Service. The Army Reorganization Act of 1920 made the Air Service a combatant arm of the Army.

The Air Corps Act of 1926 changed the Air Service to the U.S. Army Air Corps. On 1 March 1935, General Headquarters Air Force assumed command of U.S.-based Air Corps tactical units that previously existed under regional Army Corps commanders. As Germany, Japan, and Italy began to build up their armed forces, the Air Corps and the rest of the Army remained a small peacetime organization with little money for expansion or upgrades. After Adolf Hitler launched World War II by invading Poland, the Air Corps began to grow steadily, swelling from 21,000 to 354,000 members, with similar growth in the number of bases, units, and aircraft.

On 20 June 1941, the Department of War created the United States Army Air Forces. Field Manual 100-20 (*Command and Employment of Air Power,* 1943), proclaimed land and airpower were coequal and interdependent, with neither an auxiliary of the other, thereby creating a de facto air force.

By 1944, 16 numbered air forces had taken form, the first four protecting the eastern and western continental United States. In December 1941, the Philippine Department Air Force, which survived the Japanese attack on The Philippines, became Fifth Air Force, headquartered in Australia. In February 1942, Sixth Air Force was formed to defend the Panama Canal and for antisubmarine warfare. The Hawaiian Air Force became Seventh Air Force in February 1942. Also in February 1942, Eighth Air Force went to England to fly bombing raids with RAF Bomber Command. In September 1942, the new Ninth Air Force moved to Egypt. Tenth Air Force was formed in Ohio before moving in March 1942 to operate in the China-Burma-India Theater. Later, the China Air Task Force (including Claire Chennault's "Flying Tigers"), which led guerrilla-style air raids against the Japanese and later flew missions over the Himalayan Hump was designated Fourteenth Air Force. The Eleventh Air Force was formed from the Alaskan Air Force to protect the United States and Canada and to recover the Aleutian Islands from the Japanese. The Twelfth Air Force stood up in August 1942 and moved to England to participate in the invasion of North Africa. In December 1942, Thirteenth Air Force began operating out of several Pacific locations such as the Solomon Islands, New Guinea, the Philippines, the Marianas, Midway, the Caroline Islands, Iwo Jima, Japan, and the Marshall Islands. Fourteenth Air Force served mainly in China after it stood up in March 1943. Fifteenth Air Force activated in Tunisia on 1 November 1943 and began combat operations the next day. Twentieth Air Force, formed by General Henry H. "Hap" Arnold, answered directly to the Joint Chiefs of Staff. Composed of B-29 strategic bombers, its goal was breaking the Japanese Empire and setting the course for a postwar Air Force. The Twentieth changed the course of modern warfare when two of its B-29s dropped the first atomic bombs on Hiroshima and Nagasaki.

World War II was the defining moment for airpower, with its importance growing as theater commanders incorporated it into their operations. Airpower changed the way war was fought, and that power was wielded by the United States Army Air Forces. The Army Air Corps began the war with more than 2,000 members and a few hundred planes. Five years later, the Army Air Forces had nearly 2.4 million airmen and almost 80,000 aircraft. It remains the largest air force ever assembled.

Based on USAAF success in World War II, as well as the possibilities for its future, President Harry S. Truman signed the National Security Act of 1947. The historic legislation created the National Military Establishment—it would later become the Department of Defense—with three executive departments—the Army, Navy, and Air Force. Truman signed the Act while flying on his presidential airplane—*Sacred Cow*—which was operated by the USAAF.

Diane Truluck

See also

Foulois, Benjamin D.

References

Boyne, Walter J. *Beyond the Wild Blue: The History of the United States Air Force, 1947–1997.* New York: St. Martin's, 1997.
Craven, Wesley F., and James L. Cate, eds. *The Army Air Forces in World War II, Volume 1: Plans and Early Operations, January 1939 to August 1942.* Washington, DC: Office of Air Force History, 1983.

Nalty, Bernard C., ed. *Winged Shield, Winged Sword: A History of the United States Air Force.* Vol. 1. Washington, DC: Air Force History and Museum Program, 1997.

Nalty, Bernard C., John F. Shiner, and George M. Watson. *With Courage: The U.S. Army Air Forces in World War II.* Washington, DC: Air Force History and Museum Program, 1994.

U.S. War Department. Field Manual FM 100-20, *Command and Employment of Air Power.* Washington, DC: U.S. Government Printing Office, 1944.

United States Army Air Service

Early designation for the American air forces (1918–1926). Until the spring of 1918, the U.S. Army Signal Corps retained control of military aviation. This relationship had evolved because of the Signal Corps's interest in combining observation balloons with the telegraph to provide intelligence. The growth of aviation caused a series of reorganizations within the Signal Corps: the Aeronautical Division (1907) and the Aviation Section (1914). Shortly after the U.S. Congress declared war in 1917, it passed an unprecedented appropriation bill of $64 million to build a mighty air force. President Woodrow Wilson separated aviation from the Signal Corps to solve coordination problems by creating the Bureau of Military Aeronautics in May 1918, but this agency did not control aircraft procurement. Consequently, in August 1918 Wilson appointed a civilian director of air service to coordinate both functions. After the war, a major general replaced the civilian director.

During the early postwar period, Brigadier General William "Billy" Mitchell crusaded for a separate and unified air force. He did not achieve his goal, but a greater degree of autonomy was achieved with the creation of the U.S. Air Corps by act of Congress in 1926.

Bert Frandsen

See also

Mitchell, William; U.S. Army Air Corps

References

Morrow, John H. Jr. *The Great War in the Air: Military Aviation from 1909 to 1921.* Washington, DC: Smithsonian Institution Press, 1993.

Nalty, Bernard C., ed. *Winged Shield, Winged Sword: A History of the United States Air Force.* Vol. 1. Washington, DC: Air Force History and Museum Program, 1997.

United States Army Signal Corps

Created by Congress in 1860, the Signal Corps had responsibility for all signal duty, and all books, papers and apparatus connected therewith. Under this broad mandate, the Signal Corps expanded its communications methods to include employing captive balloons as portable observation platforms. With the invention of the airplane, heavier-than-air operations also became part of the Corps's mission.

In 1907, the chief signal officer established the Aeronautical Division and issued specifications soliciting bids for a flying machine. Only the Wright brothers delivered a plane, which the Army purchased in 1909. Funding and personnel shortages hampered the Signal Corps's aeronautical efforts. Flight-training initially took place at College Park, Maryland. There the Army's earliest pilots, among them Lieutenants Frank P. Lahm, Benjamin D. Foulois, and Henry "Hap" Arnold, earned their wings. By 1913, the Signal Corps had abandoned balloon operations, and the formation of the 1st Aero Squadron received official sanction.

In July 1914, Congress established the Signal Corps Aviation Section, headed by Lieutenant Colonel Samuel Reber. The 1916 Punitive Expedition into Mexico provided aviation's first real test. General John J. Pershing expected planes to find Pancho Villa and direct troops to capture him. But the 1st Aero Squadron's fragile underpowered machines could not cope with the high altitudes and strong winds of the Mexican mountains. Although they did not find Villa, the pilots performed reconnaissance, delivered messages, and took aerial photographs.

World War I proved to be the first air war. European nations, however, possessed air forces that far surpassed the U.S. force. By placing aviation within the Signal Corps, the Army had focused on aviation's reconnaissance function rather than its combat potential. Consequently, the Army had no combat aircraft and the nation had virtually no aviation industry in April 1917. Military and government leaders mistakenly assumed that the automotive industry could quickly convert to aircraft production. Meanwhile, General John Pershing, who did not believe that aviation should be part of the Signal Corps, created the separate Air Service within the American Expeditionary Forces. Although this arrangement worked well overseas, it complicated matters at home. Promises of production went unfulfilled, and U.S. pilots remained dependent on European airframes. The one bright spot was the development of the Liberty engine.

Decentralized control and lack of clear direction proved fatal to the Signal Corps's aviation program. The Corps and its wartime chief, Major General George O. Squier, received considerable criticism and scrutiny. After several investigations, President Woodrow Wilson removed aviation from the Signal Corps in May 1918 and placed it under the secretary of war's direct control. The Signal Corps retained responsibility only for airborne radio.

Under its communications umbrella, the Signal Corps fostered the development of military aviation within the United States. But as aviation's combat role became predominant, the break from its parent Signal Corps became inevitable. Separation was the first step toward the establishment of the independent Air Force in 1947.

Rebecca Robbins Raines

See also

Arnold, Henry H. "Hap"; Foulois, Benjamin D.; Pershing, John Joseph; Reber, Samuel; Squier, George Owen

References

Chandler, Charles de Forest, and Frank P. Lahm. *How Our Army Grew Wings: Airmen and Aircraft before 1914.* Chicago: Ronald Press, 1943.

Hennessy, Juliette A. *The United States Army Air Arm, April 1861 to April 1917.* Rpt. Washington, DC: Office of Air Force History, 1985.

Raines, Rebecca Robbins. *Getting the Message Through: A Branch History of the U.S. Army Signal Corps.* Washington, DC: U.S. Government Printing Office, 1996.

United States Navy

Naval aviation officially began on 8 May 1911 when Captain Washington Irving Chambers submitted a requisition for two aircraft to be built by Glenn Curtiss.

Before that, on 14 November 1910, Eugene Ely, a civilian pilot, took off in a 50-hp Curtiss plane from a wooden platform built over the bow of the light cruiser USS *Birmingham* anchored in Hampton Roads, Virginia. On 18 January 1911, Ely, flying a Curtiss pusher, landed on a specially built platform aboard the armored cruiser USS *Pennsylvania* at anchor in San Francisco Bay.

In July 1919, the Naval Appropriations Act provided for the conversion of the collier *Jupiter* into a ship specifically designed to launch and recover airplanes at sea. It was commissioned as the USS *Langley,* the nation's first aircraft carrier. The engineering plans for this conversion were modified in November 1919 and included catapults to be fitted on both the forward and aft ends of the deck. The USS *Ranger* was the first ship of the U.S. Navy to be designed and built as an aircraft carrier; the ship was commissioned on 4 June 1934.

In addition, during the late 1920s and early 1930s the Navy introduced a rigid airship program. The Navy saw these as long-range scouts and launch platforms for Sparrowhawk fighters. The program never got up to speed because of two devastating crashes. The *Akron* crashed on 3 April 1933, killing 73 men, including Admiral William Moffett, a strong supporter of the program. The second crash, the *Macon* on 12 February 1935, took four Sparrowhawk

Boeing fighters had a pugnacious look, as exemplified by this F4B-2. (U.S. Navy)

fighters down with it; all but two of the crew survived the crash.

The development of aircraft carriers and carrier operations sparked a revolution in military affairs, completely and irrevocably changing the prosecution of war at sea. But that would not occur until 1941.

On 7 December 1941, carrier aircraft of the Japanese Imperial Navy launched a devastating attack on Pearl Harbor and the military and air installations in the area. The three aircraft carriers of the Pacific Fleet were at sea and were spared attack. With this attack, the face and philosophy of naval aviation changed forever. The great dueling battles between battleships became obsolete virtually overnight. Dramatic and historic events would follow.

In April 1942, the USS *Hornet* launched 16 B-25 bombers in an attack against the Japanese mainland led by Lieutenant Colonel James Doolittle. The famous Doolittle Raid lifted sagging American morale and shocked the Japanese. In May 1942, the Battle of the Coral Sea saw the first large-scale battle involving naval aircraft. In June 1942, at the Battle of Midway, the Japanese navy lost four carriers, one cruiser, 250 aircraft, and 3,500 personnel, most to naval aviation. The United States lost one carrier (*Yorktown*), 132 aircraft, and 300 men. Most historians say Midway marked the turning point of the Pacific War. At the Battle of the Mariana Islands, the Japanese lost two carriers and about 300 aircraft to U.S. Navy and Marine pilots.

Naval aviation was also an integral part of the island-hopping campaign waged by U.S. ground forces. Whether preceding or during a battle, Navy aircraft supported the ground forces with bombing and strafing runs.

On 3 October 1942, the Navy took delivery of the first production models of the F4U Corsair. Over the course of the next 10 years, until the last one rolled off the Chance-Vought assembly line in Dallas in December 1952, the aircraft would live up to its nickname—"Swift Ship"—although its domain was the clouds rather than the sea. During World War II, Corsair pilots downed 2,140 Japanese aircraft, achieving an 11:1 kill ratio.

The atomic age arrived over Hiroshima and Nagasaki in August 1945. USAAF generals attempted to diminish the Navy's role in aviation by declaring long-range bombers equipped with atomic weapons had made conventional forces obsolete. The National Security Act, signed by President Harry S. Truman on 18 July 1947, furthered the bomber barons' clout by creating the independent U.S. Air Force.

In postwar America, the military services engaged in debates over their respective roles and missions. By far the bitterest pitted the Navy against the Air Force. The Navy believed that the atomic mission could be carried out partially from the decks of carriers and managed to obtain funding for a 1,090-foot flush-deck supercarrier to be called USS *United States.* The Air Force argued that money for the ship would be better spent on a fleet of giant B-36 bombers.

The years following World War II also marked a time of transition for naval aviation. With dwindling defense budgets and bitter interservice rivalry, the very existence of sea-based airpower was questioned. Strategic bombing employing the atomic bomb had supplanted the Navy as the nation's first line of defense and minimized the importance of tactical aviation. The severity of the situation was such that by mid-1950 a carrier fleet that numbered 98 at the end of World War II had been reduced to 15.

The so-called revolt of the admirals essentially preserved naval aviation's role in the postwar world, yet new carriers would be needed to implement it. Experience was demonstrating that existing carriers, designed to launch and recover propeller-driven aircraft, were having difficulty handling jet aircraft. On 30 October 1950, the secretary of the Navy approved a budget that included provisions for a new large-deck carrier. In its final form, the 1,036-foot, 60,000-ton carrier possessed a look all its own, featuring a small island structure, angled deck, and more powerful steam catapults capable of operating the Navy's largest heavy bombers. On 1 October 1955, the U.S. Navy commissioned its first supercarrier, USS *Forrestal.*

On 25 June 1950, North Korean tanks and troops swarmed across the 38th Parallel into South Korea in an attack that took the world by surprise. In keeping with a subsequent resolution by the United Nations Security Council, President Harry S. Truman committed U.S. military forces to battle. On 3 July 1950, USS *Valley Forge,* in concert with the British carrier HMS *Triumph,* launched the first naval air strikes of the war, attacking facilities at Pyongyang. In this engagement, U.S. Navy F9F-2 Panthers scored naval aviation's first jet kills, shooting down two North Korean Yak-9 aircraft. Eleven large attack carriers, one light carrier and two escort carriers took part in the conflict. Navy and Marine pilots provided close ground support throughout the war.

By July 1953, when the cease-fire was signed, U.S. Navy and Marine Corps aircraft had logged 189,495 sorties. Jets had successfully demonstrated their value in combat, and the helicopter had come of age as a transport and search-and-rescue platform. Most important, the aircraft carrier had demonstrated its value as a flexible platform for power projection in a limited war, a role that continues to this day.

Though the Korean War marked the dawn of the jet age, propeller-driven aircraft like the F4U Corsair and AD Skyraider logged 75 percent of all offensive sorties flown by carrier aircraft. The Corsair lived up to its World War II reputation as a tremendous close air support platform. Ten communist aircraft fell to Corsair guns during the Korean War, including a MiG-15 jet fighter. The Skyraider demonstrated its versatility in supporting troops or knocking out significant targets. In the latter mission it was greatly aided by the fact that it could carry as much ordnance as a B-17 Flying Fortress. The two mainstays in Navy and Marine Corps jet squadrons were the F9F Panther, a rugged aircraft built by Grumman, and the F2H Banshee by McDonnell.

The Navy lost its first aircraft over North Vietnam, an F-8, during a photoreconnaissance mission. Throughout the war, carriers stationed in the Gulf of Tonkin and the South China Sea provided close air support against the Vietcong and North Vietnam. Perhaps the crowning moment for naval aviation was during the fall of Saigon in April 1972. In an 18-hour period, Marine Corps helicopter pilots air-lifted more than 7,000 American and Vietnamese civilians from the U.S. Embassy compound to carriers waiting offshore.

In the early 1970s, the Navy introduced the F-14 Tomcat, and the Marine Corps accepted the AV-8 V/STOL Harrier. At the end of the decade, a new fighter-attack aircraft, the F/A-18 Hornet, was undergoing flight-trials. The submarine threat was confronted by the addition to the fleet of the Light Airborne Multipurpose System (LAMPS), which combined shipboard electronics with the SH-2D helicopter. During the 1970s, two nuclear super carriers, *Nimitz* and *Eisenhower,* were commissioned; *Carl Vinson* was launched.

As 1980 ended, the latest LAMPS version was under test in a new naval airframe, the SH-60B Seahawk. In addition, at decade's end the Navy's latest heavy-lift helicopter, the CH-53E, was ready for acceptance by a Marine Corps squadron. They are still operational in 2001.

In 1990, during Operation DESERT SHIELD, carrier- and land-based Navy aircraft provided logistical, reconnaissance, and interdiction duties during the buildup of Coalition forces. On 16 January 1991, the beginning of Operation DESERT STORM, Navy aircraft launched from carriers in the Red Sea and Persian Gulf. DESERT STORM saw the first combat use of the Navy McDonnell-Douglas F/A-18. DESERT STORM ended on 27 January 1991, but Navy and Marine aircraft continued to patrol the no-fly zones over Iraq after the turn of the century.

As of 2001, there were 12 aircraft carriers in the Navy's fleet. Nine were nuclear-powered, and the other three were fuel oil–powered. A thirteenth carrier, USS *Ronald Reagan,* will join the fleet in 2003. Naval aviation also played a significant role during the U.S. War on terror that began in 2001.

Henry M. Holden

References

Knott, Richard. "U.S. Naval Aviation at 90." *Aviation Week and Space Technology* (9 April 2001).

Unmanned Aerial Vehicles

Conveyances maintained in flight by aerodynamic lift and directed without an onboard crew. Remotely piloted vehicles and drones are the most common types of unmanned aircraft, but missiles and satellites also fall into this category.

Unmanned aircraft, distinct from piloted machines, became feasible with technological advances in aerodynamics and engines. The United States, Great Britain, France, and Germany experimented with uninhabited aircraft before World War II, with modest success. During the war, Germany successfully developed and employed the world's first cruise missile—the F2G76 pilotless aircraft better known to the world as the V-1. The United States also experimented with unmanned aircraft, developing time-expired bombers and the JB-2, a copy of the V-1 that became the basis for America's postwar program in uninhabited vehicles.

After World War II, airpower doctrine placed emphasis on the offensive capacity of unmanned platforms, insisting that missiles and automated machines would supersede manned aircraft. Consequently, missile research and development received great impetus in the United States, Europe, and the Soviet Union. Confidence in missiles continued through the 1950s and 1960s but waned gradually in the face of changing geopolitical circumstances, military realities, and financial constraints.

By the 1970s, unmanned vehicles, aside from crude missiles, had assumed largely defensive or support roles. The United States and the Soviet Union increasingly employed satellites for communications, surveillance, and navigation. During the Vietnam War, the United States Air Force used uninhabited aerial vehicles (UAVs) for reconnaissance, as did Israel during the Yom Kipper War and the Bekaa Valley operation. In the 1990s, advances in microprocessors, communications technology, and aerodynamics allowed the development of reconnaissance UAVs with longer range, better engine performance, and less vulnerability to enemy attack.

This new generation of machines, coupled with problems associated with personnel cost and availability and political sensibilities over casualties, encouraged military strategists to incorporate more UAVs into air operations.

Confidence in offensive systems, though less prevalent than in the 1950s and 1960s, has not vanished altogether, witnessed by growing interest in uninhabited combat aerial vehicles (UCAVs). Viewed as the ultimate extension of the standoff missile system, UCAVs attracted considerable attention in the late 1990s. In 1997, the United States and Britain launched feasibility studies on UCAVs. Enhancements in sensors, microprocessors, and communications seemingly solved many of the problems associated with these automated vehicles. Many technological challenges lay ahead, however, so it could be many years before UCAVs have a place alongside manned aircraft in combat.

Daniel E. Worthington

See also

Defense Suppression; Electronic Warfare; German Rocket Development; Missiles; Satellites;; V-1 Missile and V-2 Rocket; Vietnam War; World War II Aviation; Yom Kippur War

References

Armitage, Michael. *Unmanned Aircraft.* London: Brassey's, 1988.
Collier, Basil. *The History of Air Power.* New York: MacMillan, 1974.

U.S. Air Corps Tactical School (ACTS)

Developed doctrine for tactical and strategic airpower during the interwar years. Originally the U.S. Army Air Service School, it was authorized on 25 February 1920 at Langley Field, Virginia; the school was established to train Air Service officers with the rank of major or above in air tactics and operations, air defense, bombing tactics, staff operations, logistics, aviation, and combined arms operations. World War II demonstrated profound weaknesses in this doctrine. ACTS suspended classes in 1940 and was reorganized as Air University, which operates today at Maxwell AFB, Alabama.

The school opened on 1 November 1920. The school was originally nine months long but underwent many changes in subjects covered, time spent on subjects, and the school's total length. Because no other Air Service school taught tactics and administration, the Air Service Board changed the school's name to Air Service Tactical School (ASTS) on 8 November 1922 and lifted rank restrictions—sending many junior officers to the course to train them for all levels of command and staff assignments within the Air Service. Following the establishment of the Air Corps in 1926, Langley Field was selected to host several new units. The facilities could not support new units; the ACTS moved to Maxwell Field, Alabama, in the summer of 1931.

ACTS's most important contribution was the development of strategic bombing doctrine. Members of ACTS read Giulio Douhet but rejected his theories favoring nighttime area-bombing and developed air theory favoring strategic daylight precision bombing against economic targets rather than tactical ground support. ACTS airpower theory posited that fleets of bombers unescorted by fighters would perform precision daylight bombing on communications, industrial, and transportation targets. Altitude would protect these strategic bombers from enemy antiaircraft artillery; their speed, bristling armament, and disciplined formations would protect them against enemy interceptors. Only the experiences of World War II would reveal the weakness of this theory.

The Air Corps dramatically expanded following the outbreak of war in Europe. To fill new officer vacancies, the Air Corps suspended ACTS on 30 June 1940. ACTS was succeeded by the Army Air Forces School of Applied Tactics, which opened at Orlando, Florida, on 27 October 1942. This school explored current air operations rather than theory and doctrine. At the end of World War II, the School of Applied Tactics returned to Maxwell Field and was designated Air University on 12 March 1946. Air University now serves as the premier institution for commissioned and noncommissioned officer education, technology research, and doctrinal development for the United States Air Force.

Kevin Gould

See also

Command of the Air; U.S. Air Force Academy; U.S. Air Force Doctrine; U.S. Army Air Corps; U.S. Army Air Service; United States Air Force, Organizational History; World War I Aviation; World War II Aviation

References

Finney, Robert T. *History of the Air Corps Tactical School.* Washington, DC: Center for Air Force History, 1992.
Kries, John F., ed. *Piercing the Fog: Intelligence and Army Air Forces Operations in World War II.* Washington, DC: Air Force History and Museum Program, 1996.
Wolk, Hermann S. *The Struggle for Air Force Independence, 1943–1947.* Washington, DC: Air Force History and Museum Program, 1997.

U.S. Air Force Academy

Established in 1954 at Lowry Air Force Base in Denver, Colorado; the cadet corps moved four years later to the Air Force Academy's current location along the Front Range of the Rocky Mountains just north of Colorado Springs. The campus is 7,000 feet above sea level and encompasses some 18,000 acres. A chapel constructed of stainless steel, aluminum, and glass with 17 spires rising 150 feet into the Colorado sky highlights the academy's unique architecture.

The mission is to inspire and develop outstanding young men and women to become Air Force officers of knowledge and character. The 500 military and civilian faculty members are dedicated to the intellectual, moral, and physical development of 4,000 men and women from all 50 states, territories, and several foreign countries. Cadets undertake a four-year course of study for a bachelor's of science degree and can select from 30 majors. The academy stresses four primary areas of military development: military art and science, theoretical and applied leadership, aviation science and airmanship, and military training.

The academy's vision is to be recognized as the premier developer of aerospace officers, leaders with impeccable character, and the essential knowledge needed to lead the Air Force into the twenty-first century.

Earl H. Tilford Jr.

References

Air Force Magazine 83, 5 (May 2000).

U.S. Air Force Doctrine

Formal USAF guidance on operational philosophy and how best to develop and use airpower and spacepower. Doctrine provides a common institutional perspective in operations, planning, training, and force development; however, it must be applied with flexibility and not become excessively rigid.

The USAF structures doctrine into three levels: *basic doctrine,* which provides broad guidance based on the most fundamental beliefs of the service (normally presented in the 1-series manuals); *operational doctrine,* which guides the organization and employment of large forces in a distinct environment such as a theater (normally presented in the 2-series manuals); and *tactical doctrine,* which explains the proper employment of specific weapons systems (normally presented in 3-series manuals).

Doctrine is developed primarily from the lessons of experience—combat operations complemented by exercises and simulations—and is shaped by theory, technological advances, national culture, perceived threats, and national politics and strategy. USAF doctrine rests heavily on the experiences of World War I and World War II and the theoretical developments in the Air Corps Tactical School during the interwar years.

Although USAF doctrine builds on traditional military history and military theory, the specific historical experiences, theories, and other factors that shape air doctrine emphasize basic operational characteristics that make airpower different than traditional surface forces. These characteristics—which continue to shape the nature of modern airpower doctrine—are speed, range, and flexibility stemming from the ability to move in three dimensions. Airpower leaders and theorists believed—and still believe—that to best exploit these characteristics several operational tenets should guide the employment of airpower.

A key underlying belief is that airpower is perhaps the most dominant factor in modern war. Therefore, all military operations should include control of the air as the first objective. Control of the air, as well as space, enables all other friendly air and surface operations to occur unchallenged by enemy airpower while also denying or limiting the enemy's ability to use the air and space environments. These basic characteristics give airpower the ability to rapidly concentrate firepower on key targets, leading to the belief that airpower is best used offensively.

A corollary concept states that air attacks can be decisive if focused on the right targets in a timely manner. Related to this perspective is the belief that centralized control is needed to ensure that finite air resources are focused on targets that best support national and theater objectives. This commitment to centralized control includes the belief that airpower should be organized separately from the surface forces and should be commanded by airmen who understand its advantages and limitations. The logical doctrinal extension of these concepts is the rationale for an independent air force that can directly engage the enemy country and defeat it by strategic bombardment, possibly without engagements involving surface forces.

This collection of doctrinal beliefs did not sit well with Army and Navy leaders, especially when the air arm was part of the War Department in the interwar years and during World War II. During the interwar years, Army aviation doctrine, as expressed in field manuals, emphasized the support role of the Army Air Corps in ground campaigns. Nonetheless, officers at the Air Corps Tactical School studied the potential of airpower and developed theories and operational concepts that emphasized the decisive nature of air weapons and especially the potential of strategic bombing using daylight precision-bombing tactics. This concept required the ability to understand the enemy and its economic structure, to identify the most important targets of the enemy state, and to accurately strike these targets—all leading to the collapse of the enemy economic structure, which would result in national surrender and the end of the war.

Although constrained by political realities, the concept of decisive independent strategic air operations became a core element of Air Corps and Army Air Forces institutional thinking and shaped planning before and during World War II; it also influenced the perspective of the independent United States Air Force after the war. The USAAF experience during World War II included success in both theater and strategic operations, with those efforts shaping the forces and doctrine of the USAF. The early lessons of World War II and the basic doctrinal themes described above were codified in War Department Field Manual (FM) 100-20 (*Command and Employment of Air Power,* 1943). FM 100-20 began by stating in bold capital letters: "LAND POWER AND AIRPOWER ARE CO-EQUAL AND INTERDEPENDENT FORCES; NEITHER IS AN AUXILIARY OF THE OTHER." FM 100-20 differentiated between strategic and tactical operations and established priorities within phases of theater operations, with air superiority first, followed by interdiction, and finally close air support.

The independent USAF did not immediately create new formal doctrine in the late 1940s, publishing the first basic doctrine document in 1953. Air Force Manual (AFM) 1-2, *United States Air Force Basic Doctrine,* incorporated the characteristics and core institutional beliefs that evolved before the creation of a separate service. AFM 1-2 also reflected the new technology of nuclear weapons, which strengthened the commitment to strategic offensive operations. Additionally, the security realities of the Cold War resulted in a heavy emphasis on deterrence. In 1959, the Air Force recognized the effects of missiles and space systems on military operations and used the new term "aerospace" to describe forces and operations. The Air Force renumbered the basic doctrine manual in 1964, making it AFM 1-1. This revision showed the influence of the national strategy shift to "flexible response," with an expanded discussion of aerospace operations across the spectrum of conflict, including a brief chapter on counterinsurgency operations. However, AFM 1-1 continued to emphasize the importance of deterrence, and the Air Force perspective on strategic and theater uses of aerospace power remained dominated by nuclear weapons. The service revised AFM 1-1 several times in the following 20 years, with adjustments reflecting changes in national security policy and efforts by the USAF to better explain its roles. The Air Force published a major revision of AFM 1-1 in 1992, with the new title *Basic Aerospace Doctrine of the United States Air Force.* This version followed the traditional doctrinal themes but added an extensive second volume containing a set of academic articles on military power and the application of aerospace power as a dominant force in modern warfare.

In recognition of the changes in the post–Cold War national-security environment, the Air Force created a new doctrinal structure in 1997. The new Air Force Doctrine Document (AFDD) 1, *Air Force Basic Doctrine,* continued to include the core characteristics and operational beliefs that are consistently found in the earlier versions of the service's manuals. Additionally, AFDD 1 highlighted the continuing technological improvements that significantly enhanced the combat potential of air and space forces and brought such forces to the point of reaching the potential originally conceived in World War I. The publication adds to earlier doctrinal statements by stressing the importance of the emerging area of information warfare and by emphasizing the ability of airpower and spacepower to conduct precision attacks at global ranges for strategic effects. AFDD 1 presents Air Force basic doctrine within the context of U.S. joint (multiservice) and combined (multinational) doctrine. However, the document strongly argues that recent experiences validate the traditional view of airpower advocates, proving "that air and space power does now have the potential to be the dominant and, at times, the decisive element in modern warfare." AFDD 1 further summarizes the long-standing threads of airpower doctrine by stating that "given the right circumstances, the speed, range, and stunning precision of air and space power—combined with the strategic perspective of its leaders—will allow it to dominate the entire range of military operations in the air, on land, on the sea, and in space."

Jerome V. Martin

See also

Air Interdiction; Air Superiority; AirLand Battle; Close Air Support; Field Manual 100–20; Strategic Bombing; Tactical Air Warfare; U.S. Air Corps Tactical School

References

Futrell, Robert F. *Ideas, Concepts, Doctrine: Basic Thinking in the United States Air Force, Volume 1: 1907–1984;* and *Volume 2: Basic Thinking in the United States Air Force, 1961–1984.* Maxwell AFB, AL: Air University Press, 1989.

Holley, I. B. *Ideas and Weapons: Exploitation of the Aerial Weapon by the United States During World War I; a Study in the Relationship of Technological Advance, Military Doctrine, and the Development of Weapons.* Princeton, NJ: Princeton University Press, 1953.

Lambeth, Benjamin S. *The Transformation of American Air Power.* Ithaca: Cornell University Press, 2000.

Trust, Warren A. *Air Force Roles and Missions: A History.* Washington, DC: U.S. Government Printing Office, 1998.

U.S. Aircraft Development and Production (World War I)

The first powered flight had taken place in the United States in 1903. But apart from the developmental flights by the Wright brothers and the work of Glenn Curtiss, little of consequence had taken place prior to U.S. entry into World War I. Consequently, when the United States finally declared war in 1917, its claim to greatness in aviation technology had been surrendered to the European countries.

Coming to this realization, the U.S. Congress tried to close the gap, budgeting a record $640 million appropriation for military aeronautics. The U.S. Army also sent a delegation (the so-called Bolling mission) to Europe to study aviation development and recommend steps to be taken back home.

The United States began building an aviation industry to build aircraft and engines (exactly which aircraft would have to await the recommendations of the Bolling mission); engines were another matter. Putting a handful of engineers in a hotel room for a few weeks, the United States miraculously produced a winning engine design—the Liberty—which began arriving at the front in the last few months of the war and powered U.S. aircraft (as well as some tanks) for years to come.

It was initially thought that large numbers of aircraft would be built in the United States and shipped to Europe for use by the Air Service. This plan was short-lived, however. America lacked the specialized industry needed to produce aircraft. Also, in light of the severe shortage of shipping, priority should be given to sending raw materials to Europe for conversion into finished products in French and British factories. Another reality, which argued in favor of reliance on foreign production, was the rapid pace of aeronautic design, which promised to render U.S. designs obsolete by the time they made it to the front. The decision was made, at least for the short term, to buy abroad.

Consequently, when U.S. units began making it to the front in the spring and summer of 1918, they were equipped with single-seat Nieuport 28s, SPAD VIIs and XIIIs, and Sopwith Camels along with two-seat Bréguets and Salmsons.

An exception to the buy-abroad approach was the production of the U.S. DH-4 (the license-built de Havilland D.H. 4 from Britain). U.S. DH-4s began arriving at the front in August 1918, and during the remaining months of the war several U.S. squadrons converted to them. They were the only U.S.-produced aircraft to see action in World War I.

An often overlooked area in which U.S. aviation proved successful was in the production of balloons. Goodyear and Goodrich, among other manufacturers, adapted their plants to produce the Caquot observation balloon and, by war's end, were in a position to have supplied not only U.S. needs but those of Britain and France as well had the war gone on into 1919.

James Streckfuss

See also
Bureau of Aircraft Production; Liberty Engine

References

Gorrell, Edgar S. "What—No Airplanes?" *Journal of Air Law and Commerce* 12 (January 1941).

Mauer, Mauer. *U.S. Air Service in World War I: The Final Report and a Tactical History.* Washington, DC: Office of Air Force History, 1978.

Streckfuss, James. "Balloons." In Anne Cipriano Venzon, ed. *The United States in the First World War: an Encyclopedia.* New York: Garland, 1995.

U.S. Army Aviation: Operations

Generally, aerial operations conducted by the U.S. Army in support of ground warfare.

During World War II, Army artillery employed light aircraft, mainly L-4 Piper Cubs (known as Grasshoppers), to adjust artillery fire. Air observation was made necessary because artillery could fire farther than ground observers could see. Grasshoppers proved adept in other missions as well: command and control, medical evacuation, liaison, emergency supply, direction of close air support, and reconnaissance. To support amphibious operations, the army configured LSTs as mini–aircraft launchers using the Brodie device, which enabled light aircraft to take off and land on a cable-trolley suspended over an LST. Small aircraft proved to be very survivable against enemy fighters and ground fire. After the war, aviation was extended to other Army branches.

The Korean War saw Army aviation used for the same missions as during World War II. Fixed-wing aircraft included the L-4 Cub, L-17 Navion, L-19 Bird Dog, L-20 Beaver, L-21 Super Cub, and L-23 Twin Bonanza. The L-4s and L-19s served most combat needs for observation of artillery fire, liaison, command and control, and reconnaissance. Acquiring its first helicopters in 1947, the Army found that they could perform most light airplane missions in Korea. One ubiquitous mission was medical evacuation, for which H-13s were well-suited. In 1953, the Army sent two H-19 transport helicopter companies to Korea to test their use in front-line supply and troop movement. They proved very suitable, and Army leaders planned for the organization of 12 transport helicopter battalions in the 1950s. The Army also envisioned replacing most fixed-wing aircraft with helicopters for combat operations because of their greater versatility.

The Vietnam War has been called the "Helicopter War" with good reason. After U.S. support began in 1961, few Army operations were begun without helicopter participation. To counter guerrilla ambush tactics against South Vietnamese troops, the Army sent H-21 Shawnee helicopter transport units to Vietnam in 1961. Flying South Vietnamese troops into combat, U.S. officers developed immediate response units (Eagle Flights) that used various tactics to defeat guerrillas.

Because landing zones came under enemy fire, the Army installed machine guns in H-21 doorways for suppressive fire when landing, but this was unsatisfactory. In 1962, the Army sent armed UH-1 Hueys to Vietnam to escort the H-21s and provide suppressive fire. These armed Hueys were too slow to accompany troop-carrying Hueys as they replaced the H-21s. Using Huey components, Bell Helicopter developed the AH-1 Cobra attack helicopter especially for the escort and fire-suppression roles. Critics predicted that all helicopters would be shot down, yet they proved tough and survivable.

Fixed-wing aircraft also had important missions in Vietnam. The CV-2 Caribou transport proved effective on short dirt strips for supplying Special Forces outposts. Although the Army acquired the OV-1 Mohawk for high-intensity warfare, it was also useful for surveillance in guerrilla warfare. The O-1 Bird Dog, a veteran of Korean, resumed its observation and reconnaissance roles. The U-1 Otter, U-6 Beaver, and twin-engine U-21 Ute served for utility and administration. In 1966, the Army transferred all Caribous to the Air Force, as it had claimed the fixed-wing air-supply mission for itself. In return, the Air Force dropped all claims to Army helicopter missions in the combat zone. This made possible the wider use of attack helicopters that the Air Force had opposed for impinging on the close air support mission.

President Lyndon Johnson's 1965 decision to send U.S. troops to fight the war brought a new phase to helicopter warfare. Trained in airmobile operations, the 1st Air Cavalry Division (Airmobile) demonstrated its ability to fight North Vietnamese regulars in the Ia Drang highlands. Utilizing close air support, armed Hueys, and artillery fire bases, the 1st Air Cav airlifted heliborne troops into the midst of an enemy stronghold.

The versatility of the 1st Air Cav was demonstrated in 1968 when it moved scores of miles north from An Khe to open a land route to besieged Marines at Khe Sanh. In Operation PEGASUS, the 1st Air Cav leapfrogged along Route 9, destroying enemy strongpoints and relieving the surrounded outpost. Soon after this action, the division air-assaulted into an enemy stronghold in the A Shau Valley against determined resistance. It prevailed again. In 1967, the 101st Airborne Division (Air Assault) relieved the 1st Air Cav and continued to demonstrate the effectiveness of a highly mobile division.

As Army forces in Vietnam increased, they had helicopter units attached to them in addition to their own organic aircraft. In order to control, maintain, and train these attached aviation units, the Army formed the 1st Aviation Brigade. The brigade adopted a policy of decentralized control of its units, sending them where they were needed most.

The survivability of helicopters in combat was questioned early in the war, but never as intensely as during Operation LAM SON 719. In February and March 1971, U.S. helicopters flew South Vietnamese troops into Laos to destroy huge enemy supply dumps and to disrupt enemy movements southward. The North Vietnamese countered with tanks and a sophisticated air defense. They shot down 107 helicopters, but Army leaders believed that the destruction of supplies justified the helicopter losses, set at one-fourth of 1 percent of sorties flown.

LAM SON 719 and the Easter Offensive of 1972 enabled the Army to employ helicopters as antitank weapons. Using mainly antipersonnel munitions during LAM SON 719, AH-1 Cobras destroyed six tanks and immobilized eight. After North Vietnamese armor poured across the demilitarized zone in the Easter Offensive of 1972, helicopters helped stop them. UH-1s armed with TOW missiles destroyed more than 50 tanks and other vehicles, the first major use of helicopters in the antitank role. During this offensive, North Vietnamese troops fired SA-7 heat-seeking missiles at the U.S. helicopters. This necessitated modifying helicopter exhausts to direct them upward into the rotor wash, thereby reducing the heat signature. Helicopters were also fitted with decoy flares.

In the 1980s, Army helicopters were used in two major operations. In the invasion of Grenada in 1983, UH-60 Black Hawks carried Delta Force troops to attack Richmond Hill Prison. Of the 14 Black Hawks engaged, seven were heavily damaged and one shot down, so the mission was aborted. Four Black Hawks carrying Rangers from Barbados attacked the Calvigny compound, resulting in the destruction of three upon landing due to heavy fire. They had no escort providing suppressive fire.

In the 1989 Panama invasion the Army made extensive use of helicopters already positioned at its Panamanian installations. When 82d Airborne Division units parachuted into Panama's airport, UH-60s picked them up for air assaults on key Panama Defense Force strongpoints. An AH-1 Cobra supported an air assault by two UH-60s into a prison holding political prisoners.

The 1991 Gulf War witnessed the successful use of Army aviation in midintensity warfare. Coalition strategy required a joint force to hold the southern boundary of Kuwait while an amphibious force threatened a landing on the Kuwaiti coast. Thus fixed in place to meet both threats, Iraqi forces would be unable to stop another secretly assembled joint force to the west from swinging shut like a giant door against the Euphrates River. This lightning movement would trap Iraqi forces inside Kuwait and permit their destruction in detail.

This giant Coalition door, hinged at the southern border of Iraq and Kuwait, consisted of the most mobile forces, especially VII Corps, heavy in armor, and the XVIII Airborne Corps, heavy in air-assault troops. Both corps had fighting helicopter units that had trained with their divisions.

The helicopters used included OH-58 Kiowas for scouting and targeting; AH-64 Apaches for antitank and reconnaissance missions; AH-1 Cobras for escort and antitank use; UH-60 Black Hawks for troop transport, command and control, and electronic countermeasures; and CH-47 Chinooks for troop transport, supply, and artillery placement. With their ability to fire 30mm cannons, 70mm rockets, and Hellfire laser-guided missiles, and to see through rain and dark, the Apaches had the greatest combat power.

The desert presented special problems for aviation. The trackless expanse provided few terrain features for navigation. The best navigational aids were Global Positioning System satellite receivers. Desert sand degraded rotors and engine parts, requiring frequent repairs. Hardpan was needed for forward refueling and rearming points to avoid sand stirred up in rotor wash. Heavy rains during a blowing *shamal* caused some helicopters to land and await clearer weather.

Before the ground war began, helicopter units conducted important missions. The first was to screen the assembling VII and XVIII Corps so that the enemy could not detect them. The second was to conduct reconnaissance into Iraq to find suitable places for forward refueling and rearming points. An important mission for Apaches was to destroy two Iraqi radar sites to give the Air Force a cleared airpath toward Baghdad. Flying low after dark to avoid detection, the Apaches launched missiles from a distance of 2 kilometers and destroyed the radars.

When the ground war began, Apaches and Cobras flew in advance of VII Corps to provide intelligence on enemy positions and to attack armor. Kiowas and Cobras flew flank security to warn of nearby Iraqi forces and to contact friendly units. To avoid VII Corps artillery fire, helicopters flew at least 12 miles in advance of the battle line. Apaches in advance of VII Corps had a field day killing armor and other vehicles.

The most mobile unit in the XVIII Airborne Corps was the 101st Airborne Division (Air Assault). It formed the edge of the swinging door and had to advance some 200 miles by the second day of battle. In the vanguard were Chinooks and Black Hawks, carrying troops, fuel, and ammunition. These supplies enabled Apaches to advance and close the door at the Euphrates. Near the river, Apaches of the 101st destroyed hundreds of vehicles that were backed up trying to flee Kuwait. They also blocked the causeway across the marshes with wrecked vehicles and destroyed a pontoon bridge across the river. Although a cease-fire was in effect on February 28, the Iraqi Hammurabi Division offered combat on March 1, and the Apaches destroyed its equipment. Overall, Army aviation proved indispensable in waging war against the well-armed Iraqi foe.

The fall 2001 U.S. war on terror opened a new chapter in Army aviation. The desert and mountain environment of Afghanistan provided formidable obstacles for successful Special Forces operations. The full measure of Army aviation was brought to bear against an entrenched and well-armed foe.

John L. Bell

References

Bolger, Daniel P. *Americans at War, 1975–1986: An Era of Violent Peace.* Novato, CA: Presidio Press, 1998.

Dunstan, Simon. *Vietnam Choppers: Helicopters in Battle, 1950–1975.* London: Osprey, 1988.

Hassig, Lee, ed. *Sky Soldiers.* Alexandria, VA: Time-Life, 1991.

Raines, Edgar F. Jr. *Eyes of Artillery: The Origins of Modern U.S. Army Aviation in World War II.* Army Historical Series. Washington, DC: Center of Military History, Department of the Army, 2000.

Scales, Robert H. Jr. *Certain Victory: The U. S. Army in the Gulf War.* Washington, DC: Brassey's, 1997.

Smith, Kevin, comp., and Burton Wright III, ed. *United States Army Aviation During Operations Desert Shield and Desert Storm: Selected Readings.* Fort Rucker, AL: U.S. Army Aviation Center, 1993.

U.S. Army Aviation: Origins

Established in 1942 to assist the field artillery to adjust its fire, Army aviation has evolved over the years into a combat arm.

When the United States organized the Army Air Forces in 1941, AAF commanders believed that all strategic and ground support aviation should be under AAF control. The field artillery, however, had developed doctrine for indirect fire on enemy rear areas, places that ground observers could not see well. The artillery requested its own light aircraft to observe and adjust this fire. The AAF opposed the request because it planned to fly the mission. Its specially designed airplanes were not available by 1942, and the artillery was permitted to procure and fly its own airplanes, usually Piper Cubs.

During World War II, these small airplanes performed amazing feats. Besides adjusting distant artillery fire, they conducted other missions for ground forces: liaison, command and control, reconnaissance, flank security, emergency supply, medical evacuation, and direction of close air support. Despite AAF predictions that the Grasshoppers (as they were called) would be shot down, they proved very survivable. Logistical support was provided by both the AAF and the Army, an unsatisfactory arrangement. At war's end, Army aviation was made permanent and extended to all Army combat arms for uses they could determine.

After the war, the new U.S. Air Force and the Army engaged in disputes over roles and missions. They Army wanted to increase the types of missions it flew in order to secure greater mobility, but the Air Force opposed this, arguing that it could fly the missions. Given its emphasis on strategic bombing and air superiority, however, the Air Force was not responsive to Army needs. So the Army won more missions for its helicopters and larger airplanes than it was procuring. These missions included troop transport within the combat zone, air assaults and close air support, combat-zone reconnaissance, air movement of supplies and large weapons in the combat zone, and medical evacuation.

The U.S. Coast Guard is tasked with defense readiness, law enforcement, fisheries patrol, and environmental protection. Helicopters such as this one are often employed to perform these tasks. (Walter J. Boyne)

Army aviation also became more independent of Air Force control. After establishing an aviation center at Fort Rucker, Alabama, the Army gradually gained control from the Air Force of primary pilot training and logistical support.

The Army also examined doctrine for using aviation on the nuclear battlefield. This doctrine required the rapid dispersal and concentration of units and improved reconnaissance and surveillance systems. The so-called Howze Board of 1962 demonstrated the feasibility of air-assault operations. Its ideas were tested by the 11th Air Assault Division (Test) by 1965. The doctrine, except for the use of nuclear weapons, was further refined during the Vietnam War. New organizations to utilize this doctrine also proved viable in Vietnam: for example, the 1st Air Cavalry Division (Airmobile), the 101st Airborne Division (Air Assault), and the 1st Aviation Brigade. The older combat arms came to accept Army aviation as one of its own during the war, and acceptance was formalized with the creation of the Aviation Branch in 1983.

In the 1991 Gulf War, this new combat arm demonstrated its proficiency as aviation was integrated into division and corps operations. Attack helicopters killed tanks at great distances, destroyed radar stations, screened advancing forces, provided flank security, and closed enemy routes of escape. Scout helicopters located the enemy and laser-painted targets for all kinds of laser-directed munitions. Transport helicopters rushed troops and supplies forward to keep the enemy under fire and replenish aircraft. Army aviation has thus proven itself as a valuable combat arm in all kinds of warfare.

John L. Bell

References

Bergerson, Frederic A. *The Army Gets an Air Force: Tactics of Insurgent Bureaucratic Politics.* Johns Hopkins University Press, 1980.

U.S. Coast Guard Aviation

The first practical steps toward a Coast Guard air unit occurred in 1915 when Lieutenants Elmer Stone and Norman Hall conceived of using aircraft for Coast Guard missions. The Coast Guard did not receive any money from Congress at the time to create an aviation unit. During the interwar years, the Coast Guard provided a number of important tasks, using flying boats for most of the missions.

The Coast Guard was incorporated into the Navy on 1 November 1941 and played a critical role in the defense of Greenland during World War II. Coast Guard aircraft flying from cutters helped locate German weather stations in the northern areas of Greenland. Coast Guard personnel captured the stations. Coast Guard aircraft performed rescues by flying through snowstorms and landing on the icecap to aid distressed Allied aircrews that had crashed while attempting to ferry aircraft across the Atlantic. In early 1943, the Coast Guard was tasked with developing the helicopter for antisubmarine warfare.

Today the Coast Guard is tasked with defense readiness, law enforcement, fisheries patrol, environmental protection, and homeland security. To function in these assignments, the Coast Guard flies some 200 aircraft from 27 air stations throughout the continental United States, Hawaii, Alaska, and Puerto Rico. The primary aircraft currently in the Coast Guard inventory are the HU-25A Guardian, the HC-130H Hercules, the HH-65A Dolphin, and the HH-60 Jayhawk.

Henry M. Holden

References

U.S. Coast Guard Official Website. Available online at http://www.uscg.mil/welcome.html.

U.S. Marine Corps Aviation

On 6 January 1914, Marine aviation was established as a separate unit within the U.S. Navy. At the time of U.S. entry into World War I, the Marine Aviation Section consisted of five officers, one warrant officer, and 30 enlisted men; equipment consisted of four Curtiss Type AH hydroplanes.

In August 1917, the Navy decided a naval base was needed in the Azores to extend convoy protection and to prevent German submarines from using the islands as refueling bases. The Marine Aviation Section arrived at Naval Base 13, San Miguel Island, on 21 January 1918. This unit was the first completely equipped U.S. aviation unit to leave the United States for service in the war.

Between the world wars, the only U.S. ground and aviation units actually engaged in combat were Marines. Marine aviation units served in the Dominican Republic from 1919 until July 1924; in Haiti from 1919 until 1934; and in Nicaragua from 1927 until 1933. During those deployments, Marine pilots not only experienced combat but also developed new tactics that would later revolutionize ground as well as air warfare.

In Nicaragua during 1927, Major Ross E. Rowell's unit was the first to employ dive-bombing against an organized enemy unit (Sandino's rebels). Rowell's pilots were also the first to employ air-to-ground communications in combat.

During World War II, the importance of aviation to Marine tactics was graphically demonstrated at Guadalcanal, where one of the first objectives of the assault was a partially completed Japanese airfield, later renamed Henderson Field. After the airfield had been taken, Marine aviation based on Henderson Field devastated overwhelming numbers of the Japanese air force and debunked the myth that Japanese pilots and their Zero fighters were invincible.

The most famous World War II Marine squadron, the Black Sheep, forever linked with its commanding officer, Major Gregory "Pappy" Boyington, fought in the Solomon Islands from August 1943 through January 1944. The Black Sheep counted eight aces and shot down 94 Japanese planes in addition to Boyington's 22.

The most successful Marine squadron was VMF-323, the "Death Rattlers," under the command of 23-year-old George Axtell. They shot down 124.5 Japanese planes and counted a dozen aces. In total, the Marine Corps had 24 aces who alone accounted for 362 enemy aircraft. Nine of the aces earned the Medal of Honor.

The Korean War was another testing ground for the air-to-ground team tactics, which had been developed over the preceding 50 years. During the Korean War Marine aviation began to perfect the utilization of helicopters and jet aircraft. The first Marine air offensive of the war occurred on 3 August 1950. Eight Corsairs of VMF-214 carried incendiary bombs and rockets and made numerous strafing runs on the port of Pusan.

The Chosin Reservoir campaign began on 27 November 1950 at Yudam-ni with 120,000 seasoned Chinese infantry troops surrounding approximately 17,000 troops of the 1st Marine Division and an additional 3,000 British Royal Marines. The fighting withdrawal of the 1st Marine Division from Chosin, in North Korea, along a harrowing mountainous route in sub-arctic conditions (1–9 December) is considered one of the greatest moments in the history of the Navy and Marine Corps.

From the start of the 68-mile battle to the sea, Marine aviation played a critical role. The tactical air control groups of Marine, Army, and South Korean units flew 3,703 sorties in 1,053 missions. This fierce, bloody battle, unparalleled in modern history, resulted in 15,000 allied dead or wounded. The enemy forces endured crippling losses, including 40,000 dead; thousands more went down with wounds and frostbite. One milestone for Marine aviation was its first jet squadron to see combat. VMF-311, under Lieutenant Colonel Neil McIntyre, began operations at Yonpo during the last few days of the Chosin breakout.

In the late 1950s, Marine aviation perfected the helicopter assault technique known then as "vertical envelopment." The Marine Corps and Army later employed this technique in Vietnam. Since then, Marine Corps aviation has continued to concentrate on close air support with the help of VSTOL aircraft.

Marine aviation was continuously represented in Vietnam from 1962 by the helicopter squadron of Task Unit Shufly. Up to 1964, helicopter squadrons of the 1st Marine Air Wing (MAW) had been rotated to Shufly about every four or five months. By the time the escalation of U.S. forces began in early 1965, the 1st MAW had considerable experience in the tactics and operation of helicopter troop lifts in Vietnam combat.

In 1965, the first short airfield for tactical support (SATS) was created at Chu Lai. SATS was a Marine aviation concept that provided a field complete with carrier deck–type arresting gear, a catapult, and a surface of interlocking lightweight metal alloy planking. The concept also included a tactical airfield fuel-dispensing system. By the end of May 1965, 4,000 feet of usable surface was down, and the first trap of an A-4 into the gear was made on 1 June. With the use of jet-assisted takeoff bottles, the first combat mission was launched from Chu Lai.

After Vietnam, Marine aviation took on a new look. In the late spring of 1971, the AV-8A, the British-built Hawker-Siddeley Harrier with VTOL capability, joined the Marine inventory. The second version, AV-8B built by McDonnell Douglas, joined the inventory in the mid-1980s. The Harrier allows a new approach to the operation of tactical aircraft not only from small ships in the amphibious force but also from relatively unprepared and dispersed sites ashore.

In the mid-1980s, Marine aviation began replacing its F-4 series fighter-attack aircraft with the F/A-18 Hornet. This agile fighter is an accurate attack weapons platform and is currently deployed on land and fleet aircraft carriers. The Marines also use the F-14 Tomcat, and the A-6F, an all-weather attack aircraft, increased capability.

The Marines currently have AH-1T Cobra attack helicopters, H-60 Seahawks, and upgraded CH-46 helicopters in inventory. The CH-53E Super Stallion, now in the inventory, is the world's most capable heavy-lift helicopter.

The MV-22A Osprey tiltrotor promises to exceed by a wide margin the best performance figures of any of the current helicopters. However, until apparent bugs are eliminated the Osprey is not operational; limited Osprey operations have been resumed.

Henry M. Holden

References

Grosnick, Roy A., with contributions from William J. Armstrong et al. *United States Naval Aviation, 1910-1995.* 4th ed. Washington, DC: United States Navy, Naval Historical Center, 1997.

USMC Historical Office. Available online at http://www.usmc.mil/historical.nsf/nav1.

U.S. Navy, Chief of Naval Operations (CNO)

The Office of the Chief of Naval Operations was established by Congress on 3 March 1915; it functions under the command of the secretary of the Navy and is responsible for fleet operations as well as preparation and readiness plans for use during times of war.

The coordination and management of the various departments of the Navy necessary to fulfill these duties included implementing decisions concerning what, how, and when material would be purchased from the private sector. Initially, the various Navy bureaus argued that only the secretary of the Navy possessed the authority to issue orders to them even though they cooperated with the CNO. One area of agreement between the bureaus and the CNO involved logistical support and building programs. The bureaus followed the recommendation of the CNO concerning issues such as modernization, scheduled repair of ships, and the appropriate number of officers and enlisted men. Any officer, captain or above, was qualified to be the chief naval officer until 1916, when the rank was raised to admiral. The first CNO, appointed on 11 May 1915, was Admiral William Sims Benson. Benson's reputation and the raging war in Europe persuaded the reluctant secretary of the Navy, Josephus Daniels, to rely on the judgment and expertise of the CNO. By 1917, the increased planning and procurement process elevated the CNO to a respected position with expanded responsibilities.

In the immediate post–World War I period, controversies arose over the authority of the CNO with concerns raised about civilian control. Congress created the position of undersecretary of the Navy to oversee and recommend changes for reasons of efficiency and economy and to maintain a stronger civilian presence. In 1924, the Navy, during a reorganization phase, added a Regulation granting the CNO authority over repairs and alterations to vessels and the supply of personnel to ensure readiness. The bureaus challenged the legality of these expanded powers, although continuing to cooperate with the CNO, until the beginning of World War II.

At the onset of that war, President Franklin D. Roosevelt signed Executive Order No. 8984 outlining the duties of the commander in chief of the U.S. Fleet, assigning overall authority to Admiral Ernest J. King, who in turn issued orders to the other commanders in chief. In December 1941, Admiral Chester W. Nimitz and Thomas C. Hart commanded the Pacific and Asiatic Fleets, respectively. CNO Admiral Harold R. Stark coordinated efforts with the commander in chief of the U.S. Fleet (Cominch), who assumed some of the functions of the CNO beginning in January 1942. An issue arose over the chain of command after the creation of that position, with King arguing that it should be under the authority of the CNO. President Roosevelt responded by issuing Executive Order No. 9096, combining the responsibilities of the CNO and the new position in one person. Interim CNO changes involved logistical functions with responsibilities divided between fleet maintenance, base maintenance, and the naval vessels and aircraft divisions.

The so-called Booz study, concluded in March 1943, recommended the implementation of additional changes within the logistical departments. Rejecting the traditional staffing procedures, which relied on line officers, the commission suggested that technical experts from the staff corps and Marine Corps within the various bureaus be assigned additional duty with the CNO. The officers would possess the advantage of knowing exactly where to obtain information quickly within their own bureau, thereby eliminating the lengthy correspondence process. Although the system worked well most of the time, there were a few occasions when logistical personnel disagreed with their bureau chiefs, calling into question the proper chain of command. The system continued throughout the war as the CNO relied on the bureaus to carry out the specifics such as purchasing and awarding contracts while the CNO focused on coordination efforts involving ships, aircraft, men, and supplies.

An attempt by Admiral King to reorganize the CNO met with resistance by Roosevelt but did yield one positive change. In August 1943, the secretary of the Navy established the post of deputy Chief of Naval Operations (Air; DCNO [Air]) responsible for policy, plans, and logistics of naval aviation. The DCNO (Air) operated under the vice Chief of Naval Operations. Other departments that operated under the CNO during the war included the Office of Naval Intelligence, Pan-American Division, Naval Communications Division, Hydrographic Office, the Naval Observatory, the Board of Inspection and Survey, Naval Transportation Service, and the Navy Inventory Control Office. On 15 March 1945, the General Board created the Ship Characteristic Board to handle issues involving the features of the ships, a task continued after the conclusion of the war.

After the Japanese surrender in August 1945, the CNO remained responsible for the demobilization of officers and enlisted men along with the Bureau of Naval Personnel. Admiral King argued that CNO functions transferred to Cominch during the war should be returned to the CNO. After Secretary of the Navy James Forrestal finally agreed with King, the two men met with President Harry S. Truman, who signed Executive Order No. 9635, placing responsibility for administrative, military, and business and industrial matters under the authority of the CNO. A recommendation was then made by Admiral King that Admiral Nimitz replace him as CNO. Secretary Forrestal favored Admiral Richard S. Edwards, but King argued that Nimitz had been the principal naval commander during the war and therefore should not be passed over in favor of Edwards. Admiral Nimitz became CNO on 15 December 1945. The overall impact of the war substantially increased the authority of the Office of the Chief of Naval Operations.

Since the end of the war the CNO, as the Navy's senior flag officer, continues to represent the Navy on the Joint Chiefs of Staff and is the principal naval adviser to the president and the secretary of the Navy. The CNO functions under the authority of the secretary and remains responsible for issuing commands, overseeing the use of resources, and coordinating the operation of the Navy.

Cynthia Clark Northrup

See also

U.S. Navy, Office of the Secretary

References

Furer, Julius Augustus. *Administration of the Navy Department in World War II.* Washington, DC: U.S. Government Printing Office, 1959.

U.S. Navy, Office of the Secretary

U.S. Navy office that was first established in 1798 and continues through the present day.

Attacks by Barbary pirates on American vessels in the Mediterranean resulted in Congress approving appropriations for the construction of two frigates, *Constellation* and *Constitution,* in 1794. The lack of attention devoted by the secretary of war to the shipbuilding program resulted in the creation of the Department of the Navy with the secretary of the Navy as the chief officer on 30 April 1798. According to the statute, the secretary executed all orders from the president of the United States pertaining to the purchase of naval stores and materials, as well as the construction, armament, equipment, and employment of Navy war vessels. On 7 February 1815, Congress approved the appointment of the Board of Navy Commissioners, which handled matters pertaining to the construction, repair, and outfitting of ships; the secretary retained authority over military functions and command.

After the creation of the Office of the Chief of Naval Operations (CNO) in 1915, the role of the secretary of the Navy reversed. The CNO assumed control, under the secretary's command, of logistical planning while the secretary's staff focused on policy, business management, and other administrative matters. Policy, generated from the bureaus or other subordinates, reaches the office of the secretary for approval. After reviewing the recommendations and deciding on the appropriate policy, the secretary issues a directive to all departments providing the necessary guidance for implementation. The secretary, as a member of the president's Cabinet, advises the president, consults with Congress, and maintains regular contact with the secretary of defense and secretary of state. The secretary of the Navy also interacts daily with his subordinates, including the CNO, the commander in chief of the U.S. Fleet, the bureau chiefs, and the commandant of the Marine Corps.

Designed to ensure civilian control over the military, the Office of the Secretary of the Navy has been occupied by nonmilitary men throughout its history. Until World War II, 47 men held the position, but only a few had any naval experience. Throughout American history appointments to this office have been based on political considerations. Many of the early secretaries had been involved in shipping and brought civilian expertise to the military. Lawyers have dominated the position since the Civil War, and since the end of World War II businessmen with political skills, as well as business and engineering expertise, have filled the office. Their contacts in the private sector provided an opportunity for the quick addition of experts during times of war, as was the case during World War II.

Under the United States Code, the secretary of the Navy continues to conduct all functions of the Navy, including recruitment, organization, supply, equipment, training, mobilization, and demobilization, in addition to overseeing the construction, repairs, and outfitting of the Navy's ships.

Cynthia Clark Northrup

See also

U.S. Navy, Chief of Naval Operations

References

Furer, Julius Augustus. *Administration of the Navy Department in World War II.* Washington, DC: U.S. Government Printing Office, 1959.

U.S. Postal Air Mail Service

Early aerial trailblazing service (1918–1927). The U.S. Post Office Department officially took over the Air Mail Service from the Army Signal Corps in August 1918 following a string of embarrassing and deadly accidents. Under the leadership of the newly appointed superintendent, Benjamin Lispner, the legendary airmail pilots dealt with the hazards of inclement weather, unreliable engines, inadequate aircraft instrumentation, and nonexistent navigational aids to establish mail routes that connected the East and West Coasts of the continental United States. Flying war-surplus open-cockpit biplanes day and night in all kinds of weather, this club of courageous and highly skilled aerial mailmen captured the attention of the nation, much as the Pony Express riders had eight decades earlier.

By 1925, the Post Office had proven the practicality of flying the mail and, as originally planned, handed it over to private contractors. The Air Mail Act became law in February 1925, and by the summer of 1927 the Postal Air Mail Service was all but history. A staggering one-sixth of the pilots hired by the Post Office died flying the mail, but these intrepid pioneers paved the way for the safe day and night aerial cross-country navigation that would become so important in the future.

Steven A. Ruffin

References

Lipsner, Benjamin. *The Airmail: Jennies to Jets.* Chicago: Wilcox and Follett, 1951.

Shamburger, Page. *Tracks Across the Sky: The Story of the Pioneers of the U.S. Air Mail.* New York: Lippincott, 1964.

U.S. Strategic Bombing Survey (SBS)

A fact-finding and evaluation team envisioned by USAAF leaders and chartered by President Franklin D. Roosevelt to study the effects of strategic bombing on Germany and Japan. Employing more than 1,000 individuals—approximately one-third of whom were civilians—the SBS team compiled a huge mass of statistical data and wrote detailed reports of their findings that were published in 1945–1946.

Planning for the SBS began in early 1943, and teams began arriving in London before D-Day in preparation for a move to the continent. Franklin D'Olier, senior executive officer of Prudential Insurance, was selected as chairman. D'Olier then named noted civilians as his key subordinates and organized the SBS into several divisions that corresponded to target categories: oil, munitions, aircraft, transportation, morale, and so on. As the Allies moved across Europe, SBS teams followed, collecting material captured from German factories and government files, making on-site appraisals, taking thousands of photographs, and interviewing local officials, managers, workers, and inhabitants. The overall task of the SBS was to determine the effects of strategic bombing on the enemy's economy and, if possible, comment on the effectiveness of that bombing. In short, was a particular target actually destroyed and, if it was, what impact did that destruction have on the German war machine?

The Pacific SBS was also headed up by D'Olier, with Paul Nitze, another veteran of the European team, as deputy. The Pacific team, however, was plagued by interservice rivalry between the USAAF and Navy. Because the Navy had played no role in the bomber offensive against Germany, there was no reason to include naval officers on the European team. In the Pacific, however, the Navy had played a part—accounting for nearly 5 percent of the bomb tonnage dropped on Japan. As a result, naval officers were included on the Pacific team. The problems were immediate and continuous.

It was obvious to all that one of the major outcomes of the Pacific SBS would be to set the stage for the postwar U.S. defense establishment. The USAAF hoped to become a separate service based around a strategic bombing force employing atomic weapons. If the SBS reflected favorably upon the strategic bombing of Japan, this would further the airmen's goal. The Navy was adamantly opposed to a separate Air Force and therefore sought a report that reflected negatively on strategic bombing.

There were also systemic problems with the SBS teams and their methodology. The civilians who dominated the SBS included an excellent mix of bankers, industrialists, and economists. One of the division chiefs was even a specialist in public-polling techniques, invaluable in drawing up and conducting the thousands of SBS interviews. It did not, however, include any labor or union officials. Given the emphasis on determining the effect of bombing on worker morale, this was a serious oversight. Similarly, the armed forces of Germany and Japan were a major center of gravity in their own right, but there were no senior ground officers on the SBS team to lend their views of bombing's effect on this key target set.

Both the European and Pacific reports concluded that strategic bombing played a key role in victory but questioned some of the targeting decisions made by air leaders. For example, the SBS argued strongly for attacks on specific industries—oil, transport, chemicals, and utilities—rather than area-bombing of urban areas. Even so, the SBS painstakingly documented the enormous destruction that bombing caused to the economies of Germany and Japan. In addition, the Pacific team paid special attention to the effects of the two atomic strikes, as well as the subsequent Japanese decision to surrender.

Overall, the SBS reports are an extremely valuable historical resource. Altogether, 208 volumes were published on the European theater alone, another 108 for the Pacific. Most of these reports—examining strikes on specific factories, marshaling yards, utility plants, and the like—are extremely detailed and complete with maps, charts, and diagrams. Unfortunately, the sheer volume and detail make them so daunting they have been largely overlooked by historians. The two summary volumes are the most popular researchers and often quoted out of context. For example, the summary statement that airpower "was decisive in the war in Western Europe" has been cited on countless occasions, as has the statement in the Pacific summary that Japan "would have surrendered" by 1 November 1945 without the atomic strikes, without an Allied invasion of the home islands, and without Soviet intervention. Both statements are hotly debated even today.

The SBS remains the most detailed, accurate, and important source for the conduct and results of Allied strategic bombing in World War II.

Phillip S. Meilinger

References

Gentile, Gian P. "Shaping the Past Battlefield 'For the Future': The United States Strategic Bombing Survey's Evaluation of the American Air War Against Japan," *Journal of Military History* 64 (October 2000).

MacIsaac, David. *Strategic Bombing in World War II: The Story of the United States Strategic Bombing Survey.* New York: Garland, 1976.

Nitze, Paul H. *From Hiroshima to Glasnost: At the Center of Decision.* New York: Grove Weidenfeld, 1989.

V

V-1 Missile and V-2 Rocket

The well-known German *vergeltungswaffen* (vengeance or retaliation or revenge weapons) were a last-ditch stand to stave off defeat in 1944–1945 by means of pilotless bombs that could be launched against London and other Allied targets. They reflected an interservice rivalry, with the later Luftwaffe V-1 missile project being launched out of concern over the V-2 army-controlled rocket program that was seen as endangering the Luftwaffe's strategic role. The Nazi SS seized overall control of both programs in early 1945.

The V-1 missile was a flying bomb, far cheaper and simpler than the V-2 rocket already under development, though in service both would carry similar 1-ton warheads. The Argus reaction propulsion jet engine, first flown in early 1941, had a loud "on-off" roar that inadvertently provided up to a five-minute warning to targeted populations. Design work on the airframe of what became the V-1 (the Fieseler Fi 103) began in March 1942, and it first flew with a Siemens guidance system at the end of 1942, launched from an aircraft over the Baltic Sea. It was referred to as an antiaircraft weapon to throw off spies and intelligence. Tests in 1943 were often frustrating failures.

Numerous production delays due to varied priorities, design and implementation problems, and Allied bombing of test and manufacturing sites meant that large numbers did not come off production lines until late 1944. The delay helped in one way, however, as intended launch complexes were simplified to portable 150-foot catapults. The V-1 was first launched into combat on 13 June 1944 (six of the 10 launched actually reached Britain), with nearly 140 French launch sites nearing completion. Soon, more than 100 per day were launched, though many failed to reach their targets. A piloted version was tested but never used in combat (the pilot would have bailed out before the final descent). The Allied invasion shut down the French launch sites, though final launches came from sites in Holland in March 1945.

All told, more than 32,000 V-1s were manufactured. Some 6,000 V-1s were fired at Britain, 3,400 of them at London alone. The British destroyed nearly 4,000 (1,847 by RAF fighters—including 400 mph Gloster Meteor jets—1,878 with antiaircraft guns, and 232 by cables attached to barrage balloons).

The V-2 rocket grew out of German experimentation and civilian rocket clubs in the 1930s. Active development of what became the V-2 weapon began in late 1938 after testing was conducted on several smaller versions. Development was slow due to shifting military priorities and the complex guidance and propulsion systems involved. Production of early V-2s required nearly 13,000 man-hours of effort, a figure that dropped with mass production. The long-range A-4 (later the V-2) experienced several failed launches before the first successful test flight of more than 100 miles over the Baltic Sea on 3 October 1942. More failed launches followed, and continuing development prevented mass production until late 1943. Extensive use was made of slave labor and underground manufacturing sites. Range slowly grew from 140 miles to more than 200 (some versions flew nearly 300). A projected but not built A9/A10 version would have true intercontinental range to bomb U.S. targets from German launch facilities.

Unlike the V-1, whose engine noise announced its presence, the V-2 struck with no warning at supersonic speed. The first combat launch against London came on 7 September 1944. Rockets were delivered by rail to forward launch points within range of London. The camouflaged rockets could be launched about 90 minutes after arrival even from an unprepared site.

All told, more than 6,500 V-2s were manufactured through April 1945. Many were destroyed at factories or on

In response to the overwhelming superiority of Allied forces over the Luftwaffe, the Germans put their energy into making superweapons like the V-1 Flying Bomb, seen here. (U.S. Air Force)

supply trains. Of the nearly 3,200 launched, slightly more than 1,400 were launched at Britain (mostly London) before operations ceased in early 1945. Some 1,600 were aimed at Antwerp and its suburbs. Lesser numbers targeted other sites.

Both the V-1 missile and the V-2 rocket came too late to effect the war's outcome, though damage and loss of life was extensive. More than 15,000 lost their lives and another 47,000 were wounded by these weapons. Both were area weapons used for terror, as neither could be accurately aimed at specific military targets. Neither weapon was used against the Eastern or Italian Fronts but instead were focused on major Allied cities and staging areas in the west. Capture of surviving copies helped fuel the postwar missile race.

Christopher H. Sterling

See also
Peenemünde; Speer, Albert; von Braun, Werhner

References
Cooksley, Peter G. *Flying Bomb: The Story of Hitler's V-Weapons in World War II.* New York: Scribners, 1979.
Dornberger, Walter. *V-2.* New York: Viking, 1954.
Garliski, Jósef. *Hitler's Last Weapons: The Underground War Against the V1 and V2.* New York: Times Books, 1978.
Hölsken, Dieter. *V-Missiles of the Third Reich: The V-1 and V-2.* Sturbridge, MA: Monogram Aviation, 1994.

Valencia, Eugene A. (1921–)

U.S. Navy commander; World War II Pacific ace. Eugene A. Valencia was born in 1921 in San Francisco. He entered naval service as an aviation cadet in 1941. Training lasted until April 1942. Between April 1942 and his subsequent assignment to USS *Essex* in February 1943, he served as an instructor-pilot. Aboard the *Essex* in November 1943, he scored four kills—three over the Japanese stronghold of Rabaul and one over Tarawa.

The events of 16 February 1944 proved to be a turning point in his career. After becoming separated from his wingman over Truk, he was jumped by several Japanese Zeros. After a lengthy running fight in which the Zeros expended a considerable amount of ammunition without hitting his F6F Hellcat, Valencia turned on his attackers. He quickly shot down three of the Zeros. After landing, the jubilant Valencia stated about his Hellcat, "I love this airplane so much that if it could cook, I'd marry it."

After returning from the Pacific for further training, Valencia developed his "Mowing Machine" method of combat. Over Truk he had noticed a flaw with Japanese fighter tactics that he could exploit. Three pilots were recruited and put through a grueling training program. In March 1945 they joined VF-9 ("The Cat o'Nines") flying off the new *Yorktown* (part of Task Force 58), after a brief but profitable stint on the new *Lexington,* where Valencia's "Flying Circus" used his new tactics and shot down six Japanese planes on their first combat mission.

Task Force 58 was involved in the Okinawa campaign from March to June 1945. An excellent example of Valencia's Mowing Machine tactics was 17 April during a combat air patrol. The four-plane Flying Circus engaged an enemy force of 40-plus aircraft that were attacking the fleet. By using Valencia's signature move, they were able to score 17 confirmed kills and four probables, with Valencia getting six himself.

They added 11 on another sortie and 10 more on 11 May. Eugene Valencia had 23 confirmed kills and was awarded the Navy Cross.

Scott R. DiMarco

References

Barrett, Tillman. *Hellcat Aces of World War 2.* London: Osprey Aerospace, 1996.

Sims, Edward H. *Greatest Fighter Missions of the Top Navy and Marine Aces of World War II.* New York: Ballantine Books, 1962.

Vandenberg, Hoyt S. (1899–1954)

The second Air Force Chief of Staff (30 April 1948 until retirement on 30 June 1953), succeeding General Carl Spaatz. Vandenberg previously served as director of central intelligence from 10 June 1946 to 1 May 1947. Vandenberg's most significant contributions derive from his leadership at a time critical to the formation and early years of the Air Force. His exceptional managerial and organizational skills enabled the growth of the Air Force in general and the new Strategic Air Command in particular during a time of extreme budgetary competition among the services. These skills paid similar dividends during the gestation of the CIA and other U.S. intelligence collection and analysis agencies. Vandenberg was an extremely popular commander and was on equal terms with aircrews, Pentagon officials, and two presidents. Vandenberg AFB, California, is named in his honor.

Robert S. Hopkins

See also

Cold War; Strategic Air Command; Truman, Harry S.

References

Meilinger, Phillip S. *Hoyt S. Vandenberg: The Life of a General.* Bloomington: Indiana University Press, 1989.

Vang Pao (1929–)

Major general in the Royal Laotian Army (RLA); an effective commander and the only member of the Hmoung ethnic group to attain the rank of general officer. Born in Nong Het, Laos, in 1929, Vang Pao first entered military service in the French colonial army in the late 1940s. He fought as an enlisted man, reportedly attaining the rank of sergeant, during the French-Indochina War.

The Geneva Agreement of 1954, which granted the kingdom of Laos independence as a neutral nation, also provided for a period of transition during which the French military trained the RLA. Accordingly, the French tapped Vang Pao to attend the Royal Military Academy at Dong Hene, where upon graduation he received a commission.

Vang Pao rose in rank and by 1960 was commander of an army of Hmoung irregulars. The Central Intelligence Agency noticed the military prowess of the Hmoung units far exceeded that of the rest of the RLA and sent U.S. Army "White Star" Special Forces teams to train and rearm Vang Pao's forces. The Hmoung operated primarily in the rugged mountainous areas north of the capital of Vientiane dubbed Military Region II, encompassing the strategic Plain of Jars and extending west to the border of North Vietnam.

From his mountain headquarters at Long Tieng, Vang Pao led a force of less than 22,000 guerrillas. The Hmoung kept North Vietnamese forces, numbering up to seven divisions, at bay throughout the war. In 1975, after the United States had pulled out of Southeast Asia, the coalition government collapsed and the communist Pathet Lao took over. Vang Pao moved to the United States to become the titular leader of the Hmoung in exile. He currently resides in California.

Earl H. Tilford Jr.

References

Dommen, Arthur J. *Conflict in Laos: The Politics of Neutralization.* New York: Praeger, 1971.

Hamilton-Merritt, Jane. *Tragic Mountains: The Hmoung, the Americans, and the Secret Wars for Laos, 1942–1992.* Bloomington: Indiana University Press, 1993.

VARSITY (1945)

Allied code name for the largest and most successful airborne operation in history; marked the end for Germany as Allied airborne troops mounted the final barrier and crossed the Rhine in 1945. By March 1945, only the Rhine separated the Allies from the German homeland. Plans were under way to cross the Rhine and capture the Ruhr, Germany's industrial center.

The area chosen by the Allies to make the amphibious crossing was between the German cities of Emmerich and Wesel. The 17th Airborne Division and 6th British Airborne Division assisted the crossing by seizing several important objectives in a massive daylight airborne assault. Six parachute battalions, including Canadians of the 6th Airborne division supported by glider troops from the Air Landing Brigade, dropped on 24 March 1945 as a complete force, avoiding the mistakes of Arnhem. Together with the U.S. 17th Airborne Division, the aim of the operation was to secure and deepen the bridgehead cast of the Rhine and then advance across country to the Baltic coast, 350 miles away.

Their initial objectives were the high ground overlooking the crossing point at Diersfordter Wald and the road and rail bridges over the River Issel at Hamminkeln. Flying in tight formation, 540 U.S. Dakotas carried 12 parachute battalions: five British, one Canadian, and six U.S., all closely followed by 1,300 gliders packed with troops. The Germans expected the invasion, and fighting on the drop zones was heavy. By the end of the first day's action, 1,078 men of the 6th Airborne Division had been either killed or wounded, with 50 aircraft and 11 gliders shot down. Weather for the drop was perfect, and almost everyone landed on their respective drop zone, although some ended up in the trees and were cut down by German machine guns as they fought to free themselves.

The 5th Parachute Brigade suffered heavily from casualties as mortar fire exploded in the skies around them during the drop. On the ground, the enemy had occupied almost all of the nearby houses, but by late afternoon the brigade's three battalions had cleared them. Within 24 hours, all objectives for the brigade had been achieved; as planned, ground forces of the Twenty-first Army Group joined the division across Germany. The bridges over the river were secured and the village of Hamminkeln captured. All objectives were achieved within 24 hours.

Albert Atkins

V-Bombers

Trio of British-built jet bombers of unique design. By the 1950s, Britain was able to design, test, produce, and field what was known as the V-Bomber Force of jet bombers—the Avro Vulcan, Handley Page Victor, and Vickers Valiant. Each featured engines buried in the wing roots and had a crew of five.

First to fly was the Vickers Valiant on 18 May 1951. A total of 49 were introduced into RAF service. These four-engine aircraft were of relatively conventional design with a tapered cylindrical fuselage with raised cockpit, shoulder-mounted semiswept wings, and a swept empennage with a mid-mounted horizontal stabilizer. Four 10,000-pound/thrust Rolls-Royce Avon 201 turbojets gave the aircraft a top speed of 567 mph at 30,000 feet and a maximum range of 4,500 statute miles. The Valiant was capable of conventional or nuclear operations and had a maximum bombload of 21,000 pounds.

The Valiants flew their first operational missions in the conventional role during the Anglo-French intervention in Egypt (October-November 1956). Britain's first atomic bomb drop occurred during a test on 11 October 1956, when a Valiant dropped a bomb over Maralinga in southern Australia. This was followed by Britain's first hydrogen bomb drop in the Pacific on 15 May 1957, during Operation GRAPPLE. These aircraft served in 10 RAF squadrons until January 1965, when metal fatigue resulted in the RAF withdrawing the Valiants from service and scraping them.

The second V-Bomber, the Avro Vulcan, was by far the most radically designed and longest-tenured of the V-Bomber Force. These aircraft had large triangular wings with a tapered circular cross-sectioned fuselage, a raised cockpit extending forward, and a large vertical tail. The Vulcan became the first large bomber in the world to employ a delta-wing planform. This configuration offered excellent load-carrying capabilities at high altitudes. Coupled with the wing's thickness-to-chord ratio, the aircraft was capable of carrying a large military payload and fuel internally.

The prototype Vulcan first flew on 30 August 1952. On 11 July 1957, RAF No. 83 Squadron became the first operational unit to be equipped with Vulcans. In 1959, the first successful inflight refueling experiments with the Vulcan was conducted with a Valiant K.1 tanker. Over time, increased engine thrust from Olympus engines improved performance. A total of 45 Vulcan B.1s served in six Bomber Command squadrons.

The Vulcan B.2 prototype made its first flight on 31 August 1957. A feature started with the second prototype B.2 was the tailcone extension, which housed electronic countermeasures gear. Power for the B.2s was supplied by either 17,000-pound/thrust Olympus 201 or 20,000-pound/thrust Olympus 301 turbojets, offering a top speed of 645 mph and a cruising speed of 620 mph at 55,000 feet. These Vulcans were capable of low-level penetration missions with new terrain-following radar, installed after 1966. The B.2's range was 4,600 statute miles, which was increased to 5,750 statute miles with one aerial refueling. Its offensive armament consisted of nuclear weapons or up to 21 1,000-pound conventional bombs carried internally, or a Blue Steel standoff bomb carried semiexternally. The Blue Steel was deleted from the inventory in 1969. A total of 89 B.2s were built and served in 11 bomber squadrons.

Britain's third V-bomber was the Handley Page Victor. The first production aircraft flew on 1 February 1956, and the first operational unit began receiving Victors in April 1958. These aircraft had a bulbous, double-lobed fuselage cross-section and a scimitar-wing planform. Four 11,000-pound/thrust Armstrong Siddley Sapphire 200 turbojets powered the aircraft to a top speed of 680 mph at 20,000 feet and 650 mph at 40,000 feet. Its range was in excess of 3,000 statute miles. These aircraft were capable of conventional or nuclear operations. Victor B.1s were converted into K.1 tankers and became operational in February 1965. Victor

B.1s equipped four bomber squadrons; K.1s served in four squadrons.

The Victor B.1s were superseded by the B.2s starting in February 1962. This series had a greater wingspan and was equipped with four 19,750-pound/thrust Rolls-Royce Conway turbofan engines. The Victor B.2s had a top speed in excess of 600 mph at 40,000 feet and a range of 4,600 statute miles. They had a top speed of 640 mph at 40,000 feet and a maximum range of 4,600 miles. The aircraft was capable of carrying up to 35 1,000-pound conventional bombs or nuclear weapons internally. In addition, the B.2s could carry one Blue Steel standoff bomb semiexternally. The latter weapon was carried on the Victor B.2 BS, which was a low-level penetrator. The aircraft had an aerial refueling capability. A crew of five manned the Victors. Although the bomber versions of the Victor were removed from service in late 1968, 27 were returned to Handley Page for conversion into K.2 tankers. The K.2s carried 30 percent more fuel than the K.1s. The Victor B.2 BSs continued in service until 24 May 1974.

Alwyn T. Lloyd

References

Bowyer, Michael J.F. *Bombing Colours: RAF Bombers, Their Markings and Operations, 1937–1973.* Cambridge, UK: Patrick Stephens, 1973.

Thetford, Owen. *Aircraft of the Royal Air Force Since 1918.* London: Putnam, 1979.

Verdun, Battle of (1916)

The first major campaign (February-July 1916) in which aircraft were deployed in a strategic instead of a purely tactical manner. Both sides brought large numbers of machines to the Verdun sector, although the French quickly outnumbered the Germans and retained the numerical advantage throughout the battle. Verdun was also the first battle in which massed groups of aircraft supported the infantry's movements.

The German airmen fought defensively throughout the battle. Their main strategy was an aerial blockade in which pairs of aircraft patrolled defined sectors of the lines to prevent French intrusion into German airspace. In practice, the Germans did not have the quantities of aircraft or pilots to make the blockade effective; the planes were spread too thin and the French could cross the German lines at will. Alternatively, the French deployed their aircraft offensively; the fighters hunted for German planes while unescorted two-seaters flew reconnaissance and artillery-spotting missions, trusting the fighters to prevent enemy attacks.

At this time most of the German pursuit pilots at Verdun were still flying obsolete Fokker Eindecker monoplanes, whereas France had introduced the fast and agile Nieuport 11 in January 1916. Rockets attached to the Nieuport's struts were responsible for bringing down five German observation balloons in one day. The French had two famous fighter squadrons at Verdun, the Groupe des Cigognes (Storks) and the Escadrille Américaine (later, Lafayette Flying Corps), but the Germans had not yet begun to organize the *jagdstaffeln* (fighter squadrons) that would prove effective at the Somme later in the year.

Critics have noted that the Germans failed to use their bombers to destroy French supply lines like the Voie Sacrée or the bridges over the Meuse. However, if indeed the Germans' plan was to bleed the French white, then allowing French troops and supplies to flow into Verdun was a strange strategy indeed.

Suzanne Hayes Fischer

References

Cruttwell, C.R.M.F. *A History of the Great War, 1914–1918.* London, Granada, 1982.

Versailles Treaty

The treaty that brought about the Armistice of World War I and set the table for German humiliation, resentment, and rearmament. Under the articles of the Versailles Treaty, signed on 28 June 1919, Germany was forbidden from having any kind of military aviation, save for 100 unarmed hydroplanes to be used in the search for submarine mines. Furthermore, a ban on production of civilian aircraft until June 1920 went into effect and was extended until all aircraft equipment had been turned over to the Allies. It was not until 5 May 1922 that Germany was again allowed to produce aircraft on its soil.

Despite such restrictions, the German General Staff (operating under the code name *Truppenamt* due to treaty restrictions) went about laying the groundwork for a new air force. The planning process, led by General Hans von Seekt, came to include tactics, psychology, and theoretical plans. Most important among these was the notion of an air force separate from the army. In addition, the limitations the Versailles Treaty imposed on a 100,000-strong army actually helped the General Staff select the cream of the crop from thousands of applicants.

Air officers, including war veterans, were spread among the General Staff and army and infantry offices. As of 1925, thanks to the German-Soviet Rapallo Treaty of 1922, pilots were also able to train at a German army base in Lipetsk, Soviet Union, where some 300 men were secret employees of the German army. For lack of flying in Germany, though, many officers often worked on promoting aeronautics among civilians, encouraging, for example, the development of gliding as a sport.

Another impact of Versailles, which restricted powered flight until the 1926 Paris Air Agreement, was the reversion to gliding for the training of pilots. During the Weimar Republic, Germans took to designing, testing, and competing in glider meetings. The result was the discovery of ascendant currents (warmer air layers), as well as the maintenance of flying know-how among younger pilots.

Following the beginning of treaty enforcement, which included Allied inspections on German soil, the German High Command began to consider ways to circumvent the treaty without risking sanctions. One option was to establish aircraft factories outside of Germany. For example, the Dornier aircraft factory, spun off from the Zeppelin concern, established a testing ground and assembly plant at Altenrhein, on Lake Constance across from the German bank, and another in Italy. The Junkers company also established a factory in Fili outside Moscow, which operated from 1924 through 1927 but never achieved solvency due to underproduction.

The permission to develop civil air routes was smartly exploited, as the German government heavily subsidized a series of airline ventures the Junkers company developed as far as Iran, China, and Bolivia. The competition among local German routes was such that the government forced a merger in 1925, which led to the creation of the first Deutsche Lufthansa, active until 1945.

Overall, then, the Versailles Treaty had limited long-term effect on Germany's airpower capability. Some historians argue that its terms actually encouraged German military planners to think creatively: studying foreign air forces, avoiding their mistakes, and coming up with new ideas.

Guillaume de Syon

See also

German Air Force (Luftwaffe); Goering, Hermann; Paris Air Agreement; Udet, Ernst

References

Corum, James S. *The Luftwaffe: Creating the Operational Air War, 1918–1940.* Lawrence: University Press of Kansas, 1940.

Fritzsche, Peter. *A Nation of Fliers: German Aviation and the Popular Imagination.* Cambridge: Harvard University Press, 1992.

Vertol (Piasecki) H-21

Military helicopter manufactured by Piasecki Aircraft and Vertol. Its prototype, the HRP-2, entered U. S. Navy service in 1950. Characteristics of the H-21 included a rear-mounted piston engine, tandem three-blade rotors, tricycle landing gear, twin vertical fins, and a bent fuselage that earned it the nickname "Flying Banana." In 1954, the U.S. Air Force and Army began receiving the H-21. The Air Force procured the H-21A Workhorse mainly for transport and search and rescue in the Arctic. The Army procured the more powerful H-21C Shawnee for troop movement and supply in the combat zone. The Shawnee could carry about 15 combat loaded troops or sling load about two tons. In 1956 the Shawnee was the first helicopter to fly non-stop across the U. S.

The French Army flew the H-21C in the Algerian War, 1956–1962, and the U. S. Army flew it in the Vietnam War from 1961 until it was phased out with the advent of the UH-1 Huey. The U. S. sold over 50 H-21C's to the French to test their use in combat against guerillas and develop military characteristics for a follow-on transport helicopter. The Shawnee proved survivable under direct fire. Many characteristics were proposed, including greater lift, wider doors, improved radios, self-sealing fuel tanks, and armor plate. In Vietnam the Shawnees were found to need machineguns in both doors for suppressive fire at the landing zone. Piasecki and Vertol produced at least 707 "flying bananas."

John L. Bell

References

Headquarters, U. S. Military Assistance Command, Vietnam. *Evaluation of Helicopter Tactics and Techniques Report.* San Francisco: U.S. Army Military Assistance Command, Vietnam, 8 October 1962, 12 January 1963.

"Pisgah IV: Army Summer Study. Proposed Long Range Research and Development Program for the Army, 1960–1970." Volume 7: The Role of Army Aviation. Bethesda, MD: Operations Research Office, 1957.

Verville, Alfred (1890–1970)

Aircraft designer. Alfred Verville was born in Michigan in 1890. His R–3 racer became one of the most advanced aircraft in the world.

Verville learned electrical engineering through a correspondence course, a humble start to a career as one of American aviation's most famous "backroom boys." These were the engineer-designers who, far from the limelight, drew their dream planes on paper, supervised their construction, then let the pilots shake out the bugs. His first aviation experience came with Glenn Curtiss's firm in Hammondsport, New York. Curtiss needed good engineers, and Verville worked on the experimental flying boat *America.*

In early 1915, Verville opened the General Aeroplane Company in Detroit. A year later he produced a beautiful fly-

Designed by Alfred Verville and built in the Sperry plant, the Verville Sperry was years ahead of its time with its low cantilever wing and retractable landing gear. Inadequate testing kept it from entering service. (U.S. Air Force)

ing boat. Sensing the imminence of war, he also put together an experimental pusher plane that mounted a machine gun—an American adaptation of the British "gun bus." Unfortunately, it skidded out of control on frozen Lake St. Clair and crashed. In 1917, Verville closed his shop and went to work for the Fisher Body Division of General Motors. His first task was to adapt the British de Havilland D.H. 4 for production as the DH-4.

At war's end, the Army Air Service invited Verville to join an inspection tour of France to see the latest designs in fighter aircraft. He returned to the Army's flight research center at McCook Field enthusiastic about the latest SPADs he'd seen in France. His first design for the Army, the VCP-1, derived from them. It was relatively fast but not maneuverable. Verville next adapted the VCP-1 into the VCP-R (Racer). Powered by a 600-hp Packard engine, it won the 1920 Pulitzer Trophy with an average speed of 156.5 mph.

Verville designed several notable aircraft, including the Sperry Messenger, a small aircraft for liaison and artillery-spotting. However, his most important design was a streamlined low-wing monoplane with retractable landing gear—the R-3 racer, three of which were built for the Pulitzer Trophy race.

Built by Sperry, the R-3 was handicapped when it was powered by a Wright engine, which vibrated so badly that it kept the R-3s from reaching their maximum performance in the 1922 Pulitzer race. It was not until 1925 that a Curtiss-powered R-3 won the Pulitzer with a speed of 215 mph.

In 1925, Verville resigned to enter private business. His company produced several very handsome aircraft but failed to win significant orders.

Henry M. Holden

References

Who's Who in Aviation, 1942–1943. Comp. Wrighter's Program. Chicago: Ziff-Davis, p. 442.

Vian, Philip L. (1894–1968)

Admiral of the British Fleet. Sir Philip Vian, born on 13 June 1894 in London, entered the Royal Navy in 1910. He served in destroyers and cruisers during World War I and the interwar years.

When World War II began Vian was commanding a destroyer flotilla. He distinguished himself during the next three years as an aggressive and effective leader of light forces, which led to his early promotion to rear admiral in July 1941.

In 1943, Vian commanded a squadron of five escort carriers charged with providing fighter cover and close air support for the Allied landings at Salerno, Italy. Force V, operating in light winds and confined waters, provided more than half of all air support during the operation's first four days. This success was tempered by Vian's inexperience in carrier operations, reflected in extraordinarily high operational losses.

Vian then led the Eastern Task Force covering the Normandy invasion before taking command of the British carrier squadron destined for the Pacific. After preliminary strikes against oil refineries in Sumatra, the carriers joined the U.S. Pacific Fleet in March 1945 at Okinawa. After two months of operations the British Pacific Fleet withdrew for refit before rejoining the U.S. Third Fleet for the final attack on the Japanese home islands. Vian's adaptability to carrier-warfare requirements supported the integration of U.S. practices into the Royal Navy; his drive was manifest in the fleet's accomplishments.

After World War II Vian served ashore and afloat until his retirement in 1952, when he was specially promoted to Admiral of the Fleet. He died at Ashford Hill, Berkshire, 27 May 1968.

Paul E. Fontenoy

See also

Fleet Air Arm; Kamikaze Attacks; Mediterranean Theater of Operations; Okinawa; Salerno, Battle of; Task Force 38/58

References

Brown, J. David. *Carrier Operations in World War II: The Royal Navy.* London: Ian Allan, 1968.

Smith, Peter C. *Task Force 57.* London: William Kimber, 1969.

Vian, Sir Philip. *Action This Day.* London: Mullee, 1960.

Vichy French Air Force

Air force that operated under German occupation. Under the terms of an armistice signed with Germany on 22 June 1940, France was divided into an occupied German zone covering two-thirds of French territory, and an autonomous zone under the control of Marshall Philip Pétain, based in Vichy. Although the new state displayed collaborationist tendencies early on, it initially sought to maintain a modicum of autonomy and argued against certain German demands for disarmament.

Contrary to popular belief, the French air force led by General Joseph Vuillemin on 22 June still had almost 600 fighters, 300 bombers, and 200 reconnaissance aircraft, most based in France's North Africa colonies. Impressive as the numbers were, each squadron was incomplete, lacking spare parts, operational orders, and sometimes personnel.

General Jean-Marie Joseph Bergeret, who took part in the negotiations with Germany, sought to preserve the aircraft potential in Vichy territory and obtained from German and Italian authorities the specific term that planes stationed in France would be taken apart and stored rather than destroyed. Thus began a two-year period during which a part of the former French air force survived but undertook a different role.

Morale in the Vichy air force was a key element to survival. Many pilots were convinced that together they had shot down almost 1,000 enemy planes by the time of the armistice. This myth of 1,000 victories was carefully nurtured throughout Vichy's existence (the reality may be closer to 500 planes, but it is difficult to determine). The myth also helped convince the French that the 40 percent casualty rate among officers and 20 percent rate among NCOs and draftees incurred during the battle of 1940 was not in vain: France had not lost the air war; the fault lay elsewhere, or so did Vichy representatives present the facts. The blame was placed on England, and many French pilots who had thought of signing on with the RAF changed their minds following the British attack on the French fleet at Mers el-Kébir (an operation carried out to prevent Germany from using the ships.)

Domestically, the air force claimed that the poor quality of its machines was due to sabotage and paybacks (manufacturing was still slow, and many planes flew without quality checks because the air ministry had ordered quick acceptance due to war conditions). Consequently, Marcel Bloch (later Dassault), Emile Dewoitine, and Paul-Louis Weiller (a major air-transport manager) were all arrested. Meanwhile, General Bergeret was made secretary of the new Vichy air force in fall 1940.

The Vichy air force was assigned to train within the confines of the new French state and to protect its assets. This included defending the French navy fleet based at Mers el-Kébir in Algeria. This led to fighting between French and British fighters in July 1940 as the Royal Navy destroyed the French fleet. Ironically, having flown some 216 missions of all types within a week under difficult weather and conditions, French pilots had actually proven the need to maintain an air force and thus helped buy time with the Germans, who agreed to let the air force defend remaining French colonies.

Air Force engagements at Dakar, Gibraltar, and Syria against the Free French (who fought with the RAF) further affirmed the Vichy's plans for a new air arm. The planes used were the same as during the 1940 campaign against Germany but with different markings, as required by the Axis to help distinguish the French symbol from the RAF one.

Although the Vichy air force sought to maintain neutrality in its relations with Germany, there was in fact collaboration on several levels, in particular in the eastern Mediterranean, where German fighters used French bases while the latter were able to use the German phone system.

The end of the Vichy air force came in two acts. First, in fall 1942, the Allied landings in North Africa (Operation TORCH) led to a regrouping of French forces that had initially fought each other. In November, the chief of Vichy's North African arm announced to his troops that soon they would fight again, this time on the side of the Allies and using French and British aircraft.

In France proper, the German army invaded the so-called Free Zone, turning Vichy into a complete puppet government while destroying what was left of the air force there.

The Vichy air force thus became a dark page in the history of French airpower, whereby barely 10 percent of the 1940 air force followed the Free French and fought against them on several occasions. The dynamic of its operations depended heavily on Germany's willingness to let it operate, which was done only when the Germans felt they could gain a tactical advantage over the Allies.

Guillaume de Syon

See also
French Air Force

References

d'Abzac-Epezy, Claude. *L'armée de l'air des années noires.* Paris: Economica, 1998.

Vickers Aircraft

British aircraft manufacturer. Vickers got its start in aviation with the *Mayfly,* an airship built for the British Admiralty in 1911. The humor in the nickname was well-timed, for the *Mayfly* broke in two as it was being moved from its hangar.

Other Vickers airships were much more successful, including the famous series of blimps used for antisubmarine patrol, as well as the successful R-100 in which the famous Barnes Wallis and author Neville Shute Norway had a part.

It was aircraft in which Vickers excelled, however, producing in World War I such notable designs as the FB.5 Gunbus and the Vimy, which made many notable postwar flights. The Vimy's success in conquering the Atlantic and flying to Australia paved the way for a long series of large Vickers biplanes that included the Vernon, Virginia, Valentia, and Vanguard. In 1929, Vickers acquired Supermarine but allowed it to retain its own identity.

Although not successful with fighter prototypes, Vickers did very well with single-engine bombers and torpedo-planes, producing the Vildebeest and the Vincent, both of which served in combat during World War II. The principal Vickers contribution to that war was the magnificent Wellington, in which Barnes Wallis again had a hand. The Wellington was the heaviest and best of the twin-engine bombers that the RAF could deploy when it entered the war; it was Bomber Command's mainstay until the arrival of the four-engine bombers. The Wellington featured geodetic construction, which could endure a great deal of battle damage without failure. There were 11,461 Wellingtons built, and they served in a variety of roles.

In the postwar years, Vickers produced a series of twin-engine transports that were widely used and included the Viking, Valetta, and Varsity. However, it was the four-turbo-prop Viscount that made history, for it became a very popular airliner and was purchased for use in the United States. On the military side, Vickers had great success with the four-jet Valiant, the first of Bomber Command's V-bombers.

In 1960, Vickers became part of British Aircraft Corporation and lost its identity as a manufacturer.

The last airplane designed and constructed solely by Vickers was the very advanced VC-10. It first flew on 29 June 1962 and featured four engines mounted on the aft fuselage. Only 56 were built, but they were well-liked by the public, and some were later converted to tankers for the RAF.

Walter J. Boyne

See also
V-Bombers

References

Andrews, C. F. *Vickers Aircraft Since 1908.* New York: Funk and Wagnalls, 1969.

Vickers Valiant

Britain's first V-bomber. Designed to a slightly lower specification level, it entered service more quickly than the more complicated Victor and Vulcan. Although aerodynamically simpler, the Valiant did feature some innovations, such as the electric-drive undercarriage and flaps.

Prototype flying began in May 1951 with service deliveries beginning in 1954, when they replaced the obsolete Avro Lincoln. The bomber version was followed into service by a reconnaissance model designated the Valiant B(PR)1, which was exclusively by No. 543 Squadron. With tanker capabilities added to the airframe, this became the B(PR)K.1, capable of bombing, reconnaissance, and aerial refueling duties. It was followed into service by the BK.1, which removed the reconnaissance capability.

The Valiant saw action during the Suez Crisis in October-November 1956. Aircraft from Nos. 138, 148, 207, and 214 Squadrons flying from RAF Luqa, Malta, dropped high explosive bombs on designated targets. One last very important bombing mission was Operation GRAPPLE. This was the deployment of the first British atomic weapon, released over Maralinga, western Australia, on 11 October 1956.

Production ceased with the delivery of the last of 104 ordered aircraft at the end of August 1957. The Valiant remained in service until August 1964, when the fleet was hastily grounded after the discovery of extensive wing cracks in the rear wing spar. The majority were quickly scrapped, although a handful remained in use for test purposes. One aircraft still survives in the Royal Air force Museum at Hendon.

Kev Darling

References

Brookes, Andrew. *V Force.* London: Jane's Information Group, 1982.

Jackson, Robert. *V-Bombers.* London: Ian Allan, 1981.

Vietnam War

America's longest war; also, predominantly an air war in terms of resource allocation. Of the more than $200 billion expended while fighting the Vietnam War, fully half went to support air operations. Although occasionally pivotal, especially in support of ground operations, airpower was never decisive, and the role that airpower played remains controversial.

Some contend that if airpower had been used properly it could have produced a decisive victory. Airpower advocates point to results of Operation LINEBACKER II, the so-called Christmas Bombing of December 1972, as proof. Others contend that the United States used airpower to devastate the serene Southeast Asia landscape and decimate peace-loving peoples. Their claims that Hanoi and Haiphong were subject to carpet-bombing by B-52s and that napalm rained on villages are not supported by the facts.

Yet between 1962 and 1973 the United States dropped nearly 8 million tons of bombs on targets in Indochina. South Vietnam received about half that tonnage, making it the most bombed country in the history of aerial warfare. Nearly 3 million tons fell on Laos, and slightly less than 1 million tons were dropped on North Vietnam; Cambodia got hit with a 500,000 tons. The U.S. Air Force lost 2,257 aircraft to enemy action and accidents. Total U.S. air losses for the Army, Navy, Air Force, and Marines amount to 8,588 fixed and rotary-wing aircraft.

Airpower played a larger role than blasting enemy troop concentrations, railyards, petroleum storage facilities, and bridges in North Vietnam. Helicopters came into their own, and the Bell UH-1 Huey became the enduring symbol of U.S. operations. Indeed, choppers of all sorts provided unprecedented mobility for U.S. and South Vietnamese forces. They hauled troops, artillery, and supplies to dispersed locations throughout Vietnam and Laos. Medevac helicopters moved thousands of wounded soldiers from the battlefield to rear-area hospitals and life-saving surgery. Air Force transports moved troops and supplies throughout South Vietnam to keep far-flung outposts supplied even when isolated and besieged by enemy forces.

Innovation was key to the air war in Vietnam. Perhaps the most innovative application of airpower was the use of air-refuelable helicopters in search-and-rescue operations. The introduction of side-firing propeller-driven gunships for interdiction along the Ho Chi Minh Trail in Laos and their use in support of ground forces in South Vietnam, Laos, and Cambodia was another significant innovation. Revamped World War II–era propeller-driven aircraft like the North American A-26 and the Douglas Skyraider—with ruggedness, good loiter capabilities, and tremendous firepower—proved valuable for counterinsurgency as well as the more conventional role of close air support.

Throughout the Vietnam War, the preponderance of the air effort went to support ground operations. In this role, airpower was overwhelmingly successful in application and results. Indeed, superior firepower, especially in the ability of U.S. and allied forces to deliver high quantities of aerial explosives, kept allied combat deaths below 50,000 while accounting for much of the estimated 3 million in enemy killed.

Despite the dramatic accomplishments of airpower during the Vietnam War, the war itself remains an example of its misapplication and ultimate failure. Largely, the way airpower was used ran counter to the tenets of U.S. Air Force doctrine. Air Force generals argued in favor of a strategic bombing campaign against North Vietnam despite the fact that there was no industrial base to bomb and the diplomatic and political situation was such that terror-bombing, like that inflicted on Japan and Germany in World War II, was not a viable option. Indeed, one also can argue that the role airpower played in South Vietnam was strategically counterproductive. Vivid images of napalm engulfing village huts, of forests ravaged by Agent Orange defoliants, and of bombs cascading from the bellies of B-52s all seemed to support the claims of the antiwar movement. The case can also be made that the huge U.S. airpower capability, unprecedented mobility, and on-call close air support actually prolonged the war by perpetuating a strategic stalemate.

Although South Vietnam was the focus of aerial operations, so-called out-country operations accounted for an almost equal amount of effort. There were three major air campaigns aimed at North Vietnam, one of which, Operation ROLLING THUNDER, lasted almost four years (March 1965–November 1968). Laos, a nation of less than 3 million, received about 3 million tons of aerially delivered munitions. Most of this fell on North Vietnamese infiltration corridors (the Ho Chi Minh Trail) in sparsely populated eastern parts of the country. Cambodia was the target of secret bombing campaigns from late 1968 to early 1970 as well as B-52 raids until August 1973. The 500,000 tons of bombs that were dropped on Cambodia mostly fell into North Vietnamese base areas along the border.

Despite the magnitude of the bombing, only Operation LINEBACKER I, the airpower response to North Vietnam's Easter Offensive in 1972, was an unqualified success. The rest of the bombing either failed to achieve the stated objectives or the results are subject to conflicting interpretations.

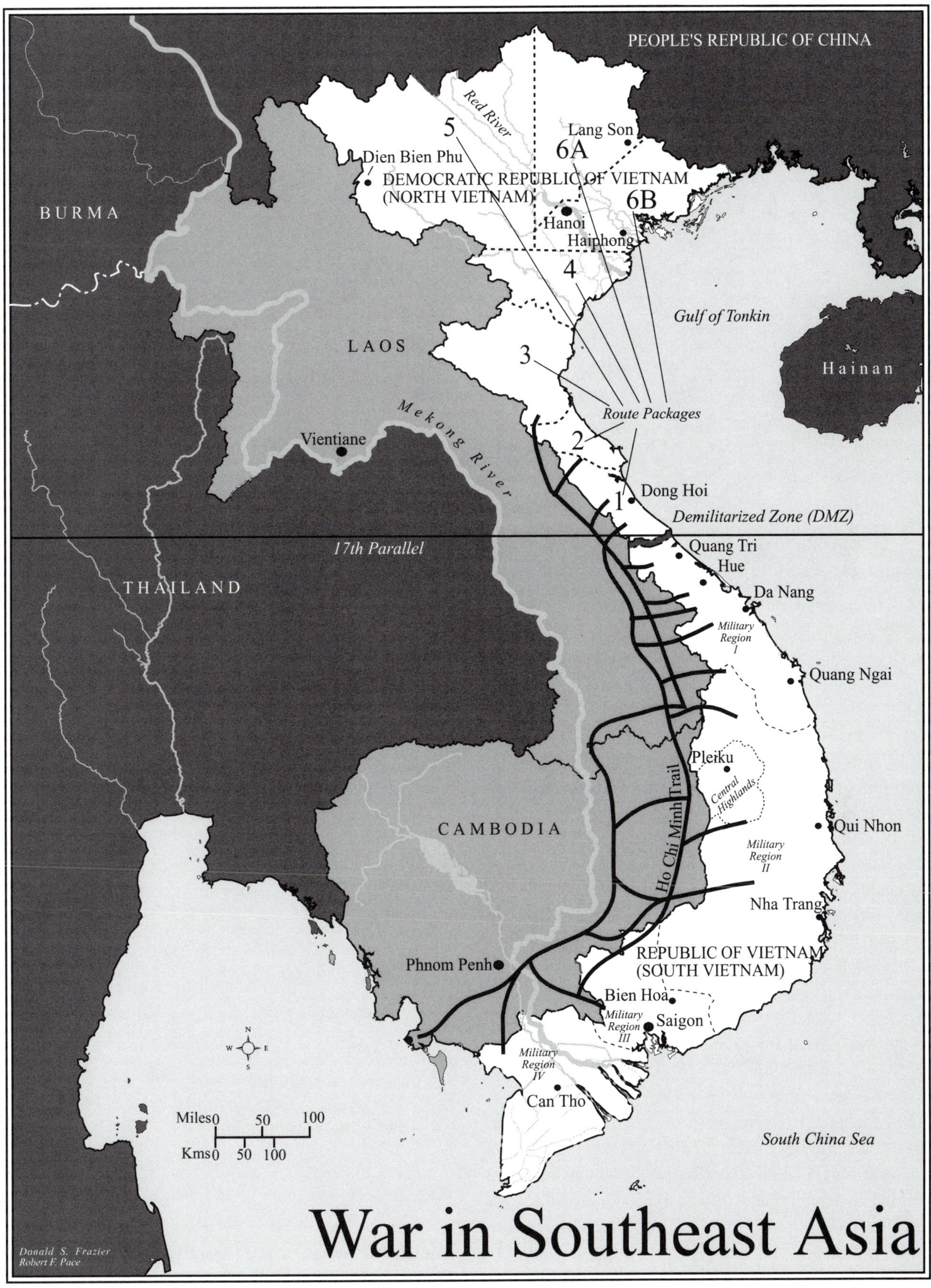
PEOPLE'S REPUBLIC OF CHINA
Red River
5
Lang Son
6A
Dien Bien Phu
DEMOCRATIC REPUBLIC OF VIETNAM
(NORTH VIETNAM)
6B
BURMA
Hanoi
Haiphong
4
Gulf of Tonkin
LAOS
3
Hainan
Route Packages
Mekong River
Vientiane
2
Dong Hoi
1
Demilitarized Zone (DMZ)
17th Parallel
Quang Tri
Hue
THAILAND
Da Nang
Military Region I
Quang Ngai
Pleiku
Central Highlands
Ho Chi Minh Trail
CAMBODIA
Qui Nhon
Military Region II
Nha Trang
REPUBLIC OF VIETNAM
(SOUTH VIETNAM)
Phnom Penh
Bien Hoa
Military Region III
Saigon
N
W
E
S
Military Region IV
Can Tho
Miles 0 50 100
Kms 0 50 100
South China Sea
War in Southeast Asia
Donald S. Frazier
Robert F. Pace

The role played by helicopters in Vietnam was so substantial that they became the symbol of American combat operations during the war. As well as hauling troops, artillery, and supplies to widely spread locations throughout Vietnam and Laos, they also served as medical evacuation helicopters. (Walter J. Boyne)

Perhaps the most controversial use of airpower was Operation ROLLING THUNDER, the longest bombing campaign ever conducted by the U.S. Air Force. Its objectives were to compel North Vietnam to stop supporting the Vietcong insurgency in South Vietnam and to stem the flow of troops and supplies moving to southern battlefields. It failed on both accounts. Despite U.S. efforts to compel North Vietnam to negotiate by escalating the bombing, Hanoi did not agree to begin talks until the United States stopped the bombing, which it did in late 1968. Bombing during ROLLING THUNDER also failed to interdict supply lines running into the South; in fact, the flow of troops and supplies doubled each year during ROLLING THUNDER.

In the wake of the Vietnam War, airpower advocates could also point to Operation LINEBACKER II as a success. Indeed, the bombing of military targets in and around Hanoi and Haiphong, when B-52s delivered 15,000 tons of bombs and fighter-bombers added another 5,000 tons, did achieve the limited objective of compelling North Vietnam to return to the Paris peace talks and, ultimately, led to the signing of the Paris Peace Accords of 23 January 1973. But what was gained at Paris—the return of U.S. POWs and the withdrawal of all U.S. forces from South Vietnam—hardly constituted an unambiguous victory; no great nation goes to war so it can retreat and get its prisoners back.

The air war in Vietnam remains controversial even today.

Earl H. Tilford Jr.

References

Clodfelter, Mark. *The Limits of Airpower: The American Bombing of North Vietnam.* New York: Free Press, 1989.

Futrell, Robert F. *The United States Air Force in Southeast Asia: The Advisory Years to 1965.* Washington, DC: Office of Air Force History, 1981.

Schlight, John. *South Vietnam: The Years of the Offensive, 1965–1968.* Washington, DC: Office of Air Force History, 1988.

Tilford, Earl H. Jr. *Crosswinds: The Air Force's Setup in Vietnam.* College Station: Texas A&M University Press, 1993.

Van Staaveren, Jacob. *Interdiction in Southern Laos, 1960–1968.* Washington, DC: Center for Air Force History, 1993.

Vietnamese Air Force (North)

Part of an air defense system that included antiaircraft guns, missiles, and radars. Outnumbered and technologically outclassed, the North Vietnamese Air Force (NVAF) inflicted many losses and forced the United States to divert valuable assets from strike missions to support missions.

NVAF inventory rose from about 30 aircraft in 1965 to 75 in 1968. By 1972, the NVAF had 93 MiG-21s, 33 MiG-19s, and 120 MiG-17s. These MiGs were small, highly maneuverable, and armed with heavy cannons as well as (on MiG-21s) two to four Atoll heat-seeking missiles. Under rigid ground control, MiGs lurked in the path of U.S. strike missions. MiGs used hit-and-run tactics, such as diving from high altitude at supersonic speeds through U.S. formations to fire a missile before escaping. U.S. aircraft were often forced to jettison their bombs, after which they could rarely accelerate fast enough to engage the nimble MiGs.

The NVAF exploited the U.S. rules of engagement. Airbases and surface-to-air missile (SAM) sites were built near so-called sanctuary areas (Hanoi, Haiphong, the Chinese border) that could not be attacked. Washington gradually lifted this restriction (1965–1968), but MiGs could always escape into Chinese airspace. The rule that MiGs could not be attacked without visual identification negated U.S. long-range air-to-air missile advantages and allowed MiGs to hide in clouds. President Lyndon Johnson's personal control of target selection caused U.S. forces to attack predictably and permitted the NVAF to concentrate defenses and establish ambushes. Finally, the United States could not attack the command-and-control system that was the key to the whole air defense network.

In air-to-air combat, the NVAF lost a total of 195 MiGs; the U.S. lost 77 aircraft. The NVAF was finally overwhelmed in 1972—bombers plastered NVAF airbases and U.S. fighters achieved a 5:1 kill ratio over the MiGs. However, the NVAF's true effectiveness should not be gauged by air-to-air losses but instead by comparison of the total offensive and defensive systems. Guns, missiles, and MiGs imposed heavy costs: from 1965 to 1968, the United States lost 800 men and 990 aircraft and spent $10 for every $1 in damage inflicted on North Vietnam. Moreover, the NVAF forced the United States to accompany each strike aircraft with many support aircraft (escorts, jammers, SAM suppression, tankers, airborne early warning, reconnaissance, combat search and rescue). This raised the cost of each mission and reduced the number of aircraft available to strike North Vietnam. In short, the NVAF was another component of Hanoi's successful overall strategy of attrition.

James D. Perry

References

Cooling, Benjamin Franklin, ed. *Case Studies in the Achievement of Air Superiority.* Washington, DC: Center for Air Force History, 1994, esp. chap. 10, "Southeast Asia."

Futrell, Robert F. *Ideas, Concepts, Doctrine: Basic Thinking in the United States Air Force, Volume 2: Basic Thinking in the United States Air Force, 1961–1984.* Maxwell AFB, AL: Air University Press, 1989.

Tilford, Earl H. Jr. *Setup: What the Air Force Did In Vietnam and Why.* Maxwell AFB, AL: Air University Press, 1991.

Vietnamese Air Force (South)

Originated in the air component set up to support the French-sponsored South Vietnamese Army in 1951. Initial equipment comprised a handful of Morane-Saulnier MS500 observation aircraft assigned to the 1st Aerial Observation Squadron. Further units were formed for similar purposes, with some receiving the Dassault MD-315 Flamant. The collapse of the French forces at Dien Bien Phu in May 1954 allowed the North Vietnamese to negotiate a favorable settlement. This also halted the expansion of the South's air force.

The South Vietnamese Air Force (SVAF) came into existence on 1 July 1955 as an independent branch, more in name than reality, as it had 58 aircraft available for operations and some 1,300 personnel. Initial equipment was Cessna L-19s and a handful of Douglas C-47s.

As part of its anticommunist policy, the United States began to back the government of Ngo Diem. First aircraft deliveries were via French advisers still in-country, but with their withdrawal the United States began to supply directly under the auspices of the Military Assistance Program with assistance via the U.S. Military Assistance Advisory Group Vietnam.

By 1960, the strength of the SVAF consisted of one squadron of F-8F Bearcats, two of C-47s, two with the L-19, one with the Sikorsky H-19, and a mixture of other types including trainers. The failure of the reunification election led the North to begin insurgent attacks into the South. As these escalated, the state of the SVAF aircraft became perilous; they were literally falling apart.

This led the United States to supply a batch of refurbished Douglas Skyraiders; spare parts problems led to grounding, and the old workhorses were replaced by North American T-28D Trojans. To support the SVAF, the USAF created the 4400th Combat Crew Training Squadron, which rapidly brought aircraft and crews up to a reasonable standard.

A change of government by coup in late 1963 was to lead to a greater expansion of the SVAF. The prime strike aircraft became the Douglas A-1 Skyraider with other types being supplied in sufficient numbers to make a difference. These included the Cessna 0–1 and the Douglas C-47.

Jet aircraft were to make an appearance on the front line in 1967. The types supplied included the Northrop F-5A/B and the Cessna A-37. There was even a combined unit flying the Martin B-57, although they were soon returned to USAF. The gunship concept made its first appearance during the Vietnam War, and so it comes as no surprise to find the

SVAF receiving quantities of the AC-47 and the Fairchild AC-119. Transport types were also upgraded from U.S. sources with versions of the C-7, C-47, C-119, and C-130 Hercules entering service. Observation and utility types were also replaced, the squadrons upgrading to the U-6 Beaver and various versions of the Bell UH-1 helicopter.

A negotiated cease-fire in 1973 had resulted in the South Vietnamese displaying some ire at being left out. In an effort to placate them and prepare the country for the imminent withdrawal of U.S. forces, Operations ENHANCE and ENHANCE PLUS were put into effect, with massive amounts of aid arriving for the air force. This included Northrop F-5s, Cessna A-37s, C-123s, and more C-130s.

All of the extra aid was in vain, as many aircraft were grounded due to lack of spares. This situation and the general corrupt nature of the government led the North Vietnamese to begin a concerted attack against the South. Although the pilots of the SVAF fought valiantly, losses mounted and their retreat continued. On 22 April 1975, the town of Xuan Loc was captured, and for all practical purposes the war was over. Some offensive sorties were flown by the SVAF, although more effort was expended on escaping the country. Some of the abandoned aircraft were later to see further service with the renamed the Vietnamese People's Air Force.

Kev Darling

References

Francillon, Rene J. *Vietnam Air War.* London: Aerospace, 1987.

Vimy Ridge, Battle of (1917)

During World War I, the general theory was that Vimy Ridge held the key to victory in France. If the heights of Vimy could be ascended by Allied forces, the army could break through and destroy the enemy. The war would at last be over. Had the Russians been more a problem to the Germans in the east, and had the British better exploited their victory, the theory might have proven correct.

Nevertheless, capturing Vimy, an effort that arguably made Canada a nation, proved immensely important the following year, when continued possession by the Germans may have been enough to have made their offensive a war winner.

At Vimy, aerial cooperation in spotting for the artillery, despite the heavy snow, proved crucial to the creeping barrage that paved the way for the infantry attack—a hint of the combined arms doctrine that would continue to develop the following year.

James Streckfuss

References

Cruttwell, C.R.M.F. *A History of the Great War 1914–1918,* 2nd ed. Chicago: Academy Chicago, 1991.

Vo Nguyen Giap (1912–)

Vietnamese general and minister of defense. Born in 1912 in the province of Quang Binh, Giap joined the Indochinese Communist Party in the 1930s. When the Communist Party was outlawed in 1939, he fled to China, where he became a military aide to Ho Chi Minh, helping to shape the Vietminh movement.

Giap became the Vietminh's foremost military commander during the war with the French (1946–1954), planning and directing the military operations that culminated in the 1954 defeat of the French at the Battle of Dien Bien Phu. Giap became North Vietnam's minister of defense and commander in chief of the People's Army of Vietnam (PAVN). As such, he planned the 1968 Tet Offensive and the 1972 Easter Offensive, both tactical disasters for the communists.

His reputation tarnished by these successive failures, General Giap was eased from power in favor of his protégé, PAVN Chief of Staff and Senior General Van Tien Dung. It was Dung, and not Giap, who planned and commanded the final offensive that defeated South Vietnam in 1975. Giap retired from politics in 1982.

James H. Willbanks

See also

Vietnam War

References

Currey, Cecil B. *Victory at Any Cost: The Genius of Viet Nam's Gen. Vo Nguyen Giap.* Washington, DC: Brassey's, 1997.
Davidson, Phillip B. *Vietnam at War: The History, 1946–1975.* Novato, CA: Presidio Press, 1988.
Vo Nguyen Giap. *Dien Bien Phu.* Hanoi: Foreign Languages, 1962.

Voisin Aircraft

French aircraft manufacturer founded by Gabriel Voisin (1880–1973), one of the great French aviation pioneers. He started to build sailplanes in 1905, then in 1907 he created the first flyable French biplane (the Delagrange No. 1, named after its buyer). Many derivatives followed until 1910, when they were supplanted by the Canard. This was selected by the French and Russians as pusher types that reached Escadrille V.14 in 1913. The metallic-tube structure was revolutionary, generating low weight with ruggedness, and was later found on all Voisin designs. The pusher formula made it possible to put a gunner in the front cockpit; this became the Voisin canon design.

At the beginning of World War I, only two escadrilles possessed some Voisins. The Type III made history when, on 5 October 1914, the two-man crew achieved the first official aerial victory against an Aviatik B.1. It was as a bomber that the Voisin Type V became famous, being able to launch 220 pounds of bombs. Big raids, with as many as 75 planes, started over Germany in May 1915, but heavy losses obliged the airmen to operate at nighttime only. Produced in great numbers, the Voisin pushers were also used by the British, Italian, Russian, and Belgian services. Improved models like the Type VIII reached the front in November 1916, and some new Type Xs were in use in 1918. A total of 3,470 were produced in France during World War I, plus 112 in Italy, 1,120 in England, and several hundred in Russia.

Immediately after the war, Gabriel Voisin left the aeronautical business to launch a much more peaceful car factory. The mechanical genius of Gabriel Voisin had found another and more peaceful field of expression.

Stéphane Nicolaou

References

Voisin, Gabriel. *Mes 10000 cerf-volants* (My 10,000 Kites). Paris: La Table Ronde, 1960.

Voskhod

A temporary replacement for the Soviet Union's Vostok program; the circumstances of its creation pertain directly to the space race. In the wake of President John F. Kennedy's challenge to land a man on the moon, Soviet premier Nikita Khrushchev had hoped to initiate a swiftly successful program of his own. However, informed that such a project would take several years, he reportedly approached rocket designer Sergei Korolyov about beating the United States in placing several people into space in one shot.

Korolyov came back with Voskhod: a Vostok capsule with the ejection seat removed and replaced with two or three seats. Added support equipment raised the capsule's weight to more than 5,200 kilograms, which exceeded the lifting thrust of the booster used to date, the A-1 (a modified R-7 ICBM). Consequently, an improved booster, the A-2, was developed, which included an upper stage, Venus, designed to reach higher orbits.

Voskhod 1 involved the first multiple-crew flight when on 12–13 October 1964 cosmonauts Vladimir Komarov, Boris Yegorov, and Konstantin Feoktistov boosted into orbit. The cramped conditions in the capsule prevented them from wearing their pressure suits, which also explains why Korolyov was intent on having the men remain aloft no more than 24 hours. A second Voskhod mission in March 1965 carried two cosmonauts, Pavel Belyayev and Aleksei Leonov, and demonstrated the feasibility of extravehicular activity (EVA) when Aleksei Leonov left the cabin briefly.

Although further Voskhod flights were planned, including one in which female cosmonaut Valentina Tereshkova would have performed an EVA, none materialized, and Soviet manned space activities stopped until April 1967. The Voskhod missions are generally viewed as the equivalent of the U.S. Gemini program, undertaken for the purposes of gaining experience in preparation for sending men to the moon. Indeed, construction and testing of a new vehicle, Soyuz, was under way to replace Voskhod and lay the basis for an expedition to the moon. Testing first took place in November 1966 and February 1967 in the form of KOSMOS flights.

Guillaume de Syon

See also

Korolyov, Sergei; Soyuz Space Vehicle; Vostok

References

Newkirk, Dennis. *Almanac of Soviet Manned Spaceflight.* Houston, TX: Gulf, 1990.
Oberg, James. *Red Star in Orbit.* New York: Random House, 1981.
Siddiqi, Asif A. *Challenge to Apollo: The Soviet Union and the Space Race, 1945–1974.* NASA SP-2000-4408. Washington, DC: NASA/U.S. Government Printing Office, 2000.

Voss, Werner (1897–1917)

German World War I ace. Voss transferred to aviation in 1915, having already won the Iron Cross, second class, with his Hussar regiment on the Eastern Front. Arriving at Jasta 2 late in 1916, Voss had time to form a friendship with Manfred von Richthofen prior to the latter's transfer the following January. When Voss's score began to rise in the new year, a friendly competition developed between the two, and Voss became Richthofen's chief competitor for the top spot on the aces' list.

By September, Voss was leader of Jasta 10, part of Richthofen's Flying Circus, and his score stood at 48. On the evening of 23 September, in an attempt to make it 50, Voss encountered RAF No. 56 Squadron's B Flight under the command of James McCudden. In what many consider the epic aerial combat of World War I, Voss was killed as he fought alone against seven SE 5as.

James Streckfuss

See also

German Air Force (Luftwaffe)

References

Franks, Norman L.R., Frank W. Bailey, and Russell Guest. *Above the Lines: The Aces and Fighter Units of the German Air Service, Naval Air Service, and Flanders Marine Corps, 1914–1918.* London: Grub Street, 1993.

McCudden, James. *Five Years in the Royal Flying Corps.* Bath, UK: Cedric Chivers, 1965.

Vostok

The first Soviet manned space program. It successfully launched Cosmonaut Yuri Gagarin on 12 April 1961 and concluded with *Vostok 6* in 1963, which carried the first woman in space, Valentina Tereshkova. The capsule, designed by Sergei Korolyov's OKB-1 design bureau, consisted of two parts. A reentry sphere, thus shaped because of known speed range, widest internal volume for a given external surface, and the option of shifting the center of gravity (removing the need for attitude-control rockets), contained the cosmonaut, the survival gear, and the ejection seat. The other part, a service module, contained the electrical batteries, thrusters to orient the machine, and the retro rocket.

Several empty test capsules were launched in 1960 and failed, but on 19 August of that year a machine identified alternately as *Korabl Sputnik 2* or *Sputnik 5* fitted with a heat shield and parachute system carried two dogs, rats, mice, and fleas. The test went well, and a fourth rocket was sent up. But the new RO-7 engine, built into the third stage of the modified Semyorka booster, failed. The dogs on board survived the fall.

Another three test capsules were fired, the last one, *Korabl Sputnik 5/Sputnik 10*—carrying a dummy in a spacesuit and a dog in March 1961—flew successfully and cleared the way for *Vostok 1* on 12 April 1961. *Vostoks 3* and *4,* as well as *5* and *6,* carried out double flights; although they were not designed for docking, they succeeded in coming within a few kilometers of each other.

Vostok was essentially a low-orbit manned program, which nonetheless gave the Soviet Union an advantage in the space race as well as the basis for the development of multiple-crew programs, such as Voskhod and Soyuz. In addition, modified Vostok capsules were used to orbit reconnaissance satellites that could function for up to 10 days in orbit. Thus, an entire camera system was placed where the cosmonaut would have been. The first successful launch of this modified Vostok was *Kosmos 4* on 26 April 1962.

Guillaume de Syon

See also

Gagarin, Yuri; Korolyov, Sergei; Soyuz Space Vehicle; Sputnik; Voskhod

References

Harford, James. *Korolev.* New York: Wiley, 1997.

McDougall, Walter. *The Heavens and the Earth: A Political History of the U.S. Space Program.* Baltimore: Johns Hopkins University Press, 1997 [1985].

Peebles, Curtiss. *Guardians: Strategic Reconnaissance Satellites.* Novato, CA: Presidio Press, 1987.

Siddiqi, Asif A. *Challenge to Apollo: The Soviet Union and the Space Race, 1945–1974.* NASA SP-2000-4408. Washington, DC: NASA/U.S. Government Printing Office, 2000.

Vought A-7 Corsair II

Conceived as a replacement for the Douglas A-4 Skyhawk; it ran counter to the "faster is better" trend of the 1950s and 1960s. The Navy's requirement was purposefully kept subsonic in order to minimize costs. At first glance the A-7 gives the appearance of being a stubby F-8 Crusader, resulting in the nickname "Sluf" (Short little ugly fellow). The A-7 first flew on 27 September 1965 and was followed by 395 A-7As and A-7Bs.

In order to secure Pentagon permission to begin the development of the F-X (what became the F-15), the Air Force agreed to purchase A-7s as its primary attack aircraft. Although intending to order a minimal-change version of an existing type, the Air Force soon specified a more powerful engine, better avionics, new guns, and additional external weapons. The A-7D thus emerged as a much more capable platform than the early Navy variants. The first flight was on 5 April 1968; a total of 459 A-7Ds were produced.

The Navy was impressed and ordered 597 slightly modified A-7Es, although the first 67 were produced as A-7Cs without the new engine. Fifty retired A-7A/Bs were rebuilt into two-seat TA-7C trainers, and 31 A-7Ds were converted into similar A-7Ks. Exports were limited to 60 A-7Hs and five TA-7H two-seaters purchased by Greece in 1975 (later supplemented with 36 former Navy A-7As and TA-7Cs), as well as a number of A-7As and TA-7Cs that were rebuilt and supplied to Portugal as A/TA-7Ps.

Dennis R. Jenkins

References

Wagner, Ray. *American Combat Planes.* 3rd ed. Garden City, NY: Doubleday, 1982.

Vought Aircraft

U.S. manufacturer of attack, fighter, reconnaissance, and scout-bomber aircraft for the U.S. Navy and Marines.

Chauncey M. "Chance" Vought (1888–1931) and Birdseye B. Lewis (1888–1917) founded the Lewis and Vought Corporation in New York on 18 June 1917. Lewis left for France shortly afterward as a member of General John J. Pershing's staff and later perished in an airplane accident. Thus, Vought managed the firm from the beginning and subsequently dropped Lewis from the company's name.

The son of a sailboat designer, Vought often applied terms of the sea to his aircraft. He studied engineering at several schools before being attracted to aviation by the Long Island Air Meet of 1910. In the seven years preceding U.S. entry into World War I, Vought became chief engineer for the Aero Club of Illinois and editor of *Aero and Hydro* magazine. He also served as engineer with Glenn H. Curtiss, Orville Wright, and Glenn L. Martin before establishing the partnership with Lewis.

Vought's seventh design with his own company, the VE-7, proved successful. After testing the two-seat tractor-style biplane at McCook Field (later Wright-Patterson) in March 1918, the U.S. Army Air Service contracted serial production with Vought. More important for the company's future, the U.S. Navy purchased 129 advanced versions of the VE-7 as its primary fighter after World War I. As a result, the VE-7 would be the first airplane to fly from the deck of a U.S. aircraft carrier (the USS *Langley*) in October 1922. The same year, Vought constructed an observation plane (UO-1) that incorporated the newly designed Lawrance radial engine, precursor to the Wright Whirlwind. Used as the standard catapult plane for U.S. Navy battleships and cruisers, the land model flew with the U.S. Marines. The improved O2U held world records in 1927 for speed, altitude, and endurance for Class-C seaplanes. It was also the first U.S. Navy plane to have an official nickname—"Corsair."

By the time Corsair II (O3U) appeared in 1931, United Aircraft and Transport Corporation (later, United Technologies) had purchased Vought Aircraft Corporation. Vought moved from New York to Connecticut and eventually occupied the facility and shared the name of another United subsidiary, Sikorsky. Based on the work of Igor I. Sikorsky, Vought-Sikorsky became the first U.S. company to mass-produce military helicopters (the R-4, R-5, and R-6). Meanwhile, during the course of the 1930s Vought moved toward building all-metal low-wing monoplanes such as the Vindicator scout-bomber (SB2U). In 1938, a team led by Rex Beisel designed the definitive Corsair (F4U), a high-performance fighter built around a Pratt and Whitney Double-Wasp engine. Arguably one of the best fighter aircraft of World War II, the plane then served as a tactical weapon in the Korean War and remained in production until December 1952.

With the start of the Cold War, security concerns prompted the U.S. government to insist that aircraft companies disperse from the Northeast; Vought moved to Dallas in 1950. Four years later, to avoid antitrust suits, the company broke away from United to become Chance Vought Aircraft, Inc. By that point, the corporation had merged its airframe designs with turbojets. In 1953, Vought won a contract for a prototype of the U.S. Navy's first Mach 1 fighter. Tested in 1955, the Crusader (F-8) achieved high-speed flight while maintaining low-speed characteristics for carrier operations via a hydraulically operated variable-incidence wing. The design won the prestigious Collier Trophy in 1957. After joining the Ling-Temco-Vought conglomerate in 1961, the firm signed a U.S. Navy contract in 1963 to produce the last Corsair, a subsonic attack plane designated the A-7. Four hundred durable A-7s were manufactured; they supplied close support for U.S. ground forces during the Vietnam War. It could not produce another winning Corsair design. As a result, the Dallas facility manufactured components for other airframe companies such as subassemblies for the McDonnell Douglas (Boeing) C-17 military transport. Northrop Grumman bought the plant in September 1994, then sold it in July 2000 to the Carlyle Group, which resurrected the Vought name for the facility.

James K. Libbey

See also

Curtiss, Glenn Hammond; Martin Aircraft; Pershing, John Joseph; Sikorsky, Igor I.; U.S. Marine Corps Aviation; United Aircraft Corporation; United States Navy, and Aviation; USS Langley; Vought A-7 Corsair II; Vought F4U Corsair; Vought F-8 Crusader; Vought VE-7; Wright, Orville

References

Lawson, Robert L., ed. *The History of U.S. Naval Air Power.* New York: Military Press, 1985.

Moran, Gerard P. *Aeroplanes Vought. 1917–1977.* Temple City, CA: Historical Aviation Album, 1978.

Schoeni, Arthur L. "Vought Aircraft Production: 1917–1947." *American Aviation Historical Society Journal* 44 (Winter 1999).

Swanborough, Gordon, and Peter M. Bowers. *United States Navy Aircraft Since 1911.* Annapolis, MD: Naval Institute Press, 1990.

Vought F4U Corsair

U.S. World War II fighter. Rex B. Beisel and his team designed the F4U around Pratt and Whitney's 18-cylinder R-2800 radial engine and the large propeller necessary to absorb its power. The type's most characteristic feature, its inverted gull wing, allowed use of a shorter, stronger undercarriage than required by a straight wing and also reduced aerodynamic drag. The prototype exceeded 400 mph during official trials, a first in the U.S. Navy.

Design began in 1938, and the prototype made its first

The distinctive shape of the Chance Vought F-4U made it a favorite with the public, and its performance made it a favorite with the U.S. Navy and Marine pilots who flew it. (U.S. Navy)

flight on 29 May 1940. Production commenced a year later, and the last of 12,582 aircraft, an F4U-7 for France, was delivered in December 1952.

Despite the Corsair's stellar performance, the Navy initially confined F4U operations to shore-based squadrons, because undercarriage bounce and restricted forward view were undesirable characteristics for deck landings. In the hands of Navy and Marine aviators, as well as New Zealanders, Corsairs proved themselves ashore in the Southwest Pacific. Royal Navy carrier operations vindicated the Corsair, so it deployed aboard U.S. carriers from late 1944.

During World War II, Corsairs excelled both as interceptors and in ground attack. Postwar, jets took over interception, but F4Us became important as night-fighters and retained the ground attack role. In Korea, Corsairs shone in both missions. French Navy Corsairs also saw action in Indochina, Algeria, and at Suez. Corsairs went to Argentina, and some fought each other during the so-called Soccer War between Honduras and El Salvador.

The Corsair was among the best Allied fighters of World War II and certainly the finest carrier fighter of its era.

Paul E. Fontenoy

See also

Boyington, Gregory; Dien Bien Phu, Battle of; Fleet Air Arm; French Naval Air Force; Suez Crisis; U.S. Marine Corps Aviation; United States Navy, and Aviation; Vought Aircraft

References

Kinzey, Bert. *F4U Corsair in Detail and Scale.* 2 vols. Carrollton, TX: Squadron/Signal, 1998.

Tillman, Barrett. *The F4U in World War II and Korea.* Annapolis, MD: Naval Institute Press, 1979.

Vought F-8 Crusader

U.S. fighter of the 1950s and 1960s. The F-8 Crusader exceeded Mach 1.0 on its first flight (March 1955) and had a significant performance advantage over its land-based contemporaries, largely as a result of imaginative engineering design and extensive use of magnesium alloy and titanium. The first fighter version of the Crusader, the F8U-1 (F-8A), entered service with the U.S. Navy in December 1956, followed in 1958 by the RF-8A, which had the armament and fire-control system replaced by cameras and additional fuel. The F-8C and F-8D both had improvements to the power plant and radar, and the F-8E had an improved radar and ground attack capability.

The F-8 was a hot aircraft for its time, capable of reaching

40,000 feet less than three minutes after brake release. It required skill and judgment to fly, particularly from an aircraft carrier, and had spectacular stall and spin characteristics. It was a dangerous opponent in a dogfight; very maneuverable, it could take battle damage and had very good fuel reserves. During the Vietnam War, the F-8 had the highest kill-to-loss ratio of any U.S. aircraft. A total of 1,261 Crusaders were produced in fighter, photoreconnaissance, and fighter-bomber versions.

Andy Blackburn

See also

Aircraft Carriers, Development of; Vietnam War

References

Gillcrist, Paul T. *Crusader! Last of the Gunfighters.* Atglen, PA: Schiffer, 1995.

Michel, Marshall L. III. *Clashes: Air Combat Over North Vietnam, 1965–1972.* Annapolis, MD: Naval Institute Press, 1997.

Vought VE-7

Originally designed by the Lewis Vought Company as a two-seat advanced trainer that could be used to instruct U.S. pilots during World War I. It was the first aircraft extensively tested by the U.S. Army. Although the first plane was delivered on 11 February 1918, full production did not begin until after the end of the Armistice, by which time the need for advanced trainers had been reduced. At the time of its introduction, the VE-7, which was powered by a 150-hp Hispano-Suiza engine, received high praise and was considered to be one of the finest training aircraft yet produced.

In 1919, a VE-7 entered in the New York–Toronto Air Race and placed first in its class. This brought it to the attention of the U.S. Navy, then seeking an aircraft that was suitable for shipboard use. The Navy issued an initial order of 20 planes, stipulating they be equipped with the improved 180-hp Hispano engine that the Wright Aeronautical Corporation was producing under license.

The Navy introduced a single-seat fighter version, designated the VE-7S, in 1921. The redesignated VE-7SH was later converted for catapult use by replacing the undercarriage with a centerline float. A carrier version, the VE-7SF, had flotation equipment and arresting gear fitted. One of the latter was flown from USS *Langley*'s flight deck for the first time on 17 October 1923 by Lieutenant Commander Virgil C. "Squash" Griffin.

Thomas Wildenberg

References

Wagner, Ray. *American Combat Planes.* 3rd ed. Garden City, NY: Doubleday, 1982.

Variations of the Huck starter were used all over the world, some up through World War II. Here it is being prepared to crank up a Vought VE-7. (U.S. Navy)

Wake Island, Battles of (1941–1945)

U.S. outpost in the central Pacific Ocean captured by the Japanese shortly after the attack on Pearl Harbor and held until the Japanese surrender. Shortly before Pearl Harbor, a squadron of PBY Catalina patrol planes and Marine Fighter Squadron 211 (VMF-211) flying Grumman F4F-3 Wildcats had reinforced Wake's tiny garrison of Marines. Despite a warning message and diligent patrol efforts, the initial Japanese air raid caused considerable damage to the poorly equipped garrison, especially the fighter squadron, which suffered more than 50 percent personnel casualties. The remaining fighters were instrumental in repulsing the initial Japanese landing effort on 12 December 1941. This triumph, including the destruction of several Japanese ships, gave the United States a tremendous boost in morale.

Rear Admiral Husband Kimmel, commander in chief of the Pacific Fleet, hoped to reinforce and hold Wake, perhaps even trapping the Japanese fleet in a naval battle that would avenge Pearl Harbor, but on 17 December he was removed from command. His temporary replacement, Vice Admiral William Pye, decided that reinforcing Wake was not worth the risk to his reduced forces. He aborted the Wake relief mission to the dismay and scorn of more aggressive Navy and Marine Corps officers. The Japanese then reinforced their invasion force with aircraft carriers returning from Pearl Harbor. On 22 December, VMF-221 lost its last fighter. Despite the conversion of squadron personnel into infantrymen, the garrison, with Japanese troops on the island, surrendered on 23 December. Its garrison entered captivity for the remainder of the war.

As the United States assumed the offensive in the Pacific, the Japanese garrison prepared to fight to the end, but U.S. airpower and naval power made an invasion unnecessary. U.S. forces simply bypassed Wake, cutting off virtually all supply routes. U.S. Army and Navy aircraft pounded the Wake garrison, but starvation hurt the Japanese more than the air attacks. Following the Japanese surrender, Wake Island returned to U.S. control.

Grant Weller

See also

Consolidated PBY Catalina; Fletcher, Frank Jack; Grumman F4F Wildcat; Halsey, William F.; Japanese Army Air Force, Imperial; Japanese Naval Air Force, Imperial; Prisoners of War; U.S. Army Air Forces; U.S. Marine Corps Aviation; United States Navy, and Aviation

References

Schultz, Duane. *Wake Island.* New York: St. Martin's, 1978.

Warden, John A. III (1943–)

U.S. Air Force colonel John Ashley Warden III was born in McKinney, Texas, on 21 December 1943. He earned a bachelor's degree from the U.S. Air Force Academy in 1965, a master's degree from Texas Tech University in 1975, and graduated from the National War College in 1985. He has more than 3,000 flying hours in aircraft such as the F-15, F-4, and OV-10 and flew 266 combat missions as a forward air controller during the Vietnam War. After serving as commander of the 36th Tactical Fighter Wing at Bitburg AFB, Germany, Colonel Warden headed the Air Staff's Warfighting Deputy Directorate.

In this capacity, his team developed alternative airpower strategies to the existing USAF doctrine, and Generals Norman Schwarzkopf and Colin Powell have credited him as the strategic architect of the 1991 Gulf War air campaign. Warden's ideas on the application of airpower have influenced USAF thought throughout the 1990s.

He served as special assistant to the vice president of the United States and as commandant at the USAF's Air Command and Staff College. Following retirement in 1995, he has developed new approaches to business and war strategy—the so-called Prometheus process. Colonel Warden's decorations include the Distinguished Service Medal, Defense Superior Service Medal, Legion of Merit, Distinguished Flying Cross, and the Air Medal with 10 Oak Leaf Clusters.

John Andreas Olsen

References

Reynolds, Richard T. *Heart of the Storm: The Genesis of the Air Campaign Against Iraq.* Maxwell AFB, AL: Air University Press, 1995.

Warden, John A. *The Air Campaign: Planning for Combat.* Washington DC: National Defense University Press, 1988.

______. *Winning in FastTime.* New York: HarperCollins, 2001.

Warning Systems

Ground-based and airborne air defense systems designed to detect and track incoming aircraft. By the end of World War I, early warning had evolved from rudimentary beginnings to a series of well-organized and reasonably effective systems. These generally relied on human observers to report aircraft sightings to a central information center, which would in turn direct resources to respond to the threat. Though the Mark I Eyeballs and simple radio transmitters of World War I would be supplemented in later years with a succession of technologically more complex systems, this would remain the basic model of air defense command and control throughout the twentieth century.

In World War II, radar revolutionized air defense. For the first time there was at least a realistic possibility of intercepting large formations of incoming aircraft before they reached their target. The most dramatic example of the importance of radar—and of warning systems in general—was the successful air defense system deployed by the British during the Battle of Britain. Later in the war, Germany and Japan were forced to form extensive early warning systems of their own, prompting U.S. and British strategic bombing forces to develop a variety of exotic technological countermeasures to confuse enemy detection devices. Engineers and physicists were proving as important as soldiers and airmen in this new kind of wizards' warfare.

Of course the ultimate technological innovation to emerge from World War II was the atomic bomb, and the advent of nuclear weapons raised the stakes enormously. Whereas in the past destroying 5–10 percent of attacking aircraft would be considered a success, with nuclear weapons every single bomber not intercepted could mean the loss of an entire city. Despite these odds the United States, driven by deep fears of a nuclear Pearl Harbor, led the way in creating a series of early warning systems deployed across the top of North America and later in space. In the 1950s, the United States and Canada deployed a series of early warning radar chains such as the Mid-Canada, Pinetree, and Distant Early Warning radar networks. Yet even the detection—let alone interception—of every incoming bomber during an intercontinental attack remained a dubious proposition at best.

In response to the threat of ICBM attacks, the United States in the 1960s deployed a second generation of early warning systems, including the Ballistic Missile Early Warning System and a variety of satellites. Though attempts were made at creating antimissile defenses, realism dictated that the primary role of air defense control centers, such as the massive North American Air Defense Command complex buried within Cheyenne Mountain, Colorado, would be primarily one of generating warnings sufficient only to initiate retaliation, not conduct a successful defense. The era of mutual assured destruction had arrived.

Partially as a result of its own devastating experience with surprise attack during World War II—the German invasion of 22 June 1941—the Soviet Union suffered from a similar sensitivity to surprise nuclear attack. Though it was hampered by a smaller economic and technological base than the United States, the Soviet Union eventually was able to field its own series of early warning systems throughout the 1960s and 1970s. Geography and limited resources prevented other nuclear powers such as Britain and France from creating warning systems as elaborate as those of the superpowers, but each could hope to generate at least enough warning to make its second-strike capability secure.

During the later years of the Cold War, and especially in the post–Cold War era, warning systems designed primarily for tactical use grew in importance. During the Vietnam War aircraft began mounting large search radars and using inside controllers to direct the interception of enemy aircraft. The extremely lopsided success of the Israeli air force in combat with Syrian aircraft over Lebanon in 1982 owed much to Israeli use of E-2 airborne early warning (AEW) aircraft, an example repeated by the Coalition's use of E-3 AEW aircraft during the 1991 Gulf War with Iraq. Just as the tactical early warning problem appeared to have been mastered by such systems, however, the United States threatened the long-term dominance of radar and other early warning methods with its introduction of stealthy aircraft designed to evade radar and other standard means of detection.

David Rezelman

See also

Airborne Early Warning; Ballistic Missile Early Warning System; Britain, Battle of; College Eye Task Force; Defense Support

Program, and Missile Detection; Distant Early Warning; Electronic Warfare; KOSMOS; Mutual Assured Destruction; Radar; SAGE Defense System; Satellite Command and Control; Satellites; Signals Intelligence

References

Buderi, Robert. *The Invention That Changed the World: How a Small Group of Radar Pioneers Won the Second World War and Launched a Technological Revolution.* New York: Simon and Schuster, 1996.

Jones, Reginald Victor. *The Wizard War: British Scientific Intelligence, 1939–1945.* New York: Coward, McCann, and Geoghegan, 1978.

Nordeen, Lon O. Jr. *Air Warfare in the Missile Age.* Washington, DC: Smithsonian Institution Press, 1985.

Warsaw Pact Aviation

Generally, the air forces of Albania (1949–1968), Bulgaria, Czechoslovakia, East Germany, Hungary, Poland, Romania, and the Soviet Union, which was the pivot of airpower. The Soviets were also the main source of weaponry, munitions, repair, parts, supplies, and training during the pact's existence (1955–1991).

Since World War II, Moscow directed and supplied the creation, reorganization, and expansion of aviation in its Eastern European satellites (in Bulgaria, Hungary, and Romania, air forces were forbidden under the 1947 peace treaties). Top-ranking Soviet air officers even commanded Polish and Hungarian air forces until 1956.

The air forces of non-Soviet members were organized as tactical air forces and equipped by the end of the 1980s mostly by Soviet-made aircraft. These included MiG-17, -21, -23, -27, and -29 fighter/fighter-bombers; Su-7, -20, and -25 ground attack aircraft; Mi-24 helicopter gunships; Tu-134, -154, Il-14, An-2, -24, and -26 transport aircraft; and Mi-2, -4, -6, -8, and Ka-26 helicopters. There were also widely distributed Czech trainers (L-29, L-39), Polish-made helicopters (Poland and Czechoslovakia), and some French Puma and Alouette helicopters (Romania).

Organization and force structure varied among non-Soviet nations. Air/air-defense forces of Bulgaria, Czechoslovakia, Hungary, and Romania formed one component within their armies. The East German army air/air-defense force consisted of three main arms of service. The Polish air force (the largest in Eastern Europe) and air defense developed into a unitary service in the late 1980s.

Czechoslovakia's aviation was usually most modern within the pact, while East Germany's had the closest operational subordination to the Soviet allies. The pact also experimented in the 1950s with an integrated Bulgarian-Hungarian-Romanian fighter regiment, and beginning in 1962 the air defense systems of East Germany, Poland, and Czechoslovakia were fully integrated with the Soviets' air defense.

At its height, the total combat airpower of non-Soviet members was 2,346 aircraft and 393,000 men. Additionally, Poland had 57 aircraft and 2,300 troops in naval aviation. In the event of war in Europe, most of these forces and their infrastructure had to be operationally subordinated to the command of Soviet tactical aviation deployed in East Germany, Poland, Czechoslovakia, and Hungary. They also had to be supported by the Soviet Long Range Aviation.

Despite the formidable numbers, about 91 percent of non-Soviet aviation was obsolete, its electronic systems and combat characteristics far less advanced than those in NATO. Nevertheless, Warsaw Pact–era aircraft remain in service in all the former member states; even Germany inherited some from East Germany.

Peter Rainow

See also

Antonov Aircraft; Ilyushin Aircraft; Mikoyan-Gurevich Aircraft; Mil Aircraft; Poland, Aircraft Development and Production; Polish Air Force; Soviet Air Force; Soviet Aircraft Development and Production; Tupolev Aircraft

References

Green, William, and John Fricker. *The Air Forces of the World. Their History, Development, and Present Strength.* New York: Hanover House, 1958.

Miller, David. *The Cold War: A Military History.* New York: St. Martin's, 1998.

Simon, Jeffrey. *NATO–Warsaw Pact Force Mobilization.* Washington, DC: National Defense University Press, 1988

Washington Naval Conference

The 1921–1922 series of meetings between the United States, Great Britain, Japan, France, and Italy; arguably the first modern international arms-limitation effort. It produced three major agreements, all of which set limits on the production of naval weapons and territorial aggrandizement, but otherwise they helped create the environment that led to the outbreak of World War II. The Five Power Naval Treaty defined the ratio of battleships among the signatories, halted territorial expansion (especially in the Pacific), and limited the development of U.S. and British bases in the Pacific, heightening Japan's importance in the region. The Four Power Pacific Treaty (which excluded Italy) guaranteed the security of each signatory's Pacific island territories but refused to go beyond diplomatic efforts to resolve potential disputes. The Nine Power Pacts (which added Belgium, the Netherlands, China, and Portugal) reaffirmed the Open Door Policy in China. It was primarily an economic declaration, and none of the signatories agreed to defend China if attacked.

As a whole, these three agreements succeeded by constraining the construction of capital ships. Unfortunately, the agreements failed to account for Japanese imperial designs, especially toward China. From Tokyo's point of view, Western unwillingness to act decisively in protecting Pacific territories and defending a pathetically weak China from invasion served as a green light for establishing the Greater East Asia Co-prosperity Sphere. As such, the Washington Naval Conference inadvertently facilitated the start of World War II.

Robert S. Hopkins

References
Buckley, Thomas H. *The Washington Conference, 1921–1922.* Knoxville: University of Tennessee Press, 1970.
Roskill, Stephen. *Naval Policies Between the Wars, Volume 1: The Period of Anglo-American Antagonism.* New York: Collins, 1968.

Weapons Systems

According to the official dictionary of the U.S. Air Force, a weapons system (WS) is an instrument of combat, such as a bomber or guided missile, together with all related equipment, supporting facilities, and services, required to bring the instrument upon its target or another location.

This explanation, when applied to a single unit of striking power built around an air vehicle such as a fighter airplane, refers not only to the immediately visible components (airframe, power plants, fire-control system, machine guns and/or cannons, missiles, navigation equipment, radar system, rockets, and other devices that are known to be aboard) but also to the entire system; the air vehicle is only the carrier.

The first established weapons system (WS) designation was the one issued to the Boeing B-47 Stratojet as WS-100A/L, which included all of its systems. The "A" suffix meant that the weapons system number (-100A) was for a standard B-47 model bombardment aircraft. The "L" suffix (-100L) denoted that it was a photographic reconnaissance version of the B-47 designated RB-47—the "RB" prefix meaning photographic reconnaissance bomber. The second WS number issued was WS-101A/L, which identified the Boeing B-52 and RB-52 Stratofortress aircraft and all of their respective systems.

Beginning in the early to mid-1950s, then, many WS-numbered designations have been assigned to attack, bomber, fighter, and interceptor aircraft, as well as to strategic missile systems such as the General Dynamics (Convair) SM-65 Atlas—America's first operational ICBM, or WS-107A.

Weapons-system classifications are ongoing; for example, the more recent Boeing North American B-1 B Lancer is WS-139A. A much higher WS-number (WS-464L) identified the Boeing X-20 Dyna-Soar program. (There were no WS-1 through WS-99 designations.)

Steve Pace

References
Air Force ROTC. *Fundamentals of Aerospace Weapon Systems.* Washington, DC: U.S. Government Printing Office, May 1961.
Knaack, Marcelle Size. *Encyclopedia of U.S. Air Force Aircraft and Missile Systems, Volume 2: Post-World War II Bombers, 1945–1973.* Washington, DC: U.S. Government Printing Office, 1988.

Welch, Larry D. (1934–)

U.S. Air Force general and Chief of Staff. Larry Welch was born on 9 June 1934 in Guymon, Oklahoma, and enlisted in the Kansas National Guard in October 1951. In November 1953, he entered the aviation cadet program, received his pilot's wings and commission as a second lieutenant, and served for a time as a flight instructor. His assignments included a stint as operations officer for the 389th Tactical Fighter Squadron stationed at Phan Rang Air Base in South Vietnam. While in Vietnam he flew combat missions in F-4Cs over North Vietnam, South Vietnam, and Laos. From July 1972 to September 1974, he served as deputy commander for operations, then as vice commander, 35th Tactical Fighter Wing, at George Air Force Base, California. After receiving his first star in 1977, he became inspector general, Tactical Air Command. In November 1982, he went to Headquarters U.S. Air Force in Washington, D.C., as deputy Chief of Staff for programs and resources and in August 1984 became vice Chief of Staff of the U.S. Air Force. From August 1985 to June 1986, he served as commander in chief, Strategic Air Command, and director, Joint Strategic Target Planning Staff, at Offutt Air Force Base, Nebraska. He became chief of Staff of the U.S. Air Force on 1 July 1986.

At the outset of his tenure as chief, General Welch was concerned with the U.S. strategic deterrent force's lack of ability to retaliate promptly against "hardened Soviet nuclear forces" and command-and-control assets. He made the strategic force issue one of his top priorities. He saw the B-1B as a superb bomber that would serve for future years initially as a penetrating bomber and then as a cruise-missile carrier.

When the Soviet Union professed a more open attitude toward the West as expressed by Gorbachev's policies of glasnost and perestroika openness and restructuring, General Welch urged that the United States remain strong in order to continue pressing the Kremlin. He also saw that the federal deficit was becoming a major national concern and that a smaller defense budget could help reduce that deficit.

On 30 June 1990, General Welch retired.

George M. Watson Jr.

References

Boyne, Walter J. *Beyond the Wild Blue: A History of the U.S. Air Force, 1947–1997.* New York: St. Martin's, 1997.

Nalty, Bernard C., ed. *Winged Shield, Winged Sword: A History of the United States Air Force, Volume 2: 1950–1997.* Washington, DC: Air Force History and Museum Program, 1997.

Watson, George M. Jr. *Secretaries and Chiefs of Staff of the United States Air Force: Biographical Sketches and Portraits,* Washington, DC: Air Force History and Museum Program, 2001.

Wells, Edward C. (1910–1986)

Boeing's chief engineer on the B-17 and other U.S. bomber programs. Edward C. Wells was born to a middle-class family in Boise, Idaho. The family moved to Portland, Oregon, where Wells completed high school. He started college at Willamette University and went on to Stanford, where he earned a degree in mechanical engineering in 1931. Wells gained a summer job at Boeing during his junior year in college and permanent employment upon graduation.

At the age of 24 he began work on the Model 299—the B-17 prototype. Complex mechanical systems were his forte. When the airplane became a formal program, Wells became its chief engineer, earning him the title father of the B-17. He was also placed in charge of the B-29 program.

After World War II, Wells headed Boeing's engineering force in developing the B-47, B-52, KC-135, 707, 757, 767, SST, and numerous space programs. He retired in 1972 but remained a member of the board of directors until 1986.

Alwyn T. Lloyd

References

Geer, Mary Wells. *Boeing's Ed Wells.* Seattle: University of Washington Press, 1992.

Wells, Herbert George (1866–1946)

British author who inspired many aviation pioneers with his sci-fi works. Born in Bromley, Kent, on 21 September 1866, H. G. Wells is most famous for authoring such novels as *The Time Machine* (1895) and *The War of the Worlds* (1898). Although briefly schooled, he was mostly self-taught. Beginning in 1901, he wrote about future technologies in his novels. *The War in the Air* (1908) even contributed to the first round of "Zeppelinitis" in England, where rumored airship incursions caused brief mass hysteria. Wells also wrote editorial pieces on airpower in April 1914, arguing that new technologies, not established strategies, would determine the winner. Wells was not always on the mark: While predicting atomic bombs, he dismissed submarines; he also described World War I as the "war to end all wars." After the conflict, his interests shifted, but his work inspired writers who projected air-war scenarios in the 1940s. Wells survived the London Blitz and died in his sleep on 13 August 1946.

Guillaume de Syon

References

Batchelor, John. *H. G. Wells.* New York: Cambridge University Press, 1985.

Westland Lynx

One of three helicopters types designed for use by the armed forces of Britain and France, the others being the Gazelle and the Puma. All were authorized by a joint agreement signed in February 1967.

Led by Westland, the first development Lynx started flight trials in March 1971. The first in-service use by the Fleet Air Arm began in September 1976, at which time they began to replace the earlier Westland Wasp. A similar deployment program was put in place for the French navy.

The naval Lynx has proven popular with the navies of many overseas countries, serving with Denmark, Germany, Holland, South Korea, and others. A version destined for the Royal Air Force was later cancelled, its place being taken by the more useful Gazelle.

The British army also operates the Lynx in the antitank role, replacing the earlier Westland Scout. The first variant deployed was the AH.1, although subsequent developments have seen the version number rise to the current AH.9 standard.

Each helicopter unit flies a number of Lynx for the attack role; spotting tasks and communications are the province of the Gazelle.

Kev Darling

References

James, Derek N. *Westland Aircraft Since 1915.* London: Putnam, 1981.

Westland Lysander

Forever known as the "Lizzie"—the British plane developed to replace the venerable Hawker Hector biplane in the army cooperation role. The contract was placed in the 1935, the first prototype flying in June 1936. An initial contract for 140 production aircraft was placed in the same year, with service deliveries beginning in 1938.

With the outbreak of hostilities in Europe, five squadrons of Lysanders deployed as part of the air component. Their duties included artillery-spotting and reconnaissance. During these operations, a Lysander succeeded in shooting down a Heinkel He 111 over British Expeditionary Forces territory. When the forces in France suffered their reversal, the air component acted in support of the troops at Dunkirk. Their roles included dropping supplies and attacking German forward positions. The Lysanders of No. 4 Squadron were the last aircraft to return to the United Kingdom.

Overseas the Lysanders based in the Middle East took part in operations in Egypt and Greece before moving on to India. In support of operations in both the Far East and Europe, a special-duties version was produced. It featured an extra external fuel tank and an access ladder fixed to the outside to allow for egress and ingress by special agents.

After the retreat from Dunkirk, the Lysanders based in Britain were temporarily equipped with sponsons on the wheel spats for carrying light bombs. As the RAF received newer aircraft, the duties of the Lysander changed to that of air-sea rescue and target-towing.

The last active-duty Lysanders retired from No. 367 (Special Duties) Squadron in 1945 and was finally declared obsolete in 1946.

Kev Darling

References

James, Derek N. *Westland Aircraft Since 1915.* London: Putnam, 1981.

Wever, Walter (1887–1936)

First chief of Luftwaffe General Staff (1933–1936). Wever was born in Whilelmsort, West Prussia, on 11 November 1887 and died in the crash of his Heinkel He 70. Wever had only recently learned to fly and was a relatively inexperienced pilot for a sophisticated aircraft like the He 70. The cause of the crash was pilot error—he had failed to release the control lock.

Wever entered the German army in 1905 and became a lieutenant in 1906 and a captain on 18 June 1915. After 1918, he spent six months in the War Historical Department of the General Staff and also as an officer in field commands. Promoted to major in 1926, he became a lieutenant colonel on 1 April 1930 and a full colonel on 1 February 1933. He did well in assignments as company commander from 1924 to the beginning of 1927 and as a battalion commander from October 1929 to September 1931. During this time, he held positions in the secret air branch of the Reichswehr ministry. He was chief of the army's training department from 1 March 1932 to 31 August 1933.

On 1 September 1933, he was appointed chief of the Air Command Office, the secret general staff of the still-clandestine Luftwaffe. Like many others, he studied the ideas of Italian airpower pioneer Giulio Douhet. Originally opposed to an air force as an independent service, he sympathized with Hitler's political aim of reestablishing a powerful Germany, including a strong independent bomber force.

Wever grasped the importance of a strategic bomber fleet to deter potential enemies during the German rearmament phase and ordered the development of a four-engine bomber dubbed the "Uralbomber." It was his view that the Soviet Union was a possible adversary, but he did not adopt Douhet's theory of the primacy of the strategic bomber. Aware of Germany's geostrategic position in the center of Europe, he knew that a tactical bomber forcer was needed above all. On 6 May 1936, Wever ordered that the fast medium bomber should have priority over all heavy bomber projects.

Wever was one of the first Reichswehr officers who thought about the combined operation of tanks and aircraft. Under him, the first German paratroop force was created and the dive-bomber introduced. Promoted to one-star general on 1 October 1934 and given the second star a half-year later, Wever did not live long enough to see the fruits of his labors. Had he lived longer, the strategic bomber force might have received priority if political and military conditions had called for it. They could not be pursued simultaneously in strength for material reasons.

Horst H. Boog

References

Boog, Horst H. *Die Deutsche Luftwaffenfuerung.* Fuehrungsprobleme-Spitzengliederung-Generalstabausbildung. Stuttgart: Deutsche Verlags-Anstalt, 1982.

Corum, James S. *The Luftwaffe: Creating the Operational Air War, 1918–1940.* Lawrence: University Press of Kansas, 1997.

Weyland, Otto P. "Opie"

U.S. Army general; during 36 years of service, he mastered tactical operations as a theorist and as a practitioner. Born in Riverside, California, he graduated from Texas A&M University and entered the U.S. Army Aviation Service in 1923. He spent his early career as a fighter and observation pilot. Named deputy director of air support at USAAF headquarters at the outbreak of World War II, Weyland developed tactics, techniques, and equipment for tactical air operations. In 1943, he went to Europe to lead the 84th Fighter Wing and soon commanded the XIX Tactical Air Command. In the latter position he directed fighter-bombers for Operation OVERLORD and teamed with General George S. Patton to spearhead the breakout from Normandy. Weyland introduced armor-column liaison officers—USAAF fighter pilots who rode with lead tanks (later called forward air controllers). Additionally, he perfected battlefield air-interdiction tactics, permitting airpower to cover Patton's southern flank during the Third Army's drive across France.

In July 1950, Weyland became vice commander for operations of the Far East Air Forces (FEAF), where he coordinated attack efforts to save the United Nations troops hemmed in along the Pusan perimeter. Later he focused USAF efforts to interdict enemy rail and communications lines in the Korean War. In 1951, he became FEAF and UN Air Force commander. He directed the continued interdiction efforts and the air superiority struggles over MiG Alley. Weyland also directed the strategic campaign against the Korean electrical power system and Korean irrigation dams. After the Korean War, he reorganized Japan's air defense and aircraft industry.

After his return to the United States in 1954, Weyland battled for tactical operations in an Air Force dominated by the Strategic Air Command. He became commander of the Tactical Air Command, where he introduced the Composite Air Strike Force and furthered overseas deployment capability. He retired in 1959.

John Farquhar

References

Bright, Charles D., ed. *Historical Dictionary of the U.S. Air Force.* New York: Greenwood Press, 1992.

Futrell, Robert F. *The United States Air Force in Korea, 1950–1953.* Rev. ed. Washington, DC: Office of Air Force History, 1983.

White, Thomas Dresser (1901–1965)

U.S. Air Force Chief of Staff. Thomas Dresser White was born on 6 August 1901 in Walker, Minnesota. He attended St. John's Military Academy in Delafield, Wisconsin, from 1914 to 1918. He graduated from the U.S. Military Academy in 1920, one of the youngest graduates in its history. He became interested in airplanes and transferred to the Air Service, earning his wings in 1925. Assigned to Washington, D.C., with the 99th Observation Squadron, he enrolled at Georgetown University to study the Chinese language. He was sent to China in 1927 to continue his language study and was able to convince his superiors to allow him to observe the fighting between Chiang Kai-shek and the communists. The reports that he sent back were so thorough that his superiors allowed him to stay longer. He also began his study of Russian that would serve him well when, after a stint at Air Corps Headquarters in 1931, he was assigned to the Soviet Union as assistant military attaché for air in February 1934.

A series of attaché assignments in Italy, Greece, and Brazil further developed his talents not only as a first-rate intelligence officer but also as an accomplished linguist. During these tours he became fluent in Chinese, Russian, Italian, Greek, Portuguese, and Spanish. Promoted to captain in August 1935, he returned to the United States in May 1938 to attend the Air Corps Tactical School at Maxwell Field, Alabama, and the Army Command and General Staff School at Fort Leavenworth, Kansas.

Following his tour at Fort Leavenworth, he was again assigned staff duty in the office of the chief of the Air Corps. Shortly thereafter, he was promoted to major and sent to Brazil as military attaché. After World War II began, White was recalled to the United States in 1942 to serve as assistant Chief of Staff of Operations and then Chief of Staff of the Third Air Force at Tampa, Florida, whereupon he was promoted to brigadier general. In January 1944, he was reassigned to Army Air Forces Headquarters, where he became assistant Chief of Staff of intelligence. In this post he helped formulate plans for the D-Day invasion.

His request for combat duty was finally honored in September 1944 when he went to the Pacific as deputy commander of the Thirteenth Air Force and took part in the New Guinea, southern Philippines, and Borneo campaigns. In June 1945, White became commanding general of Seventh Air Force in the Marinas and led it in island-hopping to Okinawa, where it played an important role in bringing about the Japanese surrender. Promoted to major general in 1946, he was called to Tokyo as Chief of Staff of the Pacific Air Command. One year later, he assumed command of the Fifth Air Force in Japan.

General White returned to the United States in 1948 to serve as director of USAF legislation and liaison. He was promoted to lieutenant general in 1951, and for more than a decade he held a succession of top-level posts in Headquarters USAF. General Nathan F. Twining selected him as his vice Chief of Staff in 1953. In that position, General White was largely responsible for domestic issues such as the air defense buildup.

When General White replaced General Twining as Chief of Staff of the Air Force in 1957, his major challenge was to interweave a complex array of missiles, space-based systems, and atomic weapons into the nation's arsenal. Believing that the Air Force ought not devote its resources overwhelmingly to a single weapons system, he called for a mixed force of strategic bombers; intercontinental and medium-range ballistic missiles; tactical aircraft; installations and reliable and secure communications; an advanced reconnaissance system; a modernized cargo fleet; and advanced space systems. During his tenure, the Air Force made its initial deep move into space, launching satellites for reconnaissance, weather forecasting, communications, and as space probes.

When he retired in 1961, the National Geographic Society honored him by designating a space award to be given annually in his name. Later, President John F. Kennedy appointed him to the General Advisory Committee of the Arms Control and Disarmament Agency, which was extended by President Lyndon Johnson. Although suffering from the initial stages of leukemia in 1965, he was called upon to chair a special advisory committee appointed by Secretary of the Air Force Eugene M. Zuckert to investigate the cadet honor system and the athletic program at the U.S. Air Force Academy. It was his final mission for the Air Force and his country; he died on 22 December 1965.

George M. Watson Jr.

References

Futrell, Robert F. *Ideas, Concepts, Doctrine: Basic Thinking in the United States Air Force, 1907–1984.* 2 vols. Maxwell AFB, AL: Air University Press, 1989.

Watson, George M. Jr. *Secretaries and Chiefs of Staff of the United States Air Force: Biographical Sketches and Portraits,* Washington, DC: Air Force History and Museum Program, 2001.

Whittle, Frank (1907–1996)

First person to think of the modern aviation gas-turbine engine; recognized as an independent coinventor of the turbojet. He was born to working-class parents in Coventry, England, on 1 June 1907 and entered the Royal Air Force in 1923, graduating from its Aircraft Apprentices Wing in 1926. He also graduated from RAF College–Cranwell in 1928 and from Cambridge University in 1936.

Whittle was fascinated with the idea of aviation gas turbines from an early age and discussed them in his 1928 thesis, "Future Developments in Aircraft Design." He then expanded his original ideas and in 1930 applied for his first gas turbine–related patent, which outlined the concept for the modern turbojet engine. Forming a private company in 1936, Power Jets Ltd., Whittle began running a prototype engine on 12 April 1937. His first flightworthy engine, designated the W.1, took to the sky on 15 May 1941, powering an experimental Gloster E.28/39 aircraft. Whittle's company was nationalized by the British government in 1944, and shareholders were compensated at bargain-basement prices. He retired from the RAF in 1948 with the rank of air commodore and was knighted by King George VI. Whittle then became a consultant. In 1976, he came to the United States and served on the faculty of the U.S. Naval Academy.

Stanley W. Kandebo

See also

Gloster Aircraft; von Ohain, Hans Joachim Pabst

References

Boyne, Walter J., and Donald S. Lopez, eds. *The Jet Age.* Washington, DC: Smithsonian Institution Press, 1979.

Golley, John. *Whittle: The True Story.* Washington, DC: Smithsonian Institution Press, 1987.

Whittle, Sir Frank. *Jet.* New York: Philosophical Library, 1954.

Wild Weasel

Air-suppression tactic. Over Southeast Asia during the Vietnam War, North Vietnamese radar-guided SA-2 Guideline surface-to-air missiles (SAMs) were a major problem for U.S. fliers. The first SAM downed an F-4C in July 1965, and others followed. Because most of the SAM sites were off-limits in Hanoi and Haiphong Harbor, U.S. aircraft adjusted their tactics, flying beneath detectability by the SAMs. This approach made the planes vulnerable to antiaircraft and small-arms fire and cost 50 Air Force and Navy aircraft. Evasion was but a weak workaround; until aircraft carried their own electronic countermeasures, the solution was the EC-66 and the Wild Weasel.

Brigadier General K. C. Dempster held a seminar that produced the solution with two pieces of equipment. The first was the APR-25 Radar Homing and Warning System, an IR-133 panoramic receiver to analyze the APR-25 signals and determine the origin—antiaircraft, ground-control intercept radar, or SAM site. The second was the APR-26 launch-warning receiver to detect the increased power indicating a SAM launch. Wild Weasel teams included an ace pilot and an equally ace electronic-warfare officer. The first aircraft selected for the task was the North American F-100F, armed with 20mm cannons, 2.75-inch rockets, and later Shrike missiles tuned to home in on the SAMs. The Weasel tactic was to precede the attacking jets by 5 minutes, get the SAM to reveal itself, then attack with missiles and conventional weapons.

The suppression of enemy air defense carried out by the Wild Weasel crews was one of the most important and certainly the most dangerous missions of the Vietnam War. The Republic F-105s had to tank up going in and coming out. (U.S. Air Force)

On 21 November 1965, the first Wild Weasels were at Korat AFB, Thailand. They were the 624th Tactical Fighter Wing (Wild Weasel Detachment) of the 388th Tactical Fighter Wing and were given the mission code-named IRON HAND. Wild Weasels flew in four flights with F-105 escorts, and their motto was "first in—last out." The first year, seven attacks got seven sites with two aircraft lost and five damaged beyond repair.

By 1966, the Weasels upgraded to F-105s. On 20 December, Captains John Pitchford and Robert Trier were in the first Wild Weasel ever to be shot down. The first success came during Operation ROLLING THUNDER with Captains Al Lamb and Jack Donovan as crew members.

The Wild Weasels helped reduce the loss rate of aircraft. In 1965, 11 aircraft were lost to 194 SAMs; by 1972 49 were lost to 4,244 SAMs, a decline in the SAM success rate from 5.7 percent to 1.15 percent. After 1966, U.S. aircraft had their own electronic countermeasures, but the Wild Weasel and EC-66 continued to play a role.

John Barnhill

References

Berger, Carl, ed. *The United States Air Force in Southeast Asia, 1961–1973: An Illustrated Account.* Washington, DC: Office of Air Force History, 1984.

Boyne, Walter J. *Beyond the Wild Blue: History of the United States Air Force, 1947–1997.* New York: St. Martin's, 1997.

Williams, Robert R. (1918–)

U.S. Army Lieutenant general. Born in Evanston, Wyoming, he graduated from West Point in 1940 and entered the field artillery. Lieutenant Colonel William W. Ford selected

Williams, a private pilot since 1935, to be his operations officer when organizing the test detachment for organic aviation in the field artillery in December 1941. During the next 33 years, Williams was at the forefront of efforts to make the greatest possible use of organic air in the Army.

As a member of the air staff (December 1944–December 1945), Williams was one of the coauthors of a series of reports on the effectiveness of field artillery aircraft in combat, essential events in the 1945 decision to expand the program to the other ground combat arms. In the 1940s and 1950s, he was a central figure in an informal group of mid-level Army officers who were convinced that the Army was not exploiting its aerial vehicles to their full potential and who worked behind the scenes to make it so. He played a key role in the establishment of the so-called Howze Board and the implementation of its recommendations. Williams was responsible for the testing and evaluation of the Army's first airmobile division (August 1963–June 1965). Other important assignments included commander and commandant of the Army Aviation Center and School (1961–1963), the director of aviation on the Army staff (1966–1967), commander of the 1st Aviation Brigade in South Vietnam (1967–1968), and assistant Chief of Staff for force development on the Army staff (1970–1972). After retiring in 1974, he became president of Bell Helicopter International.

Williams had greater cumulative impact upon the scope and purpose of Army aviation during its first 30 years than any other individual.

Edgar F. Raines Jr.

References

Bergerson, Frederic A. *The Army Gets an Air Force: Tactics of Insurgent Bureaucratic Politics.* Baltimore: Johns Hopkins University Press, 1980.

Galvin, John R. *Air Assault: The Development of Airmobile Warfare.* New York: Hawthorne, 1969.

Raines, Edgar F. Jr. *Eyes of Artillery: The Origins of Modern U.S. Army Aviation in World War II.* Army Historical Series. Washington, DC: Center of Military History, Department of the Army, 2000.

Wind Tunnels

Research and design tools used extensively in the aircraft and missile industries. Wind tunnels can save many hours of flight-testing and are a vital resource when investigating transonic and supersonic performance. They are used to gather aerodynamic data, to perform flutter testing, and for airflow and shockwave visualization to determine where the airflow separates from a smooth flow around the test model.

Most wind tunnels are subsonic, built as a closed, sectioned, tubular structure with a fan or propeller to produce airflow. A scale model of an aircraft or missile is placed in a narrow working section, and air enters through a constriction that increases the speed of the airflow in the working section and makes it more uniform. Calibrated balances measure the lift, drag, and side forces and the rolling, pitching, and yawing movements experienced by the model under test.

High-speed (transonic and supersonic) wind tunnels usually require a reservoir of compressed air to provide the motive power. The air is allowed to blow through a convergent-divergent nozzle to create a supersonic flow, then through the (typically very small) working section, and finally exhausts into the atmosphere. Clearly, high-speed tunnels can run at a constant speed only for a very short period of time, but Mach numbers of 4 or more can be reached.

Historically, supersonic wind tunnels have encountered difficulty as the airspeed approaches the speed of sound, as the airflow through the working section tends to be choked by the formation of unwanted shockwaves. This is particularly difficult to overcome at transonic speeds (Mach 0.85–Mach 1.1). Supersonic wind tunnels were available well before transonic tunnels, and many early jet aircraft experienced difficulty in the transonic region because of lack of reliable experimental data.

Andy Blackburn

References

Shevell, Richard S. *Fundamentals of Flight.* New York: Prentice-Hall, 1989.

Winter War (1939–1940)

The Soviet-Finnish conflict in the winter of 1939–1940, mostly over strategically important territories of the Karelian Isthmus. The air operations demonstrated the abilities and constraints of airpower in action in severe weather and over difficult and heavily wooded terrain. At the outbreak of hostilities, the Soviet air force had assembled about 900 aircraft, expecting an easy and quick campaign. Then Finnish air force had 162 mostly obsolete aircraft of all types.

Enjoying permanent air superiority in the course of the war, the Red Air Force was able to secure vulnerable rear areas from air strikes but failed to eliminate in a surprise strike the dispersed Finnish combat aircraft on the ground. Soviet airpower was engaged primarily in close support, air cover, and airlifting of assaulting troops in the Karelian Isthmus, some limited air operations in the Arctic area, as well as bombing raids on more than 160 rear targets.

Despite large-scale employment of bombers in daytime

The large wind tunnel at Langley proved to be invaluable in refining aircraft design. (NASA)

and clear-weather raids, the Soviets were unable to undermine Finnish defenses, economic life, supply traffic, and morale. This was due to wintertime navigation problems, bombing inaccuracy, and the fierce Finnish air defense, which claimed 275–314 Soviet air losses (more than half of them bombers).

The Finns also used fighters energetically and adapted to winter conditions: They equipped fighters with skis for takeoffs and landings on ice and snow. Their pilots demonstrated a higher level of combat skills compared to the Russian pilots. During the war, Finland received 240 aircraft of all types as well as volunteer pilots from Western countries, but massive aid was compromised by politics and logistical difficulties.

The Soviets massed reinforcements (1,500–2,000 planes) in January-February 1940 and introduced some operational and tactical changes (nighttime and poor-weather bombing raids as well as fighter escorts). Nevertheless, the war was won by the Soviets mostly on the ground due to the dramatic disparity of forces involved. Moreover, the evident failure of the Soviet air campaign was one of the primary reasons the war went on for as long as it did. The total Russian war losses were 594 aircraft; the Finnish air force lost 62 planes from all causes.

Peter Rainow

See also

Bristol Aircraft; Finland, and Air Operations During the "Continuation War"; Finnish Air Force (Early Years); Fokker Aircraft (Post-World War II); Polikarpov, Nikolai N.; Smushkevich, Yakov "General Douglas"; Soviet Air Force; Tupolev

References

Engle, Eloise, and Lauri Paanen. *The Winter War: The Russo-Finnish Conflict, 1939–1940.* New York: Charles Scribner's Sons, 1990.

Luukanen, Eino. *Fighter over Finland: The Memoirs of a Fighter Pilot.* London: Macdonald, 1963.

Women Airforce Service Pilots

The female component of the U.S. air forces, known as the WASPs. Three years before the United States entered World War II, one of America's prominent women pilots, Jacqueline Cochran, suggested that women pilots could serve in noncombat flying roles to free men for emergency war-preparedness duty. Because there was no pressing manpower problem, the Army demurred.

By 1942, however, the supply of aviation cadets could not meet demand. In September 1942, President Franklin D. Roosevelt appointed Cochran director of the Woman's Flying Training Detachment (WFTD). Cochran's job was to supervise and coordinate the training of women pilots for assignment to the Women's Auxiliary Ferrying Squadron (WAFS) of the Air Transport Command. WAFS's job was to ferry new fighters and bombers to air bases throughout the United States. In 1943, the WFTD merged with WAFS to form the Women's Airforce Service Pilots (WASP), with Cochran as director and Nancy Love as executive commander.

By 1944, combat losses were below predictions, and large numbers of USAAF pilots were rotating home to take over stateside duties. General Henry H. "Hap" Arnold, who had gone on record that "women can fly as well as men," announced the WASP program would end on 20 December 1944. WASPs were summarily sent home without military benefits. However, on 23 November 1977 President Jimmy Carter signed legislation giving the WASPs veterans' benefits—more than 30 years after they had been disbanded.

WASPs delivered 12,650 planes of 77 different types. They ferried more than 50 percent of all the high-speed pursuit planes. More than 25,000 women applied to WASP; of the 1,830 women admitted, 1,074 graduated. They flew more than 60 million miles; 38 lost their lives in accidents.

Henry M. Holden

References

Holden, Henry M., and Lori Griffith. *Ladybirds: The Untold Story of Women Pilots in America.* St. Paul, MN: Black Hawk, 1991.

Women in Air Combat

Only since the 1990s have women consistently been allowed to serve in direct air combat roles in most Western militaries. Though women flew in a variety of noncombat capacities in the United States and other nations during World War II, and even in three air combat wings in the Soviet Union, in postwar years these practices were sharply curtailed.

The U.S. military, by virtue of its size and prestige, has in recent decades played the most influential role in opening doors to women in air combat. The process began in 1973 with the transition to an all-volunteer force and its attendant increase in demand for qualified personnel. That same year, for the first time six women earned the status of naval aviator, followed shortly by women earning their wings in the Army (1974) and the Air Force (1977). Though after 1976 women were allowed into the three U.S. military academies, their continued restriction to noncombat roles remained a serious career obstacle. By the 1980s, it had become increasingly clear that U.S. women were already participating in missions that involved combat in all but name, holding the lives of millions in their hands as ICBM launch-control officers, and coming under fire as helicopter pilots during the 1989 invasion of Panama.

The 1990–1991 Gulf War demonstrated to the American public how integral women had become to U.S. airpower. They loaded laser-guided bombs onto F-117s, directed from AWACS aircraft F-15s as they intercepted and destroyed Iraqi MiG-29s, commanded Patriot missile batteries as they engaged incoming SCUD missiles, and flew refueling and supply aircraft, often deep into Iraqi airspace. Two women were taken as prisoners of war, including Major Rhonda Cornum, a flight surgeon on a Black Hawk helicopter downed while attempting the rescue of a fellow pilot behind enemy lines. Thirteen women were killed during Operation DESERT STORM, including a Chinook helicopter pilot, Major Marie T. Rossi, even though women were restricted to noncombat roles.

Entering the post–Gulf War era, the final frontier for women in air combat was fighter and bomber aircraft. In 1988, Canada quietly led the way when two women joined operational CF-18 squadrons for the first time. In December 1991, all U.S. legal impediments to women flying combat missions were removed, but the various services succeeded in delaying a final decision until the 1992 election. The Bill Clinton administration, under pressure from the unfolding Tailhook scandal, finally settled the matter on 28 April 1993 when Defense Secretary Les Aspin announced that virtually all remaining restrictions on women pilots were lifted. By 2000, U.S. women pilots were fully integrated into their respective services, having flown numerous combat missions over Iraq and the former Yugoslavia. Women pilots today fly in the armed forces of pioneering nations like the United States, Canada, and Denmark and in many other Western air forces as well.

David Rezelman

See also

Gulf War; Soviet Women's Combat Wings; Women Airforce Service Pilots (WASP); Women in the Air Force; Women's Auxiliary Air Force; Women's Auxiliary Ferrying Squadron

The first all-female aircrew of the U.S. Air Force. (U.S. Air Force)

References

Holm, Jeanne. *Women in the Military: An Unfinished Revolution.* Rev. ed. Novato, CA: Presidio Press, 1992.

Spurling, Kathryn, and Elizabeth Greenhalgh, eds. *Women in Uniform: Perceptions and Pathways.* Canberra: University College, Australian Defence Force Academy, 2000.

Women in the Air Force (WAF)

Between 1948 and 1976, the U.S. services were gender-defined. There were Women Marines, WAVES (Navy), WAC (Army), and WAF, Army Air Force, Air Force). Women had served in the military nurse's corps from 1902; thousands flew during World War II in the nonmilitary Women's Auxiliary Ferrying Squadron (WAFS) and the Women's Airforce Service Pilots (WASP). Under the defense reorganization of 1948, the services began accepting women with restrictions: no more than 2 percent of the force; highest rank would be colonel; many career fields would be off-limits, including flying and combat. Over the next two decades, the Air Force had difficulty filling even its 2 percent ceiling, averaging just more than 1 percent during that time; by the mid-1960s, fields that had been open in the 1940s and 1950s were closed to women.

Colonel Jeanne M. Holm took over WAF in 1965, doubling its size, modernizing uniforms, and expanding career opportunities. She became the first female Air Force brigadier (1971) and major general (1973). Women's rights grew in the 1970s. Women entered the ROTC in 1972, the Air Force Academy in 1976. Seven percent of the veterans of DESERT STORM are women; by the mid-1990s, women competed for 99 percent of Air Force slots, excluding only direct combat.

John Barnhill

References

Haynesworth, Leslie. *Amelia Earhart's Daughters.* New York: William Morrow, 1998.

Holm, Jeanne. *Women in the Military: An Unfinished Revolution.* Rev. ed. Novato, CA: Presidio Press, 1992.

Women in the Aircraft Industry (World War II)

During World War II, women worked in the aircraft industries of each of the major combatants. Though Nazi propaganda prevented the mass employment of German women until late in the war, Germany did force women drawn from throughout the occupied territories of Europe to work in wartime industries. In Japan, traditional restrictions on the role of women were relaxed as war fortunes waned, and by 1944 millions of women and even schoolgirls were working to produce war material. Probably no nation so nearly approached the "total war" ideal of mobilizing an entire society as did the Soviet Union; many women were integrated into the aircraft industry, just as they were integrated into almost every facet of the Soviet war effort. In Britain, women were already present in the prewar workforce in large numbers, but the nature of their employment was dramatically altered by the war. From 1939 to 1943, the number of women working in wartime manufacturing increased by 1.5 million; statistically these women were older and far more likely to be married. Changes in the area of aircraft motor production and repair were typical for engineering as a whole, with the number of women workers growing from less than one in 10 before the war to more than one in three by 1943.

It was in the United States, however, that the image of the wartime female worker would become the most famous, exemplified by the popular propaganda figure Rosie the Riveter. Women had worked in the U.S. aircraft industry since at least the 1920s, but during World War II their numbers rose dramatically. According to one survey, the number of women in the aircraft industry increased from 143 in April 1941 to 65,000 in October 1942. By 1944, approximately 40 percent of workers in Los Angeles–area aircraft plants were women, a percentage typical for the nation as a whole. Images of women defense workers abounded: Popular movies of 1943 included *Swing Shift Maisie* and Ginger Rogers's *Tender Comrade,* both set in aircraft factories; songs of the era in-

"Rosie the Riveter" symbolized the dedication of women to the war effort. Employers were agreeably surprised to find that women not only did as well as male workers, they often did better. (U.S. Air Force)

cluded "The Lady at Lockheed" and "We're the Janes Who Make Planes." Perhaps the best example of all this is the song "Rosie the Riveter" (written in 1942 by Redd Evans and John Jacob Loeb and popularized the following year by the Four Vagabonds): "Keeps a sharp lookout for sabotage, sitting up there on the fuselage, that little girl can do more than a male can do, Rosie the Riveter."

These popular images have led to some misconceptions and exaggerations, however. The majority of American women during the war stayed at home, and wartime factories usually employed more men than women. Among those women who did join the industrial workforce, fewer than 10 percent had husbands in the service; as in Britain, about half of women defense workers had already been in the national workforce for years—it was just that now they were allowed into occupations formerly reserved for men. Wartime pressures resulted in the breaking of racial barriers as well as sexual ones, as this period saw tremendous increases in the number of African American and Hispanic women participating in defense industries. Still, it was the massive success of the Rosie the Riveter campaign that has had the most lasting impact, and it is the image of the white former homemaker that is most firmly planted in American historical memory.

Women working in defense industries faced a variety of obstacles. One in three had children at home under the age of 14, yet formal child care programs were rare. Though the amount of money women could make often increased dramatically compared to prewar jobs, they were often paid far less than the men working alongside them. In theory, racial discrimination was prohibited in all defense industries by President Franklin D. Roosevelt's 1941 Executive Order 8802, but in practice African Americans were often given the most menial jobs available—or even rejected outright by potential employers. The majority of women workers polled in 1944 planned to continue working after the end of the war, and partly as a result of this government and corporate ad campaigns of this time increasingly emphasized the importance of women returning to the home at war's end. The massive postwar defense industry layoffs hit women especially hard; in the Los Angeles area, for example, the proportion of aircraft work being done by women fell from its wartime high of 40 percent to 18 percent by 1946 and 12 percent by 1948.

Despite these problems, in retrospect the glass was probably at least half-full for the some 300,000 American women that worked in the aircraft industry during World War II. Postwar attempts to return Rosie to her happy home were only partially successful. By the early 1950s, the percentage of women working in the Los Angeles–area aircraft industry had rebounded back to 25 percent. Although most Rosies did return home in postwar years, their outlook was forever broadened, and the wartime experiences of these women played an important if hard to quantify role in generating the discontent of the 1950s that manifested itself in the feminist movements of the 1960s and 1970s. Not surprisingly, women workers in World War II have received much historical attention in the last few decades, both scholarly and popular. Of particular note is the Rosie the Riveter Revisited oral history project, conducted by Sherna Berger Gluck in the Los Angeles area in the early 1980s, and the creation in October 2000 of the Rosie the Riveter World War II Home Front National Historical Park in Richmond, California.

David Rezelman

See also

Soviet Women Pilots; Soviet Women's Combat Wings; Women Airforce Service Pilots; Women in Air Combat; Women in the Air Force; Women's Auxiliary Air Force; Women's Auxiliary Ferrying Squadron; World War II Aviation

References

Erickson, Ethel. *Women's Employment in Aircraft Assembly Plants in 1942.* Bulletin No. 192-1, Women's Bureau, Department of Labor. Washington, DC: U.S. Government Printing Office, 1942.

Gluck, Sherna Berger. *Rosie the Riveter Revisited: Women, the War, and Social Change.* Boston: Twayne, 1987.

Honey, Maureen. *Creating Rosie the Riveter: Class, Gender, and Propaganda During World War II.* Amherst: University of Massachusetts, 1984.

Women's Auxiliary Air Force

The women's auxiliary component of the British air forces. On 1 April 1918, the Royal Air Force combined the Royal Naval Air Service and the Royal Flying Corps. At the same time, the Women's Royal Air Force (WRAF) formed with recruits from the other women's services. For the rest of the war, 9,000 women drove, cooked, clerked, and filled other support roles. After the war, the WRAF disbanded. In the interwar years an alumni association remained active.

In the summer of 1939, the Women's Auxiliary Air Force (WAAF) came into being. As in World War I, women served alongside the men. With some 1,700 members at the outbreak of war, the WAAF grew to roughly 180,000 by 1943. WAAF jobs included catering, meteorology, transport, telephony and telegraphy, codes and ciphers, intelligence, and security. WAAF members were among the 1,570 ground crews who lost their lives.

The WAAF reformed into the WRAF in 1949 and fully integrated into the RAF in 1994. Women are not part of the regular fighting force but do train in the use of weapons for defense. Women are loadmasters, and they pilot transports as well as single-seat and two-seat jet aircraft. Although restrictions remain, most women do the same work as men, attend the same schools, and compete equally for promotion.

John Barnhill

References

Escott, Beryl. *Our Wartime Days: The WAAF in World War II.* Alan Sutton, 1995.

______. *Women in Air Force Blue.* Wellingborough, UK: Patrick Stephens, 1989.

Women's Auxiliary Ferrying Squadron

The women's auxiliary component of the U.S. air forces formed during World War II. When war broke out in Europe in 1939, two notable women aviators, Jacqueline Cochran and Nancy Harkness Love, proposed separate military flight-training programs. Love proposed using women pilots holding commercial licenses to fly noncombat flying positions in the United States to deliver or ferry military aircraft. Cochran proposed a military flight-training program for women holding private pilot licenses.

In 1942, when manpower requirements became critical, both plans were implemented. Love was put in charge of the Women's Auxiliary Ferrying Squadron, Cochran the Women's Flying Training Detachment. After some advanced training, Love's group began ferrying fighters and bombers from factories to bases throughout the United States. Cochran's group trained at Sweetwater, Texas, completely segregated from male training groups.

In September 1943, the two groups were merged into the Women Airforce Service Pilots—the famous WASPs. Cochran remained in charge of the training program and Love the ferry squadron. WASP was disbanded on 20 December 1944.

Henry M. Holden

References

Holden, Henry, and Lori Griffith. *Ladybirds: The Untold Story of Women Pilots in America.* St. Paul, MN: Black Hawk, 1991.

Worden, Hector (1885–1916)

The first pilot of Native American ancestry. Hector Worden was born in White Plains, New York, on 4 February 1885. He worked with John Les Clark of the Indian Exhibit Company and always retained an admiration and interest in his Cherokee ancestry. In the spring of 1911, Worden enrolled in Blériot's aviation school in Pau, France; after crashing his plane he left without a license, unable to pay the damages. He obtained his license on 14 November 1911 upon returning to America. Worden often flew exhibition flights with the Moisant school but found his true calling in military aviation, becoming the first aviator to participate in warfare in the Western Hemisphere.

In 1911, Francisco I. Madero commissioned Worden a captain in his Mexican army to fly reconnaissance and bombing missions against the revolutionaries in Mexico. He served under General Victoriano Huerta for two years. Worden's success encouraged the Mexican government to send three army officers to the Moisant school on Mineola, Long Island, for training in 1912. Worden died on 5 May 1916 from injuries suffered in a crash while attempting to loop-the-loop.

Wendy Coble

References

Worden, Hector. Biographical file CW-902500-National Air and Space Museum, Smithsonian Instutiton, Washington, DC.

______. File at the Library of Congress, box 129, in the AIAA files.

World War I Aviation

Prior to the outbreak of World War I, France, Germany, and Great Britain had each thought about the role that aviation would play in their strategy. Airplanes had participated in prewar practice maneuvers; based on the performances, each power concluded that if the airplane had any value it would be for reconnaissance. They were quickly proven right. On the Western Front, a French aircraft spotted the critical turn of the German army that allowed troops to be rushed forward to what would become the First Battle of the Marne, thereby setting up the race to the sea, the end of the war of movement, and the beginning of trench warfare. Along the Eastern Front, aircraft proved equally significant, giving the Germans the first report of oncoming Russian forces, allowing them to prepare the plan for the Battle of Tannenburg, later prompting Hindenburg to say that without the airplane there would have been no Tannenburg.

Reconnaissance

Once fighting settled into the trenches, aerial reconnaissance began to specialize. Eventually, three branches developed. The first, *strategic reconnaissance,* consisted of continuously photographing enemy territory, interpreting the photographs for their intelligence value, issuing prints to local commands, and printing maps based on the photos. As this branch developed, it was responsible for introducing

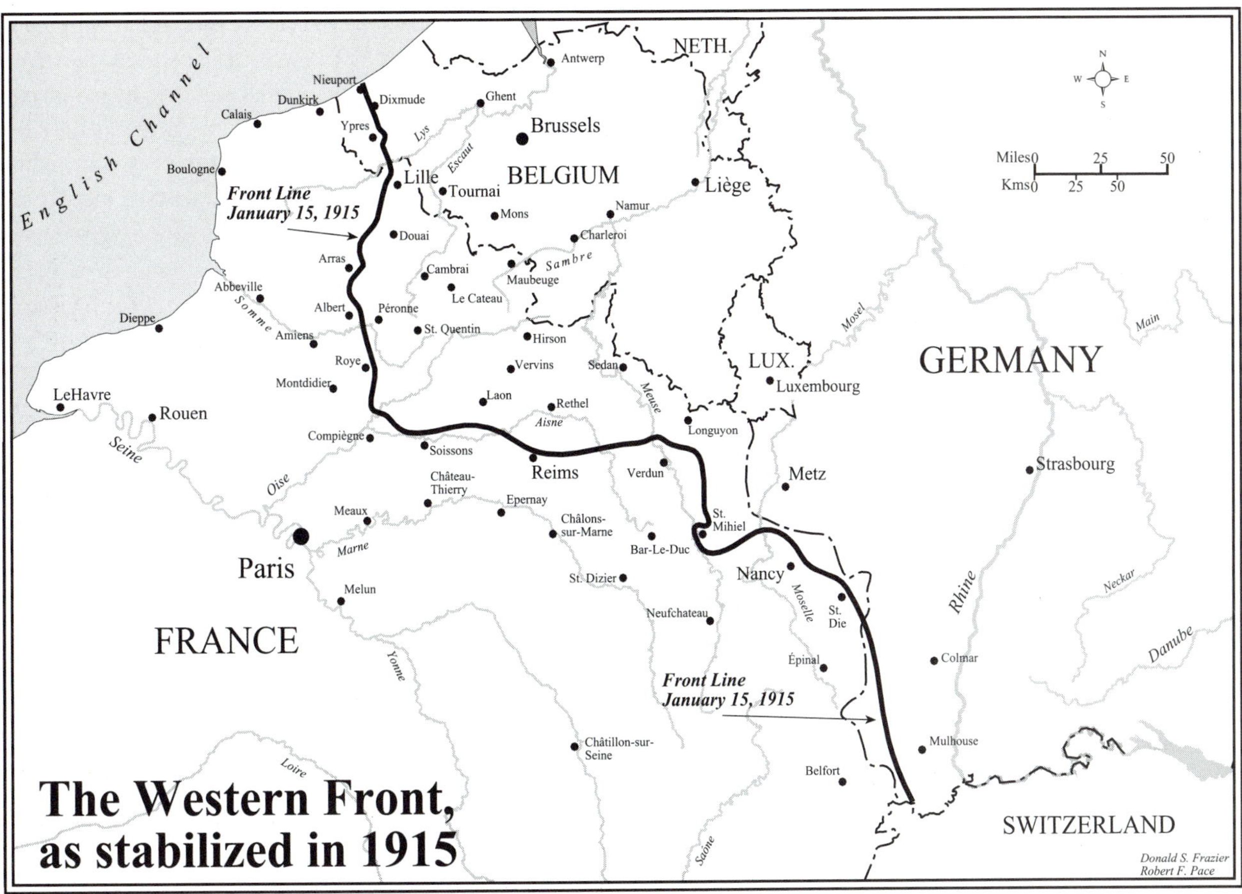

several new pieces of technology. The serial camera, which automatically clicked off exposures as the aircraft flew in a straight line over the target in order to facilitate mapmaking, represented a major development in the art of aerial espionage. And as it became necessary to fly higher to avoid hostile defense measures, other bits of new equipment were perfected. Thus were seen the first use of breathing oxygen and heated flight suits to protect the crews from the physical dangers of operating at high altitude. The development of engine superchargers improved overall performance.

The second area, *tactical reconnaissance,* included flying over the enemy during periods of active fighting to report movements and the location of friendly troops. This activity was particularly important given the state of communications technology during World War I. During periods of inactivity, a commander could keep in touch with his troops by telephone. The state of the art, however, was a huge complex of wires connected by telephone exchanges. This system broke down instantly once an attack was under way and troops began to move from friendly territory onto enemy-occupied ground that had been wired for communications. In the absence of wireless communications, troops were located by aircraft, the information being forwarded by one-way radio transmitters, signal lamps, pigeons, or weighted message bags dropped over the local command post. Troops were equipped with signal panels—white strips of cloth that were supposed to be laid out at the most forward position for the airmen to see. This seldom worked, however, as troops were reluctant to lay the panels out for fear of alerting enemy aircraft. As a result, aircrews on contact patrol were forced to fly low enough to distinguish the color of uniforms—a risky proposition because troops on both sides tended to fire on any enemy aircraft they saw.

The third area, *artillery-spotting,* was the regulation and correction of fire by aircraft observing the fall of shot and reporting the results to friendly artillery batteries. One important difference between this and other forms of aerial reconnaissance was that performance was not limited to airplanes. In fact, throughout the war most artillery-spotting was still done by putting someone at the top of a hill overlooking the area to be shelled. Because the German army controlled the majority of high ground for most of the war, however, the Allied nations were forced to use aircraft for a great deal of this work. This included airplanes as well as tethered observation balloons.

The two big advantages balloons offered over heavier-than-aircraft when it came to spotting for the guns were duration and ease of communications. Balloons could remain aloft for hours, even all day, working with one or more batteries. Communicating from the balloon basket was far easier than from the rear seat of an airplane, as the balloon observer could be connected directly to artillery commanders by telephone.

Bombardment

Aerial bombing in World War I was primarily tactical: Favorite targets were troop and supply concentrations, railyards and stations, and munitions dumps within easy reach of the front. Strategic bombing had been the subject of theory, but early experiments in its practical application were largely beyond the state of the technological art in World War I. Because of the relatively small lifting power of even the most robust aircraft engines, bombloads and striking range were miniscule by World War II standards. Zeppelins, which promised a great deal in this area at the outset of war due to their extended range, proved a disappointment. The primitive state of aerial navigation often led to airships becoming lost in their search for targets in Britain and dropping their bombs over open fields or on relatively unimportant buildings. And as the war progressed, the development of more effective defensive measures (better antiaircraft guns, fighters with increased ceilings and speeds, and incendiary ammunition capable of setting the large gas bags on fire) forced the Zeppelins to operate at increasingly higher altitudes where precision bombing became even more challenging as crew performance decreased with oxygen deprivation and subzero temperatures.

Air-to-Air Combat

Fighters have dominated the attention of historians for decades. But it needs to be remembered that the development of the fighter was a purely *defensive* measure. Judged in isolation, the dogfight in which a Triplane bested a Camel or vice versa had little objective military value or purpose. They were necessary not to fight each other but to eliminate the reconnaissance aircraft and, to a lesser extent, the bombers that threatened ground operations. Their value during the war as a diversion from the horrors of the trenches and as a morale builder to inspire the home front; during the interwar years the allure of fighters enticed new recruits into the cockpits for World War II; and in the years since fighters have lured fledgling historians into the study

One of the last fighter planes developed for World War I, the Fokker D.VIII saw limited service. (U.S. Air Force)

of this fascinating field. Their bravery in the cockpit and long-lasting historical influence cannot be underestimated.

Ground Attack

Ground attack operations developed late, not coming into general use until the spring of 1917, a year too late for the Battle of Verdun. Had the Germans attacked the single Verdun supply route—the Sacred Way—from the air in full force, aviation might have had a war winning impact on the outcome of the conflict. But this conclusion, like many others, reflects nothing more than the newborn status of military aviation in World War I. The better understanding of the uses of airpower that could have led the Verdun commanders to this realization would not come along for another generation.

Naval Operations

The use of aircraft in connection with naval operations centered on reconnaissance tasks, especially scouting patrols for submarines. Aircraft flying ahead of Allied convoys in the last years of the war saved countless tonnage from destruction by German U-Boats. This work led to the development of the so-called Spider Web, an organized network of imaginary grids laid over the North Sea between which aircraft routinely patrolled.

It's fair to conclude that the birth and adolescence of airpower between 1914 and 1918 brought fundamental changes to the conduct of war, changes that would not be fully appreciated or developed until the conflict renewed in 1939.

James Streckfuss

See also

German Air Force (Luftwaffe); Royal Flying Corps/Royal Naval Air Service/Royal Air Force; U.S. Aircraft Development and Production (World War I)

References

Raleigh, Sir Walter, and H. A. Jones. *The War in the Air: Being the Story of the Part Played in the Great War by the Royal Air Force.* 6 vols. Oxford: Clarendon Press, 1922–1937.

World War II Aviation

Although it cannot be said that airpower won World War II, it is fair to state that airpower made possible and accelerated the Allies' victory over the Axis powers. If airpower had been removed entirely from the equation, it is possible that the end result might have been exactly the same; given the difference in resources between the Allies and the Axis, however, it is fairly certain that the war would have lasted much longer with much greater loss of life. Airpower proved to be the great advantage of the Allies.

Summary of the Air War: Timing, Technology, Scale

One of the ironies is that the Axis nations chose airpower as a tool for aggression, but the Allied nations made better and far more extensive use of airpower to achieve final victory. The reason for this turnabout was that airpower in World War II turned entirely on three major issues: timing, technology, and scale. The Allies were able to exploit these issues to a far greater degree.

In the beginning, the Axis powers made excellent use of timing and technology. The timing of the war was almost solely of their choosing, and they chose to strike when their air forces were at the peak of modernization, equipped with first-rate aircraft in numbers deemed necessary for victory. Italy has been left out of this equation because its military services were totally unprepared for modern warfare in equipment, training, and morale. It was Italy's misfortune to have a leader, Benito Mussolini, who was so greedy for the spoils of war that he ignored Italy's blatant military deficiencies. In doing so, he sacrificed many brave and capable soldiers, sailors, and airmen.

Democratic Allied powers, because they were democracies, found themselves in a typical position: unprepared for war because politicians had refused to risk electoral defeat by voting to raise taxes necessary for defense. In the Soviet Union—an accidental Ally as a result of the German invasion—the situation was different. Great sums had been spent on the military, including the Soviet air force, but the armed forces were paralyzed with fear as a result of Stalin's insane purges. They left the military bereft of leadership, with the great majority of senior officers executed, the remainder afraid to take any action for fear of arrest and a quick death.

Germany and Japan were thus able to prepare first-class air forces, equipped with the most modern equipment and sufficiently strong to win almost all of their initial objectives. Both nations considered an air force of 3,000–5,000 aircraft, flown by well-trained, well-motivated crews, to be sufficient for their purposes. When Germany initiated the war on 1 September 1939, and when Japan entered the war on 7 December 1941, both nations had bent timing and technology to their will.

However, neither nation had any concept of the scale of effort that airpower required. As a result, their production would soon lag behind that of the Allies. When they finally perceived the scale of the task at hand, they were in no position to achieve it.

Only two nations did. The Soviet Union was one, and it formulated airpower projections in the same way it created divisions and employed infantry, artillery, and tanks: on a grand scale—far beyond the concepts of either the German or the Japanese leaders. In fact, even when properly informed of the scale of the Soviet effort, German leaders refused to believe it.

Even more remarkable was the Soviet ability to relocate the aircraft industry from European Russia to behind the Urals. There they not only instituted mass production in amazingly short order but also introduced new and more effective types of aircraft. It was a magnificent effort, totally beyond the comprehension of the Nazi leaders, Adolf Hitler in particular. In terms of industrial miracles, the Soviet effort corresponded fully to the renaissance of the U.S. aviation industry during the war.

The United States was the other nation to correctly estimate the scale of effort that would be required. The fact that it did so was improbable, as was the method by which grandiose estimates were made and accepted.

The United States, nurtured in its isolation by two oceans and still resenting the events in Europe and Asia following World War I, had let its armed forces be reduced to a bare minimum. In January 1939, the U.S. air forces had a nominal strength of some 1,700 aircraft, 1,000 officers, and 18,000 enlisted personnel. Most of the aircraft were obsolescent, and none were equivalent to their European and Asian counterparts. Only one year later, President Franklin D. Roosevelt would call on Congress to permit the building of 50,000 aircraft per year. It seemed an impossible assignment, but it was the clarion call that brought forth the plan conceived by four brilliant young officers: Lieutenant Colonels Harold Lee George and Kenneth N. Walker and Majors Haywood S. Hansell and Laurence S. Kuter. These four men—all future general officers—created the plan for U.S. airpower in World War II during nine hectic days in August 1941. Their audacious plan—AWPD-1—would prove to be uncannily accurate in concept and fulfillment.

In large part this was due to the permissive and aggressive leadership of the U.S. air forces, personified by Major General Henry H. "Hap" Arnold and Brigadier General Carl A. "Tooey" Spaatz, backed up by the president of the United States. In stark contrast, the Luftwaffe was under the command of a dissolute dilettante: *Reichsmarschall* Herman Goering, who had selected a fellow dilettante, *Generaloberst* Ernst Udet, to supervise the technical development of the service. The chief of state, Hitler, was too preoccupied with the army to do more than treat the Luftwaffe with benign neglect.

AWPD-1 was subsequently modified, but not to a significant extent. The final plan called for 207 groups of aircraft, 68,416 operational aircraft (including 3,740 Consolidated B-36 bombers, a design that was still on the drafting boards). The officer force was to be expanded to 179,398 while enlisted personnel would number almost 2 million. Monthly attrition was estimated at 2,133 aircraft—more than existed in the entire USAAF at the time. Also included were requirements for training, factories, targets, sorties, fuel, bombs, and all the other materiel that an air force of almost 70,000 aircraft would require.

At any other previous moment in history, the tender of such an extravagant plan would have been considered insane. It would have been rejected forthwith, and the careers of the men who made it would have been over. But the planners' timing was impeccable. As grand as it was, their plan was accepted on its merits and implemented with blinding speed. In 1939 in the United States, annual aircraft production of all types had barely reached 3,000, mostly small, simple aircraft. By 1944, the United States was producing aircraft at the rate of 100,000 per year, including some of the largest and most sophisticated aircraft in history. When the war ended, the United States Army Air Forces possessed some 70,000 operational aircraft and had suffered almost exactly the predicted rate of attrition.

In stark contrast, the Axis powers had based their plans on a series of short wars quickly won by the superior technology and numbers of their aircraft working in coopera-

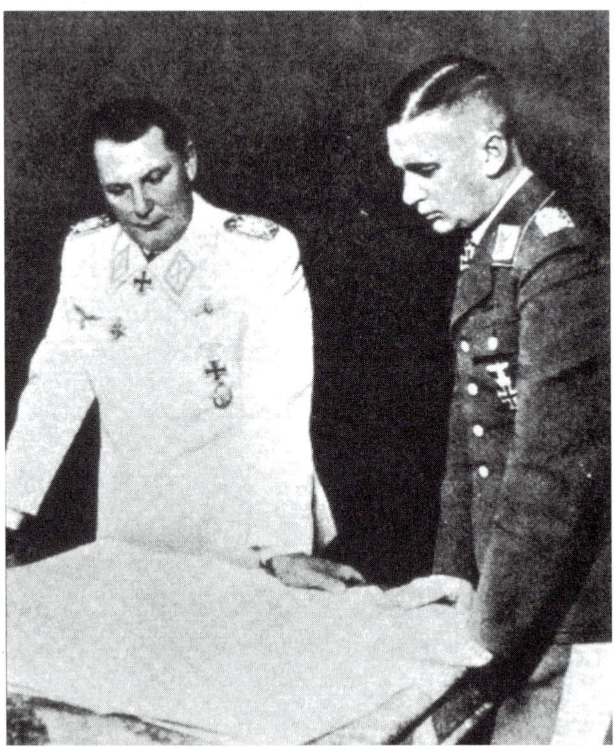

In spite of strong support by Hermann Goering (seen here with Hans Joeschennek), the German Luftwaffe failed to live up to expectations. (Smithsonian Institution)

tion with land and naval forces. A production level of 3,000–5,000 aircraft per year was considered adequate in both nations. When the war grew long, both Germany and Japan made valiant and determined efforts to expand aircraft production. Both succeeded to a remarkable degree, with Germany manufacturing some 40,000 aircraft in 1944, at the height of the Allied bombing raids. In the same year, Japan manufactured 24,000 aircraft, approximately six times its 1939 figure. If the leaders of the two nations had the foresight to make such an effort in 1939 and 1940 rather than in 1943 and 1944, the war might have taken a very different turn.

However, timing now worked against them. They were locked into manufacturing aircraft types that had begun the war and were largely obsolete by 1943. Both nations would introduce new and improved models, including such radical advances as the Messerschmitt Me 262 and Arado Ar 234 jets. These would prove too little, too late.

The Allies reflected the mirror image. Although the Allied forces suffered early defeats in every theater, they endured and were then able to begin large-scale production of more modern types. Thus, in Great Britain the late-model Supermarine Spitfire was supplemented by Hawker Typhoon and Tempest aircraft, and the RAF bomber force moved quickly from twin-engine bombers to the superb four-engine Avro Lancaster and the sensational twin-engine de Havilland Mosquito multirole fighter-bomber. In the United States, production saw multiple modified versions of the Boeing B-17 and Consolidated B-24 bombers, complemented by the introduction of the B-29—the best bomber of the war. Fighter production was originally concentrated on the obsolescent Curtiss P-40, soon replaced by the Lockheed P-38, Republic P-47, and the best U.S. fighter of the war, the North American P-51.

The forced draft of the war effort stoked the fires of technology in all the combatant countries, especially Great Britain, Germany, and the United States. Such technological advances as airborne radar, electronic counterwarfare methods, pressurized cabins, advanced fire-control systems, and jet engines were found in all three countries. Germany, in desperation, leaped ahead in some areas, including rocket and missile technology. Japan lagged behind in almost all areas, for its economy was incapable of expanding production while also conducting extensive research in new disciplines. The Soviet Union lagged as well, but primarily because it was concentrating on the basic weapons necessary to defeat Nazi Germany in the ground war. When the time came—particularly after the acquisition of German engineering data—Soviet technology moved rapidly ahead.

By 1944, timing and technology had turned against the aggressor nations on a scale the likes of which the world had never seen. Japan and Germany reacted like typical militaristic dictatorships: They allowed the discrepancy between their forfeited airpower and the overwhelming airpower to be made up by the blood of their people—soldiers as well as civilians. Axis leaders knew there was no way to win this war, their powerful opponents now fully armed and growing stronger every day, yet they forced their populations to fight on to the very end. In Germany that end came when Allied forces met their Soviet counterparts on the River Elbe. In Japan that end came with the union of the B-29 and the atomic bomb. This combination represented, for the first time, absolute airpower, and the destruction of Hiroshima and Nagasaki finally forced even the Japanese militarists to realize the war was lost.

The following contains year-by-year summaries of air warfare in World War II:

1939

The Luftwaffe paved the way for Germany's victory over Poland, demonstrating blitzkrieg tactics in which aircraft and armor cooperated to penetrate enemy positions. The Allies remained cautious and inactive on the Western Front: The few bombing raids that they did conduct met with failure, and a great deal of effort was expended on utterly pointless leaflet drops. The Germans were careful not to antagonize the Allies at first, in the hope that the war could be ended quickly. In November, the Soviet Union invaded Finland. The Finns resisted valiantly, and their small air force took a heavy toll of Soviet aircraft. In Asia, the Japanese air forces continued to operate over China with little opposition.

1940

By February, after having suffered heavy losses, the Soviet Union exhausted the Finns and a peace was concluded. In April, Germany used airpower to overwhelm Denmark and Norway, offsetting German inferiority at sea. On 10 May, Germany invaded the Low Countries, its Luftwaffe again spearheading the attacks in the Battle for France. The inadequate Allied air forces caused the Germans some casualties, but they were defeated in the air and on the ground. Luxemburg, Belgium, and Holland were quickly overrun. In late May, the Royal Air Force succeeded in preventing the Luftwaffe from interfering with the evacuation at Dunkirk. This was the first defeat the German air force had suffered. By 21 June, France had surrendered. Great Britain upped the ante in the air war, sending bombers to attack targets in Germany, particularly in the Rhineland.

After his lightning victories, Adolf Hitler offered Great Britain peace—but at too great a price. The United Kingdom was now led by Prime Minister Winston Churchill, a longtime supporter of airpower and a man who was determined

The Heinkel He 111 was one of the most commonly used aircraft in the Luftwaffe. This German all-metal monoplane was just one of the many innovations developed in World War II. (U.S. Air Force)

never to surrender. He was exactly the right man for the job, for he brought the United Kingdom back from the brink of despair and set about building a bombing force that he hoped would punish Germany.

In the meantime, Germany attempted to establish air superiority over England in the Battle of Britain. It was here that timing and technology first began to work against the Germans, for the aircraft (Messerschmitt Bf 109s, Heinkel He 111s, Dornier Do 217s, and Junkers Ju 87s and Ju 88s) that had been perfect for a continental campaign were now too few in numbers and technologically inadequate for a strategic bombing campaign. Timing and technology worked instead for Great Britain, whose factories were churning out hundreds of Hurricanes and Spitfires and whose radar system formed the core of an integrated command-and-control system that would enable the RAF to decisively defeat the Luftwaffe. Defeated in the Battle of Britain, Germany realized that invasion was impossible and turned to nighttime bombing of British cities even as the Nazis reorganized their forces for an invasion of the Soviet Union. Events in Europe had served to alert the United States that it was necessary to increase production capacity, and Allied investment in the U.S. aviation industry aided this effort. Large orders for combat aircraft were placed by England and France (with smaller orders being placed by other countries), which prompted an expansion of the U.S. aviation industry—critically important in the coming years. Japan began the occupation of French Indochina in an effort to move closer to the vital oil and mineral resources of Southeast Asia. On 28 October, Italy invaded Greece from its Albanian bases. The invasion was inadequately prepared, and the Greeks proved to be tough adversaries who promptly forced the Italians back beyond the Albanian frontiers. Great Britain sent troops and aircraft to Greece, beginning a relatively small but politically important air battle there.

1941

German bombing of the United Kingdom continued through May 1941 but on a reduced scale. In Africa, very limited British forces were able to maul Italian armies in Libya and in Eritrea and Ethiopia. The defeats in Libya would cause Hitler to send the Afrika Korps, with limited but very effective air components, to rescue the Italians. This would begin the long, bitter North African campaign. In eastern Africa, there were dogfights between biplane opponents, with Gloster Gladiators contesting Fiat Falcos in a World War I–type atmosphere. Air attacks on Malta began to build in intensity. The United States moved closer to open warfare by announcing its Lend-Lease plan, whereby it would provide arms to Great Britain on a massive scale. On 6 April, Germany began its Balkan campaign, which was massively successful and ended with the evacuation of Greece by British forces and the occupation of Crete. It had the effect, however, of delaying the German invasion of the Soviet Union, which many observers feel was critical to the outcome of the 1941 campaign. On 22 June, German launched Operation BARBAROSSA, its invasion of the Soviet Union. The Soviet air force was virtually destroyed on the ground, but once again the scale of German air effort was hopelessly inadequate, and despite overwhelming success, the fighting ground down in the winter snows. The Soviet Union began a massive relocation effort that saw no less than 1,523 factories moved beyond the Urals.

On 7 December, imperial Japan began a whirlwind air campaign with the attack on Pearl Harbor and the Philippines. Japanese airpower would soon seem to be invincible as it swept through Southeast Asia, sinking HMS *Prince of Wales* and *Repulse* in passing. It would be dominant for the next six months of the war. Germany declared war on the United States on 11 December.

1942

The Japanese forces, employing relatively small but highly effective elements of airpower, conquered some 20 million square miles of territory, including the Philippines, Malaya, the Dutch East Indies, and Burma, along with critical Pacific islands such as Wake and Guam, by March 1942. The only ray of hope came in the famed 18 April Doolittle Raid on Tokyo, the first of many. In Europe, the RAF became increasingly aggressive with daylight fighter and bomber sweeps over occupied territories. In March, RAF Bomber Command began its new offensive, intensifying the nighttime bombing of Germany. The United States would join Great Britain in the Combined Bomber Offensive, which would grow from modest beginnings to an overwhelming force over the next three years. In the Atlantic, German U-boats began a war against shipping that would become known as the Battle of the Atlantic; they would succeed for more than a year because of inadequate Allied airpower.

The war in the Pacific took a sudden and surprising turn in favor of the Allies following the Battle of Midway in early June. On August 7, the United States would invade Guadalcanal, beginning a bloody six-month battle that would literally turn on the possession of a single facility—Henderson Field. In Russia, German advances continued to the south toward Stalingrad and the Caucasus. In Africa, Germany would suffer a major defeat at El Alamein in October, then be confounded by the massive U.S. invasion of North Africa on 8 November. Allied airpower in every theater was causing the tide of war to shift.

1943

The fortunes of war turned irreversibly against the Axis powers in 1943, beginning with the catastrophic German losses in the Battle of Stalingrad. The Luftwaffe could still attain local air superiority at specific spots along the Eastern Front, but the Soviet opposition was gaining both in numbers and tactics. The effectiveness of Soviet airpower and the decline in the Luftwaffe's strength was demonstrated in the Battle of Kursk, the largest tank battle in history. Germany also suffered defeat in the Battle of the Atlantic, where the combination of land- and carrier-based aircraft shut down all areas of operation by the U-boats and, in cooperation with surface ships, caused prohibitive losses. The Germans were also defeated in North Africa, which was followed by defeats throughout the entire Mediterranean Theater with the loss of Sicily and the invasion of Italy. At the same time, the Combined Bomber Offensive grew in intensity and effectiveness over Europe, exemplified by the destruction of Hamburg. The Luftwaffe was still capable of dealing out tremendous punishment, however, as in the air battles over Regensburg, Schweinfurt, and Berlin.

In the Pacific, the defeat at Guadalcanal forced the Japanese on the defensive throughout the theater as Allied forces followed a two-axis strategy. The first was a step-by-step advance toward the Philippines by the forces of General Douglas MacArthur, the second an island-hopping advance under the direction of Admiral Chester Nimitz. The island-hopping campaign was characterized by bitter battles such as Tarawa.

1944

Allied airpower came into its own in Europe with the introduction of long-range escort fighters and a new philosophy that was aimed at destroying the Luftwaffe. By March 1944, the Luftwaffe had been soundly beaten; although it was occasionally able to muster strength for savage attacks, it was never again able to secure daytime air superiority. However, in the same month the Luftwaffe did defeat the RAF in its nighttime-bombing campaign against Berlin. The combined USAAF/RAF forces focused on preparing the European continent for an invasion; the 6 June 1944 D-Day operation was so successful that it was virtually unopposed by the Luftwaffe. The air battle over Germany intensified and was regarded as a "second front" by no less an observer than Albert Speer even before the D-Day landings.

In the Pacific, the airpower of the U.S. Army and Navy proved superior to the Japanese at every point. The Japanese were now desperately short of trained pilots, so much that their remaining aircraft carriers were sometimes forced to sortie as mere decoys without any aircraft aboard. They incurred massive defeats in the Marshall Islands and the Philippines and were forced to resort to kamikaze suicide tactics.

In the last days of 1944, the Germans took advantage of bad weather, which hampered Allied air operations, to launch their final offensive of the war in the West—the Battle of the Bulge. As soon as the weather cleared a bit, however, Allied airpower reasserted itself.

1945

Airpower played itself out in Europe; useful targets disappeared by April, and the Germans surrendered in May. In the Pacific, true airpower came into being for the first time in the B-29 fire-bombing of Japan, which reduced major cities to ashes. The Japanese militarists still refused to surrender until the application of absolute airpower in the form of atomic weapons on Hiroshima and Nagasaki.

It is worth noting that the final application of airpower in both the European and Pacific theaters was compassionate, with the dropping of food, clothing, and medical supplies to POWs still held in the defeated enemies' camps.

Walter J. Boyne

See also

Arnold, Henry H. "Hap"; Atlantic, Battle of the; Atomic Bomb; BARBAROSSA; Blitzkrieg; Britian, Battle of; Bulge, Battle of the; Combined Bomber Offensive; Crete, Battle of; Dunkirk; El Alamein, Air Battles of; France, Battle for; German Air Force (Luftwaffe); Goering, Hermann; Guadalcanal; Guam, Battles of; Hamburg Bombing Campaign; Hiroshima; Kamikaze Attacks; Kursk, Battle of; Malta, Siege of; Mediterranean Theater of Operations; Midway, Battle of; Nagasaki; Nimitz, Chester William; North African Campaign; Philippines; Spaatz, Carl Andrew; Stalingrad, Battle of; Tarawa, Battle of; Tokyo Air Raids; Wake Island, Battles of

References

Boyne, Walter J. *Clash of Titans: World War II at Sea.* New York: Simon and Schuster, 1995.

_______. *Clash of Wings: World War II in the Air.* New York: Simon and Schuster, 1994.

Goralski, Robert. *World War II Almanac, 1931–1945.* New York: Bonanza, 1981.

World War II Conferences

Generally, the 1943 wartime conferences of Allied leaders that helped shape airpower practice and operations.

The Casablanca Conference (code name SYMBOL) took place during 12–23 January 1943. President Franklin D. Roosevelt and Prime Minister Winston Churchill met with their chiefs of staff to formulate joint policies. Earlier differences on the invasion of Europe were resolved in favor of a landing on Sicily to take Italy and a delay to prepare for a cross-channel assault in northern France. Roosevelt's demand for unconditional surrender of the Axis and steps to reduce the German U-Boat menace gained British acceptance. They also discussed nuclear bomb research, as well as matters of French leadership in the war against the Axis.

General Henry H. "Hap" Arnold, U.S. Air Corps Chief of Staff, a member of the Joint Combined Chiefs of Staff assigned to develop an Allied air strategy, was embarrassed by the size and preparation of the British air staff delegation and immediately flew in General Ira Eaker of the Eighth Air Force, the most knowledgeable officer in bomber command. The British proposed that Americans join in the nighttime bombing of Germany. Eaker argued that U.S. crews trained for daylight bombing faced great losses in transitioning to night attacks. Arnold and Eaker convinced Churchill that the daylight bombing attracted German fighters that were then destroyed and provided round-the-clock bombardment, giving Germany no relief from air attack. They agreed on the Combined Bomber Offensive (CBO): The British would bomb industrial areas at night while Americans would seek precision targets during daylight bombing; Allied air forces thus assumed independent strategic missions complemented by tactical support of theater forces. It was resolved that when the new B-29 bombers became available they would be assigned to England, rejecting the British choice of North Africa, to bomb Germany.

The Casablanca Conference also took up the air war against Japan in detail. FDR insisted China be kept in the war, despite the problem of flying over the Hump from India to China, until a land connection to China was reestablished. The British accepted the U.S. explanation for a strong course of action against Japan and agreed to resolve the problems of China-Burma-India (CBI) support. George C. Marshall, grappling with the disagreement on China policy between Lieutenant General Joseph W. Stilwell and Major General Claire L. Chennault, believed that Japanese industrial production could be crippled under air assault. FDR agreed, convinced that bombing Japan would uplift Chinese morale, and he unrealistically proposed sending 200–300 planes to China despite the acknowledged logistics problems. Marshall did not share this view. After the conference, FDR wired Chiang Kai-shek that Arnold would visit China to discuss air aid to Chennault's Fourteenth Air Force to increase the offensive against Japan in China and to deliver FDR's letter promising air support. On 10 April 1943, Chiang wrote to FDR requesting that General Chennault return to Washington to present his ideas for an air offensive against Japan. Arnold yielded to a fuller airing of the Stilwell-Chennault feud. In May 1943, a few days before the so-called Trident Conference was to open in Washington, D.C., Arnold had a heart attack and was unable to attend the proceedings.

The Trident Conference took place during 15–25 May 1943. FDR, Churchill, and their chiefs of staff met to plan war strategies; Chennault and Stilwell were brought in to present their respective cases. The challenge of the CBI theater was compounded by Stilwell and Chennault's disagreement on overall strategy. General Stilwell, known as "Vinegar Joe" for his acerbic temperament, was U.S. theater commander and Chief of Staff to Chiang Kai-shek, and General Chennault commanded the newly formed Fourteenth Air Force.

Chennault went to China as air adviser to Chiang in 1937 and had trained Chinese pilots as well as an international squadron of mercenaries in effective tactics to support Chinese ground troops and challenge Japanese air units in China. Prior to Pearl Harbor, he had created, with the clandestine support of FDR, the American Volunteer Group—the famous Flying Tigers. Chennault, prone to exaggeration, proposed to drive Japan out of China with an air force of 500 planes if properly supplied and maintained.

Stilwell, an infantry officer whose forces were earlier driven out of Burma, proposed to equip and train a large Chinese army to recapture Burma and open a supply road to China. Chennault countered that the supplies necessary to equip the Chinese armies would effectively halt most of his air logistics. As the British wished not to risk a massive effort in Burma, they supported Chennault's views.

Chennault called for an increased airlift to supply the Fourteenth Air Force so that his bombers could push the Japanese back and destroy Japanese merchant shipping off the Chinese coast, then retake Hong Kong as a port for supplies to enter China. This approach depended on Allied control of the China Sea, including the Philippines and Formosa (Taiwan) to be used as bases, something not scheduled until 1947. Stilwell retorted that the Chinese armies under Chiang could not hold the eastern airbases around Guilin (Kweilin) once the Japanese retaliated for the increased air attacks on them. Without clear resolution, it was determined to assign more aircraft to boost supplies over the Hump to 10,000 tons per month by 1 September 1943. Asia would again be taken up in the Quebec Conference at the end of the summer.

Following discussion of CBI issues, attention turned to the European theater. The CBO plan was refined at Trident and designated Operation POINTBLANK, its goal to destroy German industries essential to the manufacture of weapons and war activity. In addition to formalizing the strategic bomber offensive against Germany, the principals agreed to a plan for a cross-channel invasion of Europe through France for 1 May 1944.

The Quadrant Conference (Quebec I) took place during 14–24 August 1943. U.S. military planners sought to thwart Churchill's earlier demand that the Allies drive through Italy in the wake of Mussolini's collapse. U.S. Secretary of State Henry L. Stimson stiffened FDR's resolve to limit U.S. deployment into Italy after Sicily (HUSKY) in order to prepare for the cross-channel invasion into France. Roosevelt and Churchill also discussed drawing the Soviet Union fully into the Western Allies' war plans, and Charles de Gaulle was designated the representative of all Free French forces.

Since Trident, U.S. planners focused on the pending deployment of the new B-29 bomber against Japanese homeland targets. At Quadrant, Arnold submitted the plan of Major General Laurence Kuter, called SETTING SUN, which proposed the destruction of Japan's war industries by B-29s flying from Chinese bases within 1,500 miles of Japanese targets. The plan predicted with remarkable effectiveness that 70 B-29s, each flying five missions per month, could destroy Japan by August 1945.

The plan was sent to Churchill, Chennault, and Stilwell for consideration. Stilwell argued that limited port facilities in Calcutta and the difficulties of getting supplies from India to China made it unworkable. He proposed a plan called TWILIGHT, which would base the B-29s in the Calcutta rear area and fit some B-29s with bomb-bay tanks for use as tankers over the Hump. The rest of the fuel and supplies could be flown over the Hump by cargo planes. This would eliminate the need for a supply port on the Chinese Sea and allow bombing operations to begin by April 1945, with 10 B-29 groups flying an average of 500 sorties per month. The Combined Chiefs' interest in the plan waned when Stilwell insisted that he be given provisions to equip and train 50 Chinese divisions to defend the forward eastern bases. Chennault maintained that with appropriate supplies, the Fourteenth Air Force and the Chinese army could protect the bomber bases that he proposed to place along the Kweilin-Changsha railroad. It was decided to use the B-29s to haul fuel in bomb-bay tanks as Stilwell proposed and to place the planes in forward bases in Chengtu, China. Operation MATTERHORN, the first bombing of Japan by B-29s from Chinese bases, was tentatively scheduled for 1 May 1944. The various wartime conferences had immediate effect on the conduct of the war, as well as long-range postwar effects not perceived at the time.

Richard C. DeAngelis

References

Byrd, Martha. *Chennault: Giving Wings to the Tiger.* Tuscaloosa: University of Alabama Press, 1987.

Daso, Dik A. *Hap Arnold and the Evolution of American Airpower.* Washington, DC: Smithsonian Institution Press, 2000.

Wedemeyer, Albert C. *Wedemeyer Reports!* New York: Henry Holt, 1958.

Wright, Orville (1871–1948)

Inventor, with brother Wilbur (1867–1912), of the airplane. He was born in Dayton, Ohio. At Kitty Hawk, North Carolina,

Transportability was a major requirement in the contract calling for a military airplane, and the Wrights demonstrated it with ease. (U.S. Air Force)

on 17 December 1903, Orville Wright became the first person to sustain a controlled flight of a man-operated, motor-driven aircraft. Building on the previous work of Otto Lilienthal, Octave Chanute, and Samuel Langley, the Wright brothers began building gliders in 1900. In late 1902, after more than 1,000 flights, they designed and built a plane with a light (150 pounds), powerful (12 horsepower at 2,000 rpm) engine and hand-carved propellers. In 1903 at Kitty Hawk, Orville flew the *Flyer I* 12 seconds and 120 feet. In 1905, *Flyer III* became the world's first practical airplane. It was maneuverable and could remain airborne for more than half an hour. The Wrights received a patent for the airplane on 22 May 1906. In 1908 at Fort Myers, Virginia, Orville won a competition for the world's first military airplane. Later that year, he became the first pilot to kill his passenger (Lieutenant Thomas Selfridge).

After Wilbur died of typhoid fever in 1912, Orville continued flying actively until 1915. He sold his interest in the Wright Company for $1.5 million, then retired to serve on the National Advisory Committee for Aeronautics and continued inventing household gadgets. Wright never married.

John Barnhill

References

Combs, Harry. *Kill Devil Hill: Discovering the Secrets of the Wright Brothers.* Boston: Houghton Mifflin, 1979.

Howard, Fred. *Wilbur and Orville: A Biography of the Wright Brothers.* New York: Knopf, 1987.

Wright, Orville. *How We Invented the Airplane.* Edited and with commentary by Fred C. Kelly; drawings by James MacDonald. New York: McKay, 1953.

Wright, Wilbur (1867–1912)

Inventor, with brother Orville (1871–1948), of the airplane. Wilbur, the older of the two aviation pioneering brothers, was born on 16 April 1867 on a small farm near Millville, Indiana. His father had a strong influence over Wilbur and all his siblings. He and younger brother Orville did not smoke, drink, or get married. Neither brother got more than a partial high school education. In many respects, Wilbur and Orville, like Thomas Edison of a previous generation, developed their careers very much in the tradition of the classic American inventive tinkerers who employed instinct, intuition, and endless intelligent effort to fashion new machines and innovative theories.

After the family moved to Dayton, Ohio, Orville Wright became an expert bicyclist. In the late 1880s, as the brothers became adults, they decided to make their living in the bicycle business. They were also fascinated by gliders and closely followed the career of the famous German glider pioneer Otto Lilienthal. By the time Lilienthal was killed in 1896, both brothers had become students of flying.

By 1899, the Wrights were convinced they could combine their interests and expertise to create a machine-driven heavier-than-air aircraft. By the fall of 1903, the brothers had constructed a fragile and elegant airplane with a 40.5-foot wingspan weighing 750 pounds with the pilot. Among the most important design features was wing warping (the ancestor of ailerons), which enabled them, with the elevators and a moveable rudder, to have three-axis control.

Only 10 days before they planned to make experimental flights near Kitty Hawk, North Carolina, Samuel Langley had failed in his second very public attempt to fly. The Wrights had selected Kitty Hawk because of its wide-open sand dunes and strong winds. It had been perfect for glider-testing, and now they hoped it would help them fly their powered aircraft.

On 17 December 1903, on Kill Devil Hill, near Kitty Hawk, Orville Wright made what has been credited as the world's first flight in a powered, manned, heavier-than-air machine. The aircraft flew 120 feet in 12 seconds. The distance is about half the length of the wingspan of a modern C-5 Galaxy transport. With only a handful of spectators present to witness the historic event, the brothers made three more flights that day. The longest flight, by Wilbur, measured 852 feet and lasted 59 seconds.

Over the next several years they worked, mostly in the Dayton area, to perfect what later became known as the Wright Flyer. Still, many people did not believe that they had flown. In late 1905, the editors of *Scientific American* magazine suggested in one article that the Wrights' claim was a hoax. That same year, as if to prove their critics wrong, Wilbur made a very public 24-mile flight lasting more than 30 minutes. In 1906, they also received patents for many of the important features they had developed for their plane.

Of course, the primary purpose of building the aircraft was to sell it and make money. The most likely buyer was the U.S. Army. On 10 February 1908, the Wrights negotiated a contract to sell a heavier-than-air flying machine to the U.S. Army Signal Corps. Initial flying trials began on 3 September and unfolded with remarkable success. However, they came to an abrupt halt on 17 September when one of the new wooden propellers split at 125 feet and the Flyer crashed. Orville was seriously injured; his passenger, Lieutenant Thomas Selfridge, became the first person to die in a powered aircraft crash.

The trials resumed the next summer and officially lasted from 29 June to 30 July 1909. They exceeded all expectations. During test flights, Orville flew the pusher-style aircraft to a record altitude of 500 feet and once made a 10-mile cross-country flight, with Lieutenant Benjamin D. Foulois, at the "unbelievable" speed of 42.5 mph. On 2 August 1909, the Army accepted what became known as Signal Corps Flyer Number One and paid the Wrights $25,000. That aircraft is currently on exhibit at the National Air and Space Museum.

On 30 May 1912, Wilbur Wright died of typhoid fever during an epidemic that struck Dayton. Orville was devastated and soon all but retired from the aviation business. Even though he won the 1913 Collier Trophy and remained active with the National Advisory Committee for Aeronautics, by 1915 Orville had sold his holdings in the Wright Aircraft Company.

William Head and Brian Head

References

Combs, Harry. *Kill Devil Hill: Discovering the Secrets of the Wright Brothers.* Boston: Houghton Mifflin, 1979.

Crouch, Tom D. *The Bishop's Boys: The Life of Wilbur and Orville Wright.* New York: W. W. Norton, 1989.

Head, William P. *Every Inch a Soldier: Augustine Warner Robins and the Building of U.S. Airpower.* College Station: Texas A&M University Press, 1995.

McFarland, Marvin W., ed. *The Papers of Wilbur and Orville Wright.* Rev. ed. New York: McGraw-Hill, 2000.

Wright-Patterson Air Force Base

U.S. Air Force base located approximately 10 miles northeast of Dayton, Ohio. It is one of the largest military installations, having more than 500 buildings on a property area of 8,143 acres. Main active runway 05L/23R is 12,600 feet long and 300 feet wide. Employment exceeds 20,000 combined military and civilian personnel in more than 70 different units. Headquarters of the U.S. Air Force Material Command (AFMC), with major tenant units being the Aeronautical Systems Center, Air Force Research Laboratory, Air Force Institute of Technology, National Air Intelligence Center, and Air Force Museum. AFMC organizations located at other bases across the country include product centers, test centers, and logistics centers performing the integrated management of research, development, test, acquisition, and support of aerospace weapons systems.

Wright-Patterson AFB developed from four earlier military installations: Wilbur Wright Field, Fairfield Air Depot, McCook Field, and Wright Field. Wilbur Wright Field began operations on 28 June 1917 as a training installation. The field was named in honor of the late Wilbur Wright, who with brother Orville invented the airplane. The property area of Wilbur Wright Field included Huffman Prairie, where the

McCook Field, the birthplace of experimental aviation in the United States. There was a sign on the field saying "This Field is Small, So Use it All"—still good advice today for any pilot. The Xs on the rooftops are directional signals to various cities. (U.S. Air Force)

Wright brothers conducted their flying activities after their initial successful experiments at Kittyhawk, North Carolina.

In the fall of 1917, construction began for the Fairfield Air Depot, located adjacent to Wilbur Wright Field and near the village of Fairfield. The depot provided logistics support to U.S. Army Signal Corps aviation installations in the Midwest. Although the two installations initially were administered independently, beginning 10 January 1919 they were merged. A name-change took place on 1 July 1931 when the complex became Patterson Field in honor of Lieutenant Frank S. Patterson, who died in a flight-test accident.

McCook Field opened on 4 December 1917 as the U.S. Army Signal Corps's home of the Airplane Engineering Division. The field was located immediately north of downtown Dayton on 254 acres. Its name honored the McCook family of Dayton. The facilities and projects at the field included engineering laboratories and flight-testing for the advancement of military aeronautical technology. The technical staff performed engineering developments in virtually all subjects, including aircraft design, engines, propellers, materials, parachutes, flight clothing, and aerial photographic equipment. The pilots assigned to flight testing included several notable personalities, among them Major Rudolph W. Schroeder, Lieutenant James H. Doolittle, and Lieutenant John A. Macready. These men compiled an impressive list of aviation achievements, establishing records for altitude, speed, and distance.

McCook Field is remembered for the sign painted on the main hanger that proclaimed "THIS FIELD IS SMALL—USE IT ALL." The single paved runway was only 1000 feet long and 100 feet wide. The small size and urban setting of McCook Field ultimately rendered the facility unsuitable for aviation activities.

Construction began on 16 April 1926 for a new installation 8 miles east of Dayton to replace McCook Field. At the formal dedication on 12 October 1927, it was given the name Wright Field to honor the Wright brothers. The transfer of all personnel and equipment from McCook Field was completed by May 1929. Wright Field was the headquarters of the Material Division, with responsibility for research, engineering, supply, procurement, and maintenance. Today, it is headquarters for the Aeronautical Systems Center, which directs procurement of aeronautical systems, and for the Air Force Research Laboratory, which has facilities at Wright Field and other installations around the country. The Air Force Museum is located on a portion of the deactivated flying field.

During World War II, Patterson Field and Wright Field added facilities and expanded the workforce to a size several times greater than prewar levels. New hangers, shops, laboratories, and warehouses were constructed. For the years 1942–1944 the combined military and civilian personnel strength exceeded 45,000 each year. Patterson Field was a major wartime logistics center, and Wright Field was the center of aeronautical research, development, and procurement. Nevertheless, the demands of the war and the increasing complexity of military aircraft necessitated moving some functions to other locations. For example, experimental flight test moved to Muroc Field (now Edwards AFB), and armament testing projects moved to Eglin AFB. In the 1950s, most propulsion and wind-tunnel testing moved to the new Arnold Engineering Development Center near Manchester, Tennessee.

Patterson Field and Wright Field continued as separate installations through World War II. After the war a plan to establish joint administration of the two was approved. Wright-Patterson AFB became a single base on 13 June 1948. Aircraft operations continued using the runways at both fields until 1976, when the Wright Field runways were deactivated. All flight operations now are conducted from the Patterson Field aerodrome.

Squire L. Brown

References

Wacker, Lois E., and Shelby E. Wickam. *From Hoffman Prairie to the Moon.* Washington, DC: U.S. Government Printing Office, 1985.

Y

Yakovlev, Aleksandr S. (1906–1989)

Russian aircraft designer. Aleksandr Sergeevich Yakovlev was born in Moscow on 19 March 1906. He began designing mainly light aircraft in the 1920s under the sponsorship of Sergei Ilyushin. His first combat aircraft were the Yak-4 light bomber, which flew in 1939, and the Yak-1 fighter of 1940. The Yak-4, sleek-looking but underpowered and plagued with structural problems, was total failure and withdrawn from service almost immediately after the start of war. The Yak-1 made Yakovlev's reputation and established him as Stalin's favorite designer, though other Soviet designers accused him of being a back-stabber and toady. Of mixed metal and wood construction, the Yak-1 was fast and maneuverable, and the approximately 400 examples produced by June 1941 were the only fighters capable of meeting the German aircraft on near-equal terms. Even after introduction of the evolved Yak-7, Yak-9, and Yak-3, the Yak-1 remained in production until 1944, with 8,670 examples produced, and several Yak aces expressed a preference for the earlier model. The Yak-7 and Yak-9 were heavier versions, with greater power and longer range, while the Yak-3 was a lightweight low-altitude fighter, possibly the best dogfighter of the war. By Victory Day, 32,361 Yak fighters of all types had been produced; after the war the Yak-9P was produced, bringing total production to more than 36,300 Yaks, the second-most produced combat aircraft in history after the 39,000 Il-2 Shturmovik variants.

The Yak-3 also served as the basis for the Soviets' first generation of jet fighters, the Yak-15 and Yak-17, of which 710 were produced from 1946 to 1948. Essentially basic Yak airframes fitted with a Jumo jet engine, they lost out to the more modern MiG-15, and Yakovlev never regained his preeminence. Another derivative of the wartime fighters was the Yak-11 trainer, the basic Yak airframe equipped with a lower-power radial engine. The success of this aircraft led to a series of other propeller-driven trainers, the Yak-12, Yak-18 and Yak-52, which were produced in large quantities and used for training throughout the communist world and by Third World nations; they have recently appeared in the West as sporting aircraft.

During the early 1950s, Yak built a few examples of the tandem-rotor Yak-24 helicopter, but it was not very successful, and further helicopter development was abandoned to Mil and Kamov. Yakovlev produced one more successful combat aircraft family. The Yak-25 Flashlight entered service in 1953. A strange-looking swept-wing jet with two engines under the wings and a bulbous nose housing a radar, it was used only as an interceptor. The 547 examples produced served only with the Soviet air defense units, were not exported, and never saw combat before being retired in the early 1960s. However, in 1959 an unarmed high-altitude reconnaissance version, the Yak-25 RV Mandrake, was introduced, able to reach 64,000 feet.

Also introduced in 1959 was a much more modernized aircraft of obvious lineage, the Yak-28 Brewer family. The Brewer, produced in 837 copies, served as a tactical bomber and reconnaissance aircraft and later as an electronic-warfare platform. Also members of the family were 160 Yak-27 Mangrove reconnaissance aircraft and 437 examples of the Yak-28P Firebar all-weather interceptor. Like the Flashlight, none of these aircraft were exported or saw combat, but the Brewers proved long-lived, the last examples remaining in Ukrainian service as late as 2000.

From 1973 to 1988, Yakovlev also produced a series of 231 VTOL jets, the Yak-38 Forger, for operation from aircraft carriers, but this aircraft gained an evil reputation with crews.

Aleksandr Yakovlev died on 22 August 1989.

George M. Mellinger

References

Gordon, Yefim, and Dmitrii Khazanov. *Soviet Combat Aircraft of the Second World War.* Vol. 1. Leicester, UK: Midland Counties, 1998.

Gunston, Bill. *The Encyclopedia of Russian Aircraft, 1875–1995.* Osceola, WI: Motorbooks International, 1995.

Kerber, L. L. *Stalin's Aviation Gulag.* Washington, DC: Smithsonian Institution Press, 1996.

Yamaguchi, Tamon (1892–1942)

Imperial Japanese Navy rear admiral. Born in 1892, Tamon Yamaguchi graduated from the Japanese Naval Academy in 1912 and from the Naval War College in 1925. He spent three tours in the United States, including one as naval attaché (June 1934–August 1936). He also attended Princeton University. He was one of Japan's most passionate advocates of naval airpower. The pilots he commanded admired him and considered him one of their own. One Japanese author called him "the bravest officer in the Japanese Navy." He was promoted to rear admiral in 1938 and to command of the Second Division of the main Japanese carrier strike force in 1940.

Yamaguchi, unlike most Japanese admirals of his time, had an aggressive and decisive style and personality. Some describe him as "impulsive" or "devil-may-care." He was a very close confidant of Admiral Isoroku Yamamoto, and many historians consider him Japan's most gifted wartime carrier officer. He was the most outspoken supporter of Yamamoto's plan to attack Pearl Harbor and later his plan to attack Midway. He and the carrier commander, the cautious Vice Admiral Chuichi Nagumo, were often at odds and nearly came to blows on several occasions.

Originally, left out of the Pearl Harbor operation because of concerns over fuel consumption and range, Yamaguchi demonstrated such a devotion to the plan that Yamamoto was convinced he should include Yamaguchi's carriers. During the Pearl Harbor operation, Yamaguchi commanded the Second Division, consisting of *Soryu* and the flagship *Hiryu.* It was Yamaguchi who urged Nagumo to make follow-up strikes on Pearl Harbor facilities and to seek out and destroy the U.S. carriers that had not been present on 7 December 1941. Upon returning to Japan, Yamaguchi's carriers were sent to support Japanese operations against Wake Island.

From 31 March to 10 April 1942, he again commanded the Second Division during successful Indian Ocean operations against the British. Seven weeks later, Yamaguchi and the Second Division participated in the pivotal Battle of Midway.

Again, Yamaguchi and Nagumo disagreed on tactics. When the Japanese discovered the USS *Yorktown,* Yamaguchi advocated an immediate attack and search for other carriers. Nagumo hesitated, trying to decide whether to attack Midway again or the carriers. His delay left the Japanese carriers vulnerable to air attacks. On 4 June 1942, three of the four Japanese carriers were fatally bombed by U.S. Navy dive-bombers. At 10:30 A.M., with his carrier *Akagi* sinking, Nagumo transferred command of air operations to Yamaguchi.

Yamaguchi immediately launched 18 dive-bombers and six fighters against the *Yorktown.* Although only eight returned, they hit the *Yorktown* three times, leaving it dead in the water. An hour later *Yorktown* was under way, only to be struck again by a second wave of 10 Kate torpedo-bombers and six fighters. Eight more Japanese planes were lost, but two torpedoes struck the *Yorktown,* leaving it listing and dead in the water. Despite efforts to save the carrier, a Japanese submarine later sank it.

As a third strike with only 10 planes was prepared by Yamaguchi, 24 dive-bombers from the USS *Enterprise* and *Yorktown* attacked the *Hiryu* at about 5:00 P.M., mortally wounding it. Steeped in samurai tradition, Yamaguchi assumed blame for the ship's loss and refused to leave. At 2:30 A.M. on 5 June, the 800 survivors of *Hiryu* abandoned ship. Two hours later, the last officers also departed. Yamaguchi was last seen reciting poetry and sipping tea. The ship was scuttled at 5:10 A.M. but did not sink until 9:00 A.M.

Many believe that had Yamaguchi been in command the Japanese might have been more decisive in launching strikes against U.S. carriers. Considering the effect that *Hiryu's* limited strikes had on the *Yorktown,* the argument has at least some merit. Some blame for the defeat must fall on Admiral Yamamoto's excessively complex battle plan. But the excellence of Japan's enemy had more to do with their defeat at Midway than poor military decisionmaking.

William Head

References

Dull, Paul S. *A Battle History of the Imperial Japanese Navy.* Annapolis, MD: Naval Institute Press, 1978.

Dunnigan, James F., and Albert A. Nofi. *The Pacific War Encyclopedia.* 2 vols. New York: Facts on File, 1998.

Fuchida, Mitsuo, and Masatake Okumiya. *Midway: The Battle That Doomed Japan.* Annapolis, MD: Naval Institute Press, 1955.

Ienaga, Saburo. *The Pacific War: World War II and the Japanese, 1931–1945.* New York: Pantheon Books, 1978.

Prange, Gordon W. *At Dawn We Slept: The Untold Story of Pearl Harbor.* New York: Penguin Books, 1981.

———. *Miracle At Midway.* New York: McGraw-Hill, 1982.

Yamamoto, Isoroku (1884–1943)

Imperial Japanese Navy (IJN) admiral; mastermind behind the Pearl Harbor operation. Isoroku Yamamoto was born on 4 April 1884 in Nagaoka, Japan. He graduated from the

Japanese Naval Academy in 1904 in time to fight during the Russo-Japanese War (1904–1905). After the war he attended the Imperial Naval War College. From 1919 to 1921, he attended Harvard University.

In the early 1920s Yamamoto, a carrier pilot himself, became a proponent of naval airpower. Generally considered an expert, he used his growing authority to effect the design, construction, and deployment of first-class naval aircraft. In 1925, Captain Yamamoto served as the naval attaché in the Japanese embassy in the United States. During this time, he observed the industrial power of America and also came to realize that carriers were eclipsing battleships in strategic importance.

Between 1936 and 1940, he earned the disdain of the Japanese right wing because he opposed war with the United States. He openly denounced the Axis Tripartite Pact, fearing Japan's aggressive foreign policy would incite America to war. He believed U.S. industrial might could lead to disaster and defeat for Japan. In 1940, he told one cabinet minister, "In the first six to 12 months of the war with the United States and Great Britain I will run wild and win victory upon victory. But then if the war continues after that, I have no expectations of success."

In August 1941, still opposing war with the United States, he was made commander in chief of the entire Imperial Japanese Navy and ordered to prepare the Combined Fleet for war. Yamamoto planned and led what he hoped would be a decisive blow. Although the 7 December 1941 attack on Pearl Harbor sunk five U.S. battleships, the U.S. carriers were not present and the results were far from decisive.

For five months the IJN roamed the Pacific unchecked. The Battle of the Coral Sea in May 1942 halted the advance. The Doolittle Raid against Tokyo (18 April 1942) pushed Yamamoto into an attack on Midway Island to secure the eastern sea approaches to Japan. At Midway Yamamoto created a complex plan involving naval air attacks against U.S. installations at Midway, decisive engagements with U.S. carriers, an amphibious landing on Midway, and a diversionary attack on the Aleutians. The IJN lost four carriers and most of its best pilots during the June battle. It was the turning point in the Pacific War.

He continued as Combined Fleet commander, leading his forces against the United States during the naval battles around Guadalcanal and the Solomon Islands. In an effort to improve morale and combat performance, Yamamoto conducted an inspection of Japanese airfields in southern Bougainville. When U.S. code breakers intercepted his itinerary, a plan was formulated to ambush his plane. On 18 April 1943, exactly one year after the Doolittle Raid, the Thirteenth Air Force intercepted Yamamoto's G4M Betty bomber just outside Kahlil Field, Buin, and shot it down, killing Yamamoto.

Yamamoto was given a state funeral and posthumously promoted to Admiral of the Fleet. Most experts believe that Yamamoto's death had a devastating impact on his forces and nation. Others, viewing his repeated mistakes, feel that his death benefited Japan, although the Japanese never perceived this.

William Head

References

Agawa, Hiroyuki. *The Reluctant Admiral: Yamamoto and the Imperial Navy.* American ed. trans. James Besten. New York: Harper and Row, 1979 [Rev. ed. 2000].

Yeager, Charles E. (1923–)

U.S. Air Force general. Charles E. "Chuck" Yeager was born in Myra, West Virginia, on 13 February 1923. He graduated from high school in Hamlin, West Virginia. He enlisted in the U.S. Army Air Corps in September 1941, was accepted for pilot training under the flying sergeant program in July 1942, and received his pilot wings and appointment as a flight officer in March 1943 at Luke Field, Arizona.

During World War II, Yeager distinguished himself in aerial combat over France and Germany during the years 1943–1945 by shooting down 13 enemy aircraft, five during one mission alone. He was also one of the first to down Germany's new jet-powered fighter, the Messerschmitt Me 262. On 5 March 1944, he was shot down over German-occupied France but escaped capture when elements of the French Maquis helped him to reach the safety of the Spanish border. He then returned to combat.

He returned to the United States in February 1945 to attend the instructor-pilot course, after which he served as an instructor pilot. In July 1945, he went to Wright Field, Ohio, where he received his first experimental flight-test work. His assignment there led to his selection as pilot of the nation's first dedicated research airplane, the rocket-powered Bell X-1, at Edwards AFB, California, where he served from mid-1947 to late 1954. Yeager made world history on 14 October 1947 when he became the first person to fly faster than the speed of sound while flying the Bell XS-1 (later X-1) rocket-powered airplane at Edwards AFB.

During 1952 he attended the Air Command and Staff College. He also became the second person to fly at more than twice the speed of sound while piloting the improved Bell X-1A on 12 December 1953. He was the nation's leading test pilot for nine years.

He returned to Europe in October 1954 and became commander of the 417th Fighter Squadron at Hahn Air Base, Germany, in May 1955. He remained in that position when his squadron was reassigned to Toul-Rosieres Air Base,

Strangely enough, Chuck Yeager received no publicity when he broke the sound barrier on 14 October 1947; the mission was too classified. It was many years later before he became the folk hero he is today. (U.S. Air Force)

France, in April 1956. Upon his return to the United States in September 1957, he was assigned to the 413th Fighter Wing at George AFB, California, and in April 1958 he became commander of the 1st Fighter Squadron.

Yeager graduated from the Air War College at Maxwell AFB, Alabama, in June 1961 and became commandant of the Aerospace Research Pilot School at Edwards AFB in July 1962. During the July 1966–June 1973 period, Yeager had numerous high-profile assignments, including commander of the 405th Fighter Wing at Clark Air Base in the Philippines. While commander of the 405th, he flew 127 missions in South Vietnam.

Yeager earned numerous decorations and awards during his tenure in the USAF. He is a command pilot and has flown more than 10,000 hours in 155 different types of military aircraft. He was awarded the MacKay Trophy in 1948, the Collier Trophy in 1948, and the Harmon Trophy in 1954.

He was promoted to brigadier general effective 1 August 1969, with date of rank 22 June 1969. He retired on 1 March 1975. The Tom Wolfe book *The Right Stuff* portrayed Yeager in a very positive light and gave him much greater fame than all his flying exploits had previously achieved. He continued flying and has had a successful career in industry and as a products spokesman.

Steve Pace

References

Bright, Charles D., ed. *Historical Dictionary of the U.S. Air Force.* New York: Greenwood Press, 1992.
United States Air Force Biography Service

Yom Kippur War (October War)

Arab-Israeli conflict that occurred in October 1973 during Yom Kippur. After some 25 years of unparalleled air superiority in the Middle East, the Israeli Air Force (IAF) found itself dangerously vulnerable during the opening days of the Arab-Israeli October War. Egyptian and Syrian mobile SA-6 Gainful surface-to-air missiles (SAMs) limited the IAF's ability to support ground forces. The SA-6s took a heavy initial toll of Israeli aircraft because their electronic countermeasures (ECM) equipment was ill-suited to the frequency-hopping SA-6. Losses of Israeli McDonnell Douglas F-4Es prompted the United States to transfer a number of U.S. F-4Es from Europe to the Israelis, provoking Arab claims that U.S. pilots were flying combat missions on behalf of Israel.

Prompt Israeli ECM development efforts limited the SA-6's effectiveness. IAF aircraft then turned to Israeli ground operations, which regained large portions of the Golan Heights, the Sinai, and portions of Egypt and surrounded the Egyptian Third Army.

The October War influenced the evolution of aerial warfare. It was the first post-Vietnam conflict that relied heavily upon electronic warfare, especially SAM suppression. It led to a critical diplomatic confrontation between the United States and Soviet Union, linking regional tactical warfare with global strategic dynamics. It created the mistaken image of the importance of global aerial resupply, as the vaunted U.S. airlift to Israel did not even begin until 14 October, the day after the Israelis had reversed the tide of battle. The war ultimately damaged the reputation of the IAF as invincible, which contributed to Syria's willingness to fight Israel again in 1982.

Robert S. Hopkins

See also

Defense Suppression; Electronic Warfare; Israeli Air Force; Israel–Middle East Conflicts; Israel–Middle East Wars; NICKEL GRASS; Syrian Air Force

References

Dupuy, Trevor N. *Elusive Victory.* New York: Harper and Row, 1978.
Nordeen, Lon. *Fighters over Israel.* New York: Orion Books, 1990.
Norton, Bill. *Fifty Years on the Edge.* Leicester, UK: Midland Counties, 2000.
Yonay, Ehud. *No Margin for Error.* New York: Pantheon, 1993.

Y-Service

Units that engage in the interception and exploitation of the patterns and substance of an enemy's low-grade signals traffic. Intelligence gained through the Y-service is typically used in the reconstruction of the enemy's order of battle and movements; however, it also provides important strategic intelligence. For example, on 20 May 1942 the Royal Air Force Y-service in North Africa learned that the total amount of enemy aviation fuel in the whole of Libya was only a paltry 3,283 tons.

This information enabled the RAF to gauge the effect of its interdiction campaigns and helped to predict enemy combat capability. More important to operations was the interception of enemy radio messages that contained intelligence on the locations of enemy units, early warnings of enemy air raids, as well as enemy tactics. This intelligence was intercepted, interpreted, passed along to the group controller and to Headquarters Northwest African Tactical Air Force, and aided in focusing Allied airpower against the most profitable targets.

Brad Gladman

References

Clayton, Aileen. *The Enemy is Listening.* London: Hutchinson, 1980.
Gladman, Brad. "Air Power and Intelligence in the Western Desert Campaign, 1940–1943." *Intelligence and National Security* 13, 4 (Winter 1998).
Public Record Office. AIR 40/2345 *'Y' Daily Reports Middle East for 20 May 1942.*
Public Record Office. AIR 23/1710. *Memorandum entitled Wireless Intelligence circulated by the Chief Intelligence Officer, NWATAF, 13 May 1943.* Public Record Office, Kew, Surrey.

Z

Zeppelin, Ferdinand Von (1838–1917)

Airship pioneer. As an army officer during the nineteenth century, Graf (Count) Ferdinand von Zeppelin had observed balloons during the U.S. Civil War. Upon retirement he turned his energies to the development of airships for military use. Struggling with delays occasioned by lack of funds and the destruction of his ship by fire, Zeppelin eventually sparked the imagination and national pride of the German people. He was able to hang on, and a number of his rigid airships were built for the army and navy prior to the outbreak of war.

Zeppelins became famous during the raids on England during the years 1915–1918, but by this time the count had turned his attention to the development of the *Riesenflugzeug* (giant aircraft) that would, in company with the Gothas, succeed his airships as the primary bomber against England in the last year of the war. His name will forever be synonymous with the great airships of World War I.

James Streckfuss

See also

Airships

References

Grosz, Peter M., and George W. Haddow. *The German Giants: The Story of the R-planes, 1914–1919.* London: Putnam, 1962.

Robinson, Douglas. *The Zeppelin in Combat.* London: G. T. Foulis, 1962.

Zero-Length Launcher

Rocket system designed to reduce the vulnerability of tactical air forces to airfield attacks, especially nuclear strikes. The zero-length launcher (ZEL) comprised a rocket-assisted takeoff system for fighter aircraft developed by the USAF during the 1950s. The ZEL system was designed to allow aircraft to take off from a mobile truck-mounted ramp or from a fixed ramp in a hardened aircraft shelter. This capability would allow aircraft to be launched even if the runways at an airfield had been damaged. The ZEL system was designed to ensure survival of the fighter force through protection (in the hardened shelters) or dispersal (atop the truck-mounted system). A similar launch system was used on the operational Matador, Mace, Regulus (ship- or submarine-launched), and Snark cruise missiles.

The ZEL system was successfully tested on Republic F-84G and North American F-100D fighters, but enough operational concerns existed that the capability was never deployed. The West German Bundesluftwaffe sponsored ZEL experiments with a Lockheed F-104G in the mid-1960s but did not develop an operational capability. The USAF also developed a complementary alternative landing system for use if airfield runways were too damaged for landings. This mat-landing (MAL) system used the standard aircraft tailhook and a mobile ground system composed of an arresting cable and a pneumatic mat for cushioning that could be deployed in any open field. The combined launch-and-recovery system was referred to as "ZELMAL." The MAL landing system was tested on several F-84G flights but was quickly abandoned due to physical stresses on the pilot. Although the ZELMAL effort was not successful, continuing USAF concerns over airfield vulnerability produced engineering designs that made airfields and aircraft more survivable and led to specialized aircraft designs, such as the swing wings on the General Dynamics F-111 and the V/STOL capabilities of the British and U.S. Harrier jumpjets.

Jerome V. Martin

References

Knaack, Marcelle Size. *Post–World War II Fighters, 1945–1973.* Washington, DC: U.S. Government Printing Office, 1985.

Wagner, Ray. *American Combat Planes.* 3rd ed. Garden City, NY: Doubleday, 1982.

Zuckert, Eugene M. (1911–2000)

Prominent public servant in various capacities; secretary of the U.S. Air Force. Born on 9 November 1911 in New York City, Eugene M. Zuckert attended public elementary and high schools in suburban New York. After prep school he obtained a degree from Yale University in 1933, then entered the combined Yale Law School–Harvard Business School course sponsored by William O. Douglas. Zuckert became a member of the Connecticut and New York bars and eventually that of the District of Columbia.

In 1940, after a three-year stint an as attorney for the U.S. Securities and Exchange Commission, he became an instructor in government and business relations at the Harvard Graduate School of Business Administration, where he subsequently became assistant dean. While at Harvard he also served as a special consultant to the commanding general of the Army Air Forces in developing statistical controls.

It is rare when two leaders of very strong character and personality pose together with smiles and mean it. In this case it is true: Gene Zuckert and Curtis LeMay liked each other and got along well. (U.S. Air Force)

In 1944, Zuckert entered the U.S. Navy as a lieutenant (junior grade) and worked in the office of the Chief of Naval Operations, where he was assigned to the Navy's inventory-control program. In September 1945, he was released from the Navy to become executive assistant to the administrator of surplus property administration under W. Stuart Symington. When Symington became assistant secretary of war for air in February 1946, Zuckert became his special assistant.

With the passage of the National Security Act in 1947 and Symington's subsequent appointment as the first secretary of the Air Force, Zuckert took the oath as assistant secretary of the Air Force. His principal duties were in the field of management. In this capacity, he helped institute Symington's program of management control through cost control. Zuckert represented the Air Force in the formulation of the fiscal year 1950 budget, the first joint Army–Navy–Air Force budget in U.S. history.

According to Zuckert, the accomplishment that gave him the most professional satisfaction stemmed from President Harry Truman's directive in 1948 requiring the armed services to abolish segregation. Working with General Idwal H. Edwards, head of Air Force personnel, Zuckert oversaw implementation of the integration program. When he left as assistant secretary in February 1952 to become a member of the Atomic Energy Commission, he left an Air Force cost-control system that had established a new standard for sound business administration within the military establishment, and he secured a personal reputation as one of the top-flight young career officials in government.

In December 1960, Robert McNamara, President-elect John F. Kennedy's designated secretary of Defense, recommended to Kennedy that Zuckert be appointed Air Force secretary. Zuckert was nominated and confirmed in January 1961. With nearly six years of Air Force experience, he was well prepared for the duties of secretary of the Air Force. Zuckert was involved in the controversies associated with the B-70, Skybolt, and TFX (later the F-111) weapons systems and had direct participation in the Vietnam War. Both he and Air Force Chief of Staff General Thomas D. White opposed an administration decision to cut the B-70 bomber. Zuckert later admitted he erred in promoting the bomber because of its increasing vulnerability to enemy defenses.

The TFX was a tactical fighter-bomber designed and built for both the Air Force and Navy. In negotiations over the development of this weapon, Zuckert supported the administration, which wanted the plane, against the Air Force, which did not. In so doing, he strained his relationship with the Air Force and lost a measure of confidence. Zuckert often found himself as the man in the middle, at times supporting the Air Force against the secretary of defense and the administration. Both the Air Force and the secretary of defense agreed upon one of Zuckert's ideas, however: Project Forecast. This study, initiated in May 1963, was prompted by Zuckert's observation that the Air Force ought to take a look at the technologies that would have some bearing upon future aerospace military operations.

Shortly after Zuckert left office in September 1965, the Air Force instituted the Zuckert Management Award, given each year on 30 September to a general officer or high-level civilian for outstanding management performance.

He returned to the practice of law and headed the firm of Zuckert Scoutt and Rasenberger, where he stayed until retirement in 1988. He served as director of several small technically oriented companies and as a member of the board of Washington Gas Light and Martin Marietta Corporation. Zuckert died on 5 June 2000.

George M. Watson Jr.

References

Watson, George M. Jr. *The Office of the Secretary of the Air Force, 1947–1965.* Washington, DC: Center for Air Force History, 1993.

Watson, George. "Eugene M. Zuckert: The Man in the Middle." *Airpower Historian* 36, 2 (summer 1989).

Zuckert, Eugene M. "The Service Secretary: Has He a Useful Role?" *Foreign Affairs* (April 1966).

BIBLIOGRAPHY

Agawa, Hirouki. *The Reluctant Admiral: Yamamoto and the Imperial Navy.* Tokyo: Kodansha International, 1979.

Allen, H. R. *The Legacy of Lord Trenchard.* London: Cassell, 1972.

Allen, Thomas B., and Norman Polmar. *Code-Name Downfall: The Secret Plan to Invade Japan and Why Truman Dropped the Bomb.* New York: Simon and Schuster, 1995.

Andrews, Allen. *The Air Marshals: The Air War in Western Europe.* New York: Morrow, 1970.

Andrews, William F. *Airpower Against an Army: Challenge and Response in CENTAF's Duel with the Republican Guards.* Maxwell AFB, AL: Air University Press, 1998.

Appleman, Roy, James M. Burns, Russell E. Gugeler, and John Stevens. *United States Army in World War II: Okinawa, the Last Battle.* Washington, DC: Center for Military History, 1993.

Arnold, Henry H. "First Report of the Commanding General of the Army Air Forces to the Secretary of War." (Also Second Report and Third Report.) *The War Reports of General of the Army George C. Marshall, Chief of Staff, General of the Army H. H. Arnold, Commanding General, Army Air Forces; and Fleet Admiral Ernest J. King, Commander in Chief, United States Fleet and Chief of Naval Operations.* Philadelphia: Lippincott, 1947.

______. *Global Mission.* New York: Harper and Brothers, 1949.

Ball, Desmond, and Jeffrey Richelson. *Strategic Nuclear Targeting.* Ithaca: Cornell University Press, 1986:

Ballard, Jack S., et al. *The United States Air Force in Southeast Asia, 1961–1973: An Illustrated Account.* Washington, DC: Office of Air Force History, 1984.

Barlow, Jeffrey G. *Revolt of the Admirals: The Fight for Naval Aviation, 1949–1950.* Washington, DC: Naval Historical Center, 1994.

Belote, James H., and William Belote. *Titans of the Seas: The Development of the Japanese and American Carrier Task Forces During World War II.* New York: Harper and Row, 1975.

Bergquist, Ronald E. *The Role of Airpower in the Iran-Iraq War.* Maxwell AFB, AL: Air University Press, 1988.

Boggs, Charles W., Jr. *Marine Aviation in the Philippines.* Washington, DC: Historical Division, Headquarters, U.S. Marine Corps, 1951.

Bowers, Ray L. *The United States Air Force in Southeast Asia: Tactical Airlift.* Washington, DC: Office of Air Force History, 1983.

Boyne, Walter J. *Clash of Wings: World War II in the Air.* New York: Simon and Schuster, 1994.

______. *Clash of Titans: World War II at Sea.* New York: Simon and Schuster, 1995.

______. *Beyond the Wild Blue: The History of the United States Air Force, 1947–1997.* New York: St. Martin's, 1997.

______. *The Smithsonian Book of Flight.* Washington, DC: Smithsonian Institution Press, 1986.

Bradin, James W. *From Hot Air to Hellfire: The History of Army Attack Aviation.* Novato, CA: Presidio. 1994.

Bright, Charles D., ed. *Historical Dictionary of the U.S. Air Force.* New York: Greenwood Press, 1992.

Brodie, Bernard, ed. *The Absolute Weapon: Atomic Power and World Order.* Freeport, RI: Books for Library Press, 1972.

Broughton, Jack. *Going Downtown: The War Against Hanoi and Washington.* New York: Orion Books, 1988.

Bruce, J. M. *British Aeroplanes, 1914–1918.* London: Putnam, 1957.

Cannon, M. Hamlin. *U.S. Army in World War II: Leyte, the Return to the Philippines.* Washington, DC: Office of the Chief of Military History, 1954.

Carter, Kit C., and Robert Mueller, eds. *The Army Air Forces in World War II: Combat Chronology, 1941–1945.* Washington, DC: Office of Air Force History, 1991.

Chandler, Charles DeForest, and Frank Lahm. *How Our Army Grew Wings: Airmen and Aircraft Before 1914.* New York: Arno, 1979.

Chang, Gordon H. *Friends and Enemies: The United States, China, and the Soviet Union, 1948–1972.* Stanford: Stanford University Press, 1990.

Chant, Christopher. *A Compendium of Armaments and Military Hardware.* London: Routledge and Kegan Paul, 1987.

Chesnau, Roger. *Aircraft Carriers of the World, 1914 to the Present: An Illustrated Encyclopedia.* 2nd ed. London: Arms and Armour Press, 1992.

Chinnery, Philip D. *Vietnam: The Helicopter War.* Annapolis, MD: Naval Institute Press, 1991.

Christienne, Charles, and Pierre Lissarrague. *A History of French Military Aviation.* Washington, DC: Smithsonian Institution Press,1986.

Churchill, Winston S. *The Second World War.* 6 vols. Boston: Houghton Mifflin, 1948–1953.

Clark, Alan. *The Fall of Crete.* New York: Wm. Morrow, 1962.

_______. *Barbarossa: The Russian-German Conflict, 1941–1945.* New York: Wm. Morrow, 1965.

Clodfelter, Mark. *The Limits of Airpower: The American Bombing of North Vietnam.* New York: Free Press, 1989.

Coffey, Thomas M. *Iron Eagle: The Turbulent Life of General Curtis LeMay.* New York: Crown Publishers, 1986.

Cole, Jean Hascall. *Women Pilots of World War II.* Salt Lake City: University of Utah Press, 1992.

Cooksley, Peter G. *Flying Bomb: The Story of Hitler's V-Weapons in WW II.* New York: Charles Scribner's Sons, 1979.

Cooling, Benjamin Franklin. *Case Studies in the Development of Close Air Support.* Washington, DC: Office of Air Force History, 1990.

_______. *Case Studies in the Achievement of Air Superiority.* Washington, DC: Center for Air Force History, 1994.

Cooper, Malcolm. *The Birth of Independent Airpower: British Air Policy in the First World War.* London: Allen and Unwin, 1986.

Copp, DeWitt S. *Forged in Fire.* Garden City, NY: Doubleday, 1982.

Coyne, James P. *Airpower in the Gulf.* Arlington, VA: Air Force Association, 1992.

Crane, Conrad C. *Bombs, Cities, and Civilians: Amerian Airpower Strategy in World War II.* Lawrence: University Press of Kansas, 1993.

_______. *American Airpower Strategy in Korea, 1950–1953.* Lawrence: University Press of Kansas, 2000.

Craven, Wesley Frank, and James Lea Cate, eds. *The Army Air Forces in World War Two.* 7 vols. Washington, DC: Office of Air Force History, 1983.

Cuneo, John R. *Winged Mars.* 2 vols. Harrisburg, PA: Miitary Services Publishing, 1945, 1947.

Davies, R.E.G. *A History of the World's Airlines.* London: Oxford University Press, 1964.

Davis, Benjamin O., Jr. *Benjamin O. Davis Jr., American: An Autobiography.* New York: Plume, 1992.

Davis, Richard G. *Carl A. Spaatz and the Air War in Europe.* Washington, DC: Center for Air Force History, 1993.

Day, George E. *Return with Honor.* Mesa, AZ: Champlin Museum Press, 1989.

Deichmann, Paul. *Spearhead for Blitzkrieg: Luftwaffe Operations in Support of the Army, 1939–1945.* London: Greenhill Books, 1996.

De Seversky, Alexander P. *Victory Through Air Power.* New York: Simon and Schuster, 1962.

Donald, David, ed. *U.S. Air Force, Air Power Directory.* London: Aerospace Publishing, 1992.

Donnelly, Thomas, Margaret Roth, and Caleb Baker. *Operation Just Cause.* New York: Lexington, 1991.

Doolittle, James H., with Carroll V. Glines. *I Could Never Be So Lucky Again: An Autobiography.* Atglen, PA: Schiffer Military/Aviation History, 1995.

Dorr, Robert F. *Air War Hanoi.* London: Blandford Press, 1988.

Dorr, Robert F., and Warren Thompson. *The Korean Air War.* Osceola, WI: Motorbooks International, 1994.

Douglas, Sholto, with Robert Wright. *Sholto Douglas: Combat and Command: The Story of an Airman in Two World Wars.* New York: Simon and Schuster, 1966.

Douhet, Giulio. *The Command of the Air.* Washington, DC: Office of Air Force History, 1991.

Dunmore, Spencer. *Wings for Victory: The Remarkable Story of the British Commonwealth Air Training Plan in Canada.* Toronto: McClelland and Stewart, 1994

Edmonds, Walter D. *They Fought with What They Had: The Story of the Army Air Forces in the Southwest Pacific, 1941–1942.* Washington, DC: Center for Air Force History, 1992.

Eschmann, Karl J. *Linebacker: The Untold Story of the Air Raids over North Vietnam.* New York: Ballantine Books, 1989.

Flanagan, John F. *Vietnam above the Treetops.* New York: Praeger, 1992.

Flintham, Victor. *Air Wars and Aircraft: A Detailed Record of Air Combat, 1945 to Present.* New York: Facts on File, 1990.

Foulois, Benjamin D., with Carroll V. Gilnes. *From the Wright Brothers to the Astronauts: The Memoirs of Major General Benjamin D. Foulois.* New York: McGraw Hill, 1968.

Francillon, Rene J. *Japanese Aircraft of the Pacific War.* Annapolis, MD: Naval Institute Press, 1979.

Frank, Benis M., and Henry I. Shaw Jr. *History of U.S. Marine Corps Operations in World War II, Volume 5: Victory and Occupation.* Washington, DC: Historical Branch, Headquarters, U.S. Marine Corps, 1968.

Frankland, Noble. *The Bombing Offensive Against Germany.* London: Faber and Faber, 1965.

Frankland, Noble, gen. ed. *The Encyclopedia of Twentieth Century Warfare.* New York: Crown, 1989.

Fredette, Raymond H. *The Sky on Fire: The First Battle of Britain, 1917–1918.* Washington, DC: Smithsonian Press, 1991.

Freeman, Roger A. *The Mighty Eighth: A History of Units, Men and Machines of the U.S. 8th Air Force.* Osceola, WI: Motorbooks International, 1991.

Friedman, Norman. *U.S. Aircraft Carriers: An Illustrated Design History.* Annapolis, MD: Naval Institute Press, 1983.

_______. *British Carrier Aviation: The Evolution of the Ships and Their Aircraft.* Annapolis, MD: Naval Institute Press, 1988.

Fuchida, Mitsuo, and Masatake Okumiya. *Midway: The Battle That Doomed Japan.* Annapolis, MD: Naval Institute Press, 1955.

Futrell, Robert Frank. *Ideas, Concepts, Doctrine: A History of Basic Thinking in the United States Air Force, 1907–1964.* Maxwell AFB, AL: Air University Press, 1971.

_______. *The United States Air Force in Korea, 1950–1953.* Washington, DC: Office of Air Force History, 1983.

_______. *Ideas, Concepts, Doctrine: Basic Thinking in the United States Air Force, 1907–1960.* Vol. 1. Maxwell AFB, AL: Air University Press, 1989.

_______. *Ideas, Concepts, Doctrine: Basic Thinking in the United States Air Force, 1961–1984.* Vol. 2. Maxwell AFB, AL: Air University Press, 1989.

Galland, Adolf. *The First and the Last.* New York: Holt, 1954.

Gantz, Kenneth F., ed. *The United States Air Force Report on the Ballistic Missile.* New York: Doubleday, 1958.

Gaston, James C. *Planning the American Air War: Four Men and Nine Days in 1941.* Washington, DC: National Defense University Press, 1982.

Geust, Carl-Fredrik. *Under the Red Star: Luftwaffe Aircraft in the Soviet Air Force.* Shrewsbury, UK: Airlife, 1993.

Gorn, Michael H. *Harnessing the Genie: Science and Technology Forecasting for the Air Force, 1944–1986.* Washington, DC: Office of Air Force History, 1988.

Gorrell, Edgar S. *The Measure of America's World War Aeronautical Effort.* Northfield, VT: Norwich University Press, 1940.

Gray, Peter, and Owen Thetford. *German Aircraft of the First World War.* London: Putnam, 1962.

Green, William. *Warplanes of the Third Reich.* New York: Galahad Books, 1990.

Gross, Charles Joseph. *Prelude to the Total Force: The Air National Guard, 1943–1969.* Washington, DC: Office of Air Force History, 1985.

Groves, Leslie R. *Now It Can Be Told: The Story of the Manhattan Project.* New York: Harper and Brothers, 1962.

Gunston, Bill. *World Encyclopedia of Aircraft Manufacturers.* Northamptonshire, UK: Patrick Stephens, 1993.

Gurney, Gene. *Vietnam: The War in the Air—A Pictorial History of the U.S. Air Forces in the Vietnam War: Air Force, Army, Navy, and Marines.* New York: Crown, 1985.

Halberstadt, Hans. *The Wild Weasels: History of U.S. Air Force SAM Killers, 1965–Today.* Osceola, WI: Motorbooks International, 1992.

Hall, George M. *The Fifth Star.* New York: Praeger, 1994.

Hall, R. Cargill. *Missile Defense Alarm: The Genesis of Space-Based Infrared Early Warning.* Chantilly, VA: NRO History Office, July 1988.

Hallion, Richard P. *Strike from the Sky: The History of Battlefield Air Attack, 1911–1945.* Washington, DC: Smithsonian Institution Press, 1989.

_______. *Storm over Iraq.* Washington, DC: Smithsonian Institution Press, 1992.

Halsey, William F. and Bryan J. Halsey. *Admiral Halsey's Story.* New York: McGraw Hill, 1947.

Hammel, Eric. *Air War Europa: America's Air War Against Germany in Europe and North Africa—Chronology 1942–1945.* Pacifica, CA: Pacifica Press, 1994.

_______. *Air War Pacific: America's Air War Against Japan in East Asia and the Pacific—Chronology, 1941–1945.* Pacifica, CA: Pacifica Press, 1998.

Hardesty, Von. *Red Phoenix.* Washington, DC: Smithsonian Institution Press, 1982.

Harris, Arthur. *Bomber Offensive.* London: Collins, 1947.

Harrison, Marshall. *A Lonely Kind of War: Forward Air Controller, Vietnam.* Novato, CA: Presidio Press, 1989.

Hastings, Max. *Bomber Command.* New York: Simon and Schuster, 1989.

Holley, I. B., Jr. *Ideas and Weapons.* Washington, DC: Office of Air Force History, 1983.

Hudson, James J. *Hostile Skies: A Combat History of the American Air Service in World War I.* Syracuse, NY: Syracuse University Press, 1968.

Hunsaker, Jerome C. *Aeronautics at the Mid-Century.* New Haven: Yale University Press, 1952.

Hurley, Alfred F. *Billy Mitchell: Crusader for Air Power.* New York: Franklin Watts, 1964.

Hurley, Alfred F., and Robert C. Ehrhart, eds. *Air Power and Warfare.* Washington, DC: Office of Air Force History, 1979.

Jentschura, Hansgeorg, Dieter Jung, and Peter Mickel. *Warships of the Imperial Japanese Navy, 1869–1945.* London: Arms and Armour Press, 1977.

Jones, R. V. *Most Secret War.* London: Hamish Hamilton, 1978.

Kennett, Lee. *A History of Strategic Bombing.* New York: Charles Scribner's Sons, 1982.

Kerr, E. Bartlett. *Flames over Tokyo: The U.S. Army Air Forces' Incendiary Campaign Against Japan, 1944–1945.* New York: Donald I. Fine, 1991.

King, Ernest J., and Walter Muir Whitehill. *Fleet Admiral King: A Naval Record.* New York: W. W. Norton, 1952.

Kingston-McLoughry, E. J. *War in Three Dimensions: The Impact of Air Power upon the Classical Principles of War.* London: Jonathan Cape, 1949.

Lambeth, Benjamin S. *The Transformation of American Air Power.* Ithaca: Cornell University Press, 2000.

Lauer, Timothy M., and Steven L. Llanso. *Encyclopedia of Modern U.S. Military Weapons.* New York: Berkley Books, 1995.

LeMay, Curtis E., with Mackinlay Kantor. *Mission with LeMay.* New York: Doubleday, 1965.

Littauer, Raphael, and Norman Uphoff, eds. *The Air War in Indochina.* Boston: Beacon Press, 1972.

Lloyd, Alwyn T. *A Cold War Legacy—A Tribute to Strategic Air Command, 1946–1992.* Missoula, MT: Pictorial Histories, 2000.

Loftin, Laurence K., Jr. *Quest for Performance: The Evolution of Modern Aircraft.* Washington, DC: National Aeronautics and Space Administration, 1985.

Lundstrom, John B. *The First Team: Pacific Naval Air Combat from Pearl Harbor to Midway.* Annapolis, MD: Naval Institute Press, 1984.

_______. *The First Team and the Guadalcanal Campaign.* Annapolis, MD: Naval Institute Press, 1994.

Mark, Eduard. *Aerial Interdiction in Three Wars.* Washington, DC: Center for Air Force History, 1994.

Maurer, Maurer, ed. *The U.S. Air Service in World War I.* 4 vols. Washington, DC: Office of Air Force History, 1978.

______. *Aviation in the U.S. Army, 1919–1939.* Washington, DC: Office of Air Force History, 1987.

McCall, Gene H. *New World Vistas: Air and Space Power for the 21st Century. Summary Volume.* Washington, DC: Department of the Air Force, 1995.

McCarthy, James R., and George B. Allison. *Linebacker II: A View from the Rock.* Maxwell AFB, AL: Airpower Research Institute, 1979.

McDonald, Robert A. *Corona Between the Sun and the Earth: The First NRO Reconnaissance Eye in Space.* Bethesda, MD: American Society for Photogrammetry and Remote Sensing, 1997.

McFarland, Stephen L., and Wesley Phillips Newton. *To Command the Sky: The Battle for Air Superiority over German, 1942–1944.* Washington, DC: Smithsonian Institution Press, 1991.

Meilinger, Philip S. *Hoyt Vandenberg: The Life of a General.* Bloomington: Indiana University Press, 1989.

Mersky, Peter, and Norman Polmar. *The Naval Air War in Vietnam.* Annapolis, MD: Nautical and Aviation, 1981.

Mesko, Jim. *Airmobile: The Helicopter War in Vietnam.* Carrollton, TX: Squadron/Signal, 1984.

Mets, David R. *Master of Airpower: General Carl A. Spaatz.* Novato, CA: Presidio Press, 1988.

Miller, Ronald, and David Sawers. *The Technical Development of Modern Aviation.* New York: Praeger, 1970.

Momyer, William W. *Air Power in Three Wars: WWII, Korea, Vietnam.* Washington, DC: Department of the Air Force, 1978.

Moody, Walton S. *Building a Strategic Air Force.* Washington, DC: Air Force History and Museums Program, 1996.

Morison, Samuel Eliot. *History of United States Naval Operations in the Second World War II.* 15 vols. Boston: Atlantic–Little Brown, 1947–1962.

Morrocco, John. *Thunder From Above: Air War, 1941–1968.* Boston: Boston Publishing, 1984.

Morrow, John H., Jr. *The Great War in the Air: Military Aviation from 1909 to 1921.* Washington, DC: Smithsonian Institution Press, 1993.

Morse, Stan, ed. *Gulf Air War Debrief: Described by the Pilots That Fought.* London: Aerospace Publishing, 1991.

Mrozek, Donald J. *The U.S. Air Force after Vietnam: Postwar Challenges and Potential for Responses.* Maxwell AFB, AL: Air University Press, 1988.

Murphy, Paul, ed. *The Soviet Air Forces.* Jefferson, NC: McFarland, 1984.

Murray, Williamson. *Luftwaffe.* Baltimore: Nautical and Aviation, 1985.

______. *Air War in the Persian Gulf.* Baltimore: Nautical and Aviation, 1995.

Nalty, Bernard C., ed. *War in the Pacific: Pearl Harbor to Tokyo Bay.* London: Salamander, 1991.

Neufeld, Jacob. *The Development of Ballistic Missiles in the United States Air Force, 1945–1960.* Washington, DC: Office of Air Force History, 1990.

______. *Reflections on Research and Development in the United States Air Force.* Washington, DC: Center for Air Force History, 1993.

Nordeen, Lon O., Jr. *Air Warfare in the Missile Age.* Washington, DC: Smithsonian Institute Press, 1985.

Overy, R. J. *The Air War, 1939–1945.* New York: Stein and Day, 1981.

Parrish, Thomas. *The Ultra Americans: The U.S. Role in Breaking the Nazi Codes.* Briarcliff Manor, NY: Stein and Day, 1986.

Parton, James. *Air Force Spoken Here: General Ira Eaker and the Command of The Air.* Betheseda, MD: Adler and Adler, 1986.

Penrose, Harald. *British Aviation: The Great War and Armistice.* New York: Funk and Wagnalls, 1969.

Pocock, Rowland F. *German Guided Missiles of the Second World War.* New York: Arco, 1967.

Pogue, Forrest C. *George C. Marshall: Ordeal and Hope, 1939–1942.* Vol. 1. New York: Viking Press, 1966.

Polmar, Norman, and Timothy Laurer. *Strategic Air Command.* Baltimore: Nautical and Aviation, 1970.

Powaski, Ronald E. *Return to Armageddon: The United States and the Nuclear Arms Race, 1981–1999.* New York: Oxford University Press, 2000.

Price, Alfred. *Instruments of Darkness.* London: Jane's Information Group, 1982.

Raleigh, Walter, and H. A. Jones. *The War in the Air.* Vols. 1–6. Oxford: Clarendon, 1922–1937.

Ravenstein, Charles A. *The Organization and Lineage of the United States Air Force.* Washington, DC: Office of Air Force History, 1986.

Reynolds, Clark G. *The Fast Carrier: The Forging of the Air Navy.* Annapolis, MD: Naval Institute Press, 1992.

Richards, Denis. *Portal of Hungerford.* London: Heineman, 1978.

Richards, Denis, and Hilary St. G. Saunders. *Royal Air Force, 1939–1945.* 3 vols. London: Her Majesty's Stationery Office, 1953, 1954, 1955.

Roskill, S. W. *The War at Sea, 1939–1945.* London: Her Majesty's Stationery Office, 1954.

Saunders, Hilary St. G. *Per Ardua: The Rise of British Air Power, 1911–1919.* New York: Arno, 1972.

Schaffel, Kenneth. *The Emerging Shield: The Air Force and Continental Air Defense, 1945–1960.* Washington, DC: Office of Air Force History, 1998.

Schaller, Michael. *Douglas MacArthur: The Far Eastern General.* New York: Oxford University Press, 1989.

Scharr, Adela Rick. *Sisters in the Sky: The WAFS.* Gerald, MO: Patrice, 1986.

Schlight, John. *The War in South Vietnam: The Years of the Offensive, 1965–1968.* Washington, DC: Office of Air Force History, 1988.

Sherrod, Robert. *History of Marine Corps Aviation in World War II.* Washington, DC: Combat Force Press, 1952.

Slessor, John. *The Central Blue.* London: Cassell, 1956.

Sloan, James J., Jr. *Wings of Honor: American Airmen in World War I.* Atglen, PA: Schiffer, 1994.

Speer, Albert. *Inside the Third Reich.* New York: Macmillan, 1970.

Strategic Air Command History Office. *From Snark to Peacekeeper: A Pictorial History of Strategic Air Command Missiles.* Offut AFB, NE: Office of the Historian, Headquarters Strategic Air Command, 1990.

Sturm, Thomas A. *The USAF Scientific Advisory Board: Its First Twenty Years, 1944–1964.* Washington, DC: Office of Air Force History, 1986.

Suchenwirth, Richard. *The Development of the German Air Force, 1919–1939.* Montgomery, AL: USAF Historical Division, 1968.

Swanborough, Gordon, and Peter M. Bowers. *United States Navy Aircraft since 1911.* New York: Funk and Wagnalls, 1968.

_______. *United States Military Aircraft since 1909.* Washington, DC: Smithsonian Institution Press, 1989.

Sweetman, Bill, and Bill Gunston. *Soviet Air Power.* London: Leisure Books, 1978.

Taylor, Theodore. *The Magnificent Mitscher.* New York: W. W. Norton, 1954.

Tedder, Arthur. *With Prejudice.* London: Cassell, 1966.

Termena, Bernard J., Layne B. Peiffer, and H. P. Carlin. *Logistics: An Illustrated History of AFLC and Its Antecedents, 1921–1981.* Dayton, OH: Headquarters Air Force Logistics Command.

Terraine, John. *A Time for Courage.* New York: Macmillan, 1985.

Thompson, Jonathan. *Italian Civil and Military Aircraft, 1930–1945.* Los Angeles: Aero, 1963.

Tilford, Earl H., Jr. *Search and Rescue in Southeast Asia, 1961–1975.* Washington, DC: Office of Air Force History, 1980.

_______. *Setup: What the Air Force Did in Vietnam and Why.* Maxwell AFB, AL: Air University Press, 1991.

Tolson, John J. *Vietnam Studies: Airmobility, 1961–1971.* Washington, DC: Department of the Army, 1973.

USAF Historical Studies. *The Development of Air Doctrine in the Army Air Arm, 1917–1941.* Historical Studies no. 89. Washington, DC: USAF Historical Division, 1955.

Van Staaveren, Jacob. *Interdiction in Southern Laos, 1960–1968.* Washington, DC: Center for Air Force History, 1993.

Wagner, Ray, ed. *The Soviet Air Force in World War II: The Official History.* Trans. Leland Fetzer. Garden City, NY: Doubleday, 1973.

Warden, John A. III. *The Air Campaign: Planning for Combat.* Washington, DC: National Defense University Press, 1988.

Watson, George M., Jr. *The Office of the Secretary of the Air Force, 1947–1965.* Washington, DC: Center for Air Force History, 1993.

Webster, C., and Noble Frankland. *The Strategic Air Offensive Against Germany, 1939–1945.* London: Her Majesty's Stationery Office, 1961.

Weisgall, Jonathan M. *Operation Crossroads: The Atomic Tests at Bikini Atoll.* Annapolis, MD: Naval Institute Press, 1994.

Werrell, Kenneth P. *The Evolution of the Cruise Missile.* Maxwell AFB, AL: Air University Press, 1985.

_______. *Archie, Flak, AAA, and SAM: A Short Operational History of Ground-Based Air Defense.* Maxwell AFB, AL: Air University Press, 1988.

Wolf, Richard I. *United States Air Force Basic Documents on Roles and Missions.* Washington, DC: Office of Air Force History, 1987.

Wolk, Herman S. *Planning and Organizing the Postwar Air Force, 1943–1947.* Washington, DC: Office of Air Force History, 1984.

Wood, Derek, with Derek Dempster. *The Narrow Margin.* London: Arrow Books, 1969.

Y'Blood, William T. *The Little Giants: U.S. Escort Carriers Against Japan.* Annapolis, MD: Naval Institute Press, 1987.

Yonay, Ehud. *No Margin for Error: The Making of the Israeli Air Force.* New York: Pantheon Books, 1993.

CONTRIBUTORS

Gregory Alegi
Italian Air Force Academy/LUISS
Rome, Italy

William Althoff
West Central,NJ

David C. Arnold, USAF
United States Air Force Academy
Colorado Springs, CO

Bruce Ashcroft
Air Education and Training Command
Randolph Air Force Base, TX

Albert Atkins
Embry-Riddle Aeronautical University/
University of Phoenix
Colton, CA

John H. Barnhill
Defense System Information Agency
Oklahoma City, OK

John L. Bell Jr.
Western Carolina University

Andy Blackburn
Author/Historian
Windsor, England

Carl Bobrow
National Air and Space Museum
Washington, DC

Horst Boog
Professor
Munich, Germany

Walter J. Boyne
Author/Historian
Ashburn Farms, VA

Squire Brown
Author/Historian
Dayton, OH

Robert Bunker
Institute of Land Warfare
Association of the United States Army
Washington, DC

Shawn Cafferky
University of Victoria

Donald Caldwell
Author/Historian
Lake Jackson, TX

Brian Carpenter
University of Tennessee

Michael S. Casey
Dean, Graceland University
Lamoni, Iowa

Gary Mason Church
Texas A&M University
Dallas, TX

Craig T. Cobane
Culver-Stockton College
Canton, MO

Wendy M. Coble
Naval Historical Center
Washington, DC

Kenneth Collinge
Historian
Trumbull, CT

Ann Cooper
Author/Historian
Beavercreek, OH

Major General Charles S. Cooper III,
USAFR (Ret.)
Author/Historian
Beavercreek, OH

Sherwood Cordier
Western Michigan University

Kazimiera J. Cottam
Independent Scholar
Ottawa, Ontario, Canada

Conrad Crane
Research Professor of Military Strategy
Strategic Studies Institute, U.S. Army
War College
Carlisle Barracks, PA

Thomas M. Culbert
Aviation Information Research
Corporation
Alexandria, VA

Douglas G. Culy
Author/Historian
Tempe, AZ

Kev Darling
Author/Historian
United Kingdom

R.E.G. Davies
Curator of Transport
National Air and Space Museum
Washington, DC

Richard DeAngelis
Fairfield University
Fairfield, CT

Scott R. DiMarco
Director of Library Services
Herkimer County Community College
Kerkimer, NY

David Dorando
Western Carolina University
Cullowhee, NC

Major Braxton R. Eisel, USAF
The Pentagon
Washington, DC

Jeffrey A. Engel
University of Wisconsin
Madison, WI

Lieutenant Colonel John T. Farquhar, USAF
United States Air Force Academy
Colorado Springs, CO

Susan Hayes Fischer
Author/Historian
Indianapolis, IN

Santiago Flores
Author/Historian
Tijuana, Mexico

Paul E. Fontenoy
Curator of Maritime Research and Technology
North Carolina Maritime Museum
Beaufort, NC

Lieutenant Colonel Bert Frandsen, USA (Ret.)
Author/Historian
Auburn University
Montgomery, AL

Colin Fries
National Aeronautics and Space Administration

Rafael J. Garcia Jr.
Author
Alexandria, VA

Major Paul G. Gillespie, USAF
United States Air Force Academy
Colorado Springs, CO

Brad Gladman
University of Calgary
Calgary, Alberta, Canada

Kevin Gould
American Military Institute
Manassas, VA

John F. Graham
University of North Dakota
Grand Forks, ND

Mark Grandstaff
Brigham Young University
Provo, UT

James L. Green
Author/Historian
Silver Spring, MD

First Lieutenant Troy Hammond, USAF
Whiteman Air Force Base, MO

William Hartley
University of Tennessee
Knoxville, TN

Brian Head
Warner Robins, GA

William Head
Chief WR-ALC Office of History
Robins Air Force Base, GA

Henry H. Holden
Author/Historian
Randolph, NJ

Robert S. Hopkins III
Author/Historian
Oak Creek, WI

Renjia Hua (deceased)
Professor, Air Force Command College
People's Repubic of China

J. D. Hunley
Former Chief Historian
Dryden Flight Research Center, NASA
Greenbelt, MD

David Isby
SPARTA, Inc.
Washington, DC

B. M. Jain
Rajasthan University
Jaipur, India

Dennis Jenkins
Author/Historian
Cape Canaveral, FL

Frederick A. Johnsen
Historian
Tehachapie, CA

Randy Johnson
Dean, College of Aviation
Embry-Riddle Aeronautical University
Daytona Beach, FL

Stephen B. Johnson
University of North Dakota
Grand Forks, ND

Major Ben Jones, USAF
United States Air Force Academy
Colorado Springs, CO

Mark Kahn
National Aeronautics and Space Administration
Washington, DC

Stanley Kandebo
Aviation Week and Space Technology
New York, NY

Jeremy R. Kinney
Curator for Aero Propulsion
National Air and Space Museum
Washington, DC

Gary Kuhn
Latin American Aviation Historical Society

William M. Leary
University of Georgia
Athens, GA

W. David Lewis
Auburn University
Auburn, AL

James K. Libbey
Embry-Riddle Aeronautical University
Daytona Beach, FL

Michael Little
Offutt Air Force Base, NE

Alwyn T. Lloyd
Boeing Company
Bellevue, WA

D. Y. Louie
Aviation Enthusiast
Statesboro, GA

Jerome Martin
Peru State College
Peru, NE

Jeffrey J. Matthews
University of Puget Sound
Tacoma, WA

Birch Matthews
Author/Historian
Rolling Hills Estates, CA

Emerson Thomas McMullen
Georgia Southern University

Phillip Meilinger
Author/Historian
Patomac Falls, VA

George Mellinger
Author/Historian
Sioux Falls, SD

Malcolm Muir
Austin Peay State University
Clarksville, TN

Frank Nickell
Southeast Missouri State University
Cape Girardeau, MO

Stéphane Nicolaou
Curator
Musée de l'Air et de l'Espace
Paris, France

Guy Noffsinger
Author/Historian
Defense Intelligence Agency School
Washington, DC

Cynthia Clark Northrup
University of Texas
Arlington, TX

John Andreas Olsen
Royal Norwegian Air Force Academy
Oslo, Norway

Mark A. O'Neill
Tallahassee Community College
Tallahassee, FL

Steve Pace
Author/Historian
Tacoma, WA

James D. Perry
Science Applications International Corporation
McLean, VA

Lieutenant Colonel James M. Pfaff, USAF
Marysville, IL

David Pluth
Historical Research
Chaska, MN

Raymond L. Puffer
Historian
Air Force Flight Test Center
Edwards Air Force Base, CA

Edgar F. Raines
U.S. Army Center of Military History
Washington, DC

Rebecca C. Raines
U.S. Army Center of Military History
Washington, DC

Peter Rainow
Author/Historian
San Mateo, CA

David Rezelman
Author/Historian
Virginia Beach, VA

Daniel Ruffin
Bellbrook, OH

Colonel Steven A. Ruffin, USAF
Bellbrook, OH

Frank Schumacher
University of Erfurt
Erfort, Germany

Noel Shirley
Author/Historian
San Jose, CA

Jerry D. Snead
Auburn University
Auburn, AL

J. J. Snyder
Agricultural Aviation Consultant
Kingsburg, CA

Christopher H. Sterling
Professor of Media and Public Affairs and of Telecommunications
George Washington University
Washington, DC

Erich Streckfuss
Cincinnati, OH

James Streckfuss
President
League of World War I Aero Historians
Cincinnati, OH

Rick W. Sturdevant
Deputy Director of History
Headquarters Air Force Space Command
Colorado Springs, CO

William Suit
Wright-Patterson Air Force Base
Dayton, OH

Guillaume de Syon
Albright College
Reading, PA

Christopher Terry
President and CEO
Canada Science and Technology Museum Corporation
Ottawa, Ontario, Canada

Roger M. Thomas
Jacksonville University
Jacksonville, FL

Warren Thompson
Author/Historian
Germantown, TN

Earl H. Tilford Jr.
Grove City College
Grove City, PA

William F. Trimble
Auburn University
Auburn, AL

Diane Truluck
Warner-Robins Air Logistics Command
Robins Air Force Base, GA

Frank E. Watson
Richmond, VA

George M. Watson Jr.
Chief, Special Projects
Air Force History Support Office
Bolling Air Force Base
Washington, DC

Captain Grant Weller, USAF
United States Air Force Academy
Colorado Springs, CO

Colonel Darrel Whitcomb, USAF (Ret.)
MARC Corporation
Fairfax, VA

Thomas Wildenberg
Author/Historian
Silver Spring, MD

James H. Willbanks
U.S. Army Command and Staff College
Fort Leavenworth, KS

Mark D. Witzel, USAF
United States Air Force Academy
Colorado Springs, CO

Daniel Worthington
Harpweek LLC
Norfolk, VA

INDEX

(Major references are in boldface.)

SOUTH ORANGE PUBLIC LIBRARY
3 9507 00112800 7